Fundamentals of Health Law

Fifth Edition

BY

BARRY D. ALEXANDER, ESQUIRE
BERNADETTE M. BROCCOLO, ESQUIRE
ANTHEA R. DANIELS, ESQUIRE
SANDRA M. DIVARCO, ESQUIRE
CYNTHIA B. HUTTO, ESQUIRE
CAROL COLBORN LOEPERE, ESQUIRE
DAVID E. MATYAS, ESQUIRE
THOMAS WM. MAYO, ESQUIRE
JOHN J. MILES, ESQUIRE
ELI A. POLIAKOFF, ESQUIRE
ROSS E. SALLADE, ESQUIRE
MICHAEL F. SCHAFF, ESQUIRE
SUSAN O. SCHEUTZOW, ESQUIRE
DANIEL J. SCHWARTZ, ESQUIRE
KERRIN B. SLATTERY, ESQUIRE

AMERICAN HEALTH LAWYERS ASSOCIATION

AMERICAN HEALTH LAWYERS ASSOCIATION
1620 Eye Street, NW, 6th Floor,
Washington, DC 20006-4010
Web site: www.healthlawyers.org
E-Mail: info@healthlawyers.org

Printed in the United States of America
ISBN: 978-1-4224-8962-8
978-1-4224-8961-1 (Members)

RECENT TITLES FROM HEALTH LAWYERS

False Claims Act & The Healthcare Industry: Counseling & Litigation, Second Edition with 2011 Cumulative Supplement
© 2011, perfect bound

Healthcare Compliance Legal Issues Manual, Third Edition
© 2011, perfect bound

Healthcare Entity Bylaws and Related Documents: Navigating the Medical Staff/Healthcare Entity Relationship, Third Edition
© 2011, perfect bound

The Law of Health Information Technology, First Edition
© 2011, perfect bound

AHLA's Guide to Healthcare Legal Forms, Agreements, and Policies, First Edition with November 2010 Supplement with CD-ROM
© 2010, looseleaf

Physician Recruitment and Compensation Arrangements Practice Guide, Third Edition
© 2010, perfect bound

AHLA's Federal Healthcare Laws & Regulations, August 2010 Healthcare Reform Update to 2009-2010 Edition with CD-ROM
© 2010, perfect bound

Institutional Review Boards: A Primer, Second Edition
© 2010, perfect bound

Deciphering Codes: Fraud & Abuse for Coders and Coding Insight for Healthcare Lawyers, First Edition
© 2010, looseleaf

Peer Review Guidebook, Fourth Edition with CD-ROM
© 2010, perfect bound

Peer Review Hearing Guidebook, First Edition 2010 Case Law Update
© 2010, perfect bound

Healthcare Labor and Employment Practice Guide, First Edition
© 2010, perfect bound

Legal Issues in Healthcare Fraud and Abuse: Navigating the Uncertainties, 2009 Cumulative Supplement
© 2009, perfect bound

Representing Physicians Handbook, Second Edition
© 2009, perfect bound

AHLA's Federal Healthcare Laws & Regulations 2009-2010 Edition with CD-ROM
© 2009, perfect bound 3-volume set

Practical Guidance for Patient Safety Organization Implementation
© 2009, perfect bound

Ambulatory Surgery Centers, First Edition with CD-ROM
© 2009, perfect bound

Healthcare Capital Finance: In Good and Challenging Times, First Edition with CD-ROM
© 2009, perfect bound

Enterprise Risk Management for Healthcare Entities, First Edition with CD-ROM
© 2009, perfect bound

Fifty State Survey of Certificate of Need and Licensure: Nursing Homes, Assisted Living, Home Health and Hospice, First Edition with CD-ROM
© 2009, perfect bound

The Complete "Connected" Stark Laws & Regulations, Second Edition
© 2009, CD-ROM

Corporate Governance Implications of Nonprofit Executive Compensation, First Edition
© 2009, perfect bound

Preface

In the last several decades, health law has emerged as a growing and evolving area of practice. Even since the publication of the first edition of *Fundamentals of Health Law* in 1995, dramatic changes have occurred in terms of the types of persons and entities that provide healthcare services, how these services are paid for, and the ways in which they are delivered. As a result, a great wealth of information exists which is commonly referred to as "health law."

Today, a health lawyer's practice encompasses a wide variety of legal issues, and includes a correspondingly diverse group of clients. Health lawyers may represent hospitals, physicians, and other traditional healthcare providers—or their practices may represent more exotic clients such as pharmaceutical entities, healthcare Internet companies, insurance companies, or persons involved in bioethics. Despite the breadth of this spectrum, a fundamental core curriculum of health law issues exists, about which anyone practicing any aspect of health law should be knowledgeable.

This fifth edition addresses the fundamental legal issues that need to be understood by a practicing health lawyer, regardless of the area or specialty in which she may practice. The topics in this book address not only the fundamental legal issues a health lawyer may face, but also the structural and operational issues affecting healthcare providers and payors. In addition, this book provides a basic understanding of how healthcare is rendered. Some of the key legal topics addressed in this book are an understanding of tax and tax-exempt issues, federal and state fraud and abuse issues, self-referral laws, false claims issues, antitrust issues, confidentiality, and Medicare and Medicaid reimbursement issues. Our goal in preparing this book is to provide lawyers new to the health law arena with a fundamental resource to aid them in developing their practice, as well as to provide a basic education of health law.

In compiling this book, Health Lawyers has selected experienced practitioner authors and each chapter concentrates on a fundamental aspect of health law written by an expert in that subject area. We would like to thank the authors for participating in this project and for lending their expertise.

We hope that this book will serve as a useful tool in your endeavors in health law and the healthcare industry.

About the Authors

Barry D. Alexander, Esquire (Chapter 3, Medicare) is a partner with the firm of Nelson Mullins Riley & Scarborough LLP and chair's the firm's National Healthcare Practice Group. Mr. Alexander specializes in Medicare and Medicaid reimbursement matters and mergers acquisitions and private equity transactions exclusively in the healthcare arena. He provides legal and regulatory counseling on federal and state fraud issues, including corporate compliance, anti-kickback, self-referral, false claims and health information privacy matters. His broad experience includes representation of regional and national providers in matters related to Medicare reimbursement disputes before various Medicare contractors, state Medicaid agencies, and the Centers for Medicare and Medicaid Services (CMS). In addition, he has represented hospitals and healthcare systems, advanced diagnostic imaging suppliers, medical device manufacturers, radiation therapy, medical oncology, durable medical equipment suppliers and specialty pharmaceutical providers in a wide range of transactions and joint ventures, Medicare coverage, billing and other disputes with the U.S. Department of Justice and CMS, resolved potential civil exclusionary actions, and negotiated and implemented corporate integrity agreements with the Department of Health and Human Services Office of the Inspector General (OIG). Mr. Alexander is a member of the American Health Lawyers Association (AHLA), where he currently serves as chair of the Regulation, Accreditation and Payment Practice Group and is a resident of the Nelson Mullins' Raleigh, North Carolina, office.

Bernadette M. Broccolo, Esquire (Chapter 5, Tax-Exempt Issues) is a partner in the Chicago office of McDermott Will & Emery LLP and has been counseling health industry organizations for more than 30 years on leading edge health industry relationship formation and realignments (*e.g.*, hospital and physician alignment, governance restructurings, and institutional affiliations and strategic partnerships); health information technology acquisitions, electronic health information networks, electronic data warehouses and tissue repositories to support translational research and personalized medicine; conflict of interest compliance; comprehensive programs for human subject research; and overall corporate compliance programs. Her specialties include the full scope of legal and regulatory compliance in the areas of federal taxation of exempt organizations and not-for-profit corporate governance, privacy, human subject protection and technology contracting. Bernadette is a frequent speaker and author on topics in her areas of practice. She is co-author of *Tax-Exempt Status of Health Care Organizations*, which is part of BNA's *Health Law & Business Series*. She has served in numerous leadership positions for organizations serving the health industry and the legal profession, including the Board of Directors of the American Health Lawyers Association (AHLA) and she is an AHLA Fellow. She has been selected by her peers to be included in *The Best Lawyers in America* for her expertise in healthcare law for the past 20 years and was named *Best Lawyers'* Chicago Health Care Lawyer of the Year for 2010. Bernadette is listed as a leading individual in healthcare in *Chambers USA: America's Leading Lawyers for Business*, as an *Illinois Super Lawyer* and as one of the top women business lawyers in Illinois in *Leading Lawyers Network*.

Anthea R. Daniels, Esquire (Chapter 11, Healthcare Transactions and Contracting) focuses on healthcare, corporate and non-profit law, and is co-chair of the Health Care and Life Sciences Practice Group at Calfee, Halter & Griswold in Cleveland, Ohio. She provides counsel to health systems, academic medical centers, hospitals, long-term care facilities, insurance companies, clinics, surgery centers, professional management companies and physician groups. She represents healthcare providers involved in mergers, acquisitions, joint ventures and integrated delivery systems. Anthea reviews managed care regulatory and contracting issues, mergers and acquisitions, corporate HIPAA compliance issues, fraud and abuse, OIG and DOJ investigations, Stark, Medicare and Medicaid reimbursement matters, and tax-exempt issues for public charities and private foundations. Anthea is the past president of the American Health Lawyers Association and is an AHLA Fellow. She is also past president of the Northeast Ohio Chapter of the Healthcare Financial Management Association and a recipient of its Founders, Merit and Muncie Gold Awards. She is a past recipient of *Crain's Cleveland Business* Forty Under Forty, the YWCA Women of Professional Excellence, and *Cleveland Magazine*'s 50 Most Interesting People. She formerly chaired the Cleveland Bar Association's Health Care Law Council, as well as the American Bar Association's Young Lawyers Division's Healthcare Law Committee and Delivery of Legal Services to the Elderly Committee.

Sandra M. DiVarco, Esquire (Chapter 8, Regulation of Hospitals) is a partner in the law firm of McDermott Will & Emery LLP and is based in the Firm's Chicago office. Sandy focuses her practice on the representation of hospitals and health systems. She has counseled healthcare facility and system clients regarding all aspects of health law transactions and health system restructurings. As a registered nurse, Sandy regularly advises clients on the legal aspects of clinical issues and policy/procedure matters. Sandy also has significant experience in assisting clients with regulatory, licensure and accreditation issues, including state-level and CMS survey responses, formulation of successful Plans of Correction, Joint Commission complaint responses, and EMTALA/regulatory investigations. She is also co-leader of the firm's Hospitals and Health Systems affinity group.

Cynthia B. Hutto, Esquire (Chapter 3, Medicare) is a partner in the Charleston Office of Nelson Mullins Riley & Scarborough, L.L.P. Ms. Hutto practices in the firm's National Healthcare Practice Group in the areas of healthcare and administrative law with an emphasis on operational, regulatory, and patient privacy issues for healthcare providers. She represents providers and suppliers including hospitals, long term care facilities, and ancillary service providers. Her operational experience includes advising clients on state and federal Medicare survey and certification issues, changes of ownership (CHOW), state licensing and permitting issues, reimbursement requirements for government, and private payor programs, EMTALA, and medical staff relations. Ms. Hutto also advises healthcare clients regarding issues involving patient privacy and security under the Health Insurance Portability and Accountability Act of 1996 (HIPAA), Health Information Technology for Economic and Clinical Health Act (HITECH), and state privacy laws and regulations (including analysis of data breach issues), information systems agreements, provider transactions, and state and federal referral legislation (including the Medicare and Medicaid Anti-Kickback Statute and Stark). Ms. Hutto has been a speaker for AHLA on sentinel event issues and the South Carolina Bar's Health Law Committee on physician referral issues. She also collaborated on the "Medicare: Overview, Program Administration, Reimbursement, Eligibility, Coverage, Certification, Payment, Assignment & Reassignment, Appeals" Chapter for the previous edition of AHLA's *The Fundamentals of Health Law*.

Carol Colborn Loepere, Esquire (Chapter 10, Post-Acute Providers and Suppliers) is the co-chair of Reed Smith's Life Sciences Health Industry Group, practicing in the area of healthcare regulatory law. Since joining the firm in 1984, she has practiced exclusively in healthcare law, providing ongoing counseling on regulatory and legislative initiatives affecting life sciences and healthcare companies, including Medicare and Medicaid coverage and reimbursement issues, survey and certification, and contractual arrangements. In addition, she has extensive experience in the fraud and abuse area advising clients on various business transactions and arrangements for compliance with physician self-referral and anti-kickback laws and representing clients in criminal and civil proceedings and investigations. Carol also assists pharmaceutical and device manufacturers, providers, and suppliers to develop and implement corporate compliance programs and comply with Corporate Integrity Agreements (CIAs). She also assists public companies in the preparation and review of documents filed with the Securities and Exchange Commission. Carol specializes in advising clients on the regulatory requirements and business considerations in connection with healthcare transactions. She has represented issuers in public offerings, companies and investors in financing transactions, and buyers and sellers in major acquisitions in the life sciences and healthcare industry, focusing on due diligence, change of ownership (CHOW) issues, and related regulatory issues.

David E. Matyas, Esquire (Chapter 4, Fundamentals of Health Law Fraud and Abuse) is a member of Epstein Becker & Green's Health Care and Life Sciences Practice in the firm's Washington, DC office. He practices in the firm's Health Care Fraud Practice Group, which focuses on federal and state fraud issues such as anti-kickback, self-referral, false claims, and regulatory compliance. Mr. Matyas also practices in the firm's Third-Party Payment Practice Group, which concentrates on legal and regulatory matters arising under Medicare, Medicaid, and other third-party payment programs. Mr. Matyas represents an array of healthcare providers including hospitals and health systems, pharmaceutical and medical device manufacturers, academic medical centers, retail and specialty pharmacies, ambulatory surgery centers, home health agencies, and physician organizations. He also advises investors and other financial institutions that invest in or support the healthcare industry. From 2002 to 2008, Mr. Matyas served as a member of the Board of Directors for the American Health Lawyers Association, and he continues to chair the association's Fundamentals of Health Law Program. In 2005 and 2010, Mr. Matyas was selected by the editors of *Nightingale's Healthcare News* as one of the "Outstanding Fraud & Compliance Lawyers." Mr. Matyas is also listed in the District of Columbia Healthcare category of Chambers USA and in *Washington, D.C. Super Lawyers* magazine. He is a frequent speaker and author on the subjects of healthcare fraud, corporate compliance programs, Stark Law, mergers and acquisitions in the healthcare industry, and other health-related topics. Mr. Matyas is the co-author of *Legal Issues in Healthcare Fraud and Abuse: Navigating the Uncertainties*, of which the 3rd edition was published in 2006.

Thomas Wm. Mayo, Esquire (Chapter 12, Bioethics) is an Associate Professor in the Dedman School of Law at Southern Methodist University, Adjunct Associate Professor of Internal Medicine at the University of Texas–Southwestern Medical School, and Of Counsel, Haynes and Boone, all in Dallas. He teaches courses in torts, legislation, nonprofit organizations, healthcare law, and bioethics and law, as well as a literature course for medical students and law students together (titled, unsurprisingly, "Law, Literature & Medicine"). He currently serves on five hospital ethics committees, including Parkland Memorial Hospital (co-chair since 1992) and Children's Medical Center (co-chair since 2001). He is co-founder of the North Texas Legal Hospice, Texas' first pro bono legal clinic for persons with HIV disease and persons with terminal illnesses; the 2002 recipient of the Dallas County Medical Society's Health Award for outstanding leadership and service to medicine and to the community of Dallas; the recipient of SMU's award for the outstanding member of the tenured faculty; and the long-time poetry columnist for the *Dallas Morning News*.

John J. (Jeff) Miles, Esquire (Chapter 6, Antitrust Law) is a shareholder in the Washington, D.C. office of Ober|Kaler, where he limits his practice to antitrust law. Most of his work focuses on provider mergers, joint ventures, contracting networks, exclusionary practices, and government antitrust investigations. Jeff earned his B.S. and M.A. degrees in economics from Virginia Tech, and his law degree from the Washington & Lee University School of Law. Prior to entering private practice, he served as the Assistant Attorney General in charge of the Virginia Attorney General's Antitrust Unit, and then as a Trial Attorney with the Antitrust Division of the U.S. Department of Justice, focusing on healthcare antitrust matters. Jeff is a former member of AHLA's Board of Directors and former chair of its Antitrust Practice Group. He wrote and updates the six-volume *Health Care & Antitrust* treatise, published by Thompson/West, and he authored the fourth edition of the ABA Section of Antitrust Law's *Antitrust Health Care Handbook*, published in 2010. He also serves as an Adjunct Professor of Law at the Washington & Lee University School of Law, where he teaches antitrust law.

Eli A. Poliakoff, Esquire (Chapter 3, Medicare) is an attorney in the Charleston, South Carolina office of Nelson Mullins Riley & Scarborough LLP and practices in the firm's National Healthcare Practice Group. He advises clients on a variety of healthcare regulatory and compliance matters including state and federal referral, fraud and abuse issues; privacy and information security obligations under HIPAA, the HITECH Act, and the HIPAA Breach Notification Rules; and corporate and operational issues related to the healthcare industry and transactions within the healthcare industry. He is a frequent author on the Medicare Secondary Payer program and regularly advises healthcare providers, mass-tort litigants, and medical equipment suppliers and manufacturers on compliance with the MSP program and associated regulations and administrative guidance. Mr. Poliakoff is a graduate of Harvard University and the University of South Carolina School of Law.

Ross E. Sallade, Esquire (Chapter 3, Medicare) is a partner in the Raleigh office of Nelson Mullins Riley & Scarborough LLP. Mr. Sallade practices in the firm's National Healthcare Practice Group in healthcare law with an emphasis on regulatory, operational, reimbursement, and compliance matters for healthcare providers and suppliers in a wide variety of settings. Mr. Sallade advises clients on a variety of healthcare regulatory and operational matters (including Medicare and Medicaid enrollment, survey and certification, reimbursement, and state and federal licensure, provider based, and change of ownership matters), state and federal referral matters (including the Medicare and Medicaid Anti-Kickback Statute and Stark), corporate transactions (including the structure and formation of joint ventures, professional service agreements, management service agreements, and the like), and finance transactions. Mr. Sallade also advises clients regarding state and federal patient privacy and security laws (including HIPAA).

Michael F. Schaff, Esquire (Chapter 9, Representing Physicians) is department chair of the Health Care and Corporate Groups at Wilentz, Goldman & Spitzer, PA, resident in its Woodbridge, New Jersey, Office. Michael is on the Board of Directors and the Executive Committee of the American Health Lawyers Association and previously was chair of its Physician Organizations Substantive Law Committee and editor of its newsletter. Michael is a past chair of the New Jersey State Bar Association Health and Hospital Law Section. Michael is also an Adjunct Associate Professor at the University of Medicine and Dentistry of New Jersey (UMDNJ) and at St. John's University. Michael is vice-chair of the editorial board for the *New Jersey Lawyer* Magazine and was the special editor of its issues on Health Law and on Patient Rights. Michael has spoken on numerous national teleconferences and seminars and has published extensively. His practice concentrates on providing legal counsel and advice to healthcare professionals and facilities. Mr. Schaff is listed in *The Best Lawyers in America* (2003 through 2011 editions) and *SUPER Lawyers* (2005 through 2010 editions Top 100 Attorneys).

Susan O. Scheutzow, Esquire (Chapter 2, Patient Care) is head of Kohrman Jackson & Krantz's new Healthcare Group. One of Susan's major accomplishments includes a book that she wrote titled *Ohio Health Care Provider Law*, which is still used by health law attorneys across the state. She is a fellow of the American Health Lawyers Association, a distinction granted for her contribution to healthcare law. She taught the first health law course offered by Cleveland State University's Cleveland Marshall College of Law and served on the Board of Directors of the American Health Lawyers Association. She has received many awards, including Distinguished Women in Healthcare from the Visiting Nurse Association and has authored numerous law review articles and monographs. Susan has practiced healthcare law for 25 years, most recently serving as in-house counsel for Southwest General Health Center in Cleveland. Susan continues to represent Southwest General on matters.

Daniel J. Schwartz, Esquire (Chapter 7, The Source of Payment: The State and Federal Regulation of Private Healthcare Plans) is a Shareholder in the St. Louis, Missouri, law firm of Greensfelder, Hemker & Gale, PC. He has practiced primarily in the employee benefits area since 1977, during which he has provided advice on all facets of employee benefits and has represented clients in court in ERISA litigation matters. He is the author of a BNA Tax Management Portfolio entitled *Employee Benefits for Tax-Exempt Organizations*, and a chapter editor of the treatise *Employee Benefits Law*, published by BNA. Mr. Schwartz was named to the IRS Advisory Committee on Tax Exempt and Government Entities (ACT) by the United States Department of Treasury and served as an advisor to the IRS during 2006, 2007, and 2008. The ACT is a formal body of external stakeholders in the specialized areas of tax-exempt organizations, employee retirement plans, tax-exempt bonds, and federal, state, local, and Indian tribal governments. He is frequently invited to speak on employee benefits topics. In 2000, Mr. Schwartz was elected as a Charter Fellow of the American Academy of Employee Benefits Counsel. Mr. Schwartz received his undergraduate degree from the University of Missouri-Columbia (1974, Phi Beta Kappa) and his law degree from the University of Missouri-Kansas City (1977, Law Review).

Kerrin B. Slattery, Esquire (Chapter 8, Regulation of Hospitals) is a partner in the law firm of McDermott Will & Emery LLP and is based in the firm's Chicago office. She is the partner-in-charge of the Health Industry Advisory practice in Chicago. Kerrin maintains a general health law practice, focusing on the representation of hospitals and health systems. She has significant experience in all aspects of health law transactions, including mergers, acquisitions, affiliations, joint ventures, and system restructurings for hospitals, physician groups, nursing homes, and other healthcare providers. Kerrin also advises hospital and health system clients on regulatory compliance with licensure, accreditation, and other state and federal regulatory matters. She is ranked as a leading lawyer in healthcare law in *Chambers USA: America's Leading Lawyers for Business* (2008, 2009, and 2010).

Table of Contents

1

Terminology[*]

1.1 GLOSSARY

AAPCC: Adjusted average per capita cost. The CMS's best estimate of the amount of money it costs to care for Medicare recipients under fee-for-service Medicare in a given area. The AAPCC is made up of 142 different rate cells; 140 of them are factored for age, sex, Medicaid eligibility, institutional status, working age, and whether a person has both part A and part B Medicare. The two remaining cells are for individuals with end-stage renal disease.

AAPPO: American Association of Preferred Provider Organizations. A trade organization for PPOs.

Abuse: A manner of operation that results in excessive or unreasonable costs to the Medicare or Medicaid programs.

Accelerated benefits option: Life insurance provision under which terminally ill persons with life expectancies of less than a year or persons confined to a nursing home can choose to have a certain portion of life insurance proceeds paid out before death to use as they deem appropriate.

Access: The ability to obtain needed medical care. Access is frequently affected by availability of insurance, cost of care, and the geographic location of providers.

Accountable Care Organization (ACO): A network of healthcare providers that offer the full continuum of healthcare services for patients. The network would receive payment for all care provided to a patient and would be held accountable for the quality and cost of care provided. New programs in Medicare and Medicaid included in the new healthcare reform law provide financial incentives for these organizations to improve quality and reduce costs by allowing them to share in any savings achieved as a result of these efforts.

Accreditation: Granting of approval or credentials to an agency or facility, based on that agency or facility demonstrating (usually by passing a specific survey or inspection) that standards prescribed by the accrediting body have been met.

Accrete: The term used by the CMS for the process of adding new Medicare enrollees to a plan.

Accrual: The amount of money that is set aside to cover expenses. The accrual is the plan's best estimate of what those expenses are and (for medical expenses) is based on a combination of data from the authorization system, the claims system, the lag studies and the plan's history.

[*] Gillian I. Russell updated this Chapter for the Fifth Edition. AHLA wishes to thank her for this valuable contribution.

ACEs: Accelerated-compensation events. These are medically caused injuries that should not occur. ACEs do not cover all injuries, just classes of adverse outcomes that are usually, although not invariably, avoidable through good medical care.

Actuarial assumptions: The assumptions that an actuary uses in calculating the expected costs and revenues of the plan. Examples include utilization rates, age, and sex mix of enrollees and cost of medical services.

Actuarial Value: A measure of the average value of benefits in a health insurance plan. It is calculated as a percentage of benefit costs a health insurance plan expects to pay for a standard population, using standard assumptions and taking into account cost-sharing provisions. It represents an average for a population, and does not necessarily represent the actual cost-sharing of an individual.

ADG: Ambulatory diagnostic group. These offer a method of categorizing outpatient episodes. There are 34 possible ADGs.

Administrative law judge (ALJ): An employee of the Department of Health and Human Services who presides over civil fraud and abuse administrative hearings brought by the Office of Inspector General. The ALJ's decision is final and binding 30 days after it is served on the parties, unless the decision is appealed to the Departmental Appeals Board (DAB) or the DAB grants an extension of time to file an appeal.

Advance directives: Written instructions executed by decisionally capable adults that pertain to the future medical treatment preferences or values of the party executing the document. These directives take effect only if the patient is decisionally incapacitated at the time that specific decisions need to be made.

Adverse selection: The problem of attracting members who are sicker than the general population (specifically, members who are sicker than was anticipated when the budget for medical costs was developed).

Affordable Health Care for America Act: The health reform bill created by the House of Representatives in November 2009. This bill was never passed by the Senate. The bill that was passed by the Senate is the Patient Protection and Affordable Care Act. The House abandoned this bill in 2010 in favor of amending the Senate bill in the form of the Health Care and Education Reconciliation Act of 2010.

AHIP: America's Health Insurance Plans. The trade organization that represents all forms of MCOs. Created in 2003 by the merger of AAHP and HIAA. Based in Washington, D.C., AHIP focuses heavily on lobbying, educational activities, and service to member plans.

Allowed Charge: Discounted fees that insurers will recognize and pay for covered services. Insurers negotiate these discounts with providers in their health plan network, and network providers agree to accept the allowed charge as payment in full. Each insurer has its own schedule of allowed charges.

ALOS: *See* LOS.

Ambulatory surgical center (ASC): A freestanding, self-contained facility providing outpatient surgical services to patients who do not require inpatient hospitalization.

American Recovery and Reinvestment Act of 2009 (ARRA): Commonly referred to as the "Stimulus", this is the economic stimulus package intended to create jobs and promote investment and consumer spending during the recession. A portion of this money went toward many healthcare programs such as Medicaid, health information technology, COBRA, health research and construction, community health centers, and more.

Annual Benefit Limit: Insurers place a ceiling on the amount of claims that the insurer will pay for an individual in a given year. After an individual reaches this ceiling during the course of the year, the individual must pay the full cost for all subsequent claims. However, beginning in 2010, annual benefit limits will be restricted. By 2014, annual benefit limits will be prohibited under the health reform laws.

Anti-Kickback Statute: A provision of the Social Security Act that forbids any knowing and willful conduct involving the solicitation, receipt, offer or payment of any kind of remuneration in return for referring an individual for any Medicaid- or Medicare-covered item or service or for recommending or arranging the purchase, lease or order of an item or service that may be wholly or partially paid for through the Medicare or Medicaid programs. Violation of the anti-kickback provision can result in a fine of up to $25,000 for each violation and/or imprisonment for up to five years. The law also mandates exclusion or suspension from government healthcare programs following a conviction under this statute.

Antisupplementation provision: A provision of the Social Security Act that makes it a criminal offense to charge a higher amount than the Medicaid rate for a covered service provided to a Medicaid beneficiary. Violation of this provision can subject an individual to a fine of up to $25,000 and up to five years imprisonment.

APG: Ambulatory patient group. A reimbursement methodology developed by 3M Health Information Systems for the CMS. APGs are to outpatient procedures what DRGs are to inpatient days. APGs provide for a fixed reimbursement to an institution for outpatient procedures or visits and incorporate data regarding the reason for the visit and patient data. APGs prevent unbundling of ancillary services. *See also* ACG and ADG.

ASO: Administrative services only; sometimes referred to as an administrative services contract (ASC). A contract between an insurance company and a self-funded plan where the insurance company performs administrative services only and does not assume any risk. Services usually include claims processing but may include other services, such as actuarial analysis, utilization review and so forth. *See also* ERISA.

Assignment of benefits: The payment of medical benefits directly to a provider of care rather than to a member. Generally requires either a contract between the health plan and the provider or a written release from the subscriber to the provider allowing the provider to bill the health plan.

AWP: Any willing provider. This is a form of state law that requires an MCO to accept any provider willing to meet the terms and conditions in the MCO's contract, whether the MCO wants or needs that provider or not.

AWP: Average wholesale price. Commonly used in pharmacy contracting, the AWP is generally determined through reference to a common source of information.

Balance billing: The practice of a provider billing a patient for all charges not paid for by the insurance plan, even if those charges are above the plan's UCR or are considered medically unnecessary. Managed care plans and service plans generally prohibit providers from balance billing except for allowed copays, coinsurance and deductibles. Such prohibition against balance billing may even extend to the plan's failure to pay at all (for example, because of bankruptcy).

Basic Health Plan: Beginning in 2014, the health reform law will give states the option of creating a basic health plan to provide coverage to individuals who have incomes between 133 and 200% of poverty instead of having these individuals enroll in the health insurance exchange and include the essential health benefits as defined by the health reform law. Cost-sharing under this plan would be limited. In addition, if states choose to offer this plan, the federal government will provide states 95% of what it would have paid to subsidize these enrollees in the health insurance exchange.

Benefit Package: The set of services that are covered by an insurance policy or health plan. Services include physician visits, hospitalizations, and prescription drugs. The benefit package specifies cost-sharing requirements for services, limits on particular services, and annual or lifetime spending limits.

Blue Cross: Nonprofit (usually) membership corporation providing protection against the cost of hospital care in a limited geographical area.

Blue Shield: Nonprofit (usually) membership corporation providing protection against the cost of hospital care in a limited geographical area.

California Collaborative Healthcare Reporting Initiative (CCHRI): Sponsored by the Pacific Business Group on Health (*see* entry), this program represents the collective interests of health plans, purchasers and provider organizations. CCHRI collects, analyzes, and reports performance data; promotes the use of accurate and comparable quality measures; and designs and engages in collaborative improvement projects.

Capitation: A method of reimbursement where the provider, hospital, or health plan is paid a fixed per patient amount, and is expected to provide all necessary covered services at no additional charge.

Carrier fraud control unit: A fraud control unit housed within a Medicare carrier that receives referrals of potential fraud and abuse cases and conducts case reviews.

Carve-out: Refers to a set of medical services that are carved out of the basic arrangement. In terms of plan benefits, may refer to a set of benefits that are carved out and contracted for separately; for example, mental health/substance abuse services may be separated from basic medical-surgical services. May also refer to carving out a set of services from a basic capitation rate with a provider (*e.g.*, capitating for cardiac care but carving out cardiac surgery and paying case rates for that).

Case management: An approach to managing the provision of healthcare to members with high-cost medical conditions. The goal is to coordinate the care to improve both continuity and quality of care and to lower costs. This generally is a dedicated function in the utilization management department. The official definition, according to the Certification of Insurance Rehabilitation Specialists Commission, is as follows: "Case management is a collaborative process which assesses, plans, implements, coordinates, monitors, and evaluates the options and services required to meet an individual's health needs, using communication and available resources to promote quality, cost-effective outcomes" and "occurs across a continuum of care, addressing ongoing individual needs" rather than being restricted to a single practice setting. When focused solely on high-cost inpatient cases, it may be referred to as large case management or catastrophic case management.

Catastrophic Coverage: Insurance coverage option that offers limited benefits a high deductible, intended to only protect against medical bankruptcy due to unforeseen illness or injury. These plans are generally for young adults in relatively good health. While these plans usually did not cover preventative care, under health reform, insurers will be required to exempt some preventative services from the deductible.

Case mix: Refers to the mix of illness and severity of cases for a provider.

Certificate of coverage: Refers to the document that a plan must provide to a member to show evidence that the member has coverage and to give basic information about that coverage. Required under state regulations.

Certification: Granting of approval or credentials to an individual professional, based upon that professional demonstrating (usually through education, experience and specific examination performance) that the standard prescribed by the certifying body has been met.

CHAMPUS: Civilian Health and Medical Program of the Uniformed Services (now known as TRICARE). The federal program providing healthcare coverage to families of military personnel, military retirees, certain spouses and dependents of such personnel and certain others.

Children's Health Insurance Program (CHIP): A federal-state program enacted in 1997 that provides healthcare coverage for uninsured low-income children who are not eligible for Medicaid. States have the option of administering the CHIP through their Medicaid programs, through a separate program, or a combination of both. The Federal government matches state spending for CHIP but Federal CHIP funds are capped.

Churning: The practice of a provider seeing a patient more often than is medically necessary, primarily to increase revenue through an increased number of services. Churning may also apply to any performance-based reimbursement system where there is a heavy emphasis on productivity (in other words, rewarding a provider for seeing a high volume of patients, whether through fee-for-service or through an appraisal system that pays a bonus for productivity).

Civil investigative demand: The attorney general has the authority to serve a civil investigative demand on a person who may be in possession of any documents or information relating to a false claims investigation. A demand imposes a broader range of requests than an Office of Inspector General subpoena, including producing documents, providing responses to written interrogatories or giving oral testimony concerning documentary material.

Civil Monetary Penalty Law (CMP)**:** Under this law, the Office of Inspector General (OIG) may bring administrative actions against providers who submit false or fraudulent claims to the United States or its agent for a medical item or service. The OIG need only demonstrate that the person knew or should have known that the claim was false or fraudulent. The penalty for violation of this law can be a fine of up to $10,000 for each item or service that is submitted in violation of the CMP Law, an assessment of up to three times the amount claimed for each item or service, or a fine of $50,000 for violations regarding patient stabilization and appropriate transfers. In addition, the provider can be terminated from Medicare, Medicaid or other state healthcare programs.

Claim fraud: Use of various means (material misrepresentation, exaggeration of an injury, alteration of medical bills and so on) to obtain benefits to which an insured or a physician is not entitled.

Claim lag: Time incurred between date of a claim and its submission to the insurer for payment; also, the time between claim incurred and payment (check or draft issue or redemption).

Clinical Laboratory Improvement Amendments of 1988 (CLIA): A federal law subjecting nearly all clinical laboratories operating in the United States—whether they are located in hospitals, physicians' offices or independent—to comprehensive federal quality regulation.

Closed panel: A managed care plan that contracts with physicians on an exclusive basis for services and does not allow those physicians to see patients for another managed care organization. Examples include staff and group model HMOs. Could apply to a large private medical group that contracts with an HMO.

CMS: Centers for Medicare & Medicaid Services, formerly the Health Care Financing Administration (HCFA). A branch of the Department of Health and Human Services that is responsible for administering the Medicare and Medicaid programs.

COA: Certificate of authority. The state-issued operating license for an HMO.

COB: Coordination of benefits. Method of integrating benefits payable under more than one health insurance plan so that the insured's benefits from all sources do not exceed 100% of allowable medical expenses or eliminate appropriate patient incentives to contain costs. For example, a husband may have Blue Cross and Blue Shield through work, and the wife may have elected an HMO through her place of employment. The COB agreement gives the order for what organization has primary responsibility for payment and what organization has secondary responsibility for payment.

COBRA: Consolidated Omnibus Budget Reconciliation Act. Federal statute requiring employers with more than 20 employees to make group healthcare coverage available for 18 months, at employee expense, to employees who leave the employer for any reason other than gross misconduct. Another portion eases a Medicare recipient's ability to disenroll from an HMO or CMP with a Medicare risk contract. *See also* Conversion. The American Recovery and Reinvestment Act (ARRA) provided a temporary subsidy of 65% of the premium cost for the purchase of COBRA coverage to people who have lost their job between September 1, 2008 and May 31, 2010.

Coinsurance: A provision in a member's coverage that limits the amount of coverage by the plan to a certain percentage, commonly 80%. Any additional costs are paid by the member out of pocket.

Cold claim: A claim for medical services received by the plan for which no authorization has been received; that is, it arrives "cold."

Collective knowledge doctrine: A doctrine attributing liability to a corporation for the separate actions of several employees who are operating independent of one another. The corporation is considered to have acquired the collective knowledge of its employees and is held responsible for their failure to act lawfully.

Commission: The money paid to a sales representative, broker or other type of sales agent for selling the health plan. May be a flat amount of money or a percentage of the premium.

Commissioner of Insurance: Chief state official responsible for matters related to insurance regulation.

Common law: Judge-made or court-made law, as opposed to statutes, which are laws enacted by legislative bodies. (Compare with Statute.)

Community Living Assistance Services and Supports (CLASS) Program: The CLASS program establishes a voluntary insurance program for purchasing non-medical services and support necessary for individuals with functional limitations to maintain community residence. Enrollment begins in January 1, 2011 and will target working adults who will be able to make voluntary premium contributions either through payroll deductions through their employer or directly. The first benefits will be paid out to eligible beneficiaries in 2016.

Community rating: The rating methodology required of federally qualified HMOs, HMOs under the laws of many states, and occasionally indemnity plans under certain circumstances. The HMO must obtain the same amount of money per member for all members in the plan. Community rating does allow for variability by allowing the HMO to factor in differences for age, sex, mix (average contract size) and industry factors; not all factors are necessarily allowed under state laws, however. Such techniques are referred to as community rating by class and adjusted community rating. *See also* Experience Rating.

Competitive medical plan (CMP): A federal designation, limited to the § 1876 Medicare cost program, that allows a health plan to contract for a Medicare risk contract without becoming a federally qualified health maintenance organization (HMO). Like an HMO, a CMP provides healthcare on a prepaid basis. However, a CMP differs from a federally qualified HMO because services must be provided primarily through the CMP, a CMP may be able to limit the scope of some of the services it is required to offer, and a CMP can require higher copayments and deductibles.

CON: Certificate of need. The requirement that a healthcare organization obtain permission from an oversight agency before making changes. Generally applies only to facilities or facility-based services.

Concurrent review: Refers to utilization management that takes place during the provision of services. Almost exclusively applied to inpatient hospital stays.

Consumer-Directed Health Plan: Plans that seek to increase consumer awareness about healthcare costs and provide incentives for consumers to consider costs when making decisions about healthcare. These plans usually have high deductibles along with a consumer-controlled savings account for healthcare services. The two types of savings accounts are: Health Savings Accounts (HSAs) and Health Reimbursement Arrangements (HRAs).

Consolidated Omnibus Budget Reconciliation Act (COBRA): *See* COBRA.

Continuing care retirement community (CCRC): Self-sufficient life-care community in which residents, for a substantial entry fee plus a monthly maintenance fee, enter into a contractual relationship with the community that can last a lifetime.

Contract year: The 12-month period for which a contract for services is in force. Not necessarily tied to a calendar year.

Contributory plan: A group health plan in which the employees must contribute a certain amount toward the premium cost, with the employer paying the rest.

Conversion: The conversion of a member covered under a group master contract to coverage under an individual contract. This is offered to subscribers who lose their group coverage (for example, through job loss, death of a working spouse and so forth) and who are ineligible for coverage under another group contract. *See also* COBRA.

Coordination of benefits (COB): *See* COB.

Copayment: The portion of a claim or medical expense not covered by insurance that a patient must pay for him- or herself.

Corporate compliance program: A program designed, implemented, and enforced by a corporation to detect and prevent violations of the fraud and abuse laws.

Corporate integrity agreement (CIA): An agreement that a healthcare company has entered into with the government as part of a global settlement of a government investigation.

Corporate death sentence: A penalty that may be imposed under the federal Guidelines for Sentencing of Organizations on a corporation that does not take effective measures to prevent wrongdoing among its employees. If a death sentence is imposed on the corporation, the corporation will be fined an amount sufficient to divest it of all net assets.

Corporate practice of medicine acts or statutes: State laws that prohibit a physician from working for a corporation; in other words, a physician can only work for himself or herself or another physician. Put another way, a corporation cannot practice medicine. Often created through the effort on the part of certain members of the medical community to prevent physicians from working directly for managed care plans or hospitals.

Cost sharing: Any form of coverage in which the member pays some portion of the cost of providing services. Usual forms of cost sharing include deductibles, coinsurance and copayments.

Cost shifting: When a provider cannot cover the cost of providing services under the reimbursement received, the provider raises the prices to other payors to cover that portion of the cost. Some of the costs are shifted to and absorbed by private health insurance.

Credentialing: The most common use of the term refers to obtaining and reviewing the documentation of professional providers. Such documentation includes licensure, certifications, insurance, evidence of malpractice insurance, malpractice history, and so forth. Generally includes both reviewing information provided by the provider and verification that the information is correct and complete. A less frequent use of the term applies to closed panels and medical groups and refers to obtaining hospital privileges and other privileges to practice medicine.

Current Procedural Terminology, 4th Edition (CPT-4) coding: A set of five-digit codes corresponding to medical services that are frequently used for billing purposes.

Custodial care: Care provided to an individual that is primarily the basic activities of living. May be medical or nonmedical, but the care is not meant to be curative or as a form of medical treatment, and it is often lifelong. Rarely covered by any form of group health insurance or HMO.

CVO: Credentialing verification organization. This is an independent organization that performs primary verification of a professional provider's credentials. The managed care organization may then rely on that verification rather than requiring the provider to provide credentials independently. This lowers the cost of credentialing. The NCQA has issued certification standards for CVOs. *See also* NCQA.

CWW: Clinic without walls. *See* GPWW.

Date of service: Refers to the date that medical services were rendered. Usually different from the date a claim is submitted.

DAW: Dispense as written. The instruction from a physician to a pharmacist to dispense a brand-name pharmaceutical rather than a generic substitution.

Days per thousand: A standard unit of measurement of utilization. Refers to an annualized use of the hospital or other institutional care. It is the number of hospital days that are used in a year for each thousand covered lives.

DCI: Duplicate coverage inquiry. A document used in COB when one plan contacts another to inquire about dual coverage of medical benefits.

Death spiral: An insurance term that refers to a spiral of high premium rates and adverse selection, generally in a free-choice environment (typically, an insurance company or health plan in an account with multiple other plans or a plan offering coverage to potential members who have alternative choices, such as through an association). One plan, often the indemnity plan competing with managed care plans, ends up having continually higher premium rates such that the only members who stay with the plan are those whose medical costs are so high (and who cannot change because of provider loyalty or benefits restrictions, such as preexisting conditions) that they far exceed any possible premium revenue. Called the death spiral because the losses from underwriting mount faster than the premiums can ever recover, and the account eventually terminates coverage, leaving the carrier in a permanent loss position.

Deductible: The portion of a subscriber's (or member's) healthcare expenses that must be paid out of pocket before any insurance coverage applies, commonly $100 to $300. Common in insurance plans and PPOs, uncommon in HMOs. May apply only to the out-of-network portion of a point-of-service plan. May also apply only to one portion of the plan coverage (for example, there may be a deductible for pharmacy services but not for anything else). Under health reform starting in 2014, deductibles for new plans sold in the small group insurance market will be limited to $2,000 for individual policies and $4,000 for family policies.

Defensive medicine: Physician use of extensive laboratory tests, increased hospital admissions and extended hospital stays for the principal purpose of reducing the likelihood of malpractice suits by patients or providing a good legal defense in the event of such lawsuits.

Deficit Reduction Act of 2005 (DRA): Legislation affecting, among other things, Medicare and Medicaid. The DRA provides states with flexibility to reform their Medicaid programs, Also encourages states to enact their own version of the false claims act.

Delete: The term used by the CMS for the process of removing Medicare enrollees from a plan. *See also* Accrete.

Departmental Appeals Board (DAB): In a civil action brought by the Office of Inspector General, a party may appeal an ALJ's decision to the DAB. The DAB's decision is final and binding 60 days after the parties are notified of the decision. Any petition for review of the DAB's decision must be filed with the appropriate U.S. Court of Appeals before the 60-day period has expired.

Department of Health and Human Services (DHHS): Through the Centers for Medicare & Medicaid Services, DHHS administers the Medicare and Medicaid programs, and is the federal agency primarily concerned with healthcare fraud. Also referred to as HHS.

Department of Justice: The agency responsible for the enforcement of healthcare fraud and abuse at the federal level. Healthcare fraud may be prosecuted by the antitrust, civil, and/or criminal divisions.

Dependent: A member who is covered by virtue of a family relationship with the member who has the health plan coverage. For example, one person has health insurance or an HMO through work, and that individual's spouse and children, the dependents, also have coverage under that contract.

DMO: Dental health maintenance organization. An HMO organized strictly to provide dental benefits.

Diagnosis coding: A numerical coding system, such as the International Classification of Diseases, Ninth Edition, Clinical Modification (ICD-9-CM), that is used to specify diseases, conditions, injuries, services and items provided to patients. Medicare and many other insurance programs require the use of ICD-9-CM codes on most claims for payment.

Diagnosis-related group (DRG): *See* DRG.

Direct contracting: A term describing a provider or integrated healthcare delivery system contracting directly with employers rather than through an insurance company or managed care organization. A superficially attractive option that occasionally works when the employer is large enough. Not to be confused with direct contract model (*see* entry below).

Direct contract model: A managed care health plan that contracts directly with private practice physicians in the community rather than through an intermediary, such as an IPA or a medical group. A common type of model in open-panel HMOs.

Discharge planning: That part of utilization management that is concerned with arranging for care or medical needs to facilitate discharge from the hospital. It includes a system of expediting transfer of a patient to a more cost-effective healthcare facility.

Disease management: The process of intensively managing a particular disease. This differs from large case management in that it goes well beyond a given case in the hospital or an acute exacerbation of a condition. Disease management encompasses all settings of care and places a heavy emphasis on prevention and maintenance. Similar to case management but more focused on a defined set of diseases.

Disenrollment: The process of termination of coverage. Voluntary termination would include a member quitting because he or she simply wants out. Involuntary termination would include a member leaving the plan because of changing jobs. A rare and serious form of involuntary disenrollment in which the plan terminates a member's coverage against the member's will. This is usually only allowed (under state and federal laws) for gross offenses such as fraud, abuse, nonpayment of premium or copayments or a demonstrated inability to comply with recommended treatment plans.

Disproportionate Share Hospital (DSH) Payments: Payments made by Medicaid or a State's Medicaid program to hospitals designated as serving a "disproportionate share" of low-income or uninsured patients. These payments are in addition to the regular payments that hospitals receive for providing inpatient care to Medicare and Medicaid beneficiaries. States have some discretion in determining how much eligible hospitals receive, but the amount of federal matching funds that a state can use to make payments to DSH hospitals is capped at an amount specified in the federal Medicaid statute. Health reform will reduce the amount of both Medicare and Medicaid DSH funds distributed by the Federal government as more people become insured.

DME: Durable medical equipment. Medical equipment that is not disposable (*e.g.*, used repeatedly) and is only related to care for a medical condition. Examples include wheelchairs, home hospital beds and so forth. An area of increasing expense, particularly in conjunction with case management. DME is covered under Medicare Part B.

Doughnut Hole: The gap in prescription drug coverage under Medicare Part D. The gap begins after beneficiaries enrolled in Part D plans pay 100% of their prescription drug costs after their total drug spending exceeds the initial coverage limit until they qualify for catastrophic coverage. The coverage gap will be gradually phased out under health reform, so that by 2020, beneficiaries will be responsible for 25% of all prescription drug costs up to the catastrophic level.

Dread disease policy: A type of health insurance that only covers a specific and frightening type of illness, such as cancer.

DRG: Diagnosis-related group. A statistical system of classifying any inpatient stay into groups for the purposes of payment. The DRG classification system divides possible diagnoses into more than 20 major body systems and subdivides them into almost 500 groups for the purpose of Medicare reimbursement. Factors used to determine the DRG payment amount include the diagnosis involved as well as the hospital resources necessary to treat the condition. Also used by a few states for all payors and by many private health plans (usually non-HMO) for contracting purposes. Hospitals are paid a fixed rate for inpatient services corresponding to the DRG group assigned to a given patient. CMS in August 2007 issued an inpatient prospective payment system final rule that created 745 new severity-adjusted DRGs to better account for severity of illness.

DRG creep: The placement of patients in a higher-value DRG than is warranted by the patient's condition to receive increased Medicare reimbursement.

DRG payment window: The period of time before a patient's admission to the hospital when the services provided to the patient are eligible for Medicare reimbursement. Between the advent of a prospective payment system in 1983 and 1990, hospitals were eligible for reimbursement for outpatient services performed in the 24 hours prior to admission. In 1990, Congress expanded the DRG payment window to include services provided during the three days prior to admission and expanded services to include not only outpatient services, but services furnished by any entity wholly owned or operated by the hospital.

DSM-IV: Diagnostic and Statistical Manual of Mental Disorders, fourth edition. The manual used to provide a diagnostic coding system for mental and substance abuse disorders. Far different from ICD-9-CM. *See also* ICD-9-CM.

Dual choice: Sometimes referred to as Section 1310 or mandating. That portion of the federal HMO regulations that required any employer with 25 or more employees that resided in an HMO's service area, paid minimum wage, and offered health coverage to offer a federally qualified HMO as well. The HMO had to request it. This provision was "sunsetted" in 1995. Another definition, unrelated to the previous one, pertains to point of service. *See also* POS.

Dual Eligibles: A term used to describe an individual who is eligible for Medicare and for some level of Medicaid benefits. To promote better coordination of Medicare and Medicaid services for dual eligibles, health reform creates a new Federal Coordinated Health Care Office within the Centers for Medicare and Medicaid Services.

Dual option: The offering of both an HMO and a traditional insurance plan by one carrier.

Duplicate claims: When the same claim is submitted more than once, usually because payment has not been received quickly. Can lead to duplicate payments and incorrect data in the claims file.

DUR: Drug utilization review.

Durable medical equipment (DME): *See* DME.

EAP: Employee assistance program. A program that a company puts into effect for its employees to provide them with help in dealing with personal problems, such as alcohol or drug abuse, mental health or stress issues and so forth.

Effective date: The day that health plan coverage goes into effect or is modified.

Eligibility: When an individual is eligible for coverage under a plan. Also used to determine when an individual is no longer eligible for coverage (for example, a dependent child reaches a certain age and is no longer eligible for coverage under his or her parent's health plan).

ELOS: *See* LOS.

Employee Retirement Income Security Act of 1974: *See* ERISA.

Employer Health Care Tax Credit: An incentive mechanism designed to encourage employers to offer health insurance to their employees. The tax credit enables employers to deduct an amount, usually a percentage of the contribution they make toward their employees' premiums, from the federal taxes they owe. The tax credits are typically refundable so they are available to non-profit organizations that do not pay federal taxes. The health reform law includes a tax credit for small employers that provide health coverage to their employees. The credit is available to employers with 25 or fewer employees and average annual wages of less than $50,000.

Employer Mandate: An approach that would require all employers, or at least all employers meeting size or revenue thresholds, to offer health benefits that meet a defined standard, and pay a set portion of the cost of those benefits on behalf of their employees. Currently, Hawaii is the only state in the United States to have an employer mandate.

Employer Pay-or-Play: An approach that would require employers to offer and pay for health benefits on behalf of their employees, or to pay a specified dollar amount or percentage of payroll into a designated public fund. The fund would provide a source of financing for coverage for those who do not have employment-based coverage. Currently, Massachusetts, Vermont, and the City of San Francisco impose pay-or-play requirements on employers.

Encounter: An outpatient or ambulatory visit by a member to a provider. Applies primarily to physician office visits but may encompass other types of encounters as well. In fee-for-service plans, an encounter also generates a claim. In capitated plans, the encounter is still the visit, but no claim is generated. *See also* Statistical claim.

Enrollee: An individual enrolled in a managed healthcare plan. Usually applies to the subscriber or person who has the coverage in the first place rather than to their dependents, but the term is not always used that precisely.

Entitlement Program: Federal programs, such as Medicare and Medicaid, for which people who meet eligibility criteria have a federal right to benefits. Changes to eligibility criteria and benefits require legislation. The federal government is required to spend the fund necessary to provide benefits for individuals in these programs, unlike the discretionary programs for which spending is set by Congress through the appropriations process. Enrollment in these programs cannot be capped and neither states nor the Federal government may establish waiting lists.

EOB: Explanation of benefits. A statement mailed to a member or covered insured explaining how and why a claim was or was not paid; the Medicare version is called an explanation of Medicare benefits or EOMB. *See also* ERISA.

Episode of Care: An episode of care refers to all the treatments and services related to the treatment of a condition. For acute conditions (such as a concussion or a bone fracture), the episode refers to all treatment and services from the onset of the condition to its resolution. For chronic conditions, the episode refers to all services and treatments received over a given period of time, commonly one year. Some payment reform proposals include basing payment on episodes of care, rather than on each service rendered. The intent is to increase the accountability of the provider for the care of the patient. The health reform law calls for pilot programs to test this method of payment reform in Medicare and Medicaid.

EPO: Exclusive provider organization. An EPO is similar to an HMO in that it often uses primary physicians as gatekeepers, often capitates providers, has a limited provider panel and uses an authorization system. It is referred to as exclusive because the member must remain within the network to receive benefits. The main difference is that EPOs are generally regulated under insurance statutes rather than HMO regulations. Not allowed in many states that maintain that EPOs are really HMOs.

EPSDT: The Early and Periodic Screening, Diagnostic and Treatment mandate of the Medicaid Act. It requires states to provide any service that Medicaid offers and a physician has deemed "medically necessary." Treatment is available to Medicaid-eligible children under the age of 21. EPSDT will also include follow-up diagnostic and treatment services to correct conditions identified during a screening, without regard to whether the state Medicaid plan covers those services for adult beneficiaries.

Equity model: A term applied to a form of for-profit vertically integrated healthcare delivery systems in which the physicians are owners.

ERISA: Employee Retirement Income Security Act of 1974. One provision of this act allows self-funded plans to avoid paying premium taxes, complying with state-mandated benefits, or otherwise complying with state laws and regulations regarding insurance, even when insurance companies and managed care plans that stand risk for medical costs must do so. Another provision requires that plans and insurance companies provide an explanation of benefits statement to a member or covered insured in the event of a denial of a claim, explaining why the claim was denied and informing the individual of his or her rights of appeal. Numerous other provisions in ERISA are important for a managed care organization to know.

Essential Health Benefits: A benchmark level of benefits created by the health reform law that is meant to ensure a health plan provides a comprehensive set of services. Plans both within and outside of the health insurance exchange will be required to offer at least this level of coverage. Cost-sharing will be limited to the current HSA limits ($5,950 for individuals and $11,900 for families). The Secretary of Health and Human Services will be required to define and annually update the benefit package.

Ethics in Patient Referrals Act: The official name for the laws that have become known as the Stark Laws or Stark I and Stark II. *See* Stark I and Stark II.

Evidence of insurability: The form that documents whether an individual is eligible for health plan coverage when the individual does not enroll through an open enrollment period. For example, if an employee wants to change health plans in the middle of a contract year, the new health plan may require evidence of insurability (often both a questionnaire and a medical examination) to ensure that it will not be accepting adverse risk.

Experience rating: The method of setting premium rates based on the actual healthcare costs of a group or groups. Experience rating will be prohibited under the health reform law beginning in 2014.

Experimental medical procedure: Medical practice, procedure, or treatment still in a trial stage—that is, being tested on humans or animals. (*See* Investigational medical procedure for distinction in meaning.)

Extracontractual benefits: Healthcare benefits beyond what the member's actual policy covers. These benefits are provided by a plan to reduce utilization. For example, a plan may not provide coverage for a hospital bed at home, but it is more cost-effective for the plan to provide such a bed than to keep admitting a member to the hospital.

False Claims Act (FCA): The criminal FCA makes it illegal to present a claim upon or against the United States that the claimant knows to be false, fictitious, or fraudulent. The civil FCA provides that any person who knowingly presents or causes to be presented, to the U.S. government a false or fraudulent claim for payment or approval; knowingly makes, uses or causes to be made or used, a false record or statement to get a false or fraudulent claim paid or approved by the government; or conspires to defraud the government by getting a false or fraudulent claim allowed or paid violates the act. The act also has *qui tam* provisions. Under the civil provisions of the FCA, a defendant can be assessed a penalty of at least $5,000 and as much as $10,000 per claim, plus three times the damages incurred by the federal government in its prosecution and investigation of the case. The criminal provisions provide for a fine of $25,000 and up to five years imprisonment upon conviction.

False statements statute: A statute that prohibits any false, fictitious, or fraudulent statement to the United States or any government agency. This statute is often used to prosecute healthcare providers who make false Medicare or Medicaid claims.

FAR: Federal acquisition regulations. The regulations applied to the federal government's acquisition of services, including healthcare services. *See also* FEHBARS.

Favored nations discount: A contractual agreement between a provider and a payor stating that the provider will automatically provide the payor the best discount it provides anyone else.

Federal Bureau of Investigation (FBI): As the federal government's law enforcement agency, the FBI investigates federal crimes, including healthcare fraud.

Federal Employee Health Benefits Program (FEHBP): *See* FEHBP.

Federal Medical Assistance Percentage (FMAP): The statutory term for the federal Medicaid matching rate—*i.e.*, the share of the costs of Medicaid services or administration that the federal government bears. In the case of covered services, FMAP varies from 50% to 76% depending upon a state's per capita income; on average, across all states, the federal government pays 57% of the costs of Medicaid. The American Recovery and Reinvestment Act (ARRA) provides a temporary increase in the FMAP through December 31, 2010, and additional legislation partially extends this funding through June 30, 2011.

Federal qualification: Applies to HMOs and CMPs. It means that the HMO/CMP meets federal standards regarding benefits, financial solvency, rating methods, marketing, member services, healthcare delivery systems, and other standards. An HMO/CMP must apply for federal qualification and be examined by the OMC, including an on-site review. Federal qualification does place some restrictions on how a plan operates but also allows it to enter the Medicare and FEHBP markets in an expedited way. Federal qualification is voluntary and not required to enter the market.

Federally qualified health centers (FQHC): An entity that has entered into an agreement with CMS to meet Medicare program requirements and is receiving a grant under Sections 329, 330, or 340 of the Public Health Service Act or is receiving funding from such a grant pursuant to a contract with the grant recipient and meets the grant requirements; based on the recommendation of the Public Health Service, is determined by CMS to meet the requirements for receiving such a grant; was treated by CMS as a comprehensively federally funded health center as of January 1, 1990; or is an outpatient health program or facility operated by a tribe or tribal organization under the Indian Self-Determination Act or by an urban Native American organization receiving funds under Title V of the Indian Healthcare Improvement Act.

Federally qualified health maintenance organization (HMO): An HMO that has met federal standards delineated in the federal HMO Act for legal and organizational status, financial viability, marketing, and health service delivery systems. Federally qualified HMOs are required to provide or arrange for basic necessary services with no limitation as to time, cost, frequency, extent or kind of services actually provided. Federal qualification under the HMO Act is voluntary.

Fee-for-service: Method of charging whereby a physician or other provider bills for each visit or service rendered.

Fee schedule: May also be referred to as fee maximums or a fee allowance schedule. A listing of the maximum fees that a health plan will pay for certain services based on CPT billing codes.

FEHBARS: Federal Employee Health Benefit Acquisition Regulations. The regulations applied to OPM's purchase of healthcare benefits programs for federal employees.

FEHBP: Federal Employees Health Benefits Program. The health insurance program for federal employees and their families. The FEHBP is administered by the U.S. Office of Personnel Management. *See also* OPM.

Flexible benefit plan: When an employer allows employees to choose a variety of options in benefits up to a certain total amount. The employee then can tailor his or her benefits package among health coverage, life insurance, child care, and so forth to optimize benefits for his or her particular needs.

Forensic medicine: Specialty area of medicine concerned with the investigation, preparation, preservation, and presentation of medical opinion and other evidence in courts and other legal, correctional, or law enforcement settings.

Formulary: A listing of drugs that a physician may prescribe. The physician is requested or required to use only formulary drugs unless there is a valid medical reason to use a nonformulary drug.

Foundation: A nonprofit form of integrated healthcare delivery system. The foundation model is usually formed in response to tax laws that affect nonprofit hospitals or in response to state laws prohibiting the corporate practice of medicine. The foundation purchases both the tangible and intangible assets of a physician's practice, and the physician then forms a medical group that contracts with the foundation on an exclusive basis for services to patients seen through the foundation. *See also* Corporate practice of medicine acts or statutes.

Foundation for Accountability (FACCT): This nonprofit organization was created in 1995 to bring the consumer perspective to quality assessment of healthcare. It emphasizes outcome measures but also endorses process measures.

Foundation model: Refers to an integrated healthcare delivery system in which a nonprofit foundation is responsible for providing the income to a medical group that is exclusive with the foundation. The foundation is usually, but not necessarily, associated with a nonprofit hospital and is often found in states with corporate practice of medicine acts.

FPP: Faculty practice plan. A form of group practice organized around a teaching program. It may be a single group encompassing all the physicians providing services to patients at the teaching hospital and clinics, or it may be multiple groups drawn along specialty lines (for example, psychiatry, cardiology, or surgery).

Fragmented claims: Billing separately for procedures rather than using a global billing code covering all of these services, when billing separately results in a higher payment rate.

Fraud: Knowing and willful deception or misrepresentation or a reckless disregard of the facts, with the intent to receive an unauthorized benefit.

Fraud Alerts: During the past few years, the OIG has issued Fraud Alerts as a way of informing the healthcare industry about prohibited practices. The alerts are generally brief documents that describe conduct that the OIG perceives as violating the fraud and abuse laws.

FTE: Full-time equivalent. The equivalent of one full-time employee. For example, two part-time employees are 0.5 FTE each, for a total of 1 FTE.

Full capitation: A loose term used to refer to a physician group or organization receiving capitation for all professional expenses, not just for the services it provides itself; does not include capitation for institutional services. The group is then responsible for subcapitating or otherwise reimbursing other physicians for services to its members. *See* Global capitation.

Gatekeeper: An informal, although widely used, term that refers to a primary care case management model health plan. In this model, all care from providers other than the primary care physician, except for true emergencies, must be authorized by the primary care physician before rendered. This is a predominant feature of almost all HMOs.

Generic drug: A drug that is equivalent to a brand-name drug but usually less expensive. Most managed care organizations that provide drug benefits cover generic drugs but may require a member to pay the difference in cost between a generic drug and a brand-name drug or pay a higher copay, unless there is no generic equivalent.

Global billing codes: Billing codes used by Medicare to pay for surgical services that cover not only the surgery itself, but also the usual pre- and postoperative services.

Global capitation: A capitation payment that covers all medical expenses, including professional and institutional expenses. May not necessarily cover optional benefits *(e.g.*, pharmacy). Sometimes called total capitation.

GPWW: Group practice without walls. A group practice in which the members of the group come together legally but continue to practice in private offices scattered throughout the service area. Sometimes called a clinic without walls (CWW).

Gramm-Leach-Bliley Act: Signed into law on November 12, 1999, the act provided for sweeping changes in the regulation of the financial industry allowing, among other things, for affiliations among banks, securities firms and insurance companies that were previously not permitted.

Grandfathered Plan: A health plan that was in place on March 23, 2010, when the health reform law was enacted, is exempt from complying with some parts of the health reform law, so long as the plan does not make significant changes to its policy, such as eliminating or reducing benefits to treat a specific disease or condition, significantly increasing cost-sharing, or reducing the employer contribution toward the premium, among others. Once a health plan makes such a change to their policy, it becomes subject to all the requirements of health reform.

Group: The members who are covered by virtue of receiving health plan coverage at a single company.

Group model HMO: An HMO that contracts with a medical group for the provision of healthcare services. The relationship between the HMO and the medical group is generally close, although there are wide variations in the relative independence of the group from the HMO. A form of closed-panel health plan.

Group practice: The American Medical Association defines group practice as three or more physicians who deliver patient care, make joint use of equipment and personnel and divide income by a prearranged formula.

Group purchasing organization (GPO): An entity authorized to act as a purchasing agent for a group of individuals or entities who are furnishing services payable by Medicare or a state healthcare program, and who are neither wholly owned by the GPO nor by subsidiaries of a parent corporation that wholly owns the GPO (either directly or through another wholly owned entity).

Guarantee Issue/Renewal: Requires insurers to offer and renew coverage, without regard to health status, use of services, or pre-existing conditions. This requirement ensures that no one will be denied coverage for any reason. Beginning in 2014, the health reform law will require guarantee issue and renewability.

HCFA-1500: A claims form used by professionals to bill for services. Required by Medicare and generally used by private insurance companies and managed care plans.

HCPCS: HCFA Common Procedural Coding System. A set of codes used by Medicare that describes services and procedures. HCPCS includes CPT codes but also has codes for services not included in CPT, such as DME and ambulance. Although HCPCS is nationally defined, there is provision for local use of certain codes.

HCPP: Healthcare prepayment plan. A form of cost contract between the HCFA and a medical group to provide professional services but does not cover Medicare Part A institutional services.

Health Care and Education Reconciliation Act of 2010: A law that was enacted by the House of Representatives, by means of the reconciliation process, in order to amend the Patient Protection and Affordable Care Act. It was signed into law in March 2010. The law is divided into two titles, one addressing healthcare reform and the other addressing student loan reform.

Health Care Financing Administration: *See* CMS.

Healthcare Integrity and Protection Data Bank (HIPDB): A national data collection program for healthcare fraud and abuse, formed in October 1999 pursuant to the Health Insurance Portability and Accountability Act of 1996 (HIPAA). The HIPDB is intended to complement the National Practitioner Data Bank.

Healthcare Quality Improvement Program (HCQIP): In 1992, HCFA established this program, which promotes partnerships between PROs (now QIOs) and hospitals, health plans and physicians. These partnerships profile patterns of medical care, identify areas in which treatment could be improved, assist in the development of quality improvement efforts, and measure improvement.

Health Information Technology for Economic and Clinical Health Act (HITECH): Part of the American Recovery and Reinvestment Act of 2009 (ARRA) that addresses the privacy and security concerns associated with the electronic transmission of health information, much like HIPAA.

Health Insurance Exchange/Connector: An arrangement through which insurers offer smaller employers and individuals health insurance plans for purchase. Under health reform, state-based health insurance exchanges will be established to set standards for what benefits are to be covered, how much insurers can charge, and the rules insurers must follow in order to participate in the insurance market. Individuals and small employers will then be able to select their coverage within this organized arrangement. An example of this arrangement is the Commonwealth Connector, created in Massachusetts in 2006. The state-based exchanges under health reform are legislated to begin operation in 2014.

Health Insurance Portability and Accountability Act of 1996 (HIPAA): This statute addresses the availability of private insurance to persons with preexisting medical conditions, among other topics. Its "Administrative Simplification" provisions have impacted the privacy and security of personal health information.

Health maintenance organization (HMO): A system of healthcare delivery that not only pays for the care, but also arranges for the provision of services. In order for the HMO to pay for the cost of healthcare, members must receive care from a participating provider who has contracted with the HMO. In most HMOs, members choose a primary care physician from a panel of physicians affiliated with the HMO. The primary care physician serves as a gatekeeper, authorizing all visits to a specialist.

Health Reimbursement Arrangement (HRA): A tax-exempt account that can be used to pay for current or future qualified health expenses. HRAs are established benefit plans funded solely by employer contributions, with no limits on the amount an employer can contribute. HRAs are often paired with a high-deductible health plan, but do not have to be.

Health Savings Account (HSA): A tax-exempt savings account that can be used to pay for current or future qualified medical expenses. Employers may make HSAs available to their employees or individuals can obtain HSAs from most financial institutions. Employers and employees can contribute to the plan. In order to open an HSA, an individual must have health coverage under an HSA-qualified high-deductible health plan. These HSA-qualified high-deductible health plans must have deductibles (the amount of healthcare costs that must be paid for by the consumer before the insurance plan begins to pay for services) of at least $1,200 for an individual and $2,400 for a family in 2010.

HEDIS: Health Plan Employer Data Information Set. Developed by the NCQA with considerable input from the employer community and the managed care community, HEDIS is an ever-evolving set of data reporting standards. HEDIS is designed to provide some standardization in performance reporting for financial, utilization, membership, and clinical data so that employers and others can compare performance among plans and across organizational structures. A voluntary system, HEDIS uses primarily process measures but also includes some outcome and structural measures. It covers preventive care, acute care, and chronic care.

High-Deductible Health Plan: Health insurance plans that have higher deductibles (the amount of healthcare costs that must be paid for by the consumer before the insurance plan begins to pay for services), but lower premiums than traditional plans. Qualified high-deductible plans that may be combined with a health savings account must have a deductible of at least $1,200 for single coverage and $2,400 for family coverage in 2010.

High-Risk Pool: State programs designed to provide health insurance to residents who are considered medically uninsurable and are unable to buy coverage in the individual market. As of early 2009, high-risk pools operated in 34 states but varied by eligibility requirements, cost-sharing requirements, availability of premium subsidies, and funding sources. The health reform law creates temporary high risk pools in each state (referred to as the Preexisting Condition Insurance Plan) to provide coverage for those with pre-existing conditions who are uninsured. These temporary pools will provide coverage until 2014.

HMO: *See* health maintenance organization.

Hospice: Concept of care provided to terminally ill patients and their families that emphasizes emotional and spiritual needs and coping with pain and death rather than cure.

Iatrogenic injuries: Injuries caused by the medical treatment itself, not the underlying disease.

IBNR: Incurred but not reported. The amount of money that the plan should accrue for medical expenses that it knows nothing about yet. These are medical expenses that the authorization system has not captured and for which claims have not yet hit the door. Unexpected IBNRs have torpedoed more managed care plans than any other cause.

ICD-9-CM: International Classification of Diseases, Ninth Revision, Clinical Modification. The classification of disease by diagnosis codified into six-digit numbers. The ICD-10 will use alphanumeric codes and is scheduled for publication soon.

IDS: Integrated delivery system; also referred to as an integrated healthcare delivery system. Other acronyms that mean the same thing include IDN (integrated delivery network), IDFS (integrated delivery and financing system) and IDFN (integrated delivery and financing network). An IDS is a system of healthcare providers organized to span a broad range of healthcare services. Although there is no clear definition of an IDS, in its full flower an IDS should be able to access the market on a broad basis, optimize cost and clinical outcomes, accept and manage a full range of financial arrangements to provide a set of defined benefits to a defined population, align financial incentives of the participants (including physicians) and operate under a cohesive management structure. *See also* IHO, IPA, PHO, MSO, Equity model, Staff model HMO, and Foundation model.

IHO: Integrated healthcare organization. An IDS that is predominantly owned by physicians.

Illegal drug distribution statute: A federal law that is applicable when a healthcare scheme is accompanied by a narcotics distribution not in the proper course of medical treatment by a licensed professional.

Illegal remuneration statute: Another term for the Anti-Kickback Statute. *See* Anti-Kickback Statute.

Income-Related Premium: Premiums for Medicare Part B and Part D that apply to higher-income Medicare beneficiaries. The Medicare Modernization Act of 2003 established an income-related Part B premium that took effect in 2007, requiring higher-income Medicare beneficiaries to pay a greater share of average Part B costs (35% to 80%, depending on their income). Beneficiaries are required to pay the income-related Part B premium if their income is equal to or greater than $85,000 for an individual and $170,000 for a couple in 2010. The health reform law freezes the threshold for the income-related Part B premium at 2010 levels through 2019, effective in 2011. The health reform law also creates an income-related Part D premium, effective in 2011, using the same surcharge percentages (35% to 80%) and income thresholds ($85,000 for an individual and $170,000 for a couple in 2010) as for Part B. Similar to the Part B premium provision, the income thresholds for the Part D income-related premium are not indexed to increase annually.

Incurred but unpaid claims: Claims that may not have been paid as of some specific date. May include reported and unreported claims. *See also* Lag study.

Indemnification: Obligation, established by contractual agreement or imposed as a matter of tort law, in which one party is required to reimburse another for losses of a particular type.

Independent Payment Advisory Board: A board of 15 members appointed by the President and confirmed by the Senate for six-year terms. The board is tasked with submitting proposals to Congress to reduce Medicare spending by specified amounts if the projected per beneficiary spending exceeds the target growth rate. If the Board fails to submit a proposal, the Secretary of the Department of Health and Human Services is required to develop a detailed proposal to achieve the required level of Medicare savings. The Secretary is required to implement the Board's (or Secretary's) proposals, unless Congress adopts alternative proposals that result in the same amount of savings. The Board is prohibited from submitting proposals that would ration care, increase taxes, change Medicare benefits or eligibility, increase beneficiary premiums and cost-sharing requirements, or reduce low-income subsidies under Part D.

Individual Insurance Market: The market where individuals who do not have group (usually employer-based) coverage purchase private health insurance. This market is also referred to as the non-group market.

Individual Mandate: A requirement that all individuals obtain health insurance. Massachusetts was the first state to impose an individual mandate that all adults have health insurance. There is an individual mandate to obtain health insurance in the health reform law that applies to all Americans with some hardship and income-based exemptions beginning in 2014.

Informed consent: Legal right of all adults, with no upper age limit, to make their own decisions regarding medical, financial, and daily living matters.

Institutional review board: Panel that prospectively reviews and approves biomedical or behavioral protocols involving human subjects that are supported with federal funds. Mandated by the National Research Act of 1973.

Integrated (carve-out) plan: Method of combining two or more benefit plans to prevent duplication of benefits or overinsurance.

Investigational medical procedure: Ongoing clinical observation of an approved agent with respect to immediate and long-term effectiveness, complications, consequences and care. (*See* Experimental medical procedure for distinction in meaning.)

IOM: Institute of Medicine. This organization is part of the National Academy of Sciences in Washington, D.C.

IPA: Independent practice association. An organization that has a contract with a managed care plan to deliver services in return for a single capitation rate. The IPA in turn contracts with individual providers to provide the services either on a capitation basis or on a fee-for-service basis. The typical IPA encompasses all specialties, but an IPA can be solely for primary care, or it may be a single specialty. An IPA may also be the "PO" part of a PHO.

Joint Commission: Formerly the Joint Commission on Accreditation of Healthcare Organizations (JCAHO). A nonprofit organization that performs accreditation reviews primarily on hospitals, other institutional facilities, and outpatient facilities. Most managed care plans require any hospital under contract to be accredited by the Joint Commission.

Lag study: A report that tells managers how old the claims are that are being processed and how much is paid out each month (both for that month and for any earlier months, by month) and compares these with the amount of money that was accrued for expenses each month. A powerful tool used to determine whether the plan's reserves are adequate to meet all expenses.

Licensure: Permission granted by a state, under requirements and conditions established by statute, to an individual or entity to engage in a particular type of activity (for example, practice medicine, nursing, or social work or operate a hospital, nursing facility, or home health agency).

Life care at home (LCAH): Concept of healthcare finance and delivery program models that resemble a CCRC while allowing an elderly person to live at home instead of at a centralized location.

Lifetime Benefit Maximum: A cap on the amount of money insurers will pay toward the cost of healthcare services over the lifetime of the insurance policy. Lifetime benefits maximums are prohibited under health reform.

Line of business: A health plan *(e.g.*, an HMO, EPO, or PPO) that is set up as a line of business within another, larger organization, usually an insurance company. This legally differentiates it from a freestanding company or a company set up as a subsidiary. It may also refer to a unique product type *(e.g.*, Medicaid) within a health plan.

Loading factor: Amount added to the net premium rate determined for a group insurance plan to cover the possibility that losses will be greater than statistically expected because of older average age, hazardous industry, large percentage of unskilled employees, or adverse experience.

Long term care: Continuum of maintenance, custodial and health services to the chronically ill, disabled or retarded. Services may be provided on an inpatient, outpatient or at-home basis.

LOS/ELOS/ALOS: Length of stay/estimated length of stay/average length of stay.

Loss ratio: *See* Medical loss ratio.

MAC: Maximum allowable charge (or cost). The maximum, although not the minimum, that a vendor may charge for something. This term is often used in pharmacy contracting; a related term, used in conjunction with professional fees, is fee maximum.

Magnuson-Moss Warranty-Federal Trade Commission Improvement Act: A federal law governing warranties that protects buyers of any consumer product, any person to whom the product is transferred during the duration of the implied or written warranty and any other person who is entitled under the terms of the warranty or state law to enforce the obligations contained in the warranty.

Mail fraud statute: A federal law prohibiting anyone who has devised a scheme to defraud from using the mails to further that scheme.

Major medical expense insurance: Form of health insurance that provides benefits for most types of medical expense up to a high maximum benefit. Such contracts may contain internal limits and usually are subject to deductibles and coinsurance.

Managed care: A broad term used to describe a system of healthcare delivery that tries to manage the cost of the healthcare, the quality of healthcare, and access to healthcare. Now the term encompasses a variety of healthcare delivery organizations, including HMOs, preferred provider organizations (PPOs), and physician/hospital organizations (PHOs).

Mandated benefits: Benefits that a health plan is required to provide by law. This is generally used to refer to benefits above and beyond routine insurance type benefits, and it generally applies at the state level (where there is high variability from state to state). Common examples include in-vitro fertilization, defined days of inpatient mental health or substance abuse treatment and other special condition treatments. Self-funded plans are exempt from mandated benefits under ERISA.

Master group contract: Also known as a master policy, this is the actual contract between a health plan and a group that purchases coverage. The master group contract provides specific terms of coverage, rights, and responsibilities of both parties.

Material misrepresentation: A false or misleading statement on an application for an insurance policy that influences the insurer's decision as to the prospective insured's insurability. These statements may create the basis for rescinding the policy.

Maximum daily hospital benefit: Maximum amount payable for hospital room and board per day of hospital confinement.

Maximum out-of-pocket cost: The largest amount of money a member will ever need to pay for covered services during a contract year. The maximum out-of-pocket cost includes deductibles and coinsurance. Once this limit is reached, the health plan pays for all services up to the maximum level of coverage. Applies mostly to non-HMO plans such as indemnity plans, PPOs, and POS plans.

McCarren-Ferguson Act (Public Law 15): Legislation stipulating that federal law would apply to the insurance business only to the extent that it was not regulated by state law.

M+C: *See* Medicare Advantage.

MCE: Medical care evaluation. A component of a quality assurance program that looks at the process of medical care.

MCO: Managed care organization. A generic term applied to a managed care plan. Some people prefer it to the term HMO because it encompasses plans that do not conform exactly to the strict definition of an HMO (although that definition has itself loosened considerably). May also apply to a PPO, EPO, IDS, or OWA.

Medicaid: A federal and state-funded program administered by participating states that finances healthcare for the poor. States receive federal matching funds and are free to design their programs as long as they cover certain federally mandated services and run their programs within federal parameters. Demonstration projects, especially for managed care, may get waivers from certain requirements imposed by the federal government. Most individuals are eligible for Medicaid because they receive cash assistance through federal or federally assisted welfare programs, such as Aid to Families with Dependent Children (AFDC) or Supplemental Security Income (SSI). Medicaid also covers some low-income children and pregnant women without regard to their eligibility for cash assistance programs.

Medicaid fraud control unit (MFCU): Entities located in 49 states and the District of Columbia funded jointly by state and federal money that are charged with investigating and pursuing convictions against healthcare providers who defraud the Medicaid program. These units are usually affiliated with the state Attorney General's office and directed by an assistant attorney general. An MFCU's authority is concurrent with the OIG at the DHHS.

Medicaid Waivers: Authority granted by the Secretary of Health and Human Services to allow a state to continue receiving federal Medicaid matching funds even though it is no longer in compliance with certain requirements of the Medicaid statute. States can use waivers to implement home and community-based services programs, managed care, and to expand coverage to populations who are not otherwise eligible for Medicaid.

Medical Information Bureau (MIB, Inc.): System for exchange of underwriting information among insurers writing life and health insurance.

Medical loss ratio: The ratio between the cost to deliver medical care and the amount of money that was taken in by a plan. Insurance companies often have a medical loss ratio of 92% or more; tightly managed HMOs may have medical loss ratios of 75% to 85%, although the overhead (or administrative cost ratio) is concomitantly higher. The medical loss ratio is dependent on the amount of money brought in as well as on the cost of delivering care; thus, if the rates are too low, the ratio may be high even though the actual cost of delivering care is not really out of line.

Medically necessary: Term used by insurers to describe medical treatment that is appropriate and rendered in accordance with generally accepted standards of medical practice.

Medical policy: Refers to the policies of a health plan regarding what will be paid for as medical benefits. Routine medical policy is linked to routine claims processing and may even be automated in the claims system; for example, the plan may only pay 50% of the fee of a second surgeon or may not pay for two surgical procedures done during one episode of anesthesia. This also refers to how a plan approaches payment policies for experimental or investigational care and payment for noncovered services in lieu of more expensive covered services.

Medical Review Criteria: Systematically developed statements that can be used to assess the appropriateness of specific healthcare decisions, services and outcomes.

Medicare: The federal health insurance program that provides coverage for most Americans over age 65, the permanently disabled and people with end-stage renal disease. Medicare is divided into four parts. *See* Chapter 3 **Medicare** for a description of each part.

Medicare Advantage (MA): Formerly known as Medicare+Choice (M+C) prior to the passage of the MMA, a private healthcare plan for Medicare beneficiaries created by the Balanced Budget Act of 1997. It offers a full range of Medicare coverage options by providing a choice between the traditional fee-for-service program or enrollment in a HMO, preferred-provider organization, point-of-service plan, provider sponsored-organization, or an insurance plan operated in conjunction with a medical savings account.

Medicare and Medicaid Patient and Program Protection Act (MMPPPA): A 1987 federal law that broadened the grounds for excluding healthcare providers from participation in the Medicare and Medicaid programs. This statute also granted the OIG the authority to exclude from Medicare and state healthcare program participation individuals or entities that violate the law, even if there has been no criminal conviction.

Medicare-Medicaid Antifraud and Abuse laws: Federal laws designed to control and punish fraud and abuse in connection with claims for payment under the Medicare and Medicaid programs.

Medicare Modernization Act (MMA): Signed into law on December 8, 2003, as the Medicare Prescription Drug, Improvement, and Modernization Act of 2003, the MMA brought about the most sweeping changes to the federal health insurance program for the elderly and disabled since it was created nearly 40 years ago, including adding a prescription drug benefit under Medicare Part D. Providers, physicians, payers, manufacturers, suppliers, employers, and beneficiaries all have been affected profoundly by these changes.

Medicare secondary payor statute: A federal statute providing that when payment sources in addition to Medicare are available, those sources are primary payors and Medicare is a secondary payor.

Medicare SELECT: A 50-state Medicare demonstration program that permits Medicare supplemental insurance companies (Medigap insurers) to offer a preferred provider organization policy to Medicare recipients. Medicare SELECT policies may waive or reduce deductible and coinsurance payments if the plan participant uses a network provider. Plan participants are free to choose a nonnetwork provider, but the Medicare SELECT policies may restrict or eliminate payment of deductibles and coinsurance that the policy would otherwise cover.

Medigap: Private insurance designed to supplement Medicare coverage by paying for medical costs that Medicare does not pay, such as deductibles and coinsurance.

Member: An individual covered under a managed care plan. May be either the subscriber or a dependent.

Member months: The total of all months for which each member was covered. For example, if a plan had 10,000 members in January and 12,000 members in February, the total member months for the year to date as of March 1 would be 22,000.

MeSH: Medical staff-hospital organization. An archaic term. *See* PHO.

MET: Multiple employer trust. *See* MEWA.

MEWA: Multiple employer welfare association. A group of employers who band together for purposes of purchasing group health insurance, often through a self-funded approach to avoid state mandates and insurance regulation. By virtue of ERISA, such entities are regulated little, if at all. Many MEWAs have enabled small employers to obtain cost-effective health coverage, but some MEWAs have not had the financial resources to withstand the risk of medical costs and have failed, leaving the members without insurance or recourse. In some states, MEWAs and METs are no longer legal.

Military suspension: Interruption of insurance coverage while a covered person is in military service.

Minimum Creditable Coverage: The minimum level of benefits that must be included in a health insurance plan in order for an individual to be considered insured. Minimum creditable coverage standards have been established in Massachusetts as part of that state's health reform law.

MIS: Management information system (or service). The common term for the computer hardware and software that provides the support for managing the plan or a department or group that administers and maintains such computer hardware and software.

Mixed model: A managed care plan that mixes two or more types of delivery systems. This has traditionally been used to describe an HMO that has both closed panel and open panel delivery systems.

MLP: Midlevel practitioner. Physician's assistants, clinical nurse practitioners, nurse midwives, and the like. Nonphysicians who deliver medical care, generally under the supervision of a physician but for less cost.

MMA: *See* Medicare Modernization Act.

Modified risk: Person who cannot meet the normal health requirements of a standard health insurance policy.

Money laundering statute: A federal statute that prohibits any monetary transaction in excess of $10,000 where the money was obtained from certain specified unlawful activities, including theft of federal funds or mail or wire fraud.

Morbidity: Frequency and severity of sicknesses and accidents in a well-defined class or classes of persons.

Morbidity table: Actuarial statistics showing the expected average frequency and duration of disability, illness, and sometimes accidents.

Mortality: Death rate in a group of people as determined from prior experience.

Mortality table: Exhibit showing the incidence of death in various age groups.

MSO: Management-service organization. A form of integrated health-delivery system. Sometimes similar to a service bureau, the MSO often actually purchases certain hard assets of a physician's practice and then provides services to that physician at fair market rates. MSOs are usually formed as a means to contract more effectively with managed-care organizations, although their simple creation does not guarantee success. *See also* Service bureau.

Multispecialty group: Just what it sounds like; a medical group made up of different specialty physicians. May or may not include primary care.

NAHMOR: National Association of HMO Regulators.

National Association of Insurance Commissioners (NAIC): National organization of state officials charged with regulating insurance. It has no official power but wields tremendous influence. The association was formed to promote national uniformity in insurance regulations.

NCQA: National Committee on Quality Assurance. A nonprofit organization that performs quality-oriented accreditation reviews of HMOs and similar types of managed care plans. The NCQA also accredits CVOs and produces HEDIS standards.

NDC: National drug code. The national classification system for identifying prescription drugs.

Negligence: An unintentional, but legally blameworthy, tort.

Net revenue: For a hospital, total revenue less deductions for bad debts, charity, and contractual adjustments. Net revenue is the amount of money actually received by the hospital resulting from charges for services provided. Network-based programs: Insurer arrangements with healthcare providers (such as HMOs, PPOs, and point-of-service programs) under contracts to provide services aimed at managing healthcare costs.

Network model HMO: A health plan that contracts with multiple physician groups to deliver healthcare to members. Generally limited to large single-specialty or multispecialty groups. Distinguished from group model plans that contract with a single medical group, IPAs that contract through an intermediary and direct contract model plans that contract with individual physicians in the community.

Nonpar: Short for nonparticipating. Refers to a provider that does not have a contract with the health plan. Nonprofit insurers: Corporations organized under special state laws to provide medical benefits on a not-for-profit basis (for example, Blue Cross/Blue Shield, dental service corporations).

OBRA: Omnibus Budget Reconciliation Act. What Congress calls the many annual tax and budget reconciliation acts. Most of these acts contain language important to managed care, generally in the Medicare market segment. Occupancy rate: Measure of inpatient health facility use, determined by dividing available bed days by patient days. It measures the average percentage of occupied beds in a hospital, either for the entire institution or for one department or service.

Occupational rate: Variation in premium based upon occupational class, due to differences among occupations in the incidence of accidents or illness.

Occupational schedule: Method of insurance listing under which persons are insured for an amount based on their job classifications.

OCR: The Office for Civil Rights under DHHS. Among other duties, this branch is responsible for developing and disseminating technical-assistance materials designed to help Covered Entities comply with the HIPAA privacy rule. It also is charged with enforcement of that rule.

Office for Civil Rights: *See* OCR.

Office of Audit: The branch of the OIG that performs audits of large healthcare entities to ensure that they are filing accurate cost reports. The Office of Audit also identifies specific areas of waste or abuse in CMS's administration of these programs.

Office of Evaluations and Inspections: The branch of the OIG that analyzes particular reimbursement or systems issues and produces reports on various topics.

Office of Inspector General (OIG): Every federal agency has an Inspector General who is responsible for ferreting out waste, fraud and abuse in that agency's programs. The DHHS OIG is responsible for enforcing most fraud and abuse civil penalties and programs exclusions. The OIG's office is divided into three sections: (1) the Office of Audit, (2) the Office of Evaluations and Inspections, and (3) the Office of Investigations. The Office of Personnel Management's OIG oversees the FEHB program. The Defense Contracting Investigative Service located in the Department of Defense oversees the CHAMPUS program. Finally, the Railroad Retirement Board's OIG oversees the Medicare program for railroad retirees.

Office of Investigations: The branch of the OIG responsible for investigating healthcare fraud and abuse cases.

OIG subpoena: One of the primary ways that investigators and prosecutors obtain information in healthcare fraud and abuse cases. The OIG subpoena power permits the OIG to compel only documentary information and not testimonial information. The OIG subpoena may request documents for use in criminal, civil or administrative investigations. The OIG may also serve a subpoena on parties who have no immediate connection with the HHS. *See also* Civil investigative demand.

Onset of condition: Date an illness or disease first manifested itself—generally when medical treatment and advice were first sought or when symptoms were such that an ordinarily prudent person would seek diagnosis, care, or treatment.

Open enrollment period: The period when an employee may change health plans; usually occurs once per year. A general rule is that most managed care plans will have around half their membership up for open enrollment in the fall for an effective date of January 1. A special form of open enrollment is still law in some states. This yearly open enrollment requires an HMO to accept any individual applicant (that is, one not coming in through an employer group) for coverage, regardless of health status. Such special open enrollments usually occur for one month each year. Many Blue Cross and Blue Shield plans have similar open enrollments for indemnity products.

Open panel HMO: A managed care plan that contracts (either directly or indirectly) with private physicians to deliver care in their own offices. Examples include direct contract HMOs and IPAs.

Operating a continuing criminal enterprise: A federal statute that is applicable in the healthcare fraud area where physicians and/or pharmacists are involved in repeated drug violations involving numerous people.

Operation Restore Trust: A two-year healthcare fraud demonstration project instituted by the OIG on May 3, 1995, targeting nursing home, home health, and DME providers in California, Florida, Illinois, New York, and Texas. Under this program, the OIG has issued four to eight Special Fraud Alerts in the first six months to let the public know about healthcare fraud schemes, established a new fraud and waste reporting hotline, and created a voluntary disclosure program for providers targeted by the initiative.

OPL: Other party liability. *See* COB.

OPM: Office of Personnel Management. The federal agency that administers FEHBP. This is the agency with which a managed care plan contracts to provide coverage for federal employees.

Original source: In *qui tam* actions, the term refers to an individual who has direct and independent knowledge of the information on which the allegations are based and has voluntarily provided the information to the government before filing an action.

Outlier: Something that is well outside an expected range. May refer to a provider who is using medical resources at a much higher rate than his or her peers or to a case in a hospital that is far more expensive than anticipated.

Out-of-pocket expense: Those medical expenses that an insured must pay that are not covered under the insurance contract.

Out-of-Pocket Maximum: A yearly cap on the amount of money individuals are required to pay out-of-pocket for healthcare costs, excluding the premium. The health reform law requires new plans offered beginning in 2014 to include an out-of-pocket maximum set at the current HSA level or $5,950 for an individual policy or $11,900 for a family policy in 2010.

Overhead expense insurance: Form of health insurance for business owners designed to help offset continuing business expenses during an insured's total disability.

OWA: Other weird arrangement. A general acronym that applies to any novel and bizarre managed care plan that has thought up a new twist.

Pacific Business Group on Health (PBGH): This is a nonprofit organization of large healthcare purchasers in California and Arizona created in 1989 to improve the quality of healthcare and address rising costs. One of its projects is the California Collaborative Healthcare Reporting Initiative, which represents the collective interests of health plans, purchasers and provider groups.

Package pricing: Also referred to as bundled pricing. An MCO pays an organization a single fee for all inpatient, outpatient and professional expenses associated with a procedure, including preadmission and postdischarge care. Common procedures that use this form of pricing include cardiac bypass surgery and transplants.

Par provider: Shorthand term for participating provider (that is, one who has signed an agreement with a plan to provide services). May apply to professional or institutional providers.

PAS norms: The common term for Professional Activity Study results of the Commission on Professional and Hospital Activities. Broken out by region; the western region has the lowest average LOS, so that it tends to be used most often to set an estimated LOS. Available as *LOS: Length of Stay by Diagnosis*, published by CPHA Publications, Ann Arbor, Michigan.

Patient Protection and Affordable Care Act: The major health reform bill passed by the Senate, signed into law in March 2010. Its purpose was to expand healthcare coverage to 31 million currently uninsured Americans through a combination of cost controls, subsidies, and mandates.

Patient Self-Determination Act: Congressional act mandating that all Medicare- and Medicaid-certified provider organizations notify patients of their rights to make decisions concerning medical treatment and the right to formulate advance directives.

Pay and pursue: A term in OPL that refers to a plan paying for a benefit first, then pursuing another source of payment (for example, from another plan). Also referred to as "pay and chase." *See also* Pursue and pay.

Pay for Performance: A healthcare payment system in which providers receive incentives for meeting or exceeding quality and cost benchmarks. Some systems also penalize providers who do not meet established benchmarks. The goal of pay for performance programs is to improve the quality of care over time.

Payment Bundling: A form of provider payment where providers or hospitals receive a single payment for all of the care provided for an episode of illness, rather than per service rendered. Total care provided for an episode of illness may include both acute and post-acute care. The health reform law establishes pilot programs in Medicare and Medicaid to pay a bundled payment for episodes of care involving hospitalizations.

PCCM: Primary care case manager. This acronym is used in Medicaid managed care programs and refers to the state designating PCPs as case managers to function as gatekeepers, but reimbursing those PCPs using traditional Medicaid fee-for-service as well as paying them a nominal management fee, such as $2 to $5 PMPM.

PCP: Primary care physician. Network physician designated by an employee (and each of his/her dependents) to serve as that employee's entry into the healthcare system. The PCP often is reimbursed through a different mechanism (such as capitation) than other network providers. This physician sometimes is referred to as the gatekeeper. Generally applies to internists, pediatricians, family physicians, and general practitioners, and occasionally to obstetricians/gynecologists.

Peer review organization (PRO): *See* QIO.

Pending claim: Claim that has been reported but on which final action has not been taken.

Per cause deductible: Flat amount that an insured must pay toward the eligible medical expenses resulting from each illness before the insurance company will make any benefit payments.

Percentage participation: *See* Coinsurance.

***Per diem* reimbursement:** Reimbursement of an institution, usually a hospital, based on a set rate per day rather than on charges. *Per diem* reimbursement can be varied by service *(e.g.*, medical-surgical, obstetrics, mental health, and intensive care) or can be uniform regardless of intensity of services.

PHO: Physician/hospital organization. These are legal (or perhaps informal) organizations that bond hospitals and their attending medical staff. Frequently developed for the purpose of contracting with managed care plans. A PHO may be open to any member of the staff who applies, or it may be closed to staff members who fail to qualify (or who are part of an already overrepresented specialty).

PMG: Primary medical group. A group practice made up of primary care physicians, although some may have obstetrician/gynecologists as well.

PMPM: Per member per month. Specifically applies to a revenue or cost for each enrolled member each month.

PMPY: Per member per year. The same as PMPM, but based on a year.

POD: Pool of doctors. This refers to the plan grouping physicians into units smaller than the entire panel but larger than individual practices. Typical PODs have between 10 and 30 physicians. Often used for performance measurement and compensation. The POD is often not a real legal entity but rather a grouping.

Policyholder (also policy owner): The owner of a health insurance policy. In group insurance, the legal entity (employer, union, trustee, creditor) to whom an insurer issues a contract.

Policyholder (self) administration: Situation whereby a group policyholder maintains all records and assumes responsibility regarding insureds covered under its insurance plan, including preparing the premium statement for each payment date and submitting it with a check to the insurer. The insurance company, in most instances, has the contractual prerogative to audit the policyholder's record.

Portability: Characteristic of an insurance policy that allows an insured to accumulate and transfer insurance benefits from one employer to another or from an employer to a nongroup or personal policy.

POS: Point-of-service. A plan in which members do not have to choose how to receive services until they need them. The most common use of the term applies to a plan that enrolls each member in both an HMO (or HMO-like) system and an indemnity plan. Occasionally referred to as an HMO swingout plan, an out-of-plan benefits rider to an HMO or a primary care PPO. These plans provide a difference in benefits (for example, 100% coverage rather than 70%) depending on whether the member chooses to use the plan (including its providers and in compliance with the authorization system) or to go outside the plan for services. Dual choice refers to an HMO-like plan with an indemnity plan, and triple choice refers to the addition of a PPO to the dual choice. An archaic but still valid definition applies to a simple PPO where members receive coverage at a greater level if they use preferred providers (albeit without a gatekeeper system) than if they choose not to do so.

PPA: Preferred provider arrangement. Same as a PPO but sometimes used to refer to a somewhat looser type of plan in which the payor (that is, the employer) makes the arrangement rather than the providers. Archaic term.

PPM: Physician practice management company. An organization that manages physicians' practices and in most cases either owns the practices outright or has rights to purchase them in the future. PPMs concentrate only on physicians, not on hospitals, although some PPMs have also branched into joint ventures with hospitals and insurers. Many PPMs are publicly traded.

PPO: Preferred provider organization. A plan that contracts with independent providers at a discount for services. The panel is limited in size and usually has some type of utilization review system associated with it. A PPO may be risk bearing, like an insurance company or non-risk-bearing, like a physician-sponsored PPO that markets itself to insurance companies or self-insured companies via an access fee.

PPS: Prospective payment system. A generic term applied to a reimbursement system that pays prospectively rather than on the basis of charges. Generally it is used only to refer to hospital reimbursement and is applied only to DRGs, but it may encompass other methodologies as well.

Practice guidelines: Systematically developed statements to assist practitioner and patient decisions about appropriate healthcare for specific clinical circumstances.

Precertification: Also known as preadmission certification, preadmission review, and precert. The process of obtaining certification or authorization from the health plan for routine hospital admissions (inpatient or outpatient). Often involves appropriateness review against criteria and assignment of length of stay. Failure to obtain precertification often results in a financial penalty to either the provider or the subscriber.

Preemption: Federal law preempts any state law that is inconsistent with federal law.

Preexisting condition: A medical condition for which a member has received treatment during a specified period of time before becoming covered under a health plan. May have an effect on whether treatments for that condition will be covered under certain types of health plans.

Preexisting conditions limitation: Restriction on payments for those charges directly resulting from an accident or illness for which the insured received care or treatment within a specified period of time (for example, three months) prior to the date of insurance. Pre-existing condition exclusions are prohibited by the health reform law beginning in 2010 for children and in 2014 for adults.

Preferred provider organization (PPO): Entities that supply networks of healthcare providers to employer health benefit plans and health insurance carriers. Providers contracting with PPOs typically agree to abide by procedures designed by the PPO to control the utilization and cost of health services and to accept the PPO's reimbursement structure and payment levels. PPOs provide incentives for enrollees to use network providers. Individuals may choose a nonparticipating provider and still receive coverage, although they will pay a higher coinsurance or deductible amount.

Premium: The amount paid, often on a monthly basis, for health insurance. The cost of the premium may be shared between employers or government purchasers and individuals.

Premium Subsidies: A fixed amount of money or a designated percentage of the premium cost that is provided to help people purchase health coverage. Premium subsidies are usually provided on a sliding scale based on an individual's or family's income. The health reform law provides premium subsidies through refundable pre-tax credits to individuals with incomes between 133% and 400% of the federal poverty level who purchase policies through the health insurance exchanges beginning in 2014.

Preventive Care: Healthcare that emphasizes the early detection and treatment of diseases. The focus on prevention is intended to keep people healthier for longer, thus reducing healthcare costs over the long term. The health reform law requires new qualified health plans and Medicare to provide coverage without cost-sharing for certain preventive services. The law also includes incentives for states to offer the same coverage in their Medicaid programs.

Primary care: First contact and continuing healthcare, including basic or initial diagnosis and treatment, health supervision, management of chronic conditions, preventive health services, and appropriate referral.

Primary care physician (PCP): *See* PCP.

Private inurement: Situation in which a nonprofit business operates in such a way as to provide more than incidental financial gain to a private individual; for example, if a nonprofit hospital pays too much money for a physician's practice or fails to charge fair market rates for services provided to a physician. The IRS frowns heavily on this.

Procedure coding: Coding services, treatments, and procedures to file an insurance, Medicare, or Medicaid claim for payment.

Professional Standards Review Organization (PSRO): Organization responsible for determining whether care and services provided were medically necessary and meet professional standards regarding eligibility for reimbursement under the Medicare and Medicaid programs.

Profile: Longitudinal or cross-sectional aggregation of medical care data. Patient profiles list all services provided to a particular patient during a specified period of time. Physician, hospital or population profiles are statistical summaries of the pattern of practice of an individual physician, a specific hospital or the medical experience of a specific population. Diagnostic profiles are a subcategory of physician, hospital, or population profiles for a specific condition or diagnosis.

Prognosis: Forecast or prediction of the probable course of a disease or injury.

Prospective payment system (PPS): A reimbursement system that pays a predetermined rate, rather than paying an amount that is determined retrospectively based on incurred charges. Prior to 1983, Medicare reimbursed most hospitals for the "reasonable costs" of inpatient services provided to Medicare patients. Beginning in 1983, Medicare began phasing in a PPS designed to reimburse general acute care hospitals for inpatient operating costs provided to Medicare patients.

Prospective rating: Method of renewal rating that adjusts the rates for the coming policy year in accordance with such factors as known credible past experience, insurance industry and insurance company trends, general business trends (for example, inflation, deflation), current manual rates, and so forth.

Prospective review: Reviewing the need for medical care before the care is rendered. *See also* Precertification.

Provider discounts: Element of network-based managed care programs whereby financial arrangements are negotiated with providers to reduce fees for medical services rendered.

Provider Self-Disclosure Protocol: A component of the OIG's activities that provides healthcare providers with the opportunity to self-disclose any potential fraudulent acts. Self-disclosure may reduce the possibility that the OIG will subject the corporation to a complete audit and investigation, or bring an exclusion action against the provider. In addition, the corporation might be liable for a lower amount of fines and penalties due to its cooperation with the government.

Provider Payment Rates: The total payment a provider, hospital, or community health center receives when they provide medical services to a patient. Providers are compensated for patient care using a set of defined rates based on illness category and the type of service administered.

PSA: Professional services agreement. A contract between a physician or medical group and an IDS or MCO for the provision of medical services.

PSN: Provider-sponsored network; occasionally the acronym stands for provider-service network. Also referred to as a PSO (provider-sponsored organization). A network developed by providers, whether as a vertically integrated IDS with both physicians and hospitals or as a physician-only network. Formed for the purpose of direct contracting with employers and government agencies. A PSN may even end up being an HMO, but its origins are with sponsoring providers rather than nonproviders.

PSO: Provider-sponsored organization. *See* PSN.

PTMPY: Per thousand members per year. A common way of reporting utilization. The most common example is hospital utilization, expressed as days per thousand members per year.

Public Plan Option: A proposal to create a new insurance plan administered and funded by federal or state government that would be offered along with private plans in a newly created health insurance exchange.

Purchasing Pool: Health insurance providers pool the healthcare risks of a group of people in order to make the individual costs predictable and manageable. For health coverage arrangements to perform well, the risk pooling should balance low and high risk individuals such that expected costs for the pool are reasonably predictable for the insurer and relatively stable over time.

Pursue and pay: A term used in OPL that refers to a plan not paying for a benefit until alternate sources of payment (for example, another plan) have been pursued. Also referred to as "chase and pay." *See also* Pay and pursue. QA or QM: Quality assurance (older term) or quality management (newer term).

QIO: Formerly known as peer-review organizations (PRO), quality improvement organizations are independent, private organizations, generally operating at the state level, that review medical necessity, as well as quality and cost of care for Medicare and Medicaid programs. QIOs conduct reviews primarily in connection with inpatient hospital care. Established under TEFRA.

Qualified Health Plan: Refers to insurance plans that have been certified as meeting a minimum benchmark of benefits (*i.e.*, the essential health benefits) under health reform. This will allow consumers to verify that the plan they have purchased will meet at least the minimum requirements of the individual mandate.

Quality Assurance Reform Initiative (QARI): This program, created by HCFA in 1991 to improve oversight of Medicaid managed care, has developed a uniform set of guidelines for a comprehensive, state-based system for ensuring and improving quality of care.

Quality Improvement Organization (QIO): *See* QIO.

***Qui tam* action:** Abbreviation of the Latin phrase "*qui tam pro domino rege quam pro si ipso in hac parte sequitur*," which means, "He who brings the action for the King as well as for himself." *Qui tam* provisions of a statute allow a private person to bring a civil action on behalf of both the United States and herself, and to share in part of the monetary recovery. The individual bringing the *qui tam* action can receive between 15% and 25% of whatever is recovered from the lawsuit, with the remainder going to the government.

***Qui tam* relator:** The private person who may bring a lawsuit on behalf of the U.S. government as well as herself, based on her knowledge of wrongdoing. A relator is often a current or former employee or an employee of a competitor or subcontractor of the organization accused of wrongdoing.

Racketeer Influenced and Corrupt Organization Act (RICO): A federal statute that prohibits the receipt of any income from a pattern of racketeering activity. To prove a RICO case, the government must show that the activity has an affect on interstate commerce, an association of the defendant with the enterprise and participation in its activities, and the commission of a predicate act (for example, mail or wire fraud) at least twice within 10 years.

Rate: The amount of money that a group or individual must pay to the health plan for coverage. Usually a monthly fee.

Rating: Determining the cost of a given unit of insurance for a given year.

Reasonable and customary charges (R&C): Amounts charged by healthcare providers that are consistent with charges from similar providers for identical or similar services in a given locale.

Reinsurance: Insurance purchased by a health plan to protect it against extremely high-cost cases. *See also* Stop-loss insurance. The health reform law provides for a temporary federal reinsurance program for employers that insure early retirees over age 55 who are not eligible for Medicare.

Relative value study (RVS): Guide (not a fee schedule) that attempts to show in a general way by a unit or point designation the relationship among the time, competency, experience, severity, and other factors required to perform services under usual conditions. Such a study becomes a schedule when dollar conversion factors are applied.

Renewal rating: Insurer's review of the premium rates and claim experience for a group plan from which the necessity of rate changes is determined.

Renewal underwriting: Review of the financial experience of a group case and the establishment of the renewal premium rates and terms under which the insurance may be continued.

Rescission: Voiding of an insurance contract from its date of issue by the insurer because of material misrepresentation on the application for insurance. The act of rescission must take place within the contestable period or Time Limit on Certain Defenses. The policy is treated as never having been issued and the sum of all premiums paid plus interest, less any claims paid, is refunded. Under health reform, insurers will only be able to rescind policies in cases of fraud.

Reserves: The amount of money that a health plan puts aside to cover healthcare costs. May apply to anticipated costs, such as IBNRs, or to money that the plan does not expect to have to use to pay for current medical claims but keeps as a cushion against future adverse healthcare costs.

Resource-based relative value scale (RBRVS): A fee schedule that uses a complex formula to determine the payment due a physician for patient services. Factors that are considered in determining the payment due include the resources used, practice expenses, malpractice expenses, geographic location, and whether the services were provided on an outpatient or inpatient basis. Medicare began phasing in this PPS in 1992. The practical effect has been to diminish reimbursement for procedures such as cardiac surgery and raise reimbursement for primary care office visits.

Responsible corporate officer doctrine: A doctrine holding that an officer, even without criminal intent or actual knowledge of an offense, can be convicted for the criminal acts of lower-level company employees merely because of his or her responsible share in overseeing the company's business activities and failure to correct or prevent the criminal violations.

Retrospective rating: Method of experience rating that adjusts the final premium of a risk in accordance with the experience of that risk during the term of the policy for which the premium is paid.

Retrospective reimbursement: Method of payment to providers by a third party after costs or charges have actually been incurred by insureds.

Retrospective review: Reviewing healthcare costs after the care has been rendered. There are several forms of retrospective review. One form looks at individual claims for medical necessity, billing errors, or fraud. Another form looks at patterns of costs rather than individual cases.

Risk contract: Also known as a Medicare risk contract. A contract between an HMO or CMP and CMS to provide services to Medicare beneficiaries under which the health plan receives a fixed monthly payment for enrolled Medicare members and then must provide all services on an at-risk basis.

Risk management: Management activities aimed at lowering an organization's legal and financial exposures, especially to lawsuits.

Risk pools: Method operating in some states through which persons who can afford private health insurance but who are uninsurable for medical reasons can obtain access to health insurance.

Safe harbor: Regulatory or statutory provisions that shield certain designated payment arrangements from criminal prosecution or program exclusion. Safe harbor provisions are contained in the Stark Laws and the Anti-Kickback Statute.

Safety Net: Healthcare providers who deliver healthcare services to patients regardless of their ability to pay. These providers may consist of public hospital systems, community health centers, local health departments, and other providers who serve a disproportionate share of uninsured and low-income patients.

Sarbanes-Oxley Act of 2003 (SOA): Imposes substantial obligations on publicly owned corporations to disclose and certify financial conditions.

Section 125 Plan: A section 125 plan allows employees to receive specified benefits, including health benefits, on a pre-tax basis. Section 125 plans enable employees to pay for health insurance premiums on a pre-tax basis, whether the insurance is provided by the employer or purchased directly in the individual market.

Schedule H: Accident and Health Exhibit of an insurer's Annual Statement. Its purpose is to show the profitability of various categories of health insurance business.

SCHIP: The State Children's Health Insurance Program, under Title XXI of the Social Scurity Act, is jointly funded by the Federal and State governments and administered by the States. It provides health insurance for children in need.

SCP: Specialty care physician. A physician who is not a PCP.

Second opinion: An opinion obtained from another physician regarding the necessity for a treatment that has been recommended by another physician. May be required by some health plans for certain high-costs cases, such as cardiac surgery.

Self-insured or self-funded plan: A health plan where the risk for medical cost is assumed by the company rather than an insurance company or managed care plan. Under ERISA, self-funded plans are exempt from state laws and regulations, such as premium taxes and mandatory benefits. Self-funded plans often contract with insurance companies or third-party administrators to administer the benefits. *See also* ASO.

Sentinel effect: The phenomenon that when it is known that behavior is being observed, that particular behavior changes, often in the direction the observer is looking for. Applies to the fact that utilization management systems and profiling systems often lead to reductions in utilization before much intervention even takes place simply because the providers know that someone is watching.

Service area: The geographic area in which an HMO provides access to primary care. The service area is usually specifically designated by the regulators (state or federal), and the HMO is prohibited from marketing outside the service area. May be defined by county or by ZIP code. It is possible for an HMO to have more than one service area and for the service areas to be either contiguous (that is, they actually border each other) or noncontiguous (that is, there is a geographic gap between the service areas).

Service bureau: A weak form of integrated delivery system in which a hospital (or other organization) provides services to a physician's practice in return for a fair market price. May also try to negotiate with managed care plans, but generally is not considered an effective negotiating mechanism.

Service plan: A health insurance plan that has direct contracts with providers but is not necessarily a managed care plan. The archetypal service plans are Blue Cross and Blue Shield plans. The contract applies to direct billing of the plan by providers (rather than billing of the member), a provision for direct payment of the provider (rather than reimbursement of the member), a requirement that the provider accept the plan's determination of UCR and not balance bill the member in excess of that amount, and a range of other terms. May or may not address issues of utilization and quality.

Shadow pricing: The practice of setting premium rates at a level just below the competition's rates whether or not those rates can be justified. In other words, the premium rates could actually be lower, but to maximize profit the rates are raised to a level that will remain attractive but result in greater revenue. This practice is generally considered unethical and, in the case of community rating, possibly illegal.

SHMO: Social health maintenance organization. An HMO that goes beyond the medical care needs of its membership to include their social needs as well. A relatively rare form of HMO.

Shoe box effect: When an indemnity type benefits plan has a deductible, there may be beneficiaries who save up their receipts to file for reimbursement at a later time (that is, they save them in a shoe box). Those receipts then get lost or the beneficiary never sends them in, so that the insurance company never has to pay.

Shortfall: Difference between the cost for a service charged by a hospital and the actual portion of such charges a hospital will receive as payment from a payor.

Sickness insurance: Form of health insurance providing benefits only for loss resulting from illness or disease, but excluding loss resulting from accident or injury.

Single point of entry: A relatively new term that means an individual uses the same system to access both group health medical benefits and benefits for work-related medical conditions.

Skilled nursing facility (SNF): Institution providing that step in progressive care during which a patient receives that degree of medical care required from, or under the supervision of, registered nursing personnel or a physician.

SMG: Specialty medical group. A medical group made up predominantly of specialty physicians. May be a single-specialty group or a multispecialty group.

Social Security Act: Federal law under which the federal government operates the Old Age, Survivors, Disability, and Health Insurance Program (OASDHI). Includes Medicare and Medicaid.

Socialized Medicine: A healthcare system in which the government operates and administers healthcare facilities and employs healthcare professionals.

Specialty network manager: A term used to describe a single specialist (or perhaps a specialist organization) that accepts capitation to manage a single specialty. Specialty services are supplied by many different specialty physicians, but the network manager has the responsibility for managing access and cost and is at economic risk. A relatively uncommon model as this book is being written.

Spending down: Gradual depletion of one's assets until indigent, thus qualifying for Medicaid benefits. Usually associated with nursing home or long term care.

Staff model HMO: An HMO that employs providers directly, and those providers see members in the HMO's own facilities. A form of closed panel HMO. A different use of this term is sometimes applied to vertically integrated healthcare delivery systems that employ physicians but in which the system is not licensed as an HMO.

Standard provisions: Policy provisions setting forth certain rights and obligations of insureds and insurers under health insurance policies. Originally introduced in 1912, these provisions were replaced by the Uniform Policy Provisions Law (UPPL).

Standards of Quality: Authoritative statements of (1) minimum levels of acceptable performance or results, (2) excellent levels of performance or results, or (3) the range of acceptable performance or results.

Stark I: Colloquial name for the physician self-referral prohibitions introduced to Congress in 1988 by California representative Fortney "Pete" Stark. The initial Stark Law became effective January 1, 1992, and provides that a physician or an immediate family member who has a financial relationship with an entity may not refer a Medicare patient to that entity for clinical laboratory services, unless an applicable exception exists. In addition, the law prevents an entity with which a physician has a financial relationship from billing Medicare or a beneficiary for clinical laboratory services furnished pursuant to a prohibited referral.

Stark II: The 1993 amendments to Stark I that extend the physician self-referral restrictions to Medicaid services and beneficiaries and expand the referral and billing prohibitions to 10 additional designated health services reimbursable by Medicare or Medicaid. The 10 services are (1) physical therapy, (2) occupational therapy, (3) radiology services, including magnetic resonance imaging, computerized axial tomography scans and ultrasound services, (4) radiation therapy services and supplies, (5) DME and supplies, (6) parenteral and enteral nutrients, equipment and supplies, (7) prosthetics, orthotics, and prosthetic devices, (8) home health services and supplies, (9) outpatient prescription drugs, and (10) inpatient and outpatient hospital services. Stark II became effective on January 1, 1995. The statute contains many exceptions, which can be grouped into categories applicable to all financial relationships, to ownership and investment interests, and to compensation arrangements.

Statistical claim: Another term for an encounter whereby data are entered by an MCO's claims department but no FFS payment is made. Occurs in a capitated environment.

Statute: A law enacted by an elected legislature. *Compare* with Common law.

Step-rate premium: Rating structure in which the premiums increase periodically at predetermined times, such as policy years or attained ages.

Stockholder derivative lawsuits: An action brought by a stockholder on behalf of a corporation because the corporation was caused to suffer damage but refuses to redress the act causing the damage.

Stop-loss insurance: A form of reinsurance that provides protection for medical expenses above a certain limit, generally on a year-by-year basis. This may apply to an entire health plan or to any single component. For example, the health plan may have stop-loss reinsurance for cases that exceed $100,000. After a case hits $100,000, the plan receives 80% of expenses in excess of $100,000 back from the reinsurance company for the rest of the year. Another example would be the plan providing a stop-loss to participating physicians for referral expenses greater than $2,500. When a case exceeds that amount in a single year, the plan no longer deducts those costs from the physician's referral pool for the remainder of the year.

Subacute care facility: A health facility that is a step down from an acute care hospital. May be a nursing home or a facility that provides medical care but not surgical or emergency care.

Subrogation: The contractual right of a health plan to recover payments made to a member for healthcare costs after that member has received such payment for damages in a legal action.

Subscriber: The individual or member who has health plan coverage by virtue of being eligible on his or her own behalf rather than as a dependent.

Supplemental medical insurance: Another term for Medicare Part B coverage.

Surplus: Amount by which the value of an insurer's assets exceeds its liabilities.

TAT: Turnaround time. The amount of time it takes a health plan to process and pay a claim from the time it arrives.

Tax Credit: A tax credit is an amount that a person or family can subtract from the amount of income tax that they owe. If a tax credit is refundable, the taxpayer can receive a payment from the government to the extent that the amount of the credit is greater than the amount of tax they would otherwise owe.

Tax Deduction: A deduction is an amount that a person/family can subtract from their adjusted gross income when calculating the amount of tax that they owe. Generally, people who itemize their deductions can deduct the portion of their medical expenses, including health insurance premiums, that exceeds 7.5% of their adjusted gross income. Under health reform, the threshold for deducting medical expenses increases to 10% in 2013 (this increase is waived for individuals 65 and older for tax years 2013 through 2016).

Tax Preference for Employer-Sponsored Insurance: Under the current tax code, the amount that employers contribute to health benefits are excluded, without limit, from most workers' taxable income and any contributions made by employees toward the premium cost for health insurance are made on a tax-free basis. In contrast, individuals currently who do not receive health insurance through an employer may only deduct the amount of their total healthcare expenses that exceeds 7.5% of their adjusted gross income.

TEFRA: Tax Equity and Fiscal Responsibility Act. One key provision of this act prohibits employers and health plans from requiring full-time employees between the ages of 65 and 69 to use Medicare rather than thc group health plan. Another key provision codifies Medicare risk contracts for HMOs and CMPs.

Ten-day free look: Right of the insured to examine a policy for 10 days and return it for a refund of premium if not satisfied with it. A notice of this right is required to appear on the first page of health insurance policies.

Termination date: The day that health plan coverage is no longer in effect.

Third-party administration (or administrator) (TPA): Method by which an outside person or firm, not a party to a contract, maintains all records regarding the persons covered under the insurance plan. Entity also may pay claims using the draft book system.

Third-party payor: Any organization, public or private, that pays or insures health or medical expenses on behalf of beneficiaries or recipients, such as Blue Cross and Blue Shield, commercial insurance companies, Medicare, and Medicaid. A person generally pays a premium for coverage in all such private and in some public programs. The organization then pays bills on the insured's behalf. These payments, called third-party payments, are distinguished by the separation between the individual receiving the service (the first party), the individual or institution providing it (the second party), and the organization paying for it (the third party).

Time-loss management: The application of managed care techniques to workers' compensation treatments for injuries or illnesses to reduce the amount of time lost on the job by the affected employee.

Tort: A civil wrong, leading to the imposition of liability, based on the violation of an obligation other than a breach of contract.

Total capitation: The term used when an organization receives capitation for all medical services, including institutional and professional. The more common term is global capitation.

TPA: Third-party administrator. A firm that performs administrative functions *(e.g.*, claims processing, membership and the like) for a self-funded plan or a start-up managed care plan. *See also* ASO.

TPL: Third-party liability. Also called OPL. *See* COB.

Triage: In health plans, this refers to the process of sorting out requests for services by members into those who need to be seen right away, those who can wait a little while, and those whose problems can be handled with advice over the phone.

Triple option: The offering of an HMO, a PPO, and a traditional insurance plan by one carrier.

Twenty-four-hour care: An ill-defined term that essentially means that healthcare is provided 24 hours per day regardless of the financing mechanism. Applies primarily to the convergence of group health, workers' compensation, and industrial health all under managed care.

Twisting: An agent or broker inducing a policyholder to drop an existing policy in order to take a similar policy from him or her.

UB-92: The common claim form used by hospitals to bill for services. Some managed care plans demand greater detail than is available on the UB-92, requiring hospitals to send additional itemized bills.

UCR: Usual, customary, or reasonable. A method of profiling prevailing fees in an area and reimbursing providers on the basis of that profile. One common technology is to average all fees and choose the 80th or 90th percentile, although a plan may use other technologies to determine what is reasonable. Sometimes this term is used synonymously with a fee allowance schedule when that schedule is set relatively high.

Unbundling: The practice of a provider billing for multiple components of service that were previously included in a single fee. For example, if dressings and instruments were included in a fee for a minor procedure, the fee for the procedure remains the same, but there are now additional charges for the dressings and instruments.

Uncompensated care: Healthcare rendered by providers to persons unable to pay and not covered by private or governmental health insurance plans.

Underinsured: People who have health insurance but who face out-of-pocket healthcare costs or limits on benefits that may affect their ability to access or pay for healthcare services.

Underwriting: In one definition, this refers to bearing the risk for something *(e.g.*, a policy is underwritten by an insurance company). In another definition, this refers to the analysis of a group that is done to determine rates and benefits or to determine whether the group should be offered coverage at all. A related definition refers to health screening each individual applicant for insurance and refusing to provide coverage for preexisting conditions.

Underwriting profit: Insurer's profit from its insurance operations as distinguished from its investment earnings.

Unfair Trade Practices Act (NAIC Model): NAIC regulatory model that sets certain standards for the prompt and efficient handling of claims. Used by many states as the basis for similar legislation.

Uniform Policy Provisions Law (UPPL): Statutory policy provisions of health insurance policies that specify some of the rights and obligations of the insured and the insurer. These provisions, with some modifications, are part of the insurance laws of all 50 states and the District of Columbia.

Uninsurables: High-risk persons who do not have healthcare coverage through private insurance and who fall outside the parameters of risks covered as a result of standard health underwriting practices.

Universal Coverage: A system that provides health coverage to all residents. One mechanism for achieving universal coverage (or near-universal coverage) used under health reform is the individual mandate. Single-payer proposals would also provide universal coverage.

Upcoding: Using improper billing codes to charge Medicare or Medicaid for an item or service to receive higher payments than would ordinarily be due for the treatment of a patient.

URAC: Utilization Review Accreditation Commission. A nonprofit organization that performs reviews of external utilization-review agencies (freestanding companies, utilization-management departments of insurance companies, or utilization-management departments of managed-care plans). Its sole focus is managed indemnity plans and PPOs, not HMOs or similar types of plans. States often require certification by URAC for a utilization management organization to operate.

URO: Utilization review organization. A freestanding organization that does nothing but utilization review, usually on a remote basis using the telephone and paper correspondence. It may be independent or part of another company, such as an insurance company that sells utilization review services on a stand-alone basis.

Utilization: Patterns of usage for a single medical service or type of service *(e.g.*, hospital care, prescription drugs, physician visits). Measurement of utilization of all medical services in combination usually is done in terms of dollar expenditures. Use is expressed in rates per unit of population at risk for a given period, such as number of annual admissions to a hospital per 1,000 persons over age 65.

Utilization review: Program designed to reduce unnecessary hospital admissions and to control the length of stay for inpatients through the use of preliminary evaluations, concurrent inpatient evaluations, or discharge preplanning.

Value-Based Purchasing: A payment reform under which hospitals and other providers are provided bonuses based upon their performance against quality measures. The health reform law establishes a value-based purchasing program in Medicare for hospitals and requires the development of similar programs for skilled nursing facilities, home health agencies, and ambulatory surgical centers, and the testing of pilot programs for other providers, including psychiatric hospitals, long-term care hospitals, rehabilitation hospitals, and hospice programs.

Variable deductible: Deductible amount applied to a particular sickness or injury that is the greater of either the minimum deductible stated in the policy or an amount equal to all benefit payments received from any other medical expense coverage for the same eligible expenses.

Volume discount: Premium rate reduction application to new group case coverages that is based on total case premium (for specific coverages) or total premium and premium per certificate (employee).

Volume loading: Premium rate increase applicable to new group case coverages that is based on the total case premium (for specified coverages) or total premium and premium per certificate (employee).

Well-baby care: Those medical services, physician visits, and immunizations that are recommended by the American Pediatric Association as appropriate and routine care for a normal child from birth to one year of age.

Wellness programs: Employer programs provided to employees to lessen health risks and thus avoid more serious health problems.

Whistleblower: An employee who reports the illegal or wrongful actions of his or her coworkers.

Wholesale HMO: A term occasionally used when a licensed HMO does not market itself directly, but rather contracts with another licensed HMO and accepts capitation in return. This most commonly occurs when an IDS wants to accept global capitation from an HMO, and in turn capitate other providers, since many states will only allow an HMO to capitate providers. Therefore, the IDS obtains an HMO license, but does not go directly to market to the public, and thus does not disrupt existing relationships with other MCOs.

Wire fraud statute: A federal statute that prohibits the use of wire, radio, or television communication in interstate or foreign commerce for the purpose of executing a scheme to defraud.

Workers' compensation: A form of social insurance provided through property-casualty insurers. Workers' compensation provides medical benefits and replacement of lost wages that result from injuries or illnesses that arise from the workplace; in turn, the employee cannot normally sue the employer unless true negligence exists. Workers' compensation has undergone dramatic increases in cost as group health has shifted into managed care, resulting in workers' compensation carriers adopting managed care approaches. Workers' compensation is often heavily regulated under state laws that are significantly different from those used for group health insurance and is often the subject of intense negotiation between management and organized labor.

Wraparound plan: Commonly used to refer to insurance or health plan coverage for copays and deductibles that are not covered under a member's base plan. This is often used for Medicare.

Zero down: The practice of a medical group or provider system distributing all the capital surplus in a health plan or group to the members of the group rather than retaining any capital or reinvesting it in the group or plan.

1.2 Table of Acronyms and Abbreviations

AAAHC	Accreditation Association for Ambulatory Healthcare
AABB	American Association of Blood Banks
AAFP	American Academy of Family Physicians
AAMCN	American Association of Managed Care Nurses, Inc.
AAPCC	adjusted average per capita cost
AAPHO/IHDS	American Association of Physician-Hospital Organizations/ Integrated Healthcare Delivery Systems
AAPI	American Accreditation Program, Inc.
AAPPO	American Association of Preferred Provider Organizations
ABA	American Bar Association
ACG	ambulatory care group
ACHE	American College of Healthcare Executives
ACO	Accountable Care Organization
ACP	American College of Physicians
ACR	adjusted community rating
ACS	American College of Surgeons
ADA	Americans with Disabilities Act
ADC	average daily census
ADG	ambulatory diagnostic group
ADL	activities of daily living
ADS	alternative delivery systems
AFHHA	American Federation of Home Health Agencies
AHA	American Hospital Association
AHLA	American Health Lawyers Association
AHCA	American Healthcare Association
AHCPR	Agency for Healthcare Policy and Research
AHIP	America's Health Insurance Plans
AHP	accountable health partnership
ALJ	administrative law judge
ALOS	average length of stay
AMA	American Medical Association
AMCP	Academy of Managed Care Pharmacy
AMCRA	American Managed Care and Review Association
AMPRA	American Medical Peer Review Association
ANA	American Nurses Association
AOB	assignment of benefits
APC	ambulatory payment class
APG	ambulatory patient group
APN	advance practice nurse

APR	average payment rate
AQAS	Alternative Quality Assessment Survey
ARRA	American Recovery and Reinvestment Act
ASC	ambulatory surgery center
ASHRM	American Society for Healthcare Risk Management
ASO	administrative services only contract
AVG	Ambulatory Visit Group
AWP	average wholesale price; *also* any willing provider
BBA	Balanced Budget Act of 1997
BC/BS	Blue Cross/Blue Shield Plans
BPRs	budget performance requirements
CAH	critical access hospital
CAM	catchment area management project
CAP	capitation
CARF	Commission on Accreditation of Rehabilitation Facilities
CAT	computerized axial tomography
CCN	community care network
CCP	coordinated care program; *also* corporate compliance plan
CCRC	continuing care retirement community program
CDLT	clinical diagnostic laboratory test
CERCLA	Comprehensive Environmental Response, Compensation and Liability Act; also known as SARA or Superfund
CF	conversion factor
CHAMPUS	Civilian Health and Medical Program of the Uniformed Services
CHC	community health center
CHIP	Children's Health Insurance Program
CHMIS	Community Health Management Information System
CLASS	Community Living Assistance Services and Supports
CLIA	Clinical Laboratory Improvement Amendments of 1988
CM	case management; case manager
CMHC	community mental health center
CMI	case-mix index
CMP	competitive medical plan
CMS	The Centers for Medicare & Medicaid Services, formerly HCFA
CMSA	Case Management Society of America
CNM	certified nurse midwife
Copay	copayment
COA	certificate of authority
COB	coordination of benefits
COBRA	Consolidated Omnibus Budget Reconciliation Act of 1985

COC	certificate of coverage
COI	certificate of insurance
CON	certificate of need
CoP	Conditions of Participation
COPC	community-oriented primary care
CORF	comprehensive outpatient rehabilitation facility
CPEP	Clinical Practice Expert Panel
CPI	consumer price index
CPI-MCS	consumer price index-medical care services
CPR	customary, prevailing, and reasonable
CPT-4	Physician's Current Procedural Terminology, 4th Edition
CQI	continuous quality improvement
CRC	community rating by class
CRF	comprehensive referral fund
CRI	CHAMPUS Reform Initiative
CRNA	Certified Registered Nurse Anesthetist
CSR	continued stay review
CTD	cumulative trauma disorder
CVO	credential/central verification organization
CWF	common working file
CWW	clinic without walls
DC	dual choice
DCI	duplicate coverage inquiry
DG	Documentation Guidelines
DHHS	Department of Health and Human Services (also HHS)
DME	durable medical equipment
DMEPOS	durable medical equipment, prosthetics, and orthotics supplies (or suppliers)
DMO	dental maintenance organization
DMS	demand management services
DOS	date of service
DPR	drug price review
DRA	Deficit Reduction Act of 2005
DRG	diagnosis-related group
DSA	disproportionate share adjustment
DSH	disproportionate share hospital
DSM	disease state management
DUM	drug utilization management
DUR	drug utilization review
DX	diagnosis
EACH	essential access community hospital

EAP	employee assistance program
EAPA	Employee Assistance Professionals Association, Inc.
EASNA	Employee Assistance Society of North America
EBIS	employee benefits information system
EBR	employee benefits representative
EBRI	Employee Benefits Research Institute
ECF	extended care facility
EDI	electronic data interchange
E&M	evaluation and management
EMC	electronic media claims
EMO	exclusive multiple option
EMS	emergency medical services
EMTALA	Emergency Medical Treatment and Labor Act
EOB	Explanation of Benefits
EOC	Episode of Care
E of I	evidence of insurability
EOMB	Explanation of Medicare Benefits
EPA	Environmental Protection Agency
EPCRA	Emergency Planning and Community Right-to-Know Act
EPO	exclusive provider organization
EPSDT	early and periodic screening, diagnosis and treatment
EQRO	external quality review organization
ERISA	Employee Retirement Income Security Act of 1974
ESOP	employee stock ownership plan
ESRD	end-stage renal disease
FAHS	Federation of American Health Systems
FAR	Federal Acquisition Regulations
FAS-106	Financial Accounting Standards—Rule 106
Fee Max	fee maximum
FEHBP	Federal Employee Health Benefits Program
FFS	fee-for-service reimbursement
FI	fiscal intermediary
FMAP	Federal Medical Assistance Program
FMC	Foundation for Medical Care
FP	family practice
FPL	Federal Poverty Level
FPP	faculty practice plan
FQHC	federally qualified health center
FQHMO	federally qualified HMO
FSMB	Federation of State Medical Boards

FTC	Federal Trade Commission
FTE	full-time equivalent
FWPCA	Federal Water Pollution Control Act
GAF	Geographic Adjustment Factor
GAO	Government Accountability Office (formerly Government Accounting Office)
GCM	General Counsel Memorandum
GDP	gross domestic product
GHP	group health plan
GME	graduate medical education
GP	general practitioner
GPCI	geographic practice cost index
GPWW	group practice without walls
HCBS	home- and community-based services
HCFA	Health Care Financing Administration, now CMS
HCPCS	HCFA Common Procedural Coding System
HCPP	healthcare prepayment plan
HCQIA	Healthcare Quality Improvement Act of 1986
HEDIS	Health Plan Employer Data and Information Set
HFMA	Healthcare Financial Management Association
HHA	home healthcare agency
HHPPS	home health prospective payment system
HHRG	home health resource group
HI	Hospital Insurance (Medicare Part A Trust Fund); *also* horizontal integration
HIN	health insurance network
HIPDB	Healthcare Integrity and Protection Data Bank
HIO	health insuring organization; *also* health industry organization
HIPAA	Health Insurance Portability and Accountability Act of 1996
HIPC	health insurance purchasing cooperative
HISB	Health Insurance Standards Board
HITECH	Health Information Technology for Economic and Clinical Health Act
HL	histocompatibility labs (independent)
HMO	health maintenance organization
HOI	Health Outcomes Institute
HOPPS	hospital outpatient prospective payment system
HPA	hospital-physician alliance
HPB	historic payment basis
HPNS	Healthcare Provider Networks Section of the AHA
HPSA	health professional shortage area
HRA	health risk appraisal
HRA	Health Reimbursement Arrangement

HRSA	Health Resources and Services Administration
HSA	health services agreement; *also* health savings account
HSB	health standards board
HSR	hospital specific rate
IAF	industry adjustment factor
IBNR	incurred but not reported
ICD-9-CM	International Classification of Diseases, Ninth Revision, Clinical Modification
ICF	intermediate care facility
ICFMR	intermediate care facility for the mentally retarded
ICMA	Individual Case Management Association
ICU	intensive care unit
IDS	integrated delivery system
IDTF	independent diagnostic testing facility
IFEBP	International Foundation of Employee Benefit Plans
IHPS	Institute for Health Policy Solutions
IIHI	individually identifiable health information
IMD	Institutions for Mental Disease
IME	indirect medical education
IOM	Internet-Only Manual (CMS publication); *also* Institute of Medicine
IP	inpatient
IPA	independent practice association
IPF	independent psychiatric facility
IPL	independent physiological laboratory
IPPS	inpatient hospital prospective payment system
IRB	institutional review board
IRC	Internal Revenue Code
IRF	inpatient rehabilitation facility
IRS	Internal Revenue Service
ISHA	International Subacute Healthcare Association
JCAHO	Joint Commission on Accreditation of Healthcare Organizations
JHG	Jackson Hole Group
JPA	joint powers authority
LCAH	life care at home program
LCC	lower of cost or charges
LCM	large case management
LLC	limited liability company
LMRP	local medical review policy
LOB	line of business
LOS	length of stay
LPN	licensed practical nurse

LTC	long term care
LTCH	long term care hospital
LVN	licensed vocational nurse
MA	Medicare Advantage (formerly Medicare+Choice); *also* medical assistant
MAC	Medicare Administrative Contractor; *also* maximum allowable charge
MA-PD	Medicare Advantage Prescription Drug (plan)
MAP	maximum allowable payment
MaxLOS	maximum length of stay
M+C	Medicare+Choice (now Medicare Advantage)
MCE	medical care evaluation
MCM	medical case management
MCO	managed care organization
MCP	managed care plan
MDC	major diagnostic categories
MDH	Medicare-dependent hospital
MDS-PAC	minimum data set—post acute care
MED-PAR	Medicare provider analysis and review
MEI	Medical Economic Index
MERP	medical expense reimbursement plan
MET	multiple-employer trust
MEWA	multiple employer welfare association
MFS	Medicare fee schedule
MGMA	medical group management association
MH/SA	mental health/substance abuse
MHCA	managed healthcare association
MHSS	military health services system
MIB	Medical Information Bureau
MIC	maternal and infant care
MIG	Medicare-insured group
MIP	Medicare Integrity Program; *also* managed indemnity plan
MIS	management information system
MLP	midlevel practitioner
MLR	medical loss ratio
MM	member months
MOB	maintenance of benefits plan
MOR	monthly operating report
MPP	minimum premium plan
MRI	magnetic resonance imaging
MSA	Metropolitan Statistical Area; *also* medical savings account
MSN	Medicare summary notice

MSO	management-service organization
MSP	Medicare secondary payer
MTS	Medicare transaction system
NAEBA	National Association of Employee Benefit Administrators
NAHC	National Association for Home Care
NAHDO	National Association of Health Data Organizations
NAHMOR	National Association of HMO Regulators
NAIC	National Association of Insurance Commissioners
NAMCP	National Association of Managed Care Physicians
NBCH	National Business Coalition on Health
NCCH	National Council of Community Hospitals
NCD	National Coverage Determination
NCI	nursing care institution
NCPA	National Center for Policy Analysis
NCQA	National Committee for Quality Assurance
NDC	national drug code
NDG	network design group
NHB	National Health Board
NIH	National Institutes of Health
NLR	net loss ratio
NMEP	National Medicare Education Program
NMHCC	National Managed Healthcare Congress
NonPar	nonparticipatory provider
NP	nurse practitioner
NPDB	National Practitioner Data Bank
NPI	National Provider Identifier
NPP	Notice of Privacy Practices
NPR	Notice of Program Reimbursement
NPRM	Notice of Proposed Rulemaking
NTIS	National Technical Information Service
OASIS	Outcome and Assessment Information Set
OBRA	Omnibus Budget Reconciliation Act
OCE	outpatient code editor
OCR	Office of Civil Rights (DHHS)
OGE	Office of Governmental Ethics
OHMO	Office of Health Maintenance Organizations
OMC	Office of Managed Care
OMSB	Outcomes Management Standards Board
OOA	out-of-area services
OON	out-of-network services

OOP	out-of-pocket payments
OP	outpatient
OPA	Organ Procurement Agency (independent)
OPD	outpatient department
OPHCOO	Office of Prepaid Healthcare Operations and Oversight
OPL	operational policy letter; *also* other party liability
OPM	office of personnel management
OPO	organ procurement organization
OPPS	(hospital) outpatient (department) prospective payment system
OSC	organized system of care
OSCAR	Online Survey and Certification Reporting System
OSCR	on-site concurrent review
OSHA	Occupational Safety and Health Act (or Administration)
OT	occupational therapist
OTC	over-the-counter drug
OWA	other weird arrangement
P&T	pharmacy and therapeutics committee
PA	physician's assistant
PACE	Program of All-Inclusive Care for the Elderly
PARs	participating physicians
PAS	preadmission screening program
PAS	Professional Activities Survey
PAT	preadmission testing
PBM	pharmacy benefit manager
PC	professional component
PCCM	primary care case manager
PCLR	paid claims loss ratio
PCN	primary care network
PCP	primary care physician/practitioner
PCPM	per contract per month
PCR	physician contingency reserve
PDP	Prescription Drug Plan
PE	parenteral/enteral
PET	positron emission tomography
PHCO	physician-hospital-community organization
PHO	physician-hospital organization
PHP	prepaid health plan
PIN	Provider Identification Number
PIP	periodic interim payment
PIP-DCG	principal inpatient diagnostic cost group

PLI	professional liability insurance
PHI	personal health information
PhRMA	Pharmaceutical Manufacturers Association
PMPM	per member per month
POP	premium-only plan
POS	point-of-service plan
PPI-H	producer price index-hospital
PPMP	provider-performed microscopy procedures
PPO	preferred provider organization
PPP	private practice partnership
PPS	prospective payment system
PRF	pooled risk fund
PRO	peer review organization (now QIO)
ProPAC	prospective payment assessment commission
PSA	professional services agreement
PSAO	pharmacy services administration organization
PSC	program safeguard contractor
PSN	provider-sponsored network
PSO	provider-sponsored organization
PSRO	Professional Standards Review Organization
PSV	primary source verification
PT	proficiency testing; *also* physical therapy/therapist
PTMPY	per thousand members per year
QA	quality assurance
QI	qualified individual
QIC	qualified independent contractor
QIO	quality improvement organization (formerly PRO)
QIP	quality improvement program
QM	quality management
QMB	qualified Medicare beneficiary
QRC	quality review committee
R&C	reasonable and customary charge
RAP	radiologists, anesthesiologists and pathologists; *also* request for additional payment
RBPG	risk-bearing provider group
RBRVS	resource-based relative value scale
RCF	residential care facility
RCRA	Resource Conservation and Recovery Act
Retro	retrospective rate derivation
RFI	request for information

RFP	request for proposal
RHC	rural health clinic
RHHI	regional home health intermediary
RIC	rehabilitation impairment category
RICO	Racketeer Influenced and Corrupt Organizations Act
RIMS	Risk and Insurance Management Society
RN	registered nurse
RUG	Resource Utilization Group
RVS	relative value of services
RVU	relative value unit
SAP	service assessment program
SCH	sole community hospital
SCHIP	The State Children's Health Insurance Program
SCP	specialty care physician
SCR	standard class rate
SDU	step-down unit
SEC	Securities and Exchange Commission
SGR	sustainable growth rate
SHP	state health plan
SHPDA	State Health Planning and Development Agency
SHPM	Society for Healthcare Planning and Marketing
SIC	standard industry code
SIIA	Self-Insurance Institute of America, Inc.
SIW	service intensity weights
SLMB	Specified Low-Income Medicare Beneficiary
SMG	specialty medical group
SMI	supplementary medical insurance program
SNF	skilled nursing facility
SOA	Sarbanes-Oxley Act of 2003
SOBRA	Sixth Omnibus Reconciliation Act
SPBA	Society of Professional Benefit Administrators
SSO	second surgical opinion
SSSG	similarly sized subscriber group
STD	sexually transmitted disease
SUR	statistical utilization review
TC	technical component
TEFRA	Tax Equity and Fiscal Responsibility Act of 1982
TMA	transitional medical assistance
TOP	transitional outpatient payment
TOS	type of service

TPA	third-party administrator
TPL	third-party liability
TQM	total quality management
TSCA	Toxic Substances Disposal Act
UB-92	Uniform Billing Code of 1992
UCDS	uniform clinical data set
UCR	usual, customary, and reasonable fees
UHDDS	uniform hospital discharge data set
UM	utilization management
UNAC	universal access
UPIN	Unique Provider Identification Number
UPR	unitary pricing rule
UR	utilization review
URAC	Utilization Review Accreditation Commission
URO	utilization review organization
VNAA	Visiting Nurse Associations of America
VPS	volume performance standards
WBGH	Washington Business Group on Health
WDC	weighted daily census
WEDI	Workgroup for Electronic Data Interchange
ZEBRA	zero-balanced reimbursement account

2

Patient Care

Susan O. Scheutzow, Esquire
Kohrman Jackson & Krantz, PLL

2.1 Duty to Treat; Patient Abandonment

2.1.1 Creation of a Provider/Patient Relationship; Duty to Treat; Patient Abandonment

The existence of a provider/patient relationship is fundamental to the existence of many patient rights. A physician/patient relationship usually is required prior to a patient being able to sue for malpractice; it also is necessary in order for a patient to be able to seek continual treatment from a physician (*e.g.*, a physician cannot be responsible for abandonment unless a physician/patient relationship exists.) Many patient rights to confidentiality flow from the existence of a provider/patient relationship.

Generally, the provider/patient relationship arises under the theory of implied contract.[1] A person seeks treatment from a physician or other healthcare provider, and the provider accepts the person as a patient by initially rendering treatment. A physician (or other individual healthcare provider) generally is under no legal obligation to accept any particular patient into her practice. Many physicians, however, do enter into contracts obligating them to accept certain persons as patients. Examples of such agreements include agreements with third-party payors (which, at times, require physicians to treat all patients covered by such health plans) or provisions in a hospital's medical-staff bylaws (to which physicians agree) such as those which require the physicians to treat all patients of the hospital's emergency department when the physician is "on-call". In addition, larger group practices may be subject to the same anti-discrimination restrictions as healthcare facilities (*see* Section 2.1.3).

Although no obligation generally is imposed upon a provider to provide medical care, many states have passed "Good Samaritan" laws that provide immunity from civil liability to any person who does choose to provide emergency care or treatment outside of the normal provider/patient context.[2]

Clearly if a physician treats the patient and bills for the service, a physician/patient relationship has been established. However, the law is developing as to when a physician/patient relationship may exist even if the physician never treats the patient or offers minimal services and doesn't bill.

---

1 *Childs v. Weis*, 440 S.W. 2d 104 (Ct. Cv. App. TX 1969).

2 *See, e.g.* Ohio Rev. Code § 2305.231.

Several courts have found that there is a physician patient relationship established between a physician and patient if the physician is "on-call" through an emergency department and if the physician refuses to give advice or treat the patient and the patient is harmed, the physician may be liable.[3] Whether a physician/patient relationship exists, is a factual determination dependant in large part on whether the physician was obligated to treat the patient under the medical staff bylaws. For example, at least one court has held that a physician who was on call and failed to notify the hospital that he had another physician covering for him remained responsible for patients in the emergency department and would be liable for any damage occurring to patients by his failure to respond.[4] However, in a case when a physician was contacted and refused to come in, it was held that a physician/patient relationship was not formed because the physician hadn't signed up for call but was on call "by default" because he was one of only three physicians in his specialty in the area.[5] If a physician gives advice by telephone[6] or in a quick "hallway consult"[7] a physician/patient relationship may be established even if the physician never has a face to face meeting with the patient and doesn't bill for the service.

At least one court has ruled that a physician/patient relationship may be established between a physician who supervises residents who render care and a patient treated by the resident even if the supervising physician never had direct contact with the patient and never was contacted for advice if the physician assumed an active duty to oversee the performance of the residents and familiarize himself with the condition of the patients.[8]

In an interesting case, the Georgia Court of Appeals would not grant a motion for summary judgment for a physician who had referred a patient to a specialist for care and the specialist allegedly malpracticed, stating that the physician's act of evaluating and sending the patient on for specialty care might be enough to establish a physician/patient relationship for that care.[9]

Once a physician has rendered care and the physician/patient relationship is established, the provider is under a duty to provide services for the patient until treatment is no longer necessary or either the patient terminates the relationship or the provider ends the relationship in a manner that does not constitute abandonment of the patient. Proper termination of the physician/patient relationship requires the physician both to give notice to the patient that the relationship will end and to give the patient sufficient time to secure substitute care.[10] Although the physician/patient relationship is based in contract (either expressed or implied), patient abandonment is generally characterized as a tort; be-

---

[3] *See, e.g., Milliard v. Cirrado*, Miss. Ct. App. ED Dec 14, 1999, Case No. 75420; *Hiser v. Randolph*, 126 Ariz 608, 617 P. 2d 774 (Ct. App. AZ 1980); *Mead v. Legacy Health System*, No. A130969 (Or. Ct. App. Oct. 28, 2009).

[4] *Brown v. Bailey*, No. ED 86387 (Mo Ct. App. Nov. 14, 2006). Of interest in this case is that the court found that a physician/patient relationship wasn't established; however, the physician had a duty to the patient which was sufficient for a negligence action.

[5] *Seeber v. Ebeling*, No. 94,666 (Kan. Ct. App. Sept. 1, 2006).

[6] *Kelley v. Middle Tenn. Emergency Phys. P.C.*, No. M2001-00702-SC-R11CV, 2004 Tenn. LEXIS 333 (Tenn. April 23, 2004).

[7] *Diggs v. Arizona Cardiologist, Ltd.*, 1 CA-CV 99-0508, 2000 Ariz. App. LEXIS 119 (Ariz. Ct. App., April 8, 2000).

[8] *Lawnsbury v. VanBuren*, 94 Ohio St. 3d 231 (2002).

[9] *Harris v. Griffin*, No. A 05A0576, 2005 Ga. App. LEXIS 153 (Ga. Ct. App. Feb. 21, 2005).

[10] *See, e.g., Ricks v. Budge*, 91 Utah 307, 64 P. 2d 208 (1937); *Hammonds v. Aetna Cas. & Sur. Co.*, 237 Supp. 96 (N.D. Ohio 1965).

Sample Form Letter to Terminate Physician/Patient Relationship

Dear ___________________:

cause the duty to provide continuing care exists until it is properly terminated, if the provider fails to provide the care, then a breach of a duty has occurred.

2.1.2 Requirement that Healthcare Facilities Accept Patients

As with individual providers, no general law requires institutional providers to provide services to all persons. Institutional providers, however, are subject to a wider variety of laws and regulations that affect the ability of the institutional provider to refuse care to patients.

2.1.2.1 Emergency Treatment

Almost all hospitals that offer emergency care must offer such care to all patients, regardless of a patient's ability to pay. Although this obligation exists in some jurisdictions by common law,[11] this obligation became clear with the passage of the Emergency Medical Treatment and Labor Act (EMTALA),[12] which prohibits hospitals in most circumstances from failing to provide care to stabilize patients in emergencies and active labor. (*See* Section 8.3.2 of this publication for more-detailed analysis of EMTALA.)

In addition to EMTALA, the accreditation standards of the Joint Commission (JC) and the American Osteopathic Association (AOA) require hospitals with emergency facilities to provide services to patients requiring such care. Hospitals that are exempt from federal income tax pursuant to Section 501(c)(3) of the Internal Revenue Code also may be required to provide emergency care to all patients who seek such care, or risk their tax-exempt status (*see* Section 5.2.5 of this publication for more-detailed analysis of the public-benefit requirement for attaining and maintaining federal tax-exempt status).

2.1.2.2 Non-Emergency Treatment

In non-emergency situations, hospitals and healthcare facilities have much more latitude in selecting patients. Nevertheless, a number of restrictions to this generalization apply. Similar to individual providers, healthcare facilities often contractually agree to accept certain patients. Many healthcare providers enter into agreements with third-party payors and agree to accept all patients covered by such health plans based on the facilities' available space or services.

Similarly, any healthcare facility that participates in the federal Medicare or Medicaid program agrees to accept all Medicare or Medicaid patients to the facility's capacity. Healthcare facilities that

---

This letter is to inform you that I will cease providing you medical care. Since your condition requires continued medical attention, I suggest that you secure another physician to provide medical care immediately. If you desire, I will continue to provide care to you for a period of thirty (30) days following the date of this letter, but as of ________________, I will no longer be available to provide you care.

Upon your request, I will make available your medical records to the physician that you select.

Very truly yours,

____

[11] *Wilmington Gen. Hospital v. Manlove*, 54 Del. 15, 174 A 2d 135 (1961).

[12] 42 U.S.C. §§ 1395cc, 1395dd.

have received funding for construction and modernization under the Federal Hospital Survey and Construction Act (also known as the Hill-Burton Act)[13] have an obligation to provide a "reasonable volume" of services to persons who are unable to pay for such services. Also affecting a facility's ability to refuse patients are many state property-tax exemption statutes that require healthcare facilities to provide charity care prior to qualifying for a state-tax exemption. Public hospitals also may have significant restrictions on their ability to refuse care.

Regardless of whether a healthcare facility may otherwise refuse treatment to a particular patient, most healthcare facilities are covered by a variety of federal non-discrimination statutes including Title VI of the Civil Rights Act of 1964, Section 504 of the Rehabilitation Act of 1973, Title III of the Older Americans Amendments of 1975, and the Americans With Disabilities Act of 1990, which prohibits healthcare facilities from discriminating on the basis of a protected classification such as race, color, national origin, age, or handicap.

2.1.3 Conscience Laws

Most states have some type of conscience law which provides that a provider does not need to provide care which violates the provider's conscience, such as providing abortion or sterilization services. Case law developing in this area focuses on the responsibility of the provider to provide information to a patient to allow the patient the opportunity to receive care from another provider.[14]

2.2 Consent to Medical Treatment

2.2.1 Generally

The right of every individual to be free of undesired personal contact from another is a fundamental tenet of American law, and the United States courts have jealously guarded this right. In the words of the Supreme Court:

> No right is held more sacred, or is more carefully guarded by the common law, than the right of every individual to the possession and control of his own person, free from all restraint or interference of others, unless by clear and unquestionable authority of law.[15]

From this concept of individual autonomy and self-determination flows the doctrine of informed consent. The doctrine of informed consent has two components: first, that the right of a person to determine what may be done to her body includes the right to consent to medical care; and second, that true consent cannot be given unless the patient is given all relevant information and has an opportunity to evaluate the available risks involved.[16] Therefore, if a physician or other healthcare professional renders medical treatment without a patient's consent, it is actionable as a tort.

---

[13] 42 U.S.C. §§ 291 *et seq.*

[14] *See, e.g.*, *Brownfield v. Daniel Freeman Marina Hosp.*, 208 Cal App 3d 405 (1989) regarding hospital's failure to provide a patient with information regarding the "morning after" contraceptive medication.

[15] *Union Pac. R.R. Co. v. Botsford*, 141 U.S. 250, 251, 11 S. Ct. 1000, 1001, 351 L. Ed. 734, 735 (1891).

[16] *See, e.g.*, *Canterbury v. Spence*, 464 F.2d 772 (D.C. 1972).

Historically, an action based on a lack of informed consent was brought as an action for the intentional tort of battery; unless effective consent was given, rendering medical treatment constituted an unconsented touching or a battery. The requirement of informed consent became so accepted that it is now considered the standard of care and the failure to obtain informed consent now also constitutes negligence or malpractice. In some instances, failure to give complete information may also give rise to an action for misrepresentation or fraud. The characterization of a lack of informed consent as the intentional tort battery or as negligence may have implications for statutes of limitations, insurance coverage, and the ability of a plaintiff to recover punitive damages; as punitive damages are generally not permitted for negligence claims, and insurance policies generally refuse coverage for intentional acts.

The legal standard for proper informed consent is the disclosure to the patient of:

1. the patient's condition;
2. the nature of the proposed treatment;
3. the benefits reasonably expected from a proposed treatment, together with the material risks and dangers of the proposed treatment; and
4. treatment alternatives, as well as the risks and benefits of such alternatives.[17]

The current development in the law regarding informed consent has focused on whether the standard for information to be given to the patient is what a "reasonable physician" should provide or what a "reasonable patient" would want to have. Under a "reasonable physician" standard, the patient must be given information that would customarily be given by physicians in the same specialty, in the same circumstances; under the "reasonable patient" standard, the physician must give information that would be relevant to reasonable patients in the same circumstances.[18] A small number of states have adopted a "subjective patient standard," requiring the physician to give information that the specific patient needed to know given that patient's circumstances.[19] The subjective patient standard requires physicians to have knowledge of their patients and subjects the physician to hindsight analysis of the patient's circumstances.[20]

Generally, consent may be oral or written, although some state statutes provide for statutory presumptions that appropriate informed consent was obtained if state-dictated written-consent forms are completed. The responsibility to obtain informed consent historically has rested with the physician. However, at least one court has stated that if the hospital is responsible for the physician's malpractice on a vicarious liability theory, the hospital may also be held liable for the physician's failure to obtain informed consent.[21]

---

[17] *See, e.g., Nickell v Gonzalez*, 17 Ohio St. 3d 136, 477 N.E.2d 1145 (1985); *Dries v. Grecor*, 424 N.Y.S. 2d 561, 72 A.2d 231 (1980); D. Louisell & H. Williams, *Medical Malpractice* § 2201 (1974); *Holt v. Nelson*, 11 Wash. App. 230, 523 P. 2d 211 (1974).

[18] *See, e.g., Ketchup v. Howard*, 247 Ga. App 54 (2000), which contains a survey of other states' laws regarding informed consent.

[19] *See, e.g., Scott v. Bradford*, 606 P. 2d 554 (Okla. 1979).

[20] For a state by state analysis of the various standards used, *see* King & Moulton, *Rethinking Informed Consent: The Case for Shared Medical Decision Making*, Am. J. of L. & Med, 32 (2006): 429–501.

[21] *Mueller v. Auker* No, CV-04-399-S-BLW (D. Idaho, April 14, 2006).

While hospitals or other healthcare facilities historically have had no independent duty to secure consent,[22] it is important for hospitals to have policies requiring informed consent, as the JC and AOA accreditation guidelines for hospitals require hospitals to have consent policies; further, state-licensing statutes may also require hospital consent procedures. The federal government has also established guidelines for informed consent and documentation regarding informed consent.[23] The revised Interpretive Guidelines of the federal law published by the Centers for Medicare and Medicaid became effective on April 13, 2007.[24] These regulations apply to obtaining informed consent for patients being treated at hospitals certified for participation in the federal Medicare and Medicaid programs.

2.2.1.1 *Requirements for Consent Form*

Informed consent is a process and is not limited to whether or not a form has been signed. The decision to accept or reject all medical treatment is to be based on informed consent. Generally when a patient signs an admission consent form the patient consents to testing for diagnosis and general hospital care, but specific medical treatment requires additional explanation and consent. Notwithstanding the legal requirement that the patient give informed consent for *all* medical treatment, CMS, the JC and AOA require *written* consent forms for specific procedures such as surgeries and other invasive procedures.[25] Many states provide a statutory presumption that informed consent was given if a consent form is signed that complies with statutory requirements.[26]

Written consent forms are not practical for all medical care but providers should obtain signed consent forms when required by law or an accrediting organization and should also consider consent forms for high risk activities. Regardless of whether a signed consent form is obtained, physicians and other providers should always take care to document in their records that they provided the patient with the relevant information and that the patient consented.

2.2.1.2 *Disclosure of Special Risk Factors of Providers*

Generally, informed consent involves informing the patient of the risks and benefits associated with various treatment alternatives. Recently, however, some courts have begun to recognize that a healthcare provider may need to disclose specific risks inherent with having a particular provider render the care. In *Johnson v. Kakemoor*,[27] the Wisconsin Supreme Court held that, in order to make an informed decision, a patient may need to have all relevant information presented, and that information regarding a surgeon's experience and skill may be considered relevant for a patient to know in order to give informed consent. When the patient specifically asks the physician about his or her experience or credentials and the physician does not provide all of the relevant information, or was not truthful in

---

22 *See, e.g., Bedel v. University OB/GYN Assocs.*, 76 Ohio App. 3d 742, 603 N.E.2d 342 (1991); *Gibson v. Methodist Hosp.*, 822 S.W. 2d 95 (Tex. App. 1991).

23 42 C.F.R. § 482.13(b)(2) relative to consent; 42 C.F.R. § 482.24(c)(2)(v) relative to documentation in the medical record; and 42 C.F.R. § 482.51(b)(2) relative to surgical services.

24 *See* http://www.cms.hhs.gov/SurveyCertificationGenInfo/downloads/SCLetter07-17.pdf.

25 42 CFR § 482.51 (b)(2).

26 *See e.g.* Ohio Rev. Code § 2317.54

27 *Johnson v. Kakemoor*, 199 Wis 2d 615, 545 N.W. 2d 495 (Wis. 1996); *Housel v. James*, No. 25031-8-111 (Wash Ct. App., Nov. 15, 2007), holding that the plaintiff didn't show that the defendants lack of experience was relevant.

providing the information, it is easier for the patient to successfully argue that the physician's alleged experience or credentials provided the basis for the patient's consent.[28]

Although this legal theory currently is in its infancy, patients are beginning to argue that any provider-specific information (*e.g.*, a physician's own health status, any impairment by drugs or alcohol, and any research interests of the physician) should be disclosed, as well as the physician's skill and experience.[29]

2.2.1.3 *Exceptions to the Requirement to Obtain Consent*

A patient must be fully informed and give express consent to medical procedures except in three circumstances in which actual informed consent is not necessary but, rather, is implied from the circumstances: (1) when additional procedures are necessary to accomplish the initial treatment for which there was consent; (2) in emergency situations when a presumption can be made that the patient would give consent to protect her life; and (3) when giving the patient full and complete information would be harmful to the patient.[30]

Although the law consistently has recognized these exceptions to the necessity of a physician to obtain informed consent, such exceptions may not be used to violate a patient's wishes. For instance, in an emergency situation (when it is not possible to obtain informed consent), the patient's consent is implied when the treatment considered by the physician is necessary to preserve the life or health of the patient; however, if the patient has initially refused to consent to treatment and the patient's condition becomes critical, the physician may not claim that the doctrine of implied consent in an emergency has created the right to render the treatment that was previously refused.

Similarly, another exception to the requirement for informed consent is when the risk of disclosure poses a threat to the patient because the patient might become ill or so distraught that treatment is severely hindered or becomes unfeasible.[31] The physician's privilege to withhold information, however, is severely limited; such information may be withheld only when it is absolutely required for therapeutic reasons that information be withheld, and not simply when the physician fears that the patient will make a treatment decision with which the physician does not agree.

2.2.1.4 *Special Consent Statutes*

Most states provide that special consent must be obtained for specific procedures, *e.g.*, prior to a person undergoing a test to detect the human immunodeficiency virus (HIV), prior to abortion services, and prior to patients receiving a variety of mental health procedures such as electroshock therapy. State law should always be consulted for special-consent statutes.

---

[28] *See Johnson*, *id.*; *Willis v. Bender*, 596 F. 3d 1244 (10th Dist., 2010); *but see Howard v. Univ. of Medicine and Dentistry of N.J.*, 172 N.J. 537, 800 A. 2d 73 (2002).

[29] *See e.g. Schwaller v. Maguire*, No. C-020555, 2003 Ohio App. LEXIS 6227 (Ohio Ct. App. Dec. 19, 2003), where a patient unsuccessfully alleged that a physician's failure to disclose his addiction to pain killers negated the consent the patient gave for surgery.

[30] *See, e.g.*, *Leach v. Shapiro*, 13 Ohio App. 3d 393, 469 N.E.2d 1047 (1984).

[31] *See Canterbury v. Spence*, 464 F.2d 772 (D.C. 1972).

2.2.1.5 Restraint and Seclusion

The issue of whether hospitalized patients may be restrained and/or subject to seclusion gained national attention with the death of 11-year-old Andrew McClain in 1998 from asphyxiation while being restrained at a psychiatric hospital in Connecticut. A Connecticut newspaper investigated the use of restraints and concluded that 142 patient deaths occurred between 1988 and 1998 due to improper restrains or seclusion. Restraints and seclusion are almost always imposed without the patient's consent. In January 2007, Centers for Medicare and Medicaid final rule on the use of restraints became effective. Restraints are defined as any manual method (including mechanical duress) which reduces the ability of a patient to move his or her arms or legs, body or head or any medication used to manage patient's behavior or restrict freedom of movement if such is not the standard treatment or dosage for the patient's condition, and seclusion which is defined as the involuntary confinement of a person in a room or area where the person is physically prevented from leaving.[32]

The rule which applies to all Medicare participating hospitals provides that the use of restraints or seclusion must be ordered by a physician or other licensed independent practitioner responsible for the patient's care and the order must be reviewed every four hours for adults and more frequently for children, in addition to other requirements. Simultaneous use of restraint and seclusion may only be used with continual monitoring of the patient. The law imposes a high standard on hospitals utilizing restraints and seclusion to control patient's behavior.

2.2.2 Constitutional Protection

In addition to the common-law right to give informed consent prior to receiving medical treatment, the courts have recognized the patient's constitutional right to refuse medical treatment. While tort law addresses the liability of physicians and others for treating a patient without the patient's informed consent; unless the right to determine whether to receive medical treatment is recognized as a constitutional right, the state may place restrictions upon an individual's right to determine her own appropriate medical treatment. The constitutional protection of a person's choice of medical treatment has been found to flow from the United States Constitution and through many state constitutions. Some states have characterized it as a protected liberty interest; others a protected right to privacy and in certain circumstances it may be characterized as a valid exercise of one's constitutionally protected religious freedom. Because persons generally refuse medical treatment in the end-of-life context, constitutional issues usually have been addressed in this context, and have become known as the "right to die" cases.

The U.S. Supreme Court addressed the issue in *Cruzan v. Director, Missouri Dept. of Health*[33] and found the right to refuse medical treatment is the constitutionally protected liberty interest under federal law, arising from the Fourteenth Amendment. This right grants a person the right to refuse medical treatment even if that treatment will maintain the person's life. Although the Court acknowledged that many state courts have held that the right to refuse treatment is part of a generalized constitutional right of privacy, the Court reasoned that the right to refuse treatment is more properly analyzed in terms of

[32] *See* 42 C.F.R. § 582.13.

[33] *Cruzan v. Director, Missouri Dept. of Health*, 497 U.S. 261, 110 S. Ct. 2841, 111 L. Ed. 2d 224 (1990).

a Fourteenth Amendment liberty interest. This liberty interest must then be weighed against the state's interests to determine if the deprivation of the liberty interest is constitutionally permissible.

The characterization of the right to refuse treatment as a liberty interest, rather than a fundamental privacy right may have legal significance; because traditionally, a privacy interest may only be overridden by a *compelling* state interest, whereas a liberty interest may be subject to state regulation as long as it is *rationally related* to a legitimate state interest.[34] Therefore, even though the U.S. Supreme Court has characterized the right to refuse treatment as a liberty interest, which allows states to impose restrictions on the right, additional patient rights may be given in the states which characterize the right as a privacy right under their state constitutions. The constitutionally protected right to free exercise of religion also has been raised as a basis for refusal of specific medical treatment.[35]

While *Cruzan* recognized a constitutionally protected right to refuse medical treatment, it does permit a state to abridge that right and require a patient to accept medical treatment if the state has a competing interest. Generally, four possible state interests have been recognized that could counteract the individual's constitutional rights:

- protection of third parties;
- prevention of suicide;
- preservation of ethical standards of the medical profession; and
- preservation of human life.[36]

In *Cruzan*, the Court permitted the state of Missouri to exercise its interest by requiring that it be shown by clear and convincing evidence that Nancy Cruzan would have refused life-sustaining treatment. Courts have held that the state interests generally weaken and the individual's rights grow as the "degree of bodily invasion [of the procedure] increases and the prognosis dims."[37] Most of the case law has developed in the end-of-life context, as discussed in Section 2.3.

2.2.3 Incompetent's Right to Make Treatment Decisions

Incompetency may result from a person's youth, mental incompetence, illness, injury, or external influence (*e.g.*, drugs or alcohol). Whatever the reason, if a patient is unable to make his or her own treatment decisions and these decisions must be made, someone must make them for the patient.

---

[34] *See Griswold v. Connecticut*, 381 U.S. 479, 85 S. Ct. 1678, 14 L. Ed. 2d 510 (1965); *Eisenstadt v. Baird*, 405 U.S. 438, 92 S. Ct. 1029, 31 L. Ed. 2d 349 (1972); Bopp & Coleson, *Webster and the Future of Substantive Due Process*, 28 DUQ. L. REV. 271, 280 (1990).

[35] *In re Milton*, 29 Ohio St. 3d, 505 N.E.2d 255 (1987).

[36] *Cruzan*, *supra*.

[37] *In re Quinlan*, 70 N.J. 10, 40, 355 A.2d 647 (1976), *cert. denied*, sub nom. *Garger v. New Jersey*, 429 U.S. 922, 97 S. Ct. 319, 50 L.Ed. 289 (1976); *see also Leach v. Akron Gen. Med. Ctr.*, 68 Ohio Misc. 1, 22 Ohio 3d 49, 426 N.E.2d 809 (Ohio Probate 1980).

There is no clear definition of incompetency in the law for purposes of medical decision making. The key in determining mental competency for purposes of medical decisionmaking is whether the patient has the capacity to make informed decisions with respect to medical care.[38]

Historically, principles of decision making for incompetents have been extremely inconsistent. Physicians and other healthcare professionals often would make decisions based on the medical merits of each case, and might not place much weight on the wishes of the patient's family or the patient's own earlier-expressed intentions. Some early courts took the position that mentally ill patients had no right to make their own treatment decisions, and courts regularly made decisions on behalf of such patients. Alternatively, treatment decisions often were made by healthcare professionals in consultation with the family.

For years, many courts, professionals, and scholars wrestled with the issue of medical decision-making for incompetents. Public awareness of the issue increased dramatically in the mid 1970s with the case of Karen Ann Quinlan. *In re Quinlan*[39] and its progeny established that, if the personal right to choose medical treatment is to have any meaning, then a person must maintain the right during periods of incompetency, and third parties must be able to exercise it on behalf of the incompetent patient.

The court, in *Superintendent of Belchertown v. Saikewicz*, summed up the rights of incompetents to make medical decisions when it stated: "[W]e recognize a general right in all persons to refuse medical treatment in appropriate circumstances. The recognition of that right must extend to the case of an incompetent, as well as a competent, patient because the value of human dignity extends to both."[40]

It is now widely accepted that incompetents have the right to make medical-treatment decisions, although some dispute continues as to what decisions may be made, who can act in the place of the incompetent in making those decisions, and what standard of decision making should be used.

If the patient lacks the capacity to consent, then consent should be obtained from a third party. Unless the patient has a legal guardian appointed, consent is usually obtained from the patient's "next of kin." Some states have statutes authorizing consent from family members; other states established no statutory designation, and have relied on the next of kin.

2.2.4 Minors

When a patient is a minor, consent to medical treatment must be obtained from the parent or legal guardian. Exceptions to parental consent include when the child requires immediate medical care and a parent or guardian is not available,[41] and when a child is emancipated and is no longer under the control of her parents. In addition, some states have adopted a common-law "mature minor" doctrine, which has been invoked in situations where the child is sufficiently mature to make her own healthcare decisions.[42]

---

38 *See, e.g., Bartling v. Superior Ct.*, 163 Cal. App. 3d 186, 209 Cal. Rptr. 220 (1984); *In re Quakenbusch*, 156 N.J. Super. 282, 383 A.2d 785 (1978).

39 *In re Quinlan, supra.*

40 *Superintendent of Belchertown v. Saikewicz*, 373 Mass. 728, 745, 370 N.E.2d 417, 427 (1977).

41 *See, e.g.*, Miss. Code Ann. § 41-41-3; N.Y. Pub. Health Law § 2504.4.

42 *Younts v. St. Francis Hosp. & Sch. of Nursing*, 205 Kan. 292, 469 P.2d 330 (1970).

The mature-minor doctrine is at times used to protect a healthcare provider from liability for treating a minor when the minor has requested the treatment and appeared to be an adult. Without such a doctrine, the parents or guardians of the child could sue the healthcare provider for providing care without appropriate consent, because the minor would not have the legal capacity to give consent. Many states have laws authorizing minors to consent to treatment in certain circumstances, such as for treatment of venereal disease, alcoholism, drug abuse, and mental illness. State statutes must always be consulted.[43]

A parent's right to consent to treatment for her minor children is limited to decisions made in the best interest of the child. State child-neglect laws may include the parent's failure to provide necessary medical care in its definition of "neglect." A parent's religious-based objections to treatment generally do not justify a refusal of treatment of minors.[44] Particularly problematic for healthcare providers is what to do when parents disagree about treatment; in such cases, judicial intervention may be necessary.

The U.S. Supreme Court also recognized a minor's right to make the decision to have an abortion without parental consent if the minor is mature enough to make her own decision or if it is in the minor's best interest to have an abortion without her parents' consent.[45] This follows the state law decisions recognizing the rights of a mature minor to make her own decisions and requiring parents to make decisions for children not able to give their own consent based on the child's best interests. The Court also held that a state can impose restrictions on the minor's right, such as requiring her parents to be notified prior to the abortion.

2.2.5 Consent for Experimentation

Federal regulations require the approval of a hospital's Institutional Review Board (IRB) for all federally funded research involving human subjects, or research that involves drugs or devices (including clinical trials). The IRB is required to review the research proposal to ensure that the subjects are not exposed to any unnecessary risk, and to guarantee that prospective subjects have been given a sufficient opportunity to obtain information and give consent. An IRB must also ensure that individuals are not coerced into participating in the study.

Federally funded research involving human subjects is governed by regulations promulgated by the Department of Health and Human Services (DHHS). The applicable regulations require an institution to enter into an agreement called an "Assurance" with the Office of Protection for Research Risks (OPRR), under which OPPR reviews the IRB's policies.[46] Research not subject to the OPPR Assurance but involving drugs or devices is subject to Food and Drug Administration (FDA) regulations, which provide for audits by the FDA to guarantee compliance with the regulations.[47] Although some differ-

---

[43] *See, e.g.*, ARIZ. REV. STAT. §§ 44-132.01, 44-133.01.

[44] *See, e.g. Penn. v. Nexon*, 761 A. 2d 1151. (Sup. Ct. Penn., 2000), upholding parents' conviction of involuntary manslaughter and endangering the welfare of a child based on parents' refusal to seek medical treatment and instead treating their child with prayer.

[45] *Planned Parenthood of Cent. Mo. v. Danforth*, 428 U.S. 52, 96 S. Ct. 2831, 49 L. Ed. 2d 788 (1976).

[46] 45 C.F.R. pt. 46.

[47] 56 Fed. Reg. 28,025 (1991).

ences exist between OPPR and FDA regulations, they are substantially similar in requiring patients to be informed that the study involves research, the risks of the study, its anticipated benefits, a disclosure of alternatives, the extent to which confidentiality will be maintained, information regarding how the patient could withdraw from the study, and costs of the study.

2.3 End-of-Life Decisionmaking

2.3.1 Competent Person's Right to Refuse Life-Sustaining Medical Treatment

Based upon the common-law right of informed consent and constitutional protection, an adult patient who has the capacity to understand the risks and benefits of medical treatment (competent patient) should be able to make determinations of what medical treatment to accept or reject, even if refusal of such treatment is life-threatening. If the state has an interest (*e.g.*, the protection of third parties), then it may assert such a position in the courts. Courts have been reluctant to find that the state has a strong interest in maintaining the life of a patient, particularly when that patient has a serious illness. In *Bouvia v. Superior Court of California*,[48] a hospital sought permission to feed a competent 26-year-old woman with cerebral palsy who refused to eat in an attempt to cause her own death. The California state court found that she had a constitutionally protected privacy interest in refusing treatment, and prohibited her being fed against her wishes.

2.3.2 Incompetent Patients

Incompetent patients do not lose their right to make medical decision and forego life-sustaining treatment; however, their rights must be exercised through a surrogate decision maker. If a decision to refuse or withdraw life-sustaining treatment is to be made for an incompetent patient, then one of three standards is used: the subjective standard; the substituted-judgment standard; or the best-interest standard.

The subjective standard is evidence of the patient's subjective wishes regarding treatment. A good example of the subjective wishes of the patient would be an advance directive.[49] The substituted-judgment standard is when a proxy makes decisions based upon what she believes the patient would want. The best-interest standard permits the decisions to be made in the best interest of the patient. Different states require or permit different standards to be used, depending upon the circumstances. For instance, the best-interest standard most often is appropriate when a patient has never been competent, such as mentally handicapped patient, and there is no indication of what the patient would want in such a circumstance.[50]

The constitutional interests involved in end-of-life decisions often have arisen in the context of determining the standard that the state can require before the decision to withdraw or withhold life-sustaining treatment from an incompetent patient must be honored. In *Cruzan*,[51] Missouri law provided that care could not be withdrawn from an incompetent patient without clear and convincing evidence

48 *Bouvia v. Superior Court of California*, 225 Cal. Rptr. 297 (Ct. App. 1986).
49 *See* Section 2.3.4.
50 *See, e.g., Belchertown v. Saikewicz*; *In re Conroy*, 486 A.2d 1209 (N.J. 1985).
51 *Cruzan, supra.*

of the patient's wishes, which must have been articulated prior to the patient becoming incompetent (*i.e.*, the subjective standard). The U.S. Supreme Court recognized that the state had interests in preserving life, and permitted the state to prevent life-sustaining treatment from being withdrawn from an incompetent patient unless such a standard was met.

2.3.3 Tort Liability for Rendering Care

Despite the well-settled law that a competent person is able to refuse treatment which may cause the patient's death, courts are very inconsistent about permitting patients to recover damages when a healthcare provider preserves the life or health of the patient. Often, the courts' reasoning in refusing such compensation is that saving one's life or health is not damage and, consequently, is not compensable. This position of the courts is seen with particular frequency in cases when a patient is not terminally ill and yet refuses medical treatment that could restore the patient to health. A healthcare provider faced with a patient who is refusing treatment that might restore her to a full life may wish to weigh the potential liability that could flow from wrongfully not rendering treatment versus the liability from wrongfully treating a patient. Given the court's reluctance to grant significant (or any) damages when a person's life has been maintained, and given the significant damages that could flow from wrongful death, a provider faced with a difficult decision may wish to seek judicial intervention prior to withdrawing or withholding treatment from a competent patient who is not terminally ill.

2.3.4 Advance Directives

With the increase in the healthcare provider's technological ability to maintain patients' lives, and the growing public awareness of the possibility of having life supports and other highly invasive healthcare services at the end of life, many people began to write down their wishes about the medical care they want or do not want should they become incompetent to express their wishes. Most states have now legislatively authorized competent adults to execute advance directives regarding healthcare that can later be used if the person becomes incompetent to make those decisions.

Two types of advance directives generally are used: the living will and the durable power of attorney for healthcare. Most states have statutes that are very specific about the legal formalities of advance directives (*e.g.*, requiring witnesses or notarization). While the structure and validity of advance directives is a matter of state law, the Patient Self-Determination Act of 1990[52] requires that, at the time of admission to a federal Medicare or Medicaid participating hospital or a nursing facility, or upon enrollment in a participating home health agency, the healthcare provider must give the patient information about her rights under state law to execute advance directives. Additionally, each health maintenance organization (HMO) must give patients the same information upon a subscriber's enrollment into the HMO. For patients without advance directives, the law continues to be problematic as to who may exercise a patient's wishes and what standard of evidence is necessary, as was evident with the much publicized case of Terri Schiavo in which Ms. Schiavo's husband and parents disagreed as to the withdrawal of treatment and she had no advance directive.

---

[52] 42 U.S.C. § 1395cc.

2.3.4.1 Living Wills

Living wills are documents that specify what a person wants to transpire regarding healthcare should the patient become incompetent and unable to express her own wishes. Living wills generally are limited to the issue of whether the patient wants life-sustaining treatment withdrawn or withheld, when a patient is terminally ill or in a persistent vegetative state.

2.3.4.2 Durable Powers of Attorney for Healthcare

Durable powers of attorney for healthcare are documents designating a surrogate decision maker who is empowered to make a wide range of treatment decisions for the patient in the event that the patient is not competent. Durable powers of attorney for healthcare have greater applicability than living wills because they can be used in circumstances that do not involve life-sustaining or end-of-life treatment. Many states require that, in order for the surrogate decision maker to make decisions regarding the withdrawal or refusal of life-sustaining treatment, the patient must be in a terminal condition or persistent vegetative state, and that the durable power of attorney must specifically grant the surrogate decisionmaker the authority to refuse such treatments. State laws vary as to how end-of-life decisions may be made for incompetent patients without advance directives.

2.3.4.3 Do-Not-Resuscitate Protocols

If a patient is an inpatient in a hospital or nursing home, generally all life sustaining treatment will be rendered in the case of a patient arrest unless a physician has written an order not to resuscitate the patient. Those are known as "Do-Not-Resuscitate" (DNR) orders. Patients who had living wills or durable powers of attorney which indicated that the patient did not want life sustaining treatment have been resuscitated in hospitals in emergency situations because the advance directives were not available. In response to this perceived problem, some states have passed legislation permitting physicians to write DNR orders which individuals wear as armbands or carry as wallet cards. These actual physicians' orders to not resuscitate the patient are to be honored when a patient reaches the hospital or nursing home. The laws also address the immunity from liability for healthcare providers that follow such orders.

2.3.5 Medical Futility

While it is now well established that patients and their surrogates may refuse medical treatment, a growing area of discussion is whether a physician may refuse to provide medical treatment when the patient or her surrogates want treatment but the physician has determined that care is futile and will be of no benefit or only short term benefit. There is no comprehensive definition of medical futility, but the issue of the efficacy of continued treatment usually arises when a medical decision has been made that continued treatment will only prolong the dying process and not provide any realistic expectation of improvement in the patient's condition, or when continued treatment can be expected to continue the life of someone who has no expectation of recovery, such as with a person in a persistive vegetative state. Courts, when faced with the issue of whether the patient's or surrogate's wishes to continue treatment over the physician's request to discontinue care the physician feels is futile, have been mixed.[53]

In 1999, Texas enacted legislation which allows a physician, if supported by the hospital Ethics Committee after a due process proceeding, to withdraw treatment considered futile by the physician.[54] Under the legislation, the patient's family or representative has 10 days after the due process procedure has resulted in a decision to withdraw the care in which to find a facility which will accept and treat the patient. If no facility can be found, the futile treatment may be withdrawn. The Texas law has been invoked many times, often amidst controversy. This area of the law can be expected to develop significantly over the next few years as providers, legislators, and courts grapple with how to handle cases where patients and families want care continued which providers consider to be futile.

2.3.6 Physician-Assisted Suicide

Healthcare providers and the public alike are divided in their views as to whether a competent patient's right to choose to forego or withdraw life-sustaining medical treatment should include the right to have a physician assist in ending a person's life. Suicide—the taking of one's own life—is not a crime, although state laws vary as to whether assisting someone in a suicide is punishable. The issue of physician-assisted suicide first became a prominent legal and ethical issue with the activities of Dr. Jack Kervorkian in the 1990s.

Initiatives to legalize physician assisted suicide were first considered in the state of Washington in 1991 and by California in 1992, where neither initiative passed. In 1994 voters in Oregon passed an initiative to allow physicians, after screening patients for competency and other criteria, to either provide a patient with a prescription for a lethal overdose of medication or to start an IV which the patient could control to cause the patient's death.[55] In 2008, Washington became the second state to pass an initiative to legalize physician assisted suicide.[56]

The Supreme Court of Montana ruled late in 2009 that physicians could not be prosecuted for assisting their patients to end their own lives, thereby making Montana the third state to legalize physician-assisted suicide.[57]

In 1997 the U.S. Supreme Court addressed whether an individual has a constitutionally protected right to have a physician assist in his or her suicide. In the companion cases of *Washington v. Glucksberg*[58] and *Vacco v. Quill*,[59] the Court determined that there was no constitutionally-protected interest and state law prohibiting physician-assisted suicide does not violate a person's constitutional right to due process or equal protection. The Court determined that, unlike the decision to withdraw or refuse

---

53 *See, e.g.*, *Gilgunn v. Mass. Gen. Hosp.* No. 92-4820, Mass Super Ct (1995); *In re Helga Wanglie*, PX-91-238 Minn Dist Ct. Probate Division (1991); *In re Baby K*, 16 F.3d 590 (1990).

54 Tex. Advance Directives Act, 166 Tex. Health & Safety Code, *see* § 166.046.

55 Or. Rev. Stat §§ 127.800 to 127.897.

56 *See* the Washington Death with Dignity Act, Wa. Rev. Code, Chapter 70.245b.

57 *See Baxter v. Montana*, 2009 Mt. 449.

58 *Washington v. Glucksberg*, 117 S. Ct. 2258 (1997).

59 *Vacco v. Quill*, 117 S. Ct. 2293 (1997).

life-sustaining treatment, the ability to commit suicide is not a constitutionally protected interest, and therefore a state may prohibit individuals from assisting a person commit suicide. The Court also rejected the argument that a prohibition on physician-assisted suicide was a denial of equal protection. The proponents of physician-assisted suicide had argued that, because competent patients who had medical conditions that allowed them to die without life-sustaining treatment had a constitutionally protected right to refuse such treatment (and could therefore cause their own death by refusing or withdrawing such medical treatment), those ill patients who could not effect their own death by the withdrawal of treatment were denied equal protection by the law refusing them affirmative intervention to end their lives.

The Supreme Court decisions in *Vacco* and *Quill* left to the individual states the decision of whether physician-assisted suicide is permitted or prohibited in that state. In November 6, 2001, U.S. Attorney General John Ashcroft attempted to block Oregon's assisted-suicide law by authorizing federal agents to sanction physicians who prescribe medications to assist their terminally ill patients' death for violating the Controlled Substance Act of 1970. The U.S. Court, however, ruled that the Justice Department lacks the authority to directly counteract a state law in such a manner.[60]

The states are clearly split on the issue of physician-assisted suicide with only three states clearly permitting it, a number of states legislatively prohibiting it, and the majority of states not directly addressing the issue. In any state without specific authorization of physician-assisted suicide, however, physicians may facc charges for assisting someone in ending their lives, depending upon state criminal laws.[61]

2.4 Disclosure and Protection of Patient Medical Information

2.4.1 Patient Confidentiality

Healthcare providers are subject to a wide spectrum of laws and regulations governing the maintenance and disclosure of information. As a matter of policy or requirements imposed by licensing boards or accrediting agencies, healthcare providers kept information about their patients confidential unless release of such information is mandated by state or federal law. This created variance across the states as to how patient information was to be kept confidential. With the passage of the Health Insurance Portability and Accountability Act of 1996 (HIPAA) a comprehensive nation-wide policy came into effect regarding patient privacy.

HIPAA itself does not create a private cause of action. A patient who believes his confidentiality has been breached may file a complaint against the provider with the office of Civil Rights of the Department of Health and Human Services and the provider may be sanctioned, but HIPAA does not provide other recourse to the patient. Patients seeking damages for violations of their privacy must find a state legal theory on which to base their complaint, such as negligence or other torts or contract.

---

60 *Gonzales v. Oregon*, 543 US 1145 (2005).

61 *See People v. Kevorkian*, 205 Mich. App. 180, 517 N.W.2d 293 (1994).

Physicians and many other healthcare professionals are obligated by their licensing statutes to keep patient information confidential. Therefore, if a healthcare professional releases confidential information, the professional may be subject to professional disciplinary action, and the patient may have a cause of action for such release based either on the state statute or in tort law. Some states' licensure statutes covering hospitals and other healthcare facilities also require such facilities to keep patient information confidential and accreditation criteria of the JC and the AOA require information to remain confidential.

In addition to a general right to confidentiality, certain types of information have been subject to heightened protection. For instance, most states place significant restrictions on the release of HIV and acquired immunity deficiency syndrome (AIDS) information;[62] federal law prohibits the release of information regarding anyone receiving drug abuse or alcohol treatment, unless compliance with federal confidentiality protections is at issue;[63] and many state laws protect the release of mental-health information.[64]

Unless a specific state or federal statute governed the release of information, patients who felt their information was released improperly had to base an action either on the breach of an implied contract or an assertion of negligence. In a few instances, invasion-of-privacy or defamation actions could have been supported. In defending these cases, healthcare providers often were permitted to show that they had acted reasonably in the disclosure of the information, and that the disclosure of the information was to further the valid needs of the healthcare provider.

In recent years, a few states have recognized the tort of breach of confidence, which significantly broadens patient protection for release of information. These cases have made it clear that release of patient information, even if done for a valid purpose for the healthcare provider, will not be permitted without patient consent.

In *Biddle v. Warren General Hospital*,[65] an Ohio hospital was releasing patient information to its attorneys so that its attorneys could review the patient information and determine if payment should be sought from certain third-party payors. The Ohio Supreme Court held that, absent specific authorization by the patient, the hospital could not turn the records over to its attorneys; no Ohio statutory authority permitted an attorney to obtain confidential patient information. It should be noted that the attorney/client privilege prevents attorneys from testifying about confidential client matters, but does not address an attorney's right to access confidential information given to clients.

In light of this and other cases recognizing the right of patients' to confidentiality, healthcare providers should draft very broad patient-release forms which make it clear that healthcare providers may give information to attorneys, consultants, and others determined by the healthcare provider to need such information for the efficient operation of the healthcare provider.

---

62 *See, e.g.*, Ohio Rev. Code § 2739.02.

63 Comprehensive Alcohol Abuse and Alcoholism Prevention, Treatment, and Rehabilitation Act of 1970, 42 U.S.C. § 290dd-2; Drug Abuse Office and Treatment Act of 1972, 42 U.S.C. § 290ee-3.

64 *See, e.g.*, Ohio Rev. Code § 3793.12(c).

65 *Biddle v. Warren General Hospital*, 86 Ohio St. 3d 395 (1999).

2.4.2 Mandatory Disclosure

Healthcare providers are required to release patient information (and therefore will not be liable to the patient for such release) when such a release is mandated by law.

2.4.2.1 Judicial Disclosure

Public policy generally requires full disclosure of relevant information in litigation. Therefore, absent common law or statutes giving special protection to information, no person or entity may refuse to testify or produce documents as part of judicial process, and all relevant evidence is admissible in court and discoverable in preparation for trial.

In derogation of the rule of full disclosure of relevant information in litigation, most states have adopted a privilege for communications between healthcare professionals and their patients. Three major public-policy reasons often are cited for the physician/patient privilege:

- encouraging honest communication between patients and healthcare workers;
- protecting patient privacy; and
- protecting the ethics of the medical profession.

Because no physician/patient privilege exists under common law, each state statute has identifies those healthcare professionals covered under the privilege.[66]

Rule 501 of the Federal Rules of Evidence provides that, for civil federal cases based upon state claims, privileges are determined by state law; further, for all other federal cases, the privileges are based upon federal common law. Generally, no common-law recognition of a communication privilege exists between healthcare professionals and patients; as a result, no privilege exists for communications made to healthcare professionals in cases based upon federal claims. The Supreme Court, in *Jaffee v. Redmond*,[67] recognized a common-law privilege between psychotherapists and their patients; to date, however, the Court has not broadened the privilege to cover other professionals.

2.4.2.2 Mandatory Reporting and Duty to Warn

Healthcare providers are subject to a broad range of reporting requirements that take precedence over confidentiality requirements. Mandatory reporting requirements cover a wide spectrum of reportable events, including births, deaths, infectious diseases, child and elderly abuse, cancer, abortions, and others.

A healthcare provider may also be required to release confidential information when such information is necessary for the protection of a third party. This "duty-to-warn" doctrine generally arises in the context of a physician's duty to warn a third party of a communicable illness of the physician's patient, or the duty to warn a third party of the violent propensities of the physician's patient. The

[66] Ohio, for instance, recognizes a privilege for patient communications to their physicians, dentists, podiatrists (Ohio Rev. Code Ann. § 2317.02(B)(1)); psychologists (Ohio Rev. Code Ann. § 4732.19); and counselors and social workers (Ohio Rev. Code Ann. § 2317.02(G)).

[67] *Jaffee v. Redmond*, 518 U.S.1 (1996).

best-known case establishing the duty to warn is *Tarasoff v. Regents of Univ. of California*, in which the court determined that, when a psychiatrist determines that a patient poses a direct threat against a third party, the psychiatrist must take steps to warn or protect the third party. In this case, a voluntary outpatient told his psychiatrist that he intended to murder a readily identifiable woman. The psychiatrist did not warn the woman of the danger and, after the patient did in fact kill the woman, her parents successfully sued the psychiatrist for failing to warn her that she was in danger.[68]

2.4.3 HIPAA Privacy Rules

HIPAA established standards and requirements for healthcare providers and health plans (Covered Entities) to protect confidential patient information. The regulations implementing HIPAA's privacy standards are complex, covering a wide range of topics.[69]

HIPAA's privacy standards impacting Covered Entities and individuals can be organized into four major areas:

- administrative and training requirements;
- the requirement for policies, procedures, and forms regarding how patient information is used and disclosed;
- certain requirements regarding patient access to their own information; and
- the requirement for agreements and policies regarding how Business Associates keep information confidential.

HIPAA privacy regulations generally do not preempt state laws that are more stringent than the HIPAA privacy standards regarding patient confidentiality or reporting. HIPAA's goal to create uniform confidentiality standards across the states may, in large part, remain unrealized if states maintain or develop confidentiality laws that are more stringent than HIPAA.

2.4.3.1 Administrative Requirements and Training

Two basic administrative requirements are posed by the HIPAA privacy regulations: covered individuals and entities must designate a privacy officer; and they must train their workforce on HIPAA requirements, emphasizing privacy policies and procedures. In addition, all new employees similarly must be trained within a reasonable time of their hiring. Compliance with this requirement is to be repeated when material changes are made to the covered individual or entity's privacy policies. To this end, the privacy officer is charged with maintaining compliance with federal and state law regarding HIPAA and privacy issues.

---

[68] *Tarrasoff v. Rights of Univ. of Calif.*, 17 Cal. 3d 425, 131 Cal. Rptr. 14, 551 P.2d 334 (1976).

[69] Final rules implementing HIPAA privacy standards were originally published on December 28, 2000 (65 Fed. Reg. 82,462 (2000)) and were modified on August 14, 2002 (67 Fed. Reg. 53,181 (2002)) and again in 2009 (Pub. L. No. 111-005). Compliance was required for most Covered Entities and individuals as of April 14, 2003.

2.4.3.2 *Use and Disclosure of Protected Health Information*

The basic tenet of HIPAA's privacy-related concerns is that protected health information (PHI) may not be used or disclosed unless the disclosure is authorized by the patient or specifically permitted by HIPAA. (Information that cannot identify the patient in any way is not covered by HIPAA restrictions; it is important to note, however, that very specific rules exist as to what constitutes "de-identified" information, and such information frequently has limited uses.)

HIPAA permits PHI to be used without patient consent for treatment, payment, or healthcare operations. The basic standard of HIPAA, however, is that the use of PHI must be limited to the minimum amount necessary to accomplish the purpose of the disclosure. An exception to this "minimum necessary" standard is where the disclosure is made for treatment purposes. Therefore, if a Covered Entity is disclosing PHI to another provider involved in the patient's treatment, or is making an internal disclosure for treatment purposes, then HIPAA permits full disclosure in the interest of the patient's safety and care. If the Covered Entity is using the information internally for payment or operation's purposes, or is disclosing information to others for any reason other than treatment purposes, then care must be taken to release only the information that is necessary. This means that, even within an institutional healthcare provider, access to patient information should be limited to those having a need to know the information. Consistent with the training requirement of the Privacy Rules, a provider's workforce therefore needs to be trained to limit the sharing of information between staff.

Release of information for any purpose other than treatment, payment, and healthcare operations may be made only with the patient's specific authorization unless otherwise permitted by HIPAA. The disclosures permitted under HIPAA are generally related to disclosures required by law (such as mandatory reporting to state agencies), to law enforcement in special circumstances and for certain litigation purposes. Providers may not condition the provision of services on the execution of such an authorization.[70]

To comply with the privacy regulations, healthcare providers should review carefully and develop policies regarding release of information to family, friends, clergy, and government personnel (upon request), pursuant to mandatory reporting laws and pursuant to subpoenas. The privacy regulations have tried to be neutral with respect to minors' rights to privacy, and providers should carefully review state law regarding minors in light of the privacy regulations. The regulations also address

[70] The privacy regulations are quite specific about the contents of authorizations. Authorizations are required to contain the following:

1. description of the information to be used or disclosed;
2. identification of the persons or class of persons authorized to make the disclosure of the PHI;
3. identification of the persons or class of persons to whom the Covered Entity is authorized to make the disclosure;
4. description of each purpose of the disclosure;
5. an expiration date or expiration criteria;
6. signature and date, or statement of authorization for someone signing on behalf of the patient;
7. statement that the patient may revoke the authorization in writing, and directions as to how that may occur (with a reference to the Covered Entity's notice of privacy practices);
8. statement that treatment, payment, and other benefits may not be conditioned on the execution of the authorization (or, if an exception under the privacy regulations is met, a statement of the repercussions of any refusal to execute the authorization); and
9. statement that the PHI may be redisclosed by the recipient.

how covered individuals and entities may use patient identity and information for marketing and fundraising purposes.

2.4.3.3 Patient Rights Under HIPAA

Patients are provided with very specific rights under HIPAA relative to their own information. Patients are permitted to request restrictions on how their information is to be used (although Covered Entities may not need to agree to such restrictions), the right to inspect and copy their patient information, the right to request amendments to their patient information, the right to receive an accounting of how their information has been disclosed (except for treatment, payment and healthcare operations) and the right to receive the Covered Entities Notice of Privacy Practice.

2.4.3.4 Notice of Privacy Practices

The privacy regulations contain specific requirements for Covered Entities to notify patients of the privacy practices of the Covered Entity. This notice is to be presented when the patient initially obtains services from the provider. If these practices change, patients must be notified of such changes. Additionally, providers with a direct-treatment relationship with the patient must make a good-faith effort to obtain the patient's written acknowledgement of receipt of the provider's notice of privacy practices.

Final modifications of the regulations require the patient's acknowledgement be in writing, but give no other direction concerning its form. Providers may adopt whatever form best suits their practices; DHHS has stated that it will not develop model notices or acknowledgements.

The notice requirement may be particularly problematic, because the first encounter with a patient may be by telephone, in an emergency, or another manner in which presentation of the notice may not be feasible. DHHS has provided the following potentially helpful guidance:

- if the first treatment encounter is by telephone, then the provider may satisfy the notice provision by mailing notice to the patient no later than the day of that service, and may include an acknowledgement form to be returned by the patient;
- an initial contact to schedule an appointment does not trigger the notice or acknowledgement requirements;
- if a provider renders services electronically, then DHHS expects it to give notice and obtain an acknowledgement in that form;
- if a provider revises its notice form, then a new patient acknowledgement is not required unless the patient requests a copy of the revised notice; and
- notice and acknowledgement forms may be included in other mailings to patients, so long as a notice and an authorization are not combined.

2.4.3.5 Business Associate Agreements and Policies

HIPAA regulations address the situation of PHI being released from a covered individual or entity to another entity or individual, and provide that the information should not lose its protected nature. The government has extended the protections given the information when maintained by Covered Entities and individuals by requiring that such Covered Entities and individuals enter into contracts with their Business Associates, requiring their Business Associates to keep information confidential and subject the information to the same protections required by the initial Covered Entity. To accomplish this, providers and other Covered Entities must enter into contracts with their Business Associates requiring their Business Associates to maintain the information in a manner similar to the Covered Entity or individual.

While Covered Entities and individuals are free to develop their own Business Associate Agreements, DHHS has provided sample agreements in the Privacy Regulations for the use of Covered Entities and individuals may use. Covered Entities and providers need to enter into agreements with their Business Associates covering the release of PHI. These agreements must be in writing, even if the underlying agreement with the Business Associate is an oral agreement.

2.4.3.6 Sanctions and Enforcement

Enforcement authority for HIPAA's privacy regulations has been placed with the DHHS' Office of Civil Rights (OCR). Criminal penalties and civil monetary penalties alike exist for violations. For unintentional violations, a $100 penalty per occurrence may be assessed, to a maximum of $25,000 per year for the same type of violation. No penalties will be assessed if failure to comply is due to reasonable cause, rather than willful neglect, provided that the person or entity takes action to correct the failure during the first 30 days following either actual knowledge or imputed knowledge of the non-compliance. The OCR is also granted the right to conduct compliance reviews of providers.[71] There is no private right of action for a HIPAA violation,[72] although there may be a private right of action under state law and HIPAA regulations may be cited as the standard of care.

Criminal penalties, including imprisonment, have been established for obtaining information under false pretenses, as well as obtaining information with the intent to sell, transfer, or use the information. The Secretary of DHHS also is authorized to perform compliance audits. One of the biggest current concerns of observers and practitioners is that HIPAA requirements will set the standard for maintaining health information, and that private malpractice suits may be brought for HIPAA violations.

2.5 Conclusion

Patient-care issues continue to be timely and significant, with hospital ethics committees, courts, and politicians addressing related concerns. In large part, these issues are governed by state law; the practicing attorney must take care to know the law of the applicable state.

---

[71] *See* enforcement guidelines, 70 Fed. Reg. 20,227–29 (Apr. 18, 2005).

[72] *See, e.g., Rigaud v. Garofalo*, No. Civ A. 04-1866, 2005 U.S. Dist. LEXIS 8735 (ED Pa. May 2, 2005).

3

Medicare

Barry D. Alexander, Esquire*
Cynthia B. Hutto, Esquire
Eli A. Poliakoff, Esquire
Ross E. Sallade, Esquire
Nelson Mullins Riley & Scarborough LLP

3.1 Introduction

Healthcare in America has been and continues to be big business. Healthcare spending consumed approximately 16.2% of the total U.S. gross domestic product (GDP) in 2008[1] and, by 2019, is expected to comprise 19.6% with actual healthcare spending projected to reach $4.6 trillion.[2] The Centers for Medicare and Medicaid Services (CMS) is one of the largest purchasers of healthcare services in the world. CMS administers or oversees administration of the Medicare, Medicaid and State Children's Health Insurance Programs providing healthcare for one in four Americans. Medicare enrollment has increased from 19 million in 1966 to approximately 47 million beneficiaries in 2010.[3]

In fiscal year 2010, CMS outlayed approximately $729.1 billion (net of offsetting receipt and Payments to the Health Care Trust Funds), of which total Medicare benefits alone were approximately $503.6 billion.[4] Total outlays spent by Medicare represent approximately 13% of total Federal outlays—only the Social Security Administration outlayed more at $754.2 billion.[5] CMS now predicts that Medicare, which in 2006 comprised 3.5% of total GDP in 2009, will increase to 6.4% by 2084.[6]

* The authors wish to provide thanks to Elizabeth Lippincott who provided additional editorial guidance and suggestions relating to the Medicare Part C and Part D sections of this Chapter.

1 Centers for Medicare & Medicaid Services, *National Health Care Expenditures 2008 Highlights*, at www.cms.hhs.gov/NationalHealthExpendData/downloads/highlights.pdf.

2 Centers for Medicare & Medicaid Services, *National Health Care Expenditure Projections 2009–2019*, at www.cms.hhs.gov/NationalHealthExpendData/downloads/NHEprojects2009to2019.pdf.

3 Centers for Medicare & Medicaid Services, *Financial Report, Fiscal Year 2010*, at www.cms.hhs.gov/CFOReport/Downloads/2010_CMS_Financial_Report.pdf.

4 *Id.*

5 *Id.*

6 *2010 Annual report of the Boards of Trustees of the Federal Hospital Insurance and Federal Supplementary Medical Insurance Trust Funds*, at https://www.cms.hhs.gov/ReportsTrustFunds/downloads/tr2010.pdf.

3.1.1 The Evolution of Medicare Policy and Law

Well into the late 19th century, U.S. healthcare was delivered in a two-tiered arrangement. The first tier catered to the well-to-do, who could afford to pay for healthcare services. These individuals were treated at home by trained physicians and nursed to health by relatives. The second tier was reserved for the destitute—primarily the young, the aged, and the disabled. The destitute received medical care through a patchwork system of local charities and poorly-trained volunteers. The American public perceived the hospitals of the time to be houses of misery and death. The delivery of healthcare services, long the domain of local physicians and charities, remained largely outside of the government purview.

The period between 1870 and 1930 witnessed an evolution in public-health practices and medical technology that greatly improved health outcomes. Soon, hospitals were being transformed into places of recovery as well as centers for medical education. As a result, the locus of healthcare delivery also began to move away from the home and into the hospital. Accompanying these developments were periodic discussions on a national scale over the establishment of a government health-insurance program.

The 1930s witnessed the advent of the federal role in social-welfare issues. Sparked by the Great Depression and the need to "alleviate the unpredictable and uneven incidence of medical costs," President Franklin Roosevelt's administration gave serious consideration to launching a national health-insurance initiative.[7] Fierce opposition by the American Medical Association (AMA), however, coupled with the failure to achieve a consensus on financing the plan, ultimately caused the initiative to be dropped from the proposed social-security legislation.[8]

The role of the federal government in social-welfare issues became institutionalized with the passage of the Social Security Act in 1935.[9] Congress used Social Security to broaden and reformulate traditional public-relief coverage into distinct categories for specific population groups. Categorical eligibility quickly became a politically useful paradigm for federal policymakers to define and "solve" social-welfare problems.

At the same time, the U.S. began experimenting with the concept of voluntary health insurance. A group of Dallas schoolteachers contracted to pay Baylor Hospital a 50-cent monthly premium for a guarantee of up to 21 days of hospital care. The Baylor arrangement, which subsequently expanded to include other hospitals and employers, was later known as the "Blue Cross" plan.[10]

Federal policy during World War II prohibited salary increases but not fringe benefits to employees. This dynamic accelerated the expansion of the Blue Cross plans nationwide. As the popularity of the Blue Cross plans grew, state medical societies began offering similar physician coverage under the "Blue Shield" plan.

---

[7] U.S. Dep't of Health & Human Servs., *Overview of the Medicare and Medicaid Programs*, Health Care Fin. Rev. (Medicare & Medicaid Statistical Supp. 1998) (hereinafter *1998 Overview*).

[8] Paul Starr, *The Social Transformation of American Medicine* (1982).

[9] 42 U.S.C. §§ 301–1397jj.

[10] Blue Cross Blue Shield of Texas, *Our History*, at www.bcbstx.com/company/history.htm.

By the war's end, the U.S. employer-based model for health insurance had become fully institutionalized. Congress responded to the increased demand for healthcare services with many federal subsidies. With the adoption of the Hospital Survey and Construction Act (commonly known as Hill-Burton) in 1946, Congress made construction and modernization grants and loans available to public and nonprofit hospitals, in return for a "reasonable volume" of uncompensated medical care.[11]

The Hill-Burton subsidy greatly accelerated hospital construction and expansion in rural towns and inner cities, areas that typically were bereft of adequate healthcare facilities. Local governments quickly embraced hospital construction and expansion as key to their continued economic development.[12] Hospitals funded by Hill-Burton soon became symbols of local civic pride, as well as important sources of employment and medical care for the community. Federal policy thus spawned the dramatic rise in employer-funded healthcare plans and fueled the establishment of local community hospitals.

This further propelled the public's demand for medical services, and the cost of healthcare began to soar. By the end of the 1950s, healthcare inflation had begun to "price out" certain consumers (particularly those living on the margins or with fixed incomes) of medical care. As a result, "the widely perceived inadequacy of 'welfare medical care' under public assistance" emerged as a heated political issue on the national scene.[13] Congress responded in 1960 with the Kerr-Mills Amendments to the Social Security Act, which extended grant money to the states for the establishment of a means-tested medical-assistance program for the aged.[14]

With government subsidies of all types proliferating during this period, Congress looked to exert increasing control over programs funded by the federal government. At the same time, pressure mounted on Capitol Hill to create a national healthcare program for the elderly—one that was free from the stigma of welfare and the vagaries of state control. These factors, coupled with the federal largesse produced by the "New Frontier" and "Great Society" programs of the early 1960s, sparked a complex series of political maneuvers that culminated in the adoption of the Medicare and Medicaid programs in 1965.[15]

3.1.2 Chapter Overview

This Chapter provides an in-depth examination of the Medicare program. The initial sections of the Chapter offer an overview of the program's current organizational structure (Parts A, B, C, and D), followed by a review of features specific to the operation of the Medicare program (including eligibility and cost-sharing, coverage issues, and program administration). The Chapter next presents a detailed discussion of Medicare reimbursement principles and payment methodologies. Lastly, the Chapter ends with a description of the program's grievance and appeals processes, and closes with some prognostications about the future of the Medicare program. Additional resources are located in

---

[11] 42 U.S.C. §§ 291–291o-1. The term "Hill-Burton" refers to the sponsors of the act: Senators Lister Hill (D-AL) and Harold Burton (R-OH).

[12] Grants and loans have been made to over 6,900 facilities since Hill-Burton was implemented in 1946. *See* U.S. Dep't of Health & Human Servs., Health Resources & Servs. Admin., *The Hill-Burton Free Care Program*, at www.hrsa.gov/osp/dfcr/about/aboutdiv.htm.

[13] *1998 Overview* at 2.

[14] Social Security Amendments of 1960 (Kerr-Mills), Pub. L. No. 86-778, 74 Stat. 924 (1960).

[15] 42 U.S.C. §§ 1395–1395hhh and 1396–1396v.

the Appendix to this Chapter, including useful websites; frequently referenced acts, laws, and programs; and relevant agencies, departments, commissions, advisory committees, and participants. The Medicare program also has countless acronyms, abbreviations, and designations that dominate the industry's communications landscape. A listing of such terminology may be found under the Glossary in Chapter 1.

3.2 Overview of the Medicare Program

Established under Title XVIII of the Social Security Act, Medicare is a social health-insurance program that provides universal hospital coverage for Americans who are age 65 years or older. Originally established as "a health insurance program for aged persons to complement the retirement, survivors and disability insurance benefits under Title II of the Social Security Act,"[16] Medicare now insures the long-term disabled, those who require renal dialysis, and certain other persons who may buy into the program regardless of age.[17]

3.2.1 Medicare Basics

The "original" Medicare program consisted of just two parts, Part A (hospital insurance) and Part B (supplementary insurance). Congress has significantly expanded Medicare coverage options for beneficiaries, first in 1997 with the establishment of the MedicareAdvantage (MA) program (Part C), and again in 2003 with the creation of a voluntary outpatient prescription-drug benefit (Part D). As a result, four separate components or "Parts" currently comprise the Medicare program—Part A, Part B, Part C, and Part D. The term "Part" refers to divisions within Title XVIII of the Social Security Act.

3.2.1.1 Part A

Borrowing from the Blue Cross model, Medicare Part A covers inpatient hospital and critical access hospital (CAH) care, skilled nursing facility (SNF) care, some healthcare agency (HHA) services, and hospice care. Medicare Part A is financed through the federal Hospital Insurance (HI) Trust Fund, established at the inception of the program and funded by payroll taxes from workers and employers. The HI Trust Fund balance is dependent on the fund's total income exceeding total outlays; thus, its financial health is sensitive to economic, demographic, and healthcare cost trends. As a result, the HI Trust Fund has hovered near insolvency at several times.[18]

3.2.1.2 Part B

Borrowing from the Blue Shield model, Medicare Part B covers physician services, hospital outpatient department services, ambulatory surgical centers (ASCs), laboratory services, some home healthcare, physical and occupational therapy, and durable medical equipment, prosthetics, orthotics,

---

16 Health Care Fin. Admin. *Brief Summaries of Medicare and Medicaid, Title XVIII and XIX of the Social Security Act* (Nov. 1, 2006) at www.cms.hhs.gov/medicareprogramratesstats/downloads/medicaremedicaidsummaries2006.pdf.

17 Disability and renal dialysis were added as Medicare eligible groups in 1972. Medicare was expanded again in 1973 to include certain non-covered persons who may buy into the program under specific circumstances. U.S. Dep't of Health & Human Servs., *Overview of the Medicare and Medicaid Programs*, 22 Health care Fin. Rev. 1 (2000).

18 House Comm. on Ways and Means, 108th cong., Second Session, *2004 Green Book* (Comm. Print 2004) at waysandmeans.house.gov/.

and supplies (DMEPOS), Medicare Part B, also known as Supplementary Medical Insurance (SMI), is a voluntary program. Medicare Part A beneficiaries may elect to have Part B coverage for a monthly premium that is deducted from their Social Security checks. The remainder of Medicare Part B is financed through the SMI Trust Fund, which is funded by individual premiums (25%) and general tax revenues (75%). Because the majority of Part B coverage is financed by general revenue, bankruptcy of the SMI Trust Fund has not presented a significant concern.

3.2.1.3 Part C

The Balanced Budget Act (BBA) of 1997 established a private health-plan coverage option for Medicare beneficiaries by adding a new Medicare Part C to the Social Security Act.[19] The Medicare Advantage (MA) program (formerly known as "Medicare+Choice" (M+C)) offers Medicare beneficiaries a choice of coverage options.[20] Beneficiaries that have both Medicare Part A *and* Part B coverage may elect to receive their coverage through the "original Medicare plan" or through a Medicare-approved private managed care or fee-for-service (FFS) plan for a monthly premium. MA plans may offer lower out-of-pocket costs as well as additional benefits. At a minimum, however, every MA plan must provide beneficiaries with all of the items and services covered under Parts A and B with limited exceptions. Payments to MA organizations are financed through the HI and SMI Trust Funds. Funding is proportional and based on the actuarial value of total benefits paid under Medicare Parts A and B.[21]

MA plans serve specific geographic areas comprised of individual counties and groups of counties. These plans may be coordinated care plans (CCPs), which include health maintenance organizations (HMOs), preferred provider organizations (PPOs), special needs plans (SNPs), and provider-sponsored organizations (PSOs); private fee-for-service (PFFS) plans; and insurance plans operated in conjunction with a medical savings account (MSA). There are two types of MA plans—local and regional plans. The Medicare Prescription Drug, Improvement and Modernization Act of 2003 (MMA) provides that the Secretary of the Department of Health and Human Services (DHHS) may establish as few as 10 and as many as 50 regions covering the 50 states and the District of Columbia. Currently, DHHS has designated 26 regions, including 11 single state and 15 multi-state regions.[22] The local plans were intended to serve smaller geographic areas.[23]

---

[19] The Balanced Budget Act of 1997, Pub. L. No. 105-33, 111 Stat. 251 (1997) (hereinafter BBA). The BBA added §§ 1851–1859 to the Social Security Act establishing the M+C (now MA) program. The BBA was amended in 1999 by the Medicare, Medicaid & SCHIP Balanced Budget Refinement Act of 1999, Pub. L. No. 106-113, 113 Stat. 536, 1501A-321 (1999) (hereinafter BBRA). The BBRA provided approximately $27 billion in relief to providers over 10 years from the cuts exacted by the BBA. Amended again the following year by the Medicare, Medicaid and SCHIP Benefits Improvement and Protection Act of 2000, Pub. L. No. 106-554, 114 Stat. 2763 (2000) (hereinafter BIPA), BIPA provided approximately $35 million in relief to providers over five years from the financial blows dealt by the BBA. The BBRA and BIPA also added further refinements to the MA program.

[20] The Medicare Prescription Drug, Improvement and Modernization Act of 2003, Pub. L. No. 108-173, 117 Stat. 2066 (2003) (hereinafter MMA). The MMA's Title II effected a number of substantive changes to Medicare Part C, including changing the name to "MedicareAdvantage." Economic improvements also were made to Medicare Part C, including a significant rate increase for managed-care plans, as well as the creation of a $10 billion plan entry-and-retention stabilization fund.

[21] 42 U.S.C. § 1395w-24.

[22] Ctrs. for Medicare & Medicaid Servs., *Medicare Managed Care Manual* (Pub. 100-16) Ch. 1, § 30.2.4.

[23] In order to encourage the development of regional PPOs, the MMA placed a two-year moratorium (CY 2006–2007) on the offering of new local PPOs and on the expansion of existing local PPOs.

As of the end of fiscal year 2010, approximately one in four Medicare beneficiaries were enrolled in Medicare Part C or approximately 24% of the Medicare population.[24] As discussed in greater detail below, the Affordable Care Act of 2010 made substantial changes to Medicare's methodology for payment MA plans in an effort to curtail perceived "overpayments" to plans (payments in amounts above the costs Medicare Parts A and B would incur under the traditional FFS program) while providing bonuses to plans with high quality ratings. These changes are projected to reduce Medicare spending by $132 billion over 10 years according to the Congressional Budget Office (CBO).[25] The CBO also predicts that Medicare Advantage enrollment will *decrease* by approximately 4.8M beneficiaries or approximately 35%.[26] To the extent CBO estimates are accurate, this would lead to a decrease from 24% Medicare enrollment under Part C to approximately 14%. Whether beneficiaries upset with the loss of this relatively new Medicare enrollment offering will lead to future Congressional interaction remains unclear at the present time.

3.2.1.4 Part D

Medicare Part D is a voluntary program governing outpatient prescription drugs for Medicare beneficiaries.[27] Part D covered drugs include Medicaid-covered prescription drugs, biologicals, and vaccines. Part D, established by the MMA in 2003, became operational effective January 1, 2006.[28] Similar to Part B, the Part D prescription-drug benefit is funded through beneficiary premiums (25%) and general revenue (75%).[29]

The Part D benefit is implemented through private insurers that contract with CMS as either prescription-drug plans (PDPs) or MA plans that offer integrated prescription drug and healthcare coverage.[30] Under the Part D program, CMS makes capitated payments to plans sponsors to administer the beneficiaries' benefits under the Part D plan's CMS-approved benefit and rate structure. While there are certain minimum standards that all Part D plans must meet, each plan has a certain amount of flexibility in structuring its plans in terms of prescription drugs covered, co-pays and deductibles charged and development of its distribution network.[31] To be eligible to enroll in Part D, a beneficiary must be entitled to Part A coverage or enrolled in Medicare Part B and live in the service area of the Part D plan.[32] Medicare beneficiaries who are eligible for Part D are permitted to select among the various plans offered by the PDPs and MA plans in their service area.[33] Beneficiaries who qualify for Low Income Subsidies (LIS) pay lower cost-sharing obligations for generic and brand name drugs and low or no premium payments for their Part D coverage.

---

24 Section 4, *Medicare Chartbook*, Fourth edition, 2010 (Kaiser Family Foundation).

25 Comparison of Projected Enrollment in Medicare Advantage Plans and Subsidies for Extra Benefits Not Covered by Medicare Under Current Law and Under Reconciliation Legislation Combined with H.R. 3590 as Passed by the Senate, CBO, Mar. 19, 2010.

26 *Id.*

27 MMA, Title I; *see also* 70 Fed. Reg. at 4,194 (Jan. 28, 2005).

28 42 U.S.C. § 1395w-101(a)(2); *see also* 70 Fed. Reg. at 4194 (Jan. 28, 2005).

29 42 U.S.C. § 1395w-115; 42 C.F.R. § 423.315; *see also* 70 Fed. Reg. at 4,306 (Jan. 28, 2005).

30 42 U.S.C. § 1395w-102(e); *see also* 42 C.F.R. § 423.100 and 70 Fed. Reg. at 4,197 (Jan. 28, 2005).

31 *See* 42 U.S.C. § 1395w-102, 42 C.F.R. § 423.104 and 70 Fed. Reg. at 4,197 (Jan. 28, 2005).

32 42 U.S.C. § 1395w-101(a)(3)(A); 42 C.F.R. § 423.30.

33 42 C.F.R. §§ 423.30 and 423.32; *see also* 70 Fed. Reg. 4,201–04 (Jan. 28, 2005).

To be covered under Part D, a drug must be: (i) available only by prescription; (ii) approved by the Food and Drug Administration (FDA); (iii) used and sold in the United States; and (iv) prescribed for a medically accepted indication. Insulin, certain vaccines, biological products and medical supplies may also be covered. Part D generally does not cover drugs that may be excluded under Medicaid or certain drugs that may be eligible for Medicare Part A or Part B coverage.[34]

The definition of "Part D drug" specifically excludes those drugs or classes of drugs, or medical uses of such drugs, that may be excluded from coverage or otherwise restricted under Medicaid, with the exception of smoking cessation agents.[35] These drugs include, for example:

- drugs for anorexia, weight loss, or weight gain;
- drugs used to promote fertility;
- drugs used for cosmetic purposes or hair growth;
- drugs used for the symptomatic relief of cough and colds;
- prescription vitamins and mineral products, except perinatal vitamins and fluoride preparations;
- nonprescription drugs;
- outpatient drugs for which the manufacturer seeks to require that associated tests or monitoring services be purchased exclusively from the manufacturer as a condition of sale;
- barbiturates;[36]
- benzodiazepines;[37] and
- agents used for the treatment of sexual or erectile dysfunction except under certain conditions.

3.2.2 Private Contracts

Medicare also permits the use of "private contracts" between physicians, certain practitioners, and Medicare beneficiaries under which the parties may agree that no claims for reimbursement will be submitted to Medicare. In particular, a "private contract" is a contract between a Medicare beneficiary and a physician or other practitioner who has opted out of Medicare for two years for all covered items and services the physician/practitioner furnishes to Medicare beneficiaries. In a private contract, the Medicare beneficiary agrees to give up Medicare payment for services furnished by the physician/practitioner and to pay the physician/practitioner without regard to any limits that would otherwise apply to what the physician/practitioner could charge.[38]

---

[34] *See* Social Security Act § 1860D-2(e); *see also* 42 C.F.R. § 423.100.

[35] *See* Social Security Act § 1927(d)(2); *see also* 42 C.F.R. § 423.100.

[36] Under Section 175 of The Medicare Improvements for Patients and Providers Act of 2008 (MIPPA), for prescriptions dispensed on or after January 1, 2013, prescription drug plans must include barbiturates in their formularies for the indications of epilepsy, cancer or chronic mental health disorder.

[37] Under Section 175 of MIPPA, for prescriptions dispensed on or after January 1, 2013, prescription drug plans must include benzodiazepines in their formularies.

[38] Medicare Benefit Policy (CMS Pub. 100-02), 15, § 40.7.

Physicians and practitioners entering into such contracts must file an affidavit with DHHS affirming that, for two years from the date of the affidavit, they will not submit any claims to Medicare for items or services provided to *any* Medicare beneficiary, nor will they receive payment from Medicare, either directly or indirectly, for items or services provided to any beneficiary. The beneficiary must acknowledge in writing her unlimited personal liability for the cost of medical care rendered under the contract. A private contract also may not be executed if the beneficiary is experiencing "an emergency or urgent healthcare situation."[39]

3.2.3 Excluded Services

Medicare does not pay for custodial nursing-home services; routine physicals; or dental, eye, hearing, or foot care.[40] Cosmetic surgery, private hospital rooms, and medical care that is rendered outside of the United States also are excluded from payment by Medicare with limited exceptions.[41]

3.2.4 Beneficiary Cost-Sharing

3.2.4.1 Premiums, Co-Payments, and Deductibles

The Medicare program routinely imposes beneficiary cost-sharing mechanisms (*e.g.*, premiums, copayments, and deductibles). For example, Medicare Part A services are delivered in benefit periods, each known as a "spell of illness." A spell of illness begins the day the beneficiary is admitted to the hospital, and ends when the beneficiary has not received hospital or SNF services for 60 consecutive days.[42] Medicare charges Part A beneficiaries an out-of-pocket deductible for each spell of illness.[43] Unlike Part A, Medicare Part B beneficiaries are charged a single deductible per year.[44] Part B beneficiaries also incur copayments for certain medical services.[45] Similarly, MA organizations may require enrollees to contribute to the cost of covered services in the form of deductibles, copayments, or percentage of costs under certain conditions.[46] The new prescription drug benefit under Medicare Part D also provides for coinsurance, premiums, and deductibles.[47]

3.2.4.2 Supplemental Policies

Beneficiaries have the option of purchasing supplemental health-insurance coverage from private commercial insurers. Known as "Medigap," these policies typically offer a range of coverage options for Medicare-excluded services and help defray the cost of coinsurance and deductibles for Medicare

[39] 42 U.S.C. § 1395a; 42 C.F.R. §§ 405.400–.455.

[40] Effective January 1, 2005, the MMA authorizes an initial preventative physical examination for Medicare beneficiaries within six months of enrollment in Part B. MMA, § 611.

[41] 42 C.F.R. § 411.15.

[42] 42 U.S.C. § 1395x(a).

[43] *Id.* § 1395e(a)(1). Note that no coverage is provided for stays in excess of 150 days in a benefit period.

[44] *Id.* § 1395l(b).

[45] *Id.* § 1395l(a)(1).

[46] *Id.* § 1395d ww-21(d).

[47] *Id.* § 1395w-101.

beneficiaries.[48] Medigap policies are available only to beneficiaries who are covered under Parts and B of the program.

3.2.4.3 *Assistance for Low-Income Beneficiaries*

Financial-assistance programs are available through a combination of Medicare and Medicaid coverage for low-income Medicare beneficiaries who cannot pay their Medicare premiums, coinsurance, and deductibles. These include the Qualified Medicare Beneficiary (QMB) program, the Specified Low-Income Medicare Beneficiary (SLMB) program, and the Qualifying Individual (QI) program. Known as "dual eligibles" in Medicare parlance, beneficiaries who qualify for financial assistance must have total annual incomes that match or fall below 135% of the federal poverty level (FPL).[49]

3.2.5 The Secondary Payor Rule

Medicare does not pay for services for which Medicare is not the "primary" payer. As a result, Medicare payment for any items or services that may be covered under other insurance plans or policies (*e.g.*, workers' compensation, liability insurance, or employer health-benefit plans) or by another entity (*e.g.*, a third party's self-insurance) is prohibited with certain exceptions.[50] Under such circumstances, Medicare's liability for payment is "secondary" to that of the other payer(s).[51] Medicare can "conditionally" pay the medical expenses of a beneficiary for whom Medicare may be the secondary payer, but has authority to recover those expenses from the beneficiary's settlement with a third party or from the entity that finances that settlement.[52] Entities that pay an award or settlement to a Medicare beneficiary or assume responsibility for a beneficiary's medical expenses must disclose the arrangement to the Medicare Coordination of Benefits Contractor.[53] These reporting requirements, coupled with federal budgetary pressures, foretell renewed and enhanced enforcement of the Medicare Secondary Payer Rule and of the government's authority to recoup conditional payments.

3.2.6 Other Areas Subsidized by Medicare

Medicare subsidizes the costs associated with operating approved medical residency and allied health-education training programs for teaching hospitals.[54] Hospitals that serve a high proportion of low-income patients receive additional funding from Medicare through a disproportionate-share formula adjustment. Similarly, certain rural hospitals may receive payment from Medicare at an enhanced rate.

---

48 *Id.* § 1395ss; 42 C.F.R. §§ 403.200-.258.

49 42 U.S.C. § 1396d(p). *See also* MMA, § 101 regarding subsidies for low-income beneficiaries under the Part D drug benefit and transitional drug-card program.

50 42 U.S.C. § 1395y(b)(2)(A).

51 *Id.* § 1395y(b)(2); 42 C.F.R. §§ 411.32–.33.

52 *Id*,; 42 C.F.R. §§ 411.24, 411.37.

53 42 U.S.C. § 1395y(b)(8). The administrative guidance for the reporting program is found at http://www.cms.gov/MandatoryInsRep/.

54 *See generally* 42 C.F.R. § 412 subpt. G.

3.2.7 "Provider" vs. "Supplier"

The terms "provider" and "supplier" have special meanings within the Medicare program. Medicare defines "providers" as hospitals, SNFs, HHAs, hospices, CAHs and comprehensive outpatient rehabilitation facilities (CORFs).[55] Medicare defines a "supplier" as "any company, person, or agency that provides a medical item or service."[56] Such entities or persons include physicians, DME companies, ASCs, physical and occupational therapists, speech pathologists, clinical laboratories, and renal-dialysis facilities.[57]

3.2.8 "Provider-Based"

The term "provider-based" refers to facilities or organizations that are operated under the name, ownership, financial, and/or administrative control of a provider, typically a hospital. Such facilities/organizations may be located on or off-campus from the main provider. Provider-based entities may receive enhanced reimbursement from Medicare.[58]

3.3 Program Administration

3.3.1 Organizational Overview

Congress creates Medicare law by amendment to the Social Security Act and through the federal appropriations process. The Department of the Treasury manages the two Medicare trust funds through the Medicare Board of Trustees. Eligibility for the Medicare program is determined by the Social Security Administration (SSA). DHHS oversees the Medicare program and issues relevant regulations.

3.3.2 Centers for Medicare & Medicaid Services

3.3.2.1 Administrative History

The Social Security Administration administered the Medicare and Medicaid programs until 1977, when the newly created Health Care Financing Administration (HCFA) took over the daily operation of the programs after a reorganization of the U.S. Department of Health, Education and Welfare (now DHHS). An operating division of DHHS, the name "HCFA" was formally changed to CMS on June 14, 2001.[59]

---

[55] 42 U.S.C. § 1395x(u). *See also* 42 C.F.R. § 422.2 for the meaning of "provider" within the MA program.

[56] Ctrs. for Medicare & Medicaid Servs., *Medicare—Glossary*, at www.cms.hhs.gov/glossary/; 42 U.S.C. § 1395x(r).

[57] 42 C.F.R. §§ 431.107(a), 433.37.

[58] *Id.* § 413.65.

[59] DHHS published a final regulation that revised all references to the "Health Care Financing Administration" and "HCFA" in Chapters I, IV and V of title 42, and subtitle A, and Chapters II and III of title 45 of the Code of Federal Regulations to the "Centers for Medicare & Medicaid Services" and "CMS," respectively. The technical regulation became effective upon publication. 66 Fed. Reg. 39,451 (2001). *See also* Ctrs. for Medicare & Medicaid Servs. Prog. Mem. A-01-113 (2001). According to DHHS, the effective date of the name change was the date of the announcement by DHHS Secretary Tommy Thompson (June 14, 2001). However, the effective date of the corresponding technical revisions to the Code of Federal Regulations was July 31, 2001.

3.3.2.2 Structural Overview

Currently, CMS is organized around three primary service areas: "original" Medicare (Parts A and B); voluntary/optional coverage choices (Parts C and D); and state-administered programs *e.g.*, Medicaid and the State Children's Health Insurance Program (SCHIP)). Following the enactment of the Affordable Care Act, the Obama Administration re-organized CMS into five primary centers of operation:

- *The Center for Medicare.* This center is the largest center in the Medicare program. This center is responsible for the formulation, coordination, integration, implementation, and evaluation of national Medicare program policies and operations encompassing Parts A through D of the program. This center is responsible for identifying and proposing modifications to Medicare programs and policies. This center serves as CMS' lead for management, oversight, budget and performance issues relating to Medicare Advantage and prescription drug plans, Medicare fee-for-service providers and contractors. This center is also responsible for communication and dissemination of policies, guidance and materials to same to understand their perspectives and to drive best practices in the healthcare industry.[60]
- *The Center for Medicaid, CHIP and Survey & Certification.* This center oversees the operation of federal programs administered by the states, including Medicaid and the State Children's Health Insurance Program (SCHIP or CHIP). This Center also oversees the planning, coordination and implementation of the survey, certification and enforcement programs for all Medicare and Medicaid providers and suppliers, and for laboratories under the Clinical Laboratory Improvement Amendments (CLIA). This Center also coordinates with the Center for Program Integrity on the identification of program vulnerabilities and implementation of strategies to eliminate fraud, waste, and abuse.
- *The Center for Program Integrity.* This center serves as CMS' focal point for all national and State-wide Medicare and Medicaid programs and CHIP integrity fraud and abuse issues. This center coordinates provider/contractor audits and policy reviews, identifies program vulnerabilities, recommends modifications to programs to reduce rogram fraud, waste and abuse. This center (1) collaborates with the Office of Legislation on the development and advancement of new legislative initiatives and improvements to deter, reduce, and eliminate fraud, waste and abuse and (2) oversees all CMS interactions and collaboration with key stakeholders relating to program integrity (*i.e.*, U.S. Department of Justice, DHHS Office of Inspector General, State law enforcement agencies, other Federal entities, CMS components)
- *The Center for Medicare and Medicaid Innovation (CMMI)* The CMMI is a newly created center within CMS that was designed to test innovative payment and service delivery models to reduce program expenditures, while at the same time improving the coordination, quality and efficiency of the healthcare services offered to beneficiaries.[61] This new center is, accord-

[60] For a description of the Medicare Centers, the organization chart and current leadership, *see* http://www.cms.gov/CMSLeadership/50_OrganizationalChartASP.asp#TopOfPage.

[61] PPACA § 3021. The Patient Protection and Affordable Care Act (PPACA) was enacted on March 23, 2010 (H.R. 3590, Pub. L. 111-148). PPACA, together with the Health Care and Educational Reconcilation Act of 2010 (HCERA), enacted on March 30, 2010 (H.R. 4872, Pub. L. 111-152), constitute two separate legislative enactments that are commonly referred

ing to CMS, intended to "explore new approaches to the way we pay for and deliver care to patients so that we have better results both in terms of the quality of care and the affordability of coverage.[62]

- *The Center for Strategic Planning*. This center serves as CMS' focal point for the planning, formulation and coordination of long-term strategic plans, and future program policy and proposals for CMS. This center also: (1) collaborates with the Office of Legislation on the development and advancement of new legislative initiatives and improvements; (2) conducts environmental scanning, identifying, evaluating and reporting emerging trends in healthcare delivery and financing and their interactions with CMS programs and implications for future policy development and planning; and (3) oversees strategic, cross-cutting initiatives in coordination with other CMS components and external stakeholders.

CMS also administers the insurance reform provisions of the Health Insurance Portability and Accountability Act (HIPAA) in conjunction with the U.S. Departments of Labor and Treasury.[63]

3.3.2.3 Central and Regional Operations

Headquartered in Washington, D.C., with its principal operational functions based in Baltimore, Maryland, CMS functions with a relatively small staff of approximately 4,600. The central office for CMS directs national program policy and oversees the work of the agency's 10 regional offices.[64] Located around the country, the regional offices are responsible for ensuring that participating providers, physicians, and suppliers meet applicable federal requirements.

3.3.2.4 Administrative Guidance

In addition to publishing implementing regulations in the *Federal Register*, CMS publishes interpretative guidance though various administrative manuals. With the exception of the Provider Reimbursement Manual. The agency has transitioned to exclusive use of Internet-only manuals (IOMs). Unlike the paper-based manuals (which are segregated by provider type), the new CMS manual system is organized by functional area (*e.g.*, program integrity, eligibility, entitlement, claims processing). As a result, the IOMs also follow a new publication-numbering system.[65]

3.3.2.5 Administrator Rulings

These rulings are decisions of the Administrator of CMS, and serve as precedent final opinions and orders, as well as agency statement of policy and interpretation. According to CMS, these rulings provide clarification and interpretation of complex or ambiguous provisions of the law or regulations in the areas of Medicare and Medicaid utilization, review by quality improvement organizations

---

to as the "healthcare reform" initiative under President Barrack Obama. These two Acts significantly impact the Medicare program, and Medicare reimbursement, but without directly changing Medicare reimbursement systems.

[62] CMS Center for Innovations blog site introducing the CMMI, http://innovations.cms.gov/blog/introducing.shtml.

[63] Note that the DHHS Office for Civil Rights is responsible for implementing and enforcing the privacy provisions of HIPAA. 65 Fed. Reg. 82,381 (2000).

[64] *See* Ctrs. for Medicare & Medicaid Servs., *CMS Regional Offices*, at www.cms.hhs.gov/regionaloffices.

[65] "Crosswalks" from the paper-based manuals to the new IOMs are located in the individual IOMs at www.cms.hhs.gov/manuals/.

(QIOs, formerly called "peer review organizations"), private health insurance, and related matters. Rulings of the Administrator of CMS are binding on all CMS components, MACs, the Provider Reimbursement Review Board (PRRB), and the administrative law judges (ALJs) who hear Medicare Part B appeals.[66]

3.3.3 Medicare Administrative Contractors, Fiscal Agents

CMS contracts with private organizations (usually large commercial-insurance carriers) to process and pay Medicare claims, and to provide local administrative support for a specific geographic area. In Medicare parlance, the entity that processes Part A claims used to be known as the "fiscal intermediary" or "intermediary."[67] Similarly, the processor of Medicare Part B claims was known as the "carrier."[68] Finally, the processor of Medicare Part B durable medical equipment prosthetics and orthotics claims were carried out by the "durable medical equipment regional carriers" (or DMERCs).

The MMA eliminated the distinction between fiscal intermediaries, carriers, and DMERCs. Accordingly, certain administrative functions previously carried out by fiscal intermediaries, carriers, and DMERCS began a transition "Medicare Administrative Contractors" (or MACs).[69] Generally, MACs overlap with regions previously occupied by fiscal intermediaries, carriers and DMERCs. The transition from fiscal intermediaries, carriers, and DMERCs will be completed by 2011. MACs replacing fiscal intermediaries and carriers will cover 15 distinct regions and those replacing DMERCs will cover four distinct regions. MACs will be chosen on a competitive basis. The MACs also issue guidance regarding Medicare payment policy in the form of newsletters (many of which are available through the Internet) and published manuals.

3.3.4 Quality Improvement Organizations

CMS contracts with quality improvement organizations (QIOs) composed of healthcare professionals who audit the utilization, quality, appropriateness and necessity of the medical care that is provided to program beneficiaries by physicians, providers, suppliers and Medicare Advantage plans. QIOs also serve to educate healthcare professionals about quality of care issues. Denial of service coverage by a QIO will generally result in a loss of Medicare reimbursement to the provider or supplier. An excessive claims-denial rate by a QIO may result in the investigation of the service provider for Medicare fraud.[70]

Similarly, the states may provide for the review of Medicaid services through a contract with a peer review organization (PRO). However, the review activities performed by the PRO cannot be inconsistent with Medicare QIO review activities. The states also must provide a description of whether and to what extent the PRO determinations will be considered conclusive for Medicaid payment purposes.

---

66 Copies of the rulings are posted to the CMS website on the Internet at www.cms.hhs.gov.rulings/.

67 42 U.S.C. § 1395h.

68 *Id.* §§ 1395u, 1325m(a)(12); a directory of intermediaries and carriers may be accessed through the CMS website on the Internet at www.cms.hhs.gov/contactinggeneralinformation.

69 MMA, § 911. The transition to MACs commenced in 2006.

70 42 U.S.C. § 1320c.

3.3.5 The DHHS Office of Inspector General

The DHHS Office of Inspector General (OIG) is responsible for auditing and evaluating the Medicare program. To that end, the OIG conducts financial, performance, and management-evaluation audits and inspections to identify, document, and provide recommendations for the efficient and effective operation of the program. As the enforcement arm of DHHS, the OIG also conducts criminal and civil investigations into Medicare fraud and abuse, working in cooperation with the U.S. Department of Justice, the Federal Bureau of Investigation, and state and local law-enforcement agencies.[71] Administrative sanctions, including permanent exclusion from the Medicare program, may be imposed by the OIG against providers and suppliers that violate Medicare law.[72] Periodic policy statements, advisory opinions, enforcement actions, and model compliance guidelines also are issued by the OIG in connection with various Medicare fraud and abuse laws. Such materials may be accessed through OIG's website on the Internet.[73]

3.3.6 The Provider Reimbursement Review Board

The PRRB, established by Congress in 1972, offers hospitals and other institutional providers an independent forum outside the fiscal intermediary (now known as MACs) for resolving Medicare payment disputes involving more than $10,000.[74] The PRRB has both rulemaking and subpoena power. PRRB members are appointed by the Secretary of DHHS for a three-year term.[75] The composition of the five-member PRRB includes at least one certified public accountant and two provider representatives. PRRB decisions are subject to review by the Administrator of CMS, as well as the federal courts.

3.3.7 Independent Payment Advisory Board

The Independent Payment Advisory Board (IPAB) was established by the Affordable Care Act ostensibly to ensure that growth in Medicare spending stays within certain prescribed limits. Board is tasked with drafting proposals "containing recommendations to reduce the projected per-capita growth rate" for Medicare spending in the future, provided that such projected growth rate exceeds certain targets.[76] The IPAB must annually submit these proposals, or alternatively, advisory reports, to Congress and the President (starting in 2014 for implementation in 2015) and, annually thereafter, the IPAB must submit a draft proposal to the Medicare Payment Advisory Commission (MedPAC) and the Secretary "by not later than September 1 of the determination year." Generally, the Secretary is required to implement by regulation the proposal recommendations, and may do so under an interim final rule. In what has become a recent theme in many pieces of Medicare legislation, the Affordable Care Act provides that there No administrative or judicial review under section 1869, section 1878, or otherwise of the implementation by the Secretary under this subsection of the recommendations

---

71 48 Fed. Reg. 21,662 (1983); Ctrs. for Medicare & Medicaid Servs., *Medicare Carriers Manual* (Pub. 14) § 14002.

72 51 Fed. Reg. 34,764 (1986).

73 *See* DHHS Office of Inspector General at www.oig.hhs.gov.

74 Institutional providers include SNFs, HHAs, CORFs, rural primary-care hospitals, hospices, and outpatient physical therapy, speech pathology, and ESRD facilities.

75 42 U.S.C. § 1395oo. No member may serve more than two consecutive three-year terms of office. 42 C.F.R. § 1845.

76 PPACA, § 3403.

contained in a proposal." The IPAB is to be composed of 15 members appointed by the President for six-year terms. The IPAB is prohibited from developing proposals related to Medicare benefits, eligibility or financing.

3.4 Reimbursement Overview

Because they encompass more than just payment for medical care, items, and services, Medicare reimbursement principles are relatively complex. The key to understanding how Medicare reimburses providers and suppliers involves a thorough understanding of the basic components that comprise the Medicare reimbursement system.

REIMBURSEMENT— THE FIVE COMPONENTS	
ELIGIBILITY	Is the individual eligible for Medicare benefits?
COVERAGE	Is the item or service covered by Medicare?
CERTIFICATION	Is the provider of the item or service permitted to participate in the Medicare Program?
PAYMENT	How does Medicare pay for the item or service?
ASSIGNMENT/ REASSIGNMENT	Who is entitled to receive Medicare payment?

Each of these elements is described in Sections 3.5 through 3.16 of this Chapter.

3.5 Eligibility

The first step in analyzing the potential reimbursement issues associated with a proposed Medicare item or service is to ascertain whether the individual is eligible for Medicare benefits and, if so, when the effective date of Medicare coverage began.

3.5.1 Medicare Part A

The Medicare program provides Part A coverage to persons who qualify for Social Security retirement or survivor benefits and are age 65 years or older. Under a special transitional provision, some individuals who have reached age 65 but have not met other eligibility requirements are "grandfathered" into the program. Additionally, employees of federal, state, and local governments who are age 65 years and older may be eligible for Part A coverage if their employment was "Medicare qualified" (*e.g.*, the individual was not a temporary employee, prison inmate, or election worker). Permanent residents who have resided in the U.S. for five years and who have attained the age of eligibility, but otherwise are not entitled to Medicare benefits, may voluntarily enroll in Medicare Part A if they pay a monthly premium. Younger individuals who have received disability benefits for at least 25 consecutive months under the Social Security or the Railroad Retirement programs, may apply for Medicare Part A coverage, as well as those with end-stage renal disease (ESRD) or Lou Gehrig's Disease.[77]

[77] 42 U.S.C. § 1395c; 42 C.F.R. § 406.5(a), (b).

3.5.2 Medicare Part B

Part A beneficiaries are automatically eligible for supplementary medical insurance under Medicare Part B unless they specifically decline the coverage. It is possible, however, for a person to enroll in Medicare Part B without being entitled to, eligible for, or enrolled in Medicare Part A. Part B enrollment is voluntary, and beneficiaries are required to pay a monthly premium.[78]

3.5.3 Medicare Part C

Medicare beneficiaries who are eligible for Part A *and* enrolled in Part B may elect MA coverage during designated enrollment periods.[79] Enrollment in the MA program does not occur automatically. First, an MA plan must be operating within the electing beneficiary's geographic service area.[80] Second, an MA-eligible beneficiary must elect affirmatively to enroll in the MA program. Enrollment can be accomplished directly with the MA plan, through a licensed sales agent or broker, or through CMS' relatively new online enrollment tool located at www.Medicare.gov[81] Third, a beneficiary who has been medically determined to have ESRD may not elect coverage under an MA plan.[82]

MA organizations may not refuse enrollment to any MA beneficiary eligible for the applicable MA plan who elects MA during the program's coverage election periods. Moreover, MA-eligible beneficiaries may disenroll from an MA plan or elect another plan during such periods.[83] Special coverage rules apply as to the effective dates of coverage for beneficiaries who elect MA plans.[84]

As part of the 2006 changes to the Part D program, MA beneficiaries became subject to specific enrollment lock-in restrictions, meaning that beneficiaries must remain in a plan until the next annual enrollment period.[85] Special enrollment and disenrollment periods exist for newly eligible Medicare beneficiaries, enrollees in terminated MA plans (*e.g.*, plans that cease to operate or offer an MA plan), dual eligible enrollees, enrollees who have changed their residences, and, in certain instances, where the MA plan has committed contract violations.[86]

MA organizations may terminate an enrollee's plan election for certain causes, including late premium payments, disruptive behavior by the enrollee, or termination of the enrollee's service area by the plan. In such instances, the enrollee's coverage will revert back to FFS Medicare.[87] However,

---

78 42 U.S.C. § 1395o; 42 C.F.R. § 407.10(a).

79 42 U.S.C. § 1395w-21(a)(3); 42 C.F.R. § 422.50(a).

80 Eligible beneficiaries may obtain information on the availability of MA plans in their area by calling 1-800-MEDICARE or by consulting the Medicare consumers' information website on the Internet.

81 42 U.S.C. § 1395w-21(c); 42 C.F.R. § 422.50(a)(5).

82 An exception to this rule is made for beneficiaries who develop ESRD while enrolled in an MA plan. These individuals may continue their enrollment in MA. 42 U.S.C. § 1395w-21(a)(3); 42 C.F.R. § 422.50(a)(2).

83 42 C.F.R. §§ 422.60(a)(1)(2), 422.62 *et seq.*

84 *Id.* § 422.68(a)–(e).

85 *The Public Health Security and Bioterrorism Response Act of 2002*, Pub. L. No. 107-188, 116 Stat. 594 (2002). Section 532 effected a three-year delay in lock-in procedures for MA plans.

86 42 U.S.C. § 1395w-21(e)(4), (5). For a more detailed summary of the special enrollment periods (SEP) under Medicare Part C, *see Medicare Managed Care Manual*, Chapter 2, § 30.4 (CMS Publication 100-16).

87 42 C.F.R. § 422.74(a).

special enrollment and disenrollment rules apply to enrollees who are terminated due to a reduction in the plan's service area or the termination of the plan from the MA program.[88]

3.5.4 Medicare Part D

Medicare beneficiaries who are entitled to benefits under Medicare Part A or enrolled in Medicare Part B may elect coverage under the Medicare prescription drug benefit.[89] The beneficiaries must enroll during a specified election period.[90] Beginning January 1, 2006, beneficiaries may elect to enroll in a PDP or in an MA plan that offers prescription drug coverage (such plans are differentiated from other MA plans by use of the term MA-PD). PDP coverage is available to beneficiaries enrolled in the traditional Medicare FFS program (*e.g.*, Parts A and B) and located in an MSA. Beneficiaries enrolled in an MA-PD plan must obtain prescription coverage through that plan. Eligible beneficiaries have a choice of enrollment in at least two qualifying plans—one of which must be a PDP—in the area where they permanently reside.[91]

Initial enrollment for Part D coverage is the same as the annual, coordinated election period. Additional special enrollment periods are available when the beneficiary suffers an involuntary loss of credible coverage, errors occurred in enrollment, under certain exceptional circumstances, for certain "dual eligible" beneficiaries who are also entitled to Medicaid coverage, and if a discontinuance of MA-PD coverage occurs during the first year of eligibility.[92] PDP enrollment, disenrollment, termination and change of enrollment processes are established by the Secretary of DHHS using rules similar to, and coordinated with those established for MA plans regarding residency requirements, exercise of choice, coverage and election periods, guaranteed issue and renewal, consumer protections, marketing material, and application forms.[93]

3.6 Coverage

The next step in analyzing the potential reimbursement issues associated with a proposed Medicare service or supply is to determine whether the Medicare program covers the item or service.

3.6.1 Medicare Part A

Medicare Part A provides coverage for hospitalization, rehabilitation, and long term care. Part A beneficiaries also may receive hospice care, SNF services, and care that is provided by a home health aide, or that is furnished by an HHA on a part-time basis in the beneficiary's home by an HHA.[94]

---

88 *Id.* § 422.74(b)(3).

89 Note that the MMA established a transitional drug-card program that will remain in effect until the Part D drug benefit becomes operational in 2006. MMA, § 101, subpt. 4; 68 Fed. Reg. 69,840 (2003).

90 42 U.S.C. § 1395w-101(b)(1–3).

91 *Id.* § 1395w-103; 70 Fed. Reg. 44,194.

92 *Id.* § 1395w-100(b)(3); 42 C.F.R. § 423.30.

93 42 U.S.C. § 1395w-101(b)(1); 42 C.F.R. § 423.30-46.

94 Certain medical supplies also may be covered under Medicare Part A. 42 U.S.C. § 1395x(m).

3.6.1.1 Hospital Services

Inpatient hospital coverage includes the cost of a semi-private room, meals, regular nursing services, operating and recovery room, intensive care, inpatient prescription drugs, laboratory tests, radiology services, psychiatric hospitalization, and inpatient rehabilitation and long term care hospitalization when medically necessary, as well as all other medically necessary services and supplies provided in the hospital. A provider also may contract with outside suppliers to furnish services "under arrangements."[95] Arrangements in this context are limited to those under which the receipt of payment by the provider for the services discharges the liability of the beneficiary, or any other person, to pay for the services. The provider also must exercise professional responsibility over the arranged-for services as a condition of coverage by Medicare.[96]

3.6.1.2 Extended Care or Skilled Nursing Services

SNFs provide inpatient medical, skilled nursing, or rehabilitative services and supplies to patients in a non-acute care hospital setting.[97] Part A coverage is available for each day of extended care or SNF services up to a maximum of 100 days per spell of illness, and is subject to a coinsurance charge.[98] Medicare covers SNF services if a beneficiary has been an inpatient of a hospital for at least three consecutive calendar days and is transferred to a participating SNF within 30 days after discharge from the hospital.[99] Such services also must be certified (and subsequently recertified) as "medically necessary" by a physician, a clinical nurse, or a nurse practitioner.[100]

3.6.1.3 Home Health Services

HHAs provide certain "part-time" or "intermittent" medical, nursing, and therapy services to individuals in their places of residence.[101] Medicare covers home healthcare services that are furnished in the beneficiary's home (defined as any place in which a beneficiary resides that is not a hospital, SNF, or nursing facility), or in an outpatient setting (which may include a hospital, SNF, or rehabilitation center under certain circumstances).[102] In order to qualify for home healthcare, a Medicare beneficiary must be:

1. confined to the home;
2. under the care of a physician;

---

[95] Ctrs. for Medicare & Medicaid Servs., *Medicare General Information and Eligibility Manual* (Pub. 100-01) Ch. 5 § 10.3.

[96] 42 U.S.C. §§ 1395x(w)(1), 1395cc(a)(1)(H), 1395u(b)(6), 1395yy(e). Ctrs. for Medicare & Medicaid Servs., *Medicare Intermediary Manual* (Pub. 13) § 3007.

[97] *Id.* § 1395i-3(a), (d).

[98] *Id.* § 1395e(a)(3).

[99] 42 C.F.R. §§ 409.30–.36.

[100] *Id.* § 424.20. As a general rule, Medicare will not cover items or services that are not deemed to be "reasonable and necessary" for the diagnosis or treatment of an illness or injury (*see* 42 U.S.C. § 1395y(a)(i)); however, to avoid potential overutilization in the delivery of certain services and equipment, Medicare may require a physician's certification to explain why the service or equipment is necessary.

[101] 42 C.F.R. §§ 409.44–.45. The courts have interpreted "intermittent" to mean six or fewer days of the week, and "part-time" to mean less than eight hours per day. *Duggan v. Bowen*, 692 F. Supp. 1487 (D.D.C. 1988). However, Medicare generally will not pay for home healthcare that exceeds 28 hours per week without special documentation and/or medical justification. Ctrs. for Medicare & Medicaid Servs., *Medicare Benefit Policy Manual*, (Pub. 100-2), Ch. 7, § 40.1.

[102] 42 C.F.R. § 409.47.

3. receiving services under a plan of care established and periodically reviewed by a physician; and
4. in need of skilled nursing care on an intermittent basis, requires physical therapy or speech-language pathology, or have a continuing need for occupational therapy.

HHA-covered services do not include drugs, biologicals, housekeeping, or transportation services. HHAs also cannot provide home health visits for patients receiving venipuncture (the drawing of blood) as the only skilled nursing service.[103]

HHA services are covered under Medicare Part A and Part B. The first 100 visits for home healthcare following a beneficiary's three-day hospital or SNF stay are covered under Part A. If the first HHA visit is more than 14 days after discharge from the hospital or SNF, Part B covers the first 100 visits.[104] Under the BBA, Medicare payment for post-institutional HHA services furnished on or after January 1, 1998, for Medicare beneficiaries enrolled in both Part A and Part B during a home health stay (other than the first 100 visits) are covered under Part B.[105] Such services, however, will continue to be covered under Part A for beneficiaries who are enrolled only in Part A and qualify for the home health benefit.[106]

3.6.1.4 Hospice Services

Hospice care is a service provided to terminally ill persons with a life expectancy of six months or less who elect to forgo the standard Medicare treatment benefits to receive only hospice care.[107] Such care includes pain relief, supportive medical and social services, physical therapy, nursing services, and symptom management. A beneficiary may receive covered hospice-consultation services from a physician who is also the medical director or employee of a hospice program if the beneficiary has not elected hospice coverage and has not been seen by the physician on a previous occasion.[108]

Beneficiaries must elect to receive hospice care in "periods." Under current Medicare law, there are two 90-day hospice-benefit periods, followed by an unlimited number of 60-day periods. At the beginning of the second 90-day period and for each subsequent 60-day period, the appropriate medical professional must recertify that the beneficiary is terminally ill.[109] Beginning January 1, 2011, prior to such recertifications a hospice physician or nurse practitioner must have a face-to-face encounter with the patient to determine continued eligibility to receive hospice services.[110] By electing to receive hospice care, beneficiaries waive their rights (with exceptions) to receive Medicare benefits other than hospice.

---

[103] 42 U.S.C. §§ 1395x(m), 1395f(a)(2)(C); 42 C.F.R. §§ 409.47, .42, .49.

[104] Part A only pays for post-institutional services; Program Memorandum No. A-97-16, Dec. 1, 1997; Program Memorandum No. A-98-49, Dec 1, 1998.

[105] "A post-institutional service" follows a beneficiary's stay in a hospital or SNF for three or more days.

[106] 42 U.S.C. § 1395d.

[107] Federal regulations at 42 C.F.R. § 418.3 further clarify that an individual is considered terminally ill if he or she has a medical prognosis of a life expectancy of six months or less if "the illness runs its normal course."

[108] MMA, § 512.

[109] 42 U.S.C. § 1395x(dd)(1); 42 C.F.R. §§ 418.20–.30; 67 Fed. Reg. 70,363 (proposed Nov. 22, 2002); Centers for Medicare & Medicaid Servs. Prog. Mem. AB-03-008 (2003). BIPA clarified that the certification of terminal illness of an individual who elects hospice "shall be based on the physician's or medical director's clinical judgment regarding the normal course of the individual's illness." This clarification is effective for certifications made on or after December 21, 2000. BIPA, § 322.

[110] PPACA, § 3132.

3.6.2 Medicare Part B

Medicare Part B provides coverage for "medical and other healthcare services."[111] Part B services generally fall within one of three primary categories.

- physicians" professional services, including services and supplies that are furnished "incident to" physicians' services;
- services provided by outpatient providers and freestanding supplier entities, including suppliers of diagnostic tests; and
- services rendered by non-physician practitioners working under physician supervision or in collaboration with a physician.

"Incident to" services are services that are generally not furnished directly to the patient by the physician, but are considered an *essential element* of the physician's overall professional service. Incident to services may include the services of a non-physician practitioner working *under the direct supervision* of the physician (*i.e.*, the physician is physically present in the office suite, and immediately available to provide assistance and direction throughout the time the non-physician practitioner is performing services).[112] In order to qualify for Medicare payment, incident to services must be furnished in a non-hospital setting, such as a physician's office.[113]

Detailed rules for coverage and exclusion also apply to each of the following categories and their related subsets. Such requirements typically involve the level of physician supervision, the location of the services (*e.g.*, inpatient vs. outpatient), and the qualifications of the non-physician practitioners who provide the services.[114]

3.6.2.1 Physicians' Services

Physicians' services that may be covered under Medicare Part B include services rendered to Medicare beneficiaries by medical doctors (MDs) and doctors of osteopathic medicine (DOs). Such services include diagnosis, therapy, surgery, and consultation services, as well as the oversight of the patient's plan of care.[115] Other physicians' services that occur in hospitals and like providers (*e.g.*, anesthesiology, pathology, radiology, and laboratory services) similarly are covered. Part B coverage also is extended for services and supplies that are incident to those commonly furnished in a physician's office (*e.g.*, drugs and biologicals that cannot be self-administered), and which are included in the physicians' invoice for professional services.[116] Services provided to Medicare beneficiaries by

---

[111] 42 U.S.C. § 1395j-k.

[112] 42 C.F.R. §§ 410.26, 414.34. Ctrs. for Medicare & Medicaid Servs., *Medicare Benefit Policy Manual* (Pub. 100-2), Ch. 15, § 50. *Also see* 66 Fed. Reg. 55,246 (2001) and 67 Fed. Reg. 79,966 (2002) for further clarification.

[113] 42 C.F.R. §§ 410.20–.27; Ctrs. for Medicare & Medicaid Servs., *Medicare Benefit Policy Manual* (Pub. 100-2), Ch. 15, §§ 30 and 50. *Also see Medicare Claims Processing Manual* (CMS Pub. 100-4), Ch. 11, § 40.1.3.1. and Ch. 12, § 10. *Also see Medicare General Information Eligibility and Entitlement Manual* (CMS Pub. 100-1), Ch. 5, § 70.

[114] *See generally* 42 C.F.R. pt. 410.

[115] 42 U.S.C. § 1395x(q)–(r).

[116] Ctrs. for Medicare & Medicaid Servs., *Medicare Benefit Policy Manual* (Pub. 100-2), Ch. 15 § 50.

limited-license practitioners (*e.g.*, dentists, oral and maxillofacial surgeons, optometrists, podiatrists, and chiropractors) also are covered by Part B under the physicians' services coverage definition.[117]

3.6.2.2 *Services by Non-Physician Practitioners*

Covered services by non-physician practitioners include services that are rendered by physician assistants, nurse practitioners, and clinical nurse specialists working under physician supervision, as well as services provided by certified registered nurse anesthetists (CRNAs) and anesthesiologist assistants.[118] Outpatient physical therapy services, occupational therapy services, and speech pathology services are similarly covered under Medicare Part B if they are certified as medically necessary by the physician.[119] Part B coverage also extends to the services of qualified clinical psychologists, licensed clinical social workers, certified nurse midwives, and audiologists.[120]

3.6.2.3 *Outpatient Providers and Freestanding Supplier Entities*

Services rendered by outpatient providers and freestanding supplier entities covered under Medicare Part B include clinical laboratory services, as well as outpatient therapeutic- and diagnostic-testing services conducted by independent diagnostic testing facilities (IDTFs) and suppliers of portable diagnostic X-ray services.[121] Additionally, Part B coverage encompasses rehabilitation and related services when they are furnished in a CORF, rehabilitation agency, certified rehabilitation clinic, or a public-health agency.[122] Institutional and home dialysis equipment, supplies, and support services provided by renal dialysis providers and facilities also are covered under Part B.[123]

Medicare Part B covers primary healthcare and related services that are furnished by Federally Qualified Health Centers (FQHCs) or rural health clinics (RHCs).[124] Coverage also is extended to radiation-therapy services that are conducted in a freestanding radiation therapy center under physician supervision.[125] Similarly, surgical procedures performed in an ASC are covered, as are certain services provided in a hospital outpatient department setting.[126]

Medical equipment, supplies, and prosthetic and orthotic devices that are furnished by DMEPOS suppliers are covered if such services and supplies have been prescribed by a physician and are certified as medically necessary.[127] Ambulance services also are covered under Medicare Part B if certain conditions apply.[128] Lastly, Part B coverage is extended for partial hospitalization services that are furnished by participating community mental health centers (CMHCs), provided such services are

---

[117] *Id.* §§ 2020.1–.26; 42 U.S.C. § 1395x(r). *Also see Medicare Benefit Policy Manual* (Pub. 100-2), Ch. 15, §§ 30.1, 30.2, and *Medicare General Information Liability and Entitlement Manual* (Pub. 100-01), Ch. 5, §§ 70, 70.1.

[118] 42 U.S.C. § 1395(k)–(*l*); 42 C.F.R. §§ 410.69, .74–.76.

[119] 42 U.S.C. § 1395cc(e); 42 C.F.R. §§ 400.202, 485.701–.729.

[120] 42 C.F.R. §§ 410.32, .71, .73, .77; *Medicare Benefit Policy Manual* (Pub. 100-2), Ch. 15, § 80.3.

[121] 42 C.F.R. §§ 410.31–.33, 486.100–.110, pt. 493.

[122] *Id.* §§ 410.100–.105, .170.

[123] *Id.* § 410.50–.52.

[124] *Id.* §§ 405.2400–.2415; 410.45, pt. 491.

[125] *Id.* §§ 410.10(f), .35.

[126] *Id.* pt. 416.

[127] *Id.* § 414.200–.232.

[128] *Id.* §§ 410.40–.41.

delivered pursuant to a physician plan of treatment and are certified by the physician as medically necessary.[129]

3.6.2.4 Shared Savings Programs

The enactment of the Affordable Care Act led to the development of a new "shared savings program" in Medicare under which "Accountable Care Organizations" (ACOs) can receive payments in addition to those received as standard payments under Medicare Parts A and B, if they achieve certain quality performance standards.[130] These additional payments will be in the form of shared savings as determined by achieving certain pre-determined savings targets in the average amount of per capita Medicare expenditures realized in delivering care to beneficiaries. As of the date of this publication, CMS has not yet published interim or final regulations implementing the new ACO-payment provisions.

ACOs must be comprised of groups of providers, physicians and other suppliers who work together to manage and coordinate care for beneficiaries. Specifically, these can include: (1) physicians and certain non-physician practitioners in group practice arrangements (ACO professionals); (2) networks of individual practices of ACO professionals; (3) partnerships or joint venture arrangements between hospitals and ACO professionals; (4) hospitals employing ACO professionals; and (5) other groups of providers and suppliers as the Secretary determines appropriate.[131]

Moreover, ACOs must also meet the following requirements:

- be willing to become accountable for the quality, cost, and overall care of the Medicare fee-for-service beneficiaries assigned to it;
- enter into an agreement with the Secretary to participate in the program for not less than a three-year "agreement period";
- have a formal legal structure that would allow the organization to receive and distribute payments for shared savings to participating providers and suppliers;
- include primary care ACO professionals that are sufficient for the number of Medicare fee-for-service beneficiaries assigned to the ACO (5,000 at a minimum);
- provide the Secretary with such information regarding ACO professionals as determined necessary;
- have in place a leadership and management structure that includes clinical and administrative systems;
- define processes to promote evidence-based medicine and patient engagement, report on quality and cost measures, and coordinate care, such as through the use of telehealth, remote patient monitoring, and other such enabling technologies; and
- demonstrate that it meets certain patient-centeredness criteria, such as the use of patient and caregiver assessments or the use of individualized care plans.[132]

---

129 *Id.* § 410.110.
130 PPACA § 3022.
131 *Id.*
132 *Id.*

3.6.3 Medicare Part C

MAs offer two coverage categories to beneficiaries within the plan's service area: basic and supplemental benefits. Each year, MA organizations are required to submit their proposed plan benefits and premiums for the following year (collectively, the adjusted community rate (ACR)) to CMS for approval. Each MA organization must compute a separate ACR for each MA coordinated-care or private FFS plan offered to Medicare beneficiaries. The ACR is subject to certain adjustment factors that take into account the utilization characteristics of plan enrollees. If the ACR calculation (after adjustment) produces an excess amount, then the MA organization may contribute all or part of this amount to a stabilization fund, or use the remainder to fund additional services not covered by Medicare.[133] MA SNPs and certain RFB plans are required to offer Part D coverage, while MSA plans are prohibited from offering prescription drug coverage other than that required under Parts A and B. PFFS plans may offer Part D coverage, and MA CCPs are required to provide at least one plan with prescription-drug coverage. They may also offer plans with no drug coverage for beneficiaries who choose not to enroll in Medicare Part D.[134] The rules for Part D coverage by MA plans are similar to those for stand-alone PDPs.[135]

3.6.3.1 Basic Benefits

"Basic benefits" comprise Medicare Part A and Part B benefits plus other "additional" benefits.[136] Additional benefits may include certain reductions in the Part B premium and other beneficiary cost-sharing reductions including, among others, outpatient services with fixed copayments, inpatient benefits offered either with a percent coinsurance or a fixed per-day of per-admission inpatient copayment, subject to an annual cap on out-of-pocket costs. Benefits that are not covered by FFS Medicare must be extended to all enrollees within a plan's service area or segment on a uniform premium and cost-sharing basis. The establishment of additional benefits is subject to approval by CMS.

3.6.3.2 Supplemental Benefits

Supplemental benefits are "extra" benefits (*i.e.*, services not covered by Medicare) that either must or may be purchased by the enrollee depending on the type of benefit coverage. Common examples of supplemental benefits include dental benefits, vision care benefits (Medicare Part B does not, contrary to popular assumption, include vision benefits) and exercise facility memberships. MA allows for two supplemental-coverage categories—"mandatory" and "optional" benefits. MA enrollees may choose to decline the optional benefits, but cannot decline the mandatory coverage (even if they add to the overall cost of the premium). Supplemental benefits may be offered only by coordinated-care and PFFS plans, and are subject to approval by CMS.[137] As a practical matter, MA plans in a given market

[133] *Id.* § 422.310. The purpose of a stabilization fund is to prevent undue fluctuations in the additional benefits that are offered to plan enrollees in subsequent periods. *Id.* § 422.312.

[134] 42 C.F.R. § 422.4.

[135] MMA, § 222.

[136] Hospice services are excluded from basic benefits under MA. 42 U.S.C. § 1395w-22(a)(1); 42 C.F.R. §§ 422.2, .100, .101, .312.

[137] 42 U.S.C. § 1395w-22(a)(3); 42 C.F.R. §§ 422.2, .100, .102. Special rules on supplemental benefits apply to MSA plans. 42 C.F.R. §§ 422.103–.104(a). A Point-of-Service option may be offered by coordinated-care plans and network MSAs for a supplemental premium. *Id.* § 422.105.

offer different plans with varying levels of benefits and premiums and beneficiaries choose the plan and benefit package that meets their needs.

For an enrollee who is an inpatient when MA coverage begins, payment responsibility belongs to the original Medicare program or previous MA organization until the date of discharge, even if this date extends beyond the effective date of an enrollee's MA election. For an enrollee who is an inpatient when MA coverage *ends*, the MA organization remains responsible for payment until the date of discharge (even though no payment was received from CMS for the period after coverage had ended).[138]

3.6.4 Medicare Part D

PDP and MA-PD plans may offer "standard coverage" or its actuarial equivalent (known as "alternative coverage") as approved by CMS.[139] PDP and MA-PD plans may also offer supplemental coverage to beneficiaries, including lower out-of-pocket costs and coverage of Medicare-excluded drugs.[140] Even if a drug is excluded from basic Part D coverage, PDP and MA-PD plans can include them as a supplemental benefit as long as the drugs otherwise meet the definition of a Part D drug.[141] PDP and MA-PD plans that cover excluded drugs are not, however, allowed to pass those costs on to Medicare and are required to repay CMS if they are found to have billed Medicare in such cases.[142]

Part D also provides drug coverage for dual-eligible beneficiaries, effectively eliminating Medicaid prescription drug coverage for dual eligible beneficiaries.[143] Dual eligible beneficiaries are automatically enrolled in a PDP if they have not elected to enroll.[144] Dual eligible beneficiaries also qualify for premium and cost-sharing subsidies based on income.[145]

The Affordable Care Act made a number of changes to the Part D cost-sharing obligations incurred by beneficiaries. First and foremost, the Affordable Care Act eliminates the cost-sharing obligation for full-benefit dual eligible beneficiaries who receive services under a Medicare home and community-based waiver program, beginning no earlier than calendar year 2012.[146] In addition, premium and cost-sharing subsidies are available to low-income beneficiaries with incomes at or below 150% of the FPL.[147] The Affordable Care Act also permits PDPs to waive premiums for beneficiaries who are eligible for the low-income subsidy, effective calendar year 2011, if the premium is de minimus.[148]

The standard benefit is updated annually by CMS, based on the rate of per capita Part D spending growth.[149] In 2011, after a $310 deductible, Medicare covers 75% of a beneficiary's "incurred"

---

138 42 U.S.C. § 1395w-23(g); 42 C.F.R. § 422.264; 42 C.F.R. § 422.318.
139 *See id.* § 1395w-102(a)(1).
140 *Id.* § 1395w-102(a)(2).
141 *Id.* § 1395w-102(a)(3)–(e).
142 *See* OIG-OAS Report A-06-06-00022, Sept. 25, 2006, *Report on Medicare Drug Discount Card Program Sponsor McKesson Health Solutions*.
143 42 U.S.C. § 1395w-114(a)(3)(B)(v).
144 *Id.* § 1395w-114(c)(1).
145 *Id.* § 1395w-114; 42 C.F.R. §§ 423.286(e), 423.80, and 423.82.
146 *See* Pub. L. No. 111-148, Section 3309 (2010).
147 *Id.*
148 *See* Public L. No. 111-148, Section 3303 (2010).
149 42 U.S.C. § 1395w-102(b); 42 C.F.R. § 423.104(d)(5).

drug costs, up to $2,840 (known as the Initial Coverage Limit).[150] Thereafter, beneficiaries pay 100% of their incurred drug costs (this gap in coverage is commonly known as the "donut hole") until they reach the "catastrophic coverage limit" of $4,550 in out-of-pocket expenses (*i.e.*, $6,447.50 in total drug spending or TrOOP).[151] After the catastrophic coverage limit is reached, Medicare will pay 100% of a beneficiary's incurred drug costs, except for nominal cost-sharing equal to the greater of a $2.50 copayment for generic drugs and $6.30 for other drugs.[152] The monthly premium for Part D coverage in 2010 was estimated to average $37.25.[153]

The Affordable Care Act incrementally closes the donut hole beginning in 2011 thru a combination of reductions in cost sharing obligations on generic and brand-name drugs and discounts on brand-name drugs. In particular, starting in 2011, beneficiary cost-sharing obligations will be reduced for generic drugs by 7% each year through 2019 and 12% in 2020 for a total reduction of 75%.[154] Accordingly, by 2020, coinsurance for generic drugs in the coverage gap or donut hole will be 25%, the same co-insurance amount applicable to generic drugs during the Initial Coverage Limit. Second, in 2011, beneficiaries who reach the donut hole will be eligible to receive a 50% discount on brand-name drugs at the point of sale (the Coverage Gap Discount Program). Then, beginning in 2013, coverage is provided for brand-name drugs purchased in the donut hole with co-insurance gradually reduced to 75% of the negotiated brand name drug price by 2020. When combined with the Coverage Gap Discount Program, the Part D enrollee will have co-insurance obligations for brand-name drugs furnished in the donut hole equal to 25% of the negotiated price—the same co-insurance amount applicable to brand name drugs during the Initial Coverage Limit.[155] These three key provisions in the Affordable Care Act effectively eliminate the donut hole coverage gap when fully implemented in 2020.[156]

Covered Part D drugs include the following: federal legend drugs for a medically-accepted indication that are approved by the Food and Drug Administration (FDA); insulin and diabetic supplies;[157] prescription-based smoking cessation products; biologicals, self-administered injectable and infusion drugs, as well as those items that are administered in a home setting (so long as they are not covered under Medicare Part A or Part B); and compounded prescriptions—as long as at least one of the ingredients is covered under the Part D formulary, but Medicare Part D will only pay for that portion of the compounded prescription containing the covered medication.[158] Part D also covers a number of drugs or infusion therapy that are covered under Part B in some circumstances, but do not meet Part B cover-

150 *See id.* § 1395w-102(b) and 42 C.F.R. § 423.104(d); *see also* Medicare Advantage and Part D Payment Policies and Final Call Letter, CMS (Apr. 5, 2010).

151 *Id.*

152 *Id.*

153 *See Medicare Chart Book*, Fourth Edition, The Henry J. Kaiser Foundation, available at http://facts.kff.org/chart.aspx?cb=58&sctn=164&ch=1750.

154 *See* Pub. L. No. 111-152, Section 1101 (2010).

155 *See* PPACA, Pub. L. No. 111-148, Section 3301 (2010).

156 The Affordable Care Act requires that the 50% brand-name drug discount be paid for by pharmaceutical manufacturers who must enter into an agreement with CMS in order for their brand name drug to be eligible for coverage under Part D and offered by a plan. Participating manufacturers must make quarterly payments to Part D plan sponsors based upon CMS-supplied date from the agency's third-party administrator based upon prescription drug event data. *See* PPACA, Pub. L. No. 111-148, Section 3301 (2010).

157 These supplies covered by Part D include syringes, gauze, insulin pens, and alcohol swabs. Part D does not cover diabetic testing supplies (glucose monitors and test strips) which will continue to be covered under Part B.

158 42 U.S.C. § 1395w-102(e) and 42 C.F.R. § 423.100; *see also* 70 Fed. Reg. 4,231–32 (Jan. 28, 2005).

age or medical necessity requirements including IDPN and other infusion therapies. Additionally, the Affordable Care Act mandates Part D sponsors to offer PDPs that include all covered Part D drugs in certain categories and classes identified in the law. Until CMS establishes more specific criteria, the following categories and classes must be included in the formulary: anticonvulsants, antidepressants, antineoplastics, antipsychotics, antiretrovirals, and immunosuppressants for the treatment of transplant rejection.[159] Excluded drugs include non-prescription medications, drugs and supplies covered by Part A or Part B and drugs excluded by Medicaid.[160] Examples of drugs currently excluded by Medicaid include non-prescription drugs, drugs used for weight loss, weight gain or anorexia, prescription vitamins or minerals (except for prenatal vitamins and fluorides).[161]

PDP and MA-PD plans are not required to pay for all covered Part D drugs.[162] Rather, each PDP and MA-PD plan is permitted to establish its own formulary, or list of covered drugs for which they will make payment, as long as the formulary and benefit structure are not found by CMS to discourage enrollment by certain Medicare beneficiaries.[163] PDP and MA-PD plans can also change the drugs on their formulary during the course of the year with 60 days notice to affected parties, including direct written notice to enrollees.[164]

3.6.5 National Coverage Decisions

Medicare law lists broad categories of items and services that may be covered by the Medicare program. The Secretary of DHHS has the authority to make coverage determinations regarding specific items and services. A national coverage determination (NCD) simply is a policy statement granting, limiting, or excluding Medicare coverage for a specific item or service. Often, an NCD is written in terms of a particular patient population that may receive (or not receive) Medicare reimbursement for a particular item or service. Specifically, the law provides that an NCD is a determination made by the Secretary of DHHS with respect to whether a particular item or service is covered nationally by Medicare, but that it does *not* include a determination about which code, if any, is assigned to a particular item or service, nor does it make a determination with respect to the amount of payment.[165] An NCD itself is a formal instruction to the MACs regarding how to process claims. These instructions have a specific date dictating when claims will be processed according to the new criteria. NCDs may be issued by CMS as a manual instruction or other document (*e.g.*, a program memorandum or ruling) or notice in the *Federal Register*. After issuance, an NCD is binding on all MACs, QIOs, and MA organizations, as well as ALJs during the claims-appeal process.[166]

In the absence of a specific NCD, coverage determinations are made by local MACs within the boundaries established by Medicare law. Usually these determinations are made on a claim-by-claim basis. MACs also publish local coverage determinations (LCDs) that are contractor-specific policies

159 *See* Pub. L. No. 111-148, Section 3307 (2010).
160 42 U.S.C. § 1395w-102(e)(2); 42 C.F.R. § 423.100; *see also* 70 Fed. Reg. 4,228–31 (Jan. 28, 2005).
161 42 U.S.C. § 1396r-8(d); *see also* 70 Fed. Reg. 4,228 (Jan. 28, 2005).
162 *Id.*
163 42 U.S.C. § 1395w-104(b)(3) and 42 C.F.R. § 423.120(b).
164 42 C.F.R. § 423.120(b)(5).
165 BIPA, § 522.
166 42 U.S.C. § 1395y(a); 42 U.S.C. § 1395ff(f)(1); 42 C.F.R. §§ 405.732, .860; 64 Fed. Reg. 22,619 (1999).

that offer coverage and coding guidance for providers, physicians, and suppliers in a specific geographic area. An LCD may not conflict with an NCD, but the LCD may supplement an NCD.[167] NCDs and LCDs are posted to a CMS internet site that is updated weekly.[168]

The Benefits Improvement and Protection Act (BIPA), as amended by the MMA, made significant changes with respect to the timing and circumstances under which coverage determinations may be challenged and appealed.[169]

3.7 Certification

Another crucial step in analyzing the potential reimbursement consequences associated with a proposed Medicare item or service is determining the conditions applicable to coverage. This begins with an evaluation as to whether the individual or entity that provided the service was properly certified to do so by the Medicare program.

3.7.1 Providers

The Secretary of DHHS uses conditions of participation (CoPs) to establish a provider's eligibility for participating in the Medicare program.[170] CoPs are detailed standards and requirements to which providers must adhere in order to receive payment from Medicare. Compliance with the CoPs is determined by the state department of health or similar agency that surveys, inspects, and certifies providers for program participation under an agreement with DHHS. Certain providers may be given "deemed" status for program participation without such a state-assessment survey if they have received full accreditation from the Joint Commission (JC), DNV Healthcare (DNV), Community Health Accreditation Program (CHAP), the American Osteopathic Association (AOA), or similar private accrediting entity that surveys and inspects healthcare facilities and that has been recognized by Medicare as having authority to accredit providers.[171] In 2008, CMS announced a new accreditation program known as National Integrated Accreditation for Healthcare Organizations (NIAHO). NIAHO is the first hospital accreditation program in the United States that integrates ISO 9001 Quality Management System with the CoPs.[172]

Providers also enter into a written agreement with the Secretary of DHHS, known as the "provider agreement," wherein they agree to comply with all of the Medicare program's requirements.[173]

---

[167] BIPA, § 522(a)(2)(B). Note that LCDs were called local medical review policies (LMRPs) until December 7, 2003. *See* CMS Trans. No. 63 (2004) regarding the conversion of LMRPs by CMS to NCDs.

[168] Ctrs. for Medicare & Medicaid Servs., *Medicare Coverage Database* at www.cms.hhs.gov/med/overview.asp.

[169] BIPA, § 522; MMA, § 731; 42 C.F.R. pt. 426. For background information regarding Medicare policy on coverage determinations prior to the implementation of BIPA, *see* 67 Fed. Reg. 54,534 (proposed Aug. 22, 2002). For additional information regarding the revised coverage determination process, *see* Notice, 68 Fed. Reg. 55,634 (Sept. 26, 2003).

[170] 42 C.F.R. pts. 482–498. HHAs also are required by Medicare to obtain a surety bond. 42 U.S.C. § 1395b-5; 42 C.F.R. §§ 441.16, 489.60–.74. *See also* BBRA, § 304 (clarifies the HHA surety-bond requirements).

[171] 42 U.S.C. § 1395bb; 42 C.F.R. §§ 488.5–.6.

[172] 73 Fed. Reg. 56,588 (Sep. 29, 2008); ISO 9001 Quality Management System specifies requirements for a quality management system where an organization (i) needs to demonstrate its ability to consistently provide product that meets customer and applicable regulatory requirements and (ii) aims to enhance customer satisfaction through the effective application of the system.

[173] The basic terms of the provider agreement are contained in 42 U.S.C. § 1395cc; 42 C.F.R. §§ 489.10, .12, .53.

The provider agreement is automatically renewed each year, and may be terminated by the Secretary of DHHS for substantial noncompliance.[174] The Secretary of DHHS also may exclude providers from participation in the Medicare program for certain offenses, such as patient abuse and neglect, submission of false claims, program fraud, and financial misconduct.[175]

DHHS issues an individual provider identification number (PIN) to each Medicare-certified provider. Program rules require that the provider number appear on every claim for payment that is submitted to the Medicare program. Any correspondence from the provider to the Medicare program also must contain this number.[176]

Under the Affordable Care Act, new requirements were added to require the Secretary to establish procedures to screen and monitor potential providers and suppliers of the Medicare, Medicaid and SCHIP programs for fraud, waste and abuse activities.[177] Such screening includes licensure checks, criminal background checks, fingerprinting, site visits, data base checks and other procedures. The procedures will apply to all newly enrolling providers and suppliers on March 23, 2011 and to currently enrolled providers and suppliers on March 23, 2012.[178]

3.7.2 Physicians and Suppliers

As noted above, suppliers include physicians, DMEPOS suppliers, ASCs and IDTFs. As of May 2008, each physician, supplier, and other providers were required to obtain and use a national provider identifier (NPI).[179] The NPI replaces UPINs and other so called "legacy" numbers as a physician, supplier or provider's identifier for billing and other purposes and is intended to serve as a national identification number across all public (Medicare and Medicaid) and private (*e.g.*, commercial insurers) payors. Certain types of suppliers, including DMEPOS, IDTFs and ASCs, are also subject to on-site inspection or a survey by the applicable MAC.[180] All suppliers are required to execute a written certification statement of program compliance. Suppliers also receive a Provider Transaction Access Number (PTAN) for the purpose of communication with MACs regarding claims status, beneficiary eligibility, check status or other supplier related transactions.[181]

3.7.3 MA Organizations

CMS is responsible for determining whether an entity qualifies as an MA organization, and whether proposed MA plans meet the requirements of MA participation. As a condition of participation in the Medicare program, MA organizations are required to assume full financial risk on a prospective basis

---

174 Ctrs. for Medicare & Medicaid Servs., *Program Integrity Manual* (Pub. 100-08) Ch. 10, § 9.

175 42 U.S.C. § 1395y(e).

176 Ctrs. for Medicare & Medicaid Servs., *Regional Office Manual* (Pub. 23) § 6170. Note, this manual is now only available to CMS staff.

177 PPACA § 6401(a).

178 *See* 75 Fed. Reg. 58,204 (Sep. 23, 2010).

179 The original deadline for obtaining an NPI was May 23, 2007. CMS expanded that deadline by 12 months to May 23, 2008.

180 42 U.S.C. §§ 1395m(a), 1395x(cc)(2), 1395x(p); 42 C.F.R. §§ 424.57, 400.202. Note also that the Secretary of DHHS has established conditions for coverage with respect to determining the eligibility of certain suppliers to participate in the Medicare program.

181 *See generally* Ctrs. for Medicare & Medicaid Servs., *Program Integrity Manual* (Pub. 100-08) Ch. 10.

for the provision of healthcare services. MA organizations may obtain insurance coverage to provide for this risk, or they may make other arrangements as provided by Medicare law. Such arrangements may include the assumption of downstream risk by other healthcare professionals or institutions in the organization's provider network.[182]

In order to qualify as an MA organization, enroll beneficiaries in any MA plans, and be paid on behalf of Medicare beneficiaries enrolled in those plans, an MA organization must enter into a contract with CMS. An entity seeking to contract as an MA organization is required to provide documentation of appropriate state licensure and certification, including evidence that the entity is authorized by the state to accept prepaid capitation for providing, arranging, or paying for comprehensive healthcare services. Contracting entities also must meet certain minimum enrollment requirements, and have administrative and management arrangements satisfactory to CMS.[183] Similar to providers, certain MA organizations may be given "deemed" status if they are accredited by a private accrediting organization.[184] Each contract is for a period of at least 12 months.[185]

3.7.4 PDP Sponsors

Prospective PDP sponsors must submit bid information to CMS at the same time, and in a manner similar to the MA program.[186] CMS is directed to conduct negotiations regarding terms and conditions with the PDP. Prospective PDPs may choose to participate in Medicare Part D as a full-risk, limited-risk, or non-risk bearing fallback plan.[187] PDPs that assume the highest level of risk will receive priority by the Secretary of DHHS for participation in Medicare Part D.

The service area for a PDP consists of an entire PDP "region."[188] Medicare law provides that eligible beneficiaries must have a choice of enrollment in at least two qualifying plans (one of which must be a PDP) in the area where they reside. This requirement would not be satisfied if only one PDP sponsor, or one MA-PD plan, offers all of the qualifying plans for the area. Under such circumstances, the DHHS Secretary is permitted to approve limited-risk contracts to ensure beneficiary access to Part D coverage. In the event such access is still not available, CMS is authorized to solicit bids for a "fallback plan" which does not bear insurance risk.[189]

Every PDP sponsor must enter into a contract with CMS.[190] Such entities must be licensed under state law as risk-bearing organizations eligible to offer health insurance or health benefits in the states where their prescription-drug benefit plans are offered.[191] Similar to MA organizations, PDP sponsors

[182] 42 U.S.C. § 1395w-25(b); 42 C.F.R. §§ 422.6.
[183] 42 C.F.R. §§ 422.501(a) and (b), .502, .503, .514.
[184] *Id.* § 422.156(a).
[185] *Id.* § 422.505(b). *See also* §§ 422.506–.512 for contract non-renewal and termination.
[186] 42 U.S.C. § 1395w-111(b)(1).
[187] 42 U.S.C. § 1395w-111(b)(2).
[188] The MMA directs the Secretary of DHHS to establish and revise PDP regions in a manner that is consistent with the requirements for establishing and revising MA regions; 42 U.S.C. § 1395w-111(a).
[189] 42 U.S.C. § 1395w-103; Note, however, that certain coverage, marketing, and participation restrictions would apply to such plans.
[190] 42 U.S.C. § 1395w-112(b)(1).
[191] *Id.* § 1395w-112(a)(1). The MMA allows PDP sponsors to meet solvency standards for entities not licensed by the state in a manner similar to the process for provider-sponsored organizations under Part C.

must adhere to certain administrative and management standards, in addition to requirements regarding enrollment, marketing, contracting periods, beneficiary protections, and others applicable to participation in Medicare Part D.[192]

3.8 Payment—The Prospective Payment System

A central element in analyzing the potential reimbursement issues associated with a proposed Medicare item or service is determining the methodology Medicare uses to pay for the item or service.

3.8.1 Introduction

PPS was established by the Social Security Act Amendments of 1983, which mandated that Medicare create and implement a prospective payment system (PPS) for the reimbursement of acute inpatient hospitals.[193] Prior to this time, hospitals were paid by Medicare on a retrospective reasonable cost basis. Spiraling healthcare costs prompted a rethinking of the Medicare payment system by Congress, which resulted in a complete reformulation of the program's methodology for reimbursing hospitals.

3.8.2 PPS for Acute Inpatient Hospitals

The PPS rate for acute inpatient hospitals (IPPS) represents the nationwide average cost of treating a Medicare beneficiary according to the beneficiaries' medical condition. IPPS hospitals are paid a predetermined flat rate per discharge for inpatient care that is based on the patient's principal diagnosis.[194] The full IPPS amount is paid for each stay during which there is at least one Medicare-payable "day of care." The IPPS rate may either exceed or fall short of the hospital's full costs for treating the patient. Any costs incurred by the hospital in excess of the IPPS amount will be absorbed by the hospital.

IPPS includes certain costs and excludes others from the payment rate.[195]

Costs Included in the IPPS Rate	Costs Excluded from the IPPS Rate
Inpatient Operating	Outpatient Services
Routine Ancillary	Direct Medical Education
Intensive Care	Organ Acquisition
Malpractice Insurance	Non-Physician Nurse Anesthetists
Preadmission Services	Services Covered by Parts B, C, and D
Capital-Related[196]	Medicare Excluded Services

Beginning in FY 2005, the MMA tied annual payment updates for IPPS hospitals to the submission of quality indicators established by the Secretary of DHHS. Initially, the list was comprised of 10 such indicators, but it has been gradually expanded to include 46 measures for FY 2011.[197] Hospi-

192 42 U.S.C. § 1395w-112(b–e).
193 Social Security Act Amendments of 1983, Pub. L. No. 98-21, 97 Stat. 65 (1983); 42 U.S.C. § 1395ww(d).
194 42 C.F.R. pt. 412.
195 42 C.F.R. § 412.2(c)–(e).
196 Note that a PPS for inpatient hospital-related capital costs (*i.e.*, depreciation, interest, rent, and other property-related expenses) was phased in under a 10-year transition period that ended September 30, 2001. 42 U.S.C. § 1395ww(g); 42 C.F.R. pts. 412, 413.
197 75 Fed Reg 50,041, 50,183–84 (Aug. 16, 2010).

tals that do not submit the required quality data on a timely basis receive a 2% reduction in their factor payment update for the fiscal year in question.[198]

3.8.2.1 Diagnosis-Related Groups

The IPPS uses diagnosis-related groups (DRGs) to calculate the payment rate.[199] Developed by Yale University as a patient-care management system in 1969, the DRG method groups diseases by diagnosis, and assigns them into case types that consider, among other factors, the amount of resources needed to treat the condition. The DRGs are then organized under major diagnostic categories (MDCs) that relate both to single-organ and multiple body systems. Each DRG has a relative value (or case-mix weight) that reflects the cost of treating Medicare patients in that particular group in comparison to the treatment cost of the average Medicare case.

DRG selection is determined by the specific principal diagnosis, as well as the age of the patient. The specific principal diagnosis denotes the cause for admission, as determined after treatment and discharge (note this is not necessarily the preliminary diagnosis, but rather the actual reason for the admission).

Cases are then further subdivided based on the presence of surgery (surgical DRGs) or the absence of surgery (medical DRGs).

Surgical and medical DRGs may be further differentiated by the presence or absence of complications or co-morbidities. Complications are conditions that arise during an inpatient stay that increases the patient's overall length of stay by at least one day in approximately 75% of cases; co-morbidities are any preexisting conditions that increase the patient's length of stay by one day in 75% of cases.

Beginning in 2007, CMS overhauled the DRG system with the development of "severity-adjusted DRGs." Specifically, beginning in October 2007, CMS began to replace DRGs with "Medicare-severity DRGs" or "MS-DRGs" through a three year phase-in period that blended payment under the old DRG system and the MS-DRG system. While there are similarities between the two systems in the existence or absence of complications or co-morbidities, the MS-DRG system adds a third category—"major complications and/or co-mordities." Cases are classified into MS-DRGs for payment based on: the principal diagnosis, up to eight additional diagnoses, and up to six procedures performed during the stay. In a small number of MS-DRGs, classification is also based on the age, sex and discharge status of the patient. The diagnosis and discharge information is reported by the hospital using codes from the ICD-9-CM (the International Classification of Diseases, 9th Edition, Clinical Modification).

[198] MMA, § 501.

[199] 42 C.F.R. § 412.2(a).

3.8.2.2 Determining the IPPS Rate

Determining payment can be tricky, due to the myriad of special payments and adjustments that may figure into the calculation of a final payment amount. Also, the IPPS rate and related payment adjustments seldom remain static. The IPPS rate adjustments routinely figure into the budgetary deliberations of Congress, and are the subject of an annual rulemaking by DHHS.[200]

Similar to an income-tax return, providers prepare a "cost report" that is used to reconcile the estimated IPPS rate adjustments for the cost-reporting year on a claims-made basis.[201] The provider files the cost report with the MAC for auditing and review. A Notice of Program Reimbursement (NPR), which details the Medicare program's final determination and settlement of the provider's total allowable costs and IPPS payments, is issued to the provider by the MAC.

The following examples describe the basic mechanics involved in determining the total payment amount for acute inpatient hospital services.

1. *Determining the Basic Payment Rate.* A payment event occurs when an acute inpatient hospital submits a claim for payment to the MAC for inpatient care that was delivered to a Medicare beneficiary.
2. *The MS-DRG Assignment.* Based on the information provided on a claim, the case is assigned to a DRG. Providers may appeal their MS-DRG assignment within 60 days from the date the claim was filed.[202]
3. *The MS-DRG Weight.* An appropriate weighting factor (which represents the average resources required to care for that specific MS-DRG relative to the average resources used to treat all MS-DRGs) is assigned by the Secretary of DHHS to each MS-DRG (the MS-DRG weight). Changes to the MS-DRG weights resulting from changes in resource patterns, technology, and various other factors are published in an annual rulemaking by the Secretary of DHHS.[203]
4. *The Payment Amount.* The MS-DRG weight is then multiplied by a dollar amount that is based on the average Medicare allowable operating cost per discharge (known as the "standardized amount") for that year.[204] The MMA permanently equalized the standardized amount for all areas. Hospitals in rural and small urban areas are paid the same standardized amount as that utilized by Medicare to pay hospitals in large urban areas.[205]

---

[200] The Social Security Amendments of 1983 authorized the Secretary of DHHS to determine the rate of increase to the PPS rate, taking into account the recommendation of the Prospective Payment Assessment Commission (ProPAC). The 1983 amendments established ProPAC to advise the Secretary of DHHS on DRG classification, weight adjustments, and increases to the payment rate. Congress used the BBA to combine the functions of ProPAC and the Physician Payment Review Commission (PPRC) into a single commission called the Medicare Payment Advisory Commission (MedPAC). BBA, § 4022. MedPAC is charged with advising Congress on payment issues relating to Medicare payment issues. 42 U.S.C. § 1395 ww(e). To help fund the costs of reform initiatives in PPACA, market basket updates for inpatient services will be reduced on an annual basis from 2010 to 2019.

[201] CMS requires cost reports from *all hospitals* and their components, as well as from freestanding SNFs, HHAs, and outpatient physical-therapy providers.

[202] 42 C.F.R. § 412.60(d).

[203] Data for DRG relative weights may be obtained from the CMS website on the Internet at www.cms.hhs.gov/AcuteInpatientPPS/FFD/list.asp.

[204] 42 U.S.C. § 1395ww(d).

[205] MMA, § 401.

The standardized amount is divided into a labor and non-labor share. The non-labor component is adjusted by a cost-of-living factor. The labor component is adjusted by the wage index applicable to the area where the hospital is located.

The wage index accounts for variations in area-hospital labor costs (which is established by the Secretary of DHHS based on an annual survey of wage and wage-related costs for short-term acute-care hospitals).[206] The Secretary of DHHS also is required to make an annual determination with respect to the wage index.[207]

A hospital may request that it be reclassified or redesignated to a different geographic area for purposes of using the other area's wage index.[208] Reclassification is accomplished by appealing to the Medicare Geographic Classification Review Board (MGCRB).[209] The MMA established a one-time process for hospitals to appeal their wage-index classifications and select another area within the same (or a contiguous) state if they do not otherwise qualify for wage reclassification.[210]

Under MMA the Secretary of DHHS also established a payment adjustment recognizing the out-migration of hospital employees who reside in one county and work in a different area with a higher wage index. Hospitals eligible for this "commuting wage adjustment" must be located in a qualifying county. A "qualifying county" is a county that meets all of the following criteria: (i) hospital employees in the county commute to work in an MSA (or MSAs) with a wage index (or wage indices) higher than the wage index of the MSA or rural statewide area in which the county is located; (ii) at least 10% of the county's hospital employees commute to an MSA (or MSAs) with a higher wage index (or wage indices); and, (iii) the three-year average hourly wage of the hospital(s) in the county equals or exceeds the three-year average hourly wage of all hospitals in the MSA or rural statewide area in which the county is located.[211]

Calculation of the Payment Amount

Step 1	(Labor component) x (MS-DRG weight) x (wage index) = A
Step 2	(Non-labor component) x (MS-DRG weight) = B
Step 3	A + B = Standardized Amount

[206] This data is derived from each hospital's annual Medicare cost report, and reflects the earnings and paid hours of employment by occupational category.
[207] 42 U.S.C. § 1395ww(d)(5)(A); 42 C.F.R. § 412.64.
[208] BIPA extends the effective duration of a hospital's wage-index reclassification by the MGCRB to three fiscal years. BIPA, § 304(a).
[209] The guidelines concerning the criteria and conditions for hospital reclassification are located at 42 C.F.R. §§ 412.230–.236.
[210] The statutory deadline for hospitals to file an appeal was February 15, 2004. Reclassification is effective for three years starting April 1, 2004. MMA, § 508; 69 Fed. Reg. 661 (2004).
[211] MMA, § 505; 42 C.F.R. 412.64(i).

3.8.2.3 Case-Mix Adjustment

The Secretary of DHHS also may adjust the average standardized amount to "eliminate the effect" of coding and discharge classification changes "that do not reflect real changes in case mix" for discharges occurring on or after October 1, 2001.[212] This is done in the aggregate for all hospitals as part of the annual updating process.

3.8.2.4 Special Adjustments and Payments for Certain Costs

CMS may adjust the IPPS rate or make special payment for certain costs.[213] These include the following categories.

Treatment of Low-Income Patients

A percentage add-on payment is applied to the DRG-adjusted base payment rate for hospitals that serve a "disproportionate share" (DSH) of low-income patients. In Medicare parlance, these hospitals are referred to as "DSH hospitals." The DSH adjustment provides for a percentage increase in Medicare payment for hospitals that qualify under either of two statutory formulas designed to identify hospitals that serve a disproportionate share of low-income patients. For qualifying hospitals, the amount of this adjustment may vary based on the outcome of the statutory calculation. [214]

Beginning in fiscal year 2014, DSH payments will be equal to 25% of what otherwise is calculated, multiplied by three factors: (a) the difference in the hospital's DSH payments because of the Affordable Care Act and other reform measures; (b) the difference in the percentage change in the uninsured under-65 population from 2013 and those who are uninsured in the most recent period for which data is available; and (c) the percentage of uncompensated care provided by the hospital relative to all acute care hospitals. A portion of the 75% otherwise calculated may be paid to hospitals based on their level of uncompensated care.[215]

Indirect Medical Education

Approved teaching hospitals may receive a percentage add-on payment for each case paid through IPPS. The indirect medical education (IME) adjustment provides additional IPPS payments to hospitals for the indirect costs attributable to approved medical-education programs for physicians. The IME adjustment varies depending on the ratio of residents-to-beds under IPPS for operating costs, and according to the ratio of residents-to-average daily census under the IPPS for capital costs.[216]

---

212 BIPA, § 301(e). The term "case mix" refers to the types of cases that are treated by the hospital.

213 42 C.F.R. § 412.90.

214 42 U.S.C. § 1395ww(d)(5)(F); 42 C.F.R. §§ 412.2(f)(6), .106, .320. *See also* MMA, §§ 402, 951.

215 PPACA, § 3133.

216 42 U.S.C. § 1395ww(d)(5)(B); 42 C.F.R. §§ 412.105, .322. Note that Medicare Part B provides for a graduate medical education (GME) payment adjustment for a hospital's activities based on a prospectively determined amount per resident. 42 U.S.C. § 1395ww(h)(4); 42 C.F.R. § 413.76.

Outlier Cases

Special payment adjustments are made for cases involving extraordinarily high costs compared to most discharges classified in the same DRG.[217] The threshold criteria for determining outlier payment are published in the annual rulemaking by the Secretary of DHHS.[218]

New Technologies and Medical Services

Hospitals are eligible for an add-on payment for a new medical service or technology, if:

- the medical service or technology is new;
- the medical service or technology is costly such that the MS-DRG rate otherwise applicable to discharges involving the medical service or technology is determined to be inadequate; and
- the service or technology demonstrates a substantial clinical improvement over existing services or technologies.

The amount of the add-on payment depends on the cost incurred by the hospital for the new medical service or technology.[219]

Post-Acute Transfers

IPPS distinguishes between patient "transfers" and "discharges." Medicare considers a patient to be "discharged" when the patient is formally discharged from the hospital, expires while in the hospital, or is transferred to an excluded hospital or distinct-part unit. Activities that *do not* qualify as a "discharge" include the transfer of a patient to another IPPS hospital, or a patient's leave of absence from the hospital. "Discharging" hospitals are paid the full DRG amount.[220]

A patient is considered "transferred" by Medicare when the patient is moved:

1. to another IPPS hospital;
2. from an IPPS hospital;
3. from a hospital excluded from IPPS because of a statewide cost-control program or demonstration project; or
4. to a hospital that has not yet begun its first IPPS cost-reporting period.

The "transferring" hospital is paid a per diem rate for each day of the stay, not to exceed the full DRG payment that would have been made had the patient been discharged without being transferred. The per diem rate is determined by the full DRG divided by the average length of stay for that DRG,

---

217 42 U.S.C. § 1395ww(d)(5); 42 C.F.R. §§ 412.80–.89. Payment for day outliers was phased out of the Medicare program in 1998.

218 CMS published a final rule revising its outlier payment policies effective for discharges occurring on or after August 8, 2003, with deferred implementation of various changes until October 1, 2003. 68 Fed. Reg. 34,494 (2003).

219 42 U.S.C. § 1395ww(d)(5)(K) and (L); *see also*, 42 C.F.R. §§ 412.87–.88.

220 42 C.F.R. § 412.4(e).

multiplied by the length of stay at the transferring hospital. Certain exceptions to the payment-rate standard for transferring hospitals apply to specific DRGs and cost outliers.[221]

As of FY 2008, DHHS had designated 273 MS-DRGs that commonly require post-hospital care for payment either as "transfers" or "qualified discharges."[222] Medicare updates the DRGs subject to the postacute transfer policy every fiscal year in connection with the IPPS rulemaking.

In certain instances, a "special payment methodology" applies whereby Medicare pays qualified discharges at a "fifty/fifty" blend of the transfer/discharge rate for the first day and at the transfer rate for all subsequent days.[223] Specifically, under the special payment methodology, a hospital is paid 50% of the total IPPS payment plus the average per diem for the first day of the stay, and 50% of the per diem amount for each subsequent day of the stay, up to the full MS-DRG payment amount.[224]

ESRD Discharges

Hospitals receive a payment adjustment for ESRD discharges if these discharges equal 10% or more of the hospital's total Medicare discharges. The ESRD payment adjustment is based on the estimated weekly cost of dialysis and the ALOS of ESRD beneficiaries for the hospital.[225]

Low-Volume Hospitals

A graduated payment adjustment of up to 25% is available to "low-volume" hospitals. Medicare defines a low-volume hospital as a short-term general hospital that is located more than 25 road miles from a similar hospital, and that has less than 200 discharges (including both Medicare and non-Medicare patients) during a fiscal year.[226]

The Affordable Care Act temporarily expanded the eligibility for low-volume hospital add-on payments. During 2011 through 2012, hospitals within 15 miles and 1,600 discharges can qualify for the adjustment.[227]

Excluded (Pass-Through) Costs

Certain inpatient hospital costs are excluded from PPS, and thus, continue to be reimbursed by Medicare on a reasonable cost basis. These include, among others, hospital bad debt related to "covered services" that are derived from beneficiary deductible and coinsurance amounts; heart, liver, lung,

---

[221] *Id.* § 412.4(b), (f).

[222] 72 Fed. Reg. 47,188 (Aug. 22, 2007); 73 Fed. Reg 48,956 (Aug. 19, 2008).

[223] 42 U.S.C. § 1395ww(d)(5); 42 C.F.R. § 412.4(f)(5), (6); 65 Fed. Reg. 40,953 (1998); 68 Fed. Reg. 45,345 (2003); 72 Fed. Reg. 47,188 and 47,410 (Aug. 22, 2007).

[224] 42 C.F.R. § 412.4(f)(2); 73 Fed. Reg. 48,593 (Aug. 19, 2008).

[225] 42 C.F.R. § 412.104(a), (b)(1).

[226] 42 C.F.R. § 412.101. Note, while the statute defines low-volume hospital as hospital with 800 or fewer discharges per year (*see* 42 U.S.C. § 1395ww(d)(12)(C)(i)), the law provides that the term "discharge" refers to total discharges, and not merely to Medicare discharges and the Secretary has interpreted the law to require "an empirically justifiable adjustment formula based on the relationship between costs and discharges for these low-volume hospitals." *See* 69 FR 48,916, 49,099 (2004). Upon performing this calculation, CMS determined the discharge number should be established at 200 or fewer per year.

[227] PPACA, § 3025.

and kidney acquisition costs incurred by an approved transplant facility; and costs associated with blood-clotting factor.[228]

Value Based Purchasing

Beginning in fiscal year 2013, the Secretary of DHHS must implement a value-based purchasing program under which payment can be increased based on a provider's performance score.[229]

Hospital Acquired Conditions

Beginning in fiscal year 2015, hospitals will be ranked based on their number of hospital-acquired conditions and hospitals in the top quarter (*i.e.*, with the most HACs) will have overall inpatient payments further reduced by 1%, in addition to current payment penalties for HACs.[230]

Hospital Readmissions

Beginning in fiscal year 2013, IPPS for hospitals with readmission rates higher than their Medicare-calculated expected readmission rates will be reduced by the greater of (a) a floor adjustment factor equal to 0.99% for FY 2013, 0.98% for FY 2014 and 0.97% for FY 2015 and subsequent years, or (b) the excess readmissions ratio for the applicable federal fiscal year.[231] The excess readmissions ratio is 1 minus the ratio of the aggregate payments for excess readmissions for the hospital divided by the total aggregate payments for all discharges.

Bonus Payment for Low-Cost Hospitals

For hospitals in the top quarter of low-cost counties of adjusted Medicare Part A and B benefit spending (adjusted by age, sex and race), a bonus payment will be made. A total of $400 million is established as a pool for those payments for federal fiscal years 2011 and 2012. [232]

Community-based Care Transition Program

Beginning January 1, 2011, funding will be made available to facilities that furnish improved care transition services to high-risk Medicare beneficiaries (for example, post-discharge planning, medication administration counseling, follow-up services, etc.). Unless otherwise extended, payments under this program are available for a five-year period.[233]

---

[228] *See* 42 C.F.R. §§ 412.2(e)(5), .2(f)(8), .2(e)(2), 413.85, 415.160, 412.2(e)(4), .113(c), .113(d), .113(f)(4), .115(a).
[229] PPACA, § 3001.
[230] PPACA, § 3008.
[231] PPACA, §§ 3025, 10309.
[232] PPACA, § 1109.
[233] PPACA, § 3026.

3.8.3 Other Hospital PPS

3.8.3.1 *Rehabilitation Hospitals*

Inpatient rehabilitation facilities (IRFs) and distinct-part units are paid under an IRF PPS. IRF PPS applies to all inpatient rehabilitation facilities except Department of Veterans Affairs (VA) hospitals, hospitals subject to state cost controls (*e.g.*, Maryland hospitals), and hospitals in demonstration projects. The IRF PPS utilizes information from a patient-assessment instrument to classify patients into distinct groups based on clinical characteristics and expected resource needs. Separate payments are calculated for each group, including the application of case- and facility-level adjustments.[234]

3.8.3.2 *Long Term Care Hospitals*

Long term care hospitals (LTCHs) are paid under a separate LTCH PPS.[235] LTCH PPS applies to hospitals with an average length of stay greater than 25 days. The LTCH PPS uses information from LTCH patient records to classify patients into distinct long term care DRGs based on clinical characteristics and expected resource needs. Separate payments are calculated for each DRG. The establishment of new LTCHs are subject to a multi-year moratorium enacted by Congress.[236]

3.8.3.3 *Psychiatric Hospitals*

Inpatient psychiatric facilities (IPF PPS) are paid under a per diem-based payment system. The per diem payment amount reflects the average daily costs of inpatient psychiatric care, including capital-related costs. After adjustment for budget neutrality, the per diem amount is modified by factors for patient and facility characteristics to account for variation in patient resource use. Adjustments also are made to account for area wage levels, rural IPFs, and teaching IPFs.[237]

3.8.3.4 *Affordable Care Act Updates*

Under the Affordable Care Act, market basket updates for IRFs, LTCHs and IPFs will be reduced on a sliding scale between the years 2010 and 2019. IRFs, LTCHs and IPFs will also be required to report data on quality measures beginning fiscal year 2014, similar to what is already occurring in the hospital and SNF settings. Providers that fail to submit data on such measures will be subject to a 2% reduction in market basket updates.[238]

---

[234] 42 U.S.C. 1395ww(d); 42 C.F.R. §§ 412.500 *et seq.*; BBRA, § 123; BIPA, § 307; 67 Fed. Reg. 55,954 (2002).

[235] *Id.*

[236] Section 114(d) of the Medicare, Medicaid and SCHIP Extension Act (MMSEA), enacted December 29, 2007, established a three-year moratorium on the establishment of new LTCHs, an increase in the number of certified beds at LTCHs, or the establishment of a satellite facility by an existing LTCH. This moratorium was extended until December 28, 2012 by section 3106(a) of the PPACA.

[237] 42 U.S.C. § 1395ww(d)(1)(B); 42 C.F.R. §§ 412.400 *et seq.*

[238] PPACA §§ 3004, 10322.

3.8.4 Rural-Area Hospitals

Special payment provisions apply to hospitals identified as isolated or essential hospitals primarily located in rural areas. Such entities include critical access hospitals, sole community hospitals, rural referral centers and Medicare-dependent hospitals.[239] Each is briefly described below.

- *Critical Access Hospitals (CAHs)* — CAHs must have no more than 15 inpatient beds, offer 24-hour emergency care, and be located more than a 35-mile drive from any other hospital. CAHs are reimbursed based on what they spend for each patient, rather than on the average expected cost for specific diagnoses that most hospitals are paid.[240]
- *Sole Community Hospitals (SCHs)* — SCHs are the sole source of care in their area and are eligible for reimbursement as a SCH if they are located at least 35 miles from other similar hospitals or are located in a rural area and meet certain conditions regarding accessibility. SCHs receive the higher of a hospital-specific rate based on their costs in a base year or the IPPS Federal rate based on the standardized amount.[241]
- *Rural Referral Centers (RRCs)* — The RRC program was established to support high-volume rural hospitals that treat a large number of complicated cases. To be eligible to be a RRC, a hospital must be either located in a rural area and have more than 275 beds in use, or meet certain criteria concerning case volume and patient travel.[242]
- *Medicare-Dependent Hospitals (MDHs)* — MDHs have fewer than 100 beds, do not serve as SCHs, and at least 60% of the facility's inpatient days or discharges are for Medicare beneficiaries. An MDH receives the higher of the Federal rate or the Federal rate plus 75% of the amount by which the Federal rate is exceeded by the highest of its FY 1982, FY 1987, or FY 2002 hospital specific rate.[243] Under the Affordable Care Act, the MDH program was extended for another year through October 1, 2012.[244]

3.8.5 Hospitals Excluded from PPS

Certain hospitals are excluded from PPS primarily because the government has been unable to devise a workable PPS methodology for these hospitals. Hospitals *originally* excluded from PPS included IRFs, LTCHs, IPFs, hospitals located in any U.S. territory (except Puerto Rico), children's hospitals, cancer hospitals, VA hospitals, and CAHs.[245] Medicare traditionally reimburses PPS-exempt hospitals for "reasonable costs" subject to the limits imposed by the Tax Equity and Fiscal Responsibility Act (TEFRA), thereby the "TEFRA limit."

---

[239] *See generally* 42 U.S.C. § 1395ww(d); 42 C.F.R. §§ 412.90(a), .92 (SCHs); 42 U.S.C. §§ 1395i; 42 C.F.R. § 412.96 (RRCs); 42 C.F.R. § 412.108 (MDHs).

[240] *See generally* at 42 U.S.C. § 1395ww(d) and specifically at 42 C.F.R. § 413.70.

[241] *See generally* at 42 U.S.C. § 1395ww(d) and specifically at 42 C.F.R. §§ 412.90(a) and 412.92.

[242] *See generally* at 42 U.S.C. § 1395ww(d) and specifically at 42 C.F.R. § 412.96.

[243] *See generally* at 42 U.S.C. § 1395ww(d) and specifically at 42 C.F.R. §§ 412.90(j) and 412.108.

[244] PPACA, § 3124.

[245] *See* discussion regarding transition to IRF PPS, LTCH PPS, and IPF PPS at section 3.8.1.3. *See also* 42 C.F.R. § 413.80 regarding CAHs.

The term "reasonable cost" is defined by Medicare law as follows:

> the cost actually incurred, excluding therefrom any part of incurred cost found to be unnecessary in the efficient delivery of needed health services, and shall be determined in accordance with regulations establishing the method or methods to be used and the items to be included in determining such costs….[246]

Reasonable costs encompass "all necessary and proper expenses incurred in furnishing services" including the provider's direct and indirect costs.[247] Reasonable-cost principles contemplate that a provider will be reimbursed the actual costs of providing quality care, regardless of how widely the actual costs may vary from provider to provider and from time to time for the same provider.[248]

Cost-based providers are reimbursed subject to allowable costs. Under the allowable-cost principle, "the costs for individuals covered by the Medicare Program are not borne by others not so covered, and the costs for individuals not so covered are not borne by the Medicare Program."[249] Allowable costs are determined using the claims that are submitted by the provider, the provider's annual cost reports, or a combination of the two. If the provider's operating costs include amounts unrelated to patient care, specifically not reimbursable, or flowing from the provision of luxury items or services, then such amounts will not be deemed "allowable" for payment by Medicare.[250]

In Medicare parlance, PPS-excluded hospitals are frequently referred to as "TEFRA hospitals." These hospitals receive a *per diem* interim payment for the cost of inpatient care that is subject to a final cost-report settlement. Medicare uses the hospital's net cost amount (*e.g.*, exclusive of capital-related and medical-education costs) to determine whether such costs exceed the program's targeted cost threshold (known as the "TEFRA target amount"). Medicare imposes a "penalty payment" on hospitals that exceed the TEFRA target amount, as only a portion of the excess cost will be reimbursed to the hospital. Similarly, hospitals will receive an "incentive payment" from Medicare if their final reimbursable costs fall below the TEFRA limit.[251]

3.8.6 Hospital Outpatient Department Services

A PPS for hospital outpatient department services (HOPPS) became effective August 1, 2000.[252] Under HOPPS, only a hospital may bill Medicare for services provided to hospital outpatients pursuant to an "encounter" in the outpatient department and when furnished by the outpatient department.

---

[246] 42 U.S.C. § 1395x(v)(1)(A).

[247] Ctrs. for Medicare & Medicaid Servs., *Medicaid Management Care Manual* (Pub. 100-16), Chap. 17A, § 50.

[248] 42 C.F.R. § 413.9(c)(3). *See also GranCare, Inc. v. Shalala*, 93 F. Supp. 2d. 24 (D.D.C. 2000) regarding the court's interpretation of the "prudent buyer" principle when costs are considered "substantially out of line" with institutions in the same geographic area that are similar in size, scope of services, utilization, and the like.

[249] Ctrs. for Medicare & Medicaid Servs., *Medicaid Management Care Manual* (Pub. 100-16), Ch. 17A, § 50.

[250] 42 C.F.R. § 413.9(c)(3).

[251] Tax Equity and Fiscal Responsibility Act of 1982, Pub. L. No. 97-248, 96 Stat. 324 (1982). TEFRA hospitals are paid a target rate for their operating costs. The "cost with TEFRA limit" reimbursement scenario is set forth in 42 U.S.C. § 1395x(v), which defines "reasonable cost," and at 42 C.F.R. §§ 412.22, 413.40.

[252] 42 U.S.C. § 1395(*l*); 42 C.F.R. pt. 419. *See also* BBA, § 4523; BBRA, §§ 201–204, 402; and BIPA, §§ 401–406. Although an effective date of January 1, 1999 was established under the BBA, the implementation of the OPPS was delayed by CMS for various reasons until August 1, 2000. Additionally, the effective implementation of OPPS for provider-based facilities was delayed until October 7, 2000.

An "encounter" is defined by Medicare as a "direct personal contact between a patient and physician, or other person" who is authorized under state law or the hospital's bylaws.[253]

OPPS uses "ambulatory payment classification" (APC) groups to calculate the hospital outpatient rate.[254] Developed by 3M Health Information Systems, the APC system groups outpatient procedures into individual ambulatory payment classes. Each APC contains an aggregation of clinically related and resource-similar services.

The beneficiary coinsurance is calculated for each APC based on 20% of the national median charge for services in the APC. The coinsurance amount for an APC will not change until such time as the amount becomes 20% of the total APC payment. Regardless, no coinsurance amount can be greater than the hospital inpatient deductible in a given year.[255]

The OPPS rate is based on the median cost of the procedures contained within each APC subject to an outlier payment adjustment for high-cost cases established by the Balanced Budget Refinement Act (BBRA).[256] Further, both the total APC payment and the coinsurance amount are adjusted for geographic wage variations. Hospitals also may be paid for more than one APC per patient encounter, depending on the type of service provided.

The MMA established a new payment methodology for "specified covered outpatient drugs" furnished as part of a covered hospital's outpatient-department service. "Specified covered outpatient drugs" are drugs that were paid on a pass-through basis prior to December 31, 2002, and for which a separate APC has been established. They also include radio-pharmaceuticals. Reimbursement for these types of drugs and biologicals furnished in the hospital outpatient department setting migrated to the average sales price (ASP) methodology.[257] Now, covered Part B drugs and biologicals (including IVIG, orphan drugs, separately payable drugs and biologicals, blood clotting factors, intrathecal drugs and echocardiography contrast agents) are generally paid at the lesser of 106% of ASP or the actual charge, just as in the physician office setting.[258] In some instances, however, the payment amount differs depending upon the type of drug or biological being provided. These include the following:

- payment for drugs and biologicals, and radiopharmaceuticals before a HCPCs code is assigned will be paid at 95% of the average wholesale price (AWP);[259]
- because CMS lacks ASP data on which to base payment rates for radiopharmaceuticals, it proposes to pay for such agents in 2007 according to the following: (i) separately payable radiopharmaceuticals (those above the $55 packaging threshold)—determined from aggregate hospital mean costs for radiopharmaceuticals from 2005 claims data; and (ii) new radiophar-

253 42 C.F.R. § 410.2.
254 *Id.* §§ 419.30–.32.
255 BBA, § 4523; BBRA, § 204; 65 Fed. Reg. 18,434 (2000). *See* BIPA, § 111 for subsequent modifications to the beneficiary copayment amount; 42 C.F.R. §§ 419.42–.44.
256 BBRA, § 201; 65 Fed. Reg. 18,434 (2000). *See also* 67 Fed. Reg. 9,556 (2002).
257 70 Fed. Reg. 68,516 (Nov. 10, 2005).
258 70 Fed. Reg. 68,640, 68,648, 68,661, 68,671–72.
259 70 Fed. Reg. 68,669.

maceuticals depending on whether they have a HCPCs code (paid at 106% ASP) or not (paid at 95% AWP);[260] and

- certain vaccines, namely pneumococcal pneumonia, flu, and hepatitis vaccines will continue to be paid according to reasonable costs.[261]

3.8.6.1 The Three-Day DRG Payment-Window Rule

Diagnostic and certain non-physician therapeutic services performed on an outpatient basis during the three days immediately preceding a patient's date of admission to a PPS hospital are not billable to the Medicare program as separate services. Despite the fact that this rule commonly is known as the "72-hour DRG payment window," a literal reading of the applicable provisions indicates that three days will mean more than 72 hours in most cases. The statute and regulations refer to diagnostic and therapeutic services furnished by a hospital or by an entity wholly-owned by a hospital (*e.g.*, laboratory and radiology services) furnished during the three days "immediately preceding the date of the patient's admission."[262] The Medicare Hospital Manual, however, refers to services furnished "within three days prior to the date of the beneficiary's admission."[263] Thus, the window can be as long as 95 hours and 59 minutes—three days, plus the date of admission.

3.8.6.2 Unbundling

"Unbundling" is the improper practice of billing Medicare for separate procedures that routinely should be reported as a single claim. This practice results in an overall higher cost to the Medicare program for such services. In 1986, Congress extended the 1983 prohibition against the unbundling of hospital inpatient services to include hospital outpatient services.[264]

3.8.7 Post-Acute Care Providers

Medicare also covers certain post-hospital services (*e.g.*, SNF and hospice) for patients who are discharged to a post-acute care setting after a hospital stay, as well as for medical services that are provided to beneficiaries in their homes. Medicare reimburses such providers for post-acute care services using a PPS or fee-based payment methodology. Payment also may be tied to the satisfactory submission of certain additional requirements, such as a physician's certification of medical necessity, patient-assessment data, and/or a written plan of care.

3.8.7.1 Skilled Nursing Facilities

Medicare classifies SNFs as hospital-based, freestanding, or "swing-bed" for payment purposes. In order to be considered "hospital-based," the SNF must be an integral and subordinate part of the hospital, and be subject to the same bylaws and governance as the hospital. Swing-bed SNFs may be

---

[260] 71 Fed. Reg. 49,584.

[261] 70 Fed. Reg. 68,669, 68,670.

[262] 42 U.S.C. § 1395ww(a)(4); 42 C.F.R. §§ 412.2(c)(5), .413.40(c)(2).

[263] Ctrs. for Medicare & Medicaid Servs., *Medicare Claims Processing Manual* (Pub. 100-04), Ch. 3, § 40.3B.

[264] 42 U.S.C. §§ 1395y(a)(14), 1395cc(a)(1)(H); 42 C.F.R. §§ 410.42, 1003.102–.103; 65 Fed. Reg. 18,434 (Apr. 7, 2000).

converted to either short-term (acute care) or long-term (extended care) use, subject to need. Swing-bed SNFs also must meet specific eligibility requirements, and are subject to special payment rules.

As a condition of participation, Medicare requires all SNFs to have in effect a transfer agreement with a hospital. Medicare also excludes services furnished by SNFs from the three-day DRG payment-window rule.[265]

For cost-reporting periods occurring after July 1, 1998, a PPS *per diem* rate was phased in over a transition period that ended in 2001.[266] The initial PPS *per diem* rate was based on 1995 aggregate cost-report data and is adjusted for case-mix variation using a resident classification system called Resource Utilization Groups (RUGs). The RUGs are based on resident-assessment data (*e.g.*, health conditions, clinical characteristics, and patient service needs), and are weighted by the intensity of care and services required. Initially, 44 RUGs were established. Recently that has been expanded to encompass 53 RUGs.[267] The PPS rate is further adjusted for geographic wage variations using the hospital wage index.[268]

The Affordable Care Act requires the Secretary of DHHS to develop a plan to implement value based purchasing for SNFs by October 1, 2011.[269] Market based updates for SNFs will be reduced by a productivity adjustment in 2012, which may cause updates to go below zero.[270]

3.8.7.2 Hospice

CMS establishes payment rates for specific categories of covered hospice care (*e.g.*, routine home care, continuous home care, inpatient respite day care, general inpatient care) that are subject to a cost cap and an inflation update.[271] Under the Affordable Care Act, the Secretary of DHHS is required to promulgate regulations after October 1, 2013 implementing revisions to the methodology for the routine homecare payment rate, which may include revisions to the per diem payment amounts, and other hospice care services.[272] Medicare beneficiaries must elect to receive hospice care and be certified by a physician as terminally ill at the beginning of the initial hospice-benefit period.[273]

Payment is made for each day during which the beneficiary is eligible and under the care of the hospice, regardless of the amount of services furnished on any given day. Additionally, payment is

[265] *See* section 3.8.6.1 for a discussion of the three-day DRG payment-window rule. 42 U.S.C. §§ 1395tt, 1395x(*l*); 42 C.F.R. §§ 409.20, .32–.33, 412.2(c), .4, 413.114, .40(c); Ctrs. for Medicare & Medicaid Servs., *Medicare Claims Processing Manual* (Pub. 100-04), Ch. 3, § 40.3B.

[266] 42 C.F.R. §§ 413.335, .337; Ctrs. for Medicare & Medicaid Servs., *Medicare Program Integrity Manual* (Pub. 100-08), Ch. 6, § 6.1; *see also* BIPA, §§ 311–315 for subsequent modifications to the SNF payment methodology. Ctrs. for Medicare & Medicaid Servs. Prog. Mem. A-01-08 (Jan. 16, 2001) at www.cms.hhs.gov/transmittals/downloads/a0108.pdf.

[267] Note that under PPACA, the implementation of the RUG-IV system was delayed by one year until October 11, 2011. *See* PPACA § 10325.

[268] The hospital wage index is being used by CMS for the SNF geographic-wage adjustment because the agency lacks reliable SNF-specific data to establish a wage index for SNFs. 66 Fed. Reg. 39,562 (2001).

[269] PPACA § 3006.

[270] PPACA § 3401.

[271] 42 C.F.R. §§ 418.302(b), .308, .309. Medicare also excludes hospice services from the three-day DRG payment-window rule. *Id.* §§ 412.2(c), 413.40(c).

[272] PPACA § 3132.

[273] 42 U.S.C. § 1395d(a)(4), (d)(1); 42 C.F.R. §§ 418.200–.204.

made for only one of the categories of hospice care for any particular day.[274] The hospice cap, which runs from November 1 of each year until October 31 of the following year, is calculated by the MAC at the end of the hospice-cap period. Payments made to a hospice during the cap period that exceed the cap amount are considered overpayments, and must be refunded back to the Medicare program by the hospice.[275]

Similar to other PPS providers, hospice providers are required to report quality measures beginning in fiscal year 2014, or have their annual market basket updates reduced by 2%.[276] As was done in the context of other PPS payment systems, and to help fund the costs of reform initiatives, market basket updates for hospice services will be reduced on a sliding scale between fiscal years 2013 through 2019.[277]

3.8.7.3 Home Health Agencies

HHAs are classified by Medicare as hospital-based or freestanding for payment purposes. Effective October 1, 1997, HHAs are paid based on the physical location where the HHA services are provided, as opposed to where the HHA that provides the services is located.[278]

Prior to October 1, 1997, HHAs were reimbursed by Medicare on a per-visit cost basis subject to applicable limits. Between October 1, 1997, and September 30, 2000, HHAs were reimbursed under an interim payment system (IPS) that paid HHAs according to the "*lesser*" of (1) the agency's specific costs, (2) the Medicare per-visit limit, or (3) the agency's specific per-beneficiary limit, which is calculated using a statutory formula prescribed under the BBA.[279]

For cost-reporting periods occurring on or after October 1, 2000, HHAs are paid under a PPS. The PPS rate, which is based on data collected from a two-year (1995–1997) demonstration project, is adjusted for case-mix variation using a Home Health Resource Group (HHRG) classification system. The HHRG system classifies HHA patients into 80 case-mix groups that are adjusted for geographic wage variations.

Under PPS, HHAs are paid for each 60-day episode of care. Sixty percent of the estimated base payment for the full 60 days is paid to the HHA when the initial claim is filed with the MAC. The remaining 40% is received by the HHA at the close of the first 60-day episode of care. For subsequent episodes, the HHA receives a 50% initial payment and a 50% residual payment. Additional adjustments may be made for payment outliers, significant changes in a beneficiary's condition, low beneficiary utilization during an episode of care, or when a beneficiary changes HHAs in the middle of an

274 42 C.F.R. § 418.302(e)(2). *See also* BIPA, § 321(a)–(b) for subsequent modifications to the hospice payment methodology.
275 42 C.F.R. §§ 418.308–.309.
276 PPACA §§ 3004, 10322.
277 PPACA § 3401.
278 42 U.S.C. § 1395bbb(g).
279 *Id.* § 1395x(v)(1)(L); *see also* BBRA, §§ 301–303 for subsequent modifications to the interim payment system and PPS methodologies.

episode of care.[280] Certain items (*e.g.*, DME, oxygen, and related supplies) also are excluded from the PPS rate.[281]

Beginning in 2014, the Secretary of DHHS must re-base home health payments by a percentage determined by the Secretary to reflect the number, mix and level of intensity of home health services in an episode of care, and the average cost of providing care.[282] Re-based payments must be phased in over four-year increments not to exceed 3.5% per year.

As with hospitals and SNF's, the Secretary is required to develop a plan to implement value based purchasing for home health agencies.[283] The Affordable Care Act also reduces market based updates for HHAs by 1% for calendar years 2011 through 2013.[284] Beginning in 2015, market based updates will be further reduced by a productivity adjustment.

3.9 Payment—The Resource-Based Relative Value Scale Fee Schedule

3.9.1 Overview

Historically, physicians and other Part B suppliers were paid by Medicare on a "reasonable charge" basis. Medicare defines "reasonable charge" as the "lesser" of (i) the submitted charge; (ii) the "customary charge," which is the median of the supplier's historical charges for that service; or (iii) the prevailing charge, which is derived from what the other suppliers charge for the service in the same area.[285] Since the early 1980s, Medicare has moved progressively away from paying physicians and suppliers using the reasonable-charge methodology.

Congress established a new payment program for physicians in 1989. The new methodology, which was phased in between 1992 and 1996, pays physicians according to the lesser of the actual charge, or the amount determined from a resource-based relative value scale (RBRVS) fee schedule. Developed by the Harvard School of Public Health under the direction of William Hsiao, the RBRVS fee schedule is based on the relative value of a physician's work (*i.e.*, intensity of effort, skill, and medical judgment) as adjusted for geographic, practice, and malpractice-expense variations.[286]

3.9.2 RBRVS Fundamentals

Each medical procedure is assigned a relative value unit (RVU) for the physician work, practice, and malpractice components that is based on the individual procedure's ranking, relative to the other procedures on the scale.[287] The RVU is then multiplied by a national dollar "conversion factor" to

---

[280] 65 Fed. Reg. 41,128 (2000).
[281] BBRA, § 305; 65 Fed. Reg. 41,128 (2000).
[282] PPACA § 3131.
[283] PPACA § 3006.
[284] PPACA §§ 3401, 10322.
[285] 42 U.S.C. § 1395u(b)(3).
[286] *Id.* § 1395w-4(a); 42 C.F.R. pt. 414. Radiology and anesthesiology services are subject to separate RBRVS fee schedules. 42 C.F.R. §§ 414.22(a)(2), .46.
[287] 42 U.S.C. § 1395w-4(c); 42 C.F.R. §§ 414.20–.28. The MMA effected changes in practice-expense RVUs for drug administration costs. MMA, § 303.

determine the amount of Medicare payment.[288] Individual Geographic Practice Cost Indexes (GPCIs) are used by Medicare to adjust this number to account for geographical differences in practice costs.[289]

Annual updates to the conversion factor are derived from a market-basket index of medical service costs called the Medicare Economic Index (MEI). To control the overall growth of physician expenditures to the Medicare program, RBRVS uses a target rate (the Sustainable Growth Rate (SGR)) that is linked to the growth of the U.S. Gross Domestic Product and certain other factors.[290] Such factors include the estimated weighted percentage increase in fees for all physician services, the estimated changes in the average number of Part B beneficiaries, and the estimated change in expenditures for all physician services due to statutory and regulatory changes. The annual update to the conversion factor is tied to the SGR.

For services furnished on or after January 1, 1999, separate facility and non-facility practice-expense RVUs have been established. The lower facility-expense RVU applies to services that are delivered in a hospital, SNF, or ASC. The higher non-facility expense RVU applies to services that are furnished in a physician's office, a patient's home, or a facility that is not an ASC, SNF or hospital.[291]

Medicare participating physicians (PARs) with UPINs are paid based on the full RBRVS payment amount. Non-participating physicians (Non-PARs) are paid based on 95% of the allowable RBRVS amount, and are subject to a maximum limit on what they can charge beneficiaries over the fee-schedule amount. Non-PARs can be subject to sanctions, including civil monetary penalties and program exclusion, for repeatedly billing Medicare beneficiaries in excess of the "limiting charge."[292]

3.9.3 Coding and Documentation Standards

The RVUs have been compiled into HCPCS' common five-character coding arrangement.[293] Eighty percent of all HCPCS codes are compiled under the Practitioner's Current Procedural Terminology (CPT) for medical services that is updated annually by the AMA. The other 20% include physician and non-physician services not included in the CPT, as well as codes based on local reporting practices. CPT codes are five-digit numerical codes; the other codes are alphanumeric.

In conjunction with the AMA, CMS has developed explicit evaluation and management (E&M) guidelines to assist physicians in properly coding and documenting office visits, hospital visits, medical consultations, and other case-management services in the patient's chart. Components used in proper E&M code selection include the type of medical history taken, the category of medical examination performed, and the complexity level of medical decision making by the physician. Failure to provide adequate documentation in the patient's medical record (*i.e.*, appropriate support for the

---

288 42 C.F.R. § 414.30.

289 42 U.S.C. § 1395w-4(e); 42 C.F.R. § 414.26.

290 42 U.S.C. § 1395w-4(f). The MMA modified the formula for calculating the sustainable growth rate to include a ten-year rolling-average factor. This change applies to SGR computations starting in 2003. MMA, § 601.

291 42 C.F.R. § 414.22.

292 *Id.* § 414.20.

293 *See* cms.hhs.gov/medhcpcsgeninfo/01_overview.asp for detailed information relating to the HCPCS coding.

coding decision) can result in reduced reimbursement and/or allegations that the physician submitted "false claims" to the Medicare program.[294]

Teaching physicians who bill Medicare when services are provided in part by a medical resident are required to adhere to additional documentation standards. For example, the teaching physician must be physically present during *key* portions of the procedure. In cases involving surgery or procedures that are dangerous or complex, the teaching physician must be present during all *critical* portions of the procedure, and must be immediately available to furnish services throughout the entire procedure.[295] Documentation of the physician's presence also must be included in the patient's chart.

3.9.4 Application of RBRVS to Non-Physician Practitioners and Other Suppliers

Medicare uses the RBRVS fee schedule to reimburse limited-license practitioner services, incident to services, radiology services, outpatient physical and occupational therapy services, and certain diagnostic tests exclusive of clinical laboratory tests.[296] Physician assistants, nurse practitioners, clinical nurse specialists, nurse midwives, and CRNAs also are subject to cost limits that are based on a percentage of the RBRVS fee-schedule amount.[297]

3.9.5 Fee Schedules for Freestanding Supplier Entities

Medicare uses a combination of national fee schedules and cost-charge limitations to pay freestanding supplier entities such as clinical laboratories, DME and prosthetic and orthotic providers, screening mammography suppliers, CORFs, rehabilitation agencies and clinics, ESRD facilities, FQHCs, and RHCs.[298]

3.9.6 Ambulance Services

Payment is available according to a national fee schedule under Medicare Part B only if payment is not made under Medicare Part A, directly or indirectly, for the service.[299] There are seven levels of ambulance services, five of which apply to ground ambulances and two of which apply to air ambulances (one for fixed wing and one for helicopters). Each level of service has a slightly different payment schedule amount which is generally determined by adding a base rate to a payment rate per mile which is adjusted by a geographic adjustment factor, multiplied by the number of miles the beneficiary is transported.

---

[294] The False Claims Act creates criminal liability for anyone who presents a false, fraudulent, or fictitious claim for payment to the federal government. A violation of the act constitutes a felony offense punishable by imprisonment of up to five years, fines up to $25,000, and exclusion from participation in government healthcare programs. 18 U.S.C. § 287. *See also* 31 U.S.C. § 3729 (civil False Claims Act).

[295] 42 C.F.R. § 415.172.

[296] *Id.* §§ 410.10, .32, .59.

[297] Revisions to Payment Policies and Adjustments to the Relative Value Units Under the Physician Fee Schedule for Calendar Year 1999, 63 Fed. Reg. 58,814 (1998).

[298] 42 U.S.C. §§ 1395m, 1395k; Ctrs. for Medicare & Medicaid Servs., *Medicare Claims Processing Manual* (Pub. 100-04), Ch. 15, §§ 10.2, 20, 20.1; Ch. 18, §§ 20.2, 20.3, 20.4.

[299] 42 C.F.R. § 410.40(a)(2).

For ambulance services where the pickup point is in a rural area, there is an add-on to the mileage rate for both ground (for first 50 miles) and air transport. Further, for a period commencing July 1, 2004, and continuing through December 31, 2011, rural transports will be paid the higher of (a) the current rate payable under the national fee schedule process or (b) a blended rate that is a mix of the national fee schedule and a new, regional fee schedule. Section 414 of MMA requires the Secretary to increase the base rate for certain rural area transports.[300]

The national fee schedule is not applicable to critical access hospitals (CAH) or entities owned or operated by CAHs, which continue to be paid on a reasonable cost basis if there is no other ambulance supplier or provider within a 35-mile drive.

3.10 Payment—Blended Capitation

3.10.1 Introduction

Medicare employs a distinct payment methodology for MA organizations that ties the program's payment to the number of beneficiaries enrolled in the MA plan. CMS makes advance monthly payments to MA organizations using a per-member per-month (PMPM) methodology known as "capitation."

MA organizations receive an advance monthly payment equal to 1/12th of the annual MA capitation rate for the county or geographic area (*i.e.*, payment area) they serve.[301] Monthly payments to MA organizations reflect existing enrollees, including enrollment that is effective both before and in the month for which payment is being made. CMS can retroactively adjust (reconcile) payments to MA organizations to reflect any differences between the actual number of MA enrollees in a plan and the number on which CMS based the MA organization's advance monthly payment.[302]

---

[300] Specifically, between July 1, 2004 and 2009, MMA § 414 provides additional funding for transports that originate in a "qualified rural area." MMA § 414 also provides additional funding under the current fee schedule, for the period July 1, 2004, through January 1, 2010, for long trip mileage and rural transports attributable to low-density areas. Finally MMA § 414 provides, beginning July 1, 2004, for mileage payment increases for long trips, that is, trips in excess of 50 miles in both urban and rural areas. Sections 3105 and 10311 of the Affordable Care Act extended increases in the ambulance fee schedule amounts for covered ground ambulance transports which originated in rural areas by 3% and for covered ground ambulance transports which originated in urban areas by 2% retroactive to January 1, 2010 through December 31, 2010. The new law similarly extends the provision for air ambulance services provided in any area that was designated as a rural area for purposes of making payments under the ambulance fee schedule for services furnished on December 31, 2006. Finally, the Affordable Care Act extended, retroactive to January 1, 2010 through December 31, 2010, § 414 of the Medicare Prescription Drug, Improvement and Modernization Act of 2003 which established the super rural bonus. The Medicare and Medicaid Extenders Act of 2010 (H.R 4994, signed into law Dec. 15, 2010), further extended these provisions through December 31, 2011 or January 1, 2012 dependent upon the specific provision.

[301] 42 C.F.R. § 422.304. Special rules apply to enrollees in MSAs and RFBS plans, as well as to enrollees with ESRD. *Id.* § 422.304(c)(1)–(3).

[302] *Id.* § 422.308(f). *See* Ctrs. for Medicare & Medicaid Servs., *Medicare Managed Care Manual* (Pub. 100-16), Ch. 19, § 60 regarding CMS policy on retroactive payment adjustments.

3.10.2 Determining the MA Payment Rate

MA plans (other than medical savings accounts) are required to use a competitive-bidding system for Part A and Part B benefits. The MMA allows for competitive bidding that compares geographically-based benchmarks and bids to calculate beneficiary premiums and plan-payment amounts. Each MA organization must annually submit a monthly aggregate bid for each of its MA Plans.[303] The Secretary of DHHS will determine benchmark amounts for Part A and Part B benefits in geographic areas based on the MA capitation rates. The benchmark amounts, risk adjustment factors, and related information will be announced by the Secretary of DHHS by the first Monday in April of each year.[304]

3.11 Payment—New Competitive "Market-Based" Systems

3.11.1 Part B

A competitive acquisition program (CAP) for Part B drugs was phased in during 2006.[305] Under the competitive acquisition program as originally designed, physicians select a contractor to supply all necessary drugs and biologicals to the physician's practice. The contractor is then responsible for submitting claims for the furnished drugs and biologicals to Medicare while the physician submits a claim for administration of the drug or biological (at 106% ASP).[306] Physicians determine annually whether to participate in CAP or obtain and bill their own drugs independently. Certain drug classes are excluded from competitive bidding, including pneumococcal, influenza, and hepatitis B vaccines, drugs and biologicals (other than erythropoietin) furnished in connection with renal dialysis services, radiopharmaceuticals, intravenous immune globulin (IVIG) products. This program, however, was postponed in 2009 by CMS, and it is unclear whether or when it will be re-launched.[307]

Most recently, CMS has launched (and re-launched) a competitive acquisition program to replace the traditional payment system for DMEPOS under the Medicare fee schedule. In particular, Section 302 of the MMA requires that competitive bid payment amounts be used to *replace* the current Medicare DMEPOS fee schedule payment amounts for selected items in selected areas. Those selected items include the following 10 product categories: (1) Oxygen Supplies and Equipment; (2) Standard Power Wheelchairs, Scooters, and Related Accessories; (3) Complex Rehabilitative Power Wheelchairs and Related Accessories; (4) Mail-Order Diabetic Supplies; (5) Enteral Nutrients, Equipment, and Supplies; (6) Continuous Positive Airway Pressure (CPAP) Devices, Respiratory Assist Devices (RADs), and Related Supplies and Accessories; (7) Hospital Beds and Related Accessories; (8) Negative Pressure Wound Therapy (NPWT) Pumps and Related Supplies and Accessories; (9) Walkers and Related Accessories; and (10) Support Surfaces, including group 2 mattresses and overlays (Miami).

303 42 C.F.R. §§ 422.254–.256.

304 MMA, § 222(f).

305 MMA, § 303.

306 70 Fed. Reg. 39,022 (July 6, 2005); 70 Fed. Reg. 52,930 (Sept. 6, 2005).

307 With the implementation of the new Medicare payment rate for covered Part B drugs of ASP + 6%, the viability and need for the competitive acquisition program for drugs appears to be unnecessary. In addition, CMS encountered a number of contacting and vendor programs related to the operation of this program.

Following an initial Round I bid leading to a number of widespread complaints and Congressional scrutiny with respect to CMS' implementation of the Round I bids,[308] the agency was directed to conduct a re-bid of the Round I Competitive Bidding Program and, barring Congressional intervention, the newly selected contract suppliers will begin January 1, 2011.[309] The new Round I Competitive Bidding Program will encompass nine of the largest MSAs in the country including Charlotte, Cincinnati, Cleveland, Dallas-Fort Worth, Kansas City, Miami, Orlando, Pittsburgh, and Riverside, California. Another 91 areas throughout the U.S. will be subjected to the bidding program starting later in 2011. Although as of the eve of this publication, CMS remains committed towards moving forward with the Competitive Bidding Program, the program has been widely criticized by the DMEPOS industry on a number of grounds including errors in the processing (and denial) of certain applicants.

3.11.2 Part C

Since January 1, 2006, MA plans (other than medical savings accounts) were also moved to a competitive-bidding system for Part A and Part B benefits. *See* Section 3.10.2 above.

The most significant change to the MA program since the MMA is, undoubtedly, the Affordable Care Act. Prior to the Affordable Care Act, MA plans were paid a monthly per-capita benefits (except for hospice services) to beneficiaries who enrolled in their MA plan. Under Section 1853 of the Act, CMS was required to calculate benchmark amounts for MA plans. MA plans annually submitted bids that represented the plans estimated monthly revenue requirement for providing covered benefits for the average beneficiary in the upcoming plan year. Under prior guidelines, if the MA plan's bid equaled the CMS-determined benchmark, CMS would pay the MA organization the benchmark amount and there is no beneficiary premium to be charge. If the MA plan bid *exceeded* the benchmark, CMS would pay the MA organization the benchmark amount and the MA organization would charge the beneficiary a monthly premium based upon the difference between he bid and the benchmark amount. Likewise, if the MA plan bid was *less than* the benchmark, CMS would pay the MA organization 75% of the difference between the bid amount and the benchmark—the MA "rebate"—which could be used by the MA organization to (1) lower Medicare cost sharing obligations, (2) provide supplemental benefits (*e.g.*, vision care), or (3) reduce or eliminate monthly premiums.

The Affordable Care Act makes a number of fundamental changes to this process. First and foremost, the Act provides that benchmarks are frozen at 2010 levels. Second, the Act establishes a new MA benchmark rate methodology that is pegged to a fixed percentage of the Medicare FFS costs for the MA plan's payment area. To determine the applicable percentage, each MA payment area (*i.e.*, county) will be ranked based on its Medicare FFS costs and will be grouped into four categories rang-

---

[308] MIPPA made a number of procedural changes to the DMEPOS Competitive Bidding Program, including a requirement that competition to re-bid Round 1 occur in 2009. On January 16, 2009, CMS issued an interim final rule with comment period that incorporates into regulations those provisions of MIPPA related to the DMEPOS Competitive Bidding Program. That rule became effective on April 18, 2009.

[309] The Round 1 re-bid includes the following DMEPOS items: (1) Oxygen Supplies and Equipment; (2) Standard Power Wheelchairs, Scooters, and Related Accessories; (3) Complex Rehabilitative Power Wheelchairs and Related Accessories (Group 2); (4) Mail-Order Replacement Diabetic Supplies; (5) Enteral Nutrients, Equipment and Supplies; (6) CPAP, RADs, and Related Supplies and Accessories; (7) Hospital Beds and Related Accessories; (8) Walkers and Related Accessories and (9) Support Surfaces (Group 2 mattresses and overlays) in Miami.

ing from 95% (for areas that are ranked as high FFS cost areas) to 115% (for areas ranked as low FFS cost areas). This new methodology will be phased in using a three-tiered approach, beginning in contract year (CY) 2011, with the full methodology in effect for CY 2017 and subsequent years.[310]

For all MA plans, payments for CY 2011 will be frozen at the CY 2010 levels. Thereafter, the new methodology will be phased in over a three-year period for most MA plan payment areas. For MA plans in payment areas where the difference between the current CY 2010 payment rate and the CY 2010 projected benchmark rate (calculated under the new methodology) is $30 or more, the phase-in will occur over a four-year period. In those payment areas where the difference is $50 or more, it will occur over a six-year period. All MA plans will be paid under the new methodology beginning in CY 2017.

Of note, while the Affordable Care Act imposes substantial payment reductions as a result of these changes to the benchmark payment approach, the law also establishes new bonus payments available to MA plans that achieve a four stars or higher rating under the MA plan five-star quality rating current used by CMS. In 2012, plans achieving four stars or higher will be eligible for a 1.5% increase, in 2013 a 3% increase, and in 2014 and beyond a 5% increase. Accordingly, the ultimate impact on MA organizations will depend upon their geographic location and the ability to meet four stars or higher on the five-star quality rating system currently used by CMS.

3.11.3 Part D

The MMA also incorporates competitive-bidding and benchmark rates into the Part D payment methodology.[311] As a result, beneficiary premiums vary based on the bids of the selected PDP or MA-PD plan.

PDPs and MA-PD plans are paid for the Part D benefit through a complex scheme of subsidy payments. The PDP and MA-PD plans receive subsidies from the federal government, paid by CMS, through four payment mechanisms: (a) a direct premium subsidy; (b) reinsurance subsidies; (c) payment adjustments; and (d) additional payments for low-income subsidy individuals.[312] Except for those that qualify for a low-income subsidy or premium waiver, beneficiaries are required to pay a monthly premium in addition to their cost sharing obligations through the deductible and co-pays.[313]

The payments CMS provides to the Part D plans under the direct premium subsidy are for each Medicare beneficiary enrolled in the PDP or MA-PD plan and equal to the approved standardized bid of the individual PDP or MD-PD plan, adjusted for health status minus the monthly beneficiary premium.[314] The health status adjustment amount is based on the formula used by CMS to adjust the subsidy amount based on the overall health of a given PDP or MA-PD plan's enrollees.[315]

---

310 Pub. L. 111-152, Section 1102(b) and (c).
311 42 U.S.C. § 1395w-111.
312 42 U.S.C. § 1395w-115 and 42 C.F.R. § 423.315; 70 Fed. Reg. 4,306 (Jan. 28, 2005).
313 *See* 42 U.S.C. § 1395w-102(b), 42 U.S.C. § 1395w-114, 42 C.F.R. § 423.286, and 42 C.F.R. § 423.771.
314 42 C.F.R. § 423.329(a).
315 42 C.F.R. § 423.329(b).

CMS also provides the PDP and MA-PD plans with reinsurance and risk-sharing reimbursement.[316] Reinsurance is provided to a PDP or MA-PD plan once a beneficiary reaches their out-of-pocket threshold,[317] in the amount of 80% of the beneficiary's drug cost for the balance of the year.[318] The MMA also established risk corridors for PDP and MA-PD plans (*i.e.*, specified percentages above and below a target amount).[319] PDP and MA-PD plans are at full risk during 2008–2011 for adjusted allowable-risk corridor costs within 5% above or below the target. PDP and MA-PD plans with adjusted allowable costs above the 5% level would receive increased payments.[320] Conversely, if a PDP or MA-PD plan falls below the target, then the PDP or MA-PD is required to refund a percentage of the savings to the government.[321] CMS will establish the adjusted allowable risk corridor costs for all subsequent years; however, the risk percentage may not be less than 5%.[322] CMS may also provide additional reimbursement to a PDP or MA-PD plan if it experiences unexpected expenses not included in its competitive bid.[323]

3.12 Assignment and Reassignment

The final step in analyzing the potential reimbursement issues associated with a proposed service or supply is determining who is entitled to receive payment from Medicare.

3.12.1 Assignment

The term "assignment" is defined by Medicare as an agreement between a physician or supplier and the beneficiary. Under the terms of the assignment, the beneficiary transfers to the physician or supplier her right to benefits based on covered services specified on the assigned claim; in turn, the physician or supplier agrees to accept the approved charge determined by the MAC as the *full charge* for the items or services.[324]

3.12.1.1 Part A

Medicare Part A prohibits direct payment to beneficiaries for "covered services." Part A providers must accept direct assignment of payment from Medicare, and are prohibited from charging program beneficiaries fees in excess of the Medicare payment amount.[325]

---

316 70 Fed. Reg, at 4,306 (Jan. 28, 2005).

317 The out-of-pocket threshold is $6,447 for 2011. Medicare Advantage and Part D Payment Policies and Final Call Letter, CMS (Apr. 5, 2010).

318 *See* 42 C.F.R. § 423.336 and 42 C.F.R. § 423.343.

319 42 C.F.R. § 423.336. Note, the target amount is defined as total payments that are paid to the plan, risk-adjusted, and reduced by total administrative expenses assumed in the plan's approved bid.

320 *Id.*

321 *Id.* Note that the subsidy and risk-corridor provisions do not apply to fallback plans.

322 42 C.F.R. § 423.336(a)(2).

323 42 C.F.R. § 423.315.

324 42 U.S.C. § 1395(b)(3)(B)(ii); Ctrs. for Medicare & Medicaid Servs., *Medicare Claims Processing Manual* (Pub. 100-04), Ch. 1, § 30.3.2.

325 42 C.F.R. §§ 424.70–.90.

3.12.1.2 Part B

Unlike Part A, beneficiaries under Part B may receive direct payment from Medicare, or they may assign this benefit to their treating physician or supplier.[326] Physicians and suppliers who accept assignment from beneficiaries may not charge them more than the Medicare deductible and coinsurance amounts. A physician or supplier also may refuse to accept assignment from a Medicare beneficiary on an occasion of service basis. In any case, however, Medicare beneficiaries may not be charged over 115% of the nonparticipant fee-schedule amount by such physicians and suppliers.[327]

3.12.1.3 Part C

Except under certain circumstances (*e.g.*, payments made to healthcare providers by CMS because the MA organization failed to do so), only the MA organization is entitled to receive payment for healthcare services that are provided to MA enrollees.[328]

3.12.2 Reassignment

Subject to certain exceptions, Medicare prohibits payment for assigned benefits to anyone other than the physician or supplier who provided the items or services.[329] The MMA liberalized the reassignment rules by eliminating the site of service requirement. Effective as of December 8, 2003, physicians and suppliers may reassign payment for Medicare-covered services, regardless of where the service is furnished, as long as the physician or supplier is an employee of, or has an independent contract with, the entity that will be billing for the physician's services.[330]

An otherwise-correct Medicare payment made to an ineligible recipient under a reassignment will not constitute an overpayment. Nevertheless, the physician's or supplier's right to accept assignment may be subject to revocation for an improper assignment.[331] A violation of the reassignment prohibition also can result in exclusion from the Medicare program.[332] Exceptions include the following:

- *Payment to an Employer.* Payment to an employer of a physician or supplier pursuant to an employment agreement. The agreement must provide the employer with the right to charge and collect payment for the services of the physician or supplier. The employer also must provide CMS with acceptable evidence (*e.g.*, a W-2) of the employer/employee relationship.
- *Payment to an Inpatient Facility.* Payment to an "inpatient" facility (for services furnished in that facility) pursuant to a written agreement that is entered into between the facility and the physician or supplier. The agreement must provide the facility with the right to bill and receive payment for the services of the physician or supplier.
- *Payment to an Organized Healthcare Delivery System.* Payment to a "healthcare delivery system" (for services furnished within the system) if the system and the physician or supplier

---

326 *Id.* §§ 424.53, .55.
327 42 U.S.C. § 1395w-4(g)(2)(C).
328 42 C.F.R. § 422.268.
329 42 U.S.C. § 1395g.
330 MMA, § 952.
331 Ctrs. for Medicare & Medicaid Servs., *Medicare Claims Processing Manual* (Pub. 100-04), Ch. 1, § 30.2.
332 42 C.F.R. § 424.82(c).

enter into a contractual arrangement that allows the system to bill and receive payment for services provided by the physician or supplier. Three organization types may provide and administer healthcare through an organized delivery system—medical group clinics, university-affiliated medical faculty practice plans, and managed care organizations that provide services through a network of contracting providers.

- *Payment to an Agent.* Payment in the name of the party eligible to receive payment to an agent who furnished billing or collection services if the agent receives payment under an agreement with the physician, the agent's compensation is not related to the dollar amounts billed or dependent upon the actual collection of payment, and the agent acts under payment disposition instructions which the physician may modify or revoke at any time.
- *Payment Under Reciprocal Billing Arrangements.* Payment under reciprocal billing arrangements where the patient's regular physician submits a claim for covered visit services that the regular physician arranges to be provided by a substitute physician on an occasional reciprocal basis. The term "covered visit services" includes not only those services ordinarily characterized as a covered physician visit, but also other covered items and services furnished by the substitute physician or by others as incident to the physician's services. Reciprocal billing arrangements are limited to 60 continuous days.
- *Payment Under* Locum Tenens *Arrangements.* Payment to a *locum tenens* or substitute physician. A *locum tenens* physician substitutes for a physician who is absent from his or her professional practice due to illness, pregnancy, vacation, or continuing medical education. The *locum tenens* physician must be paid on a *per diem* or similar fee-for-time basis by the "regular" physician, and may not provide services to Medicare patients for longer than 60 continuous days.
- *Payment for Purchased Diagnostic Tests.* Payment to a physician or medical group for diagnostic laboratory tests (other than clinical) which the physician or group purchases from an independent physician, medical group, or other supplier.
- *Payment for Diagnostic Test Interpretations.* Payment to a supplier for diagnostic test interpretations if (i) the test is initiated by a physician or medical group that is independent of the entity providing the test and of the physician providing the interpretation, (ii) the supplier submits assigned or unassigned claims for both the test and the interpretation, and (iii) the physician providing the interpretation does not see the patient.
- *Payment to a Bank.* Absent a court order, Medicare payments that are due to a physician may be sent to a bank or similar financial institution for deposit in the physician's account. The physician must have sole control over the account, and the bank may not be providing any direct or indirect financing to the physician.
- *Payment to Others.* Payment also may be made pursuant to a court order; or may be made to a government agency or entity, a medical school, or a university under specific circumstances.[333]

[333] 42 U.S.C. § 1395u(b)(6); 42 C.F.R. §§ 424.73, .80; Ctrs. for Medicare & Medicaid Servs., *Medicare Claims Processing Manual* (Pub. 100-04), Ch. 1, § 30.2.

3.13 Appeals—Parts A and B

Payment disputes between Part A providers or Part B suppliers and the Medicare program may be administratively appealed. Under Part A, there are two types of appeals processes available, depending on whether a provider is appealing reimbursement for claim(s) or reimbursement under a cost report.

3.13.1 Claims Appeals—Parts A and B

On March 8, 2005, CMS published Interim Final Rules mandating changes to the Part A and B claims appeals processes.[334] The new regulations appeared at 42 C.F.R. §§ 405.900 *et seq.* and substantially changed the appeals procedures for Part A providers and Part B suppliers.[335] Among other changes, the procedures for appealing Part A and Part B claims are now equivalent. These revisions became effective January 1, 2006.

The new process for a Part A and Part B appeal is as follows:

- *Step 1—Initial Determination.* Once an initial determination has been made by the Medicare Administrative Contractor, a Provider has 120 days to file a request that the Medicare Administrative Contractor revise its determination—*i.e.*, render a redetermination. The Medicare Administrative Contractor then has 60 days in which to make such a redetermination.
- *Step 2—Redetermination.* If the redetermination continues to be adverse to the provider, the provider has 180 days to request that a "qualified independent contractor" (QIC) modify the Medicare Administrative Contractor's determination. This is called requesting a reconsideration. QICs are independent from the Medicare Administrative Contractors that make the initial determination and are not bound by LMRPs or CMS Manual provisions. The QIC must render its reconsideration within 60 days. Appeals to the QIC are "record" appeals and are not live hearings. Importantly, § 933 of the MMA requires that all evidence be presented at this point and bars submission of additional evidence at the next or higher levels of appeal, absent just cause.
- *Step 3—Administrative Law Judge.* If the QIC's reconsideration continues to be adverse to the provider, and the amount in controversy is at least $100 (and claims can be aggregated to meet this threshold), the provider may request review by an administrative law judge (ALJ) within 60 days of the QIC's action.[336] The ALJ must render his or her ruling within 90 days of the completion of the record. If the ALJ does not meet this time frame the appellants case is automatically escalated to the next level of appeal. ALJs must give "substantial deference" to LCDs, LMRPs, and CMS guidance. If the ALJ fails to do so the ALJ must provide reasons why.
- *Step 4—Medicare Appeals Council.* If the provider continues to be dissatisfied with the ALJ action, the provider may request review by the Department Appeals Board (DAB) Medicare

---

334 70 Fed. Reg. 11,420 (Mar. 8, 2005).

335 A chart summarizing the old and new appeals procedures is included at 70 Fed. Reg. 11,426.

336 The minimum amount in controversy is subject to an annual inflation factor. As of January 1, 2010, that amount was $130.74 Fed. Reg. 48,976 (Sept. 25, 2009).

Appeals Council within 60 days of the ALJ's ruling. The Medicare Appeals Council has 90 days to render its ruling.[337]

- *Step 5—Federal District Court.* If the provider continues to be dissatisfied with the ruling of the Medicare Appeals Council, and if the amount in controversy is at least $1,050, the provider may request initiate an action in federal district court within 60 days of the decision by the Appeals Council.[338] Appeals for judicial review must be for "final" determinations after all administrative appeals have been exhausted.

3.13.2 Cost Report Appeals—Part A Only

After the Medicare Administrative Contractor performs an audit of the provider's cost report, it issues an NPR, which is the Medicare Administrative Contractor's determination of allowable costs, including any underpayment owed to the provider or any overpayment owed by the provider to the Medicare program. A provider has 180 days to appeal the Medicare Administrative Contractor's determination subsequent to the issuance of the NPR. The total dollar amount in controversy generally determines where the provider must file an appeal.[339]

- *Medicare Administrative Contractor.* A reimbursement dispute involving more than $1,000 but less than $10,000 must be appealed to the Medicare Administrative Contractor where the dispute is heard by a hearing officer or a panel that is designated by the Medicare Administrative Contractor. Medicare Administrative Contractor decisions are subject to a reevaluation or "reopening" within 12 months (or four years if the provider can show good cause).[340] Medicare Administrative Contractor hearing decisions may be reviewed by the Administrator of CMS at his or her discretion or at the request of the affected provider.[341] However, such decisions are not subject to judicial review.
- *Provider Reimbursement Review Board Appeals.* A reimbursement dispute involving more than $10,000 must be appealed to the Provider Reimbursement Review Board (PRRB).[342] Decisions by the PRRB may be reviewed by the Administrator of CMS and are subject to judicial review.[343] Individual providers may aggregate their appeals for submission to the PRRB if the aggregate dollar amount in controversy exceeds $50,000 and the appeal involves a question of fact or judicial interpretation common to all providers in the appeal.[344] Medicare

337 The DAB was chartered in 1973 as the Departmental Grant Appeals Board; until the 1980s, DAB jurisdiction was limited to disputes arising under the large public assistance grants, such as Medicaid and Aid to Families with Dependent Children, as well as discretionary grant programs. In 1988, the Secretary delegated to the DAB responsibility for adjudicating civil money penalties and exclusions imposed under a wide range of fraud and abuse authorities. In 1993, the Secretary delegated to the DAB responsibility for hearing appeals in enforcement cases brought by CMS and, in 1995, the Secretary delegated to the DAB the Medicare Appeals Council function of hearing appeals in Medicare coverage and payment cases and entitlement cases. The MAC provides the final administrative review of claims for entitlement to Medicare and individual claims for Medicare coverage and payment filed by beneficiaries or healthcare providers/suppliers inclusive of claims appeals and enrollment matters (including denials and revocations).

338 Effective January 1, 2009, this amount was increased to $1060. *Id.*

339 42 C.F.R. §§ 405.1809–.1839.

340 42 C.F.R. § 405.750.

341 42 C.F.R. § 405.1875.

342 42 C.F.R. § 405.1835.

343 42 C.F.R. §§ 405.1873–.1877, 405.1878(f).

344 42 C.F.R. §§ 405.1837–.1839.

also requires providers under common ownership to aggregate their appeals to the PRRB under such circumstances.

- *Right to an Appeal Before the PRRB*. A provider who is dissatisfied with any "final determination" of the MAC or the Secretary of HHS may appeal to the PRRB. "Final determinations" include an original or revised NPR, an amended cost report provided to the Medicare Administrative Contractor before an NPR is issued, refusal to reopen a cost report, rate of payment notices, denial of requests for exception, exemption, and adjustment, including routine cost limit exceptions and TEFRA adjustments, ESRD exception requests for fiscal years ending after August 1983, denial of provider status or classification requests (*e.g.*, sole community hospitals, rural referral centers, etc.) and late NPR determinations.
- *Judicial Review*. Providers may appeal the final administrative decision (whether by the PRRB or from the CMS Administrator's review) to federal court by initiating an action within 60 days from the date of receipt of an adverse decision.[345] Providers also may bypass the hearing process and obtain an expedited judicial review of any action of a Medicare Administrative Contractor that involves the validity of a governing law, regulation or CMS ruling.[346]

3.14 Appeals—Part C

Medicare has established procedures for processing enrollee appeals regarding coverage denials, payment for services, and other grievances. An MA organization must provide appeal procedures, either directly or by delegation to another entity, for each MA plan that it offers.

3.14.1 Enrollee Grievances and Appeals

Each MA plan must establish procedures for standard and expedited MA organization determinations, standard and expedited resolution of grievances, and standard and expedited resolution of appeals.[347] The procedures described in this subsection refer to the appeals process. Disputes that do not meet the definition of an initial determination (*e.g.*, items or services to be included in an optional supplemental plan, or complaints about waiting times or inadequate facilities) are categorized as grievances and are not subject to the appeals process.[348]

MA plans are required to provide timely enrollee-coverage determinations regarding plan benefits. Such determinations must be made by an MA organization "as expeditiously as the enrollee's health condition requires," but no later than 14 calendar days after the date the organization receives the request for a standard organization determination.[349] Either the enrollee or her physician may request a 72-hour "expedited" determination in situations involving serious risk to the enrollee's life, health, or physical functioning. [350]

---

[345] 42 C.F.R. §§ 405.1875, 405.1877.

[346] *Id.* § 405.1842.

[347] Ctrs. for Medicare & Medicaid Servs. *Medicare Managed Care Manual* (Pub. 100-16) § 10.3.

[348] *Id.* § 20.2. Regulations governing grievances can be found at 42 C.F.R. §§ 422.561–.564 and more detail is located in Chapter 13 of the *Managed Care Manual.*

[349] 42 C.F.R. § 422.568.

[350] 42 U.S.C. § 1395w-22(g); 42 C.F.R. §§ 422.570.

3.14.1.1 Reconsiderations

An enrollee may request a reconsideration of an adverse organization determination from an MA organization. This request must be made within 60 calendar days from the date of the initial determination notice. The MA organization is required to complete the reconsideration "as expeditiously as the enrollee's health condition requires" or within 30 to 60 calendar days, depending on the circumstances.[351] The enrollee or the enrollee's physician (acting on the enrollee's behalf) may request a 72-hour determination, provided the same serious-jeopardy standard is met.

3.14.1.2 Independent Review

Adverse reconsiderations are referred to an independent entity for resolution and review. The independent-review process is subject to the same time frames that govern determinations and reconsiderations by MA organizations. If the enrollee, or any party other than the MA organization, is dissatisfied with the decision of the independent entity, and the amount in controversy is in excess of the annual threshold amount, then the case may be heard by an ALJ.[352] Opportunities for review of the ALJ's decision by the Medicare Appeals Council (MAC) or by a U.S. district court also are available.[353]

3.14.1.3 Judicial Review

Any party, including the MA organization, may request judicial review of an ALJ's decision if (i) the DAB denied the party's request for a review and (ii) and the amount in controversy is in excess of the annual threshold amount.[354]

3.14.1.4 Determinations During an Inpatient Stay

Special provisions apply when an MA organization determines that an authorized hospital stay is no longer necessary. MA organizations are required to provide enrollees with a formal end-of-coverage-determination notice that specifies the reasons why continued hospitalization is not considered medically necessary by the MA organization. Information regarding the appeal rights of the enrollee and the enrollee's financial liability for continuing the hospital stay also must be included in the notice. An immediate QIO review may be requested by the enrollee, and the enrollee may remain hospitalized throughout the course of the QIO review period without incurring additional financial liability for the continued hospital stay.[355]

3.14.1.5 Service Terminations

An enrollee of an MA organization has a right to a "fast-track" appeal of an MA organization's decision to terminate provider services. An enrollee must make a request for a fast-track appeal by an independent review entity (IRE) by noon of the first day after the day of delivery of the termination

[351] 42 C.F.R. § 422.590.
[352] For CY 2011, the AIC for ALJ review is $130.
[353] *Id.* §§ 422.592–.608.
[354] *Id.* § 422.612. For CY 2011, the threshold amount for judicial review is $1,300.
[355] *Id.* §§ 422.620–.622.

notice. If the IRE upholds the MA organization's decision, in whole or in part, then an enrollee may request that the IRE reconsider its original decision.[356]

3.14.2 MA Organization Contract Appeals

Contract-determination disputes between MA organizations and the Medicare program may be administratively appealed.[357] Once CMS has made a contract determination, the agency will send a written notice to the contracting applicant or MA organization stating the reasons for the determination and the right to request a reconsideration of the contract determination by CMS.

3.14.2.1 Request for Hearing

A contracting applicant or MA organization may request a hearing of an adverse contract determination (*e.g.*, termination) or intermediate sanctions by filing a written request with CMS within 15 days of receipt from the date of the contract determination or intermediate sanction.[358] The hearing officer, who is designated by CMS, and need not be an ALJ, must set the hearing date for no later than 30 days from the date the request for hearing was received by CMS. Parties to the hearing may appoint a representative for the hearing, request permission for pre-hearing discovery, and examine/cross-examine witnesses.[359] A decision of a hearing officer may be reopened and revised by another hearing officer designated by CMS within one year of the notice of the hearing decision if the hearing officer who issued the initial decision is unavailable.[360]

3.14.2.2 Request for Review by the Administrator of CMS

An MA organization that has received a hearing decision upholding a contract determination may request review by the Administrator of CMS within 15 days of receiving the hearing decision. A decision by the Administrator of CMS is final and binding. Such decisions may be reopened and revised by the Administrator of CMS, however, upon the administrator's own motion within one year of the date of the notice of determination. [361]

3.15 Appeals—Part D

A beneficiary may obtain coverage determinations, request an exception to obtain coverage of a drug that is excluded from a plan's formulary, or appeal if the beneficiary disagrees with information provided by the pharmacy.[362] Participating Pharmacies are required to provide the beneficiary with a notice containing information about the beneficiary's rights in this regard.[363] The process begins

[356] 68 Fed. Reg. 16,652 (2003).

[357] 42 C.F.R. § 422.641. *See also* Ctrs. for Medicare & Medicaid Servs., *Managed Care Manual* (Pub. 100-16) § 10.1.1.

[358] 42 C.F.R. § 422.460. A party has a right to a hearing if the applicant has been found to be unqualified to enter into a contract with CMS; if the MA organization contract is terminated or not renewed or if the organization is assessed intermediate sanctions under 42 C.F.R. § 422.572(a)–(b).

[359] *Id.* §§ 422.662–.690.

[360] *Id.* § 422.696(b).

[361] *Id.* § 422.692–.694. Note that a contract applicant is not entitled to determination review by the Administrator of CMS.

[362] 42 U.S.C. §§ 1395w-104 *et seq.*; 42 C.F.R. § 423.562(b).

[363] *Id.*

when the plan issues a coverage determination. Plans are required to notify the beneficiary of initial coverage determinations as the beneficiary's health condition requires, but no later than 72 hours after receipt of request.[364] Each PDP Sponsor must provide a meaningful process of resolving grievances.[365] The Affordable Care Act requires PDPs to use a single, uniform exception and appeals process for prescription drug coverage determinations effective January 1, 2012.[366]

A beneficiary has a process to obtain a covered drug at a more favorable costs sharing level or a covered drug not on a plan formulary. This is called the "exceptions process."[367] More specifically, a beneficiary can request an exception under the following circumstances: when the beneficiary is using a drug that has been removed from a plan formulary, a non-formulary drug is prescribed and is medically necessary, the cost-sharing status of a drug a beneficiary is using changes, or a drug covered under a more expensive cost sharing tier is medically inappropriate.[368] The plan must act within 72 hours for standard coverage determinations or 24 hours for expedited requests if the standard timeframe for making a decision may seriously jeopardize the life or health of the beneficiary or the beneficiary's ability to regain maximum function.[369] If a request is denied, a beneficiary may follow the appeals process.[370]

In addition, the statute prescribes a five-level appeals process.[371] A beneficiary must initially request a redetermination of an unfavorable coverage determination.[372] The redetermination is performed by the plan and the decision must be communicated within seven days of receipt of the redetermination request.[373] Expedited redetermination requests must be made within 72 hours.[374] If a beneficiary is dissatisfied with the redetermination, the beneficiary may request reconsideration by an Independent Review Entity (IRE).[375] The beneficiary then may appeal the IRE's decision to an administrative law judge.[376] The next level of appeal is to the Medicare Appeals Council.[377] Ultimately, the final level of review is to federal district court.[378]

3.16 Conclusion

The continued popularity of the Medicare program stands as a testament to America's long-term commitment to safeguarding the nation's elderly and disabled from medical impoverishment. The establishment of the program, however, not only increased access to medical care for these population groups but also escalated overall demand for healthcare services. As the Medicare program

364 42 U.S.C. § 1395w-104(g); 42 C.F.R. § 423.568.
365 42 U.S.C. § 1395w-104(f); 42 C.F.R. § 423.564.
366 *See* Pub. L. No. 111-148, § 3312 (2010).
367 42 U.S.C. § 1395w-104(g)(2); 42 C.F.R. § 423.578.
368 *Id.*
369 *See* 42 C.F.R. § 423.566(a) *referencing* 42 C.F.R. §§ 423.568, 423.570.
370 42 U.S.C. § 1395w-104(h); 42 C.F.R. § 423.580.
371 42 U.S.C. § 1395w-104(h); 42 C.F.R. §§ 423.580–.638.
372 42 C.F.R. § 423.580.
373 42 C.F.R. § 423.590.
374 *Id.* § 423.590(d).
375 42 C.F.R. § 423.600.
376 42 C.F.R. §§ 423.1970, .1972.
377 42 C.F.R. § 423.1974. For the ALJ amount in controversy for FY 2011, *see* note 351 *supra.*
378 42 C.F.R. § 423.1976. For the judicial review amount in controversy for FY 2011, *see* note 353 *supra.*

mushroomed in size, scope, and complexity, so has the nature, size, and number of its participating providers, physicians, and suppliers—so much so that today Medicare provides a substantial financial underpinning for the American healthcare industry.

As demonstrated by the discussions in this Chapter, many efforts have been made by federal policymakers to reduce program expenditures and to shore up the HI Trust Fund. Beginning with TEFRA target rates in 1982 and PPS for inpatient hospital care in 1983 and additional providers in subsequent years, through RBRVS for physicians in 1989 and the introduction of "market-based" payment systems in the new millennium, Medicare payment policy has attempted to shift more of the program's financial burdens and risks to providers, physicians, and suppliers. The effect of the government's actions *vis-à-vis* changes to Medicare reimbursement policy ripple throughout the healthcare industry. Other government healthcare programs—including Medicaid, the VA, FEHBP (the health benefits program for federal employees), TRICARE (the health benefits program for the Department of Defense), as well as commercial insurance carriers—tie many of their own payment methodologies and rates to the Medicare reimbursement system.

The Medicare program has evolved from a government payment system for healthcare services to a force for dictating American healthcare policy. New challenges await federal policymakers in meeting the growing demand for expanded Medicare benefits, such as plugging the "donut hole" in the prescription-drug benefit, stemming the relentless rise in healthcare expenditures, and preparing for an unprecedented increase in program beneficiaries as American "baby boomers" rapidly matriculate toward retirement age. Although the BBA stemmed the immediate hemorrhage of the HI Trust Fund, it only delayed the inevitable. Indeed, current projections indicate that the HI Trust Fund will be totally depleted within 15 years. As a result, larger premiums, increased means-testing, greater cost-sharing, and a rise in the eligibility age all loom on the horizon as the future of Medicare is debated by Congress.

The Affordable Care Act has also shifted a number of priorities within CMS. The establishment of the new CMMI is expressly intended by Congress to encourage CMS to develop new payment methodologies including bundled payment methodologies and payments that take into consideration quality of care and savings to the Medicare Program. And, at the same time, the CMS is increasingly focused on eliminating fraud, waste and abuse in what is the largest healthcare benefit provider in the world. ACOs and other new initiatives lay on the horizon as the program and its leadership work to maintain and shape the future of Medicare.

3.17 Useful Websites and other Resources

MEDICARE SPEAK

The following is a brief functional overview of the countless phrases, acronyms, abbreviations, and designations that have evolved over the years into the distinct linguistic system (commonly known as "MedicareSpeak") that dominates the communications landscape of providers:

Acts/Laws/Programs Frequently Referenced

- ARRA — American Recovery and Reinvestment Act of 2009
- BBA — The Balanced Budget Act of 1997
- BBRA — The Balanced Budget Refinement Act of 1999\
- BIPA — Benefit Improvement and Protection Act of 200
- COBRA — Consolidated Omnibus Budget Reconciliation Act of 1985
- DEFRA — Deficit Reduction Act of 1984
- DRA — Deficit Reduction Act of 2005
- HCERA — Health Care and Education Reconciliation Act of 2010
- HIPAA — Health Insurance Portability and Accountability Act
- MMA — Medicare Modernization Act of 2003
- MIPPA — Medicare Improvements for Patients and Providers Act of 2008
- OBRA '(yr) — Omnibus Budget Reconciliation Act ('86, '87, '89, '90, '93, '99 and '00)
- PPACA — Patient Protection and Affordable Care Act of 2010
- SSA — Social Security Act
- SSI — Supplemental Security Income
- Stark I & II — Physician Self Referral Laws—part of OBRA '89 and '93, respectively
- TEFRA — Tax Equity and Fiscal Responsibility Act of 1982

Relevant Agencies, Departments, Commissions and Participants

- ALJ — Administrative Law Judge
- AMA — American Medical Association
- CMS — Centers for Medicare and Medicaid Services (formerly known as the Health Care Financing Administration or HCFA)
- DAB — Departmental Appeals Board
- HHS or DHHS — U.S. Dept. of Health and Human Services (also DHHS)
- IPAB — Independent Payment Advisory Board
- MedPAC — Medicare Payment Advisory Commission
- MGCRB — Medicare Geographic Classification Review Board
- OIG — Office of Inspector General
- OMB — Office of Management and Budget
- PRO — Peer Review Organization
- PPRC — Physician Payment Review Commission (also PhyPRC)
- PRRB — Provider Reimbursement Review Board
- PSRO — Professional Standards Review Organization

Commonly Used Terms and Descriptors

- AAPCC Adjusted Average Per Capita Cost
- ACO Accountable Care Organization
- ACR Adjusted Community Rate
- ALOS Average Length of Stay
- APC Ambulatory Payment Class
- APG Ambulatory Patient Group
- AVG Ambulatory Visit Group (as opposed to average)
- CAH Critical Access Hospital
- CIA Corporate Integrity Agreement
- CF Conversion Factor
- CMHC Community Mental Health Center
- CMI Case Mix Index
- CMMI Center for Medicare and Medicaid Innovation
- CMP Competitive Medical Plan
- CoP Conditions of Participation
- CORF Comprehensive Outpatient Rehabilitation Facility
- CPI Consumer Price Index
- CPR Customary, Prevailing and Reasonable
- CPT Current Procedural Terminology
- CRNA Certified Registered Nurse Anesthetist
- DMEPOS Durable Medical Equipment Prosthetics Orthotics & Supplies
- DRG Diagnosis Related Group
- DSA Disproportionate Share Adjustment
- DSH Disproportionate Share Hospital
- E&M Evaluation and Management
- EACH Essential Access Community Hospital
- EOB Explanation of Benefits
- ESRD End Stage Renal Disease
- FFS Fee for Service
- FI Fiscal Intermediary
- FQHC Federally Qualified Health Center
- GAF Geographic Adjustment Factor
- GME Graduate Medical Education
- GPCI Geographic Practice Cost Index (pronounced "gypsy")
- HCPCS HCFA Common Procedure Coding System
- HHA Home Health Agency
- HHRG Home Health Resource Group
- HI Hospital Insurance (Part A Trust Fund)
- HMO Health Maintenance Organization
- HPB Historic Payment Basis
- HSR Hospital Specific Rate

- ICD-9-CM International Classification of Diseases, Ninth Revision, Clinical Modification
- IDTF Independent Diagnostic Testing Facility
- IME Indirect Medical Education
- IPL Independent Physiological Laboratory
- IRF Inpatient Rehabilitation Facility
- JCAHO Joint Commission on Accreditation of Healthcare Organizations
- LCC Lower of Cost or Charges
- LMRP Local Medical Review Policy
- LTAC Long Term Acute Care Hospital
- MAPDP Medicare Advantage Prescription Drug Plan
- MDC Major Diagnostic Category
- MDH Medicare Dependent Hospital
- MEI Medical Economic Index
- MED PAR Medicare Provider Analysis and Review
- MEI Medical Economic Index
- MFS Medicare Fee Schedule
- MSA Metropolitan Statistical Area; also Medical Savings Account
- NonPARs Nonparticipating Physicians
- NPI National Provider Identifier
- NPR Notice of Program Reimbursement
- NPRM Notice of Proposed Rule Making
- OPD Outpatient Departure
- OPO Organ Procurement Organization
- PARs Participating Physicians
- PC Professional Component
- PDP Prescription Drug Plan
- PIN Provider Identification Number
- POS Point of Service
- PPIS Physician Practice Information Survey
- PPO Preferred Provider Organization
- PPS Prospective Payment System
- PSO Provider Sponsored Organization
- QI Qualified Individual
- QMB Qualified Medicare Beneficiary
- RBRVS Resource Based Relative Value Scale
- RHC Rural Health Clinic
- RUG Resource Utilization Group
- RVU Relative Value Unit
- SCH Sole Community Hospital
- SGR Sustainable Growth Rate
- SLMB Specified Low Income Medicare Beneficiary

- SMI Supplemental Medical Insurance
- SNF Skilled Nursing Facility
- SSA Social Security Act
- TC Technical Component
- TPA Third Party Administrator
- UCDS Uniform Clinical Data Set
- UPIN Unique Provider Identification Number

Sources of Medicare Law

- Part A, General Provisions; Part B Peer Review of Utilization and Quality of Health Care Services; and Administrative Simplification: Social Security Act (SSA §§ 1101–1179; 42 U.S.C. §§ 1301–1320d-8)
- Health Insurance for the Aged and Disabled; Part A: Hospital Insurance Benefits; Part B—Supplemental Medical Insurance Benefits for the Aged and Disabled; Provisions Relating to the Administration of Part B, Payment for Physicians Services; Part C—Medicare Advantage Program; Part D—Voluntary Prescription Drug Program; Part E—Miscellaneous Provisions. SSA §§ 1801–1896; 42 U.S.C. § 1395)

Sources of Medicare Regulations

- 42 C.F.R. Parts 400–424; 482–494: Regulations, generally
- 42 C.F.R. Parts 409–410: Coverage, generally
- 42 C.F.R. Parts 482–493: Certification
- 42 C.F.R. Parts 412–414; 416–418; 424: Payment, generally
- 42 C.F.R. § 406: Part A Eligibility
- 42 C.F.R. § 407: Part B Eligibility
- 42 C.F.R. § 411: Exclusions from Medicare Payment *including* Stark law provisions
- 42 C.F.R. § 412: Inpatient Hospital PPS
- 42 C.F.R. § 413: End Stage Renal Disease
- 42 C.F.R. § 416: Ambulatory Surgery Services
- 42 C.F.R. § 420: Program Integrity
- 42 C.F.R. § 422: Medicare Advantage Program
- 42 C.F.R. § 423: Part D Rules and Regulations
- 42 C.F.R. § 424: Conditions for Medicare Payment
- 42 C.F.R. §§ 1000–1008: OIG Regulations including AKBS Safe Harbor Provisions

MEDICARE MANUALS

In addition to publishing implementing regulations in the Federal Register, CMS publishes additional interpretative guidelines though various administrative manuals. Medicare manuals are a repository of operating instructions, policies, and procedures to administer CMS programs. The manuals are based on interpretations of statutes and regulations and were drafted for CMS agencies, contractors, and State survey agencies. The manuals are useful for many as source of technical and professional information about the Medicare and Medicaid programs.

CMS has transitioned to Internet-only manuals (IOMs). Unlike the paper-based manuals, the new CMS manual system is organized by functional area (*i.e.*, program integrity, eligibility, entitlement, claims processing, etc.).

The IOM manuals include the following:

- Medicare General Information, Eligibility, and Entitlement Manual: CMS Pub 100-01
- Medicare Benefit Policy Manual: CMS Pub 100-02
- Medicare National Coverage Determinations Manual: CMS Pub 100-03
- Medicare Claims Processing Manual: CMS Pub 100-04
- Medicare Secondary Payer Manual: CMS Pub 100-05
- Financial Management Manual: CMS Pub. 100-06
- State Operations Manual: CMS Pub. 100-07
- Program Integrity Manual: CMS Pub 100-08
- Medicare Contractor Beneficiary and Provider Communications Manual: CMS Pub 100-09
- Quality Improvement Organization Manual: CMS Pub 100-10
- End-Stage Renal Disease Network Organizations Manual: CMS Pub 100-14
- Medicare State Buy-In Manual: CMS Pub 100-15
- Managed Care Manual: CMS Pub 100-16
- Business Partners Systems Security Manual: CMS Pub 100-17
- Business Partners Security Oversight Manual: CMS Pub 100-18
- Demonstrations: CMS Pub. 100-19
- One Time Notification Manual: CMS Pub. 100-20

The older paper based manuals include the following:

- Coverage Issues Manual: CMS Pub 6
- State Operations Manual: CMS Pub 7
- Outpatient Physical Therapy, Comprehensive Outpatient Rehabilitation Facility and Community Mental Health Center Manual: CMS Pub 9
- Hospital Manual: CMS Pub 10
- Home Health Agency Manual: CMS Pub 11
- Skilled Nursing Facility Manual: CMS Pub 12
- Medicare Intermediary Manual: CMS Pub 13
- Medicare Carriers Manual: CMS Pub 14
- Provider Reimbursement Manual: CMS Pub 15
- Peer Review Organization Manual: CMS Pub 19
- Hospice Manual: CMS Pub 21
- Regional Office Manual: CMS Pub 23
- State Buy In Manual: CMS Pub 24
- Carrier QA Handbook: CMS Pub 25

- Rural Health Clinic Manual: CMS Pub 27
- Renal Dialysis Facility Manual: CMS Pub 29
- Christian Science Sanatorium Hospital Manual Supplement: CMS Pub 32
- State Medicaid Manual: CMS Pub 45
- HMO/CMP Manual: CMS Pub 75
- Federally Qualified HMO Manual: CMS Pub 77
- End Stage Renal Disease Manual: CMS Pub 81

NATIONAL COVERAGE DECISIONS (NCDs)

NCDs set forth whether Medicare will cover specific services, procedures or technologies on a national basis based on a reasonableness standard. NCDs do not make determinations on codes assigned to a service or the amount of payment to be made for the service. An NCD is binding on all Medicare contractors, including, but not limited to, MACs, Medicare carriers, fiscal intermediaries, and QIOs. The Medicare contractor must make the coverage decision if an NCD does not specifically exclude an indication or circumstance, or if the item or service is not mentioned in an NCD or Medicare manual. NCDs are located on the CMS Medicare Coverage Homepage website at http://www.cms.gov/mcd/overview.asp?from2=overview.asp&.

IMPORTANT WEBSITES & LINKS

- Social Security Administration (SSA) — www.ssa.gov
- U.S. Dept. of Health and Human Services (HHS) — www.hhs.gov
- Centers for Medicare and Medicaid Services (CMS) — www.cms.hhs.gov
- Consumer Medicare Information — www.medicare.gov
- HHS Office of Inspector General (OIG) — www.oig.hhs.gov
- U.S. Dept. of Justice (DOJ) — www.usdoj.gov

- The Federal Register — http://www.gpoaccess.gov/fr/index.html soon to be replaced by http://www.gpo.gov/fdsys/
- Federal Register Advance Desk — http://www.archives.gov/federal-register/public-inspection/index.html

- CMS Medlearn Matters: — http://www.cms.hhs.gov/MedlearnMattersArticles/
- Congressional Budget Office (CBO) — www.cbo.gov
- General Accounting Office (GAO) — www.gao.gov
- Office of Management and Budget (OMB) — www.whitehouse.gov/omb

- House Budget Committee — www.house.gov/budget
- House Committee on Ways and Means — www.house.gov/ways_means
- House Committee on Energy and Commerce — www.house.gov/commerce
- Senate Committee on Finance — www.finance.senate.gov

4

Fundamentals of Health Law Fraud and Abuse

David E. Matyas, Esquire
Epstein Becker & Green PC

In response to reports of billions of dollars being paid each year to healthcare providers who engage in fraud, federal and state governments continue to focus significant attention on developing ways to identify and ferret out healthcare fraud. By way of example, the Health Insurance Portability and Accountability Act of 1996 (HIPAA) established a national Health Care Fraud and Abuse Control Program (HCFAC) under the joint direction of the Attorney General for the Department of Justice (DOJ) and the Secretary of the Department of Health and Human Services (HHS), acting through the Inspector General, designed to coordinate Federal, state and local law enforcement activities with respect to healthcare fraud and abuse.[1] As a result of the establishment of the HCFAC Program, it has been reported that the Program was responsible in FY 2010 for returning $4 billion in fraudulent and misspent funds and that more than $18 billion has been returned to the Medicare Trust Fund since its creation in 1997.[2] As an example of another interagency initiative, DOJ and HHS announced in May 2009 the creation of the Health Care Fraud Prevention and Enforcement Action Team (HEAT) which is designed to, among other things, "gather resources across government to help prevent waste, fraud and abuse in the Medicare and Medicaid programs, and crack down on the fraud perpetrators who are abusing the system and costing us all billions of dollars" and to "to highlight best practices by providers and public sector employees who are dedicated to ending waste, fraud and abuse in Medicare."[3]

As healthcare fraud enforcers are targeting a wide array of business arrangements and payment practices as potentially constituting fraud, this Chapter addresses the fundamental legal underpinnings of the broad spectrum of healthcare fraud and abuse laws. In particular, this Chapter provides a brief overview of the federal laws and regulations, particularly the Anti-Kickback Statute, the physician self-referral law (known as the Stark Law for its chief legislative architect), and the prohibitions against false claims and fraudulent billing practices. This Chapter also examines the importance of establishing a corporate compliance program.

1 Health Insurance Portability and Accountability Act of 1996, Pub. L. No. 104-191, 110 Stat. 1936 (1996).

2 The Department of Health and Human Services and The Department of Justice Health Care Fraud and Abuse Control Program Annual Report for Fiscal Year 2010, January 2011, available at http://oig.hhs.gov/publications/docs/hcfac/hcfacreport2010.pdf.

3 *See* HEAT initiative website at http://www.stopmedicarefraud.gov/heattaskforce/index.html.

4.1 The Federal Healthcare Program's Anti-Kickback Statute

4.1.1 Statutory Prohibition

The federal healthcare program's Anti-Kickback Statute makes it a felony to knowingly and willfully solicit or receive remuneration "in return for referring an individual to a person for the furnishing or arranging for the furnishing of any item or service" or "in return for purchasing, leasing, ordering, or arranging for or recommending purchasing, leasing, or ordering any good, facility, service, or item for which payment may be made in whole or in part under a Federal healthcare program."[4] The Anti-Kickback Statute also prohibits a person from knowingly and willfully offering or paying remuneration to any person to induce that person to refer or purchase, lease, order, or arrange for or recommend the purchasing, leasing, or ordering of items or services for which payment may be made by a federal healthcare program. Although the Anti-Kickback Statute originally applied to Medicare and Medicaid only, over the years it has been broadened to apply to any "Federal healthcare program," defined as "any plan or program that provides health benefits, whether directly, through insurance, or otherwise, which is funded directly, in whole or in part, by the United States Government" other than the Federal Employee Health Benefit Program.[5]

Each offense under the Anti-Kickback Statute is punishable by a fine of up to $25,000 and imprisonment for up to five years. Violators of the Anti-Kickback Statute also are subject to exclusion from participation in the federal healthcare programs, as well as imposition of civil monetary penalties for each violation of (i) up to $50,000, and (ii) three times the amount of the remuneration in question. In addition, As part of the Patient Protection and Affordable Care Act of 2010 along with the Health Care Education Affordability Reconciliation Act of 2010 (referred to collectively as Health Reform), Congress established conclusively that violation of the Anti-Kickback Statute is a false claim for purposes of the federal False Claims Act.[6]

In recognition of the breadth of the prohibition contained in the Anti-Kickback Statute, Congress has enacted several exceptions over the years for certain financial arrangements. Specifically, there are exceptions for:

1. discounts that are properly disclosed and reflected in the costs claimed or charges made by the provider;
2. payments by an employer to an employee for bona fide employment in the provision of covered items and services;

---

[4] 42 U.S.C. § 1320a-7b(b).

[5] 42 U.S.C. § 1320a-7(g). Examples of federal healthcare programs include, but are not limited to: Medicare (Title XVIII of the Social Security Act); Medicaid (Title XIX of the Social Security Act); Department of Defense healthcare programs (*i.e.*, CHAMPUS and TRICARE, Chapter 55 of Title 10, United States Code); programs funded by Maternal and Child Health Block Grants (Title V of the Social Security Act); programs funded by Social Services Block Grants (Title XX of the Social Security Act); a medical care program of the Indian Health Service or of a tribal organization; and a health benefit plan under § 5(e) of the Peace Corps Act.

[6] *See* Patient Protection and Affordable Care Act of 2010, Pub. L. No. 111-148, 124 Stat. 119 § 6402(f)(1) (2010) (codified at 42 U.S.C. § 1320a–7b(g)). Health Care and Education Reconciliation Act of 2010, Pub L. No. 111-152, 124 Stat. 1029 (2010).

3. amounts paid by providers to a group purchasing organization (GPO) where a written agreement is made between the providers and the GPO specifying the fee and the GPO discloses the amount of the administrative fee to providers purchasing from the GPO;
4. waivers of coinsurance amounts in connection with certain Federally Qualified Healthcare Centers (FQHC);
5. activities protected by the safe-harbor regulations (which will be described in the following section);
6. certain risk-sharing arrangements;
7. certain arrangements involving FQHCs;
8. waivers of certain cost sharing amounts under Medicare Part D; and
9. hardware, software or information technology and training services used to receive and transmit electronic prescription information.[7]

4.1.2 Judicial Interpretation

4.1.2.1 The First 25 Years of Case Law Under the Statute: Pre-Hanlester

United States v. Greber[8] is the landmark case on the scope of the Anti-Kickback Statute. In this case, the Third Circuit Court of Appeals adopted the "one-purpose" test. Dr. Greber, an osteopathic physician who was board-certified in cardiology, was president of Cardio-Med, Inc., an organization that provided diagnostic services for cardiac patients. When Cardio-Med performed a test at the request of a referring physician, Cardio-Med also forwarded a portion of the Medicare reimbursement it received to the referring physician. This fee was purportedly for "interpretations" by the referring physician. Evidence was introduced, however, that physicians received these interpretation fees even though Dr. Greber evaluated the tests. In addition, the amount paid to the physicians was more than Medicare allowed for such services. Hence, Dr. Greber was convicted of, among other transgressions, tendering kickbacks in violation of the Anti-Kickback Statute. In upholding his conviction, the Third Circuit Court of Appeals held that "if one purpose of the payment was to induce future referrals, the [Anti-Kickback Statute] has been violated."

After the *Greber* case, the issue confronting the healthcare industry was whether the broad "one-purpose" test was applicable merely to the egregious facts presented, or whether the test would be generally applicable to *all* kickback cases. For several years, no other kickback cases considered this issue until 1989, when two separate circuit courts considered the *Greber* "one-purpose" test.

In *United States v. Kats*,[9] a physician owned a 25% interest in Community Clinic, which collected blood and urine specimens and forwarded the specimens to Tech-Lab. Tech-Lab billed Community Clinic, which in turn billed the California Medicaid and Medicare programs. According to the court's description of the facts, 50% of the laboratory payments were "kicked back" to Community Clinic. The Ninth Circuit Court of Appeals followed the *Greber* holding, and upheld a jury instruction al-

---

[7] *See* 42 U.S.C. § 1320a-7b(b)(3); *see also* 42 U.S.C. § 1395w-104(e).
[8] *United States v. Greber*, 760 F.2d 68 (3rd Cir.1985), *cert. denied*, 474 U.S. 988 (1985).
[9] *United States v. Kats*, 871 F.2d 105 (9th Cir. 1989).

lowing conviction unless the payment was "wholly and not incidentally attributable to the delivery of goods and services." The Ninth Circuit stated that it is not a defense to claim that other purposes are behind the payment as long as one of the material purposes is to induce referrals.

United States v. Bay State Ambulance and Hospital Rental, Inc.[10] concerned the award of a hospital ambulance contract. Allegedly, the ambulance company made illegal payments to a hospital official who sat on the bid committee. Such payments consisted of a management-consulting contract, loans, and other consideration including automobiles and cash. The court cited with approval *Greber*'s holding that any amount of inducement is illegal under the Anti-Kickback Statute, but stopped short of explicitly adopting the Third Circuit's broad "one-purpose" test. The district court had instructed the jury that, in order to obtain a conviction under the Anti-Kickback Statute, the *primary* purpose (as opposed to an incidental or minor purpose) of the payments must be improper, and thus the less-favorable *Greber* standard was not directly challenged on appeal. The court in *Bay State Ambulance* also noted that the government was not required to prove that payments received were not reasonable for the work performed, because "the gravamen of Medicare fraud is inducement. Giving a person an opportunity to earn money may well be an inducement to that person to channel potential Medicare payments towards a particular recipient."

4.1.2.2 The Hanlester Decision

On April 6, 1995, the U.S. Court of Appeals for the Ninth Circuit issued a decision in *Hanlester Network v. Shalala*,[11] the first case in which the OIG asserted its civil-sanction authority under the Anti-Kickback Statute. Significantly, the Ninth Circuit determined that the appellants should not be excluded under the statute.

This case involved a network of three clinical laboratories that had been established as physician joint ventures by the Hanlester Network of Santa Ana, California. The joint ventures established by the Hanlester Network were organized as limited partnerships with more than 100 physicians participating as investors. The investment arrangement basically consisted of physicians as limited partners who owned between three and seven shares at $500 per share. Although no express requirement was made that physician investors refer to the laboratory, physician investors were required to sell back their shares if they retired, lost their medical license, or relocated outside the laboratory's service area. In addition, each joint-venture laboratory was operated under a management agreement with SmithKline Beecham Clinical Laboratories (SBCL). The management agreement provided the payment to SBCL of either $15,000 per month or 76% of the revenues generated by the joint-venture laboratory, whichever was greater.

In 1989, the OIG issued notices of proposed program exclusion to five individuals and five entities involved in the joint ventures.[12] The individuals and entities subject to the exclusion action requested an administrative hearing to challenge their proposed program exclusion. Initially, the Administrative

---

10 *United States v. Bay State Ambulance and Hospital Rental, Inc.*, 874 F.2d 20 (1st Cir. 1989).

11 *Hanlester Network v. Shalala*, 51 F.3d 1390 (9th Cir. 1995), *reh'g en banc denied*, No. 93-55351 (9th Cir. Nov. 15, 1995).

12 Simultaneously, the OIG announced the settlement of charges against SBCL for $1.5 million.

Law Judge (ALJ) held that the Anti-Kickback Statute was not violated unless the government demonstrated that there was an actual agreement or *quid pro quo*, whereby the referral of patients to the entity was a condition imposed on physician investors for maintaining their investment interest in the entity. Then, upon initial appeal, the Departmental Appeals Board (DAB) held that the term "inducement" contained in the Anti-Kickback Statute meant something more than "encourage," but something less than "require"—that is, "an intent to exercise influence over the reason or judgment of another in an effort to cause the referral of program-related business." The DAB subsequently remanded the case to the ALJ, who concluded that permissive exclusions were necessary for some but not all of the appellants. The defendants then appealed the DAB's decision to the U.S. District Court for the Central District of California, which affirmed the DAB's decision,[13] and then to the Ninth Circuit Court of Appeals.[14]

Although the Ninth Circuit agreed with the DAB's definition of the term "inducement," it reversed the exclusions against the appellants, apparently based on the particular facts of the case. The Ninth Circuit found that "the fact that a large number of referrals resulted in the potential for a high return on investment, or that the practical effect of low referral rates was failure for the labs, is insufficient to prove that appellants offered or paid remuneration to induce referrals" in violation of the Anti-Kickback Statute. The court noted that limited partners were paid dividends based on their ownership share, not the volume of their referrals, and that payments were made to limited partners regardless of whether they referred business to the joint venture.

The Ninth Circuit did find, however, that the Hanlester Network's Marketing Director, Patricia Hitchcock, had made representations to prospective investors that were indeed in violation of the Anti-Kickback Statute. Thus, Ms. Hitchcock apparently "crossed the line" into illegality by linking a physician-investor's personal referral pattern to his or her participation in the joint venture.

As a result of Ms. Hitchcock's conduct, the Court of Appeals further held that the Hanlester Network and joint-venture laboratories' organizational entities could be held vicariously liable under the Anti-Kickback Statute for Ms. Hitchcock's actions, regardless of the fact that Ms. Hitchcock acted in a manner contrary to the organizations' stated policies. Nevertheless, the Court of Appeals found that no remedial purpose would be served by excluding organizational entities of either the Hanlester Network' or the joint-venture laboratories' from the Medicare or Medicaid programs, because their vicarious liability arose entirely from the conduct of Ms. Hitchcock, who was no longer associated with the organizations.

The court additionally held that vicarious liability cannot extend to the individual partners in the organizational entities, and that they did not act with the requisite intent in order to constitute an independent violation of the statute. Citing U.S. Supreme Court precedent,[15] the Ninth Circuit concluded that a party may violate the Anti-Kickback Statute's *mens rea* requirement (*i.e.*, knowingly and willfully) *only* if he or she *knows* that the Anti-Kickback Statute prohibits offering or paying remuneration to induce referrals *and* engages in the prohibited conduct with the *specific intent* to disobey the law.

[13] *Hanlester v. Sullivan*, CCH Medicare and Medicaid Guide ¶ 41,076, CV-92-4552 (C.D. Cal. Feb. 10, 1993).
[14] *Hanlester Network v. Shalala*, *supra*.
[15] *See Ratzlaf v. United States*, 114 S. Ct. 655, 657, 126 L. Ed. 2d 615 (1994).

Although Ms. Hitchcock's conduct was sufficiently egregious to infer the requisite intent to violate the Anti-Kickback Statute, the Ninth Circuit found that the other partners displayed no such conduct.

Significantly, the positions held by the Ninth Circuit in the *Hanlester* case were not universally by other courts.[16] Then, in 2010 as part of Health Reform, the Anti-Kickback Statute was amended to provide that "a person need not have actual knowledge of this section or specific intent to commit a violation of this section."[17]

4.1.3 Special Fraud Alerts

Whereas the safe harbors describe conduct that is explicitly permissible, the OIG also has published various issuances over the past several years that describe conduct that the OIG views as impermissible. Specifically, the OIG issues fraud alerts as a vehicle for identifying fraudulent and abusive practices within the healthcare industry.

Although the majority of the OIG's fraud alerts are disseminated internally within the government, the OIG has issued several "Special Fraud Alerts" that are distributed directly to members of the healthcare provider community. To date, the OIG has issued Special Fraud Alerts that address the following:

- joint venture arrangements;
- routine waiver of copayments or deductibles under Medicare Part B;
- hospital incentives to physicians;
- prescription drug marketing schemes;
- arrangements for the provision of clinical lab services;
- home health fraud;
- fraud and abuse in the provision of medical supplies to nursing facilities;
- fraud and abuse in nursing home arrangements with hospices;
- fraud and abuse in the provision of services in nursing facilities;
- rental of space in physician offices by persons or entities to which physicians refer; and
- telemarketing by durable medical equipment suppliers.[18]

[16] *See, e.g., United States v. Starks*, 157 F.3d 833 (11th Cir. 1998); *United States v. Jain*, 93 F.3d 436 (8th Cir. 1996), *cert. denied*, 520 U.S. 1273 (1997); *United States v. Neufeld*, 908 F. Supp. 491, 497 (S.D. Ohio 1995); *Med. Dev. Network, Inc. v. Prof. Respiratory Care/Home Medical Equip. Servs., Inc.*, 673 S.2d 565 (Fla. Dist. App. 1996); *United States v. Mittal*, 2002 U.S. App. LEXIS 11220 (2d Cir. 2002); *see also United States v. Starks*, 157 F.3d 833 (11th Cir. 1998); *United States v. Anderson*, 85 F. Supp.2d 1047, 1065–68 (D. Kan. 1999), *rev'd sub nom.*; *United States v. McClatchey*, 217 F.3d 823 (10th Cir. 2000); *United States v. Shaw*, 106 F. Supp.2d 103 (D. Mass. 2000).

[17] *See* Patient Protection and Affordable Care Act of 2010, Pub. L. No. 111-148, 124 Stat. 119 (2010) § 6402(f)(2) (codified at 42 U.S.C. § 1320a–7b(h)).

[18] Copies of these Special Fraud Alerts can be found on the OIG's Internet site at oig.hhs.gov/fraud/fraudalerts.html. In addition to the Special Fraud Alerts that are listed and address arrangements that may violate the Anti-Kickback Statute, the OIG also has published other types of Special Bulletins and Special Alerts related to other issues (*e.g.*, in 1999, the OIG issued a "Special Bulletin" related to gainsharing arrangements, in 2003 issued a Special Advisory Bulletin entitled "Contractual Joint Ventures", and in 2005 issued a Special Advisory Bulletin entitled "Patient Assistance Programs for Medicare Part D Enrollees").

4.1.4 Advisory Opinions

In 1996, as part of HIPAA, Congress authorized DHHS to issue, upon request, advisory opinions on the applicability of the Anti-Kickback Statute, the safe-harbor regulations, and other OIG health-care fraud and abuse provisions to either a proposed or an existing financial arrangement.[19]

In order to obtain an advisory opinion, the requesting party must submit to the OIG detailed information on the circumstances of the transaction, including all background information, copies of all existing or proposed operative documents, and detailed statements of all collateral or oral understandings. In disclosing this information to the government, the OIG has confirmed that documents submitted in connection with an advisory-opinion request are subject to the Freedom of Information Act (FOIA).

In addition to the time and costs associated with the requesting party or its representatives preparing the request for an advisory opinion, the requesting party is responsible for reimbursing the OIG for costs in processing the advisory-opinion request.

In July 2008, HHS issued a Final Rule amending its policies relating to the collection and payment by individuals requesting an Advisory Opinion.[20] Under the July 2008 Rule, parties no longer are required to deposit $250 to the U.S. Treasury upon requesting an OIG Advisory Opinion. According to the OIG, this policy change eliminates the resource demands that arise when a party rescinds its request for an advisory opinion and seeks to recoup its initial deposit. The April 2008 rule also sets forth that parties can no longer pay the U.S. Treasury by way of check or money order but instead must pay for these charges directly through wire or electronic funds transfer.

The OIG is required to issue an advisory opinion within 60 days of receipt of an "accepted" request. The 60-day period does not begin until the OIG deems the request to be complete, but it may be tolled at various times.

4.2 Federal Anti-Kickback Safe-Harbor Regulations

Congress established a statutory exception for certain payment practices that the Secretary of the Department of Health and Human Services (DHHS) specifies as being "safe harbored" and therefore not subject to the Anti-Kickback Statute. An arrangement that meets the criteria of a safe harbor is fully protected from criminal and civil liabilities under the Anti-Kickback Statute; it is important to note, however, that failure to fall squarely within the terms of a safe harbor does not necessarily mean that the arrangement is illegal or that it will be investigated or prosecuted. Indeed, the OIG has stated that

> [c]ommenters should not infer that because a safe harbor provision does not specifically refer to a particular arrangement or activity, it is unlawful. Nor should [one] interpret that lack of a safe harbor to mean that the [ ] activit[y] will be subjected to heightened scrutiny. Moreover,

---

[19] 42 U.S.C. § 1320a-7d; *see also* 42 C.F.R. pt. 1008; 62 Fed. Reg. 7,350 (1997); 63 Fed. Reg. 38,311 (1998). Copies of all advisory opinions can be found on the OIG's Internet site at oig.hhs.gov/fraud/advisoryopinions.html.

[20] 73 Fed. Reg. 40,982 (July 17, 2008); 42 C.F.R. § 1008.31(b); 42 C.F.R. § 1008.36(b); 42 C.F.R. § 1008.43(d).

> safe harbors do not create affirmative obligations on individuals or entities since *compliance with the* [ ] *safe harbors is purely voluntary*. The failure to comply with a safe harbor means only that the practice or arrangement does not have absolute assurance of protection from anti-kickback liability.[21]

Thus, conduct outside the safe harbors must be analyzed based on its particular facts and circumstances to determine whether a violation exists under the Anti-Kickback Statute.

In 1991, the OIG promulgated the first set of final "safe harbor" regulations, which set forth permissible payment practices in the following 11 areas:

1. investment interests;
2. space rental;
3. equipment rental;
4. personal services and management contracts;
5. sale of a practice;
6. referral services;
7. warranties;
8. discounts;
9. employees;
10. GPOs; and
11. waiver of beneficiary coinsurance and deductible amounts for Part A inpatient hospital services and certain federally qualified and federally funded health centers and healthcare facilities.[22]

Although these 11 safe harbors were published as a "final" list, the OIG published "clarifications" to several of these safe harbors in 1999.[23]

With respect to the applicability of the Anti-Kickback Statute to certain managed-care activities, the OIG has confirmed that the Anti-Kickback Statute does, in fact, apply by adopting several managed-care safe harbors. In particular, in 1996, the OIG not only modified the safe harbor for waivers of inpatient and deductible amounts so as to include Medicare "SELECT PPOs," but also adopted safe harbors for incentives offered to beneficiaries in order to encourage the use of the preferred provider network and provider discounts offered to managed-care plans.[24] Then, in 1999, the OIG issued as an interim final rule two safe harbors related to the shared-risk exception that was added to the Anti-Kickback Statute as part of HIPAA.[25]

---

[21] 61 Fed. Reg. 2,122, 2,124 (1996) (emphasis added).

[22] 42 C.F.R. § 1001.952(a)–(k); *see also* 56 Fed. Reg. 35,952 (1991).

[23] *See* 64 Fed. Reg. 63,518 (1999); *see also* 59 Fed. Reg. 37,202 (1994).

[24] 42 C.F.R. § 1001.952 (k)–(m); *see* 61 Fed. Reg. 2,122, (Jan. 25, 1996); *see also* 57 Fed. Reg. 51,723 (1992).

[25] 42 C.F.R. § 1001.952(t)–(u); *see* 64 Fed. Reg. 63,504 (1999).

Also in 1999, the OIG finalized additional safe harbors for several different categories of ambulatory surgery centers (ASCs), for group practices, for referral arrangements for specialty services, and for cooperative hospital service organizations. The OIG also adopted several safe harbors related to financial relationships entered into by and with healthcare entities located in medically underserved areas (MUAs). Specifically, safe harbors were established for investment interests held in healthcare entities located in MUAs, for remuneration paid as part of a recruitment package in order to attract professionals to an MUA, and for obstetrical malpractice-insurance subsidies paid to a practitioner who is primarily engaged in an obstetrical practice in a designated Health Professional Shortage Area (HPSA).[26]

In 2001, the OIG established a safe harbor for ambulance arrangements with hospitals and other receiving facilities that replenish drugs and medical supplies used by the ambulance provider when transporting patients to the hospitals or receiving facilities.[27]

In August 2006, the OIG issued regulations creating two safe harbors for non-monetary remunerations involving certain electronic prescribing and electronic health records arrangements,[28] and in October 2007, the OIG published a safe harbor in order to enable FQHCs to more easily provide medical care to underserved populations.[29]

4.2.1 Investment Interest Safe Harbors

The final safe-harbor regulations published in 1991 contained two separate sets of criteria for investment interests: (1) investment interests in large, publicly held companies; and (2) investment interests held in smaller healthcare companies. In 1999, the OIG adopted a third set of criteria related to investment interests held in healthcare entities that are located in MUAs.[30]

4.2.1.1 *Large Investment Interests*

Under this safe harbor, a large publicly traded company must have at least $50 million in undepreciated net tangible assets related to the furnishing of healthcare items or services. Moreover, equity securities must be registered with the Securities and Exchange Commission, and the investment interest must be obtained "on terms equally available to the public" through trading on a registered national-securities exchange. As a result of the clarifications adopted by the OIG in 1999, language was added to this safe harbor to "clarify" that the investment interest (1) may not be subject to restrictions or limits on transferability that are not applicable to an investment held by members of the public and (2) must be obtained for the same price available to the general public.

Additional requirements under this safe harbor include that neither the entity nor any investor (nor other individual acting on behalf of the entity or any investor in the entity) may make loans or loan guarantees to investors who may be in a position to refer business to the entity. Further, dividends to investors must be in proportion to the amount of the investment, and the entity may not market or furnish its services differently to passive investors than it does to non-investors.

---

[26] 42 C.F.R. § 1001.952(n)–(s); *see* 64 Fed. Reg. 63,518 (1999); *see also* 58 Fed. Reg. 49,008 (1993).
[27] 42 C.F.R. § 1001.952(v); *see* 66 Fed. Reg. 62,979 (2001); *see also* 65 Fed. Reg. 32,060 (2000).
[28] 42 C.F.R. § 1001.952(x)–(y); *see* 71 Fed. Reg. 45,110 (2006).
[29] 42 C.F.R. § 1001.952(w); *see* 72 Fed. Reg. 56,632 (2007).
[30] 42 C.F.R. § 1001.952(a).

4.2.1.2 *Small Investment Interests*

With respect to the small entity safe harbor, each of the following eight standards must be satisfied.

1. *"60/40" Investor Rule.* No more than 40% of the value of the investment interests of each class of investments may be held in the previous fiscal year or previous 12-month period by investors who are in a position to make or influence referrals to, furnish items or services to, or otherwise generate business for, the entity. In 1999, the OIG added language to this requirement explaining that equivalent classes of equity investments may be combined.
2. *Terms of Investment.* The terms on which an investment interest is offered to a passive investor who is in a position to make or influence referrals to, furnish items or services to, or otherwise generate business for the entity must be no different than the terms offered to other passive investors.
3. *Investment Not Related to Referrals.* The terms on which an investment interest is offered to an investor who is in a position to make or influence referrals to, furnish items or services to, or otherwise generate business for the entity must not be related to the previous or expected volume of referrals, items, or services furnished, or the amount of business otherwise generated, by that investor to the entity.
4. *No Requirement to Generate Referrals.* No requirement may be made that a passive investor make referrals to, be in a position to make or influence referrals to, furnish items or services to, or otherwise generate business for the entity as a condition for remaining as an investor.
5. *Marketing Efforts.* Neither the entity nor any investor may market or furnish the entity's items or services (or those of another entity as part of cross-referral agreement) to passive investors differently than to non-investors.
6. *"60/40" Revenue Rule.* No more than 40% of the gross revenue of the entity in the previous fiscal year or previous 12-month period may come from referrals or business otherwise generated from investors.
7. *Prohibition on Loans.* Neither the entity nor any investor (nor other individual or entity acting on behalf of the entity or any investor in the entity) may loan funds to or guarantee a loan for an investor who is in a position to make or influence referrals to, furnish items or services to, or otherwise generate business for the entity if the investor uses any part of such loan to obtain the investment interest.
8. *Investment Return.* The amount of payment to an investor in return for the investment interest must be directly proportional to the amount of the capital investment of that investor.

4.2.1.3 *Investments in Entities in MUAs*

In contrast to the OIG's proposal in 1993 to adopt a safe harbor for investments held in entities that are located in "rural" areas, in 1999 the OIG expanded the scope of this safe harbor so as to apply to MUAs, which can be located in either a rural or urban area. Although many of the requirements for this safe harbor are similar to the small-investment safe harbor, this safe harbor eliminates the 60/40

Revenue Rule, and modifies the 60/40 Investor Rule to a 50/50 Investor Rule (*i.e.*, no more than 50% of the value of the investment interest of each class of investments may be held by investors who are in a position to make or influence referrals to, furnish items or services to, or otherwise generate business for the entity). In addition, the OIG has included a requirement that at least 75% of the business in the previous fiscal year or previous 12-month period be derived from services furnished to persons in an MUA or who are members of a medically underserved population (MUP).

4.2.2 Space and Equipment Rental, and Personal Services and Management Contracts

The OIG created three separate safe harbors for certain contracts related to space rental, equipment rental, and personal services and management contracts. Nevertheless, all three of these safe harbors share common requirements.[31] For example, all three safe harbors require that a written agreement be executed for a term of at least one year that specifies the aggregate payment amount, as well as the premises, equipment, or services covered. If the agreement does not contemplate full-time services, then the agreement must also specify the schedule of intervals, their precise length, and the exact charge for such intervals.

As part of the "clarifications" adopted by the OIG in 1999 and in order to "preclude schemes involving the use of multiple overlapping contracts to circumvent the one-year requirement," the OIG has added a requirement to all three safe harbors that the agreement cover *all* space, equipment, or services for the term of the agreement.

These three safe harbors also require that the payments must be based upon fair market value, and not vary on the volume or value of any Medicare-covered or state healthcare program-covered referrals or business generated between the parties. For purposes of space rental, fair market value means the value of the rental property for general commercial purposes. For purposes of equipment rental, fair market value means the value of the equipment when obtained from a manufacturer or professional distributor. The assessment of "fair market value" for space and equipment leases, however, may not include additional value for location or convenience to sources of Medicare and/or state healthcare program business. An additional requirement for personal services and management contracts is that the services performed under the agreement must not involve the counseling or promotion of a business arrangement or other activity that violates any State or federal law.

4.2.3 Sale of Practice

Although the "sale of practice" safe harbor originally only covered sales between practitioners, the OIG expanded this safe harbor in 1999 to include the sale of a practice by a practitioner in an underserved area to a hospital.[32]

With respect to the sale of a physician's practice to another practitioner, the sale must be completed within one year, and the selling practitioner cannot remain in a position to generate business for the purchasing practitioner beyond the one-year period. Thus, the safe harbor would not protect any

31 42 C.F.R. § 1001.952(b)–(d).

32 42 C.F.R. § 1001.952(e).

situation in which the physician who sells the practice is retained on its staff for any significant period of time following the purchase.

With respect to payments made to a practitioner by a hospital or other entity to purchase the practitioner's practice, the safe harbor requires that: (1) the sale be completed within three years; (2) after the sale is completed, the practitioner not be in a position to make referrals to or generate business for the purchasing entity; (3) the practice be located in a HPSA for the practitioner's specialty; and (4) the purchasing entity must, in good faith, engage in recruitment activities to find a new practitioner to take over the acquired practice.

4.2.4 Referral Services

The final sale-harbor regulations include a safe harbor for payments to "referral services."[33] Under this safe harbor, a referral service may not exclude any person or entity that meets participation qualifications. Although the safe harbor does not require inclusion of *all* physicians in a particular geographic area, the safe harbor requires that, if the referral service qualifies physicians based upon certain criteria, then such criteria must be applied equally to all participants. In addition, the referral service must disclose to persons seeking referrals how individual participants are chosen, whether a fee is paid, the relationship between the participant and the service, and any restrictions that would exclude a participant.

4.2.5 Warranties

The safe harbors protect payments or exchanges of value under certain manufacturer or supplier warranties.[34] In order to qualify for safe-harbor protection, the buyer and the manufacturer or supplier alike must comply with specified reporting standards. The buyer must report any price reduction or free item obtained as part of the warranty in its cost report or claim for payment. The supplier or manufacturer, in turn, must report such price reductions or free items on the buyer's invoice (or, if the amount is unknown, the existence of the warranty and the full documentation when known), and inform the buyer of its reporting obligations. The buyer also must furnish the invoice information to the Medicare or relevant state healthcare program on request. Additionally, the warranty can only be for the item itself, and cannot include payment to an individual or entity other than a beneficiary for any medical, surgical, or hospital expenses incurred by a beneficiary. Finally, the safe harbor not only defines the term "warranty" under the Magnuson-Moss Warranty-Federal Trade Commission Improvement Act's definition of "written warranty" at 15 U.S.C. § 2301(6) governing the sale and warranty of consumer products, but it also includes one manufacturer's or supplier's agreement to replace another manufacturer's or supplier's defective item (which is covered by a "written warranty" under that act) on terms equal to the original written warranty.

---

33 42 C.F.R. § 1001.952(f).

34 42 C.F.R. § 1001.952(g).

4.2.6 Discounts

The Anti-Kickback Statute includes several statutory exceptions, including an exception for "a discount or other reduction in price obtained by a provider of services or other entity under a Federal healthcare program if the reduction in price is properly disclosed and appropriately reflected in the costs claimed or charges made by the provider or entity...."[35] Despite the existence of a statutory exception, the OIG has adopted safe harbors related to the statutory exceptions as it has taken the position that its role is "to define innocuous arrangements that should not be prosecuted, including the statutory exceptions."[36]

In contrast to the statute, which only requires that the discount be "properly disclosed and appropriately reflected" in the entity's Medicare and Medicaid costs or charges, the safe harbor sets forth a restrictive definition of the term "discount," excluding such typical discount arrangements as discounts not applicable to Medicare or Medicaid, and those discounts given directly to beneficiaries (*e.g.*, coinsurance waivers).[37] In addition, although the safe harbor originally excluded from the definition of "discount" the provision of discounted or free items or services in exchange for the purchase of different items or services, the OIG "clarified" this exclusion so as to allow this type of discount arrangement if the goods and services are reimbursed by the same federal healthcare program using the same methodology.

The protection provided under the discount safe harbor is categorized based upon the type of party involved in the transaction (buyers, sellers, and offerors) with the safe harbor placing different requirements on the respective parties. Specifically, the safe harbor provides protection to buyers that are Medicare+Choice plans and/or Medicaid risk contractors without imposing any reporting requirements; by contrast, cost-reporting entities not only must report the discount on the cost report, but also must earn the discount within a single fiscal year and claim the benefit of the discount in that or the following fiscal year. All other purchasers, such as Part B suppliers, can only take advantage of discounts made at the time of the original sale, or the terms of the rebate must be fixed and disclosed in writing to the buyer at the time of the initial sale of the good or service.

With respect to sellers, the safe harbor provides protection for discounts given to cost-reporting entities as long as the seller reports the discount on the purchaser's invoice and reasonably notifies the buyer of its obligations to report such discount. For cost-reporting entities, the safe harbor also provides that, if the value of the discount is unknown at the time of the sale, the seller can disclose the existence of the discount program on the invoice and furnish the additional documentation later. For all other entities, the seller's obligations depend on whether the seller submits a claim or request for payment on behalf of the buyer, or whether the buyer instead submits such claims on its own behalf.

In addition to buyers and sellers, the safe harbor includes protection for offerors, who are individuals or entities who are not sellers but who promote the purchase of an item or service by a buyer at a reduced price. Similar to sellers, the ability of an offeror to qualify for safe-harbor protection depends on the offeror satisfying certain requirements that are based upon the type of purchaser.

---

35 42 U.S.C. § 1320a-7b(3)(A).

36 56 Fed. Reg. 35,952, 35,957 (1991).

37 42 C.F.R. § 1001.952(h).

4.2.7 Employees

The Anti-Kickback Statute includes a statutory exception for "any amount paid by an employer to an employee (who has a bona fide employment relationship with such employer) for employment in the provision of covered items or services."[38] Despite the significant legislative history that surrounded the enactment of this exception, in which Congress explained its intention to include a broad meaning for the term "employee," this position was rejected by the OIG as the OIG defined the term "employee" pursuant to the "usual common law rules."[39] Therefore, independent-contractor arrangements fall outside the employee safe-harbor protection, unless they otherwise qualify for the safe harbor governing personal services and management contracts described earlier.

4.2.8 Group Purchasing Organizations

The Anti-Kickback Statute includes a statutory exception for amounts paid by a vendor to a GPO as long as two conditions are satisfied:

1. the person has a written contract with each such individual or entity, which specifies the amount to be paid the person, which amount may be a fixed amount or a fixed percentage of the value of the purchases made by each such individual or entity under the contract; and
2. in the case of an entity that is a provider of services (as defined in § 1861(u)), the person discloses (in such form and manner as the Secretary requires) to the entity and, upon request, to the Secretary the amount received from each such vendor with respect to purchases made by or on behalf of the entity.[40]

Within the safe harbors, the OIG narrowed the scope of the protection offered to GPOs by excluding GPOs that are part of the same corporate family as the entities for whom the GPOs are purchasing.[41] On the other hand, although the statute requires that the agreement specify the amount the vendor pays the GPO, irrespective of the amount, the safe harbor permits the agreement to state that vendors will pay the GPO a fee of 3% or less of the purchase price of the vendor's goods. If the fee is more than 3%, the agreement must specify the amount (or, if unknown, the maximum amount) of the GPO payment by each vendor.

4.2.9 Coinsurance and Deductible Waivers

The safe harbor for waivers of coinsurance and deductible amounts pertains only to inpatient services furnished by hospitals paid under the Prospective Payment System, and, as required by statute, to certain services furnished by federally qualified health centers and similar healthcare facilities receiving Public Health Service and Title V grants.[42] Consequently, this safe harbor does not apply to waivers with respect to physician and supplier services paid under Medicare Part B. In the context of

---

[38] 42 U.S.C. § 1320a-7b(b)(3)(B).
[39] 42 C.F.R. § 1001.952(i).
[40] 42 U.S.C. § 1320a-7b(b)(3)(C).
[41] 42 C.F.R. § 1001.952(j).
[42] *Id.* § 1001.952(k).

managed care, however, this safe harbor was modified in 1996 to permit such waivers under Medicare SELECT policies.

4.2.10 Beneficiary Incentives Offered by Managed-Care Organizations

The safe harbor for beneficiary incentives offered by health plans (*e.g.*, differentials in coinsurance and deductible amounts) applies only to Medicare and Medicaid contracting health plans.[43] The term "health plan" has been defined in the safe harbor to apply to a managed care entity that:

1. has a formal contract with the Medicare or Medicaid programs;
2. charges a premium regulated by a state insurance statute or existing state statute governing health maintenance organizations (HMOs) or preferred provider organizations (PPOs);
3. is an Employee Retirement Income Security Act (ERISA) or self-funded/self-insured employer or union plan that contracts directly with healthcare providers or insurance companies; and
4. acts as an intermediary between contract healthcare providers and employers, union welfare funds, and/or insurance companies such as PPOs.

Nevertheless, no safe harbor protection exists for commercial managed-care plans that furnish coverage to Medicare eligibles on a fee-for-service basis.

Plans that qualify under the definition of a "health plan" and that have a formal Medicare or Medicaid contract also must meet other requirements, such as not discriminating in offering incentives to all potential enrollees. Consequently, these health plans must offer the same incentives to all Medicare or state healthcare program enrollees, unless otherwise approved by the federal or state program. Moreover, health plans paid on a reasonable cost or similar basis cannot claim the cost of the incentive as a bad debt, or otherwise make additional claims to the federal or state healthcare program to pay for the incentive.

4.2.11 Price Reductions Offered to Group Health Plans

The managed-care safe harbors also protect price reductions that providers offer to health plans under certain circumstances.[44] Unlike the beneficiary-incentive safe harbor, which applies only to Medicare and Medicaid contracting health plans, the price-reduction safe harbor enables non-contracting health plans to qualify for safe-harbor protection, albeit based on different safe-harbor criteria.

First, for all health plans, a contract must be created between the provider and the health plan, and such contract must be for the sole purpose of furnishing covered items and services to health plan enrollees. Thus, contracts for utilization-review or enrollment-screening services would not qualify for safe-harbor protection unless they otherwise meet the employment or personal services contracts safe harbor previously issued.

---

[43] *Id.* § 1001.952(*l*).

[44] *Id.* § 1001.952(m).

Second, the health plan must meet certain standards, depending on whether the health plan's relationship with the Medicare and Medicaid programs falls under one of the following categories:

1. risk-based health plans with formal program contracts;
2. cost-based health plans with formal program contracts cost contractors;
3. non-contracting health plans that do not pay providers on an at-risk capitated basis; and
4. health plans making capitated payments to providers.

4.2.12 Practitioner Recruitment

In 1999, the OIG added a safe harbor for physician-recruitment activities paid to a physician in order to induce the physician who has been practicing her specialty for less than one year to locate her primary practice to a HPSA for such physician's specialty as long as the following nine requirements are satisfied.[45]

1. *Written Agreement.* The arrangement must be set out in writing, specifying the recruitment benefits being provided and the respective parties' obligations.
2. *75% Revenue from New Patients.* If a practitioner is leaving an established practice, at least 75% of the revenues of the new practice must be generated from new patients.
3. *Three-Year Limitation.* The period of the agreement cannot exceed three years, and the terms of the agreement cannot be renegotiated during such three-year period.
4. *No Requirement to Refer.* There may not be any requirement that the physician make referrals to or otherwise generate business for the entity, although the entity may require physician to maintain staff privileges.
5. *No Restrictions on Staff Privileges.* The practitioner may not be restricted with respect to where the practitioner may maintain staff privileges.
6. *Amount of Benefits.* The amount of benefits provided to the physician may not vary in any manner based on the volume or volume of any expected referrals to or business generated for the entity.
7. *Agreement to Treat.* The practitioner must agree to treat patients receiving Medicare benefits or assistance from a Federal healthcare program in a nondiscriminatory manner.
8. *75% of Revenues Generated from Underserved Area.* At least 75% of the revenues of the new practice must be generated from patients who reside in a HPSA or a MUA or who are part of a MUP.
9. *Benefits Only Paid to Practitioner.* Except for the practitioner who is being recruited, no payment or exchange of anything of value given to a person or entity in a position to make or influence referrals may be made.

---

[45] *Id.* § 1001.952(n).

4.2.13 Obstetrical Malpractice-Insurance Subsidies

This safe harbor protects malpractice subsidies for obstetrical care paid by a hospital or other entity where such payment is for a practitioner (including a certified nurse-midwife) who engages in obstetrical practice as a routine part of her medical practice in a primary care HPSA.[46] Included among the criteria for this safe harbor is a requirement that at least 75% of the practitioner's obstetrical patients, who are treated under the coverage policy, reside in a HPSA or MUA or be part of a MUP. In addition, for practitioners who are not full-time obstetricians or certified nurse-midwives, the safe harbor only protects payments related to obstetrical malpractice insurance.

4.2.14 Investments in Group Practices

The OIG has adopted a safe harbor that protects returns on investments made to a solo or group practitioner investing in her own practice, as long as certain requirements are satisfied. In light of the fact that much of the day-to-day management of most physician groups is given to one physician or a practice manager, the OIG deleted its proposal to require that the group practice be composed of "active investors," and instead merely requires that the group practice be comprised of licensed professionals who practice as part of the group.

Among the other requirements are that the physician's equity interest be held in the group practice itself and not a subdivision of the group, that the group satisfy the Stark Law's requirements for being a "group practice," and that revenues from ancillary services be derived from "in-office ancillary services" that meet the applicable definition under the Stark Law. Moreover, the OIG has required that the group practice be organized "as a unified business with centralized decision-making, pooling of expenses and revenues, and a compensation/profit distribution system that is not based on satellite offices operating substantially as if they were separate enterprises or profit centers."[47]

4.2.15 Cooperative Hospital-Services Organizations

This safe harbor protects most cooperative hospital-service organizations (CHSOs) that qualify under § 501(c)(3) of the Internal Revenue Code (IRC), which operate by distributing earnings to members in accordance with the volume of services used by the member hospital.[48] The safe harbor requires that if the patron-hospital makes a payment to the CHSO, the payment must be for *bona fide* operating expenses of the CHSO. On the other hand, if the CHSO makes a payment to the patron-hospital, the payment must be for the purpose of paying a distribution of net earnings required to be made under IRC § 501(e)(2).

4.2.16 ASCs

In 1993, the OIG proposed adding a safe harbor protecting payments to surgeon-investors in ASCs who refer patients directly to the ASC and perform the surgery themselves on those patients. In contrast to other investment-interest safe harbors that limit investment by individuals in a position

46 *Id.* § 1001.952(o).
47 *Id.* § 1001.952(p).
48 *Id.* § 1001.952(q).

to refer, the proposed ASC safe harbor would have only protected entities whose investment interests were held entirely by such individuals. After the OIG received a great volume of comments on this proposed safe harbor, however, the OIG significantly revised it in 1999.

In the final regulations, the OIG created four different categories of ASC safe harbors: surgeon-owned ASCs; single-specialty ASCs; multi-specialty ASCs (*e.g.*, a mix of surgeons and specialists); and hospital/physician-owned ASCs. In addition to the surgeons, physicians, and/or a hospital that can have an ownership interest in the entity, certain other "non-tainted" investors can own an investment interest as long as they: (1) do not provide items or services to the ASC or its investors; (2) are not employed by the ASC or any investor; and (3) are not in a position to refer patients directly or indirectly to, or generate business for, the ASC or any of its investors.[49]

Applicable to all four categories of ASCs are requirements that the ASC be Medicare certified, that the ASC's operating and recovery room space be dedicated exclusively to the ASC (*i.e.*, if the ASC is located in a hospital, the ASC space must be dedicated exclusively to the ASC and not used by the hospital for the treatment of the hospital's inpatients or outpatients), and that all patients who are referred to the ASC by an investor must receive information about the investor's investment interest. In addition, all four categories include a requirement that all ancillary services be directly and integrally related to primary procedures performed at the ASC, and that none may be separately billed to Medicare or other federal healthcare programs.

With respect to the first three categories of ASC safe harbors (*i.e.*, surgeon-owned ASCs, single-specialty ASCs, and multi-specialty ASCs), each requires that physician investors satisfy the "One-Third Practice Income Test," which requires that each physician investor derive at least one-third of her medical practice income for the previous 12-month period from her own performance of procedures that require an ASC or hospital surgical setting. Moreover, a physician investor in the third category of ASC (*i.e.*, a multi-specialty ASC) must satisfy another standard whereby at least one-third of the physician's procedures that require an ASC or hospital surgical setting be performed at the ASC in which she is investing (known as the "One-Third/One-Third Test").

With respect to the fourth category (*i.e.*, a hospital/physician ASC), the OIG has included a requirement that the hospital not be in a position to make or influence referrals directly or indirectly to the ASC or to any of its physician investors—a development which, from a practical perspective, may preclude many hospital/physician ASC joint ventures from qualifying for safe-harbor protection.

4.2.17 Referral Agreements for Specialty Services

This safe harbor excludes from the purview of the Anti-Kickback Statute any "exchange of value" among individuals or entities where one party "agrees to refer a patient to other party for the provision of a specialty services" in return for an agreement that the other party will "refer that patient back at a mutually agreed upon time or circumstance" as long as certain requirements are met.[50] In particular, the safe harbor requires that the timing and circumstances for the referral back to the originating physi-

[49] *Id.* § 1001.952(r).
[50] *Id.* § 1001.952(s).

cian or entity be "clinically appropriate," that the service for which the referral is made not be within the expertise of the referring individual or entity, and that the parties neither receive any payment from each other for the referral nor share or split a global fee in connection with the referred patient. Finally, unless the parties to the agreement belong to the same group practice, the only permitted "exchange of value" is the remuneration the respective parties receive from the third-party payor or the patient for the services furnished to the patient.

4.2.18 Ambulance Replenishing/Restocking

In 2001, the OIG adopted a final regulation establishing safe-harbor protection for ambulance "restocking" or "replenishing" arrangements.[51] As described in the preamble to the safe harbor, ambulance "restocking" is the practice of hospitals, or other receiving facilities, restocking ambulance providers with drugs or supplies used during the transport of a patient to the hospital or receiving facility. Operationally, this is done to ensure that, when the ambulance departs the hospital, it is, as the OIG points out, ready for the next emergency call, fully stocked with current medications, sanitary linens, and a full complement of appropriate medications and supplies, and helps to ensure that supplies, such as intravenous tubing and catheters, are compatible with equipment used in local emergency rooms so as to expedite the transfer or critically ill or injured patients to emergency room systems.[52]

The final regulations address three categories of restocking: general restocking (either for free or for a charge); fair-market-value restocking; and government-mandated restocking. Common to all three categories of safe harbors are the following four conditions:

1. under no circumstances may both the ambulance provider and the receiving facility bill for the same replenished drug or supply, and all billing or claims submission for the replenished drugs must comply with all federal healthcare-program payment and coverage rules;
2. one of the parties will maintain records of the replenished drugs and medical supplies;
3. no ties to referrals, and
4. all parties will ensure compliance with all other federal, state, and local laws regulating ambulance services.

4.2.19 Federally Qualified Health Centers

In 2003, Congress amended the Anti-Kickback Statute and include a statutory requirement that the OIG develop a safe harbor for certain agreements involving FQHCs. On October 4, 2007, the OIG published a final rule establishing a safe harbor for FQHCs for certain goods, items, services, donations, and loans provided by individuals and entities to certain health centers funded under Section 330 of the Public Health Service Act, which is a health center program designed to assist individuals living in medically underserved areas and populations with limited access to healthcare resources.[53]

---

[51] *Id.* § 1001.952(v); *see* 66 Fed. Reg. 62,979 (2001); *see also* 65 Fed. Reg. 32,060 (2000).

[52] 66 Fed. Reg. 62,979 (2001). In the preamble, the OIG also explains that, although "restocking" is the term commonly used, the OIG uses the word "replenishing" to make clear that "the safe harbor only applies to the gifting or transfer of drugs and supplies that replace comparable drugs and supplies administered," and that the safe harbor is not applicable to "general stocking of the inventories of ambulance providers." *Id.*

[53] 42 C.F.R. § 1001.952(w); *see* 72 Fed. Reg. 56,632 (2007).

The safe harbor excludes remuneration between a health center and an individual or entity providing goods, items, services, donations, loans, or a combination of these to the health center pursuant to a contract, lease, grant, loan, or other agreement, provided that the agreement contributes to the health center's ability to maintain or increase its services to the medically underserved. The remuneration must be "medical or clinical in nature or relate directly to patient services" such as billing services, administrative support services, technology support and the like.

4.2.20 Risk-Sharing Arrangements

In 1999, the OIG issued two safe harbors for shared-risk arrangements.[54] The first safe harbor protects price reductions that are offered to "eligible managed care organizations" (EMCOs), which are defined to include HMOs and competitive medical plans (CMPs) with a risk- or cost-based contract; Medicare+Choice organizations that receive capitation payments; certain Medicaid managed care organizations (MCOs), Programs for the All Inclusive Care For the Elderly, and federally qualified HMOs.

This safe harbor is divided into two categories of requirements. The first category sets out standards for arrangements between EMCOs and any individual or entity that contracts directly with the EMCO (referred to as a "first tier" contractor). Among this safe harbor's requirements is the requirement that the EMCO and the first-tier contractor have an agreement that is set out in writing, is for a term of at least one year, specifies the items and services covered under the agreement, and specifies that the first-tier contractor cannot claim payment in any form from a federal healthcare program for items or services covered under the agreement, except for (1) HMOs and CMPs that have cost-based contracts, (2) federally qualified HMOs without a CMS contract, and (3) federally qualified health centers that claim supplemental payments from a federal healthcare program.

In addition, the safe harbor requires that, when the parties establish the financial terms of the agreement, neither party gives nor receives remuneration in return for, or to induce the provision or acceptance of, fee-for-service business reimbursed by a federal healthcare program.

The second category addresses financial arrangements between first-tier contractors and downstream contractors, or between successive tiers of downstream contractors. Although many of the requirements of this section of the safe harbor are similar to the first category, the major difference is that, under this safe harbor, the underlying agreement between the first-tier contractor and the EMCO may *not* involve an HMO or CMP with a cost-based contract, a federally qualified HMO without a CMS contract, or a federally qualified health center receiving supplemental payments.

While the first safe harbor covers most Medicare and HMO plans, the scope of the second safe harbor is very narrow. To qualify under this safe harbor, the risk-sharing arrangement must be part of a "qualified managed care plan" (QMCP), which is defined as a managed-care entity that satisfies the requirements of the definition of a "health plan" located in the managed-care safe harbor related to beneficiary incentives. Moreover, a QMCP must adopt processes and procedures to assure that the healthcare services are managed (*e.g.*, utilization-review procedures, grievance-procedure require-

---

[54] 42 C.F.R.§ 1001.952(t)–(u); *see also* 64 Fed. Reg. 63,504 (1999).

ments). The safe harbor also requires either that no more than 10% of the QMCP's beneficiary population be Medicare beneficiaries (excluding those individuals where Medicare is secondary) or that no more than 50% are Medicare beneficiaries, but only if the premium payments are made on a periodic basis and do not take into account various factors.

Similar to the safe harbor for price reductions offered to EMCOs, this safe harbor provides protection to two categories of entities: first-tier contractors and downstream providers. Both must satisfy the requirement that the applicable party (*i.e.*, the first-tier contractor or the downstream contractor) have substantial financial risk for the cost or utilization of services that it is obligated to provide. The regulations then create four payment methodologies that qualify as placing a contractor at "substantial financial risk": periodic fixed payments per patient, percentages of premiums, diagnosis-related groups (DRGs), and bonus and withhold arrangements.

With respect to the last category of payment methodologies—bonus and withhold arrangements—the OIG has further required that the target payment for individuals and non-institutional providers must be at least 20% greater than the minimum payment, whereas the target payment for an institutional provider (*e.g.*, a hospital or nursing home) must be at least 10% greater. The safe harbor further requires that the amount at risk must be in direct proportion to the ratio of the contractor's actual utilization to its target utilization. Alternatively, for contractors that are physicians, the OIG adopts the definition of "substantial financial risk" based upon CMS's requirements under the physician incentive plan regulations.[55]

4.2.21 Electronic Prescribing

In August 2006, HHS promulgated a final rule establishing an e-prescribing safe harbor,[56] and between 2005 and 2008 HHS promulgated two additional rules, which taken together establish a comprehensive and uniform set of standards for e-prescribing under Medicare Part D.[57]

The final e-prescribing safe harbor incorporates most of the language from the 2005 proposed safe harbor, but the OIG modified a few provisions in order to expand the overall scope of safe harbor protection. Whereas the proposed safe harbor would have protected arrangements relating to the transmission of electronic "drug" information, the final safe harbor protects arrangements relating to the transmission of "any" prescription information, such as information related to drugs, laboratory tests, and durable medical equipment orders.[58] In addition, the OIG has abandoned provisions from the proposed safe harbor that (1) would have imposed a cap on the amount of technology or services that an entity can donate, and (2) would have required a recipient to certify the technical or functional superiority of donated technology over technology already in the recipient's possession. The OIG also dismissed a proposal to create a separate e-prescribing safe harbor for multipurpose technology.[59]

---

55 *See* 42 C.F.R. § 417.479.
56 71 Fed. Reg. 45,110 (Aug. 8, 2006).
57 73 Fed. Reg. 18,918 (Apr. 7, 2008); 70 Fed. Reg. 67,568 (Nov. 7, 2005).
58 71 Fed. Reg. 45,114 (Aug. 8, 2006).
59 *Id.*

As proposed in 2005, the final safe harbor applies if eight conditions are met. Among these conditions, the items and services may be provided: (a) in the case of a hospital, by the hospital to physicians who are members of its medical staff; (b) in the case of a group practice, by the group practice to prescribing healthcare professionals who are members of the group practice (including not only physicians, but other healthcare professionals who are authorized to prescribe by state licensing laws); and (c) in the case of a PDP sponsor or MA organization, by the sponsor or MA organization to pharmacists participating in the network of such sponsor or organization and to prescribing healthcare professionals.[60]

Safe harbor protection applies to e-prescribing hardware, software, and information technology and training services that are necessary and used solely to receive and transmit electronic prescription information. Examples of protected products and services include electronic clinical support tools, tools that provide access to formulary information, and operating software required for hardware usage.[61]

The e-prescribing safe harbor does not protect the donation of unnecessary technology or technology that is functionally equivalent to products and services already possessed by a recipient. If the OIG discovers that a donor had actual knowledge or acted in reckless disregard or deliberate ignorance of the fact that a recipient already possessed functionally equivalent technology, then neither party can receive safe harbor protection. The final safe harbor has abandoned language from the proposed safe harbor that would have required donors to certify that donated products and services are technically or functionally superior to those already possessed by the recipient. Instead, the OIG recommends that donors make "reasonable inquiries" (which should not usually require the use of technical experts) about a recipient's existing e-prescribing capabilities before donating.[62]

Only technology used solely for e-prescribing purposes can receive safe harbor protection. For technology to serve an e-prescribing purpose, it must provide information or perform functions necessary to formulate, transmit, or receive a medically appropriate prescription for a patient. Technology that directly relates to e-prescribing, such as electronic clinical support software that identifies alternative drug therapies, drug-drug interactions, or payor formulary information, satisfies this requirement. Technology that bundles e-prescribing functions with unrelated functions, such as patient billing or scheduling, will not satisfy this requirement.[63]

Donated e-prescribing technology will not receive safe harbor protection unless it meets HHS standards for e-prescribing systems.[64] These standards, established to ensure that e-prescribing technology is interoperable, consist of rules relating to all aspects of e-prescribing, such as the electronic transmittal of information between providers and pharmacists, eligibility and benefits queries, formulary and benefit information, medication history, and network compatibility. Before being incorpo-

60 *Id.* at 45,117; 42 C.F.R. § 1001.952(x)(1).

61 71 Fed. Reg. 45,116–117 (Aug. 8, 2006); 42 C.F.R. § 1001.952(x).

62 *Id.* at 45,115, 45,123.

63 *Id.* at 45,115.

64 42 C.F.R. § 1001.952(x)(2).

rated into law, HHS tested many of these rules through pilot programs conducted at various provider and pharmacy settings throughout the country.[65]

The OIG also conditioned safe harbor protection on compliance with specific rules relating to the selection of donors and recipients. Recipients may not make the donation of e-prescribing technology a prerequisite for doing business with a donor, and neither the donor nor the recipient may directly or indirectly base selection on the volume or value of referrals or other business generated between the parties. The safe harbor permits selection based on the total number of prescriptions written by a recipient, but does not permit selection based on the value of prescriptions written by the recipient, or the volume or value of prescriptions written by a recipient that are reimbursable to any Federal healthcare program.[66]

Also, parties seeking safe harbor protection must satisfy the following additional requirements: (1) where possible, recipients must have the ability to use donated e-prescribing technology on all patients without regard to payor status;[67] (2) arrangements between donors and recipients must be written and signed by the parties;[68] (3) the donor must not take any action to restrict the compatibility of donated e-prescribing technology with other e-prescribing or electronic health record systems;[69] and (4) such arrangements must identify with specificity the items or services being provided (but do not have to specify the value of the donated technology).[70] The final e-prescribing safe harbor abandoned language from the proposed safe harbor that would have limited the aggregate value of e-prescribing technology that a donor could provide to a qualifying recipient. As a result, in the final regulations, there is no cap on the value of services that a donor can provide or a recipient can receive.[71]

4.2.22 Electronic Health Records and Community-Wide Information System

Towards promoting the development of interconnected, interoperable electronic health records (EHRs), the OIG finalized in August 2006 a safe harbor that protects the donation and receipt of the technology underlying EHR systems.[72] Both the nature and the scope of the EHR safe harbor have undergone significant modification during the rulemaking process. The final rule only bares a partial resemblance to the proposed rule. Whereas the proposed rule called for separate "pre-interoperability" and "post-interoperability" safe harbors, the final rule created a single safe harbor that will remain in effect after HHS releases final interoperability standards. The final rule's EHR safe harbor also provided more expansive safe harbor protections than the OIG had initially proposed. In addition, the OIG abandoned provisions from the proposed safe harbor that would have imposed a cap on the amount of technology or services that an entity can donate and would have restricted safe harbor protection to technologies "solely" used for EHR purposes.[73]

---

[65] 71 Fed. Reg. 45,115 (Aug. 8, 2006); Center for Medicare & Medicaid Services, http://www.cms.hhs.gov/eprescribing/.
[66] 71 Fed. Reg. 45,118 (Aug. 8, 2006).
[67] 42 C.F.R. § 1001.952(x)(4).
[68] 42 C.F.R. § 1001.952(x)(7).
[69] 42 C.F.R. § 1001.952(x)(3).
[70] 71 Fed. Reg. 45,119 (Aug. 8, 2006); 42 C.F.R. § 1001.952(x)(7).
[71] 71 Fed. Reg. 45,118, 45,119 (Aug. 8, 2006).
[72] 71 Fed. Reg. 45,121 (Aug. 8, 2006).
[73] *Id.* at 45,121, 45,122.

The EHR safe harbor protects technology necessary and used predominantly to create, maintain, and transmit or receive EHRs, such as EHR computer software and related wireless internet services, clinical support tools, electronic messaging services, and helpdesk services.[74] However, the safe harbor does not protect hardware, hardware operating software, software primarily used for non-EHR purposes, or the provision of staff services to perform EHR related tasks such as the conversion of paper medical records into EHRs.[75] The safe harbor also does not protect the donation of unnecessary technology or technology that is functionally equivalent to products and services already possessed by a recipient.[76] If the OIG discovers that a donor had actual knowledge or acted in reckless disregard or deliberate ignorance of the fact that a recipient already possessed functionally equivalent technology, then neither party can receive safe harbor protection. Although donors do not have to certify that donated products and services are technically or functionally superior to those already possessed by the recipient, the OIG recommends that donors make "reasonable inquiries" (which should not usually require the use of technical experts) about a recipient's existing EHR capabilities before donating.[77] The OIG interprets the donation of software upgrades that enhance usability or technology that enhances the interoperability of donor and recipient systems as necessary and functionally superior.[78] In contrast to the safe-harbor for e-prescribing, which only covers technology used solely for e-prescribing, the EHR safe harbor covers multi-purpose technology as long as the technology is used predominately for EHR purposes and its other uses relate to patient care. For example, EHR technologies that have secondary functions associated with patient administration, scheduling, and billing can qualify for safe harbor protection.[79]

In order to qualify for safe harbor protection, arrangements for the donation and receipt of EHR technology must also comply with interoperability requirements, which the OIG describes as the ability of systems to communicate and exchange data accurately, effectively, securely, and consistently with different information technology systems without altering the meaning of the data.[80] The OIG's decision to create only one safe harbor, instead of separate pre- and post-interoperability safe harbors, reflects progress in the development of interoperability criteria for EHR systems that occurred between the publication of the proposed and final rules. By August 2006, informal criteria for certifying the interoperability of EHRs had become available. While HHS has not yet incorporated these criteria into legally binding standards, the OIG "deems" all technology approved by certifying entities recognized by HHS as interoperable, and reviews unapproved technology on a case by case basis.[81] When reviewing unapproved technology, the OIG considers whether the technology was as interoperable as was technologically feasible at the time it was donated. The OIG has specified, however, that the safe harbor does not cover technology that is only compatible with the products of specific vendors, or technology unique to a local community or a limited number of healthcare systems. Related to these

---

74 *Id.* at 45,125; 42 C.F.R. § 1001.952(y).

75 71 Fed. Reg. 45,125 (Aug. 8, 2006).

76 *Id.* at 45,115, 45,123.

77 *Id.* at 45,123.

78 *Id.*

79 *Id.* at 45,124; 42 C.F.R. § 1001.952(x); 42 C.F.R. § 1001.952(y).

80 71 Fed. Reg. 45,126 (Aug. 8, 2006); 42 C.F.R. § 1001.952(y)(2).

81 71 Fed. Reg. 45,121, 45,127 (Aug. 8, 2006); 42 C.F.R. § 1001.952(y)(2).

interoperability requirements, the OIG also requires that EHR systems be compatible with electronic prescribing systems.[82]

The EHR safe harbor only applies to donors and recipients of EHR technology that meet the following eligibility criteria: entities that provide covered services and submit claims or payment requests to a Federal Health Care Program are eligible donors, and entities that engage in the delivery of healthcare items and services are eligible recipients. Among eligible donors, the OIG has included health plans and clinical laboratories, but not pharmaceutical, medical device, and durable medical equipment manufacturers, or research entities.[83] The EHR safe harbor does not impose a cap on the value of items or services that can be donated or received, but it does require that each recipient contribute at least 15% of the value of the donation.[84]

The OIG also conditions safe harbor protection on compliance with specific rules relating to the selection of donors and recipients. Recipients may not make the donation of EHR technology a prerequisite for doing business with a donor, and donors may not select recipients or determine the value of a donation based on the volume or value of referrals or other business generated between the parties. The OIG identifies as examples of permissible criteria for selecting a recipient selections made in a "reasonable" and "verifiable" manner based on: (1) the total number of prescriptions written by a recipient; (2) the size of a recipient's medical practice; (3) the total number of hours a recipient practices medicine; (4) the recipient's overall use of automated technology for medical care; (5) whether the recipient is a member of the donor's medical staff; and (6) the level of uncompensated care provided by the recipient.[85]

Parties seeking safe harbor protection must satisfy the following additional requirements: (1) where possible, recipients must have the ability to use donated EHR technology on all patients without regard to payor status;[86] (2) arrangements between donors and recipients must be written and signed by the parties;[87] and (3) such arrangements must identify with specificity the items or services being provided, the donor's costs of those items and services, and the recipients contribution.[88] Because the OIG expects EHRs to become widespread by 2013, it has indicated in the final rule that the EHR safe harbor will only remain in effect until December 31, 2013. After that time, all arrangements involving the donation and receipt of EHR related items and services will be subject to a case-by-case analysis under the anti-kickback statute.[89]

[82] 71 Fed. Reg. 45,126–127 (Aug. 8, 2006); 42 C.F.R. § 1001.952(y)(10).
[83] 71 Fed. Reg. 45,127, 45,129 (Aug. 8, 2006); 42 C.F.R. § 1001.952(y)(1).
[84] 71 Fed. Reg. 45,132 (Aug. 8, 2006); 42 C.F.R. § 1001.952(y)(11).
[85] 71 Fed. Reg. 45,130 (Aug. 8, 2006); 42 C.F.R. § 1001.952(y)(5).
[86] 42 C.F.R. § 1001.952(y)(8).
[87] 42 C.F.R. § 1001.952(y)(6).
[88] *Id.*
[89] 71 Fed. Reg. 45,133 (Aug. 8, 2006); 42 C.F.R. § 1001.952(y)(13).

4.3 Federal Physician Self-Referral Law

4.3.1 Statutory Prohibition

The Stark Law prohibits a physician from ordering "designated health services" (DHS) for Medicare patients from entities with which the physician (or an immediate family member) has a "financial relationship."[90] The term "financial relationship" is defined in the Stark Law to include both compensation arrangements and interests in investment and/or ownership. In addition, the term "referral" is defined more broadly than merely recommending a vendor of DHS to a patient. Instead, the term "referral" means, for Medicare Part B services, "the request by a physician for the item or service" and, for all other services, "the request or establishment of a plan of care by a physician which includes the provision of the designated health service."[91]

Although the Stark Law originally only applied to the provision of clinical laboratory services, effective January 1, 1995, the Stark Law was expanded to apply to a host of "designated health services." DHS includes clinical laboratory services as well as the following:

- physical-therapy services;
- occupational-therapy services;
- radiology, including magnetic resonance imaging, computerized axial tomography scans, and ultrasound services;
- radiation-therapy services and supplies;
- durable medical equipment and supplies;
- parenteral and enteral nutrients, equipment, and supplies;
- prosthetics, orthotics, and prosthetic devices;
- home health services and supplies;
- outpatient prescription drugs; and
- inpatient and outpatient hospital services.[92]

However, excluded from the definition of the term "DHS" are services that are reimbursed by Medicare as part of a composite, except for the services listed above that are themselves payable through a composite rate (*e.g.*, home health, outpatient hospital services).

In 2003, Congress modified the Stark Law by adopting an 18-month moratorium on the ability of physicians to own an interest in a specialty hospital.[93] Although the moratorium officially lapsed in June 2005, over the last several years, Congress has continued to monitor and debate the issue of

---

[90] 42 U.S.C. § 1395nn. The federal physician self-referral statute, as noted, often is referred to as the "Stark Law" after Congressman Fortney "Pete" Stark (D-CA), the Congressman who introduced and strongly supported the enactment of the statute.

[91] 42 U.S.C. § 1395nn (h)(5).

[92] CMS has defined certain designated health services (*i.e.*, clinical laboratory services, physical therapy, radiology, and certain other imaging services, and radiation therapy services) by publishing specific lists of the Current Procedural Terminology and HCFA Common Procedure Coding System codes that physicians and providers most commonly associate with a given service.

[93] Medicare Prescription Drug, Improvement and Modernization Act of 2003, Pub. L. No. 108-173 § 507.

whether this exception to the Stark Law should be modified. With the passage of Health Reform, Congress again placed significant limitations on physicians' ownership interests in hospitals located both in urban and rural areas.[94]

Violations of the Stark Law are subject to various penalties, including one or more of the following:

- denial of payment for the DHS provided;
- refund of monies received by physicians and facilities for amounts collected;
- payment of civil penalties of up to $15,000 for each service that a person "knows or should know" was provided in violation of the Stark Law, and three times the amount of improper payment the entity received from the Medicare program;
- exclusion from the Medicare program and/or state healthcare programs including Medicaid; and
- payment of civil penalties for attempting to circumvent the Stark Law of up to $100,000 for each circumvention scheme.

In the Phase II Regulations, CMS adopted an exception to when the government will impose penalties if an arrangement involves "temporary noncompliance." Specifically, CMS provides that a violation has not occurred if: (1) an arrangement met an exception for at least 180 consecutive calendar days preceding the date when the agreement was no longer in compliance; (2) the financial relationship fell out of compliance for reasons beyond the control of the entity; and (3) the arrangement does not violate the Anti-Kickback Statute.[95]

Then, in the 2009 IPPS Final Rule, CMS adopted a provision that allows an entity under certain circumstances to submit a claim for a DHS if the compensation arrangement between the entity and a referring physician fully complied with an applicable exception except with regard to the signature requirement. More specifically, if the failure to comply with the signature requirement was "inadvertent" and the parties obtain the required signature(s) within 90 consecutive calendar days immediately following the date on which the compensation arrangement became noncompliant, the arrangement qualifies for the exception, without regard to whether any referrals occur or compensation is paid within the 90-day period. If the failure to comply was "not inadvertent," the parties must obtain the required signature(s) within 30 consecutive calendar days following the date on which the compensation arrangement became noncompliant to enjoy the protection of the exception.[96] An entity may use the provision for alternative method for compliance with signatures only once every three years with respect to the same referring physician. CMS specifically declines to extend relief to failures to satisfy other prescribed procedural or "form" criteria of an exception such as the amount of compensation or the description of the services.

---

94 *See* Patient Protection and Affordable Care Act of 2010, Pub. L. No. 111-148, 124 Stat. 119 § 6001(a)(3) (2010) (codified at 42 U.S.C. § 1395nn).

95 42 C.F.R. § 411.353(f).

96 42 C.F.R. § 353(g); *See also* 73 Fed. Reg. at 48,705–09.

In addition to applying to the Medicare program, certain aspects of the Stark Law apply to state Medicaid programs. Specifically, the Social Security Act denies federal financial-participation payment under a Medicaid program to a state for services that would have been prohibited by Medicare under the Stark Law, if Medicare covered the services to the same extent as under the state's Medicaid plan.[97] Under the "Stark II Proposed Regulations" (as will be discussed), CMS has articulated its proposed position that individuals and entities are not precluded from referring Medicaid patients, or from billing for DHS that otherwise would be prohibited under the Medicare Stark Law prohibition. Instead, CMS has taken the position that, in these circumstances, state Medicaid programs may pay for these services even though the states will not be eligible to receive federal financial participation for these services.[98]

4.3.2 Regulations

On August 14, 1995, CMS published final regulations implementing the Stark Law's prohibition against the ordering of clinical laboratory services from an entity with which a physician has a financial relationship (the Stark I Regulations).[99] Then, on January 9, 1998, CMS published as a proposed rule for public comment the "Stark II" regulations (the Stark II Proposed Regulations).[100]

On January 4, 2001, almost three years to the day after the Stark II Proposed Regulations were issued, CMS published in the *Federal Register* "Phase I" of the Final Stark II regulations (Phase I Regulations),[101] which implemented only certain portions of the Stark Law:

1. the Stark Law's prohibition;
2. exceptions to the law that apply to both ownership and compensation arrangements;
3. the definitions of key terms included in the Stark statute; and
4. certain new regulatory exceptions.

On March 26, 2004, CMS published Phase II of the Final Stark II regulations (Phase II Regulations) as an interim final rule with comment period.[102] The comment period ended on June 24, 2004, and the Phase II Regulations became effective July 26, 2004. On September 5, 2007, CMS issued Phase III of the Final Stark regulations (Phase III Final Regulations).[103]

While traditionally CMS issued stand-alone Stark regulations, CMS has begun including extensive changes to the Stark regulations in other regulatory issuances such as the Medicare Physician Fee Schedule (MPFS) or the Hospital Inpatient Prospective Payment Systems (IPPS). For example, final Stark regulations can be found in the FY 2008 IPPS Final Rule,[104] the CY 2008 MPFS Final Rule,[105]

---

97 42 U.S.C. § 1396b(s).
98 63 Fed. Reg. 1,659, 1,672 (1998).
99 *See* 60 Fed. Reg. 41,914 (1995) (codified at 42 C.F.R. pt. 411).
100 *See* 63 Fed. Reg. 1,659 (1998).
101 66 Fed. Reg. 856 (2001) (codified at 42 C.F.R. Part 411 & 424).
102 69 Fed. Reg. 16,054 (2004).
103 *See* 72 Fed. Reg. 51,012 (2007).
104 72 Fed. Reg. 47,130 (Aug. 22, 2007). *See also* the Proposed FY 2008 IPPS rule at 72 Fed. Reg. 24,680 (May 3, 2007).
105 72 Fed. Reg. 66,222 (Nov. 27, 2007). *See also* the Proposed CY 2008 MPFS rule at 72 Fed. Reg. 38,122 (July 12, 2007).

FY 2009 IPPS Final Rule,[106] the CY 2009 MPFS Final Rule,[107] the CY 2010 MPFS Final Rule[108] and the CY 2011 MPFS Final Rule.[109]

4.3.3 Reporting Requirements

The Stark Law includes certain reporting requirements whereby any entity that provides items or services for which payment may be made under Medicare must submit certain information about the entity's financial relationship with physicians to CMS under time periods prescribed by the entity's Medicare carrier.[110] In the Phase II Regulations, CMS waived all reporting requirements for DHS entities providing fewer than 20 Part A and B services during a calendar year. Moreover, CMS decided not to require regular submission of information of other providers, but instead only requires information to be submitted upon request by CMS. [111]

As part of the Deficit Reduction Act of 2005, Congress required DHHS to develop a strategic and implementing plan to address certain issues relating to physician-owned specialty hospitals.[112] In preparing its report, CMS sent a voluntary survey to 130 specialty hospitals and 220 competitor hospitals which sought information regarding, among other things, the hospitals' ownership and investment relationships and their compensation arrangements with physicians. Then, in August 2008, CMS issued its Final Report to Congress and that it would require all hospitals to provide information on a periodic basis concerning the investment interests and compensation arrangements with physicians.[113] As a result, in 2007, CMS began its initiative to implement a survey to investigate the investment/ownership and compensation arrangements between physicians and hospitals to determine whether they are in compliance with the Stark Law and implementing regulations. Under the Paperwork Reduction Act, CMS was required to obtain clearance from the Office of Management and Budget (OMB) prior to sending out the survey. Although the DFRR was under review by OMB for several months, on April 10, 2008, OMB reported that CMS had withdrawn its request for clearance of the DFRR survey.[114] Although CMS had not reintroduced this tool, as part of Health Reform, Congress adopted another provision requiring the Secretary to collect information regarding physician ownership in hospitals.[115]

---

106 73 Fed. Reg. 48,434 (Aug. 19, 2008). *See also* the Proposed FY 2009 IPPS rule at 73 Fed. Reg. 23,528 (Apr. 30, 2008).

107 73 Fed. Reg. 69,726 (Nov. 19, 2008). *See also* the Proposed CY 2009 MPFS rule at 73 Fed. Reg. 38,502 (July 7, 2008).

108 74 Fed. Reg. 61,738 (Nov. 25, 2009).

109 75 Fed. Reg. 73,170 (Nov. 29, 2010).

110 42 U.S.C. § 1395nn(f); 42 C.F.R. § 411.361.

111 42 C.F.R. § 411.361.

112 Deficit Reduction Act of 2005, Pub. L. No. 109-171, § 5006.

113 A copy of the CMS Final Report to Congress can be found at http://www.cms.hhs.gov/PhysicianSelfReferral/06a_DRA_Reports.asp#TopOfPage.

114 *See* http://www.reginfo.gov/public/do/PRAViewICR?ref_nbr=200710-0938-003.

115 *See* Patient Protection and Affordable Care Act of 2010, Pub. L. No. 111-148, 124 Stat. 119 § 6001(a)(3) (2010) (codified at 42 U.S.C. § 1395nn(i)).

4.3.4 Definition of "Entity"

Although in the Phase I Stark II Final Regulations, CMS adopted the definition of the term "entity" as "the person or entity to which CMS makes payment for the DHS,"[116] in 2007, as part of the CY 2008 MPFS Proposed Rule, CMS proposed to revise the definition of the term "entity" to include not only the person or entity that bills for the DHS but also any person or entity that "performs" the DHS as well as any person or entity that "presented a claim or caused a claim to be presented" to Medicare for the DHS.[117]

Although CMS did not finalize its proposal in the CY 2008 MPFS Final Rule, CMS did adopt a modified definition in the FY 2009 IPPS Final Rule so as to include any person or entity that "has performed services that are billed as DHS."[118] By changing the definition of "entity" to include persons and entities that "perform" DHS, CMS specifically stated in the preamble to the regulations that it intended to include within the scope of the Stark Law those physician groups and other organizations that provide inpatient and/or outpatient services to a hospital "under arrangements."[119] Consequently, any physician who maintains a financial relationship with the "under arrangement" organization/DHS entity can only make DHS referrals to the organization if that financial relationship meets a Stark Law exception. While it may be possible to structure a physician's *compensation* arrangement with such an "under arrangement" organization to satisfy a compensation arrangement exception, only under very limited circumstances will a physician be able to maintain an *ownership* or investment interest in an "under arrangement" organization after October 1, 2009.[120]

In the FY 2009 IPPS Final Rule, CMS specifically addresses two sets of services that, in many instances, are provided to hospitals by physician organizations under arrangements: lithotripsy services and cardiac catheterization services. With respect to lithotripsy and as a result of the District of Columbia District Court decision in 2002 finding that lithotripsy is not a DHS, CMS stated in the FY 2009 IPPS Final Rule that lithotripsy services will not be subject to these principles.[121] With respect to cardiac catheterization services, CMS states that the final rule does not prohibit physicians from furnishing services, in part because "[w]here a group practice or other physician organization provides the service and bills for it, the service is not DHS and the physician self-referral statute will not apply."[122] Yet, this statement ignores the practical reality of cardiac catheterization practices as Medicare billing rules provide that cardiac catheterization services generally must be billed by a hospital.[123] As a result of this position, a group of physicians and physician-owned entities that provide cardiac catheterization services (Cath Labs) across Colorado brought a lawsuit to overturn CMS's position.[124] To stop the definitional change prior to its October 1, 2009 effective date, plaintiffs sought a declaration that the

---

116 42 C.F.R. § 411.351; *see* 66 Fed. Reg. at 943.

117 72 Fed. Reg. at 38,224.

118 42 C.F.R. § 411.351; *see* 73 Fed. Reg. at 48,721. However, in the FY 2009 IPPS Final Rule, CMS did not adopt the concept of including within the definition of "entity" those who present or cause a claim to be submitted to Medicare.

119 73 Fed. Reg. at 48,721.

120 Specifically, the only remaining ownership exception available would be the rural provider exception (*see* Section 3-4(b)(3) for a description of the rural provider exception).

121 73 Fed. Reg. at 48,730; *see also Lithotripsy Society v. Thompson*, 215 F. Supp. 2d 23 (D.C. 2002).

122 73 Fed. Reg. at 48,729–30.

123 *See* Medicare Provider Reimbursement Manual, Part I, Ch. 21, § 2118.1.

124 *Colorado Heart Institute v. Johnson*, 609 F. Supp. 2d 30 (D.D.C. 2009).

expanded definition "'is contrary to clear congressional intent, based on an impermissible construction of the Stark Law, arbitrary and capricious, and exceeds the agency's authority,' in contravention of the Administrative Procedure Act...."[125] The district judge's interpretation of the definitional change recognized that "absent an applicable exception, the Stark Law will prohibit the individual physician Plaintiffs from making referrals to their own Cath Labs." However, the court never reached a decision on the merits. The court ultimately dismissed the case for lack of subject matter jurisdiction, reasoning in its Memorandum Opinion that even though the Cath Labs were not entitled to HHS administrative review because they do not bill or receive payments from Medicare, their contracting hospitals could bring such a challenge.

4.3.5 Advisory Opinions

Prior to the passage of the BBA, neither the OIG nor CMS was specifically authorized to issue advisory opinions under the Stark Law. The Stark Law now requires the issuance of written advisory opinions concerning whether a referral relating to DHS is prohibited under the Stark Law.[126]

On January 9, 1998, CMS promulgated a "Final Rule with Comment Period" that not only sets forth the framework for how a private party can obtain an advisory opinion from CMS, but also incorporates certain limitations that have been placed on the OIG with respect to the substance of advisory opinions under the Anti-Kickback Statute and other fraud and abuse provisions. Specifically, CMS has incorporated the limitations placed on the OIG by stating that, in advisory opinions regarding the Stark Law, it will not assess fair market value for any goods, services, or property, nor will it determine whether an individual is a *bona fide* employee within the meaning of the IRC.[127] Moreover, CMS has verified that each advisory opinion issued will only be binding on the DHHS Secretary and the party or parties who requested the opinion.

In contrast to the numerous advisory opinions that have been issued by OIG under the Anti-Kickback Statute and other fraud and abuse provisions, and except for a dozen or so advisory opinions that were issued by CMS from 2004–2005 interpreting whether hospitals were "under development" for purposes of the specialty hospital moratorium, there has been a dearth of advisory opinions interpreting the Stark Law.

4.3.6 Self-Referral Disclosure Protocol

In 2009, the OIG issued an Open Letter to the healthcare community that stated the OIG would no longer accept self- disclosures of matters that only involve liability under the Stark Law without any potential liability under other similar laws (*e.g.*, the federal healthcare program anti-kickback statute).[128]

As a result, Congress included in the 2010 set forth in Health Reform legislation that DHHS was to develop a self-disclosure protocol related to Stark Law violations (referred to as the self-referral

[125] *Id.* at 34.
[126] 42 U.S.C. § 1395nn(g)(6).
[127] 63 Fed. Reg. 1,646 (1998) (to be codified at 42 C.F.R. §§ 411.370 *et seq.*).
[128] http://oig.hhs.gov/fraud/docs/openletters/OpenLetter3-24-09.pdf.

disclosure protocol or SRDP), which CMS posted on its website on September 23, 2010.[129] Then, 18 months after the SRDP is established, the Secretary must issue a report regarding the number of entities disclosing under the SRDP, the amounts collected and the nature of the issues being disclosed under the SRDP. In addition to establishing a process by which entities can self-disclose Stark Law violations, this provision authorizes the Secretary to negotiate settlements for an amount less than the amount set forth under the Stark Law. Under the SRDP, HHS can negotiate a settlement down based upon a variety of factors such as the timeliness of the disclosure, the level of cooperation, and the nature of the violation.

4.4 Stark Exceptions

The Stark Law contains several exceptions, with some applying to both ownership and compensation arrangements, some applying only to ownership arrangements, and the remainder applying only to compensation arrangements.

4.4.1 Ownership and Compensation Exceptions

Exempt from both the ownership and compensation arrangement proscriptions are the following exceptions.

4.4.1.1 Physician Services

An exception is provided for physician services provided personally by, or under the personal supervision of another physician in the same group practice as, the referring physician.[130] CMS adopted a qualifier in that, except for "physician services" defined at § 410.20(a), all other "incident to" services are excluded from the definition of "physician services."[131]

4.4.1.2 In-Office Ancillary Services

This exception relates to DHS furnished by a physician in her office, except for durable medical equipment (excluding infusion pumps) and parenteral and enteral nutrients, equipment, and supplies.[132]

In order to qualify for the in-office ancillary-services exception, the referring physician (or another physician who is a member of the same group practice) must personally furnish the services. If other individuals (*e.g.*, technicians) perform the services, then they must be directly supervised by the referring physician or another physician in the group practice.

---

[129] *See* Patient Protection and Affordable Care Act of 2010, Pub. L. No. 111-148, 124 Stat. 119 § 6409 (2010) (codified at 42 U.S.C. § 1395nn). http://www.cms.gov/PhysicianSelfReferral/Downloads/6409_SRDP_Protocol.pdf.

[130] 42 U.S.C. § 1395nn(b)(1).

[131] 42 C.F.R. § 411.355(a)(2).

[132] 42 U.S.C. § 1395nn(b)(2).

To be exempt, in-office ancillary services also must be furnished either:

1. in a "centralized" building used by the group practice for the provision of some or all of the group's clinical laboratory services, or for the centralized provision of the group's DHS (other than clinical laboratory services); *or*
2. in the "same building" in which
   a. the referring physician or group practice has an office that is normally open to their patients at least 35 hours per week, and the referring physician or group members regularly practices medicine and furnishes physician services to patients in that office at least 30 hours per week,
   b. the referring physician or group practice has an office that is normally open to patients at least eight hours per week, and the referring physician regularly practices medicine and furnishes physician services to patients in that office at least six hours per week, or
   c. the referring physician or group has an office that is normally open eight hours per week, and the referring physician or group member regularly practices medicine and furnishes physician services to patients at least six hours per week in that office (including "some" services that are unrelated to DHS) and referring physician must be present and order the DHS in connection with a patient visit during the time the office is open, or the referring physician or a group practice member is present while the DHS is furnished during the time the office is open.[133]

As part of Health Reform, Congress adopted a requirement as part of the in-office ancillary services exception that for MRI, CT, PET and any other designated health services identified by the Secretary, the provider must inform the individual in writing at the time of the referral that the individual may obtain the services from another healthcare provider and provide the patient with a written list of suppliers who furnish services in the area in which such patient resides.[134] As part of the CY 2011 MPFS Final Rule, CMS adopted regulations setting forth the substance of what is to be included in these disclosures (*i.e.*, that the physician must identify five suppliers in a 25-mile radius).[135]

Another significant issue under the in-office ancillary services exception is that the Stark Law's definition of the term "group practice."[136] First, a group practice must consist of two or more physicians who are legally organized as a single legal entity primarily for the purpose of being a physician group practice. Second, each physician who is a member of the group must provide substantially the full range of services that the physician routinely provides (including medical care, consultation, diagnosis, or treatment) through the joint use of shared office space, facilities, equipment, and personnel. Third, "substantially all" of the services of the physician group members must be provided through the group, billed in the name of the group, and treated as receipts of the group. Fourth, overhead expenses of and income from the practice must be distributed in accordance with methods previously determined by members of the group. Fifth, no physician group member may receive compensation

[133] 42 C.F.R. § 411.355(b)(2).
[134] *See* Patient Protection and Affordable Care Act of 2010, Pub. L. No. 111-148, 124 Stat. 119 § 6003 (2010) (codified at 42 U.S.C. § 1395nn).
[135] 75 Fed. Reg. at 73,443–47 (Nov. 29, 2010).
[136] 42 U.S.C. § 1395nn(h)(4).

directly or indirectly based on the volume or value of referrals by the physician, except for certain productivity bonuses. Sixth, group members collectively must personally conduct no less than 75% of the physician-patient encounters of the group practice. In addition, CMS has adopted an additional requirement that the group practice be a "unified business" that has (1) centralized decisionmaking by a body representative of the group practice that maintains effective control over the group's assets and liabilities (including, but not limited to, budgets, compensation, and salaries) and (2) consolidated billing, accounting, and financial reporting.[137]

CMS, in Phase III, revised the definition of "physician in the group practice" to "clarify" that an independent contractor must furnish patient care services pursuant to a contract made directly with the group practice in order for the physician to qualify as a "physician in the group practice." Previously, physicians with contractual arrangements could qualify as "physicians in the group" but not necessarily as "members" of the group, but the Stark regulations did not precisely dictate how the contractual arrangement should be structured, leaving open the possibility for contracting though another entity. However, in Phase III, CMS made an explicit requirement that independent contractors have a direct contractual arrangement with the group. CMS specifically said, in the preamble, that the definition of "physician in the group practice" does not extend to contractors between the group practice and another entity, such as a staffing company.[138] The significance of being a "physician in the group" is that such physicians are included for purposes of determining whether the group qualifies for Stark Law protection under several of the criteria applicable to group practices.

4.4.1.3 *Prepaid Plans*

The Stark Law includes an exemption for services furnished to enrollees of certain health plans. Such health plans include health plans with Medicare risk or cost contracts, carrier-dealing prepayment organizations, organizations that receive payments on a prepaid basis under certain demonstration projects, federally qualified HMOs, and Medicaid managed-care plans.[139]

4.4.1.4 *Academic Medical Centers*

CMS adopted an exception for services referred within academic medical centers (AMCs).[140] These requirements focus on the definition of an AMC, the conditions for how the components of an AMC operate, and the requirements on the physicians within the AMC who are making the referrals in question. For purposes of this exception, an "academic medical center" is defined as (1) an accredited medical school or accredited academic hospital; (2) one or more affiliated faculty-practice plans; or (3) one or more affiliated hospitals in which a *majority* of the hospital medical staff consists of physicians who are faculty members, and where a *majority* of all hospital admissions are made by physicians who are faculty members. In addition, AMCs need to meet the following additional requirements:

---

137 42 C.F.R. § 411.352(f).

138 72 Fed. Reg. at 51,018.

139 42 U.S.C. § 1395nn(b)(3).

140 42 C.F.R. § 411.355(e).

- all monetary transfers between "components" (defined as an affiliated medical school, faculty practice plan, hospital, teaching facility, institution of higher education or departmental professional corporation) of the AMC must directly or indirectly support the missions of teaching, indigent care, research, or community services;
- one or more written agreements, approved by the governing body of each component, must control the relationship between the components of the AMC;
- all money paid to a referring physician for research must be used solely to support bona fide research;
- the physician's compensation arrangement does not violate the Anti-Kickback Statute; and
- the exception also places limitations on its applicability to only certain referring physicians.[141]

In 2008, the Western District of Kentucky reviewed the applicability of the AMC exception.[142] *United States ex rel. Villafane v. Solinger* involved alleged Stark Law violations being bootstrapped into an FCA *qui tam* action. After the government declined intervention, the defendants moved for summary judgment on the basis that the Stark law was not violated because the arrangements fit within the AMC exception. Due to the lack of a "jurisprudential consensus about the meaning or applicability of the AMC's many elements," the judge instead, "looked to the history and evolution of the exception for its primary guidance."[143]

The two main issues in *Villafane* were whether the defendant physicians provided substantial academic or clinical services to the AMC and whether the total compensation received by the physician defendant's from the AMC was at fair market value. The regulations for the AMC exception do provide a "safe harbor" for meeting the substantial academic or clinical services requirement, however the defendants' could not meet the "safe harbor" requirements. This was not dispositive because "a physician who fails to meet this safe harbor 'is not precluded from qualifying' under this requirement."[144] The court concluded that while the defendants did not fall within the safe harbor and failed to use a time keeping system that was of high quality or accuracy, they met the "substantial" requirement because "Defendants' annual work assignments and performance reviews, as well as curricula vitae indicate they were tasked with and completed substantial academic and clinical services."[145] The judge further determined that the defendants complied with the regulations regarding calculating fair market value by "presenting a 'comparison… [to] aggregate compensation paid to physicians practicing in similar academic settings located in similar environments… demonstrating that their compensation is comparable to similarly situated academics.'"[146]

---

141 *Id.* § 411.355(e)(1).
142 *United States ex rel. Villafane v. Solinger*, 543 F. Supp. 2d 678, 687 (W.D. Ky. 2008).
143 *Id.*
144 *Id.* at 688.
145 *Id.* at 689–90.
146 *Id.* at 692.

4.4.1.5 *Implants in ASCs*

CMS adopted an exception for all prosthetic devices—including introcular lenses used as part of cataract surgery—that are implanted in a Medicare-certified ASC but which may not otherwise be included in the bundled ASC payment rate.[147] CMS created this exception, in part, in order to prevent procedures currently performed in ASCs to be shifted to what CMS considers more-costly hospital-outpatient settings. This exception, however, is limited to only a narrow field of devices, and applies only in certain settings.

4.4.1.6 *Additional Regulatory Exceptions Applicable to Both Ownership and Compensation Arrangements*

CMS also created a number of additional exceptions for both ownership and compensation arrangements concerning the provision of the following items: eyeglasses or contact lenses that are prescribed after cataract surgery; EPO and other dialysis drugs provided by or in end-stage renal disease facilities; preventive screening tests, immunizations, and vaccines; and intra-family rural referrals.[148]

4.4.2 Ownership Exceptions

Exempt from only the proscription on ownership arrangements are the following exceptions.

4.4.2.1 *Ownership in Publicly Traded Securities and Mutual Funds*

The Stark Law includes a specific exemption for ownership of publicly traded securities and mutual funds,[149] which applies to ownership of investment securities (including shares or bonds, debentures, notes, or other debt instruments) purchased on terms generally available to the public. The securities must be listed on the New York Stock Exchange, the American Stock Exchange, or any regional exchange in which quotations are published on a daily basis; foreign securities listed on a recognized foreign, national, or regional exchange in which quotations are published on a daily basis are exempted as well. Alternatively, exempt securities could be traded under an automated "inter-dealer" quotation system operated by the National Association of Securities Dealers. In order to qualify for the exemption, the corporation must have total stockholder equity exceeding $75 million at the end of the corporation's most recent fiscal year, or on average during the previous three fiscal years.

4.4.2.2 *Hospitals*

Also exempt from the ownership proscription are DHS provided by hospitals located in Puerto Rico, as well as DHS furnished by hospitals outside of Puerto Rico where the referring physician has an ownership interest in the hospital itself (and not in a subdivision of the hospital), and where the referring physician is authorized to perform services at the hospital.[150]

---

147 42 C.F.R. § 411.355(f).
148 42 C.F.R. § 411.355(g)–(j).
149 42 U.S.C. § 1395nn(c); 42 C.F.R. § 411.356(a).
150 42 U.S.C. § 1395nn(d)(1) and (d)(3); 42 C.F.R. § 411.356(c)(2) and (c)(3).

As described above, in 2010 and as part of Health Reform, Congress has now placed significant limitations on physicians' ownership interest in hospitals located both in urban and rural areas. Specifically, the Stark Law provides that a hospital cannot be owned by physicians unless the ownership interest was obtained by the physicians prior to enactment of Health Reform and that the hospital had a provider agreement in place as of December 31, 2010.[151]

With limited exceptions, Health Reform precludes a physician owned hospital from expanding the number of licensed beds, operating or procedure rooms beyond the number that existed as of the date the hospital is licensed following enactment of the law. Health Reform establishes that a facility can seek a waiver from the expansion limitation in two separate sets of circumstances: (1) a hospital, that among other things, is in a county that has percentage increase in population over the last five years that is 150% of the population growth in the state; or (2) a hospital that constitutes a "High Medicaid Facility," which is not the sole hospital in a county and, for the three most recent years, has a larger percentage of Medicaid inpatient admissions than any other hospital in the county. Health Reform establishes that the Secretary is to promulgate regulations by January 2012 that set forth the process by which a hospital can apply for one of these exceptions.

As part of these modifications, Congress imposed additional requirements in order to ensure that the physicians' ownership interests are "bona fide". For example, the terms upon which a physician is offered an ownership interest in the hospital can be no different than the terms upon which a non-physician would be offered the same interest. Congress also provided that, not only is the hospital prohibited from loaning money to a physician, but the hospital cannot guarantee a loan that a physician might obtain from a third party.

Congress also enacted a number of disclosure requirements that the hospital and physician owners must make to patients concerning the existence of the ownership interest. The Health Reform legislation requires the hospital to disclose to patients if the hospital does not have a physician onsite 24/7. Congress adopted the specialty hospital moratorium in 2003 when a number of incidents occurred at specialty hospitals allegedly because there was not adequate physician coverage. Although CMS adopted regulations a few years ago that require certain of these items to be disclosed by hospitals to patients,[152] Congress apparently saw a need to codify these requirements into the Social Security Act.

Health Reform also includes a provision requiring the Secretary to collect information regarding physician ownership in hospitals. Although the Stark Law already included a provision providing the Secretary with the authority to request information regarding physician ownership and compensation arrangements that healthcare entities may have with physicians, as discussed above, CMS has not been able to finalize a process by which it intends to collect this information.

---

[151] *See* Patient Protection and Affordable Care Act of 2010, Pub. L. No. 111-148, 124 Stat. 119 § 6001(a)(3) (2010) (codified at 42 U.S.C. § 1395nn).

[152] 42 C.F.R. § 489.20(u) – (v).

4.4.2.3 *Rural Providers*

Currently, the Stark Law exempts DHS furnished by physician-owned entities located in a rural area.[153] The exception applies only if substantially all of the DHS furnished by the entity are furnished to individuals residing in the rural area. Significantly, as part of Health Reform, the modifications to the exception for ownership in a hospital also apply to ownership interests in hospitals in rural areas.

4.4.3 Compensation Arrangement Exceptions

The Stark Law contains the following exceptions applicable only to the proscription on compensation arrangements.

4.4.3.1 *Rental of Office Space and Equipment*

The exemption for office space protects arrangements for the use of premises in which the lease is set out in writing, signed by the parties, specifies the premises (which must be used exclusively by the lessee when used by the lessee), and is for a term of at least one year.[154] The space rented or leased must not exceed that which is "reasonable and necessary" for legitimate business purposes. The lessee may make payments for the use of common areas if the payments do not exceed the lessee's pro rata share of expenses for such common space based on the ratio of space used exclusively by the lessee to the total amount of space (other than common areas) occupied by all persons using the common areas. The rental charges over the term of the lease must be set in advance, consistent with fair market value, and not determined in a manner that takes into account the volume or value of any referrals or other business generated between the parties. In addition, the lease must be commercially reasonable even if no referrals were made between the parties.

The exception for equipment rental is similar to the criteria for space rental in that the lease must be set out in writing, signed by the parties, and must specify the equipment covered by the lease. The equipment must be used exclusively by the lessee when used by that lessee. The lease term must be at least one year, and the equipment rented or leased must not exceed that which is "reasonable and necessary" for legitimate business purposes. The rental charges over the term of the lease must be set in advance, consistent with fair market value, and not determined in a manner that takes into account the volume or value of any referrals or other business generated between the parties. In addition, the lease must be commercially reasonable even if no referrals were made between the parties.[155]

Finally, although CMS has adopted certain "special" rules on compensation arrangements that allow for the payment of per-use, per-click and percentage based fees, CMS, in 2008, adopted modifications to these rules such that beginning October 1, 2009, percentage and per-check compensation methodologies are no longer permitted for rental of office space and equipment.[156]

---

[153] 42 U.S.C. § 1395nn(d)(2); 42 C.F.R. § 411.356(c)(1).

[154] 42 U.S.C. § 1395nn(e)(1); 42 C.F.R. § 411.357(a).

[155] 42 U.S.C. § 1395nn(e)(1); 42 C.F.R. § 411.357(b).

[156] 73 Fed. Reg. 48,434 (Aug. 19, 2008).

4.4.3.2 *Bona Fide Employment Relationships*

This exception protects arrangements between employers and physicians (or the immediate family members of either party who have a *bona fide* employment relationship with the employer) for the provision of services. The exception applies if the employment is for identifiable services in which the amount of payment is consistent with fair market value and is not determined in a manner that takes into account (directly or indirectly) the volume or value of any referrals by the referring physician.[157]

The last requirement—that payment made to employees not be determined based on the volume or value of referrals—does not prohibit payments in the form of productivity bonuses based on services performed personally by the employee (or immediate family member of the employee).

4.4.3.3 *Personal-Service Arrangements*

The exemption for personal-service arrangements protects compensation arrangements between a physician and an entity where the physician is an independent contractor and not an employee of the entity.[158] In order to qualify for the exemption, a written agreement must:

1. specify the services covered by the arrangement;
2. cover all of the services to be provided by the physician to the entity;
3. have a term for one year or longer;
4. provide that the aggregate services contracted for must not exceed those that are reasonable and necessary for the legitimate business purposes of the arrangement;
5. require that compensation paid over the term of the agreement is set in advance, not exceed fair market value, and not be determined in a manner that takes into account the volume or value of any referrals or other business generated between the parties; and
6. establish that the services to be performed under the arrangement not involve the counseling or promotion of a business arrangement or other activity that violates any state or federal law.

Although this exception requires that compensation paid to a physician may not be determined in a manner that takes into account the volume or value of any "referrals" or other business generated between the parties, the Stark Law includes a further "exception within an exception" for physician-compensation arrangements specifically related to physician incentive payments that satisfy certain requirements.

4.4.3.4 *Unrelated Payments*

The statute exempts payments provided by a hospital to a physician if such payments do not relate to the provision of DHS.[159]

---

[157] 42 U.S.C. § 1395nn(e)(2); 42 C.F.R. § 411.357(c).
[158] 42 U.S.C. § 1395nn(e)(3); 42 C.F.R. § 411.357(d).
[159] 42 U.S.C. § 1395nn(e)(4); 42 C.F.R. § 411.357(g).

4.4.3.5 Physician Recruitment and Retention

The physician recruitment exemption protects payments made by a hospital to a physician to induce the physician to relocate to the geographic area served by the hospital and to become a medical staff member.[160] In order to qualify for this exemption, the physician cannot be required to refer patients to the hospital, and the amount of the payment cannot be determined in a manner that takes into account, directly or indirectly, the volume or value of any referrals by the referring physician. In the Phase II Regulations, CMS provided that a hospital can make payments to an existing group in order to assist the group in recruiting the physician as long as the remuneration is passed directly through to and remain with the recruited physician, except for actual recruitment expenses. In the case of an income guarantee, the costs allocated by the physician or group practice to the recruited physician may not exceed the actual additional incremental costs attributable to the recruited physician.[161] In the Phase III Regulations, CMS revised the exception to prohibit physicians and physician practices from imposing any practice restrictions that "unreasonably restrict" the recruited physician's ability to practice medicine in the geographic area while no longer categorically prohibiting physician practices from imposing non-compete provisions.[162]

As part of the exception, the recruited physician must relocate her medical practice to the geographic area served by the hospital (the area composed of the lowest number of contiguous ZIP codes from which the hospital draws at least 75% of its inpatients) as evidenced by (1) the physician moving her medical practice at least 25 miles or (2) the physician deriving 75% of her revenues from professional services furnished to patients not previously seen by the physician during the prior three years.[163]

In addition, in the Phase II Regulations, CMS added an exception for retention payments made *directly* to a physician if the payment is to retain the physician's medical practice in the geographic area served by the hospital that is either a HPSA or is an area with a demonstrated need for the physician (as determined through a Stark advisory opinion). This exception also requires that the physician have a *bona fide* firm and written recruitment offer from an unrelated hospital that specifies the remuneration being offered and that requires the physician to move her practice at least 25 miles *and* to a location outside of the geographic area served by the hospital. Moreover, the retention payment is limited to the *lower of* the amount obtained by subtracting (i) the physician's current income from physician and related services from (ii) the income the physician would receive from comparable services in the *bona fide* recruitment offer or the reasonable costs the hospital would expend in recruiting a new physician. [164]

---

160 42 U.S.C. § 1395nn(e)(5).

161 42 C.F.R. § 411.355(e). This issue was further addressed in the Phase III Regulations. *See* 72 Fed. Reg. at 51,050.

162 *See* 72 Fed. Reg. at 51,054 (2007).

163 42 C.F.R. § 411.355(e).

164 42 C.F.R. § 411.355(t).

4.4.3.6 Isolated Financial Transactions

This exemption protects isolated transactions, such as a one-time sale of property or practice, where the amount of the payment is consistent with the fair market value and does not take into account, directly or indirectly, the volume or value of any referrals between the parties.[165] In addition, the remuneration provided must be commercially reasonable even if no referrals were made. The transaction also must meet other requirements imposed by regulation to protect against program or patient abuse.

4.4.3.7 Certain Group Practice Arrangements with a Hospital

The Stark Law contains an exception for DHS furnished "under arrangements" to a hospital by a group practice.[166] The exception is essentially a "grandfather" of certain relationships that existed prior to December 19, 1989, and that have continued in effect without interruption thereafter. This exception requires that a written agreement establishes that substantially all of the DHS furnished to patients of the hospital are furnished by the group under the arrangement; further, compensation paid over the term of the agreement will be consistent with fair market value, is fixed in advance, and is not determined in a manner that takes into account the volume or value of any referrals or other business generated between the parties.

4.4.3.8 Payments for Items and Services

This exception protects both payments made by a physician to a laboratory in exchange for the provision of clinical laboratory services, as well as payments made by a physician to an entity as compensation for items or services (other than clinical laboratory services), if the items or services are furnished at a price that is consistent with fair market value.[167] However, in the Phase III Regulations, CMS states that the expansion of the fair market value exception (discussed below) to apply not only to items purchased by a physician from DHS provider may make this exception unavailable.[168]

4.4.3.9 Fair Market Value Exception

CMS created an exception for certain fair market value arrangements that largely mirror the existing compensation-arrangement exceptions. The most significant issue raised by the fair market value exception might be the requirement that such arrangements meet a safe harbor under the Anti-Kickback Statute, be approved by the OIG under a favorable advisory opinion, or not violate the Anti-Kickback Statute.[169] In the Phase III Regulations, CMS expanded this exception to apply both to arrangements involving payments *to* physicians as well as payments *from* physicians to DHS entities.

---

165 42 U.S.C. § 1395nn(e)(6); 42 C.F.R. § 411.357(f).
166 42 U.S.C. § 1395nn(e)(7); 42 C.F.R. § 411.357(h).
167 42 U.S.C. § 1395nn(e)(8); 42 C.F.R. § 411.357(i).
168 *See* 72 Fed. Reg. at 51,056–57.
169 42 C.F.R. § 411.357(*l*).

4.4.3.10 *Non-Monetary Compensation up to $300*

In the Stark II Proposed Regulations, CMS set out a new exception titled "De Minimis Compensation" which permitted noncash items or services to be provided to a physician or her family member that did not exceed $50 per gift and an aggregate of $300 per year. In the proposed version, this exception would apply only if the entity providing the compensation makes it available to all "similarly situated" individuals, regardless of whether they referred patients to the entity. In the final regulations, CMS changed the name of this exception to "Non-Monetary Compensation Up To $300" to eliminate any "unintentional implication" that the $300 limit is inconsequential in producing referrals. In addition, in the final regulations, CMS eliminated the $50-per-gift limit.[170]

This exception provides that this amount is to be adjusted each year based upon any increases in the Consumer Price Index-Urban All Item (CPI-U) for the 12-month period ending the preceding September 30th.[171] Therefore, for the calendar year beginning January 1, 2011, the compensation limit under this exception was increased to $359 per year.[172]

4.4.3.11 *Medical Staff Incidental Benefits*

CMS created an exception that permits hospitals to furnish to their medical staffs certain incidental benefits of low value, such as parking, meals, or free computer/Internet access.[173]

4.4.3.12 *Managed-Care Risk-Sharing Arrangements*

In response to the unintended effect of the Stark Law on commercial health plans, CMS created a compensation exception for remuneration pursuant to a "risk-sharing arrangement" (including, but not limited to, withholds, bonuses, and risk pools) between a MCO and a physician for the provision of items or services to enrollees of the health plan.[174]

4.4.3.13 *Compliance Training*

Because CMS views compliance training programs as "beneficial," CMS adopted in the Stark II Final Regulations an exception for compliance training provided to physicians who practice in the DHS entity's community. [175]

4.4.3.14 *Indirect Compensation and the "Stand in the Shoes" Analysis*

CMS created an exception for indirect-compensation arrangements that satisfy the following requirements:

1. the compensation received by the physician from the person or entity with which the referring physician has the direct financial relationship is at "fair market value" for services and items

[170] *Id.* § 411.357(k).
[171] 42 C.F.R. § 411.357(k).
[172] *See* http://www.cms.gov/PhysicianSelfReferral/50_CPI-U_Updates.asp#TopOfPage.
[173] *Id.* § 411.357(m).
[174] *Id.* § 411.357(n).
[175] *Id.* § 411.357(o).

actually provided, "not taking into account" the volume or value of referrals for the entity furnishing DHS;

2. the compensation arrangement between the physician and the entity with which the physician has the direct financial relationship is set out in writing, is signed by the parties, and specifies the services covered (except for *bona fide* employment arrangements, which need not be in writing but must be for identifiable services and commercially reasonable even if no referrals are made to the employer); and
3. the arrangement does not violate the Anti-Kickback Statute or any laws or regulations governing billing or claims submission. [176]

Prior to the Phase III Regulations, financial arrangements between an intermediary physician group or other entity and a DHS entity were analyzed to determine, first, whether the arrangement constituted an "indirect compensation arrangement" under the Stark regulations definition and, second, if yes, whether the arrangement met the exception for indirect compensation arrangements. The analysis generally turned on whether the physicians at the other end of the "chain" of arrangements were paid based in any manner on the volume or value of referrals to the DHS. However, the Phase III Regulations adopted the first "stand in the shoes" concept that was designed to treat compensation arrangements between DHS entities and group practices as if the arrangements are also with the referring physicians.[177] As adopted in the Phase III Regulations, a physician is to "stand in the shoes" of his/her "physician organization" and is deemed to have the same compensation arrangement—with the same parties and on the same terms—as the physician organization.[178] The effect of this interpretation of the Stark Law and the application of the stand in the shoes was twofold. First, it rendered some arrangements that would have constituted indirect compensation arrangements to now be direct compensation arrangements that must meet a direct compensation exception. Second, arrangements that did not implicate Stark at all under the prior regulations may now be implicated. Some distinctions between the indirect exception and other potentially relevant direct exceptions is that "indirect" compensation is not subject to the requirement that it be set forth in writing and signed by both parties, or be set in advance for one year, giving parties substantial latitude in establishing and amending their arrangements to meet immediate business needs, so long as those modifications are not based on the volume or value of referrals.

As a result of numerous comments from the healthcare community, CMS explained in the FY 2009 IPPS Proposed Rule that it was revisiting the "stand in the shoes" policy and that it was looking to achieve the goal of "simplifying the analysis of many financial arrangements" while reducing program abuse. To this end, in the FY 2009 IPPS Proposed Rule, CMS proposed two new alternatives to addressing these concerns: (1) a "multi-faceted approach" to analyzing stand in the shoes arrangements; or (2) the development of a new exception for "mission support" payments, leaving the current stand in the shoes rules intact.[179]

---

[176] *Id.* § 411.357(p).

[177] 42 C.F.R. § 354(c)(3); *see also* 72 Fed. Reg. at 51,028.

[178] A "physician organization" means a physician (including a professional corporation of which the physician is sole owner), a physician practice, or a group practice that complies with the regulatory requirements for group practices. A "physician practice" as used in this definition is not defined. 42 C.F.R. § 411.351.

[179] 73 Fed. Reg at 23,686.

However, when CMS issued the FY 2009 IPPS Final Rule, it revised the "physician stand in the shoes" provisions to apply only if "the only intervening entity between the physician and the entity furnishing DHS is his or her physician organization and the physician has an ownership or investment interest in the physician organization."[180] Moreover, CMS adopted a provision in the regulations that physicians with only a "titular ownership interests (that is, physicians without the ability or right to receive the financial benefits of ownership or investment)" are not required to undergo the "stand in the shoes" analysis.[181]

4.4.3.15 *Electronic Prescribing and Electronic Health Records*

As required by MMA, CMS in 2006 created two exceptions for compensation arrangements involving certain electronic prescribing and electronic health records arrangements.[182]

The first of these exceptions applies to the provision of items or services that are necessary and used solely to receive and transmit electronic prescription information. This exception requires compliance with criteria similar to those listed under the Anti-Kickback safe harbor that protects the same arrangements.

Meanwhile, the second exception establishes the conditions under which entities furnishing DHS may donate to physicians interoperable electronic health records software, information technology and training services. In order to qualify for protection under this exception, the relevant items or services must be necessary and used predominantly to create, maintain, transmit or receive the electronic health records of the donor's or physician's patients. Additionally, this exception requires compliance with criteria similar to those listed in the electronic prescribing exception, as well as requiring cost sharing and selection of physician recipients of donated technology.

4.4.3.16 *Additional Compensation Exceptions*

In the Phase II Regulations, CMS created a number of new exceptions for:

- referral service arrangements and obstetrical medical-malpractice insurance that satisfy the requirements under the applicable safe harbors of the Anti-Kickback Statute;[183]
- professional-courtesy discounts offered to all physicians on the entity's *bona fide* medical staff, or in the local community or service area, without regard to volume or value of referrals;[184]
- technology provided as part of a community-wide information system;[185] and
- charitable donations made by physicians.[186]

---

[180] 42 C.F.R. § 411.354(c)(3); *see also* 73 Fed. Reg. at 48,693–99.
[181] *Id.*
[182] *Id.* § 411.357(v) and (w).
[183] *Id.* § 411.355(q) and (r).
[184] *Id.* § 411.355(s).
[185] *Id.* § 411.355(u).
[186] *Id.* § 411.355(j).

4.4.4 "Special Rules" for Compensation

4.4.4.1 Definition of Fair Market Value

The concept of "fair market value" is relevant to many of the Stark Law exceptions. In the Stark II Final Regulations, CMS provided additional definitional guidance for what constitutes "fair market value."[187] Fair market value means the value of a good or service in arm's-length transactions that are consistent with "general market value." In other words, fair market value for an item or service is the price that an asset would bring as the result of *bona fide* bargaining between, or the compensation in a service agreement negotiated by, well-informed buyers and sellers who are not in a position to generate business for one another. The general benchmark for fair market value is the price at which *bona fide* sales have been consummated for assets of like type, quality, and quantity in the particular market at the time of the transaction, or the compensation included in *bona fide* service agreements with comparable terms at the time of the agreement.

In this regard, CMS states that, when fair market value is included in an exception that also includes the "volume or value" standard, the parties may be precluded from relying on comparables that involve entities and physicians in a position to refer and generate business. CMS also states that the burden of establishing "fairness" rests with the parties.

With regard to the use of independent-valuation consultants to determine fair market value, CMS states that no requirement is made to use such outside sources if other "appropriate" valuation methods are available. Nonetheless, CMS states that, although internally generated surveys can be used to determine fair market value in certain circumstances, such surveys do not have "strong evidentiary value" due to their susceptibility to manipulation and absence of independent verification.

For space leases and equipment rentals, fair market value means the value for commercial purposes, not taking into account its "intended use" or its proximity to referral sources. CMS makes clear that this "intended use" limitation still allows for development upgrades and maintenance that customize premises for healthcare usages to be factored into fair market value, and allows rental payments that reflect the fair market value of the area in which the property is located (*i.e.*, medical property in a medical community). "Intended use" is taken into account only where the lessee pays inflated amounts to enhance her medical practice—that is, pays additional amounts in excess of those paid by other medical practitioners in the same building.

In the Phase II Regulations, CMS provided guidance in connection with hourly payments for a physician's personal services by using one of two possible methodologies (*i.e.*, an hourly payment that is less than or equal to the average hourly rate for emergency-room physician services in the relevant physician market; or an hourly rate based upon the 50th-percentile national compensation level for physicians with the same specialty by benchmarking against various publicly available surveys). CMS, however, eliminated this "safe harbor" for calculating fair market value in the Phase III Regulations. While noting that parties are left to choose their own methodologies, CMS stated that "[r]eference to multiple, objective, independently published surveys remains a prudent practice for evaluating fair market value."[188]

---

[187] *Id.* § 411.351.

[188] *See* 72 Fed. Reg. at 51,015 (2007).

4.4.4.2 *Compensation Methodologies*

In the Phase III Regulations, CMS confirmed that percentage compensation arrangements are deemed to be "set in advance" if the specific formula for calculating the compensation is set in advance and the compensation does not take into account the volume or value of referrals or other business generated Additionally, CMS stated that entities may continue to use unit-based (per-click) and percentage-based compensation arrangements.[189]

However, in the CY 2008 MPFS Proposed Rule, CMS proposed to modify the special rules on compensation in such a way that a percentage based formula could only be used for paying for personally performed physician services. In addition, CMS proposed to exclude per-click based payments to a physician lessor for services rendered by an entity lessee to patients who are referred to the entity by the physician lessor. CMS commented that these situations are inherently susceptible to abuse because the physician has an incentive to profit from referring a higher volume of patients to the lessee.[190]

While these proposals were not addressed in the CY 2008 MPFS Final Rule, CMS adopted a number of changes to the ability of entities to use percentage and per click arrangements when the FY 2009 IPPS Final Rule were issued. Specifically, instead of modifying the "special rules on compensation" and the definition of "set in advance," CMS revised several exceptions (*i.e.*, the office space and equipment lease exceptions, as well as the fair market value and indirect compensation arrangements exceptions) to address the use of percentage-based compensation formulae and per-click arrangement. Effective October 1, 2009, these exceptions prohibit compensation arrangements that use a formula based on either: a percentage of the revenue raised, earned, billed, collected, or otherwise attributable to the services performed or business generated in the office space or by the use of the equipment; or per-unit of services rental charges, to the extent that such charges reflect services provided to patients referred between the parties.[191]

4.4.4.3 *Physician's Compensation can be Conditioned on Referrals to a Particular Provider*

CMS expressly permits compensation paid to a physician pursuant to an employment agreement or a managed-care contract to be conditioned on the physician's referring patients to a particular provider, practitioner, or supplier.[192] Specifically, these types of "mandated referral" requirements are permissible as long as:

1. the arrangement is in writing;
2. the compensation is set in advance and is consistent with fair market value;
3. the arrangement complies with an ownership or compensation exception; and
4. the referral requirement does not apply if a patient expresses a different choice of provider, the patient's insurance decides which provider is used, or if the referral is not in the best medical interest of the patient (as determined by the physician).

---

189 42 C.F.R. § 411.354(d); *see* 72 Fed. Reg. at 51,030–31.

190 72 Fed. Reg. at 38,184.

191 42 C.F.R. §§ 357(a)(5), 357(b)(4), 357(l)(3); and 357(p)(1); *see also* 73 Fed. Reg. at 48,709–21.

192 *Id.* § 411.354(d).

4.5 Federal Criminal Prohibitions Against False Claims and Fraudulent Billing Practices

4.5.1 Social Security Act

Section 1128B of the Social Security Act sets forth criminal penalties that are to be imposed upon individuals and entities that engage in certain activities that result in the submission of false or fraudulent claims to a federal healthcare program. Specifically, the Social Security Act sets forth that it is a felony to commit any of the following:[193]

- knowingly and willfully make or cause to be made any false statement of a material fact in any application for any benefit or payment, or for use in determining rights to such payment, under a federal healthcare program;
- conceal information from or fail to disclose information to the government—specifically, information of an event affecting the initial or continued right to a benefit or payment under a federal healthcare program;
- apply to receive federal benefit or payment for the use and benefit of another and knowingly and willfully converting such payment to another use, or present (or cause to be presented) a claim for physician services knowing that the person who furnished the services is not a licensed physician, or counsel or assist an individual to dispose of assets (including by any transfer in trust) in order for an individual to become eligible for medical assistance; or
- knowingly and willfully make, cause to make, induce, or seek to induce, any false statement or representation of a material fact as to the conditions or operation of any institution, facility, or entity:
    - in order to qualify for certification or recertification as any entity for which certification is required, including a hospital, critical access hospital, skilled nursing facility, intermediate care facility for the mentally retarded, home health agency, health maintenance organization or competitive medical plan; or
    - in response to required disclosure of information under § 1124A of the Social Security Act.

Each violation of any of these provisions by a person in connection with the furnishing by that person of items or services for which payment is made under a federal healthcare program is a felony punishable by a fine of up to $25,000 and/or up to five years imprisonment. With respect to violations by all other persons, such violations are misdemeanors, and are punishable by a fine of up to $10,000 and/or up to one year of imprisonment.

4.5.2 Federal Healthcare Fraud Offenses

As part of HIPAA, the U.S. Criminal Code was amended to include several new healthcare fraud offenses.

[193] *See* 42 U.S.C. § 1320a-7b.

4.5.2.1 General Prohibition

HIPAA enacted a general prohibition that makes it a crime to knowingly and willfully execute, or attempt to execute, a scheme or artifice: (1) to defraud any healthcare benefit program; or (2) to obtain, by means of false or fraudulent pretenses, representations, or promises, any of the money or property owned by, or under the custody or control of, any healthcare benefit program.[194]

The term "healthcare benefit program" is defined as "any public or *private* plan or contract, affecting commerce, under which any medical benefit, item or service is provided to any individual, and includes any individual or entity who is providing a medical benefit, item or service for which payment may be made under the plan or contract."[195] However, the majority of cases concerning fraud offenses under HIPAA center on parties who defrauded public payors, or public payors in conjunction with private payors. For example, in *United States v. Edwards*, the United States District Court for the Northern District of Texas ordered a former medical clinic executive to serve a 30-month prison term and pay over $370,000 in restitution for filing fraudulently coded claims and diagnosis codes to Medicare, Medicaid, and private insurance companies in order to receive higher payments than those authorized by the payors, in violation of 18 U.S.C. § 1347.[196] In this case, it was alleged that the executive directed employees under her supervision to submit claims that were "upcoded" with higher level physician encounters, additional diagnoses and laboratory tests, and/or additional symptoms that were not approved by the clinician. In *United States v. Davis*, a psychologist was found to have violated 18 U.S.C. § 1347 when he used college students to do the "lion's share of his work while still billing Medicaid as if he had performed the tests himself."[197]

Violation of this statute can result in a fine and/or imprisonment for not more than 10 years; if the violation results in serious "bodily injury," then such person shall be fined and/or imprisoned for not more than 20 years. Finally, if the violation results in death, such person shall be fined and/or imprisoned for any term of years or lifetime imprisonment.

4.5.2.2 Making of False Statements

A person can be subject to a fine and/or imprisonment of up to five years when such person, in any matter involving a healthcare program, knowingly and willfully (1) falsifies, conceals, or covers up by any trick, scheme, or device a material fact or (2) makes any materially false, fictitious, or fraudulent statements or representations, or makes or uses any materially false writing or document knowing the same to contain any materially false, fictitious, or fraudulent statement or entry.[198]

---

194 18 U.S.C. § 1347.

195 18 U.S.C. § 24(b) (emphasis added). *See U.S. v. McGovern*, 329 F.3d 247 (1st Cir. 2003); *U.S. v. Whited*, 311 F.3d 259 (3d Cir. 2002).

196 *See, e.g., United States v. Edwards*, No. 5:07-cr-00076 (N.D. Tex. Mar. 14, 2008).

197 *United States v. Davis*, 471 F.3d 783, 785 (7th Cir. 2006).

198 18 U.S.C. § 1035.

4.5.2.3 Theft or Embezzlement

HIPAA also added a theft or embezzlement provision specifically applicable to healthcare. Violation of this provision can result in a fine and/or imprisonment for not more than 10 years. If the value of the property is less than $100, however, violation can result in a fine and/or imprisonment of not more than one year.[199]

4.5.3 Mail and Wire Fraud

The U.S. Criminal Code prohibits the use of the national mail system for the purpose of executing any scheme or artifice to defraud, or for obtaining money or property by means of false or fraudulent representations.[200] Violation of these provisions is a felony punishable by a fine of up to $1,000 and/or up to five years imprisonment for each violation. Healthcare providers may be prosecuted under the mail-fraud statute for submitting claims for services never rendered, filing claims for services billed at inflated rates, waiving co-payments, and billing for services that were not medically necessary.

4.5.4 Racketeering Violations

The Racketeer Influenced and Corrupt Organizations Act (RICO), enacted as part of the Organized Crime Control Act of 1970, has been applied by the federal government and private parties alike in contexts far beyond organized crime. The federal criminal RICO statute prohibits a person from receiving any income, directly or indirectly, from a pattern of "racketeering activity," which is defined as committing a predicate act (*e.g.*, mail or wire fraud) at least twice within 10 years.[201] As Medicare fraud has been recognized as a predicate act supporting a racketeering claim, healthcare providers and suppliers must be cognizant that they potentially could be prosecuted under RICO for different forms of alleged healthcare fraud.[202]

Significantly, RICO provides for a private right of action for persons injured in their business or property.[203] Successful private litigants can be awarded treble (*i.e.*, triple) damages in addition to the cost of the suit, including attorney's fees. It is important to note that the defendant need not be convicted of any predicate act; the plaintiff is required only to show that the defendant engaged in conduct that would amount to a predicate offense.

4.5.5 Money-Laundering

The U.S. Criminal Code prohibits a person from knowingly engaging or attempting to engage in a "monetary transaction in criminally derived property" greater than $10,000 and derived from "specified unlawful activity," including mail and wire fraud. The prohibition also covers theft or bribery in

---

199 18 U.S.C. § 669.
200 18 U.S.C. § 1341.
201 18 U.S.C. §§ 1961 *et seq.*
202 *See North Shore Med. Ctr., Ltd v. Evanston Hosp. Corp.*, No. 92 C 533, 1996 U.S. Dist. LEXIS 10804 (N.D. Ill. July 30, 1996).
203 18 U.S.C. § 1964(c).

programs involving federal funds, and "any act or activity constituting an offense involving a Federal healthcare offense."[204]

Although the statute provides criminal and civil penalties, it is most frequently used for its civil-forfeiture and broad civil-penalty provisions. Civil penalties (the greater of $10,000 or the value of the transaction) may be imposed against *anyone* who conducts a violative transaction, regardless of whether that person benefits from it. Consequently, this provision could be used to penalize attorneys who assist clients in secreting or moving funds.

Forfeiture can be applied to any property involved in a transaction in violation of the statute, as well as any property traceable to such property. Thus, if both "dirty" and "clean" funds are used to purchase property, the *entire* property can be subject to forfeiture. Additionally, forfeiture can occur without first obtaining a conviction. Indeed, it can occur without notice to the affected individual, based upon the government's *ex parte* application, supported by affidavit, to a district judge.

4.5.6 Other Criminal Statutes

The federal government also has in its arsenal of criminal penalties the following: conspiracy to defraud the government;[205] the submission of fictitious or fraudulent claims;[206] and conspiracy to defraud.[207]

4.6 Federal Civil Prohibitions Against False Claims and Fraudulent Billing Practices

4.6.1 The Federal False Claims Act and *Qui Tam* Actions

The federal False Claims Act (FCA) prohibits a person from "knowingly" submitting claims or making a false record or statement in order to secure payment of a false or fraudulent claim by the federal government.[208] A person found to have violated this statute is liable for a civil penalty for each such claim of not less than $5,500 and not more than $11,000, plus three times the amount of damages sustained by the federal government.

The statute specifically provides that the terms "knowing" and "knowingly" mean that a person "(1) has actual knowledge of the information; (2) acts in deliberate ignorance of the truth or falsity of the information; or (3) acts in reckless disregard of the truth or falsity of the information."[209] Therefore, no proof of specific intent to defraud is required. Under the False Claims Act, civil actions must be brought within six years after the date of the violation, or within three years after the date when material facts are known or should have been known by the government; in any event, no claims may be made more than 10 years after the date on which the violation was committed.[210]

---

204 18 U.S.C. §§ 1956–1957.
205 18 U.S.C. § 286.
206 18 U.S.C. § 287.
207 18 U.S.C. § 371.
208 31 U.S.C. §§ 3729 *et seq.*
209 *Id.* § 3729(b).
210 *Id.* § 3731(b).

In 2009, Congress enacted the Fraud Enforcement and Recovery Act of 2009 (FERA).[211] Although the primary purpose of FERA was to address fraudulent activity associated with the financial industry,[212] FERA expanded the application of the False Claims Act (FCA) which also significantly impacts the healthcare industry. For example, FERA amended the liability provisions of the FCA by broadening the scope of FCA violations as well as the types of claims that can constitute a FCA violation, which were specifically intended to override and reverse the Supreme Court's decision in *Allison Engine Co. v. U.S. ex rel. Sanders*[213] and the decision of the United States Court of Appeals for the D.C. Circuit in *United States ex rel. Totten v. Bombardier Corp.*[214] FERA also expanded the reverse false claims provision of the FCA by covering acts in which a person "has possession, custody, or control of property or money used, or to be used, by the Government and *knowingly delivers or causes to be delivered, less than all of that money or property*" as well as "*knowingly conceals or knowingly and improperly avoids or decreases an obligation to pay or transmit money or property to the government.*"[215] Congress also added a definition of the term "obligation" as being "an established duty, whether or not fixed arising from an express or implied contractual, grantor-grantee, licensor-licensee, relationship, from a fee-based or similar relationship, from statute or regulation, or from the retention of any overpayment."[216]

In addition to actions initiated by the federal government, the FCA authorizes *qui tam* actions to be brought on behalf of the federal government by a private party having direct knowledge of the fraud. These private parties, who are often referred to as *qui tam* relators, may share in the monetary recovery paid as part of the eventual settlement or disposition of the action in cases whereby the *qui tam* relator's recovery depends on whether the government has intervened in the action. The private party commences such an action in federal court by filing the complaint and relevant documentation "under seal" and serving these documents on the DOJ only. Initially, the defendant is not served. By statute, the DOJ then has at least 60 days to evaluate whether to pursue the action. If good cause can be shown, the government may obtain an extension of time beyond the 60-day period. This may result in a *qui tam* complaint pending for an extended period of time before the defendant is even aware of the action. During this time period, the government will conduct its own investigation of the fraud alleged in the complaint. If, based upon its investigation, the government decides to proceed with the action, then the government has the primary responsibility for prosecuting the action, and the *qui tam* relator has the right to remain as a party to the action. If the government decides not to proceed with the action, the *qui tam* relator may elect to proceed on her own with the action against the defendant; the government, however, may be permitted at a later time to intervene in the case.[217]

---

211 Pub. L. No. 111-21, § 4, 123 Stat. 1617, 1621–25 (2009) (codified as amended at 31 U.S.C. §§ 3729–3733).

212 *See* S. Rep. No. 111-10, at 3–4 (2009) ("This bipartisan legislation will reinvigorate our Nation's capacity to investigate and prosecute the kinds of financial frauds that have so severely undermined our financial markets and hurt so many hard working people in these difficult economic times.... The [FCA] must be corrected and clarified in order to protect from fraud the Federal assistance and relief funds expended in response to our current economic crisis.").

213 553 U.S. 662 (2008) (holding that liability may only be imposed under section 3729(a)(2) of the FCA when the Government can prove that ("a defendant intended that the government itself pay the claim.").

214 380 F.3d 488 (D.C. Cir. 2004), *cert denied*, 544 U.S. 1032 (2005) (holding that FCA liability under 3729(a)(1) requires the presentment of a false or fraudulent claim for payment directly to the government).

215 31 U.S.C. § 3729(a)(1)(D) and (G) (emphasis added).

216 *Id.* § 3729(b)(3).

217 *Id.* § 3730(c).

4.6.2 Social Security Act

In addition to its criminal provisions described earlier, the Social Security Act provides for the imposition of civil money penalties against any person who knowingly presents, or causes to be presented, a claim that is improperly filed. Specifically, the statute provides penalties for filing:[218]

- a claim for a medical item or service that the person knows or should know was not provided as claimed, including engaging in a practice of presenting a claim using a Current Procedural Terminology (CPT) code that the person knows or should know will result in greater payment than using the CPT code the person knows or should have known was applicable to the item or service actually provided;
- a claim for Medicare item or service that the person knows or should know is false or fraudulent;
- a claim for a physician's service by a person who knows or should know that the individual who provided that service was not a licensed physician, was licensed as a physician but such license was obtained through misrepresentation of a material fact, or misrepresented that the physician was certified in a medical specialty;
- a claim for a medical or other item or service furnished during a period in which the person was excluded; or
- a pattern of claims for medical or other items or services that a person knows or should know are not medically necessary.

The statute also provides civil money penalties for other activities that include, but are not limited to, knowingly giving a person information that she knows or has reason to know is false or misleading with respect to coverage of inpatient hospital services under the Medicare program, as well as a physician executing a certification that a patient meets the requirements for home health services when, in fact, the physician knows the requirements are not met.

Violation of these provisions generally results in penalties from $5,000 to $10,000 for each item or service claimed, plus an assessment of up to three times the amount claimed for each such item or service. With respect to giving false or misleading information regarding inpatient hospital services, the penalty is $15,000 for each individual with respect to whom such information was given.

4.6.3 Program Fraud and Civil Remedies Act

The Program Fraud Civil Remedies Act of 1986 provides that any person who makes, presents or submits a claim that the person "knows or has reason to know" is false, fictitious, or fraudulent is subject to CMPs of up to $5,000 per false claim or statement and up to twice the amount claimed in lieu of damages.[219] This statute goes beyond the FCA and the CMPs of the SSA to provide for penalties and assessments against those who make false statements.[220]

[218] 42 U.S.C. § 1320a-7a; *see also* 42 C.F.R. § 1003.102.

[219] 31 U.S.C. § 3801 *et seq.*

[220] *Id.* § 3802(a)(2).

Under this statute, the OIG has authority to investigate allegations of liability, and then is required to report its findings and conclusions to the "reviewing official" at DHHS. If adequate evidence exists that a violation has occurred, written notice is sent to the Attorney General who is responsible for either approving or disapproving the referral of these allegations to the "presiding officer." If a reviewing officer refers allegations of liability to a presiding officer, the reviewing officer then provides notice to the person alleged to have violated this statute. Persons so notified may request a hearing regarding these allegations.[221] The statute provides that such hearing must be commenced within six years after the date on which the false claim or statement is made.[222]

4.7 Corporate Compliance Programs

The general principle that a healthcare company should foster an environment of compliance is not novel. Nevertheless, given the increased focus on fraudulent activities by healthcare providers, the recommendation that organizations adopt a "corporate compliance program" has been widely endorsed, as a number of benefits follow from implementing an effective program. A well-established corporate compliance program can protect a healthcare company in the midst of a legal crisis by shielding the company from suffering harsher penalties or stricter sentences. Equally as important, a corporate compliance program can reduce the likelihood of potential violations by clarifying to employees what behavior is acceptable and what is intolerable. Also, an effective corporate compliance program can help management detect violations early enough to enable the company to proactively correct a potential problem. Finally, a compliance program can assist a company to gain credibility with the government as a law-abiding organization in the event of an investigation.

4.7.1 The Federal Sentencing Guidelines

"Corporate compliance programs" were originated in 1991 as part of the Federal Sentencing Guidelines as a means to determine whether a corporation's criminal penalties should be reduced. Specifically, the Federal Sentencing Guidelines provide that an organization's culpability will be lessened "if the offense occurred even though the organization had in place at the time of the offense an effective compliance and ethics program."[223]

In order to have an effective compliance and ethics program, the Sentencing Guidelines state that an organization shall "(1) exercise due diligence to prevent and detect criminal conduct; and (2) otherwise promote an organizational culture that encourages ethical conduct and a commitment to compliance with the law." Furthermore, the Sentencing Guidelines provide the following requirements to prove that an organization has adopted a program that promotes "an organizational culture that encourages ethical conduct and a commitment to compliance with the law."

1. The organization shall establish standards and procedures to prevent and detect criminal conduct.

---

221 *Id.* § 3803.
222 *Id.* § 3808(a).
223 United States Sentencing Commission, *Guidelines Manual* § 8C2.5(f).

2. (A) The organization's governing authority shall be knowledgeable about the content and operation of the compliance and ethics program and shall exercise reasonable oversight with respect to the implementation and effectiveness of the compliance and ethics program.

   (B) High-level personnel of the organization shall ensure that the organization has an effective compliance and ethics program, as described in this guideline. Specific individual(s) within high level personnel shall be assigned overall responsibility for the compliance and ethics program.

   (C) Specific individual(s) within the organization shall be delegated day-to-day operational responsibility for the compliance and ethics program. Individual(s) with operational responsibility shall report periodically to high-level personnel and, as appropriate, to the governing authority, or an appropriate subgroup of the governing authority, on the effectiveness of the compliance and ethics program. To carry out such operational responsibility, such individual(s) shall be given adequate resources, appropriate authority, and direct access to the governing authority or an appropriate subgroup of the governing authority.

3. The organization shall use reasonable efforts not to include within the substantial authority personnel of the organization any individual whom the organization knew, or should have known through the exercise of due diligence, has engaged in illegal activities or other conduct inconsistent with an effective compliance and ethics program.

4. (A) The organization shall take reasonable steps to communicate periodically and in a practical manner its standards and procedures, and other aspects of the compliance and ethics program, to the individuals referred to in subdivision (B) by conducting effective training programs and otherwise disseminating information appropriate to such individuals' respective roles and responsibilities.

   (B) The individuals referred to in subdivision (A) are the members of the governing authority, high-level personnel, substantial authority personnel, the organization's employees, and, as appropriate, the organization's agents.

5. The organization shall take reasonable steps—

   (A) to ensure that the organization's compliance and ethics program is followed, including monitoring and auditing to detect criminal conduct;

   (B) to evaluate periodically the effectiveness of the organization's compliance and ethics program; and

   (C) to have and publicize a system, which may include mechanisms that allow for anonymity or confidentiality, whereby the organization's employees and agents may report or seek guidance regarding potential or actual criminal conduct without fear of retaliation.

6. The organization's compliance and ethics program shall be promoted and enforced consistently throughout the organization through

   (A) appropriate incentives to perform in accordance with the compliance and ethics program; and

   (B) appropriate disciplinary measures for engaging in criminal conduct and for failing to take reasonable steps to prevent or detect criminal conduct.

7. After criminal conduct has been detected, the organization shall take reasonable steps to respond appropriately to the criminal conduct and to prevent further similar criminal conduct, including making any necessary modifications to the organization's compliance and ethics program.

The Federal Sentencing Guidelines also state that failure to prevent or detect the offense does not mean that the compliance program was *per se* ineffective.[224]

4.7.2 Various OIG Guidances to Particular Segments of the Healthcare Industry

While the Sentencing Guidelines provide an overall structure for an organization's assessment of compliance program effectiveness, the OIG has promulgated more-specific "industry compliance guidances" that provide specific criteria for "effectively" meeting the requirements of the Sentencing Guidelines, as well as examples of what the OIG expects an "effective" compliance program to include. To date, the OIG has issued guidance for:

1. clinical laboratories;[225]
2. home health agencies;[226]
3. hospitals;[227]
4. durable medical equipment, prosthetics, and orthotics suppliers;[228]
5. Medicare+Choice (now referred to as Medicare Advantage (MA)) organizations;[229]
6. third-party medical-billing companies;[230]
7. skilled nursing facilities;[231]
8. hospices;[232]
9. ambulance providers;[233]
10. individual physicians and small group practices;[234]
11. pharmaceutical manufacturers;[235] and
12. recipients of National Institutes of Health research grants.[236]

---

224 *United States Sentencing Commission Guidelines Manual* § 8B2.1.
225 63 Fed. Reg. 45,076 (1998).
226 63 Fed. Reg. 42,410 (1998).
227 63 Fed. Reg. 8,987 (1998); *see also* 70 Fed. Reg. 4,858 (2005) (Supplemental Guidance).
228 64 Fed. Reg. 36,368 (1999).
229 64 Fed. Reg. 61,893 (1999).
230 63 Fed. Reg. 70,138 (1998).
231 65 Fed. Reg. 14,289 (2000); *see also* 73 Fed Reg. 56,832 (2008) (Supplemental Guidance).
232 64 Fed. Reg. 54,031 (1999).
233 68 Fed. Reg. 14,245 (2003).
234 65 Fed. Reg. 36,818 (2000).
235 68 Fed. Reg. 23,731 (2003).
236 70 Fed. Reg. 71,312 (2005) (Draft OIG Program Guidance).

Each of the OIG's compliance program guidances is structured around the seven elements delineated in the Federal Sentencing Guidelines. Although adoption of a compliance plan solely based upon a compliance-program guidance generally is not mandatory, providers interested in voluntarily implementing a compliance program should incorporate these basic elements into their own individually tailored programs. Adoption of a voluntary compliance program is becoming a requirement in a few settings such as Medicare Advantage Plans as well as by state Medicaid programs (*e.g.*, New York).

Although the first document that the OIG published on corporate compliance programs (which was related to the clinical laboratory industry) referred to the document as being a "model" corporate compliance program, the OIG recognized that no one document can—or should—serve as a "model" for an entire segment of the healthcare industry. Therefore, the OIG now refers to these documents as "guidance," and has stated that the document itself is not a compliance program, but rather is a statement of the OIG's notions on the basic procedural and structural elements to be included in an organization's compliance program.

To this end, within each such guidance, the OIG sets forth its general views on the value and fundamental principles of corporate compliance programs, then provides specific elements that it believes should be considered by an organization when developing and implementing a compliance program.

4.7.3 Corporate Integrity Agreements

Even though a provider may deny that it has committed any wrongdoing in connection with a healthcare fraud investigation, the provider may agree to enter into a settlement agreement with the government in order to avoid lengthy and uncertain litigation arising out of such investigations by the federal government. As part of the settlement agreement, the OIG often will agree not to seek to exclude the healthcare provider from participation in the federal healthcare programs so long as the provider agrees to a number of obligations concerning the establishment and maintenance of a compliance program.

Originally, these compliance obligations were included as a section of a global settlement agreement among the healthcare provider, DOJ, and the OIG. Currently, however, the settlement-negotiation process is bifurcated, whereby the healthcare provider enters into two separate agreements: (1) a settlement agreement with DOJ; and (2) a CIA with the OIG. Although such agreements with the OIG are generally referred to as CIAs, some organizations have entered into similar agreements with the OIG referred to by a different name.

CIAs outline certain obligations that the healthcare provider agrees to undergo in order to establish an effective compliance program. CIAs typically address the seven core elements of an effective compliance program, which track the Sentencing Guidelines. For example, the more-comprehensive CIAs require that the organization:

- hire a compliance officer/appoint a compliance committee;
- develop written standards and policies;
- implement a comprehensive employee training program;

- review claims submitted to federal healthcare programs;
- establish a confidential disclosure program; and
- restrict employment of ineligible persons.[237]

CIAs also include a number of notification and reporting requirements, such as notification to the OIG of any ongoing investigations or legal proceedings conducted or brought by a governmental entity. When an entity subject to a CIA discovers that an overpayment may have occurred, it may be required to make certain notifications to payors and complete specific forms for submission to Medicare Carriers and/or Intermediaries. CIAs also require that if the entity determines that it has engaged in an event that would constitute a "Reportable Event," then it must disclose the event to the OIG within certain timeframes (*i.e.*, within 30 days).

Providers also are required to submit to the OIG an initial "Implementation Report" and then subsequent "Annual Reports" concerning the status of and findings regarding the entity's compliance activities. All such reports submitted to the OIG must include a certification by the organization's compliance officer that the organization is in compliance with all of the CIA's requirements, and that the information in the report being submitted is "accurate and truthful." Consequently, as this certification is being made by compliance officers "under penalty of perjury," it is extremely important that, from the inception of the CIA, the compliance officers develop procedures to ensure that they are confident that all of the CIA's requirements have been satisfied. Therefore, as CIAs generally require that all "Covered Persons" (which includes not only the healthcare entity's employees, but also its contractors/agents and [for hospitals] members of the hospital's medical staff) receive training, it will be necessary that the compliance officers have a process by which they can attest that all such covered persons have, in fact, received training.

Recent CIAs reveal that the OIG believes boards of directors of healthcare companies should be more involved in the organization's corporate compliance programs. Specifically, a number of new CIAs require that that a Board of Directors (or the relevant Board committee) meet quarterly to review and oversee the companies' compliance with federal healthcare programs requirements and laws, FDA laws and requirements, the obligations of the CIA, and the corporate compliance program. In addition, a number of recent CIAs require the Board of Directors to adopt resolutions specifying that the board or board committee has concluded, after a reasonable inquiry that the company has implemented "effective" compliance programs and that each individual member of the board or board committee must certify that he or she agrees with the board's resolution.[238]

The OIG has also begun requiring more from the Board of Directors in connection with oversight on quality of care issues. For example, a number of CIAs require the Board of Directors to: "(i) review the adequacy of the provider's system of internal controls, quality assurance monitoring, and patient care; (ii) ensure that provider's response to state, federal, internal, and external reports of quality of care is complete, thorough, and resolves the issues identified; and (iii) ensure that [the provider] adopts

[237] Copies of various CIAs are *available online at* www.oig.hhs.gov/fraud/cias.html.

[238] *See* Corporate Integrity Agreement between the OIG and Eli Lilly and Company (Jan. 2009), available at http://oig.hhs.gov/fraud/cia/agreements/eli_lilly_and_company_01142009.pdf; Corporate Integrity Agreement between the OIG and Cephalon, Inc. (Sept. 2008), available at http://oig.hhs.gov/fraud/cia/agreements/cephalon.pdf.

and implements policies and procedures that are designed to ensure that each individual cared for by a Covered Facility receives the highest practicable physical, mental, and psychosocial level of care attainable."[239]

[239] *See e.g.*, Corporate Integrity Agreement between the OIG and Corona Care Convalescent Corporation (Mar. 2008), available at http://oig.hhs.gov/fraud/cia/agreements/corona_care_convalescent_corporation_03212008.pdf.

5

Tax-Exempt Issues

Bernadette M. Broccolo, Esquire*
McDermott, Will & Emery LLP

5.1 Introduction

This Chapter focuses primarily on the requirements for obtaining and maintaining exemption from federal income tax under § 501(c)(3) of the Internal Revenue Code (the Code). The Chapter will review the fundamental rules under § 501(c)(3). It will also explore briefly the application of those fundamental rules to mainstream health industry transactions and relationships, such as physician recruitment arrangements, physician practice acquisitions, physician and executive compensation, joint operating companies, use of taxable affiliates, and participation in joint ventures. The majority of the discussion will be devoted to tax exemption for hospitals and health systems, with only brief references to the exemption considerations applicable to other types of health organizations, such as health maintenance organizations (HMOs).

The tax-exemption considerations addressed in this Chapter must be in the forefront of the legal and strategic considerations addressed in planning and implementing transactions, and for relationships involving exempt healthcare organizations and either individuals or taxable entities, as well as in the development and implementation of corporate compliance programs.

This Chapter will not address related topics such as: (1) the rules on reporting obligations (*e.g.*, Forms 990 and 990-T) and related public disclosure requirements;[1] (2) the rules governing the use of tax-exempt financing under Code §§ 103 and 145 by a § 501(c)(3) healthcare organization; (3) the ability of a § 501(c)(3) healthcare organization to qualify for exemptions from state and local taxes (*e.g.*, real estate and sales taxes); and (4) the interplay between § 501(c)(3) compliance and compliance with the federal and state fraud and abuse laws. These related topics will also need to be considered in many circumstances in which § 501(c)(3) tax-exemption issues arise.

* The author gratefully acknowledges the valuable contributions made by Lisa Schmitz Mazur, an Associate in the Health Industry Advisory Practice of McDermott Will & Emery LLP, to the updating of this Chapter.

[1] Section 5.2.3.3 of this Chapter discusses recent revisions to Form 990, *Return of Organization Exempt from Income Tax*, the annual information return filed by many § 501(c)(3) organizations, including tax-exempt healthcare organizations.

5.1.1 Benefits of Section 501(c)(3) Tax-Exempt Status

Qualifying for and maintaining tax-exempt status under Code § 501(c)(3) offers several important benefits to healthcare organizations. First and foremost, a § 501(c)(3) tax-exempt organization is exempt from paying federal income tax on its net income. Second, and also quite significant, is the eligibility to borrow funds by issuing tax-exempt bonds under § 103 of the Code, which can be more cost effective than commercial (and taxable) financing alternatives. Third, § 501(c)(3) organizations are more attractive to donors than other forms of federal tax-exempt organizations because a donor's contributions to § 501(c)(3) organizations qualify for charitable deductions. Fourth, having § 501(c)(3) status can enhance an organization's ability to qualify in some states and localities for exemption from taxes such as property tax and sales tax.

5.1.2 Public Charity Status

Every organization that is exempt under § 501(c)(3) is considered a private foundation unless it is described in § 509(a)(1), (2), (3) or (4) of the Code. Organizations described in §§ 509(a)(1), (2), (3) or (4) are commonly referred to "public charities" or "non-private foundations." Generally an organization is presumed to be a private foundation even if it meets the requirement for public charity status unless it gives timely notice to the IRS that it is not a private foundation. An organization usually gives such notice at the same time as it files for tax-exempt status under Code § 501(c)(3) (discussed further below).

Disadvantages of being classified as a private foundation include exposure to restrictions and excise taxes on net investment income, excess business holdings, and "self-dealing" between private foundations and disqualified persons; mandatory distributions of income for charitable purposes; filing with the IRS of additional and more detailed reports of financial matters and activities; and less advantageous charitable deduction rules for donors.

5.1.3 Recurring Concepts

The following are the fundamental concepts and terms that will appear frequently in this Chapter's discussion of the requirements for obtaining and maintaining § 501(c)(3) tax-exempt status: (1) exempt purpose and the "community benefit" standard; (2) unrelated business income tax (UBIT); (3) stand-alone exempt status; (4) integral-part exempt status; (5) private inurement; (6) more-than-incidental private benefit; and (7) public charity status.

5.2 Exemption Requirements—Generally

To qualify for tax-exempt status under § 501(c)(3) of the Code, an organization must be *organized* and *operated* exclusively for religious, charitable, scientific, literary, educational, or other specified purposes (the Operational Test).

5.2.1 The Organizational Test

An organization is organized exclusively for one or more exempt purposes only if its articles of organization:

(a) Limit the purposes of such organization to one or more exempt purposes;

(b) Do not expressly empower the organization to engage, other than as an insubstantial part of its activities, in activities which in themselves are not in furtherance of one or more exempt purposes;

(c) Do not expressly empower the organization to:

  (i) Devote more than an insubstantial part of its activities to attempting to influence legislation by propaganda or otherwise;

  (ii) Directly or indirectly participate or intervene in (including the publishing or distributing of statements) any political campaign on behalf of or in opposition to any candidate for public office; or

  (iii) Have objectives and engage in activities that characterize it as an "action" organization; and

(d) Permit distribution of the organization's assets, upon dissolution, only for one or more exempt purposes or to the federal, state or local government for a public purpose, or as may otherwise be determined by a court of competent jurisdiction.[2]

These organizational requirements typically are not difficult to meet, and do not become an ongoing compliance issue following the initial filing of the articles of organizations with the relevant secretary of state. However, careful drafting of the organization's articles, bylaws and other governing documents is essential.

5.2.2 The Operational Test

The operational test is more complex and comprehensive, and presents significant challenges for monitoring an organization's day-to-day activities so as to ensure continued compliance with the requirements of exempt status under Code § 501(c)(3). The Operational Test requires that: (1) the organization engage primarily in activities that further one or more recognized exempt purposes (the exempt purposes requirement);[3] (2) such activities serve a public rather than a private purpose (the public benefit requirement);[4] (3) no part of the net earnings of the organization may inure to the benefit of any private shareholder or individual (the prohibition against private inurement); and (4) the organization may not engage in political activity, and no more than an insubstantial part of its activities may be to influence legislation (the political activity prohibition and lobbying limitation).

---

[2] Treas. Reg. § 1.501(c)(3)-1(b)(1), (2), (3), and (4).

[3] Treas. Reg. § 1.501(c)(3)-1(c)(1).

[4] Treas. Reg. § 1.501(c)(3)-1(d)(1)(ii).

5.2.3 The Exempt Purposes Requirement

5.2.3.1 *Stand-Alone Exemption–The Community Benefit Standard*

Although the Code and Treasury Regulations do not identify the provision of healthcare as an exempt purpose, the Service has recognized that the provision of healthcare may further charitable purposes in certain circumstances. In 1969, the Service issued Revenue Ruling 69-545,[5] which recognized that the promotion of health is one of the purposes in the general law of charity that is deemed beneficial to the community as a whole even though the class of beneficiaries eligible to receive a direct benefit from its activities does not include all members of the community, such as indigent members of the community, provided that the class is not so small that its relief does not benefit the community.[6]

This 1969 community benefit standard remains the principal standard applied by the Service today, in determining whether a healthcare organization qualifies as "charitable."[7] The standard derives primarily from the fact pattern set out in Situation 1 in Revenue Ruling 69-545. In Situation 1, the Service concluded that the hospital was operated primarily for the promotion of health, and satisfied the community benefit standard because it: (1) operated an emergency room open to all persons regardless of ability to pay; (2) provided hospital care in non-emergency situations for everyone able to pay the cost thereof, either directly or through third-party reimbursement (*e.g.*, private health insurance or public programs such as Medicare or Medicaid); (3) was governed by a board of directors composed of independent civic leaders; (4) extended medical-staff privileges to all qualified physicians in the area; (5) conducted all transactions with its medical staff on an arm's-length basis; and (6) applied any surplus receipts to improving facilities, equipment, patient care, medical training, education, and research.[8]

An organization is not required to establish the presence of all of the factors in Revenue Ruling 69-545 for the organization to satisfy the community benefit standard. The organization must, however, establish the presence of significant factors demonstrating that the organization promotes the health of a class of persons that is broad enough so that the community as a whole benefits. One highly significant factor is an emergency room that is open to all persons, regardless of their ability to pay. In Revenue Ruling 83-157,[9] however, the IRS ruled that a hospital could be tax-exempt despite its lack of an emergency room, provided either that the appropriate governmental health agency has determined that the hospital's emergency room would unnecessarily duplicate other emergency services in the community or that the hospital is specialized and treats conditions that do not require emergency treatment.

---

[5] 1969-2 C.B. 117.

[6] *Id.*

[7] *See* Lawrence M. Brauer, Mary Jo Salins, and Robert Fontenrose, "Update on Health Care," *IRS Exempt Organizations Continuing Professional Education Technical Instruction Program for Fiscal Year 2002*, at 171.

[8] *See also* IRS Exempt Organization Handbook (IRM 7751) §§ 349.1(2), 349.2(2), and 349.4(2).

[9] 1983-2 C.B. 94.

The IRS also has identified having a board of trustees comprised of prominent citizens drawn from the community as a significant factor in determining whether hospitals and other healthcare organizations qualify for § 501(c)(3) status.[10] In the early to mid 1990s, the IRS took the position that *no more than 20%* of the governing board of a tax-exempt entity formed to operate a physician practice could be comprised of a combination of disinterested persons, including both officers and physicians. In 1996, however, the IRS liberalized its position in its announcement of the following three criteria for demonstrating appropriate community representation on the board: (a) a majority of the voting members of the organization's board are independent community members; (b) the organization has a conflict-of-interest policy applicable to transactions or arrangements with interested persons;[11] and (c) the board and all committees with board-delegated powers, as part of their systems of controls, conduct periodic reviews of the organization's activities to ensure that it is operating for community benefit, rather than private interests, in areas such as compensation arrangements, practice acquisitions, and joint ventures.[12]

At the same time, the IRS also took the following position regarding physician-controlled boards of entities created as subsidiaries of exempt parent organizations:

> "In a multi-entity hospital system, the board of a subsidiary non-profit health care organization is considered to be comprised of independent community members if it is controlled by an exempt organization whose board is comprised of a majority of voting members who are independent community members."[13]

In 2000, the IRS expanded this concept of a "derived community board" by applying it in the context of professional corporations (PCs) seeking tax-exemption in those states with strict corporate practice of medicine prohibitions. More specifically, tax-exempt hospitals located in states with strict corporate practice of medicine prohibitions had difficulty forming tax-exempt hospital affiliated group practices because the states in which such hospitals were located required such group practices to be established as PCs, but the IRS would not grant exemption to PCs because of the organizational structure of such entities. In order to rectify this problem, the IRS released a new position in which it would agree to recognize tax-exempt hospital affiliated PCs as described in § 501(c)(3) of the Code if certain conditions were satisfied. With respect to board composition, the IRS stated that while the board members of the PCs may be physicians (as required under state law), the community board of the tax-exempt parent must retain and exercise reserved powers that are sufficient to ensure that the PC's activities always accomplish charitable purposes and avoid inurement and private benefit, including the right to: (1) elect, appoint, remove and change the number of the directors; (2) amend, alter or repeal the articles of incorporation and bylaws;

[10] Rev. Rul. 69-545, 1969-2 C.B. 17.

[11] For the model conflicts policy the IRS has recommended for use by exempt organizations, *see* Instructions to Form 1023 (Rev. June 2006) at http://www.irs.gov/pub/irs-pdf/i1023.pdf, which replaces the model policy first published by the IRS in Lawrence M. Brauer and Charles F. Kaiser III, "Tax-Exempt Healthcare Organizations Revised Conflict of Interest Policy," *IRS Exempt Organizations Continuing Professional Education Technical Instruction Program for Fiscal Year 2000*, at 45 (1999).

[12] Lawrence M. Brauer and Charles F. Kaiser, "Tax-Exempt Healthcare Organizations Community Board and Conflicts of Interest Policy," *IRS Exempt Organizations Continuing Professional Education Technical Instruction Program for Fiscal Year 1997*, at 18 (1996).

[13] 1997 CPE Textbook, at 21.

and (3) approve significant actions including (a) the annual operating and capital budgets and material deviations from such budgets, (b) the sale, lease, mortgage or other transfer or encumbrance of real or certain valuable personal property; (c) the merger, acquisition, consolidation, liquidation, or dissolution; (d) the settlements of claims and litigation; and (e) the selection of auditors.[14]

In February 2008, the IRS released a set of governance guidelines for tax-exempt organizations expanding the IRS's guidelines first released in 2007,[15] which updated and clarified in a significant way the IRS's position that a well-governed charity is more likely to obey the tax laws, safeguard charitable assets, and serve charitable interests than one with poor or lax governance. In particular, the guidelines shed light on the IRS's view on important governance-related issues, including (1) the importance of an "active and engaged" board (and how such diligence can be demonstrated), (2) issues associated with boards that are either "too small" or "too large", (3) director/committee member independence, (4) the benefits associated with the adoption of formal governance policies, (5) the need for boards to exercise oversight of sophisticated investment vehicles—including both joint ventures with for profit entities, as well as complicated and sophisticated financial products or investments and use of competent financial advisors, and (6) executive compensation as a continuing area of IRS focus—including with respect to such matters as the expertise of compensation committee members, the independence of the compensation committee consultant, and the emphasis on accurate and reliable comparability data.[16]

5.2.3.2 *Stand-Alone Exemption–Charity Care as a Consideration Under the Community Benefit Standard*

Prior to 1969, a hospital's charitable purpose was based on its provision of relief to the poor. Revenue Ruling 56-185[17] sets forth the pre-1969 requirements for a hospital to qualify as a § 501(c)(3) charitable organization. The requirements included, among others, that the hospital (1) operate to the extent of its financial ability for persons who are unable to pay for hospital services rendered, and not exclusively for persons who are able and expected to pay; and (2) generally accept patients who need hospital services, but could not pay for those services. Although this ruling was replaced in 1969, a hospital's care for patients without charge or at below-cost rates remains a factor that demonstrates

[14] Fiscal Year 2000 CPE Textbook at 58.

[15] *See* "Governance and Related Topics–501(c)(3) Organizations," released February 4, 2008, available at http://www.irs.gov/pub/irs-tege/governance_practices.pdf at 1. The IRS had previously released proposed, suggested governance guidelines for tax-exempt organizations in early 2007. The proposed guidelines addressed the following nine general areas: (1) Adoption of a Mission Statement; (2) Adoption of a Code of Ethics and whistleblower policies; (3) Satisfaction for the Duty of Care/Director Diligence; (4) Satisfaction of the Duty of Loyalty/effective conflicts of interest oversight; (5) Constituent transparency; (6) Oversight of fund-raising activity; (7) Stewardship of financial affairs; (8) Payment of reasonable compensation; and (9) Adoption of a document retention policy. *See* "Good Governance Practices for 501(c)(3) Organizations," 1–4, released February 2007, available at http://www.mwe.com/info/news/IRS0207.pdf.

[16] "Governance and Related Topics," *id.* at 2–5. For additional insight into how the IRS evaluates and examines the governance practices of tax-exempt organizations, *see* "IRS Governance Check Sheet" and the supplemental "Guide Sheet" released by the IRS on December 9, 2009, which can be found at http://www.irs.gov/pub/irs-tege/governance_check_sheet.pdf. The IRS released an informative set of guidelines to assist its agents in the course of examining the governance of tax-exempt organizations. The guidelines include both a "Governance Check Sheet" to be compiled by the agent and a supplementary "Guide Sheet" for the agent to use when completing the check sheet. The new examination guidelines highlight practices likely to be viewed with suspicion or concern by the IRS, such as whether persons with conflicts of interest participate in executive compensation decisions (Question 13 of the check sheet).

[17] 1956-1 C.B. 202.

to the IRS that a hospital promotes health to benefit the community. Unless a hospital did not operate an emergency room, however, the extent to which a healthcare organization has adopted and implemented a charity-care policy has not, since 1969, been considered as a relevant criteria in determining a hospital's tax-exempt § 501(c)(3) tax-exempt status, the IRS and the courts have instead recognized not-for-profit hospitals as § 501(c)(3) organizations because they further the charitable purpose of promoting the health of the community and they do not operate as proprietary entities.[18]

Despite the absence of charity care as a criteria in Revenue Ruling 69-545, the IRS directed its examination agents in early 2001 to ask a series of questions relating to free and discounted care practices when reviewing the tax-exempt status of a hospital, including the amount of charity care that the hospital actually provides.[19] Among the questions were issues such as: (1) whether the hospital has a specific, written plan or policy to provide free or low-cost healthcare services to the poor or indigent; (2) under what circumstances might the hospital deviate (or has the hospital deviated) from its stated policies to provide free or low-cost healthcare services to the poor or indigent; (3) what directives or instructions does the hospital provide to ambulance services about bringing poor or indigent patients to its emergency room; and (4) what documents or agreements must the poor or indigent patients sign before receiving care from the hospital? Worth noting is that Revenue Ruling 69-545 is legally binding on the IRS, while the Field Service Advice Memorandum is not. Nonetheless, the Field Service Memorandum is indicative of the IRS administrative and enforcement mindset at the time it was issued.

The relevance of charity care to a hospital's tax-exempt status was addressed in various contexts since 2001, such as congressional hearings and proposals on tax exemption policy and enforcement, congressional and IRS surveys or "soft contact" audits eliciting information on charity care practices from hundreds of hospitals nation-wide, class action litigation initiated in both federal and state courts, and state attorney general inquiries into hospital charity care practices. The discussion and debate that occurred in these contexts culminated in and the IRS's recent overhaul of the Form 990 annual information return filed by tax-exempt organizations,[20] and the adoption of Code § 501(r). While Revenue Ruling 69-545 itself has not been revisited, the Form 990 changes and new § 501(r) demonstrate that charity care and other financial assistance practices will be considered administratively by the IRS in its assessment of the community benefit achieved by exempt healthcare organizations.

New Code § 501(r) was enacted as part of the Patient Protection and Affordable Care Act (PPACA), the federal health reform legislation enacted on March 23, 2010.[21] It imposes several additional requirements on exempt "hospitals" described in § 501(c)(3) of the Code.[22] Now, in addition to complying with the general requirements set forth above, tax-exempt hospitals must: (1) conduct a community health needs assessment[23] at least once every three years, adopt an implementation strategy for meeting the needs the assessment identifies, and make the assessment widely available to the public;

---

[18] "Update on Health Care," at 172–73.

[19] Field Service Advice No. 200110030 (Feb. 5, 2001).

[20] Please refer to Section 5.2.3.3 for a discussion regarding the recent revisions to Form 990.

[21] Pub. L. No. 111-148, 124 Stat. 119 (2010), § 9007. The Treasury Department requested comments regarding these new requirements by July 22, 2010. Notice 2010-39, 2010-24 I.R.B. 756.

[22] Patient Protection and Affordable Care Act, Pub. L. 111-148, § 9007(a), 124 Stat. 1035.

[23] The community health needs assessment must incorporate input from a broad cross-section of the community the hospital serves, including those with knowledge and expertise in public health.

(2) adopt, publicize and make widely available its financial assistance policy;[24] (3) restrict charges for emergency or medically necessary care provided to patients eligible under the financial assistance policy to no more than the lowest amounts generally charged to insured patients and refrain from using gross charges; and (4) take "reasonable efforts"[25] to determine if a patient qualifies for financial assistance before initiating "extraordinary" collection actions (*e.g.*, referral to collection agencies).[26] These new requirements apply for tax years beginning after PPACA's enactment date.[27] PPACA also adds § 4959 to the Code, which provides for the imposition of excise taxes for failure to meet the community health needs assessment requirement. Failure to comply with the new requirements of § 501(r) may also result in loss of exemption under § 501(c)(3) at either the entity level or at the hospital-specific level.

5.2.3.3 Stand-Alone Exemption–Application of the Community Benefit Standard to Other than Hospitals and Other than Direct Providers of Healthcare

While Revenue Ruling 69-545 involved a hospital, the community benefit standard generally applies to any healthcare organization that seeks tax-exempt status under § 501(c)(3) of the Code. Other types of healthcare organizations to which the IRS has applied the community benefit standard include HMOs,[28] physician practice organizations,[29] hospices,[30] home health agencies,[31] and fitness centers.[32]

[24] The financial assistance policy must incorporate eligibility criteria for financial assistance and address the extent to which such assistance includes free or discounted care, the basis for calculating patient charges, how to apply for financial assistance, and how the policy will be publicly publicized. It must also commit the hospital to provide non-discriminatory emergency medical care, regardless of whether the individual is eligible for assistance under the policy.

[25] The definition of "reasonable efforts" is not included in the statute and will be developed by implementing regulations.

[26] These new requirements are set forth in new Internal Revenue Code Section 501(r) and apply for tax years beginning after the Act's enactment date. For example, if a tax-exempt hospital's fiscal year ends on April 30, then these requirements would apply beginning as of May 1, 2010.

[27] For example, if a tax-exempt hospital's fiscal year ends on April 30, then these requirements would apply beginning as of May 1, 2010.

[28] *See Sound Health Ass'n v. Commissioner*, 71 T.C. 158 (1978), *acq.* 1981-2 C.B. 2. *Compare, Geisinger Health Plan v. Commissioner*, 985 F.2d 1210 (3d Cir. 1993); *IHC Health Plans v. Commissioner*, Op. No. 01-9013 (10th Cir. 2003); 82 T.C.M. (CCH) 593 (2001); Internal Revenue Manual [7.8.1] 27.8. HMOs may also qualify for tax-exemption as social welfare organizations under Code § 501(c)(4). Code § 501(m), however, precludes tax-exempt status under either § 501(c)(3) or § 501(c)(4) if the organization provides commercial-type insurance as a substantial part of its activities. *See also* "Update on Health Care," at 155–58; Lawrence M. Brauer and Roderick Darling, "Update on Health Care," *IRS Exempt Organizations Continuing Professional Education Technical Instruction Program for Fiscal Year 2001*, at 59–65 (2000); Internal Revenue Manual [7.8.7] Chapter 27.

[29] *See, e.g.*, *University of Maryland Physicians, P.A., v. Commissioner*, 41 T.C.M. (CCH) 732 (1981); *University of Massachusetts Med. Sch. Group Practice v. Commissioner*, 74 T.C. 1299 (1980); *B.H.W. Anesthesia Found. v. Commissioner*, 72 T.C. 681 (1979); Physicians Network P.C., IRS Determination Letter (Oct. 23, 1996): Marietta Health Care Physicians, Inc., IRS Determination Letter (Oct. 3, 1995); C.H. Wilkinson Physician Network, IRS Determination Letter (June 19, 1996). *See also* Charles F. Kaiser and John F. Reilly, "Integrated Delivery Systems," *IRS Exempt Organizations Continuing Professional Education Technical Instruction Program for Fiscal Year 1994* at 212 (1993).

[30] *See* Rev. Rul. 79-19, 1979-1 C.B.193.

[31] *See* Rev. Rul. 72-209, 1972-1 C.B. 148 (freestanding home health agency); Rev. Rul. 68-375, 1968-2 C.B. 246 (hospital-based home health agency).

[32] *See, e.g.*, Tech. Adv. Mem. 9803001 (June 30, 1997). *See also* "Update on Health Care," at 163–67; Virginia Richardson, Roderick Darling and Marvin Friedlander, "Health Clubs," *IRS Exempt Organizations Continuing Professional Education Technical Instruction Program for Fiscal Year 2000* at 1 (1999).

Further, the fact that an organization does not provide healthcare services will not necessarily preclude it from qualifying as a § 501(c)(3) organization under the "community benefit standard."[33] Stated otherwise, the direct provision of medical, hospital, or nursing care to individuals is *not* the exclusive means by which an organization can establish that it promotes health for the benefit of the community within the meaning of § 501(c)(3). The IRS has ruled that the following organizations promoted health for the benefit of the community within the meaning of § 501(c)(3) of the Code despite the fact that they provided no direct healthcare services: professional standards review organizations (PSROs);[34] health planning agencies;[35] an organization that constructed a hospital and leased it to a public entity to operate the hospital;[36] an organization operating a free computerized donor authorized retrieval system to facilitate the transplantation of body organs;[37] and a regional health data system formed to conduct studies and propose improvements regarding quality, utilization and effectiveness of healthcare and healthcare agencies and to educate those involved in furnishing, administering and financing healthcare.[38]

In contrast, in the mid 1990s, the IRS characterized physician-hospital organizations referred to as "PHOs" as an "independent practice association" with a hospital participant formed for the purpose of arranging with managed care payers (*e.g.*, insurance companies or employers), on behalf of the participants in the PHO, to provide physician or hospital care.[39] The IRS characterized a PHO as a "joint marketing arrangement." The IRS stated that a PHO will not qualify for *stand alone* § 501(c)(3) status because: (a) it does not engage in the practice of medicine or operate a hospital; and (b) despite

---

[33] The "community benefit standard" for exemption is set forth generally in Rev. Rul. 69-545, 1969-2 C.B. 117. In this ruling, the IRS determined the following factors may demonstrate that a healthcare organization benefits the community rather than serving private interests and, therefore, qualifies for exemption under Section 501(c)(3) of the Code: (a) operating a full-time emergency room which provides treatment regardless of patients' ability to pay; (b) providing non-emergency services to all individuals who are able to pay for those services, including Medicare and Medicaid beneficiaries; (c) having an open medical staff whose members deal with the organization only on an arms'-length basis; (d) having a board of directors composed of independent civic leaders drawn from the community (rather than physicians, administrators, or others with a private interest in the organization) (described in more detail below); and (e) using any operational surplus to further the organization's exempt purposes by improving the quality of patient care and advancing the organization's medical training, education and research programs.

[34] Rev. Rul. 81-276, 1981-2 C.B. 128 (The PSRO was formed pursuant to the mandate of the Social Security Act Amendments of 1972 and designated to review medical necessity of services billed under the Medicare program. DHHS fully funded the PSRO. The IRS ruled that the organization promoted the health of the community by reducing over-utilization and relieving the burdens of government.)

[35] Rev. Rul. 76-455, 1976-2 C.B. 150.

[36] Rev. Rul. 80-309, 1980-2 C.B. 183.

[37] Rev. Rul. 75-197, 1975-1 C.B. 156 ("[b]y facilitating the donation of organs which will be used to save lives, the organization is serving the health needs of the community and, therefore, is promoting health within the meaning of the general law of charity").

[38] Revenue Ruling 76-455 (Specifically, the organization furnished aid for the development of uniform health data record-keeping and reporting procedures, and conducted related studies and educational programs. The data gathered was useful for reviewing patient management patterns, planning for regional and community health needs, and conducting epidemiological research. The members of the organization were other not-for-profit health information organizations, but the health data system maintained by the organization was open to everyone on a free, non-discriminatory basis. The IRS ruled that organization in this ruling was exempt as an organization that was organized and operated primarily for scientific and educational purposes under Section 501(c)(3). Nonetheless, the facts and circumstances would be persuasive in making the case for exemption under the community benefit theory for exemption as a charitable organization under Section 501(c)(3)).

[39] Charles F. Kaiser, Phyllis D. Haney and T. J. Sullivan, "Integrated Delivery and Joint Venture Dissolution Update," *IRS Exempt Organization Continuing Professional Education Technical Instruction Program for Fiscal Year 1995*, 153 (1994) (hereinafter "1995 CPE Text").

the hospital's participation, the PHOs primary beneficiaries are its member-physicians rather than the community as a whole (citing Rev. Rul. 86-98, 1986-2 C.B. 74) and its activities are substantially devoted to serving those physicians' interests (and thus cannot satisfy the private inurement or private benefit prohibitions of § 501(c)(3)).[40]

5.2.3.4 *Stand-Alone Exemption–Lessening the Burdens of Government*

"Lessening the burdens of government" is an alternative basis for exemption under § 501(c)(3). While its applicability in the healthcare context is limited, it is a theory worth considering in the current, changing healthcare context.

Qualification for exemption as an organization described in § 501(c)(3) under a lessening the burdens of government rationale requires satisfaction of a two-part test. First, the organization seeking exemption must demonstrate an objective manifestation by a state or Federal government that the activities engaged in by the organization seeking exemption are a burden of government.[41] Second, the organization must demonstrate that its activities actually lessen such burden.[42]

The IRS has determined that a PSRO may qualify under § 501(c)(3) of the Code under the lessening the burdens of government theory.[43] In the ruling, the organization's membership was open without charge to all licensed physicians engaged in the practice of medicine and the composition of the organization's board of directors was not tied to membership or association in any medical society. Revenues for the organization were derived exclusively from contracts with the federal government. Based on the legislative history of the applicable federal statute, the IRS found that Congress' objectives in establishing PSROs were (i) to reduce overutilization of the health services provided under Medicare and Medicaid and (ii) to enable the medical profession to assume the federal government's responsibility for reviewing the appropriateness and quality of services provided under Medicare and Medicaid. Accordingly, the IRS determined that reviewing the appropriateness and quality of services provided under Medicare and Medicaid was a burden of government and that the organization's activities actually lessened such burden.

Most recently, the IRS began granting exemption to organizations designed to facilitate the adoption of electronic health information under a § 501(c)(3) lessening the burdens of government rationale. In reaching its conclusion that these types of organizations lessened the burdens of government, the IRS relied on statements in the legislative history of the Health Information Technology for

---

[40] This position is restated by the IRS in its 1996 CPE Text at 401. The 1995 CPE Text also states that a PHO will not qualify for *integral part exempt* status because negotiating managed care contracts for the member-physicians is a substantial activity of the PHO and such activity is not an essential service to the hospital participant in the PHO. In a tax exemption determination letter issued to a PHO affiliate of the University of Kansas Medical Center, however, the IRS granted 501(c)(3) status to a PHO with faculty practice plan characteristics. *See* Charles F. Kaiser and T. J. Sullivan, "Integrated Delivery Systems and Health Care Update," *IRS Exempt Organization Continuing Professional Education Technical Instruction Program for Fiscal Year 1996 (1995)* at 402; Peregrine, Michael W. and Broccolo, Bernadette M. *PHO Tax Planning Update*, The Exempt Organization Tax Review, Vol. 11, No. 5 (1995). The faculty practice plan characteristics of this case make it relatively unique and limit its overall applicability.

[41] Rev. Rul. 85-1, 1985-1 C.B. 178.

[42] *Id.*

[43] Rev. Rul. 81-276, 1981-2 C.B. 128. As discussed above, the IRS also determined in this ruling that the PSRO's activities promoted health for the benefit of the community within the meaning of section 501(c)(3) of the Code as well.

Economic and Clinical Health Act (HITECH) in which Congress expressly deemed such activities to lessen the burdens of government within the meaning of § 501(c)(3) of the Code.[44]

5.2.3.5 *Annual Information Return Reporting–Compliance with the Community Benefit Standard*

The redesigned Form 990 introduced by the IRS in December of 2007 elicits significantly more information that will enable the IRS to monitor and enforce a § 501(c)(3) organization's compliance with the community benefit standard and explicitly incorporates charity care as a consideration. As such, it has significant implications for reporting the information upon which the IRS will administratively determine compliance with the "community benefit" standard.[45]

The majority of the community benefit-related questions are contained in "Schedule H – Hospitals."[46] Schedule H requires disclosure of a tax-exempt hospital's charity care and other community benefits and community building activities, in addition to bad debt expenses, Medicare shortfall, debt collection practices, management companies and joint ventures.[47] In addition to providing all these required statistics, hospitals must provide supplemental narrative information describing how the hospital assesses the needs of its community, informs patients of eligibility requirements for charity care, and uses community building activities to promote the health of the residents of its service area.[48]

In addition to enacting new Code § 501(r), PPACA amends Code § 6033(b) to require that a tax-exempt hospital include in its Form 990 a description of how the organization is addressing the needs identified in each community health needs assessment, a description of any such needs that are not being addressed, and an explanation of why such needs are not being addressed.[49] Each organization must also include in the Form 990 its financial statements (or the consolidated financial statements, if applicable).[50]

The redesigned Form 990 contains an 11-page core form (Core Form) that must be completed by all filing organizations and includes eight additional sections.[51] The "Governance, Management and Disclosure" section of the Core Form[52] is a recent addition. It is generally intended to improve tax compliance by providing insight into an organization's governance structure, policies, and practices[53]

---

44 H.R. 1, S.1, American Recovery & Reinvestment Act of 2009, Health Information Technology for Economic and Clinical Health Act, §§ 13001 *et seq.* (Feb. 17, 2009).

45 For a detailed discussion of the redesign of Form 990 and the implementation of § 501(r), *see* Michael N. Fine and Christopher M. Jedrey, '*Show Me the Money'–Maintaining Hospital Tax-Exempt Status*, Journal of Taxation of Exempt Organizations, at 1–2 (Sept./Oct. 2010).

46 Schedule H of Form 990 can be found at http://www.irs.gov/pub/irs-pdf/f990sh.pdf.

47 *Id.*

48 *Id.*

49 Internal Revenue Code Section 6033(b)(15)(A).

50 Internal Revenue Code Section 6033(b)(4).

51 A copy of the redesigned Form 990 can be found at http://www.irs.gov/pub/irs-pdf/f990.pdf.

52 Part VI of the Core Form. Some of the questions in this new Part VI were previously asked on the Form 990 in several different sections, but they are now consolidated into this one part of the Core Form. A copy of the Form 990 prior to its redesign in 2007 can be found at http://www.unclefed.com/IRS-Forms/2006/f990.pdf.

53 *See* "IRS Governance Check Sheet" and "Guide Sheet for Completing the Check Sheet" for insight into the IRS's examination of governance practices of tax-exempt organizations.

and it underscores the importance that the IRS attributes to effective corporate governance by tax-exempt organizations.

In particular, this new section on governance requires the organization to disclose the number of "independent" voting directors. The corresponding instructions introduce a revised standard for determining director independence. This new standard focuses principally on whether the board member (or family member) was involved in a transaction or relationship with the organization. In general, according to the instructions, a board member will be regarded as "independent" only if three specific circumstances are satisfied at all times during the organization's tax year: (a) the board member was not compensated as an *officer* or other employee of the organization or of a *related organization*,[54] except as provided in the religious exception discussed below; (b) the board member did not receive total *compensation* or other payments exceeding $10,000 during the organization's tax year from the organization or from related organizations as an *independent contractor*, other than reimbursement of expenses under an *accountable plan* or *reasonable compensation* for services provided in the capacity as a member of the governing body;[55] and (c) neither the board member, nor any of his or her *family members*, was involved in a reportable transaction with the organization (whether directly or indirectly through affiliation with another organization) for the organization's tax year, or in a transaction with a related organization of a type and amount that would be reportable if required to be filed by the related organization. The instructions also note that a board member will not be considered to lack independence merely because of the following circumstances: (a) the board member is a donor to the organization, regardless of the amount of the contribution; (b) the board member has taken a *bona fide* vow of poverty and either (i) receives *compensation* as an agent of a *religious order* or a § 501(d) religious or apostolic organization, but only under circumstances in which the member does not receive taxable income;[56] (ii) belongs to a religious order that receives sponsorship or payments from the organization which do not constitute taxable income to the member (the "religious exception" referred to above); or (iii) the member receives financial benefits from the organization solely in the capacity of being a member of the charitable or other class served by the organization in the exercise of its exempt function, such as being a member of a § 501(c)(6) organization, so long as the financial benefits comply with the organizations terms of membership. Finally, the Final Instructions provide a series of helpful examples applying this three part independence test.

The new governance section of the Form 990 also requests information concerning business relationships and business transactions between and among directors, trustees, officers, and key employees.[57] The corresponding instructions define "business relationships" between two persons to include any of the following: (a) one person is employed by the other in a sole proprietorship or by an organization with which the other is associated as a trustee, director, officer, key employee or greater than 35% owner; (b) one person is transacting business with the other (other than in the ordinary

---

[54] *See* Form 990, Schedule R instructions.

[55] For example, a person who receives reasonable expense reimbursements and reasonable compensation as a director of the organization does not cease to be independent merely because he or she also receives payments of $7,500 from the organization for other arrangements.

[56] *See, e.g.*, Rev. Ruls.77-290, 1977 CB ___, 80-332, 1980 CB ___.

[57] Part VI, Question 2. *See* IRS Form 990 Filing Tips: Schedule L (Transactions with Interested Persons) available at http://www.irs.gov/charities/article/0,,id=215122,00.html.

course of either party's business on the same terms as are generally offered to the public), directly or indirectly, in one or more contracts of sale, lease, license, loan, performance of services, or other transaction involving transfers of cash or property valued in excess of $10,000 in the aggregate during the organization's tax year (indirect transactions are transactions with an organization with which the one person is associated as a trustee, director, officer, key employee, or greater-than 35% owner); *and* (c) the two persons are each a director, trustee, officer, or greater than 10% owner in the same business or investment entity.[58] In contrast, reportable "business transactions" between the organization and its interested persons (including its current and former officers, directors, trustees, key employees, family members thereof, and certain entities owned or controlled, in part, by those officers, directors, trustees, and key employees) include, for example, excess benefit transactions, loans between the filing organization and interested persons, and grants or other assistance to interested persons. Transactions between the organization and such person's family members or affiliated entities generally are included.[59] The business relationships and business transactions reportable in the new governance section of the Form 990 are similar in that both require the disclosure of certain contracts of sale, lease, license, and performance of services. However, each involves different reporting thresholds and exceptions set forth in their respective instructions.[60]

5.2.4 "Derivative" or "Integral Part" Theory of Exemption

As discussed in Section 5.2.3, a healthcare organization may qualify for "stand-alone" tax-exempt status if it can demonstrate that its activities are primarily charitable in nature under the community benefit standard. An organization involved in healthcare whose activities are *not* inherently charitable may nonetheless qualify for tax-exempt status under the § 501(c)(3) "derivative" or "integral part" theory of exemption if they meet *both* of the following requirements: (a) the activities of the organization are ones that could or otherwise would have been performed by another exempt organization (the essential services requirement);[61] and (b) a sufficient structural or financial relationship exists between the organization seeking exemption and such other exempt organization (the relationship requirement).[62] Although the community benefit requirement does not apply to integral-part exempt

58 *See* Form 990 Instructions, at 19–20, http://www.irs.gov/pub/irs-pdf/i990.pdf. Ownership is measured by stock ownership (either voting power or value) of a corporation, profits or capital interest in a partnership or limited liability company, membership interest in a nonprofit organization, or beneficial interest in a trust. Ownership also includes indirect ownership (*e.g.*, ownership in an entity that has ownership in the entity in question). *Id.* at 20.

59 *Id.* at 74.

60 *See* IRS Form 990 Instructions for Schedule L, available at http://www.irs.gov/pub/irs-pdf/i990sl.pdf. For example, an organization that completes Schedule L, Part IV generally is not required to report transactions with an interested person for a dollar amount that did not exceed the greater of $10,000 or 1% of the organization's total revenue for the exempt organization's tax year, whereas the similar threshold for Part VI, line 2 is simply $10,000. *See* IRS Form 990 Filing Tips: Schedule L.

61 *See, e.g.*, *Squire v. Students Book Corp.*, 191 F.2d 1018 (9th Cir. 1951); Rev. Rul. 58-194, 1958-1 C.B. 240; Rev. Rul. 67-217, 1967-1 C.B. 181; Rev. Rul. 67-291, 1967-2 C.B. 184; Rev. Rul. 69-538, 1969-2 C.B. 116; Rev. Rul. 76-336, 1976-2 C.B. 143; Gen. Couns. Mem. 39830 (Aug. 24, 1990). *See also* Gen. Couns. Mem. 39830 (Aug. 30, 1990), which states that the services must be "essential" for fulfilling the exempt purposes of the benefited organization.

62 *See, e.g.*, Treas. Reg. § 1.502-1(b); *Council for Bibliographic & Information Techs. v. Commissioner*, 63 TCM 3186 (1992); *Estate of Thayer v. Commissioner*, 24 T.C. 384 (1955); Rev. Rul. 78-41, 1978-1 C.B. 148; Rev. Rul. 71-529, 1971-2 C.B. 234; Rev. Rul. 69-572, 1969-2 C.B. 119; Rev. Rul. 75-282, 1975-2 C.B. 201; Rev. Rul. 74-614, 1974-2 C.B. 164; Rev. Rul. 58-194, 1958-1 C.B. 240. *Compare with* Rev. Rul. 69-633, 1969-2 C.B. 121; Rev. Rul. 69-528, 1969-2 C.B. 127; Rev. Rul. 72-369, 1972-2 C.B. 245; Gen. Couns. Mem. 39003 (Nov. 29, 1982). A corollary to the derivative theory of exemption is that the provision of services by one exempt organization to one or more other exempt organizations that do

organizations, the other components of the § 501(c)(3) operational test discussed in Section 5.2 do apply. Common examples of healthcare organizations that have relied on the derivative/integral part theory are parent corporations of diversified hospital systems, malpractice-insurance trusts created to pool risk among various related healthcare providers,[63] and joint-operating companies formed to implement a "virtual merger" between two previously unrelated healthcare systems.

The predominant focus of the IRS in making derivative-exemption determinations has been on the relationship requirement. In the healthcare context, the IRS has displayed a preference for a formal structural relationship, such as a parent/subsidiary relationship. As will be reflected in the following discussion of joint-operating companies, the IRS has also recognized a financial relationship as sufficient under certain facts and circumstances.

The essential services requirement was the focus, however, in the integral-part debate involved in the controversial *Geisinger Health Plan* line of cases. On remand from the Third Circuit, the Tax Court held that Geisinger Health Plan did not qualify for tax-exempt status as an integral part of the Geisinger Health System. The court based its decision on the finding that the plan did not provide services directly, either to its affiliates or to the class of beneficiaries of the charitable purposes of its affiliates, and that the subscribers to the plan included individuals who were not patients of the hospitals in the Geisinger system.[64]

The Tenth Circuit took a somewhat different approach to the essential services requirement in its decision issued in connection with the HMO affiliates of Intermountain Health Care, Inc. (IHC), focusing instead on the nexus between the IHC plans and IHC Health Services, a tax-exempt subsidiary of IHC.[65] Under the Tenth Circuit's interpretation of the integral-part doctrine, the performance of a particular activity that is not inherently charitable may nonetheless further a charitable purpose; the analysis depends on why and how the activity is being conducted. The Tenth Circuit stated that one of the factors to be considered in applying the integral-part doctrine is "whether an essential nexus exists between the organization seeking tax exemption and a tax-exempt affiliate."[66] The Tenth Circuit noted that the electric power subsidiary described in Treasury Regulations § 1.502-1(b) furnished power solely to the tax-exempt affiliate. That fact, together with the facts that the product provided is essential and that the tax-exempt affiliate exercises control over the subsidiary, "support[s] a strong inference that the subsidiary operates for the same purpose as the parent."[67] The Tenth Circuit concluded that it need not decide whether the IHC plans provided an essential service because the required

---

not satisfy this relationship requirement is not necessarily an exempt activity unless the nature of the services themselves would support a stand-alone exemption. *See, e.g.*, Tech. Adv. Mem. 98 22 004 (Nov. 10, 1997).

63 Rev. Rul. 78-41, 1978-1 C.B. 148.

64 *Geisinger Health Plan v. Commissioner*, 100 T.C. 394 (1993), *aff'd on other grounds*, 30 F.3d 494 (3d Cir. 1994). For examples of the bases upon which the IRS and the courts have found the activities of supporting organizations to be sufficient to satisfy the essential services requirement, *see* Gen. Couns. Mem. 39830 (Aug. 24, 1990); Rev. Rul. 78-41, 1978-1 C.B. 148; Gen. Couns. Mem. 39864 (Sept. 28, 1984); Gen. Couns. Mem. 39508 (May 27, 1986); Rev. Rul. 58-194, 1958-C.B. 240; Rev. Rul. 67-217, 1967-1 C.B. 181; Rev. Rul. 67-291, 1967-2 C.B. 184; Rev. Rul. 68-26, 1968-1 C.B. 272; Rev. Rul. 75-282, 1975-2 C.B. 201; University of Maryland Physicians, P.A.; University of Massachusetts Med. Sch. Group Practice; B.H.W. Anesthesia Found.

65 *IHC Health Plans v. Commissioner*, 82 T.C.M. (CCH) 593 (2001).

66 *Id.*

67 *Id.*

nexus between the activities of the IHC plans and IHC Health Services is lacking. The Tenth Circuit found that, because a substantial portion of IHC plans' subscribers received services from independent physicians, the IHC plans do not function solely to further IHC Health Services' performance of its exempt activities.[68]

5.2.4.1 Parent Corporations

In the mid 1980s, the IRS's Chief Counsel raised, but did not resolve, the issue of whether parent corporations in restructured hospital systems, which do not have an inherently charitable purpose of their own, should be able to derive § 501(c)(3) status from their exempt subsidiaries.[69] Specifically, the Chief Counsel questioned whether, under the relationship requirement, a parent may derive its exempt status from its subsidiaries, rather than vice versa. Nonetheless, the IRS thereafter has issued favorable derivative exemption rulings to parent corporations in hospital systems.[70] In October 1993, for example, the IRS issued derivative exempt status to a "Superparent" or "Grandparent" in a hospital network, even though a layer of other derivatively exempt parent corporations existed between the Superparent and the exempt hospitals from which it derived its status.[71]

5.2.4.2 Joint Operating Companies

In some cases, two or more previously unrelated health systems interested in affiliating with one another have chosen to do so using what has become known as a joint-operating agreement arrangement (JOA) rather than a formal structural affiliation under a common-parent corporation. Although the specific design components of JOAs may vary from case to case, the advantages most often associated with the JOA concept include: (a) achievement of a significant amount of integration among the hospitals, while preserving both separate identities and current hospital asset ownership (often a prerequisite for religious-sponsored and governmental healthcare entities); (b) increased attractiveness for managed-care contracting purposes (*i.e.*, allows managed-care firms to negotiate with a single entity, the JOC); (c) enhanced opportunities for efficiencies and cost savings; and (d) no disruption to the existing debt structure of the participating hospitals.

In many JOAs, the parties create a new entity, known as a "joint operating company" (JOC), to assume the direct responsibility for the management and operation of all the healthcare facilities in the affiliating health systems. In late 1996, the IRS published an essay that articulated its position concerning whether a JOC can qualify for § 501(c)(3) status under the integral-part theory.[72] The discussion in the essay differentiates between a JOC and a parent company that functions as a centralized authority

---

[68] The Tax Court had relied on the heavy use of independent physicians as the basis for determining that the IHC plans did not provide an essential service to IHC Health Services. *See IHC Care v. Commissioner*, 82 T.C.M. (CCH) 617 (2001); *IHC Group v. Commissione*r, 82 T.C.M (CCH) 606 (2001); *IHC Health Plans*.

[69] Gen. Couns. Mem. 39598 (Jan. 23, 1987) and Gen. Couns. Mem. 39508 (May 27, 1986).

[70] *See* Judith E. Kindell and T.J. Sullivan, "Health Care Update," *IRS Exempt Organizations Continuing Professional Education Technical Instruction Program for Fiscal Year 1995*, 137, 145.

[71] *See* Bernadette M. Broccolo & Michael W. Peregrine, *IRS Issues "Double Derivative" Exemption to Super Parent in Regional Health Network—A Glimmer of Hope for the Future of Integral Part Status?* The Exempt Organization Tax Review, Vol. 8, No. 4 at 731 (Oct. 1993).

[72] *See* Roderick Darling and Marvin Friedlander, "Virtual Mergers, Hospital Joint Operating Agreement Affiliations," *IRS Exempt Organizations Continuing Professional Education Technical Instruction Program for Fiscal Year 1997*, 131.

with absolute financial and structural control over the directors and assets of the organizations coming together through the affiliation. It also describes the types of facts and circumstances that will be sufficient to demonstrate a relationship that supports integral-part exemption other than one in which a common-parent entity exercises absolute financial and structural control.

The facts and circumstances articulated by the IRS focus on the delegation to the JOC of management and financial authority, the binding nature of the JOA, the dispute-resolution mechanism, and the reservation of powers by the participating systems.[73] Elements of specific JOC management authority cited by the IRS include: (a) authority to establish budgets; (b) authority by the JOA governing body to monitor and audit each participating entity's compliance with its directives; (c) authority to direct services; (d) authority to enter agreements that bind participating entities, particularly agreements with managed-care providers; (d) authority to hire and fire personnel; (e) authority to grant hospital-staff privileges; (f) authority to set or approve fees and prices; (g) authority to buy assets for and sell assets of participating entities; and (h) authority to reallocate income among the participating entities to balance income and expenses in order to ensure financial integration and achieve mutual objectives.

Other relevant factors articulated by the IRS include: (a) whether significant penalties or other hindrances are posed by potentially terminating the agreement; (b) whether mechanisms, such as direct negotiations and binding arbitration, are in place to resolve disputes among the parties; and (c) the degree to which the JOA is permanent. If the authority ceded to the JOC is merely the power to veto actions taken by participating hospitals, then the facts and circumstances necessary to establish the equivalent of a parent/subsidiary relationship would not be present. Similarly, if actions of the JOC governing body are subject to veto by the participating hospitals, then this also would negate a finding that the hospitals function as subordinates of the JOC. Retaining some authority in the governing bodies of the participating systems does not necessarily determine whether the equivalent of a parent/subsidiary relationship has been established. Examples of such authority include authority over ethical or moral issues based on religious principles.[74]

5.2.5 Public-Benefit Requirement

A § 501(c)(3) organization must also be operated for the benefit of public, rather than private, interests. Thus, the organization must establish that it is not organized or operated for the benefit of private interests, such as designated individuals, the creator or the creator's family, shareholders of the organization, or persons controlled (directly or indirectly) by such private interests.[75] It must be capable of demonstrating that any benefits that flow from its corporate activities to private interests are

[73] As a word of caution, these facts and circumstances in many cases may not be suitable for the traditional parent in a restructured hospital system, as they would require the parent to have significant direct involvement in the day-to-day affairs of the hospitals coming together under the JOA arrangement.

[74] Private letter rulings issued in the JOA context include Priv. Ltr. Rul. 200245057 (Aug. 13, 2002); Priv. Ltr. Rul. 200238051 (June 28, 2002); Priv. Ltr. Rul. 200108045-47 (Nov. 29, 2000); Priv. Ltr. Rul. 200044040 (Aug. 3, 2000); Priv. Ltr. Rul. 200036049 (June 13, 2000); Priv. Ltr. Rul. 9814039 (Jan. 5, 1998), Priv. Ltr. Rul. 9738038-9738054 (June 26, 1997); Priv. Ltr. Rul. 9722042; Priv. Ltr. Rul. 9721031 (Feb. 26, 1997); Priv. Ltr. Rul. 9714011 (Dec. 24, 1996); 9716021 (Jan. 17, 1997) and 9716026; Priv. Ltr. Rul. 9609012 (Nov. 22, 1995); Priv. Ltr. Rul. 9623011 (Feb. 29, 1996); and Priv. Ltr. Rul. 9651047 (Sept. 24, 1996).

[75] Treas. Reg. § 1.501(c)(3)-1(d)(1)(ii).

incidental, both qualitatively and quantitatively, to the public benefits derived from the activity.[76] The substantiality of the private benefit is measured in the context of the overall public benefit conferred by the activity.[77] Unlike the private-inurement prohibition, the "private benefit" prohibition is not limited to "insiders." This is commonly referred to as the private-benefit prohibition or the public-benefit requirement. Organizations that violate the public-benefit requirement jeopardize their tax-exempt status.

5.2.6 Private-Inurement Prohibition

Section 501(c)(3) of the Code and the corresponding Treasury Regulations[78] provide that no part of the net earnings of a § 501(c)(3) organization may inure to the benefit of private shareholders or individuals with an "inside" relationship to the charity. This is commonly referred to as the private-inurement prohibition. Private shareholders or individuals, typically referred to as "insiders," are "persons having a personal and private interest in the activities of the organization,"[79] and generally include officers, directors, major donors, and senior management because of their interest in and potential ability to influence the affairs of the tax-exempt organization. In the case of a healthcare provider, therefore, the IRS may take the position that certain physicians employed by, or on the medical staff of, the organization are "insiders."[80]

An organization may pay or receive "fair market value" or "reasonable compensation" for a good or service without violating the inurement prohibition.[81] If, however, a transaction results in the payment by a hospital of more than fair market value or reasonable compensation for an item or service it purchases, or the receipt of less than fair market value or reasonable compensation for an item or service it sells, then the transaction may result in private inurement.[82] The Code and its regulations do not define private inurement. As a result, whether private inurement occurs depends upon the facts and circumstances surrounding a transaction or arrangement. Organizations that violate the private inurement prohibition jeopardize their tax-exempt status.

---

[76] *See, e.g.*, Rev. Rul. 73-313, 1973-2 C.B. 174; Gen. Couns. Mem. 39598 (Dec. 8, 1986); Gen. Couns. Mem. 39498 (Apr. 24, 1986); Gen. Couns. Mem. 37789 (Dec. 18, 1978); Gen. Couns. Mem. 35268 (Mar. 14, 1973). Like private letter rulings, General Counsel Memoranda are not binding precedent. Nevertheless, they provide insights into the IRS's current policy and enforcement positions.

[77] Gen. Couns. Mem. 39598 (Dec. 8, 1986); Gen. Couns. Mem. 39498 (Apr. 24, 1986); Gen. Couns. Mem. 37789 (Dec. 18, 1978).

[78] Treas. Reg. § 1.501(c)(3)-1(c).

[79] Treas. Reg. § 1.501(a)-1(c); *American Campaign Academy v. Commissioner*, 92 T.C. 1053 (1989). *See also* Mertens, *The Law of Federal Income Taxation* 99 (1986); *Passaic United Hebrew Burial Ass'n v. United States*, 216 F. Supp. 500 (N.J. 1963), citing the *Mertens* text, *Founding Church of Scientology v. United States*, 412 F.2d 1197 (Ct. Cl. 1969).

[80] *See, e.g., Lowry Hosp. Ass'n v. Commissioner*, 66 T.C. 80 (1976); *Harding Hosp., Inc. v. United States*, 505 F.2d 1068 (6th Cir. 1974); Gen. Couns. Mem. 39498 (Apr. 24, 1986); Gen. Couns. Mem. 39862 (Nov. 22, 1991); Gen. Couns. Mem. 39670 (June 17, 1987); Gen. Couns. Mem. 39598 (Dec. 8, 1986). Compare with Rev. Rul. 69-383, 1969-2 C.B. 113; Rev. Rul. 73-313, 1973-2 C.B. 174.

[81] *See, e.g., Alive Fellowship of Harmonious Living v. Commissioner*, ¶41,011 (M) T.C.M. (1984); *World Family Corp. v. Commissioner*, 81 T.C. 958 (1983); *John Marshall Law Sch. v. United States*, 81-2 U.S.T.C ¶ 9514 (Ct. Cl. 1981); *B.H.W. Anesthesia Found., Inc. v. Commissioner*, 72 T.C. 681 (1979); Rev. Rul. 76-441, 1976-2 C.B. 147; Gen. Couns. Mem. 39498 (Apr. 24, 1986); Rev. Rul. 69-383, 1969-2 C.B. 113; Gen. Couns. Mem. 38283 (Feb. 15, 1980).

[82] *See, e.g., Birmingham Bus. College v. Commissioner*, 276 F.2d 476 (5th Cir. 1960) and *Mabee Petroleum v. United States*, 203 F.2d 872 (5th Cir. 1953), in which the courts found the compensation arrangements to be excessive, and *Anclote Psychiatric Ctr., Inc. v. Commissioner*, T.C. Memo 1998-273, *aff'd*, 190 F.3d 541, in which the court found the organization had sold assets to a for-profit company owned by former board members for less than fair market value.

5.2.7 Intermediate Sanctions and the Rebuttable Presumption of Reasonableness

5.2.7.1 *The Intermediate Sanctions Excise Taxes*

Code § 4958 contains a series of penalty excise taxes generally referred to as "intermediate sanctions." Under those rules, "disqualified persons" (that is, persons in a position to exercise substantial influence over the affairs of the organization) who receive excess benefits, and the organizational managers who approve such benefits, are subject to the imposition of penalty excise taxes.[83] No penalty excise tax applies to the organization itself. The tax on disqualified persons is a two-tier tax. The initial tax is 25% of the amount of the excess benefit.[84] An additional tax of 200% of the excess benefit is imposed if the excess-benefit transaction is not corrected within the taxable period.[85] The organization manager tax is 10% of the amount of the excess benefit,[86] up to a maximum of $20,000 per transaction.[87]

Congress intended that these excise taxes generally be imposed in lieu of a loss of tax-exempt status for organizations that violate the private-inurement prohibition. In certain circumstances, however, these penalties may be imposed in addition to loss of tax-exempt status. The applicable Treasury regulations provide guidance on the specific factors that the IRS will consider in determining whether a § 501(c)(3) organization jeopardizes its tax-exempt status by engaging in one or more excess benefit transactions. [88] In other words, these regulations address the circumstances under which the IRS would consider revoking an organization's tax-exempt status for engaging in an excess benefit transaction in addition to imposing § 4958 intermediate sanctions. The factors include: (1) the size and scope of the organization's regular exempt activities; (2) the relationship between the size and scope of the excess benefit transaction(s) and the organization's regular exempt activities; (3) whether the organization has a history of engaging in "repeated" excess benefit transactions; (4) whether the organization has adopted compliance measures intended to prevent the occurrence of future intermediate sanctions violations; and (5) whether the excess benefit transaction has been corrected (or the organization has made a good faith effort to seek correction).[89] These regulations should be consulted in analyzing any transaction or arrangement with potential intermediate-sanctions risks.

---

83 The IRS has published two detailed articles on the intermediate-sanctions excise tax in its Continuing Professional Education Texts. *See* Lawrence M. Brauer and Leonard J. Henzke, "Intermediate Sanctions (IRC 4958) Update," *IRS Exempt Organizations Continuing Professional Education Technical Instruction Program for Fiscal Year 2003* (2002), and Lawrence M. Brauer, Toussaint T. Tyson, Leonard J. Henzke, and Debra J. Kawecki, "An Introduction to I.R.C. 4958 (Intermediate Sanctions)," *IRS Exempt Organizations Continuing Professional Education Technical Instruction Program for Fiscal Year 2002*, 260 (2001). Although "An Introduction to I.R.C. 4958 (Intermediate Sanctions)" was written prior to the publication of the final regulations, much of the discussion remains relevant, and the article contains several helpful checklists. *See also* Internal Revenue Manual [7.8.1] Chapter 28.

84 I.R.C. § 4958(a)(1).

85 *Id.* § 4958(b).

86 *Id.* § 4958(a)(2).

87 *Id.* § 4958(d)(2).

88 "Standards for Recognition of Tax-Exempt Status if Private Benefit Exists," 73 Fed. Reg. 16519–25 (Mar. 28, 2008).

89 *Id.*

5.2.7.2 Excess-Benefit Transactions and the Rebuttable Presumption

For intermediate-sanctions purposes, a benefit is an "excess benefit" if it has a value in excess of the fair market value of the goods and services for which it is given.[90] A benefit will not be an excess benefit if it is reasonable. The legislative history underlying Code § 4958 contains guidelines for raising a "rebuttable presumption" of the reasonableness and fair market value of payments made to disqualified persons.[91] The final Treasury Regulations implement these guidelines by providing that payments under a compensation arrangement are presumed to be reasonable, and the transfer of property is presumed to be at fair market value, if the following three conditions are met: (1) the specific compensation arrangement, or specified terms of a property transfer, is approved in advance by an authorized body (*i.e.*, the board of directors or trustees or appropriately qualified committee thereof) that is composed entirely of individuals that do not have a conflict of interest with respect to the transaction; (2) the board or committee obtained and relied upon appropriate data as to comparability; and (3) the board or committee adequately documented the basis for its determination.[92]

Although the intermediate-sanctions rules only apply to transactions and arrangements involving disqualified persons, the process required to qualify for the rebuttable-presumption protection against intermediate sanctions is a prudent one to follow for any compensation arrangement or purchase and sale transaction involving an exempt organization and an individual or nonexempt organization.

5.2.7.3 Disqualified Persons

The final Treasury Regulations provide important guidance concerning the definition of a "disqualified person." The Treasury Regulations specify certain persons deemed to be persons in a position to have substantial influence, and certain others as persons deemed not to be in a position to have substantial influence.[93] A person is deemed to be in a position to have substantial influence over the affairs of a tax-exempt organization, and thus to be a disqualified person, if he or she: (1) serves on the organization's governing body and is entitled to vote; (2) is the president, chief executive officer, or chief operating officer of the organization;[94] or (3) is the treasurer or chief financial officer of the organization.[95] A person is deemed *not* to have substantial influence, and thus not to be a disqualified person, if (1) the person is an organization described in § 501(c)(3) or (2) the person is an employee receiving total direct and indirect economic benefits in an amount less than the amount of compensation necessary to be highly compensated as defined in § 414(q)(1)(B)(i) (currently $110,000), who is

---

[90] *Id.* § 4958(c)(1); Treas. Reg. § 53.4958-1(b); Treas. Reg. § 53.4958-4(a)(1). *See also Caracci v. Commissioner*, 188 T.C. 379 (2002) (property transfer); Tech. Adv. Mem. 200244028 (June 21, 2002) (executive compensation); Tech. Adv. Mem. 200243057 (July 2, 2002) (compensation and benefits).

[91] H. Rep. No. 506, 104th Cong., 2d Sess. 56, 57 (1996).

[92] Treas. Reg. § 53.4958-6(c). See "Intermediate Sanctions (IRC 4958) Update," at E-33-E-38; "An Introduction to I.R.C. 4958 (Intermediate Sanctions)," at 270, 327–33; Rebuttable Presumption Checklists in Appendices 4 and 5.

[93] *See* Treas. Reg. § 53.4958-3(c) and (d); "Intermediate Sanctions (IRC 4958) Update," at E-8-E-9;"An Introduction to I.R.C. 4958 (Intermediate Sanctions)," at 261–63.

[94] An individual is considered to serve in such capacity, regardless of title, if he or she has or shares ultimate responsibility for implementing decisions of the governing body or supervising the management, administration, or operation of the organization. Treas. Reg. § 53.4958-3(c)(2).

[95] An individual is considered to be the treasurer or chief financial officer, regardless of title, if he or she has or shares ultimate responsibility for managing the finances of the organization. Treas. Reg. § 53.4958-3(c)(3).

not a substantial contributor within the meaning of § 507(d)(2) or otherwise within the definition of disqualified person.[96]

In all other cases, the determination of whether a person is a disqualified person is left to a facts-and-circumstances inquiry. The Treasury Regulations set forth certain facts and circumstances "tending to show" that a person has substantial influence. These include whether the person: (1) is a founder of the organization; (2) is a substantial contributor (within the meaning of Code § 507(d)(2)); (3) is one whose compensation is based primarily on revenues derived from activities of the organization that he or she controls;[97] (4) has or shares authority to control or determine a substantial portion of the organization's capital expenditures, operating budget, or compensation; (5) manages a discrete segment or activity of the organization that represents a substantial portion of the activities, assets, income, or expenses of the organization; (6) owns a controlling interest in an entity that is a disqualified person; or (7) is a non-stock corporation controlled, directly or indirectly, by one or more disqualified persons. The regulations make clear that this list is not exclusive.[98] Therefore, a person who has managerial control over a portion of an organization or over a subsidiary of an organization may nevertheless be in a position to exercise substantial influence over the affairs of the organization.

The Treasury Regulations set forth other facts and circumstances "tending to show" that a person is not a disqualified person. These include:

1. the person has taken a *bona fide* vow of poverty as an employee, agent, or on behalf of a religious organization;
2. the person is an independent contractor (*e.g.*, an attorney, accountant or investment manager, or advisor) whose sole relationship to the organization is providing professional advice (without having decision-making authority) with respect to transactions from which the contractor will not economically benefit either directly or indirectly (aside from customary fees for the professional advice rendered);
3. the direct supervisor of the individual is not a disqualified person;
4. the person does not participate in management decisions affecting the organization as a whole or a discrete segment or activity of the organization that represents a substantial portion of the activities, assets, income, or expenses of the organization, compared to the organization as a whole; and
5. any preferential treatment a person receives based on the size of that person's donation also is offered to all other donors making a comparable contribution as part of a solicitation intended to attract a substantial number of contributions.[99]

The Treasury Regulations include 13 examples analyzing the facts and circumstances of whether a person is a disqualified person, including (among others) a for-profit hospital management company

---

[96] Treas. Reg. § 53.4958-3(d).

[97] Note that this factor does not take into account whether the activities the person controls represent a substantial portion of the overall activities of the exempt organization.

[98] *See* Treas. Reg. § 53.4958-3(e)(2).

[99] *See id.* § 53.4958-3(e)(3).

managing a whole-hospital joint venture, a hospital-employed radiologist, and the head of a hospital's cardiology department.[100]

The legislative history specifically rejects the IRS view that all physicians are insiders.[101] The Treasury Regulations include two examples involving physicians. In the first, a radiologist is deemed not to have substantial influence where the physician is employed by a large acute-care hospital, has no managerial authority over any substantial part of the hospital's operations, does not serve as a supervisor over hospital employees other than giving instructions to staff with respect to the physician's own radiology work, is compensated primarily in the form of a fixed salary, is eligible to receive an incentive award based on revenues of the radiology department, is not related to any other disqualified person at the hospital, and does not serve on the hospital board or as an officer.[102]

A second example, however, involves a cardiologist who is the head of the same hospital's cardiology department and who is deemed to be a disqualified person. Although neither a board member nor an officer, the physician has managerial authority for the cardiology department, which is a major source of patients and represents a substantial portion of the hospital's income, as compared to the hospital as a whole. The physician has authority to allocate the department's budget, including authority to distribute incentive bonuses among cardiologists according to criteria he can set.[103]

The legislative history underlying Code § 4958 states that a person could be in a position to exercise substantial influence over a tax-exempt organization even if the person was not an employee of and was not compensated directly by the tax-exempt organization, but was formally an employee of a subsidiary—taxable or tax-exempt—controlled by the parent exempt organization.[104] The Treasury Regulations make clear that, in the case of multiple organizations affiliated by common control, the determination of whether a person has substantial influence must be made separately for each applicable tax-exempt organization.[105] The Treasury Regulations also provide, however, that an economic benefit may be provided directly or indirectly, including through the use of one or more entities controlled or affiliated with an applicable tax-exempt organization. Thus, where a tax-exempt parent causes a taxable subsidiary to pay excessive compensation to, or engage in a transaction at other than fair market value with, a disqualified person of the parent, these arrangements may well fall within the definition of excess-benefit transactions.[106]

---

100 *Id.* § 53.4958-3(g). Example 5 in the disqualified-person section of the regulations demonstrates that a person who had no prior relationship with the organization prior to the transaction at issue can become a disqualified person as a result of the transaction. The effect of this position, however, is somewhat limited by the special provisions relating to initial contracts set forth in Treas. Reg. § 53.4958-4(a)(3).

101 H. Rep. No. 506 at 58, n.12.

102 Treas. Reg. § 53.4958-3(g), Example 10.

103 *Id.* Example 11.

104 H.R. Rep. No. 104-506 at 58 n.10 (Mar. 28, 1996).

105 Treas. Reg. § 53.4958-3(f).

106 *Id.* § 53.4958-4(a)(2).

5.2.7.4 Relationship to Revocation Sanction

Intermediate sanction excise tax may be imposed instead of revocation of tax exemption or, in extreme cases, intermediate sanctions may be imposed along with revocation of exemption. The first Tax Court case to interpret the intermediate sanctions provisions,[107] concluded that disqualified persons were liable for excess benefit taxes but that the tax exemption of the organization should not be revoked. The case involved several § 501(c)(3) corporations owning home health agencies that were controlled by the same family. The exempt organizations transferred all their assets and liabilities to for-profit corporations owned by the family after obtaining a valuation indicating that the exempt organizations' liabilities exceeded their assets. The Tax Court found that the transferred assets far exceeded the consideration paid and indicated that first-level excise taxes were due. The Court of Appeals, however, reversed the Tax Court decision and rendered judgment for the taxpayers, finding that as a matter of law no excess benefits were received.

5.2.8 Unrelated Business Activities

A § 501(c)(3) organization is subject to tax on income generated by its unrelated business activities. An activity is an unrelated trade or business if the conduct of the activity does not have a substantial causal relationship (other than the production of income) to the accomplishment of the organization's exempt purposes. In general, the IRS takes into account the nature of the activity; that is, whether the activity is inherently exempt or commercial in nature. If the activity is not inherently exempt, the organization must demonstrate a substantial causal relationship to the accomplishment of an exempt purpose.

An organization is considered "operated exclusively" for one or more § 501(c)(3) exempt purposes "only if it engages primarily in activities which accomplish one or more of" the exempt purposes specified in its articles of incorporation. If "more than an insubstantial part" of an organization's activities is not "in furtherance of an exempt purpose," such organization will not be regarded as operated exclusively for exempt purposes, and its exempt status may be jeopardized. The phrase "more than an insubstantial part of [an organization's] activities" is not further defined in the regulations under § 501(c)(3). Therefore, the IRS and the courts have made such determinations on a case-by-case basis.

There is no "bright line" for determining what constitutes an insubstantial portion. The IRS is likely to take into account the following five factors in determining whether a § 501(c)(3) organization's unrelated business activities are substantial:

1. the time, attention, and importance given by the officers and directors of the organization to exempt activities as compared with unrelated business activities;
2. the organization's expenditures for exempt activities as compared with expenditures for unrelated business activities;
3. the organization's income from exempt activities as compared with income from unrelated business activities;

107 *Caracci v. Commissioner*, 118 T.C. 379 (2002), *rev'd*, 456 F.3d 444 (5th Cir. 2006).

4. the organization's reasonable expectation of earning a profit; and
5. staff time spent on exempt activities, as compared with staff time spent on unrelated business activities.

An exempt organization will be subject to unrelated business income tax (UBIT) on its share of the income of a partnership or limited-liability company (LLC) taxed as a partnership to the extent that the income was generated from partnership activities that are unrelated to the exempt partner's § 501(c)(3) purposes.[108]

The IRS has found various hospital businesses to be related to the hospital's exempt function: (a) the operation of a gift shop, which is patronized by patients, visitors making purchases for patients, and employees;[109] (b) the operation of a cafeteria and coffee shop for employees and the medical staff;[110] (c) the operation of a parking lot for patients and visitors;[111] (d) the sale of pharmaceuticals by a hospital pharmacy to its "patients";[112] (e) the income received by a teaching and research hospital for the performance of pathological diagnostic tests on samples submitted by physicians associated with the hospital;[113] (f) the sale of durable medical equipment (in certain limited cases);[114] (g) the rental of pagers to staff physicians;[115] and (h) the leasing of space in a medical office building and the furnishing of services to physicians (if the lease enhances the use of diagnostic facilities, helps patient admissions, increases the availability of physicians for duty, and enhances their participation in medical education and research programs).[116]

---

108 I.R.C. § 512(c).

109 Rev. Rul. 69-267, 1969-1 C.B. 160.

110 *Id.* 1969-1 C.B. 160.

111 *Id.*

112 "Patients" may be one of six categories of individuals: (1) a person admitted as an inpatient; (2) a person receiving general or emergency diagnostic, therapeutic, or preventive health services from outpatient facilities of a hospital; (3) a person referred to a hospital's outpatient facilities for specific diagnosis or treatment; (4) a person refilling a prescription received during treatment as a patient; (5) a person receiving medical services as a part of a hospital-administered home care program; and (6) a person receiving medical care and services in a hospital-affiliated extended care facility. Rev. Rul. 68-376, 1968-2 C.B. 246; Priv. Ltr. Rul. 8206093, 8131063. Nevertheless, the sale of pharmaceutical supplies by an exempt hospital to *private patients of physicians* who have offices in a medical building owned by the hospital is an unrelated business, with income therefrom constituting UBI. Rev. Rul. 68-375, 1968-2 C.B. 245. Likewise, sales of pharmaceuticals by a hospital to the general public are UBI. To treat such income as exempt from taxation would permit hospital-owned pharmacies to unfairly compete with commercial pharmacies. *Carle Found. v. United States*, 611 F.2d 1192 (7th Cir. 1979), *cert. denied*, 449 U.S. 824 (1980).

113 *St. Luke's Hosp. of Kansas City v. United States*, 494 F. Supp. 85 (W.D. Mo. 1980); Rev. Rul. 85-109, 1985-2 C.B. 165. Thus, unless such laboratory tests are provided to hospital patients or patients of physicians on the medical staff of a teaching hospital, such services constitute UBI. An exception to this general rule is stated in Rev. Rul. 85-110, 1985-2 C.B. 166, where the service acknowledged a "unique circumstances" exception exists if alternative facilities for providing the service are not available within a reasonable distance, or if the facility is unable or inadequate to conduct such tests, or if the analysis is needed on an emergency basis. In such cases, the income generated from performing the tests is not UBI. *See also* Priv. Ltr. Rul. 9023041 (Mar. 9, 1990).

114 *See* Rev. Rul. 78-435, 1978-2 C.B. 181, in which the IRS noted that the sale of hearing aids by a hospital whose primary activity is the operation of a clinic that provides various rehabilitation services to handicapped individuals (including testing and evaluating their hearing and recommending necessary hearing aids) was not an unrelated trade or business. By selling hearing aids to such patients, maximum assistance to the patients was assured.

115 Tech. Adv. Mem. 8452011.

116 *See* Rev. Rul. 69-463, 1969-2 C.B. 131; Rev. Rul. 69-464, 1969-2 C.B. 132; LTR 8452099.

5.2.9 Political Activity Prohibition and Lobbying Limitation

5.2.9.1 *Political Activity Prohibition*

The Code absolutely prohibits tax-exempt healthcare organizations from engaging in any political campaign activity. Section 501(c)(3) of the Code defines prohibited political activity as participation or intervention in any political campaign on behalf of or in opposition to any candidate for public office. Any violation of this prohibition will result in the loss of the organization's tax-exempt status, as well as the incurrence of substantial excise-tax penalties.[117]

A candidate is defined as any individual who offers oneself, or is proposed by others, as a contestant for an elective public office, regardless of whether such office is national, state, or local. Neither the Code nor the regulations define the term "public office;" however, the IRS has identified the following as characteristics of a public office: (1) created by statute; (2) continuing; (3) not occasional or contractual; (4) has a fixed term of office; and (5) requires an oath of office.[118]

Prohibited activity includes the publication or distribution of written or printed statements on behalf of or in opposition to a candidate. A written or oral endorsement of a candidate and the rating of candidates (even on a non-partisan basis) is prohibited. A § 501(c)(3) organization also may not provide or solicit financial or other forms of support to or for candidates or political organizations.[119]

Revenue Ruling 2007-41[120] provides formal IRS guidance concerning common situations that my involve political activity, including: (a) individual activities of the leaders of the exempt organization); (b) appearances at exempt organization events by candidates in a candidate or a non-candidate capacity; (c) issue advocacy; and (d) voter education, voter registration, and get-out-the-vote drives.[121] The guidance provides a useful basis for the development of policies and procedures designed to maintain compliance with the § 501(c)(3) political activity prohibition.

5.2.9.2 *Lobbying Limitation*

In contrast to the Code's absolute prohibition against engaging in political activities, a tax-exempt healthcare organization may engage in activities with the purpose of influencing legislation, so long as those activities do not become a substantial part of the organization's activities. Unfortunately, no clear guidelines have been established as to when lobbying activities will constitute a substantial part of an organization's activities. Section 501(h) of the Code permits some tax-exempt organizations to elect to avail themselves of a special set of rules that provides specific guidelines concerning the permissible

---

[117] I.R.C. § 4962. *But see* Gen. Couns. Mem. 39414 (Sept. 25, 1985), which suggests that in some cases the IRS has excused *de minimis* political activity.

[118] Judith E. Kindell and John Francis Reilly, "Election Year Issues," *IRS Exempt Organizations Continuing Professional Instruction Program for Fiscal Year 2002*, at 335 (2001).

[119] Treas. Reg. § 1.501(c)(3)-1(c)(3)(iii).

[120] 2007-25 I.R.B. (June 18, 2007).

[121] In June 2007, the IRS released an update on the political activity prohibition enforcement activities the IRS undertook during the federal 2006 campaigns as part of its Political Activities Compliance Initiative (PACI) project, which was previously discussed in the IRS' February 2006 fact sheet entitled, "Election Year Activities and the Prohibition on Political Campaign Intervention for Section 501(c)(3) Organizations (FS-2006-17, (February 2007). *See* http://www.irs.gov/pub/irs-tege/2006paci_report_5-30-07.pdf., http://www.irs.gov/charities/article/0,id=154622,00.html.

amount of expenditures for legislative activities. This election, however, is not available to organizations controlled by a religious order.

Legislative activities include: (i) advocating the adoption or rejection of legislation; (ii) engaging in direct lobbying by communicating with legislators, their staff, and, under certain circumstances, executive-branch officials who participate in the formulation of legislation for the purpose of proposing, supporting, or opposing legislation; and (iii) engaging in "grass-roots" lobbying by urging the public to contact members of a legislative body for the purpose of proposing, supporting, or opposing legislation.[122]

Public education and advocacy are distinct from lobbying. The term "educational" includes the instruction of the public on subjects useful to the individual and beneficial to the community. An activity may be educational even though it advocates a particular position or viewpoint, so long as it presents a sufficiently full and fair exposition of the pertinent facts as to permit an individual or the public to form an independent opinion or conclusion. Therefore, engaging in and making available the results of nonpartisan analysis is study or research, not lobbying. The organization is not engaging in educational activities, however, if it merely presents unsupported opinion.

5.3 Practical Application of the Fundamental Exemption Requirements

IRS policymaking and enforcement initiatives that affect exempt healthcare organizations have focused on the application of the private-inurement prohibition and the public-benefit requirement in various contexts such as the purchase or sale of a business or other assets, compensation arrangements, physician recruitment arrangements, joint ventures, courtesy discounts, and the use of taxable affiliates.

5.3.1 Purchase and Sale of a Business or Other Assets

An exempt organization may purchase or sell a business or other asset (and pay value for that business's intangible assets such as goodwill) from or to a for-profit entity so long as the organization pays or receives no more or less than fair market value for the business or asset.[123] The transaction must be conducted at arm's length, and the amounts paid by the tax-exempt organization must be no greater than the fair market value of the assets, including intangible assets.[124]

The IRS defines fair market value as the price at which a willing purchaser and a willing seller agree, neither operating under any compulsion to buy or sell, and both having reasonable knowledge of the relevant facts.[125] In general, fair market value is determined within the framework of the business enterprise's worth to the most likely hypothetical purchaser, which is assumed to be a commercial healthcare corporation, even if the purchaser is tax-exempt. The IRS has recognized that fair market value is a question of fact, depending upon the circumstances of each case.

122 Treas. Reg. § 1.501(c)(3)-1(c)(3)(ii).
123 Rev. Rul. 76-91, 1976-1 C.B. 149, in which the IRS approves the use of the capitalization of excess earnings method set forth in Rev. Rul. 68-609, 1968-2 C.B. 327, to value the intangible assets being purchased but does not indicate that this is the only acceptable method of valuing intangible assets.
124 *Id.*
125 Rev. Rul. 59-60, 1959-1 C.B. 237.

Where an organization purchases assets from an independent third party, a presumption exists that a purchase price arrived at through arm's-length negotiations represents fair market value. Where the purchaser has a close relationship to the seller at the time of sale, however, the nature of the relationship brings into question whether the elements of arm's-length negotiations are present. The IRS has stated that, in situations where the close relationship between purchaser and seller precludes arm's-length negotiations, the fair market value of the assets acquired must be established through a valuation performed by a qualified, independent third party.[126] The IRS will not only look to see if a valuation was performed, but also will scrutinize the valuation methodology and underlying assumptions.[127]

The IRS has not released any binding guidance with respect to the valuation of businesses to be acquired or disposed of by a tax-exempt organization. However, it has released a limited amount of non-binding guidance on valuation of medical practices to be purchased by an exempt organization.[128] While this guidance addresses valuation issues only in the context of medical practice acquisitions, the guidance can be applied generally to purchase and sale transactions in which exempt organizations are involved.

The valuation guidance states that a valuation appraisal should include all recognized approaches for estimating value, including the market approach, cost approach, and income approach. Although the IRS requires an analysis of all three methodologies, it has indicated that the income approaches are the most relevant in the context of valuing a physician practice.[129] The IRS will apply two "income" approaches: (i) the "excess earnings method;"[130] and (ii) the "discounted future cash flow" method.[131] The cost and market approaches generally are used as benchmarks to determine whether the valuation reached under the income approach is reasonable. The IRS also has reiterated that a "weighting" approach is inappropriate, and that "no useful purpose is served by taking an average of several factors... and basing the valuation on the result."[132]

---

126 Rev. Rul. 76-91, 1976-1 C.B. 149.

127 The Tax Court also has indicated that it will carefully scrutinize valuation methodology and underlying assumptions. In *Caracci*, the Tax Court declined to adopt either parties' approach to the valuation completely, finding certain assumptions by both valuation experts not to be credible, and parts of each methodology flawed.

128 Much of this guidance can be found in the continuing materials that the IRS prepares for its internal continuing education programs. *See* Charles F. Kaiser, Phyllis D. Haney, and T. J. Sullivan, "Integrated Delivery Systems and Joint Venture Dissolutions Update," *IRS Exempt Organizations Continuing Professional Education Technical Instruction Program for Fiscal Year 1995*, 153 (1994); Charles F. Kaiser and Amy Henchy, "Valuation of Medical Practices," *IRS Exempt Organizations Continuing Professional Education Technical Program for Fiscal Year 1996*, 404 (1995). While the CPE Text represents non-precedential guidance, which means it may not be relied upon by taxpayers or the IRS, the CPE Text does serve as a good indication of what the IRS believes to be the correct statement of law and how the IRS would rule under a particular set of facts.

129 "Valuation of Medical Practices."

130 The excess-earnings method is described in Rev. Rul. 68-609, 1968-2 C.B. 327, and was approved for valuation of intangibles in Rev. Rul. 76-91, 1976-1 C.B. 149.

131 Raymond C. Miller, "Basic Business Appraisals," (1984); 1994 CPE Text, at 236. "Valuation of Medical Practices," at 417–38.

132 "Valuation," *1978 IRS Exempt Organizations Continuing Professional Education Technical Instruction Program*, Chapter J (1978); *see also* Rev. Rul. 59-60, 1959-1 C.B. 237. The IRS will also take into account whether the primary purpose of a medical practice acquisition is (a) a "bail-out" of a financially distressed medical practice, which is otherwise important to the success of the exempt-organization purchaser; or (b) an attempt to find a purchaser for a practice for which no conceivable market exists. "Integrated Delivery Systems and Joint Venture," at 236.

The IRS will scrutinize closely the various assumptions used in an income-approach valuation of a medical practice.[133] For example, the IRS requires the use of after-tax cash flows and will scrutinize revenue and expense projections. The projected future physician-compensation expenses used in the income-approach valuation should be based on the actual compensation that will be paid to the selling physician under a post-acquisition employment arrangement. The valuation may incorporate certain assumptions about future benefits, such as synergy, growth, or expansion; these assumptions, however, should hold true for the entity as a stand-alone business or by virtue of *any* purchaser's ability to achieve such benefits. The valuation should not include assumptions about such matters if they are unique to the particular purchaser. For example, if a hospital-purchaser is exempt from state sales tax, then the projections should not include a reduction in sales-tax expense for the seller.[134]

Although the IRS has expressed a preference for the discounted cash-flow income-valuation approach in medical practice acquisitions, it also began to recognize the validity of the market approach in late 1995. To support the validity of the market approach in a particular case, however, the IRS will insist upon detailed documentation of comparability, including information concerning actual sales of "comparable" physician practices in the same community, but the actual purchase prices must be evaluated, adjusted, and applied to the operating data of the selling practice. Moreover, factors affecting comparability should be discussed (*e.g.*, markets served; competitive position; profitability; growth prospects; risk perceptions; capital structure; physician compensation, age, health, reputation, and productivity; average revenue per physician; cost structure; and average revenue per visit or covered-life-to-revenue mix).[135]

The valuation report should include the following: an executive summary; a review of the nature of the business and history of the enterprise; the economic outlook in general, and that of the specific industry in particular; the book value of the stock and hard assets; the financial condition of the business; the earning capacity of the business; the dividend-paying capacity of the business; the estimated value of the intangible assets; a description of the subject assets; and (where applicable) a discussion of comparable enterprises and their market value.[136]

In the IRS's view, continuing a long-term relationship with the selling physicians helps to protect the exempt purchaser's investment in the anticipated future income stream to be generated by the physicians; the investment is represented by the exempt purchaser's payment for the practice.[137] The IRS has expressed no definitive position on the use of non-competition covenants in this context; however, it has expressed what may be viewed as a preference for using them in connection with practice-acquisition agreements and corresponding service relationships.[138]

---

[133] "Valuation of Medical Practices," at 409.

[134] *Id.*; *see also* "Integrated Delivery Systems and Joint Venture," at 167–68.

[135] "Valuation of Medical Practices," at 409.

[136] Rev. Rul. 59-60, 1959-1 C.B. 237.

[137] "Integrated Delivery Systems and Joint Venture," at 222.

[138] *Id.*

5.3.2 Compensation Arrangements

5.3.2.1 General Principles

A tax-exempt organization may pay reasonable compensation to its executives and its employed and non-employed physicians for the services they render without jeopardizing its tax-exempt status. The determination of whether total compensation is reasonable depends on the facts and circumstances of each case, and requires an examination of the total compensation paid, including base salary, bonuses, deferred and incentive compensation, benefits (including fringe benefits), and all other items of value (such as beneficial loans and leases) provided to the person delivering services to the organization.[139]

The compensation principles from Code § 162 provide useful guidance for evaluating the reasonableness of compensation for purposes of Code § 501(c)(3)'s private-inurement prohibition and public-benefit requirement. For purposes of Code § 162, "reasonable compensation is the amount that would ordinarily be paid for like services by like organizations in like circumstances."[140] In determining the reasonableness of compensation under Code § 162, the IRS will consider whether the compensation is comparable to what other organizations pay their employees based on the following comparability factors:

- what similar organizations pay persons of comparable experience and qualifications performing comparable services;
- the duties to be performed;
- the time devoted to the duties;
- the employee's background, experience, and knowledge of the business;
- the size of the business;
- the employee's contribution to profit-making;
- the time the employee devotes to the business;
- the character and amount of the employee's responsibility;
- the time of the year when compensation is determined;
- the working conditions;
- the prevalent economic conditions; and
- whether the negotiations for such salaries were conducted at arm's length.[141]

An exempt organization may rely on various third-party sources for data and other information needed to demonstrate comparability.[142] The legislative history underlying Code § 4958 states that an

[139] Jean Wright and Jay Rotz, "Reasonable Compensation," *IRS Exempt Organization Continuing Professional Education Technical Instruction Program for Fiscal Year 1992*, 191 (1991); "Compensation," *IRS Exempt Organization Continuing Professional Education Technical Instruction Program for Fiscal Year 1990*, 171 (1989).

[140] Treas. Reg. § 1.162-7(b)(3). The proposed intermediate-sanction regulations under Code § 4958 uses this same definition. Prop. Treas. Reg. § 1.53.4958-4(b)(2).

[141] Internal Revenue Manual 4233, § 232.2 (last revised Mar. 11, 1985).

[142] "Reasonable Compensation," lists 10 such sources.

individual need not accept reduced compensation merely because he or she is serving a tax-exempt organization.[143] Many sources of objective comparability data exist for physician compensation for a broad spectrum of specialties.[144]

5.3.2.2 *Incentive Compensation Generally*

The mere establishment of incentive compensation will not *per se* jeopardize an organization's tax-exempt status where the plan advances the exempt purpose of a hospital by improving the quality and efficiency of patient care, and is not a mere device to distribute profits.

Incentive compensation is, however, of special concern to the IRS. Its Hospital Audit Guidelines instruct IRS auditors to scrutinize closely incentive-compensation arrangements for potential inurement.[145] When reviewing incentive-compensation arrangements, the IRS seeks to determine whether the total compensation is reasonable, and whether the method by which incentive compensation is determined is acceptable. In particular, the IRS requires that incentive-compensation arrangements (a) are not either a device to distribute profits or tantamount to giving private individuals an "equity" interest in the exempt organization and (b) do not create a significant conflict between serving the personal interests of the individual involved and serving the tax-exempt purpose of the organization.

Accordingly, the IRS has approved incentive-compensation arrangements, but only with the presence of certain safeguards: (a) an arm's-length relationship; (b) contingent payments that serve a real and discernible business purpose; (c) the amount of compensation is not dependent principally on incoming revenues, but rather on accomplishment of the objectives of the compensation arrangement; (d) to the extent that compensation is related to revenues, the compensation is based on a percentage of gross or adjusted gross revenues (and not on net income); (e) actual results do not indicate abuse or unwarranted benefits; (f) presence of a ceiling or reasonable maximum amount of compensation; and (g) total compensation, including the incentive amount, is reasonable.[146]

If a compensation package satisfies these tests, then the mere fact that the compensation involves the payment of incentive compensation will not *per se* result in private inurement, impermissible private benefit, or an excess benefit for purposes of the intermediate-sanctions excise taxes.

5.3.2.3 *Physician Incentive Compensation*

In 1999, the IRS discussed the application of these safeguards in the context of physician incentive compensation, and identified the following additional factors to be considered: (a) whether the arrangement was established by an independent board of directors or independent compensation com-

---

[143] JCX-7-96, Bureau of National Affairs, Daily Tax Report L-1 (Mar. 22, 1996). The 1992 CPE Text lists five sources for comparability data drawn from for-profit businesses.

[144] For example, the Medical Group Management Association annually publishes a physician compensation survey in its *Physician Advisory Newsletter*. The Graduate Medical Education National Advisory Committee and the American Medical Association publish similar surveys. Other sources of information may include state or local medical societies, national trade associations, the "Big Five" accounting firms, healthcare consulting firms, benefits and compensation firms (*e.g.*, William Mercer, Hay Associates), and physician-recruiting firms (*e.g.*, Jackson and Coker).

[145] Examination Guidelines for Hospitals, Announcement 92-83, 1992-22 I.R.B. 59, § 333.3(6).

[146] Gen. Couns. Mem. 38,905 (Oct. 6, 1982), *citing* Gen. Couns. Mem. 32453 (Nov. 30, 1962).

mittee; (b) whether the arrangement has the potential for reducing the charitable services or benefits the organization would otherwise provide; (c) whether the arrangement takes into account data that measures quality of care and patient satisfaction; and (d) whether the arrangement rewards the physician based on services the physician actually performs.[147]

It is also important to note that the intermediate-sanction provisions of Code § 4958 includes in the definition of "excess benefit transactions" revenue-sharing arrangements that are defined by Treasury regulations as resulting in prohibited private inurement.[148] The final Treasury Regulations simply reserve that topic; currently, no such arrangements have been defined.[149]

5.3.2.4 Executive Compensation

In determining whether executive compensation is reasonable, it is necessary to examine the total compensation paid to the executive, including base salary, bonuses, fringe benefits, and other items of value provided to the executive. As discussed in the preceding section, bonuses and other incentive compensation vehicles are permitted if appropriate safeguards are present. An additional area of concern related to executive compensation is fringe benefits. In 2001, the IRS included an extensive discussion of the tax implications of fringe benefits in its Continuing Professional Education Text for Fiscal Year 2002.[150] The discussion focused on a number of issues related to fringe benefits, including how they are analyzed and valued for purposes of determining whether (1) total compensation is reasonable, (2) the benefits are provided in exchange for services, and (3) the benefits are properly reported and taxed.[151] In 2002, the IRS issued two Technical Advice Memoranda involving possible imposition of intermediate-sanctions excise taxes in the context of executive compensation.[152]

In 2004, the IRS conducted a "soft contact audit" initiative in which it sought detailed information from 2,000 exempt organizations concerning their executive compensation practices, including the amount of cash and non-cash compensation paid, the exempt organization's internal compensation review processes (including the use of outside consultants), and the nature and extent of the data supporting the reported compensation levels. The IRS also required identification and discussion of any business or financial ties between the exempt organization's disqualified persons and its independent contractors. In its 2007 summary of the results of the project, the IRS reported that, in general, there were widespread significant reporting errors or omissions for compensation paid or benefits (such as cars or cell phones) to officers or high-ranking employees, and that 31% of the organizations reviewed filed amended returns or schedules.[153]

---

147 Lawrence M. Brauer and Charles F. Kaiser III, "Physician Incentive Compensation," *IRS Exempt Organization Continuing Professional Education Technical Instruction Program for Fiscal Year 2000*, 30–33. *See also* IRS Information Letter 2002-0021 (Jan. 9, 2002).

148 I.R.C. § 4958(c)(2).

149 Treas. Reg. § 53.4958-5. The proposed intermediate sanctions regulations on this topic were abandoned.

150 "An Introduction to I.R.C. 4958 (Intermediate Sanctions)," at 291–323.

151 *Id.*

152 Tech. Adv. Mem. 200244028 and Tech. Adv. Mem. 200243057.

153 *See* "Report on Exempt Organizations Executive Compensation Compliance Project," at 5, available at http://www.irs.gov/pub/irs-tege/exec._comp._final.pdf.

This soft contact audit initiative culminated in significant revisions to the Form 990 annual information return relating to compensation paid to officers, directors, trustees, key employees and their five highest paid employees, and independent contractors.[154] Among the most notable changes are the following:

1. An organization must disclose compensation and benefits provided to the top 20 current "key employees" (*i.e.*, executives who do not fit within the fairly narrow definition of "officer"). A key employee is defined as an individual who receives $150,000 or more in compensation from the exempt organization and has certain types of responsibilities within the organization even if they do not bear an officer title. For example, physicians who chair a hospital's medical department would be treated as key employees for this purpose.
2. An organization must also report compensation paid to the five "highest compensated" employees who have certain officer-type responsibilities and who receive over $100,000 but less than $150,000 in reportable compensation.
3. An organization must report compensation paid to "former" officers, directors, trustees, key employees and five highest paid employees, reporting organizations who received compensation during a five-year lookback period.
4. If an organization disclosed any of the following on the Core Form, it must provide additional information on Schedule J to the Core Form: (a) compensation to a "former" officer, director, trustee, key employee, or five highest compensated employee; (b) more than $150,000 in compensation paid to any individual (including compensation from related organizations); or (c) participation in an arrangement in which an unrelated organization paid compensation to at least one of its officers, directors, trustees, key employees, or five highest compensated employees for services performed to the filing organization. Schedule J requires organizations to provide more detailed compensation information than included on the Core Form, such as incentive compensation, deferred compensation, nontaxable benefits, and compensation reported in a prior Form 990. It also requires additional information regarding other compensation practices, including, among others: (a) payment of "sensitive" compensation items including spousal travel, discretionary spending accounts, and tax-gross ups; (b) payment for first-class travel for any person whose compensation is being reported, including first-class upgrades on air travel (if paid for with organization funds); and (c) providing personal services for any person whose compensation is being reported (*e.g.*, payment for legal services).
5. The organization must disclose on the Core Form whether it reviews and approves executive compensation in a manner that qualifies for the IRS safe harbor under Section 4958. The IRS contemplates that a "yes" answer would be based, in part, on the use of an independent compensation consultant (or the use of data from an independent consultant).[155]

---

[154] Beginning with the 2008 Form 990, these changes are reflected in Part VII of the Core Form 990 and in Schedule J to the Core Form. On May 1, 2009, the IRS released a number of FAQs to guide organizations in their reporting of executive compensation on Part VII to the Form 990 and Schedule J. The FAQs contain responses to 11 separate questions and are available at http://www.irs.gov/pub/irs-tege/execcomptips_05_2009.pdf

[155] For this purpose, the IRS provides a fairly broad definition of independence: the consultant is independent if he or she does not have a family or business relationship with the Chief Executive Officer or Executive Director, and if a majority of

These Form 990 reporting changes signal the IRS' continuing focus on executive compensation programs and practices, and they reinforce the importance of approving executive compensation in a manner consistent with the rebuttable presumption of reasonableness, and that the market data being used by the board or board-appointed committee be "appropriate comparability data."[156] Tax-exempt organizations should pay close attention to their board-level process of reviewing and approving executive and physician compensation. A strong process led by the board or board-appointed committee, and one in which the data comparison is appropriate for the organization, will be the strongest defense against intermediate sanctions and also against a threat to exempt status.

5.3.3 Physician Recruitment Incentives

5.3.3.1 Background

The IRS has recognized that hospitals may need to offer incentives to attract qualified physicians in a particular specialty in order to provide quality healthcare to the community. The IRS historically has been concerned, however, that physician-recruitment arrangements may result in excessive private benefit to the recruited physician.[157] In the course of the past few years, the IRS has increased its scrutiny of physician recruiting activities.

The most common approach to physician recruitment is for an exempt hospital to provide financial assistance needed to bring a new physician into the community either in his or her own private practice or in the practice of an existing group practice. In such case, the hospital would not retain the physician either as an employee or as an independent contractor to provide services on the hospital's behalf.

In 1997, the IRS published Revenue Ruling 97-21,[158] providing physician-recruitment guidance to tax-exempt hospitals. The ruling applies to employed physicians, independent contractor physicians, and voluntary members of a hospital's medical staff who are establishing a private practice in the hospital's service area. The ruling states that, although the compensation of physicians providing services "to or on behalf of the hospital" is reviewed under a reasonable-compensation analysis, the compensation of physicians *not* providing services to or on behalf of the hospital should be scrutinized under a four-part analysis, including the following factors: (a) furtherance of charitable purposes; (b) potential

---

the consultant's appraisals during the same year are for other organizations, even if the consultant's firm also provides tax and audit services to the organization. This will enable many organizations that use their consultant for multiple engagements to take the position that the consultant is nevertheless independent.

[156] *Id.* at 1. The IRS has also addressed the importance of tax-exempt organizations implementing policies regarding executive compensation to maintain tax-exempt status. *See* "Governance and Related Topics – 501(c)(3) Organizations," at 3.

[157] Rev. Rul. 97-21, 1997-1 C.B. 121. The private-inurement prohibition technically does not apply to recruitment arrangements because a physician being newly recruited does not have an existing relationship that would trigger insider status. It is important in this regard, however, to distinguish between offering incentives to recruit new physicians and offering incentives to retain existing physicians. The inurement prohibition does apply to the latter. The IRS's definition of "Permissible Recruits" in the *Hermann Hospital Closing Agreement*, for example, is a "physician who either (i) is a recent graduate of a residency or fellowship program whether or not in the hospital's community or (ii) has not previously practiced in hospital's community or been affiliated with another hospital serving all or part of the hospital's community." This provision of the *Hermann Hospital Closing Agreement*, however, should be considered relative to subsequent guidance, such as Rev. Rul. 97-21 and the unpublished Priv. Ltr. Rul. dated July 31, 1998, which suggest that cross-town recruitment may be permissible in certain cases.

[158] Rev. Rul. 97-21.

for private inurement; (c) potential for excessive private benefit; and (d) potential for substantial illegal activities.[159]

The situations set forth in the ruling involved the use of a variety of recruiting incentives without a loss of exemption. The incentives include a one-time cash bonus, below-market rent for a limited number of years, a home-mortgage guarantee, start-up financial assistance, malpractice insurance and reimbursement of malpractice "tail" coverage, paid moving expenses, private-practice income guarantees for a limited number of years, and use of medical staff. These incentives were not all provided in each case.

Prior to the issuance of Revenue Ruling 97-21, the IRS's positions concerning recruitment were reflected in non-precedential guidance such as private letter rulings, general counsel memoranda, audit guidelines, and closing agreements.[160] Together with Revenue Ruling 97-21, such non-precedential guidance remains a useful source of insight into structuring recruitment arrangements.

5.3.3.2 Community Benefit Requirement

From these formal and informal sources of IRS guidance on physician recruitment emerges the clear message that the IRS will require a hospital to demonstrate and document that achieving a *bona fide* community benefit is the principal purpose of all physician recruitment arrangements (rather than increasing the hospital's market share or improving its competitive position).

The closing agreement in the case of Hermann Hospital provides the following examples of evidence of a demonstrable community need for physician: (a) a deficiency in the population-to-physician ratio for the relevant specialty (relative to the ideal ratio set forth in Graduate Medical Education National Advisory Committee reports); (b) documented demand for a particular medical service, coupled with a documented lack of availability of the service of long waiting periods for it; (c) designation of the relevant community as a "Health Professional Shortage Area;"[161] (d) demonstrated reluctance of physicians to relocate to the hospital's location in a rural or economically disadvantaged inner-city area; (e) a reasonably expected reduction in the number of physicians in a given specialty due to anticipated retirement of existing physician; or (f) documented lack of physicians serving indigent or Medicaid patients, and a commitment by the recruited physician to serve a substantial number of such patients.

In an unpublished IRS Private Letter Ruling, the IRS also provided useful guidance to tax-exempt hospitals on permissible recruitment incentives that can be extended to new physicians entering private practice. It also provides detail concerning the facts and circumstances that supported the commu-

---

[159] An example of potential illegality would be a violation of the Medicare antifraud and abuse laws. A discussion of the effect of illegal activities is outside the scope of this Chapter, but one can be found in Gen. Couns. Mem. 39862 (Nov. 22, 1991).

[160] *See, e.g.*, Gen. Couns. Mem. 39498 (Apr. 24, 1986); Gen. Couns. Mem. 39598 (Dec. 8, 1986); *Examination Guidelines for Hospitals* § 333.3(5), Announcement 92-83, 1992-22 I.R.B. 59; the *Hermann Hospital Closing Agreement* (Sept. 20, 1994), Bureau of National Affairs, "Highlights and Documents," 648 (Oct. 17, 1994). *See also* unpublished Priv. Ltr. Rul. dated July 31, 1998, in Bureau of National Affairs, Health Law Reporter 960 (June 10, 1999). (It has not been formally released by the IRS, and thus has no specific identifying number.)

[161] Health Professional Shortage Area is defined under 42 C.F.R. §§ 5.1–5.4.

nity-benefit rationale for the recruitment arrangement in that case.[162] A specific strategic focus of the hospital in recent years had been the development of a series of community health centers providing specialized non-tertiary inpatient and outpatient services. Designed to provide access to the hospital's services to a larger number of community residents, the centers were located in growing areas of the hospital's service area where a need existed for additional primary care and specialist physicians. The centers were being developed in conjunction with a primary care physician group loosely affiliated (*i.e.*, not owned or controlled by) with the hospital. The hospital's most recent community-needs assessment determined that, in order to address a shortage of primary-care physicians and certain physician specialists, additional physicians must be recruited to join the physician's group and to provide care in the communities served by the centers.

5.3.3.3 Income Guarantees

Guaranteeing the private-practice income of a newly recruited physician for a period of time is one of the most common forms of recruitment assistance provided by exempt hospitals. In such arrangements, the hospital agrees to fund the shortfall if the professional revenue generated by the physician during the guarantee period is not sufficient to support a specified level of monthly compensation and expenses. At the end of the guarantee period, the total amount of funds advanced and not repaid is converted to a loan. The following are the factors that the IRS likely would consider in evaluating an income guarantee: (a) whether the physician is relocating to the service area; (b) the reluctance of the physician or other physicians to relocate to the service area; (c) whether the period of any benefit provided is longer than two years; (d) whether sufficient evidence is present of *bona fide* community need; (e) whether the level of income guaranteed is reasonable; (f) whether a reasonable and explicit ceiling is established on the amount of any potential subsidy to be provided under the guarantee arrangement; (g) whether an unconditional obligation has been established to repay amounts advanced; and (h) if the physician's repayment obligation is forgiven in whole or in part, whether the forgiveness arrangement is demonstrably related to community benefit.[163] It is also essential that the terms and conditions of any forgiveness arrangement are structured so as to achieve the community benefit the recruitment arrangement was intended to achieve.[164]

The following are the factors that the IRS would likely consider in evaluating the loan aspects of an income guarantee: (a) whether a reasonable rate of interest (generally 1 to 2% above the prime rate) is charged; (b) whether the loan is secured by adequate assets; (c) whether the loan is approved by the board of directors, whose approval reflects consideration of the payment history of any prior loan; and (d) whether any variance between the terms of the loan and commercially available loan terms is treated and reported as compensation.[165]

---

162 Unpublished Priv. Ltr. Rul. dated July 31, 1998.

163 These factors emanate from Rev. Rul. 97-21, and the Examination Guidelines for Hospitals.

164 For example, any forgiveness of a loan is conditioned upon continued presence in private practice in the community, and is pro-ratable for no less than four years (which time period is specified at the time the loan is made); such forgiveness is supported, at the time provision for forgiveness is made, by evidence of a demonstrable need for the physician and the amount of the incentive. *Hermann Hospital Closing Agreement.*

165 *Examination Guidelines for Hospitals*, at § 333.3(10); *Hermann Hospital Closing Agreement.*

5.3.4 Joint Venture Arrangements Involving Exempt and Non-Exempt Participants

Prior to 1980, the IRS generally took the view that participation as a general partner[166] in a joint venture with a for-profit entity was *per se* inconsistent with continued tax-exempt status for a § 501(c)(3) organization.[167] The IRS's *per se* rule was based on the view that (1) the joint venture is a vehicle for sharing profits with other investors, (2) as a general partner the exempt organization has a fiduciary duty under state partnership law to further the private financial interests of its partners, and (3) as a general partner the exempt organization is exposed to unlimited liability for the debts of the partnership, which benefits its partners.

The IRS's *per se* prohibition was rejected by the Tax Court in *Plumstead Theatre Society v. Commissioner*,[168] in which a § 501(c)(3) organization acted as the sole general partner in a limited partnership with a for-profit corporation and individuals. The purpose of the partnership was to raise funds to produce a play. The Tax Court approved Plumstead's role as general partner and found that: (1) the formation of the partnership was the result of arm's length negotiations; (2) the exempt organization was not obligated to use its own funds to return any capital contributed by the limited partners; (3) the partnership had no interest in the exempt organization; (4) the limited partners had no control over the way the exempt organization managed its affairs; and (5) none of the limited partners was an officer or director of the exempt organization.

Since the Tax Court's decision in *Plumstead*, it has been the administrative position of the IRS that, under appropriate circumstances, an exempt organization may participate in a joint venture with a taxable entity without jeopardizing its tax-exempt status. The IRS's post-*Plumstead* position is generally regarded as imposing two basic requirements on an exempt organization serving as the general partner of a joint venture with for-profit participants. [169] The first requirement is that the partnership further the exempt organization's charitable purposes. The second requirement is that the partnership agreement permit the exempt organization as general partner to operate exclusively in furtherance of its exempt purposes, without regard to any state-law duty to maximize profits for other partners.

This two-part test has been interpreted and applied in many GCMs and PLRs that have added various refinements. First, the exempt general partner should receive distributions of partnership income at least in proportion to its capital contribution and its losses should not exceed its share of partnership capital.[170] Second, transactions between the partnership and its for-profit partners must be at arm's length and reflect fair market value, including reasonable compensation for services provided to the partnership.[171] Third, in determining whether the charitable purpose requirement is met, there should be evidence of community benefit such as creation of a new healthcare provider, expansion of com-

---

166 Participation by an exempt organization as a limited partner has not been raised by the IRS as a threat to exemption. The only issue in that case is whether the exempt organization's share of partnership income is subject to unrelated business income tax. Rev. Rul. 79-22, 1979-2 C.B. 236.

167 *Compare* GCM 36293 (May 30, 1975) (stating the *per se* position) with GCM 37852 (Feb. 15, 1979) (retreating somewhat from the *per se* rule).

168 74 T.C. 1324 (1980).

169 GCM 39005 (June 28, 1983). *See also* GCM 39862 (November 22, 1991); GCM 39732 (November 4, 1987); GCM 39546 (Aug. 14, 1986).

170 GCM 39732 (Nov. 4, 1987).

171 *Id.*

munity healthcare resources, improvement of treatment modalities, reduction of healthcare costs, or improvement of patient convenience and access to physicians.[172] Finally, there should be protections against conflicts of interest if insiders of the exempt organization general partner invest in the joint venture.[173]

5.3.4.1 *Whole Hospital Joint Ventures*

In March 1998, the IRS issued its first precedential guidance in this area with the release of Rev. Rul. 98-15.[174] This ruling focused on the type of joint venture referred to as a "whole hospital joint venture, which involves the transfer by an exempt hospital organization of its entire exempt operations into a joint venture in which the exempt hospital is a co-investor with a proprietary entity. The ruling emphasized the exempt organization's degree of control over the venture as a key factor in determining whether participation in the venture jeopardized the exempt organization's tax-exempt status, and expressed a clear preference that the exempt organization have majority control over the venture.

Since the issuance of Rev. Rul. 98-15, two important "whole hospital" joint venture cases have been fully adjudicated. In *Redlands Surgical Services, Inc. v. Commissioner*,[175] which the Tax Court, while not wholly adopting the views of the IRS in Rev. Rul. 98-15, also placed tremendous emphasis on the language contained in the governing documents, the ability of the tax-exempt partner to control the joint venture entity, and the role of the for-profit partners in the management of the joint venture. The case was appealed to the Ninth Circuit Court of Appeals where it was affirmed. In *St. David's Health Care System, Inc. v. United States*,[176] the District Court for the Western District of Texas rendered summary judgment in favor of the tax-exempt participant and against the government. The case, was the first to review a whole hospital joint venture and the first to approve a 50-50 joint venture. The district court's grant of summary judgment was reversed and remanded by the Fifth Circuit, which remanded the case to the district court for trial.[177] On remand, a jury rendered a verdict for St. David's.

The IRS is not bound to follow the result in *St. David's*. Moreover, the IRS is unlikely to agree that a tax-exempt organization whose primary activity is holding an interest in a joint venture retains its exemption unless the fact situation very closely adheres to the facts and circumstances the IRS described in the "good" fact pattern in Rev. Rul. 98-15. While the IRS did not ultimately prevail in result in the *St. David's* case, based on the appellate decision the IRS believes it has the support of the courts for its position.

5.3.4.2 *Ancillary Joint Ventures*

Revenue Ruling 2004-51 addresses an exempt organization's participation in an *ancillary joint venture*, which is a joint venture between an exempt organization and a for-profit entity in which the joint venture's activities represent an insubstantial portion of the total activities of the exempt partici-

---

172 GCM 39862 (Nov. 22, 1991).
173 GCM 39444 (July 18, 1985).
174 1998-1 C.B. 718.
175 113 T.C. 47 (1999), *aff'd per curiam*, 242 F.3d 904 (9th Cir. 2001).
176 (W.D. Texas), 01-CV-46 (June 7, 2002).
177 *St. David's Health Care System v. United States*, 2003-2 USTC ¶50,713 (5th Cir. 2003).

pant. Revenue Ruling 2004-51 involves the formation of a limited liability company by a tax-exempt university and a for-profit company for the purpose of offering off-campus, summer training programs for secondary school teachers using interactive video technology. The exempt university did not have majority control over the venture. Nonetheless, the Ruling concludes that the university's participation in the joint venture will not adversely affect the university's continued tax-exempt status because the activities the university is conducting through the joint venture are not a substantial part of the university's activities. The Ruling also concludes that the activities the university is conducting through the joint venture are not an unrelated trade or business and do not create UBI for the university. The key factor supporting this conclusion is the exclusive control the exempt university exercises over the important, educational aspects of the joint venture's activities that affect whether the joint venture operates in a manner consistent with the exempt organization's exempt purposes. The Ruling does not indicate how the IRS determined that the university's participation in the joint venture was an insubstantial part of its activities, and in fact there is no bright-line test for substantiality. However, the Ruling clearly indicates that majority control by the exempt organization is not essential for a favorable ruling on both issues in the context of an ancillary joint venture.

Other facts and circumstances the IRS cites in support of the favorable ruling focus primarily on: the provisions of the LLC governing documents dealing with the purposes and activities of the LLC and their compliance with the exempt status of the university; the equal voice of the members in making non-curriculum or business decisions with respect to the LLC; the allocation of profits and losses of the venture in proportion to each party's capital contribution; and the arm's-length nature and market comparability of the contractual relationships between the LLC and either of the venturers or third parties.[178]

To be able to take a position that an exempt organization's participation in the joint venture does not create unrelated business income or otherwise jeopardize the organization's exemption, the joint venture arrangement, and the associated joint venture documents, should include the following features:

- The purpose of the joint venture is to provide healthcare in a charitable manner (consistent with the community benefit standard set forth in § 501(c)(3) of the Code).
- If there is a conflict between charitable objectives and profit maximization when the joint venture board or members are making a particular decision, charitable operation will prevail over profit maximization.

[178] In connection with its consideration of the application of § 501(c)(3) to an exempt organization's participation in the Medicare Shared Savings Program (MSSP) described in § 3022 of the Patient Protection and Affordable Care Act enacted on March 23, 2010, Pub. L. 111-148, 124 Stat. 119, the IRS issued Notice 2011-20, 2011-16 I.R.B. 652, to solicit comments concerning two important exemption issues: (1) whether this prior IRS guidance on participation in a joint venture is sufficient with regard to participation in an MSSP accountable care organization, and (2) whether guidance is needed regarding the tax-exemption implications of participating in non-MSSP accountable organizations. Notably, the Notice does not address or seek comments concerning whether the nature of the activities of a joint venture organization created to implement some or all of an accountable care strategy will support a position that an exempt healthcare organization's share of the income generated by such a joint venture will qualify as related to the exempt healthcare organization's § 501(c)(3) purposes. Nor does it address or seek comments concerning the ability of a new entity created to implement an ACO strategy (in whole or in part) can qualify for stand-alone exemption.

- The joint venture may not engage in activities that would jeopardize the exempt joint venturer's tax-exempt status.
- The joint venture documents should not include a binding arbitration requirement, on the theory that the arbitrator will make decisions that are not necessarily in furtherance of charitable purposes.
- The joint venture documents should not include a non-compete provision that completely precludes the exempt joint venturer from providing a type of service. For example, the joint venture documents may provide that neither party may operate a freestanding ambulatory surgery center in a particular area but should not prohibit the exempt organization from providing outpatient surgery in its facility.
- The joint venture documents should require reformation of documents if the exempt joint venturer determines that the documents' provisions may affect tax-exempt status, be contrary to law, or preclude billing for services.

If the joint venture enters into a management agreement with a for-profit entity:

- The management agreement should not have a term longer than five years.
- The management agreement should require the manager to operate the facility in conformance with the venture's charitable purposes, and failure to comply with this requirement should be included as a basis for termination and/or non-renewal. Further, there should be an effective means of enforcing this obligation short of dissolution of the joint venture.
- If the management fee is based on a percentage of revenues, it is best that the fee be based on gross charges, not collections, so that the manager is not incentivized to limit charitable care improperly or engage in inappropriate collection practices.
- The management fee should be validated as fair market value as to methodology (*e.g.*, if a percentage of revenues, is there a dollar cap?) and amount.
- The exempt organization's approval should be required for certain key matters that could affect whether the joint venture furthers the exempt organization's charitable purposes or furthers the private interests of the non-exempt participants, such as changes in joint venture services and programs; annual capital and operating budgets or significant variations therefrom; the acquisition or disposition of healthcare facilities; appointment of joint venture executives; renewal or termination of management agreements; amendment of joint venture organizational documents; the addition of partners to the venture; calls for additional capital contributions; conflicts of interest and charity care policies; and merger, dissolution or declaration of bankruptcy by the venture.

5.3.5 Courtesy Discounts

The IRS historically has taken the position that courtesy discounts offered to physicians, nurses, clergy, members of religious orders, or other individuals may represent private inurement or more-than-incidental private benefit to the extent that they are provided without regard to financial need, unless: (1) the individual entitled to the discount is an employee or otherwise provides services to the organization, and the discounts are part of a package that constitutes no more than reasonable compensation; or (2) the organization can show that the practices are qualitatively and quantitatively incidental to advancing its exempt functions or purposes. The informally reported position of the IRS in certain of its Coordinated Examination Program (CEP) audits is consistent with this position.[179]

In addition, the amount of any actual courtesy discounts provided to an individual must be reported as income on either Form W-2 or Form 1099.

5.3.6 Donation of Electronic Health Record Technology

A recent possible private inurement situation faced by tax-exempt hospitals involved whether tax-exempt hospitals could donate electronic health record (EHR) technology items and services to healthcare providers. In response to requests by the exempt hospital community, the IRS issued a directive on May 11, 2007 (the Directive)[180] concerning exempt hospitals that provide physicians who have staff privileges at those hospitals with assistance to acquire and implement EHR items and services. The Directive states that the IRS will not treat the benefits a hospital provides to its medical staff physicians as an impermissible private benefit or inurement if the hospital meets the following requirements:

- the hospital and the participating physicians comply with the requirements of the EHR Regulations on a continuing basis;
- to the extent permitted by law, the hospital may access all of the electronic medical records created by a physician using the donated items or services;
- the hospital ensures that the donated items and services are available to all of its medical staff physicians; and
- the hospital provides the same level of subsidy to all of its medical staff physicians or varies the level of subsidy by applying criteria related to meeting the healthcare needs of the community. [181]

It is important to keep in mind that the IRS directive is also, in effect, a safe harbor. That is, a failure to fit squarely within the parameters it sets forth does not result in a *per se* tax-exemption violation. Instead, the hospital would need to develop an alternative facts and circumstances analysis to demonstrate its compliance with tax-exemption requirements. For example, it has suggested that

---

[179] For example, in the CEP audit of Baylor University Medical Center in Dallas, Texas, the IRS required Baylor to discontinue its practice of providing discounts on hospital services to members of its medical staff. Medicare Compliance Alert, May 11, 1992.

[180] IRS Memorandum, "Hospitals Providing Financial Assistance to Staff Physicians Involving Electronic Health Records" (May 11, 2007). The Memorandum and a related Question and Answer guidance document are available at http://www.irs.gov/charities/article/0,,id=171542,00.html.

[181] *Id.*

a hospital may provide access to various groups of physicians at different times according to criteria related to meeting the healthcare needs of the community and that the hospital should develop a plan for providing such access.

5.3.7 Use of Taxable Affiliates

Many healthcare systems include taxable subsidiaries and affiliates, which often are used to conduct activities that might be characterized as unrelated business activities if conducted by the § 501(c)(3) healthcare organization. The IRS has taken the position that, in certain circumstances, the activities of a taxable affiliate that violate the private-inurement or private-benefit prohibitions may be attributed to its related § 501(c)(3) organization[182] and thereby jeopardize its tax-exempt status.

The IRS has recognized that the taxable corporation is a separate legal entity and that, where a corporation is organized with a *bona fide* intention that it will have some real and substantial business function, its existence may not generally be disregarded for tax purposes.[183] The activities of a separately incorporated subsidiary cannot ordinarily be attributed to its parent organization unless the subsidiary is in reality an arm, agent, or integral part of the parent.[184] Nevertheless, where the parent corporation so controls the affairs of the subsidiary that it is merely an instrumentality of the parent, the corporate entity of the subsidiary may be disregarded.[185] In addition, the corporate entity may be disregarded if the corporation or transaction involved was a sham or fraud without any valid business purpose, or there is a true agency or trust relationship between the entities.[186]

Merely showing that one corporation is wholly owned by another is not, in and of itself, sufficient to allow attribution.[187] The IRS has indicated that the activities of a separately organized subsidiary generally will not be attributed to the parent where the day-to-day management of the subsidiary is separate from the parent and a majority of the subsidiary's directors are unrelated to the parent.[188] Other factors that the IRS has considered in determining whether activities of a taxable affiliate may be attributed to a § 501(c)(3) organization are: (1) whether costs related to shared assets, facilities, or services are allocated between the entities according to proportionate use; (2) whether corporate formalities are observed; (3) whether funds are commingled; (4) whether transactions between the taxable affiliate and the § 501(c)(3) organization reflect arm's-length negotiations; (5) whether the entities have common officers or employees; and (6) whether the funding for the taxable affiliate comes in whole or in part, directly or indirectly, from the § 501(c)(3) affiliate.[189]

---

182 *See, e.g.*, Gen. Couns. Mem. 39646 (June 30, 1987); Gen. Couns. Mem. 39598 (Jan. 23, 1987); Gen. Couns. Mem. 39326 (Jan. 17, 1985).

183 *Moline Properties, Inc. v. Commissioner*, 319 U.S. 436, 438 (1943); *Britt v. United States*, 431 F.2d 227, 234 (5th Cir. 1970).

184 *Id. See also* Gen. Couns. Mem. 39326.

185 *Krivo Indus. Supply Co. v. National Distillers & Chem. Corp.*, 483 F.2d 1098, 1106 (5th Cir. 1973).

186 Gen. Couns. Mem. 39598; Tech. Adv. Mem. 200208027 (Oct. 4, 2001). *See Commissioner v. Bollinger*, 485 U.S. 340 (1988) and *National Carbide Corp. v. Commissioner*, 336 U.S. 422 (1949) for a discussion of the six factors identified by the Supreme Court for determining whether an agency relationship exists.

187 Gen. Couns. Mem. 39598; Priv.. Ltr. Rul. 200130048 (Apr. 19, 2001); Priv. Ltr. Rul. 199941051 (July 22, 1999).

188 Gen. Couns. Mem. 39598; Priv. Ltr. Rul. 200130048. Gen. Couns. Mem. 39598 clarifies that complete overlap between the directors of the § 501(c)(3) organization and the taxable affiliate is not alone, however, a sufficient basis for attribution.

189 Gen. Couns. Mem. 39646; Gen. Couns. Mem. 39326. *See also* Priv. Ltr. Rul. 200037050 (June 20, 2000); Priv. Ltr. Rul. 199941048 (July 20, 1999); Priv. Ltr. Rul. 9819046 (Feb. 11, 1998): Priv. Ltr. Rul. 9817034 (Jan. 28, 1998).

5.4 Section 509(a) Public Charity Status

5.4.1 Section 509(a)(1) Public Charities

Some organizations qualify for § 509(a)(1) public charity status on the basis of their principal function rather than on the basis of their financial support. Such organizations include a church, a hospital or a medical research organization operated in connection with a hospital, an organization operated for the benefit of certain state and municipal colleges and universities, a governmental unit or a publicly supported organization. Each of these functions is specifically defined under the applicable treasury regulations. For example, "hospital" is broadly defined to include a principal purpose or function of providing hospital or medical care, whether physical or mental, inpatient or outpatient. Thus, the IRS has granted public charity status as a "hospital" to ambulatory surgical centers, psychiatric hospitals, rehabilitation institutions, outpatient clinics, and community mental health and drug treatment centers. Convalescent homes and homes for children or the aged or institutions whose principal purpose or function is to train handicapped individuals to pursue some vocation do not qualify as a "hospital."

Other organizations qualify for § 509(a)(1) public charity status on the basis of their sources of financial support. Specifically, an organization may qualify as such if it meets the "public support test" of Code § 170(b)(1)(A)(vi). This test generally requires that the organization receive more than one-third of its total support from a governmental unit and/or from contributions made directly or indirectly by the general public. Contributions made by one individual, trust or corporation—other than from a governmental unit or another § 509(a)(1) organization described in 170(b)(1)(A)(vi)—are counted as public support only to the extent they do not exceed 2% of an organization's total support. The public support test typically is calculated as a four-year moving average. Alternatively, the public support test can be met on a facts and circumstances basis if the organization normally receives at least 10% public support and it organization demonstrates it can attract new and additional public support on a continuous basis. Relevant factors include the amount by which the organization's support exceeds 10%, the extent to which an organization makes its facilities or services available to the public, the variety of an organization's supporters and the composition of its governing board.

5.4.2 Section 509(a)(2) Public Charities

An organization qualifies as a § 509(a)(2) public charity if it meets a two-part public supported test. First, more than one-third of the organization's total support must be from gifts, grants, contributions, membership fees, and gross receipts from admissions, sale of merchandise, performance of services or furnishing of facilities in an activity that is not an unrelated trade or business. Support is counted as public support only if it is from persons who are not disqualified persons, from organizations described in § 509(a)(1) or from governmental units. In addition, amounts received from persons in excess of both $5,000 and 2% of total contributions in a given year are totally excluded. Second, an organization may not receive more than one-third of its support from the sum of gross investment income and any net unrelated business income (less taxes paid on that income).

5.4.3 Section 509(a)(3) Public Charities

An organization qualifies as a § 509(a)(3) public charity if it is a "supporting organization" for one or more §§ 509(a)(1) or 509(a)(2) public charities. To qualify, the organization must be organized and at all times thereafter operated exclusively for the benefit of, to perform the functions of, or to carry out the purposes of one or more specified §§ 509(a)(1) or (2) organizations (referred to as the "organizational and operational test");[190] the organization must be operated, supervised or controlled by or in connection with one or more §§ 509(a)(1) or (2) organization (referred to as the "relationship test"); and the organization must not be controlled directly or indirectly by disqualified persons (other than foundation managers of §§ 509(a)(1) or (2) organizations).

5.4.3.1 *Organizational Test*

An organization is organized exclusively to support or benefit one or more specified publicly supported organizations only if its articles (a) limit its purposes to the purposes permitted under § 509(a), (b) do not expressly empower the organization to engage in activities that are not in furtherance of those purposes, (c) state the specified publicly supported organizations on whose behalf the organization is operated,[191] and (d) do not expressly empower the organization to operate to support or benefit any organization other than the specified publicly supported organizations.[192]

5.4.3.2 *Operational Test*

An organization is operated exclusively to support one or more specified publicly supported organizations only if it engages solely in activities that support or benefit its specified supported organizations. These activities may include making payments to or for the use of or providing services or facilities for individual members of the charitable class benefited by the specified supported organizations.[193] A supporting organization is also operated exclusively to support one or more specified supported organizations when it makes payment indirectly through another unrelated organization to a member of a charitable class benefited by a specified publicly supported organization, but only if the payment constitutes a grant to an individual rather than a grant to an organization.[194] A supporting organization need not pay over its income to its supported organizations; it may satisfy the operational test by carrying on an independent activity or program that supports or benefits its supported organizations. It may also engage in fund-raising activities on behalf of its supported organizations or the charitable class benefited by such organizations.[195]

---

[190] Treas. Reg. § 1.509(a)-4(b).

[191] The degree of specificity with which the supported organizations must be named depends on which of the three relationship tests the organization meets. Treas. Reg. § 1.509(a)-4(d)(2)(i)(a) and (b).

[192] Treas. Reg. § 1.509(a)-4(c). Note, Treasury Regulations also provide that a supported organization may engage in activities that support organizations other than the named supported organizations so long as such other organizations are organized and operated to support the same supported organizations. Treas. Reg. § 1.509(a)-4(e)(1).

[193] Treas. Reg. § 1.509(a)-4(e)(1).

[194] *Id.*

[195] *Id.* § 1.509(a)-4(e)(2).

5.4.3.3 Relationship Test

There are three categories of 509(a)(3) supporting organizations,[196] referred to as "Type I Supporting Organizations," "Type II Supporting Organizations," and "Type III Supporting Organizations." These three categories are based on which of three relationship tests the § 509(a)(3) supporting organization meets. Those three relationships have historically been referred to, respectively, as "operated, supervised or controlled by," supervised or controlled in connection with," and "operated in connection with."[197]

A Type I relationship is defined as comparable to that of a parent and subsidiary, in which the subsidiary is under the direction of and accountable or responsible to, the parent organization. This relationship is established by the fact that the supported organization(s)' governing body, members of the governing body, officers acting in their official capacity, or members officers supported organization appoint or elect a majority of the officers, directors or trustees of the supporting organization.[198]

A Type II relationship is established through common supervision or control by the persons supervising or controlling both the supporting organization and the supported organization. To meet this standard, the control or management of the supporting organization must be vested in the same persons that control or manage the publicly supported organization.[199]

To establish a Type III relationship, the supporting organization must meet both the responsiveness test and the integral part test. The responsiveness test requires either that: (a) one or more officers, directors, or trustees of the supporting organization are elected or appointed by the officers, directors, trustees or membership of the supported organizations; (b) one or more of the members of the governing bodies of the publicly supported organizations are also officer, directors, or trustees of, or hold other important offices in, the supporting organization; or (c) the officers, directors, or trustees of the supporting organization maintain a close and continuous working relationship with the officers, directors, or trustees of the supported organizations; *and* that, by reason of one of the foregoing, the officers, directors, or trustees of the publicly supported organizations have a significant voice in the investment policies of, the timing and manner of making of grants by, and the selection of grant recipients by the supporting organization and in otherwise directing the use of the income or assets of the supporting organization. [200] The integral part test requires that the supporting organization maintains a significant involvement in the operations of one or more publicly supported organizations that depend on the supporting organization for the type of support that it provides. The supporting organization must demonstrate either that (a) it engages in activities for or on behalf of the publicly supported organizations that are in furtherance of the functions or purposes of its supported organizations, and, but for the involvement of the supporting organization, that are ones that would normally be engaged in directly by the publicly supported organizations or (b) make payments of substantially all of its income (85% or more) to or for the use of one or more of its supported organizations, in circumstances in which

---

196 These three categories were established by the Pension Protection Act of 2006 (the PPA). P.L. 109-280, 120 Stat. 780, located at http://www.dol.gov/ebsa/pdf/ppa2006.pdf.

197 Treas. Reg. § 1.509(a)-4(f)(2).

198 Treas. Reg. § 1.509(a)-4(g)(1)(i).

199 Treas. Reg. § 1.509(a)-4(h)(1).

200 Treas. Reg. § 1.509(a)-4(i)(2).

(i) the amount received by one or more of such supported organizations is sufficient to ensure the attentiveness of such publicly supported organizations to the operations of the supporting organization and (ii) a substantial amount of the total support of the supporting organization goes to those supported organizations that meet the attentiveness requirement.[201]

There are also two subcategories of Type III Supporting Organizations—those that are *functionally integrated*, and those that are *not functionally integrated*, with the organizations they support. Internal IRS guidance issued in late 2007 sets forth the requirements the IRS will apply to determine whether an organization is "functionally integrated" in the interim until final regulations are published.[202] The guidance also indicated, however, that compliance with these requirements is not a guarantee of recognition by the IRS if the IRS finds an organization to be "potentially abusive." Further, any recognition of functionally integrated status granted prior to issuance of the final regulations will also have to comply with the final regulations. An organization that does not meet these requirements is still eligible to receive classification as a Type III supporting organization at this time, but its determination letter will be silent with respect to whether it is functionally integrated or non-functionally integrated status.

The internal IRS guidance stated that the IRS will only issue determination letters classifying Type III supporting organizations as "functionally integrated" if the supporting organizations satisfy three requirements: the "but for" test, a new expenditure test, *and* a new asset test. A supporting organization satisfies the "but for" test if "the activities engaged in [by the supporting organization] for or on behalf of the [public charities it supports] are activities to perform the functions of, or to carry out the purposes of, such organizations, and, but for the involvement of the supporting organization, would normally be engaged in by the [public charities] themselves." The IRS has indicated, however, that it *anticipates* that the final regulations will allow certain organizations that oversee the operation of "integrated systems," such as hospital systems, to qualify as functionally integrated Type III supporting organizations by satisfying only the "but for" test. The new expenditure test requires the supporting organization to use substantially all of the lesser of (a) its adjusted net income or (b) 5% of the aggregate fair market value of all its assets (other than assets that are used, or held for use, directly in supporting the charitable programs of the public charities) directly for the active conduct of activities that directly further the exempt purposes of the public charities it supports. The new asset test requires the organization to devote at least 65% of the aggregate value of all its assets directly for the active conduct of activities that directly further the exempt purposes of the public charities it supports.

5.4.3.4 Control Test

To satisfy the Control Test, the supporting organization must demonstrate that (a) the disqualified persons may not, by aggregating their votes or positions of authority, require the organization to perform or prevent it from performing any act that significantly affects its operations (*e.g.*, the right of any substantial contributor (or spouse of a substantial contributor) to designate annually the recipients from among the publicly supported organizations of the income attributable to his or her contribution

201 Treas. Reg. § 1.509(a)-4(i)(3).

202 IRM 7.20.7, Exempt Organizations Determination Letter Program, IRC 509(a)(3) Supporting Organizations Guide Sheet (Oct. 1, 2007), available at http://www.irs.gov/pub/irs-tege/irm7_20_7_509a3guidesheet.pdf.

to the supporting organization is considered control for these purposes) and (b) one or more disqualified persons do not possess 50% or more of the total voting power of the organization's governing body or the right to exercise veto power over the actions of the organization.[203]

5.4.4 Effect of the Pension Protection Act of 2006

The Pension Protection Act of 2006 (the PPA) added several private foundation-like provisions affecting Type III supporting organizations, particularly non-functionally integrated supporting organizations. For example: (a) § 509(a)(3) supporting organizations are not eligible to receive contributions from individual retirement accounts, unlike other public charities; (b) Type III § 509(a)(3) supporting organizations that are not functionally related may not receive private foundation grants unless expenditure responsibility is exercised; (c) Type III § 509(a)(3) supporting organizations that are not functionally related are subject to the private foundation excess business holding rules; (d) the Department of the Treasury is directed to promulgate regulations requiring Type III § 509(a)(3) supporting organizations that are not functionally related to annually distribute prescribed amounts to a supported organization; (e) Type III § 509(a)(3) supporting organizations may not support a foreign charity; (f) payment of compensation by a § 509(a)(3) supporting organization to its substantial contributors or related parties thereof is an automatic excess benefit transaction subject to intermediate sanctions under Code § 4958, regardless of its reasonableness; (g) private non-operating foundations will be able to count donations to the Type III parent and fundraising foundation towards their required minimum annual distributions; and (h) § 509(a)(3) supporting organizations must file a From 990 annual information return regardless of its income level. The PPA also added provisions that will affect Type I and Type II supporting organizations. These and the other provisions of the PPA could have a potentially significant effect the operations and funding of parents and fundraising foundations in a restructured hospital system.

[203] Treas. Reg. § 1.509(a)-4(j).

6

Antitrust Law

John J. Miles, Esquire
Ober/Kaler

6.1 Introduction

Federal and state antitrust laws can affect so many activities of participants in the healthcare sector that a basic understanding of antitrust principles is crucial to the practice of health law today.[1] The courts have specifically held that the antitrust laws are fully applicable to healthcare-sector industries, and the Obama administration has taken aggressive antitrust action against both providers and health plans.[2] This Chapter is an overview of the purpose of the antitrust laws, the antitrust statutes and their application, exemptions from antitrust coverage, and antitrust enforcement, particularly as they affect firms in the healthcare sector.[3]

6.1.1 Purpose of the Antitrust Laws

The antitrust laws protect and promote competition as the primary method by which this nation allocates its economic resources.[4] More specifically, the antitrust laws are a "consumer welfare prescription."[5] They are designed to protect consumers, not competitors *per se*.[6] They protect competitors only when the challenged conduct reduces the number of competitors to the extent that the market

---

1 For a much more in-depth treatments of numerous antitrust issues arising in the healthcare sector, *see* 1-6 John J. Miles, *Health Care & Antitrust Law* (1992 and Supp); ABA Section of Antitrust Law, *Antitrust Health Care Handbook* (2010); Federal Trade Comm'n & U.S. Dep't of Justice, *Improving Health Care: A Dose of Competition* (2004).

2 *See, e.g.*, *Boulware v. Nev.*, 960 F.2d 793 (9th Cir. 1991).

3 To aid in understanding application of the antitrust laws to several particular issues arising in the healthcare sector, the Department of Justice and Federal Trade Commission, in 1996, issued their *Statements of Antitrust Enforcement Policy in Health Care*, at http://www.usdoj.gov/atr/public/guidelines/1791.pdf. These statements discuss hospital mergers, hospital joint ventures, providers' communicating non-fee information to payers, providers' communicating fee-related information to payers, competitor exchanges of price and wage information, group-purchasing arrangements, and provider-controlled contracting networks.

4 *See generally Northern Pac. Ry. v. United States*, 356 U.S. 1, 4 (1958); *City of Lafayette v. Louisiana Power & Light Co.*, 435 U.S. 389 (1978) ("[i]n enacting the Sherman Act…, Congress mandated competition as the polestar by which all must be guided in ordering their business affairs").

5 *Reiter v. Sonotone Corp.*, 442 U.S. 330, 343 (1979); *see also Glen Holly Entm't Inc., v. Tektronix, Inc.*, 343 F.3d 1000 (9th Cir. 2003) ("customers are the intended beneficiaries of competition").

6 *See generally Brunswick Corp. v. Pueblo Bowl-O-Mat, Inc.*, 429 U.S. 477 (1977); *Metro Net Servs. Corp. v. US W. Communications*, 329 F.3d 986 (9th Cir. 2003).

as a whole does not perform in a competitive manner, and consumers suffer as a result. As a result, a plaintiff always must show harm not merely to itself, but harm to market-wide competition.[7]

The antitrust laws protect consumers by attempting to shield them from "market power." Seller market power is the ability of a single firm, or a group of firms acting in concert, to raise price above (or lower quality below) the competitive level without losing so many sales that the price increase (or decrease in quality) is unprofitable and thus must be rescinded.[8] A seller, or group of sellers acting jointly, exercises market power by restricting output, which increases price, misallocates resources,[9] and inappropriately transfers income from buyers to sellers.

Buyer market power, of equal concern to the antitrust laws, is the ability of a purchaser, or group of purchasers acting jointly, to depress the price they pay for a product or service below the competitive level by restricting the amount of that product or service they purchase. Called "monopsony power," buyer market power also misallocates resources and inappropriately transfers income from sellers to buyers.[10] Providers frequently allege that health plans exercise monopsony power in their contracting relationship.

Even if the challenged conduct creates market power, it may also achieve offsetting benefits to competition that justify it. These offsetting benefits are usually referred to generally as "efficiencies"—more technically, "productive efficiencies," which refer to the ratio of a firm's outputs to its inputs.[11] Efficiencies usually result from some type of "economic integration" among firms, *i.e.*, the combination of resources, functions, and operations among firms in a way so that "the whole is greater than the sum of its parts."[12] Efficiency benefits include any benefits from the integration that benefit consumers, including lower prices, higher quality, greater innovation, higher output, and improved access.

Antitrust analysis, conceptually and at its most basic level, requires identifying, assessing, and balancing the market-power and efficiency effects of the conduct under examination. In general, if the conduct generates no market-power effects, it raises no antitrust concern, regardless of its efficiency effects. If it generates, maintains, or increases market power but not efficiencies, it usually is unlawful. The most difficult situation is that where the conduct generates both effects, and balancing them becomes necessary. In some situations, that can be done quantitatively through econometric analysis,

---

[7] *E.g.*, *Benson v. St. Joseph's Reg'l Health Ctr.*, 575 F.3d 542 (5th Cir. 2009); *Four Corners Nephrology Assocs., P.C. v. Mercy Med. Ctr.*, 582 F.3d 1216 (10th Cir. 2009) ("Plaintiff must show not only that he was harmed by [defendant's] conduct, but that the injury he suffered involved harm to competition.... After all, it is the 'protection of competition or prevention of monopoly[ ] which is plainly the concern of the Sherman Act,' not the vindication of general 'notions of fair dealing,' which are the subject of many other laws.") (citation omitted); *Perry v. Rado*, 343 Fed. App'x 240 (9th Cir. 2009).

[8] *See, e.g.*, *Eastman Kodak Co. v. Image Technical Servs., Inc.*, 504 U.S. 451 (1992) (explaining that market power is the ability of a seller to restrict output and thus raise price). For excellent discussions of market power and how it is identified, *see* IIB Phillip E. Areeda, Herbert Hovenkamp & John L. Solow, *Antitrust Law* Chs. 4A, 4B, and 5 (3d ed. 2007); William Landes & Richard Posner, *Market Power in Antitrust Cases*, 94 Harv. L. Rev. 937 (1981).

[9] *See generally* Dennis W. Carlton & Jeffrey M. Perloff, *Modern Industrial Organization* Ch. 4 (4th ed. 2005).

[10] Monopsony is analytically the same as monopoly, but on the buyer side rather than the seller side. *See Weyerhaeuser Co. v. Ross-Simons Hardwood Co.*, 549 U.S. 312 (2007). For a full discussion of monopsony power, *see* Roger D. Blair & Jeffrey L. Harrison, *Monopsony: Antitrust Law and Economics* (2nd ed. 2010); *see also* Mark V. Pauly, *Managed Care, Market Power, and Monopsony*, 33 Health Servs. Research 1439 (1998).

[11] *See generally* Herbert Hovenkamp, *Federal Antitrust Policy* § 2.3c at 75 (3d ed. 2005) ("A firm that produces a product valued at $100 and requires inputs valued at $80 is more efficient than a firm that produces a product valued at $100 but requires inputs valued at $90.").

[12] *See generally Broadcast Music, Inc. v. Columbia Broadcasting Sys.*, 441 U.S. 1 (1979).

but doing so is extremely complex and expensive (and in many cases, impossible).[13] This is often especially true in healthcare-sector antitrust cases because quality improvements are often the primary efficiency, and they are notoriously difficult to measure.

6.1.2 Relevant-Market Definition

It is usually impossible to assess whether particular firms have market power, or to determine the effect of a practice on competition, without first determining the markets that the conduct affects, *i.e.*, the "relevant market."[14] In general, a relevant antitrust market consists of a firm, or the smallest group of firms acting together, that could exercise market power if it or they attempted to.[15] In other words, if a firm is able to exercise market power by itself, *e.g.*, significantly raise price and sustain its price increase, it is the only firm in the relevant market. If the presence of competitors constrains it from exercising market power, then they must be included in the relevant market. Thus, the purpose and methodology for defining the relevant market are to identify and include in the relevant market those firms that could prevent or constrain a hypothetical monopoly from profitably raising prices.[16]

Several sources of potential constraints on firms attempting to exercise market power exist, based primarily on (1) substitute products and (2) more-distant substitute suppliers, to which consumers could turn to escape the seller's hypothetical price increase. Examining these two factors results in defining the "relevant product market" and the "relevant geographic market," which together constitute the relevant market. In essence, the relevant market consists of those firms with the ability to take significant amounts of business away from one another.[17]

If a seller attempts to exercise market power by increasing the price of its product, consumers might substitute other products for that product. If they do in sufficient volume, the seller would be forced to rescind its price increase because it would be unprofitable.[18] Thus, the relevant product market includes all products that are "reasonably interchangeable" with one another (sometimes referred

---

[13] *See* Herbert Hovenkamp, *Federal Antitrust Policy* § 5.6c at 259 (2d ed. 1999) (explaining that courts are ill-equipped to balance effects); Robert Pitofsky, *A Framework for Antitrust Analysis of Joint Ventures*, 74 Geo. L.J. 1605, 1623 (1986) (noting that "except in rare cases, it is almost impossible, at least at the present state of economic learning, to quantify efficiencies").

[14] *E.g.*, *Little Rock Cardiology Clinic, PA v. Baptist Health*, 591 F.3d 591 (8th Cir. 2009) ("Without a well-defined relevant market, a court cannot determine the effect that an allegedly illegal act has on competition.").

[15] *See generally* U.S. Dep't of Justice & Federal Trade Commission, *Horizontal Merger Guidelines* § 4 (2010) (*Merger Guidelines*), at http://www.justice.gov/atr/public/guidelines/hmg-2010.pdf; *FTC v. Whole Foods Mkt., Inc.*, 548 F.3d 1028 (D.C. Cir. 2008).

[16] *See generally Ky. Speedway, LLC v. Nat'l Ass'n of Stock Car Auto Racing, Inc.*, 588 F.3d 908 (6th Cir. 2009) ("This test measures whether increasing a product's price—usually by five percent—results in a substantial number of consumers purchasing an alternative product."); *Geneva Pharms. Tech. Corp. v. Barr Labs., Inc.*, 386 F.3d 485 (2d Cir. 2004) ("The goal in defining the relevant market is to identify the market participants and competitive pressures that restrain an individual firm's ability to raise prices or restrict output."); *Rebel Oil Co. v. Atl. Richfield Co.*, 50 F.3d 1421 (9th Cir. 1995) ("'A market' is any grouping of sales whose sellers, if unified by a monopolist or hypothetical cartel, would have market power in dealing with any group of buyers.... If the sales of other producers substantially constrain the price-increasing ability of [these firms], these other producers must be included in the market."); *FTC v. Cardinal Health, Inc.*, 12 F. Supp. 2d 34, 46 (D.D.C. 1998) ("definition of the relevant market rests on a determination of available substitutes"). For an excellent discussion, *see* Jonathan B. Baker, *Market Definition: An Analytical Overview*, 74 Antitrust L.J. 129 (2007).

[17] *Gordon v. Lewiston Hosp.*, 373 F. Supp.2d 393 (M.D. Pa. 2003), *aff'd*, 423 F.3d 184 (3d Cir. 2005).

[18] *See generally Merger Guidelines* § 4.1.1; *FTC v. Whole Foods Mkt.*, 548 F.3d 1028 (D.C. Cir. 2008); *United States v. Oracle Corp.*, 331 F. Supp. 2d 1098 (N.D. Cal. 2004).

to as "demand substitutability").[19] The degree of interchangeability between two products or services is determined by examining their price "cross-elasticity of demand"—*i.e.*, the percentage change in quantity demanded of Product B for a given percentage change in the price of Product A.[20] A high price cross-elasticity of demand between two products, *e.g.*, a relatively large increase in the quantity demanded of Product B resulting from a relatively small increase in the price of Product A, indicates that Products A and B are in the same relevant product market because it suggests that consumers of A would readily substitute B if the producer of A attempted to exercise market power by increasing its price. In hospital-merger cases, for example, several courts have determined that the price cross-elasticity of demand between inpatient acute-care hospital services and outpatient services is low and that, therefore, the two types of services are not in the same relevant product market.[21]

In addition to demand substitutability, courts also consider supply substitutability in defining relevant product markets. Supply substitutability (or price cross-elasticity of supply) measures the degree to which firms not producing Product A at present would quickly do so if producers of A attempted to increase its price. Elasticity of supply is high (and those firms are included in the relevant market) if they would significantly increase supply of the relevant product quickly as a result of the attempted exercise of market power.[22]

In some situations, products that are neither demand substitutes nor supply substitutes can be "clustered" into a single relevant market for antitrust purposes because they are sold or purchased together as a package. In hospital-merger cases, for example, most courts have clustered most types of inpatient acute-care hospital services into a single relevant product market even though they are poor substitutes for one another (*e.g.*, hernia and open-heart surgeries), rather than examining each as a separate relevant product market. This is largely because health plans typically do not contract separately for the different types of inpatient services but rather purchase them as a "cluster."[23]

Once the relevant product market is defined, the relevant geographic market must be delineated. Broadly stated, the relevant geographic market is the "area of effective competition."[24] More specifically, it is the area in which the sellers under examination operate, plus those areas (and thus more distant suppliers) to which purchasers practicably would turn for the relevant product if sellers in that area attempted to exercise market power by raising price.[25] As in defining the relevant product market,

---

19 *See generally Eastman Kodak Co. v. Image Technical Servs.*, 504 U.S. 451 (1992); *Brown Shoe Co. v. United States*, 370 U.S. 294 (1962); *Little Rock Cardiology Clinic, PA v. Baptist Health*, 591 F.3d 591 (8th Cir. 2009); *Reifert v. S. Cent. Wis. MLS Corp.*, 450 F.3d 312 (7th Cir. 2006); *Nat'l Hockey League Players Ass'n v. Plymouth Whalers Hockey Club*, 419 F.3d 462 (6th Cir. 2005); *Queen City Pizza, Inc. v. Domino's Pizza, Inc.*, 124 F.3d 430 (3d Cir. 1997).

20 *See generally United States v. E.I. du Pont de Nemours & Co.*, 351 U.S. 377 (1956).

21 *E.g., United States v. Rockford Mem'l Corp.*, 898 F.2d 1278 (7th Cir. 1990); *Evanston Nw. Healthcare Corp.*, 2007-2 Trade Cas. (CCH) ¶ 75,814 (FTC 2007).

22 *See, e.g., United States v. Columbia Steel Co.*, 334 U.S. 495 (1948); *Geneva Pharms. Tech. Corp. v. Barr Labs., Inc.*, 386 F.3d 485 (2d Cir. 2004); *AD/SAT v. Associated Press*, 181 F.3d 216 (2d Cir. 1999) (explaining that "cross-elasticity of supply… depends on the extent to which producers of one product would be willing to shift their resources to producing another product in response to an increase in the price of the other product"); *Blue Cross & Blue Shield v. Marshfield Clinic*, 65 F.3d 1406 (7th Cir. 1995) (holding that "products are in the same market if producers can easily shift production from one to the other").

23 *E.g., United States v. Carilion Health Sys.*, 892 F.2d 1042 (4th Cir. 1989) (*per curiam*) (*unpublished op. reprinted at* 1989-2 Trade Cas. (CCH) ¶68,859); *Cal. v. Sutter Health Sys.*, 130 F. Supp. 2d 1109 (N.D. Cal. 2001); *Green Country Food Market, Inc. v. Bottling Group, LLC*, 371 F.3d 1275 (10th Cir. 2004) ("A 'cluster market' exists where a seller provides a full line of products or services that create a separate product market consisting of the 'cluster' of products or services.")

24 *United States v. Philadelphia Nat'l Bank*, 374 U.S. 321 (1963).

25 *E.g., Tampa Elec. Co. v. Nashville Coal Co.*, 365 U.S. 320 (1965); *see also E.I. du Pont de Nemours & Co. v. Kolon Indus.*, 637 F.3d 435 (4th Cir. 2011); *Little Rock Cardiology Clinic, PA v. Baptist Health*, 591 F.3d 591 (8th Cir. 2008)

the goal is to identify those firms (here, more-distant firms) that would constrain the ability of a seller to raise prices profitably, because many of its customers would switch their purchases to more distant firms.[26] So, for example, if two cardiology practices in Town A merge, cardiology practices in Town B would be included in the relevant geographic market if health plans and their enrollees would substitute those practices for the merged Town A group if it attempted to exercise market power post-merger by raising its prices.

6.1.3 Market Share, Market Concentration, and Effect on Competition

Market definition is not an end in itself, but rather one tool for helping to assess an action's effect on competition.[27] It identifies competitors and thus is a necessary step in calculating a firm's market share and the level of market concentration, which permit predictions and inferences of market power. All else equal, the larger a firm's market share, the greater its market power and the greater the potential adverse effect on relative sizes of firms in the relevant market. The greater the level of market concentration, the easier and more likely that firms in a market will engage in coordinated conduct—either express collusion or interdependent coordinated interaction.[28]

In some situations, however, an adverse effect on competition can be shown directly—*e.g.*, by higher-than-competitive prices, lower-than-competitive output, or lower-than-competitive quality. In those situations, some courts have held that formal proof of the relevant market is unnecessary or can be defined in very rough fashion.[29] Where, for example, economic evidence shows that a consummated hospital merger has resulted in hospital reimbursement higher than would have resulted absent the merger, it may not be necessary for a plaintiff to prove the relevant market.[30]

6.2 The Substantive Antitrust Statutes and Their Analyses

The basic antitrust statutes are sections 1 and 2 of the Sherman Act,[31] section 7 of the Clayton Act,[32] section 5 of the Federal Trade Commission Act (FTC Act),[33] and the Robinson-Patman Act (which is part of the Clayton Act).[34] Each requires that a plaintiff allege and prove, in addition to the

("The end goal in this analysis is to delineate a geographic area where, in the medical setting 'few patients leave… and few patients enter.'") (citation omitted); Gordon *v. Lewistown Hosp.*, 423 F.3d 184 (3d Cir. 2005); *FTC v. Tenet Health Care Corp.*, 186 F.3d 1045 (8th Cir. 1999).

[26] For a helpful discussion of the appropriate methodology, *see Cal. v. Sutter Health Sys.*, 130 F. Supp.2d. 1109 (N.D. Cal. 2001); *FTC v. Arch Coal Co.*, 329 F. Supp. 2d 109 (D.D.C. 2004) ("If buyers would respond to the [price increase] by shifting to products produced *outside* the proposed geographic market, and this shift were sufficient to render the [price increase] unprofitable, then the proposed geographic market would be too narrow.").

[27] *E.g., Law v. NCAA*, 134 F.3d 1010 (10th Cir. 1998).

[28] *E.g., FTC v. Arch Coal Co.*, 329 F. Supp 109 (D.D.C. 2004) (explaining that "in a market with few rivals, firms are able to coordinate behavior, 'either by overt collusion or implicit understanding' to restrict output and achieve anticompetitive profits").

[29] *E.g., Republic Tobacco Co. v. N. Atl. Trading Co.*, 381 F.3d 717 (7th Cir. 2004) (indicating that "it is unnecessary to prove that the defendant wielded market power in a properly defined market" when plaintiff can adduce "direct evidence of anticompetitive effects").

[30] *See Evanston Nw. Health Care Corp.*, 2007-2 Trad Cas. (CCH) ¶ 75,814 (FTC 2007), & Rosch, Comm'r, concurring).

[31] 15 U.S.C. §§ 1, 2.

[32] *Id.* § 18. Not discussed here is section 7A of the Clayton Act, 15 U.S.C. § 18a, the Hart-Scott-Rodino premerger notification provisions. For an overview of them, *see* 1 ABA Section of *Antitrust Law*, 388–96 (6th ed. 2007).

[33] 15 U.S.C. § 45.

[34] *Id.* §§ 12–27; 29 U.S.C. § 52.

other elements, some connection between the parties or their actions and an effect on interstate commerce.[35] In addition, almost every state has a set of state antitrust laws, most of which mirror, and are interpreted in conformance with, the federal antitrust laws. The antitrust statutes are few in number but extremely broad and ambiguous in language. As the Supreme Court has explained, the antitrust statutes are akin to constitutional provisions that supply the "skeleton" to which the courts add "meat."[36]

6.2.1 Section 1 of the Sherman Act

Section 1 of the Sherman Act prohibits agreements that unreasonably restrain competition. It is the most important and most frequently invoked antitrust law. The essential elements of a section 1 violation are (1) an agreement (or other form of concerted action) between two or more entities legally capable of agreeing that (2) unreasonably restrains competition.[37] Importantly, it is the agreement itself that is unlawful, and thus the agreement need not be implemented or successful for a violation to result (although it would need to be both implemented and successful for a plaintiff to suffer injury and thus recover damages).[38]

6.2.1.1 Agreement

Unilateral action *never* violates section 1, regardless of its effect on competition.[39] Determining if section 1's agreement requirement is met usually requires answering two questions: (1) whether the alleged co-conspirators are legally capable of agreeing; and, if so, (2) whether, as a factual matter, the challenged conduct resulted from concerted action, rather than unilateral action.

As to the first question, the Supreme Court, in *Copperweld Corp. v. Independence Tube Corp.*,[40] held that the individual components of a single, integrated enterprise are incapable of conspiring for antitrust purposes even if, as a technical matter, they are separate entities. The *Copperweld* decision, itself, held only that a parent corporation and its wholly-owned subsidiaries are a single entity, and thus legally incapable of entering an agreement between themselves for purposes of the antitrust laws.

---

[35] For discussions of the interstate-commerce requirement, *see Summit Health, Ltd. v. Pinhas*, 500 U.S. 322 (1991); *McLain v. Real Estate Bd.*, 444 U.S. 232 (1980); *Hosp. Bldg. Co. v. Trustees of Rex Hosp.*, 425 U.S. 738 (1976); *Villare v. Beebe Med. Ctr., Inc.*, 630 F. Supp. 2d 418 (D. Del. 2009).

[36] *See Appalachian Coals, Inc. v. United States*, 288 U.S. 344 (1933) (comparing the breadth of lack of detail in the antitrust laws to constitutional provisions); *BCB Anesthesia Care, Ltd. v. Passavant Mem'l Area Hosp. Ass'n*, 36 F.3d 664 (7th Cir. 1994) ("The Sherman Act is perhaps the quintessential delegation by the Congress to the courts of the task of fashioning a legal structure to govern conduct.").

[37] *E.g., Realcomp II, Ltd. v. FTC*, 635 F.3d 815 (6th Cir. 2011); *Golden Bridge Tech., Inc. v. Motorola, Inc.*, 547 F.3d 266 (5th Cir. 2008); *Expert Masonry, Inc. v. Boone County*, 440 F.3d 336 (6th Cir. 2006); *Gordon v. Lewistown Hosp.*, 423 F.3d 184 (3d Cir. 2005); *Willman v. Heartland Hosp.*, 34 F.3d 605 (8th Cir. 1994).

[38] *E.g., Summit Health, Ltd. v. Pinhas*, 500 U.S. 322 (1991) (explaining that "the essence of any violation of § 1 is the illegal agreement itself—rather than the overt acts performed in furtherance of it"); *United States v. United States Gypsum Co.*, 438 U.S. 422 (1978) *United States v. Rose*, 449 F.3d 627 (5th Cir. 2006) ("[C]onspiracies under the Sherman Act are not dependent on any overt act other than the act of conspiring."); *Blades v. Monsanto Co.*, 400 F.3d 562 (8th Cir. 2005) ("The mere act of agreeing to raise prices, even if the undertaking is 'wholly nascent or abortive,' violates… section 1 of the Sherman Act.").

[39] *E.g., Bell Atl. Corp. v. Twombly*, 550 U.S. 544 (2007) (noting that § 1 does not prohibit all restraints on competition but only those resulting from concerted action); *Fisher v. City of Berkeley*, 475 U.S. 260 (1986); *Abraham v. Intermountain Health Care, Inc.*, 461 F.3d 1249 (10th Cir. 2006); *Am. Chiropractic Ass'n v. Trigon Healthcare, Inc.*, 367 U.S. 212 (4th Cir. 2004); *Capital Imaging Assocs., P. C. v. Mohawk Valley Med. Assocs., Inc.*, 996 F.2d 537 (2d Cir. 1993).

[40] 467 U.S. 752 (1984).

Numerous decisions hold the same.[41] The rationale of *Copperweld*, however, applies to many other relationships as well. For example, "sister" corporations of the same corporate "parent" are legally incapable of conspiring among themselves or with their parent,[42] and the unincorporated divisions of the same corporation are incapable of conspiring among themselves or with the corporation.[43] The courts have emphasized that in determining whether two entities are a single entity or separate entities for purposes of the antitrust laws, the analysis should focus on the substance of the relationship between the them rather than its form.[44]

The key issue in determining whether two entities are single or separate entities for purposes of the antitrust laws is whether they have a single, unified economic interest or, conversely, whether their interests do or might diverge.[45] Thus, if two firms completely integrate all their operations in such a way that they have no economic incentives to compete with each other, or if all their action is in their joint best interests, then they are deemed to be one entity for antitrust purposes. The same is true if, as in *Copperweld Corp*., one entity completely controls the other.

As the structural and operational relationship between the alleged co-conspirators becomes more attenuated, the question of whether they have the capacity to conspire becomes more difficult to answer and may require in-depth discovery and factual analysis. Typically, a business entity is incapable of conspiring with its own employees, officers, and/or directors,[46] although some circuits apply an exception when the employee has an "independent personal stake," separate from his or her employer, in the success of the conspiracy.[47]

The case law is not in complete accord about the ability of less-than-wholly-owned subsidiaries to conspire with their parents[48] or the ability of separate corporations owned by the same individuals to conspire with each other or their owners.[49] Some courts hold that total, or almost total, ownership

---

41 *E.g., Total Benefits Planning Agency, Inc. v. Anthem Blue Cross & Blue Shield*, 552 F.3d 430 (6th Cir. 2008).
42 *E.g., Advanced Health-Care Servs. v. Radford Cmty. Hosp.*, 910 F.2d 139 (4th Cir. 1990); *Gonzalez-Maldonado v. MMM Healthcare, Inc.*, 2011-1 Trade Cas. (CCH) ¶ 77,315 (D.P.R. 2011).
43 *E.g., Gregory v. Ft. Bridger Rendezvous Ass'n*, 448 F.3d 1195 (10th Cir. 2006) ("The general rule, sometimes termed the 'single-entity rule'… is that coordinated activity within a corporation does not represent the plurality of actors necessary to establish concerted action."); *Alvord-Polk, Inc. v. F. Schumacher & Co.*, 37 F.3d 996 (3d Cir. 1994).
44 *See, e.g., Am. Needle, Inc. v. NFL*, 130 S.Ct. 2201 (2010); *Copperweld Corp. v. Independence Tube Corp.*, 467 U.S. 752 (1984); *Deutscher Tennis Bund v. ATP Tour, Inc.*, 610 F.3d 820 (3d Cir. 2010).
45 *See, e.g., Am. Needle, Inc. v. NFL*, 130 S.Ct. 2201 (2010); *Jack Russell Terrier Network v. Am. Kennel Club, Inc.*, 407 F.3d 1027 (9th Cir. 2005); *City of Mt. Pleasant v. Associated Elec. Co-Op., Inc.*, 838 F.2d 268 (8th Cir. 1988).
46 *E.g., Solla v. Aetna Health Plans*, 182 F.3d 901 (2d Cir. 1999) (Table); *Nurse Midwifery Assocs. v. Hibbett*, 918 F.2d 605 (6th Cir. 1990); *Am. Chiropractic Ass'n v. Trigon Healthcare, Inc.*, 258 F. Supp. 2d 461 (W.D. Va 2003). *But cf. Reddy v. Puma*, 2006-2 Trade Cas. (CCH) ¶ 75,497 (E.D.N.Y. 2006) (noting that, depending on facts, hospital-employed physicians may be capable of conspiring among themselves and with their hospital: "Due to the tangled economic relationships that exist among employers and employees in the medical field, the intra-corporate conspiracy doctrine will not always apply.").
47 *E.g., Stark v. Ear, Nose & Throat Specialists*, 185 Fed. App'x 120 (3d Cir. 2006); *St. Joseph's Hosp. v. Hospital Corp. of Am.*, 795 F.2d 948 (11th Cir. 1986); *New York Medscan LLC v. New York Univ. Sch. of Med.*, 430 F. Supp.2d 140 (S.D.N.Y. 2006). Other courts reject the exception. *Am. Council of Certified Podiatric Physicians & Surgeons v. Am. Bd. of Podiatric Surgery, Inc.* 185 F.3d 606 (6th Cir. 1999).
48 Compare *Square D Co. v. Schneider S.A.*, 760 F. Supp. 362 (S.D.N.Y. 1991) (parent can conspire with partially owned subsidiary) with *Bell Atl. Bus. Sys. Servs. v. Hitachi Data Sys. Corp.*, 849 F. Supp. 702 (N.D. Cal. 1994) (no conspiracy possible between parent and 80%-owned subsidiary).
49 Compare *Century Oil Tool Corp. v. Production Specialties, Inc.*, 737 F.2d 1316 (5th Cir. 1984) (conspiracy not possible) with *Fishman v. Wirtz*, 807 F.2d 520 (7th Cir. 1986) (conspiracy possible).

is necessary,[50] while other courts require only a controlling interest by one company in the other or control as a factual matter.[51]

The activities of joint ventures usually are deemed to result from a combination among the venturers (and thus are subject to section 1), rather than from unilateral action undertaken by a single entity,[52] unless the venturers cease competing against one another and completely integrate the lines of business involved in the venture.[53] This is a very uncertain area of antitrust law at present. For example, it is frequently difficult to determine whether certain types of joint ventures between hospitals and physicians constitute a single entity or separate entities for antitrust purposes.

Intra-enterprise conspiracy issues arise frequently in healthcare cases. In staff-privilege antitrust cases, for example, most courts hold that hospital medical staffs are combinations of their members,[54] but that the hospital and its medical staff, when engaging in peer review, are a single entity because the medical staff acts as the hospital's agent when conducting peer review.[55] Additionally, a partially integrated provider-controlled network (*e.g.*, an independent practice association (IPA)), is a combination of its members, rather than a single entity; thus, section 1 applies to its activities—as it does to most activities of any organization controlled by competitors.[56] On the other hand, if two parties completely integrate, such as medical practices or hospitals—through, *e.g.*, a merger, asset or stock acquisition, or consolidation—they become a single entity for antitrust purposes and are no longer capable of conspiring amongst themselves for purposes of the antitrust laws. Fully integrated medical groups constitute single entities for purposes of the antitrust laws.[57]

If the parties are capable of conspiring, the question becomes whether the challenged conduct resulted from unilateral action or concerted action as a factual matter. Technically, a "conspiracy" for antitrust purposes is a conscious commitment by two or more parties to a common scheme designed to achieve an unlawful objective, or a "meeting of the minds" in an unlawful agreement.[58] As a practical matter, however, any agreement or understanding meets section 1's concerted-action requirement; no

---

[50] *E.g.*, *Aspen Title & Escrow, Inc. v. Jeld-Wen, Inc.*, 677 F. Supp. 1477 (D. Ore. 1987) (holding that *Copperweld* doctrine applies only if parent owns 100% or a de minimis amount less than 100% of the subsidiary).

[51] *E.g.*, *Livinston Downs Racing Ass'n v. Jefferson Downs Corp.*, 257 F. Supp. 2d 819 (M.D. La. 2002) (indicating that mere majority control suffices for corporations to constitute a single entity).

[52] *Am. Needle, Inc. v. NFL*, 130 S.Ct. 2201 (2010); *NCAA v. Bd. of Regents*, 468 U.S. 85 (1984).

[53] *Texaco, Inc. v. Dagher*, 547 U.S. 1 (2006); *HealthAmerica Pennsylvania v. Susquehanna Health Sys.*, 278 F. Supp.2d 423 (M.D. Pa. 2003).

[54] *E.g.*, *Oksanen v. Page Mem'l Hosp.*, 945 F.2d 696 (4th Cir. 1991) (en banc); *Wesley v. Howard Univ.*, 3 F. Supp. 2d 1 (D.D.C. 1998).

[55] *E.g.*, *Oksanen v. Page Mem'l Hosp.*, 945 F.2d 696 (4th Cir. 1991) (*en banc*); *Nurse Midwifery Assocs. v. Hibbett*, 918 F.2d 605 (6th Cir. 1990); *Nanavati v. Burdette Tomlin Mem'l Hosp.*, 857 F.2d 96 (3d Cir. 1988); *Rowell v. Valley Health Sys.*, 2010-2 Trade Cas. (CCH) ¶ 77,214 (N.D. Cal. 2010). A minority of courts hold otherwise. *E.g.*, *Crosby v. Hosp. Auth.*, 93 F.3d 1515 (11th Cir. 1996); *Fox v. Good Samaritan Hosp.*, 2008-1 Trade Cas. (CCH) ¶ 76,008 (N.D. Cal. 2007).

[56] *N. Tex. Specialty Physicians v. FTC*, 528 F.3d 346 (5th Cir. 2008) ("When an organization is controlled by a group of competitors, it is considered to be a conspiracy of its members."); *Capital Imaging Assocs., P.C. v. Mohawk Valley Med. Assocs., Inc.*, 996 F.2d 537 (2d Cir. 1993) ("As members of the [IPA], the doctors are not staff physicians employed by the HMO…, that is, they are not agents of the HMO. Instead, these healthcare professionals are independent practitioners with separate economic interests."); *see also Podiatrist Ass'n, Inc. v. La Cruz Azul*, 332 F.3d 6 (1st Cir. 2003); *Perinatal Med. Group, Inc. v. Children's Hosp.*, 2010-1 Trade Cas. (CCH) ¶ 77,078 (E.D. Cal. 2010).

[57] *E.g.*, *Georgandellis v. Holzer Clinic, Inc.*, 2009-1 Trade Cas. (CCH) ¶ 76,651 (S.D. Ohio 2009).

[58] *E.g.*, *Am. Tobacco Co. v. United States*, 328 U.S. 781 (1946); *W. Penn Allegheny Health Sys. v. UPMC*, 627 F.3d 85 (3rd Cir. 2010) ("an agreement exists when there is a unity of purpose, a common design and understanding, a meeting of the minds, or a conscious commitment to a common scheme).

formal agreement is necessary.[59] Indeed, the terms "contract," "conspiracy," "combination," "agreement," and "understanding" are synonymous, meaning generally any type of concerted action.[60] The point worth emphasizing is that, for antitrust purposes, the concept of "agreement" is quite broad and that juries have significant leeway in finding (even by inferring) an agreement from circumstantial evidence.[61]

The conspiracy-in-fact analysis tends to be quite fact-intensive and fact-specific. Where the evidence of conspiracy is circumstantial and ambiguous, the range of permissible inferences from ambiguous evidence in antitrust cases is limited.[62] Thus, even at the summary-judgment stage, the plaintiff must present evidence tending to exclude the possibility that the defendants acted independently.[63] A number of courts have held, for example, that, if the inference of unilateral action is as justified from the evidence as that of concerted action (*i.e.*, the evidence is in "equipoise"), a jury cannot infer that the challenged action resulted from an agreement.[64] Indeed, the Supreme Court has indicated that even at the motion-to-dismiss stage, a plaintiff must plead facts plausibly suggesting that the challenged action resulted from concerted, and not unilateral, action.[65]

When the evidence whether the challenged conduct resulted from an agreement or from unilateral action is circumstantial (and thus inherently ambiguous, requiring inferences to reach the relevant conclusion), courts examine a number of factors, none of which is independently determinative, in assessing whether the challenged action was concerted or unilateral or whether to permit the jury to decide this question. These include whether:

1. the defendants had a motive to conspire;[66]
2. they had the opportunity to conspire, or met or communicated frequently;[67]

---

[59] *E.g.*, *United States v. Beaver*, 515 F.3d 730 (7th Cir. 2008).
[60] *See generally In re Ins. Brokerage Antitrust Litig.*, 618 F.3d 300 (3d Cir. 2010).
[61] *See, e.g.*, *Flat Panel Antitrust Litig.*, 385 F.3d 350 (3d Cir. 2004).
[62] *E.g.*, *Matsushita Elec. Indus. Co. v. Zenith Radio Corp.*, 475 U.S. 574 (1986); *see also Omincare, Inc. v. UnitedHealth Group, Inc.*, 627 F.3d 697 (7th Cir. 2010).
[63] *E.g.*, *Monsanto Co. v. Spray-Rite Serv. Corp.*, 465 U.S. 574 (1984); *see also Nitro Distrib., Inc. v. Alitor Corp.*, 565 F.3d 417 (8th Cir. 2009); *Golden Bridge Tech., Inc. v. Motorola, Inc.*, 547 F.3d 266 (5th Cir. 2008); *Abraham v. Intermountain Health Care, Inc.*, 461 F.3d 1249 (10th Cir. 2006); *Mitchael v. Intracorp, Inc.*, 179 F.3d 847 (10th Cir. 1999).
[64] *E.g.*, *Blomkest Fertilizer, Inc. v. Potash Corp.*, 203 F.3d 1028 (8th Cir. 2000) (*en banc*); *Thompson Everett Co. v. Nat'l Cable Adver.*, L.P., 57 F.3d 1317 (4th Cir. 1995).
[65] *Bell Atl. Corp. v. Twombly*, 550 U.S. 544 (2007); *In re Text Messaging Antitrust Litig.*, 630 F.3d 622 (7th Cir. 2010).
[66] *E.g.*, *Collins v. Associated Pathologists, Ltd.*, 844 F.2d 473 (7th Cir. 1988).
[67] *E.g.*, *Todorov v. DCH Healthcare Auth.*, 921 F.2d 1438 (11th Cir. 1991).

3. they engaged in consciously parallel behavior, and whether parallel behavior would be expected in the circumstances absent an agreement[68] (*i.e.*, "whether the defendants' actions, if taken individually, would be contrary to their economic self-interest");[69]
4. they put forth a legitimate explanation and justification for their individual actions;[70]
5. the plaintiff's theory of conspiracy makes any economic sense;[71] and
6. the plaintiff shows that justifications put forth by the defendants for the action are a pretext.[72]

Importantly, even consciously parallel behavior by the defendants is not, by itself, sufficient to prove that they reached an agreement.[73] Indeed, if the plaintiff alleges merely that all the defendants took the same action believing that their competitors would do the same, the court should grant the defendants' motion to dismiss for failure to state a claim.[74]

Typically, however, one party's mere acceptance of another's recommendation does not constitute a conspiracy or agreement between the two[75]—as when, for example, a hospital board follows the recommendation of its medical staff not to grant staff privileges to a practitioner.[76]

6.2.1.2 *Unreasonable Restraint on Competition*

If the challenged activity results from an agreement, the question becomes whether the agreement unreasonably restrains competition. Section 1 does not prohibit every restraint on competition, but

---

[68] "Consciously parallel action" occurs when parties act knowing or believing that their competitors will take the same action. Their action may be "interdependent"—that is, not successful in achieving their goal unless all take the same action—as in an oligopoly. In an oligopoly, competitors hesitate to lower their prices because they know that the competitors will do the same and that they will lose any competitive advantage they might gain from the price reduction. As a result, even absent a price-fixing agreement, prices remain above competitive levels through what some courts call "tacit collusion." *Compare generally Interstate Circuit, Inc. v. United States*, 306 U.S. 208 (1939) ("[i]t was enough that, knowing that concerted action was contemplated and invited, the [alleged conspirators] gave their adherence to the scheme and participated in it") *with Theatre Enters., Inc. v. Paramount Film Distrib. Corp.*, 346 U.S. 537 (1954) (consciously parallel action, by itself, is not sufficient to prove conspiracy). For more recent discussions, *see Bell Atl. Corp. v. Twombly*, 550 U.S. 544 (2007) (emphasizing that a conspiracy cannot be inferred from consciously parallel action by itself); *In re Flat Panel Glass Antitrust Litig.*, 385 F.3d 350 (3d Cir. 2004) (discussing the factors in addition to consciously parallel action that a plaintiff must prove); *Williamson Oil Co. v. Phillip Morris USA*, 346 F.3d 1287 (11th Cir. 2003).

[69] *Nat'l Hockey League Players Ass'n v. Plymouth Whalers Hockey Club,* 419 F.3d 462, 475 (6th Cir. 2005) ("A showing that defendants' actions, taken independently, would be contrary to their economic self-interest will ordinarily 'tend to exclude the likelihood of independent conduct'").

[70] *E.g., Cooper v. Forsyth County Hosp. Auth.*, 789 F.3d 278 (4th Cir. 1986); *see also City of Tuscaloosa v. Harcros Chems.*, Inc., 158 F.3d 548 (11th Cir. 1998); *Fleischman v. Albany Med. Ctr.*, 728 F. Supp. 2d 130 (N.D.N.Y. 2010); *Merck-Medco Managed Care, Inc. v. Rite-Aid Corp.*, 22 F. Supp. 2d 447 (D. Md. 1998), *aff'd per curiam*, 201 F.3d 436 (4th Cir. 1999) (Table).

[71] *E.g., JTC Petrol. Co. v. Piasa Motor Fuels, Inc.*, 179 F.3d 1073 (7th Cir. 1999).

[72] *E.g., Re/Max Int'l, Inc. v. Realty One, Inc.*, 173 F.3d 995 (6th Cir. 1999); *Boczar v. Manatee Hosp. & Health Sys.*, 993 F.2d 1514(11th Cir. 1993).

[73] *E.g., White v. R.M. Packer Co.*, 635 F.3d 571 (1st Cir. 2011); *In re Text Messaging Antitrust Litig.*, 630 F.3d 622 (7th Cir. 2010) (explaining that "[p]arallel behavior… is… a symptom of price fixing, though standing alone it is not proof of it").

[74] *E.g., Bell Atl. Co. v. Twombly*, 550 U.S. 544 (2007).

[75] *E.g., Abraham v. Intermountain Health Care, Inc.*, 461 F.3d 1249 (10th Cir. 2006); *Gordon v. Lewistown Hosp.*, 423 F.3d 184 (3d Cir. 2005); *Untracht v. Fikri*, 454 F. Supp. 2d 289 (W.D. Pa. 2006), *aff'd*, 249 Fed. App'x 268 (3d Cir. 2007); *Veesom v. Atchison Hosp. Ass'n,* 2006 WL 2714265 (D. Kan. 2006).

[76] *E.g. Mathews v. Lancaster Gen. Hosp.*, 87 F.3d 624 (3d Cir. 1996).

rather only those that "unreasonably" restrain competition.[77] In assessing the agreement's effect on competition, the first question is the standard or analytical methodology that applies—the *per se* rule, the full-blown rule of reason, or some standard in between, sometimes referred to as the "quick-look" or "truncated" rule of reason.[78] Perceived important factors other than competition (*e.g.*, other social goals, public-health goals, and public-welfare goals) are irrelevant in antitrust analysis.[79]

Agreements that, by their nature, are so obviously anticompetitive that no analysis of their actual effect on competition is necessary are "*per se* illegal":[80] a plaintiff need not prove any actual or likely anticompetitive effect from the agreement, and the defendants may not proffer any justifications for it. Rather, the *per se* rule has the force and effect of a statutory command that the challenged practice is unlawful.[81] It creates a conclusive presumption that the agreement unreasonably restrains competition without further analysis.[82]

The *per se* rule applies to agreements among competitors that facially appear to be of a type that always (or almost always) tends to restrict competition by decreasing output or increasing prices, rather than designed to increase economic efficiency or to otherwise generate procompetitive effects.[83] In general, the *per se* rule applies only to naked horizontal price-fixing, market-allocation, and other agreements not to compete, including bid-rigging agreements,[84] where the parties have not integrated their operations in ways likely to achieve efficiencies.[85]

---

77 *E.g.*, *Bell Atl. Corp. v. Twombly*, 550 U.S. 544 (2007); *Texaco, Inc. v. Dagher*, 547 U.S. 1 (2006) (noting that the Court has never taken a "literal approach" to section 1's language); *NYNEX Corp. v. Discon, Inc.*, 525 U.S. 128 (1998) (the Sherman Act's prohibition of "[e]very agreement in 'restraint of trade,'… prohibits only agreements that unreasonably restrain trade"); *W. Penn Allegheny Health Sys. v. UPMC*, 627 F.3d 85 (3d Cir. 2010) ("Despite its seemingly absolute language, section 1 has been construed to prohibit only *unreasonable* restraints of trade.").

78 For the analytical framework applied by the Antitrust Division and Federal Trade Commission in analyzing the lawfulness of agreements among competitors under section 1, *see* Federal Trade Comm'n & U.S. Dep't of Justice, *Antitrust Guidelines for Collaborations Among Competitors* (2000). For an excellent discussion of the relationship between the three standards, *see* Herbert Hovenkamp, *Federal Antitrust Policy* § 5.6b at 255–59 (3d ed. 2005).

79 *E.g.*, *National Soc'y of Prof'l Engr's v. United States*, 435 U.S. 679 (1978); *Schering-Plough Corp. v. FTC*, 402 F.3d 1056 (11th Cir. 2005) ("A restraint on competition cannot be justified solely on the basis of social welfare concerns.").

80 *See, e.g.*, *Ariz. v. Maricopa County Med. Soc'y*, 457 U.S. 332 (1982); *California v. Safeway, Inc.*, 615 F.3d 1171 (9th Cir. 2010); *Total Benefits Planning Agency, Inc. v. Anthem Blue Cross & Blue Shield*, 552 F.3d 430 (6th Cir. 2008) ("The *per se* standard recognizes that there are some methods of restraint that are so inherently and facially anti-competitive that an elaborate and burdensome inquiry into a demonstrable economic impact on competition in a relevant market is not required.").

81 *FTC v. Superior Court Trial Lawyers Ass'n*, 493 U.S. 411 (1990); *In re Cardizem CD Antitrust Litig.*, 332 F.3d 896 (6th Cir. 2003).

82 *Arizona v. Maricopa County Med. Soc'y*, 457 U.S. 332 (1982); *InterVest, Inc. v. Bloomberg*, L.P., 340 F.3d 144 (3d Cir. 2003).

83 *E.g.*, *Texaco, Inc. v. Dagher*, 547 U.S. 1 (2006) ("*Per se* liability is reserved for only those agreements that are 'so plainly anticompetitive that no elaborate study of the industry is needed to establish their illegality.'"); *Broadcast Music, Inc. v. Columbia Broad. Sys.*, 441 U.S. 1 (1979); *Nitro Distrib., Inc. v. Alitor Corp.*, 565 F.3d 417 (8th Cir. 2009); *Paycom Billing Servs., Inc. v. MasterCard Int'l, Inc.*, 467 F.3d 283 (2d Cir. 2006) ("The *per se* label is applied '[o]nce experience with a particular kind of restraint enables the Court to predict with confidence that the rule of reason will condemn it.'"); *Nat'l Hockey League Players Ass'n, v. Plymouth Whalers Hockey Club*, 419 F.3d 462 (6th Cir. 2005) ("The *per se* rule is appropriate where the challenged practice is 'entirely devoid of redeeming competitive rationales.'").

84 *E.g.*, *In re Ins. Brokerage Antitrust Litig.*, 618 F.3d 300 (3d Cir. 2010).

85 Until June 2007, vertical minimum price-fixing agreements, by which, for example, a supplier and retailer agree on the price at which the retailer will resell the product, were *per se* unlawful. In *Leegin Creative Leather Products, Inc. v. PSKS, Inc.*, 551 U.S. 877 (2007), the Supreme Court held that the rule-of-reason standard, rather than the *per se* standard, applies to all vertical price-fixing agreements when analyzed under section 1 of the Sherman Act. Whether the same will be true when these agreements are challenged under state antitrust laws is unclear.

Where the agreement is not obviously anticompetitive, courts apply a more lenient standard—the "rule of reason." Broadly stated, the question under full-blown rule-of-reason analysis is whether, after identifying and weighing an agreement's procompetitive and anticompetitive effects, the agreement on balance results in substantial or significant anticompetitive effects. If it does, the agreement is unlawful.[86] Although the analysis, is typically quite expensive and time-consuming,[87] the rule of reason is the accepted standard for testing whether an agreement unreasonably restrains competition. Application of the *per se* rule is limited to those agreements that always or almost always restrict competition without providing any offsetting procompetitive benefits.[88]

In recent years, many courts, in applying the rule of reason, have adopted a broad three-step "burden shifting" framework. First, the plaintiff must prove that the agreement has or would have a substantial anticompetitive effect. If the plaintiff sustains this burden, the burden of going forward shifts to the defendants to show that the agreement has significant procompetitive effects. "Procompetitive effects" is a broad term, generally encompassing any effect that benefits consumers.[89] If the defendants carry their burden, then the burden shifts back to the plaintiff to show that those could have been achieved in a manner less restrictive of competition or that, on balance, the agreement's anticompetitive effects significantly outweigh its procompetitive effects.[90] The ultimate burden of persuasion always remains on the plaintiff.

As a threshold matter, proving anticompetitive effects usually requires the plaintiff to show that the defendants have significant market power, or that their agreement would result in their obtaining market power. Indeed, some courts have held explicitly that no violation of section 1 can result under rule-of-reason analysis absent proof that the defendants have market power.[91] Anticompetitive effects include increased prices, reduced output, or lower quality resulting from the exercise of market power.[92]

A plaintiff can prove the requisite anticompetitive effect or market power (*i.e.*, meet its initial burden) by direct or circumstantial evidence.[93] Direct evidence includes proof of supracompetitive

---

[86] *E.g.*, *N. Tex. Specialty Physicians v. FTC*, 528 F.3d 346 (5th Cir. 2008) (noting that under rule-of-reason analysis, the fact-finder decides, under all the relevant circumstances, whether the agreement imposes an unreasonable restraint on competition); *Flegel v. Christian Hosp.*, 4 F.3d 682 (8th Cir. 1993); *Bhan v. NME Hosps.*, 929 F.2d 1404 (9th Cir. 1991).

[87] *E.g.*, *Cal. v. Safeway, Inc.*, 615 F.3d 1171 (9th Cir. 2010) (explaining that "[f]ull rule of reason review is data-intensive, and, consequently, expensive for litigants; it also consumes large amounts of courts' time and resources").

[88] *E.g.*, *Leegin Creative Leather Prods., Inc. v. PSKS, Inc.*, 551 U.S. 827 (2007).

[89] *See generally California v. Safeway, Inc.*, 615 F.3d 1171 (9th Cir. 2010) ("Procompetitive effects include efficiency gains, the development or improvement of products and other benefits to consumers and society.").

[90] *See, e.g.*, *In re Ins. Brokerage Antitrust Litig.*, 618 F.3d 300 (3d Cir. 2010); *In re Ciprofloxacin Hydrochloride Antitrust Litig.*, 544 F.3d 1323 (Fed. Cir. 2008); *Nilavar v. Mercy Health Sys.*, 244 Fed. App'x 690 (6th Cir. 2007); *In re Tamoxifen Citrate Antitrust Litig.*, 466 F.3d 187 (2d Cir. 2006); *Gordon v. Lewistown Hosp.*, 423 F.3d 184 (3d Cir. 2005); *Schering-Plough Corp. v. FTC*, 402 F.3d 1056 (11th Cir. 2005); *Levine v. Cent. Fla. Med. Affiliates, Inc.*, 72 F.3d 1538 (11th Cir. 1996); *Capital Imaging Assocs., P.C. v. Mohawk Valley Med. Assocs., Inc.*, 996 F.2d 537 (2d Cir. 1993).

[91] *E.g.*, *Menasha Corp. v. News Am. Mkting. In-Store, Inc.*, 354 F.3d 661 (7th Cir. 2004) ("The first requirement in every suit based on the Rule of Reason is market power...."); *Digital Equip Corp. v. Uniq Digital Tech., Inc.*, 73 F.3d 756 (7th Cir. 1996) (noting that in the Seventh Circuit, substantial market power is an ingredient of every claim under the rule of reason); *see also E. Food Servs., Inc. v. Pontifical Catholic Univ. Servs. Ass'n*, Inc., 357 F.3d 1 (1st Cir. 2004) (explaining that "absent market power there is ordinarily no detriment and no reason to engage in any weighing").

[92] *E.g., W. Penn Allegheny Health Sys. v. UPMC*, 627 F.3d 85 (3d Cir. 2010).

[93] *E.g.*, *Republic Tobacco Co. v. N. Atl. Trading Co.*, 381 F.3d 717 (7th Cir. 2004) (explaining that "there are some circumstances where to establish a violation of the antitrust laws it is unnecessary to prove that defendant wielded market power in a properly defined product and geographic market, and plaintiff may rely instead on direct evidence of anticompetitive effects"); *Levine v. Cent. Fla. Med. Affiliates, Inc.*, 72 F.3d 1538 (11th Cir. 1996); *Peoria Day Surgery Ctr. v. OSF*

prices, sub-competitive output, or sub-competitive quality. Under this approach, the plaintiff need not prove the relevant market, the defendants' market share, or the existence of entry barriers.[94] Under the circumstantial-evidence approach, those factors are precisely what the plaintiff must prove—the relevant market, that the defendants have a substantial share of that market, typically 40% or more, and that entry and expansion barriers prevent new firms from entering the market, as well as incumbent firms from expanding their output.[95]

As a general rule, the quick-look version of the rule of reason—a standard between the *per se* and full-blown rule-of-reason standards—applies to agreements among competitors that clearly would, all else being equal, restrict their output or increase prices, but which may have significant procompetitive justifications.[96] The court presumes that the defendants have the necessary market power for a violation and takes a "quick look" at the purported justifications to determine whether they are plausible.[97] If they are not and the potential anticompetitive effects of the agreement are obvious, then the agreement is condemned summarily, as under the *per se* rule, without any examination of relevant markets, market power, or the agreement's actual effect on competition. If the justifications are plausible, however, the court applies a more in-depth rule-of-reason analysis.[98]

The quick-look rule of reason has significant applicability to healthcare antitrust issues. For example, in examining whether the joint pricing of physician services by partially integrated, provider-controlled contracting networks (such as IPAs) constitutes a *per se* unlawful price-fixing agreement, it frequently is necessary to first examine whether the physicians have substantially integrated their practices through the network through risk sharing or clinical integration. If so, this may provide the

---

Healthcare Sys., 2010-1 Trade Cas. (CCH) ¶ 76,870 (C.D. Ill. 2009); *Minn. Ass'n of Nurse Anesthetists v. Unity Hosp.*, 5 F. Supp. 2d 694 (D. Minn. 1998), *aff'd*, 208 F.3d 655 (8th Cir. 2000).

[94] *See generally FTC v. Ind. Fed'n of Dentists*, 476 U.S. 477 (1986); *see also Angelico v. Lehigh Valley Hosp.*, 184 F.3d 268 (3d Cir. 1999).

[95] *E.g., Rebel Oil Co. v. Atl. Richfield Co.*, 51 F.2d 1421 (9th Cir. 1995); *United States v. Brown Univ.*, 5 F.3d 658 (3d Cir. 1993); *Gordon v. Lewistown Hosp.*, 272 F. Supp.2d 393 (M.D. Pa. 2003), *aff'd*, 423 F.3d 184 (3d Cir. 2005).

[96] For development and application of the quick-look rule of reason by the Supreme Court, *see Cal. Dental Ass'n v. FTC*, 526 U.S. 756 (1999); *FTC v. Ind. Fed'n of Dentists*, 476 U.S. 447 (1986); *NCAA v. Bd. of Regents*, 468 U.S. 85 (1984); *Broadcast Music, Inc. v. Columbia Broad. Sys.*, 441 U.S. 1 (1979).

[97] For examples or discussion of quick-look analysis, *see N. Tex. Specialty Physicians v. FTC*, 528 F.3d 346 (5th Cir. 2008) (applying quick-look analysis to price fixing by an IPA), *granting petition for review in part and remanding*, 2005-2 Trade Cas. (CCH) ¶ 75,032 (FTC 2005) (FTC decision holding that IPA's joint negotiations and other conduct constituted horizontal price fixing); *FTC v. Polygram Holding, Inc.*, 416 F.3d 29 (D.C. Cir. 2005); *Gordon v. Lewistown Hosp.*, 423 F.3d 184 (3d Cir. 2005) ("The [quick-look rule of reason] applies where *per se* condemnation is inappropriate but where no elaborate industry analysis is required to demonstrate the anticompetitive character of an inherently suspect restraint.... Rather, the competitive harm is presumed and the defendant must set forth some competitive justification for the restraints."); *Continental Airlines, Inc., v. United Airlines, Inc.*, 277 F.3d 499 (4th Cir. 2003); *Law v. NCAA*, 134 F.3d 1010 (10th Cir. 1998); *Retina Assocs., PA. v. S. Baptist Hosp.*, 105 F.3d 1376 (11th Cir. 1997) (*per curiam*).

[98] *See Cal. Dental Ass'n v. FTC*, 526 U.S. 726 (1999) (rejecting application of quick-look analysis to dental association's restraints on advertising because the restraints were not obviously anticompetitive on balance and their effect on competition could not be determined without further analysis); *In re Ins. Brokerage Antitrust Litig.*, 618 F.3d 300 (3d Cir. 2010) (explaining that "[u]nder a quick look analysis..., competitive harm is presumed and the defendant must set forth some procompetitive justification for the restraints.... If no plausible justification is forthcoming, the restraint will be condemned.... 'If the defendant offers sound procompetitive justifications, however, the court must proceed to weigh the overall reasonableness of the restraint....'") (citations and internal quotation marks omitted; *Deutscher Tennis Bund v. ATP Tour, Inc.*, 610 F.3d 820 (3d Cir. 2010).

In fact, there is no bright-line distinction between the three different standards. Rather, there is a continuum. The quest is simply to determine how much information a court needs before it can determine whether the agreement unreasonably restrains competition. *See* Herbert Hovenkamp, *Federal Antitrust Policy* § 5.6b at 255 (3d ed. 2005).

plausible competitive justification for applying the rule of reason, rather than the *per se* rule, to the physicians' joint negotiations of prices, which constitute a form of price-fixing agreement.

6.2.1.3 Agreements with Potential Section 1 Ramifications

Agreements can be horizontal (*i.e.*, among actual or potential competitors), vertical (*i.e.*, between firms at different levels in the chain of production or distribution), or conglomerate (among firms with no discernable economic relationship). Horizontal agreements are the primary concern of the antitrust laws because, since they are among competitors, they have the greatest potential to affect competition directly and adversely.[99]

6.2.1.3.1 Horizontal Price-Fixing Agreements

A horizontal price-fixing agreement is any type of agreement among competitors that directly affects the prices they charge (seller price fixing) or pay (buyer price fixing) for their goods or services.[100]

The breadth of conduct constituting price fixing is sweeping. It encompasses much more than the classic image of a meeting in a smoke-filled hotel room where the competitors, all undoubtedly wearing trench coats, hats, and dark glasses, explicitly agree on the specific prices they will charge. Rather, price-fixing agreements include such activities as the use of a single agent by competitors to negotiate their prices[101] and agreements on profit margins, pricing formulae, ranges of prices, discounts, output, and the like.[102]

"Naked" horizontal price-fixing agreements are *per se* unlawful, regardless of whether engaged in by sellers or buyers[103] and are frequently prosecuted criminally by the Antitrust Division of the U.S. Department of Justice. "Ancillary" price-fixing agreements are analyzed under the rule of reason. A price-fixing agreement is "naked" if it is not closely connected to a venture in which competitors have economically integrated their operations and thus there is no likelihood of any significant procompetitive effects. A price-fixing agreement is ancillary if it:

1. is related to and implemented in connection with a larger venture that itself is likely to generate procompetitive effects because the parties have significantly integrated their operations;

---

[99] For the analytical framework the federal antitrust enforcement agencies apply in analyzing horizontal restraints, *see* Federal Trade Comm'm & U.S. Dep't of Justice, *Antitrust Guidelines for Collaborations Among Competitors* (2000), at http://www.ftc.gov/os/2000/04/ftcdojguidelines.pdf.

[100] *See generally United States v. Socony-Vacuum Oil Co.*, 310 U.S. 150 (1940) (noting that a horizontal price-fixing agreement is any agreement or understanding among competitors that increases, decreases, pegs, or stabilizes the prices at which they sell their products).

[101] *See New York v. St. Francis Hosp.*, 99 F. Supp. 2d 399 (S.D. N.Y. 2000) (applying the *per se* rule to an agreement among hospitals to negotiate contracts jointly with managed-care plans).

[102] For a list of the types of conduct that courts have held constitute price fixing, *see* 1 John J. Miles, *Health Care & Antitrust Law* § 3:2 at 3-5 through 3-9 (Supp. 2010).

[103] *See Arizona v. Maricopa County Med. Soc'y*, 457 U.S. 332 (1982); *Omnicare, Inc. v. UnitedHealth Group, Inc.*, 629 F.3d 697 (7th Cir. 2011) (alleged buyer price-fixing agreement); *Freeman v. San Diego Ass'n of Realtors*, 322 F.3d 1133 (9th Cir. 2003) ("No antitrust violation is more abominated than the agreement to fix prices."); *All Care Nursing Servs., Inc. v. High Tech Staffing Servs., Inc.*, 135 F.3d 740 (11th Cir. 1998) ("That price fixing is equally violative of antitrust laws whether it is done by buyers or sellers is... undisputed."); *Doe v. Ariz. Hosp. & Healthcare Ass'n*, 2009-1 Trade Cas. (CCH) ¶ 76,591 (D. Ariz. 2009) (same); *N. Jackson Pharm., Inc. v. Caremark Rx, Inc.*, 385 F. Supp.2d 740 (N.D. Ill. 2005) (same).

2. significantly promotes, or is reasonably necessary to, the venture's achievement of those procompetitive effects; and
3. no obvious method exists for achieving those procompetitive effects that would have a significantly less restrictive effect on competition.[104]

The ultimate question is whether the parties are merely a "cartel" that fixes prices, or, on the other hand, whether they are a joint venture and the agreement on price is reasonably necessary for the venture to achieve its procompetitive effects.[105]

The "naked"/"ancillary" price-fixing distinction is particularly important in determining whether partially integrated, provider-controlled contracting networks (*e.g.*, IPAs, preferred-provider organizations, accountable care organizations, and physician/hospital organizations) can themselves establish fee-for-service prices for their providers' services in contracting with commercial health plans without running afoul of the *per se* rule against price fixing, or whether they must use some form of "messenger-model" arrangement through which each provider-member of the network independently establishes its own prices in dealing with third-party payors.[106] In 1996, the Federal Trade Commission and Antitrust Division issued their Statements of Antitrust Enforcement Policy in Health Care, two of which address provider-controlled contracting networks.[107] They provide that economic integration sufficient to permit the network to establish prices without committing a *per se* violation of section 1 includes either (1) the provider members' sharing substantial financial risk by contracting with payors on an at-risk basis[108] or (2) their "clinically integrating" with one another by ensuring that the network has strong and effective utilization-review, quality-assurance, reporting, monitoring, case-management, and credentialing programs.[109] The FTC has issued four staff-advisory opinions discussing the

---

[104] This definition of "ancillary restraint" is a synthesis of numerous sources. The seminal decision is *United States v. Addyston Pipe & Steel Co.*, 85 F. 271 (6th Cir. 1898), *modified and aff'd*, 175 U.S. 211 (1899). Other important decisions discussing when a restraint is ancillary include *Major League Baseball Props., Inc. v. Salvino*, 542 F.3d 290 (2d Cir. 2008) (Sotomayor, J., concurring); *Freeman v. San Diego Ass'n of Realtors*, 322 F.3d 1133 (9th Cir. 2003); *SCFC ILC, Inc. v. Visa U.S.A., Inc.*, 36 F.3d 958 (10th Cir. 1994); *Rothery Storage & Van Co. v. Atlas Van Lines, Inc.*, 792 F.2d 210 (D.C. Cir. 1986); *Nat'l Bancard Corp. v. VISA U.S.A.*, 779 F.2d 592 (11th Cir. 1986); *Polk Bros. v. Forest City Enters.*, 776 F.2d 185 (7th Cir. 1985); and *Gen. Leaseways, Inc. v. Nat'l Truck Leasing Ass'n*, 744 F.2d 588 (7th Cir. 1984); *see also* Federal Trade Comm'n & U.S. Dep't of Justice, *Antitrust Guidelines for Collaboration Among Competitors* § 3.2 (2000). For a helpful discussion in the context of an FTC challenge to a physician-controlled contracting network's allegedly negotiating prices in contracts with payors on behalf of its members challenged by the FTC, *see N. Tex. Specialty Physicians*, 2005-2 Trade Cas. (CCH) ¶ 75,032 (FTC 2005), *petition for review granted in part and remanded*, 528 F.3d 346 (5th Cir. 2008).

[105] *Compare Ariz. v. Maricopa County Med. Soc'y*, 457 U.S. 332 (1982) (cartel) *with Broadcast Music, Inc. v. Columbia Broad. Sys.*, 441 U.S. 1 (1979) (joint venture in which the price-fixing agreement was ancillary because it was necessary for the joint venture product to be offered at all).

[106] For a discussion of the antitrust ramifications of provider-controlled networks, *see* John J. Miles, *Joint Venture Analysis and Provider-Controlled Health Care Networks*, 66 Antitrust L.J. 127 (1997). For a discussion of the antitrust issues raised by messenger-model networks, *see* Jeff Miles, *Ticking Antitrust Time Bombs: A Message to Messed-Up Messenger Models*, AHLA Health Lawyers News, Nov. 2002 (Vol. 6, Number 11), at 4.

[107] U.S. Dep't of Justice & Federal Trade Comm'n, *Statements of Antitrust Policy in Health Care* (1996) ("*Health Care Statements*").

[108] For a helpful discussion of the antitrust ramifications of shared financial risk in the context of provider-controlled contracting networks, *see* Susan A. Creighton, Director, Bureau of Competition, FTC, "Diagnosing Physician-Hospital Organizations," Prepared Remarks Before the AHLA Program on Legal Issues Affecting Academic Medical Centers and Other Teaching Institutions (Jan. 22, 2004), at http://www.ftc.gov/speeches/other/creightonphospeech.shtm.

[109] *See* U.S. Dep't of Justice & Federal Trade Comm'n, *Statements of Antitrust Enforcement Policy in Health Care Statements* 8 & 9 (1996), at http://www.justice.gov/atr/public/guidelines/1791.pdf.

antitrust ramifications of clinically integrated provided-controlled contracting networks.[110] The FTC and Antitrust Division have brought numerous actions challenging alleged price-fixing agreements among providers, particularly physicians, for jointly refusing to contract, or threatening to refuse to contract, with health plans absent reimbursement increases.[111] But even if a network is sufficiently integrated and its joint negotiations are reasonably necessary to achieve the efficiencies from its integration, a second step—rule-of-reason analysis—is necessary because its joint negotiations are still unlawful if it can increase its participants' reimbursement by exercising market power. Whether a network has market power is largely a function of two variables: (1) whether the network includes a large percentage of all area providers of the services offered by the network, and (2) whether the network is "exclusive" in the sense that participating providers are not permitted to contract with health plans through mechanisms other than the network.[112]

The Accountable Care Act, part of the Obama administration's healthcare reform legislation, directs the Secretary of the Department of Health and Human Services, through its Center for Medicare and Medicaid Services (CMS), to establish a "shared-savings program" through the creation of accountable care organizations, or ACOs, to manage and coordinate the care of Medicare beneficiaries in the fee-for-service program.[113] ACOs would share in cost savings to Medicare they generate if they meet certain quality performance and cost-saving goal, and distribute the money they receive with their participating providers.

ACOs are, in effect, clinically integrated provider-controlled contracting networks that likely will contract not only with Medicare but also with commercial health plans by negotiating contracts jointly on behalf of their provider participants. CMS has issued a proposed rule that would govern their creation and operation.[114] Because joint negotiations by ACOs with commercial health plans potentially raise significant antitrust issues, the FTC and Antitrust Division have issued a proposed Statement of Antitrust Policy Regarding Accountable Care Organizations Participating in the Medicare Shared Savings Program.[115] The Statement provides that ACOs meeting CMS's eligibility criteria are deemed sufficiently clinically integrated so that their joint negotiations are tested under the rule of reason rather than summarily condemned under the per se rule. The market-power analysis under the Statement focuses on the ACO's market shares in the services provided by its participating providers in their

---

[110] FTC Staff Advisory Opinion to TriState Health Partners, Inc. (Apr. 13, 2009), at http://www.ftc.gov/os/closings/staff/090413tristataoletter.pdf; FTC Staff Advisory Opinion to Greater Rochester Independent Practice Association (Sept. 17, 2007), at http://www.ftc.gov/bc/adops/gripa.pdf; FTC Staff Advisory Opinion to Suburban Health Organization (Mar. 28, 2006), at http://www.ftc.gov/os/2006/03/suburbanhealthorganizationstaffadvisoryopinion03282006.pdf; FTC Staff Advisory Opinion to MedSouth Inc. (Feb. 19, 2002), at www.ftc.govfbc/adops/medsouth.htm.

[111] *See, e.g.*, *Sw. Health Alliances, Inc.*, File No. 091 0013 (FTC May 10, 2011) (proposed consent order); *Minn. Rural Health Coop.*, Dkt. No. C-4311 (FTC Jan. 4, 2011) (consent order); *United States v. Idaho Orthopaedic Soc'y*, 2010-1 Trade Cas. (CCH) ¶ 77,142 (D. Idaho 2010) (consent decree and competitive impact statement); *Boulder Valley Individual Practice Ass'n*, Dkt. No. C-4285 (FTC Apr. 2, 2010) (consent order); *Roaring Fork Valley Physicians I.P.A., Inc.*, Dkt. No. C-4288 (FTC Apr. 5, 2010).

[112] *Health Care Statements*, Statements 8.A, 9.B.

[113] Patient Protection and Affordable Care Act, Pub. L. 111-148, § 3022, as amended by the Health Care and Education Reconcilation Act of 2010, Pub. L. 111-152.

[114] Notice of Proposed Regulation, Medicare Program; Medicare Shared Savings Program: Accountable Care Organizations, 76 Fed. Reg. 19,528 (Apr. 7, 2011).

[115] U.S. Dep't of Justice & Federal Trade Comm'n, *Proposed Statement of Antitrust Enforcement Policy Regarding Accountable Care Organizations Participating in the Medicare Shared Savings Program*, 76 Fed. Reg. 21,894 (Apr. 19, 2011).

primary service areas. If any of an ACO's market shares exceeds 50%, as a condition of participation in the shared-savings program, it must obtain a review letter from either the FTC or Antitrust Division stating that the agency does not intend to challenge its actions on antitrust grounds.

6.2.1.3.2 *Horizontal Agreements to Exchange Pricing Information*

Agreements among competitors to exchange price information can raise three issues under section 1. First, they may be the first step toward a horizontal price-fixing agreement that is *per se* unlawful.[116] Second, they are probative circumstantial evidence of a *per se* unlawful price-fixing agreement.[117] And third, even short of a resulting price-fixing agreement, they can result in price stabilization and thus violate section 1.[118] On the other hand, the exchange or dissemination of pricing information can be procompetitive by facilitating more-informed business decisions.[119]

Horizontal agreements to exchange price information are analyzed under the rule of reason.[120] The exchange is more likely to have an unlawful effect on prices when:

- the relevant market is highly concentrated;
- the price information exchanged concerns present or future prices, as opposed to historical prices;
- the price information exchanged is firm- or transaction-specific;
- the products or services that the firms sell are fungible; and
- demand for the product or services is price-inelastic[121] (*i.e.*, an increase in the product's price results in a less than proportional decrease in quantity demanded).[122]

Statement 6 of the *Statements of Antitrust Enforcement Policy in Health Care* discusses "provider participation in exchanges of price and cost information," specifically providing an "antitrust safety zone" for competitor price and cost exchanges if the program meets certain requirements. The antitrust rules and principles governing agreements among competitors to exchange information about the prices they charge apply equally to agreements among competitors to exchange the prices they pay for their inputs, *e.g.*, an agreement among competing hospitals to exchange information about their wage

---

116 *See, e.g., Morton Salt Co. v. United States*, 235 F.2d 573 (10th Cir. 1956); *Jung v. Am. Ass'n of Med. Colls.*, 300 F. Supp. 2d 119 (D.DC. 2004).

117 *E.g., Fleischman v. Albany Med. Ctr.*, 728 F. Supp. 2d 130 (N.D.N.Y. 2010).

118 *E.g., United States v. Container Corp. of Am.*, 393 U.S. 333 (1969); *Omnicare, Inc. v. UnitedHealth Group*, Inc., 629 F.3d 697 (7th Cir. 2011) (noting that "[i]nformation exchange can help support an inference of a price-fixing agreement")

119 *Int'l Healthcare Mgmt. v. Haw. Coalition for Health*, 332 F.3d 600 (9th Cir. 2003).

120 *E.g., United States v. Citizens & S. Nat'l Bank*, 422 U.S. 86 (1975).

121 *See generally United States v. United States Gypsum Co.*, 438 U.S. 422 (1978).

122 For an excellent explanation of price-elasticity of demand, *see* Robert S. Pindyck & Daniel L. Rubinfeld, *Microeconomics* 32-42 (6th ed. 2005).

levels for nurses or their participation in a third-party survey of wage levels.[123] The FTC and Antitrust Division have issued numerous advisory opinions discussing price surveys by healthcare providers.[124]

6.2.1.3.3 *Horizontal Market-Allocation Agreements*

A horizontal market-allocation agreement is an agreement among competitors by which they allocate among themselves designated geographical areas, the sale of particular goods or services, or particular types of customers, agreeing not to compete along those dimensions. For example, two hospitals might agree that one will provide open-heart surgical services and the other will establish a cancer center of excellence and that they will not compete against each other to provide those services. Market-allocation agreements destroy competition along all competitive dimensions, not just price.[125] "Naked" market-allocation agreements are *per se* unlawful,[126] but "ancillary" market-allocation agreements (*i.e.*, those that are part of an efficiency-enhancing cooperative effort and that are reasonably necessary for the venture to function effectively) are tested under the rule of reason.[127]

In healthcare, market-allocation-agreement problems usually arise in the context of agreements among competing hospitals by which they agree about which hospital will provide particular services—efforts to reduce "unnecessary duplication," such as two open-heart programs, neither of which is operating at capacity.[128] Two of the federal antitrust enforcement agencies' *Health Care Statements* discuss the issue: Statement 2, dealing with "hospital joint ventures involving high technology or other expensive health care equipment and includes a safety zone;" and Statement 3, dealing with "hospital joint ventures involving specialized clinical or other expensive health care services" but includes no safety zone. The Statements indicate that, in many instances, the agencies will assess horizontal market-allocation agreements in these contexts under the rule of reason unless "the joint venture arrangement is… one that uses the joint venture label but is likely to merely to restrict competition and

---

[123] For examples of enforcement actions in healthcare involving the exchange of price information, *see United States v. Utah Soc'y for Health & Human Res. Admin.*, 1994-2 Trade Cas. (CCH) ¶ 70,845 (D. Utah 1994) (consent decree); *United States v. Burgstiner*, 1991-1 Trade Cas. (CCH) ¶ 69,422 (S.D. Ga. 1991) (consent decree). Because wages are the prices paid for inputs, exchanges of wage information among competing employers also can raise serious antitrust issues. *See generally Todd v. Exxon Corp.*, 275 F.3d 191 (2d Cir. 2001); *see also Fleischman v. Albany Med. Ctr.*, 728 F. Supp. 2d 130 (N.D.N.Y. 2010); *Jung v. Ass'n of Am. Med. Colls.*, 226 F.R.D. 7 (D.D.C. 2005) (rejecting plaintiff's motion to amend complaint alleging numerous graduate education programs agreed to fix the stipends paid medical residents), *aff'd*, 184 Fed. App'x 9 (D.C. Cir. 2006); *Reed v. Advocate Health Care*, No. 06 C 3337 (N.D. Ill. complaint filed June 20, 2006) (one of six class-action suits alleging hospitals in various areas of U.S. fixed the wages paid).

[124] *See, e.g.*, FTC Staff Advisory Opinion to Medical Group Management Association (Nov. 3, 2003), at http://www.ftc.gov/bc/adops/mgma031104.pdf; FTC Staff Advisory Opinion to PriMed, Inc. (Feb. 6, 2003), at http://www.ftc.gov/bc/adops/030206dayton.shtm; Antitrust Division Business Review Letter to Washington State Medical Association (Sept. 23, 2002), at http://www.usdoj.gov/atr/public/busreview/200260.pdf.; *see also United States v. Prof'l Consultants Ins. Co.*, 2005-2 Trade Cas. (CCH) ¶ 75,031 (D.D.C. 2005) (consent decree and competitive impact statement) (Antitrust Division enforcement action challenging allegedly unlawful information sharing).

[125] *Blue Cross & Blue Shield v. Marshfield Clinic*, 65 F.3d 1406 (7th Cir. 1995) ("It would be a strange interpretation of antitrust law that forbade competitors to agree on what price to charge, thus eliminating price competition among them, but allowed them to divide markets, thus eliminating all competition among them.").

[126] *E.g.*, *Palmer v. BRG of Ga.*, 498 U.S. 46 (1990) (per curiam); *In re Ins. Brokerage Antitrust Litig.*, 618 F.3d 300 (3d Cir. 2010); *Nitro Distrib., Inc. v. Alitor Corp.*, 565 F.3d 417 (8th Cir. 2009); *Kentuckiana Med. Ctr. LLC v. Clark County*, 2008-1 Trade Cas. (CCH) ¶ 76,011 (S.D. Ind. 2006).

[127] *E.g.*, *Polk Bros. v. Forest City Enters.*, 776 F.2d 185 (7th Cir. 1985).

[128] *See New York v. St. Francis Hosp.*, 94 F. Supp. 2d 399 (S.D.N.Y. 2000) (applying the *per se* rule to an agreement among hospitals as to the services each would and would not offer).

decrease output."[129] But the Antitrust Division has challenged several market-allocation agreements between hospitals.[130]

6.2.1.3.4 Horizontal Concerted Refusals to Deal or Group Boycotts

A concerted refusal to deal or "group boycott" is an agreement among competitors not to deal with another firm (usually a competitor of the boycotting parties).[131] Conduct of this description is ubiquitous throughout the economy, and certainly is prevalent in healthcare—for example, a medical staff including competitors of an applicant for staff privileges may recommend against granting the applicant staff privileges, preventing the applicant from competing; similarly, a provider network may deny membership to a provider who wishes to join.[132]

Until 1985, many courts stated that group boycotts are *per se* unlawful, although they frequently found ways not to apply the strict *per se* rule.[133] In 1985, however, the Supreme Court, in *Northwest Wholesale Stationers, Inc. v. Pacific Stationery & Printing Co.*[134] held specifically that, at a minimum, the boycotting parties must have market power before the *per se* rule applies. Moreover, courts almost uniformly permit defendants to justify their group boycotts on procompetitive grounds.[135] In practice, most courts, in practical effect, now apply the rule of reason to group boycotts,[136] and this is particularly true in cases involving the healthcare sector,[137] but some courts continue to use the *per se* label in discussing group boycotts.[138]

6.2.1.3.5 Tying Agreements

A tying agreement results when a seller and buyer agree that the seller will sell the buyer one product or service (the "tying" product), but only if the buyer purchases a second separate product or service (the "tied" product) as well.[139] The antitrust concern from tying agreements is that competitors

---

129 *Health Care Statements*, Statement 2 n.5.

130 *See United States v. Charleston Area Med. Ctr.*, 2006-1 Trade Cas. (CCH) ¶ 75,313 (S.D.W.Va. 2006) (consent decree and competitive impact statement); *United States v. Bluefield Reg'l Med. Ctr., Inc.*, 2005-2 Trade Cas. (CCH) ¶ 74,916 (S.D. W.Va. 2005) (consent decree and competitive impact statement).

131 *E.g.*, *Bogan v. Hodgkins*, 166 F.3d 509 (2d Cir. 1999); *Balaklaw v. Lovell*, 14 F.3d 793 (2d Cir. 1994).

132 *See generally Reifert v. S. Cent. Wis. MLS Corp.*, 450 F.3d 312 (7th Cir. 2006) ("A group boycott traditionally occurs when a particular group or individual is prohibited from joining an organization."); *Doctor's Hosp. v. Se. Med. Alliance*, 123 F.3d 301 (5th Cir. 1997) (hospital expulsion from PPO); *Levine v. Cent. Fla. Med. Affiliates*, 72 F.3d 1538 (11th Cir. 1996) (refusal to permit physician to join a PPO).

133 *E.g.*, *FMC v. Aktiebolaget Svenska Amerika Linien*, 390 U.S. 238 (1968) (holding that "[u]nder the Sherman Act, any agreement by a group of competitors to boycott a particular buyer or group of buyers is illegal *per se*").

134 472 U.S. 284 (1985).

135 *E.g.*, *Gregory v. Ft. Bridger Rendezvous Ass'n*, 448 F.3d 1195 (10th Cir. 2006); *Palladin Assocs., Inc. v. Mont. Power Co.*, 328 F.3d 1145 (9th Cir. 2003); *Hassan v. Independent Practice Assocs.*, P.C., 698 F. Supp. 679 (E.D. Mich. 1988).

136 *See, e.g.*, *Tunica Web Adver. v. Tunica Casino Operators Ass'n*, 496 F.3d 403 (5th Cir. 2007).

137 *E.g.*, *Cohlmia v. Ardent Health Servs., LLC*, 448 F. Supp. 2d 1253 (N.D. Okla. 2006) ("Although group boycotts have frequently been cited as examples of a *per se* antitrust violation, not all group boycotts are predominantly anticompetitive.... '[C]ourts have generally applied the rule of reason, holding that a hospital must be allowed, in conjunction with its medical staff, to exclude individual doctors on the basis of their lack of professional competence or unprofessional conduct.'"); *Welchlin v. Tenet Healthcare Corp.*, 366 F. Supp. 2d 338 (D.S.C. 2005) ("As a threshold matter, the court notes that "[a] group boycott is not... always a *per se* violation.'"); *see also Health Care Statements*, Statement 9.B.2.c (providing that the rule of reason applies to exclusion of providers by provider-controlled contracting networks).

138 *E.g.*, *Campfield v. State Farm Mut. Auto. Ins. Co.*, 532 F.3d 1111 (10th Cir. 2008).

139 *E.g.*, *Eastman Kodak Co. v. Image Technical Servs., Inc.*, 504 U.S. 451 (1992); *Jefferson Parish Hosp. Dist. No. 2 v. Hyde*, 466 U.S. 2 (1984).

in the market for the tied product may be foreclosed from that market, raising the possibility that the seller of the tying product may obtain market power in the tied-product market.

In the healthcare context, tying arrangements arise most frequently when a hospital enters into an exclusive contract with a single group of hospital-based physicians by which that group is the only provider of specified services permitted to provide those services at the hospital. In that situation, the plaintiff's argument is that, to purchase hospital services (the "tying" service), the patient must purchase the professional services offered by the exclusive group (the "tied" service), excluding other groups for competing for those patients.[140] Another example is a hospital's conditioning the sale of certain hospital services (such as trauma care) to health plans on the condition that they also contract for the hospital's less sophisticated services. This may or may not foreclose the hospital's competitors selling the latter services, depending on whether the health plan is willing to contract with other hospitals as well. As hospitals continue to employee physicians, tying issues may arise where the hospital conditions its sale of hospital services on a health plans's also contracting for its employed physicians' services.

Traditionally, courts have held that tying agreements violate section 1 if a plaintiff proves:

1. the existence of separate tying and tied products;
2. a requirement (or coercion) by the seller forcing the purchaser to buy the tied product, either from it or from a source designated by it, as a condition for purchasing the tying product;
3. that the seller has market power in the market for the tying product (including definition of the relevant market for the tying product); and
4. an effect from the tying arrangement on a "not insubstantial" volume of interstate commerce in the tied product.[141]

In most circuits, the plaintiff must also show that the seller of the tying product has a direct economic interest in the sale of the tied product,[142] a condition usually not met when hospitals enter into exclusive contracts with non-employee hospital-based physicians.[143] In addition, more recent decisions also require the plaintiff to prove an adverse effect on competition in the market for the tied product or service[144]—that is, significant foreclosure from the market of competitors selling the tied

---

[140] *E.g.*, *Jefferson Parish Hosp. Dist. No. 2 v. Hyde,* 466 U.S. 2 (1984); *Beard v. Parkview Hosp.*, 912 F.2d 138 (6th Cir. 1990).

[141] *See generally Eastman Kodak Co. v. Image Technical Servs., Inc.*, 504 U.S. 451 (1992); *Palmyra Park Hosp., Inc. v. Phoebe Putney Mem'l Hosp.*, 604 F.3d 1291 (11th Cir. 2010); *Michigan Div. v. Mich. Cemetery Ass'n*, 524 F.3d 726 (6th Cir. 2008); *Cascade Health Solutions v. PeaceHealth*, 515 F.3d 883 (9th Cir. 2008); *Gordon v. Lewistown Hosp.*, 423 F.3d 184 (3d Cir. 2005); *Warren Gen. Hosp. v. Amgen, Inc.*, 2010-1 Trade Cas. (CCH) ¶ 77,043 (D.N.J. 2010).

[142] *E.g.*, *Abraham v. Intermountain Health Care, Inc.*, 461 F.3d 1249 (10th Cir. 2006); *U.S. Philips Corp. v. Int'l Trade Comm'n*, 424 F.3d 1179 (Fed Cir. 2005); *CTUnify, Inc. v. Nortel Networks, Inc.*, 115 Fed. App'x 831 (6th Cir. 2004); *White v. Rockingham Radiologists*, 820 F.2d 98 (4th Cir. 1988).

[143] For an example, *see Healow v. Anesthesia Ptrs.*, 92 F 3d 1192 (9th Cir. 1996) (*per curiam unpublished opinion reprinted at* 1996-2 Trade Cas. (CCH) ¶ 71,567).

[144] *E&L Consulting, Ltd. v. Doman Indus., Ltd.*, 472 F.3d 23 (2d Cir. 2006); *CTUnify, Inc. v. Nortel Networks, Inc.*, 115 Fed. App'x 831 (6th Cir. 2004) ("More importantly, [plaintiff] has not concretely alleged any anticompetitive effect that the defendant's tying agreement has had on the tied market."); *Highland Capital, Inc. v. Franklin Nat'l Bank*, 350 F.3d 558 (6th Cir. 2003).

products or service.[145] For example, if the seller forces the purchaser to purchase the tied product, but the purchaser would not have purchased the tied product from anyone absent the tying agreement, no competitors are foreclosed from the tied-product market.[146] The Supreme Court has recognized that many tying arrangements are competitively benign.[147]

6.2.1.3.6 *Exclusive-Dealing Agreements*

An exclusive-dealing contract results when a buyer and seller agree either (1) that the seller will sell to only one buyer, and not to that buyer's competitors; or (2) that a buyer will buy only from that seller, and not from its competitors (*e.g.*, a "requirements contract").[148] The antitrust concern is the same as that with tying agreements—competitor foreclosure from the market and thus potential market power of a participant in the contract.

Exclusive contracts are always analyzed under the rule of reason.[149] The plaintiff must: (1) define the relevant market affected by the exclusive contract;[150] (2) show that the contract forecloses a significant percentage of that market;[151] and (3) show that the duration of the exclusive relationship is sufficiently long that, given the percentage of foreclosure from the contract, it likely will have a significant anticompetitive effect because the party with the contract will be able to exercise market power by excluding its competitors from the market.[152] Importantly, the court must consider any offsetting procompetitive benefits from the contract,[153] and subjectively balance the procompetitive and anticompetitive effects to determine which resulting impact predominates.

---

[145] *See, e.g.*, *Blough v. Holland Realty, Inc.*, 574 F.3d 1084 (9th Cir. 2009) (holding that no tying violation results absent foreclosure of competition in the tied-product market); *Reifert v. S. Cent. Wis. MLS Corp.*, 450 F.3d 312 (7th Cir. 2006).

[146] *Jefferson Parish Hosp. Dist. No. 2 v. Hyde*, 466 U.S. 2 (1984).

[147] *Ill. Tool Works, Inc. v. Independent Ink, Inc.*, 547 U.S. 28 (2006) ("Many tying arrangements... are fully consistent with a free competitive market.").

[148] *E.g.*, *Allied Orthopedic Appliances, Inc. v. Tyco Health Group, LP*, 592 F.3d 991 (9th Cir. 2010).

[149] *Jefferson Parish Hosp. Dist. No. 2 v. Hyde*, 466 U.S. 2 (1984); *Tampa Elec. Co. v. Nashville Coal Co.*, 365 U.S. 320 (1961); *Imaging Ctr., Inc. v. W. Md. Health System, Inc.*, 158 Fed. App'x 413 (4th Cir. 2005); *Natchitoches Parish Hosp. Serv. Dist. v. Tyco Int'l*, 2009-2 Trade Cas. (CCH) ¶ 76,815 (D. Mass. 2009).

[150] *E.g.*, *Chuck's Feed & Seed Co. v. Ralston Purina Co.*, 810 F.2d 1289 (4th Cir. 1987).

[151] *E.g.*, *Allied Orthopedic Appliances, Inc. v. Tyco Health Group, LP*, 592 F.3d 991 (9th Cir. 2010); *B&H Med., L.L.C. v. ABP Adm'rs, Inc.*, 526 F.3d 257 (6th Cir. 2008); *Geneva Pharms. Tech. Corp. v. Barr Labs., Inc.*, 386 F.3d 485 (2d Cir. 2004) ("Exclusive dealing is an unreasonable restraint of trade and a § 1 violation only when the agreement freezes out a significant fraction of buyers or sellers from the market."); *Republic Tobacco Co. v. N. Atl. Trading Co.*, 381 F.3d 717 (7th Cir. 2005) ("Exclusive dealing arrangements violate the antitrust laws only when they foreclose competition in a substantial share of the line of commerce at issue."); *Stop & Shop Supermarket Co. v. Blue Cross & Blue Shield*, 373 F.3d 57, (1st Cir. 2004) (indicating that the exclusive contract must foreclosure some 30% or 40% of the market or more to raise antitrust concern); *Morales-Villalobos v. Garcia-Llorens*, 316 F.3d 51 (1st Cir. 2003); *U.S. Healthcare, Inc. v. Healthsource, Inc.*, 986 F.2d 589 (1st Cir. 1993) (explaining that substantial foreclosure is a threshold element in proving an exclusive contract unlawful); *United States v. Microsoft Corp.*, 87 F. Supp. 2d 30 (D.D.C. 2000) (holding that unlawfulness requires a 40% foreclosure percentage), *rev'd in part on other grounds*, 253 F.3d 34 (D.C. Cir. 2001) (per curiam); *Colonial Med. Group, Inc. v. Catholic Healthcare W.*, 2010-1 Trade Cas. (CCH) ¶ 77,039 (N.D. Cal. 2010) (noting that '"[f]or exclusive dealing, foreclosure levels are unlikely to be of concern where they are less than 30 or 40 percent'") (citation omitted); *Natchitoches Parish Serv. Dist. v. Tyco Int'l*, 2009-2 Trade Cas. (CCH) ¶ 76,815 (D. Mass. 2009) (same).

[152] *E.g.*, *Imaging Ctr., Inc. v. W. Md. Health Sys., Inc.*, 158 Fed. App'x 413 (4th Cir. 2005) ("The inquiry into exclusive dealing arrangements focuses on whether the arrangement forecloses competition among producers or suppliers in a substantial share of the affected market."); *Omega Envtl.., Inc. v. Gilbraco, Inc.*, 127 F.3d 1157 (9th Cir. 1997); *Rome Ambulatory Surgery Ctr., LLC v. Rome Mem'l Hosp.*, 349 F. Supp. 2d 389 (N.D.N.Y. 2004).

[153] *E.g.*, *Jefferson Parish Hosp. No. 2 v. Hyde*, 466 U.S. 2 (1984) (O'Connor, J., concurring) (listing several efficiency benefits from exclusive contracts); *Barr Labs. v. Abbott Labs.*, 978 F.2d 98 (3d Cir. 1992) (court must consider legitimate

Exclusive-dealing contracts are common in the healthcare sector. Examples include hospital exclusive contracts with hospital-based physicians; health maintenance organization exclusive contracts with a single provider group in some specialties; and group purchasing organization single-source contracts with vendors of hospital supplies.[154] But no violation results when a party merely replaces one exclusive dealer with another.[155]

For the contract to constitute an exclusive contract, it need not spell out exclusivity specifically.[156] For example, in its United Regional Health Care System enforcement action,[157] the Antitrust Division alleged that a large hospital offered health plans a substantially lower price if they refused to contract with a competing hospital than if they excluded that hospital from their provider panels, which resulted in a de facto exclusive contract. And in its Blue Cross and Blue Shield of Michigan enforcement action,[158] the Division alleged that Blue Cross' use of a most-favored-nations clause in contracts with health plans effectively foreclosed competing health plans from markets—another form of de facto exclusive dealing arrangement.

6.2.2 Section 2 of the Sherman Act

Section 2 of the Sherman Act prohibits monopolization, attempted monopolization, and conspiracies to monopolize.[159] In general, the monopolization and attempted-monopolization provisions apply to single firms with substantial market power that engage in conduct preventing other firms from encroaching on that power (*i.e.*, "exclusionary" or "predatory" conduct that forecloses competitors from the market). Both violations usually require, preliminarily, definition of the relevant market.[160] Of course, a firm cannot monopolize or attempt to monopolize a market in which it is not a competitor.[161]

6.2.2.1 Monopolization

Monopolization requires proof of two essential elements: (1) monopoly power and (2) the willful acquisition or maintenance of monopoly power by "predatory" or "unreasonably exclusionary" conduct, as opposed to a superior product, business acumen, historical accident, or competition on the merits.[162] Importantly, a "monopoly" or monopoly power, by itself, is not unlawful. To constitute

---

business justifications for the exclusive contracts).

[154] *See, e.g., Stop & Shop Supermarket Co. v. Blue Cross & Blue Shield*, 373 F.3d 57 (1st Cir. 2004); *Woman's Clinic, Inc. v. St. John's Health Sys.*, 252 F. Supp. 2d 857 (W.D. Mo. 2002).

[155] *E.g., NicSand, Inc. v. 3M Co.*, 507 F.3d 442 (6th Cir. 2007).

[156] *See generally LePage's, Inc. v. 3M*, 324 F.3d 141 (3d Cir. 2993) (*en banc*).

[157] Compl., *United States v. United Reg'l Health Care Sys.*, No. 7:11-cv-00030 (N.D. Tex. filed Feb. 11, 2011).

[158] Compl., *United States v. Blue Cross & Blue Shield*, No. 10-cv-14155-DPH-MKM (E.D. Mich. Filed Oct. 18, 2010).

[159] The conspiracy-to-monopolize violation is not discussed here. The essential elements are (1) a conspiracy or agreement, (2) specific intent to monopolize, and (3) an overt act in furtherance of the agreement. *E.g., Stewart Glass & Mirror, Inc., v. U.S. Auto Glass Discount Centers*, 200 F. 3d 307 (5th Cir. 2000) (discussing an auto-glass preferred-provider network).

[160] *E.g., M&M Med. Supplies & Serv., Inc. v. Pleasant Valley Hosp.*, 981 F.2d 160 (4th Cir. 1992) (*en banc*); *Levine v. Cent. Fla. Med. Affiliates, Inc.*, 72 F.3d 1538 (11th Cir. 1996).

[161] *E.g., Lucas v. Citizens Commc'ns Co.*, 244 Fed. Appx 744 (9th Cir. 2007); *RxUSA Wholesale, Inc. v. Alcon Labs., Inc.*, 661 F. Supp. 2d 218 (E.D.N.Y. 2009), *aff'd without published opinion*, 2010 U.S. App. LEXIS 18200 (2d Cir. Aug. 30, 2010).

[162] *United States v. Grinnell Corp.*, 384 U.S. 563 (1966); *Allied Orthopedic Appliances, Inc. v. Tyco Health Group, LP*, 592 f.3d 991 (9th Cir. 2010); *HDC Med., Inc. v. Minntech Corp.*, 474 F.3d 543 (8th Cir. 2007).

monopolization, that power must have been acquired or maintained competitively inappropriate—that is, "predatory"—conduct.[163]

The legal definition of "monopoly power" is "the power to control prices or exclude competition."[164] As a matter of economics, monopoly power is simply a substantial degree of market power,[165] and the terms are often used interchangeably.[166] As in the case of market power, monopoly power can be proved either directly or circumstantially.[167] Direct evidence of monopoly power includes proof of supracompetitive pricing or restricted output.[168] To prove monopoly power by circumstantial evidence—the usual mode of proof—a plaintiff must prove:

- that the relevant market allegedly monopolized;
- that the defendant has a dominant share of the relevant market (usually at least 65%);[169]
- that significant entry barriers prevent new competitors from entering the market; and
- that significant barriers to expansion prevent incumbent competitors from expanding their output.[170]

Section 2 prevents firms with substantial market power from engaging in unnecessarily exclusionary conduct that prevents other competitors or potential competitors from challenging their power—in antitrust jargon, "predatory conduct." In general, conduct is predatory if it has significantly exclusionary effects on the defendant's actual or potential competitors *and* promotes none of the values that competition is meant to promote (*i.e.*, lower prices, greater efficiency, higher quality, greater choice, and increased innovation).[171] Conduct is not predatory if the defendant can show that it has a "legiti-

---

163 *E.g., Pac. Bell Telephone Co. v. linkLINE Commc'ns, Inc.*, 129 S.Ct. 1109 (2009); *Verizon Communications, Inc. v. Law Offices of Curtis V. Trinko, LLP*, 540 U.S. 398 (2004) ("The mere possession of monopoly power, and the concomitant charging of monopoly prices, is not... unlawful.... [T]he possession of monopoly power will not be found unlawful unless it is accompanied by an element of anticompetitive conduct."); *Rambus, Inc. v.* FTC, 522 F.3d 456 (D.C. Cir. 2008); *Christy Sports, LLC v. Deer Valley Resort Co.*, 555 F.3d 1188 (10th Cir. 2009) ("Under both types of § 2 claims, [plaintiff] must... plead both power in a relevant market and anticompetitive conduct."); *Gulf States Reorg. Group, Inc. v. Nucor Corp.*, 466 F.3d 961 (11th Cir. 2006) ("The antitrust laws allow legal monopolies to compete vigorously on the merits..., even if such competition drives out competitors."); *Total Renal Care, Inc. v. W. Nephrology & Metabolic Bone Disease, P.C.*, 2009 U.S. Dist. LEXIS 80821 (D. Colo. Aug. 21, 2009).

164 *United States v. E.I. du Pont de Nemours & Co.*, 351 U.S. 377, 391 (1957); *Four Corners Nephrology Assocs. P.C. v. Mercy Med. Ctr.*, 582 F.3d 1216 (10th Cir. 2009). Of course, a seller cannot "control prices" unless it can "exclude competition."

165 *E.g., Queen City Pizza, Inc. v. Domino's Pizza, Inc.*, 124 F.3d 430 (3d Cir. 1997) ("Monopoly power under § 2 requires 'something greater' than market power under § 1.").

166 *See* Robert S. Pindyck & Daniel L. Rubinfeld, *Microeconomics* 340 n.1 (6th ed. 2005).

167 *E.g., Geneva Pharms. Tech. Corp. v. Barr Labs., Inc.*, 386 F.3d 485 (2d Cir. 2004).

168 *Harrison Aire, Inc. v. Aerostar Int'l, Inc.*, 423 F.3d 374 (3d Cir. 2005) ("Monopoly power can be demonstrated with either evidence of supracompetitive pricing and high barriers to entry..., or with structural evidence of a monopolized market.... Plaintiffs relying on market share as a proxy for monopoly power must plead and produce evidence of a relevant product market, of the alleged monopolist's dominant share of that market, and high barriers to entry."); *Rebel Oil Co. v. Atl. Richfield Co.*, 51 F.3d 1421 (9th Cir. 1995).

169 *See generally Cal. v. Safeway, Inc.*, 615 F.3d 1171 (9th Cir. 2010) (noting that a market share between 60 and 70% was sufficient to establish monopoly power); *United States v. Aluminum Co. of Am.*, 148 F.2d 416 (2d Cir. 1945) (stating the classic standard: A 90% market share "is enough to constitute a monopoly; it is doubtful whether sixty or sixty-five per cent would be enough; and certainly thirty-three percent is not").

170 *Image Technical Servs., Inc. v. Eastman Kodak Co.*, 125 F.3d 1195 (9th Cir. 1997).

171 *Cf. Wichita Clinic, P.A. v. Columbia/HCA Healthcare Corp.*, 45 F. Supp. 2d 1164 (D. Kan. 1999) ("Predatory practices are illegal only if they impair opportunities of rivals, are not competition on the merits or go beyond reasonable competition, and appear reasonably capable of contributing significantly to creating or maintaining monopoly power.").

mate business justification" or "valid business reason" for the conduct,[172] although some courts require a balancing of procompetitive and anticompetitive effects of the conduct.[173]

Distinguishing between anticompetitive predatory conduct and merely very aggressive procompetitive conduct is often quite difficult. The latter can exclude competitors but benefit consumers. One example is an efficient firm, even one with monopoly power, charging very low, but not below cost, prices. The focus in determining whether conduct is predatory is its effect on the defendant's competitors, not its customers. For example, a firm with legitimately obtained monopoly power (*e.g.*, because it "built a better mousetrap")[174] can lawfully charge any price the market will bear, including the monopoly price.[175] High prices do not exclude or foreclose competitors from the market; indeed, they invite new entry into the market and competitors to undercut those prices.

Although difficult to define precisely, predatory conduct is conduct that permits a firm to obtain or maintain its substantial market power but generates no consumer benefits—exclusionary conduct not constituting competition on the merits.[176] It can include predatory pricing (*i.e.*, pricing below cost to destroy competitors, and then recouping the losses by later charging the monopoly price),[177] "bundled" discounts that competitors cannot match (*i.e.*, pricing a package of goods or services below the prices at which they would be sold separately,[178] some refusals by firms with market power to deal with their competitors,[179] a firm's refusal to provide competitors with access to an "essential facility" or relationship necessary for effective competition,[180] assertion of a fraudulently obtained patent,[181] "sham" litigation,[182] and leveraging.[183] These are not the only forms of conduct that can be predatory,[184] but they are the most frequently alleged. Of these, the type of predatory conduct alleged most often is some type of refusal of the firm with market power to deal or provide some type of support to its

---

[172] *E.g., Eastman Kodak Co. v. Image Technical Servs.*, Inc., 504 U.S. 451 (1994); *Gordon v. Lewistown Hosp.*, 423 F.3d 184 (3d Cir. 2005); *United States v. Dentsply Int'l, Inc.*, 399 F.3d 181 (3d Cir. 2005).

[173] *E.g., United States v. Microsoft Corp.*, 253 F.3d 34 (D.C. Cir. 2001) (per curiam).

[174] *See, e.g., Morgan v. Ponder*, 892 F.2d 1355 (8th Cir. 1989).

[175] *E.g., Ocean State Physicians Health Plan v. Blue Cross & Blue Shield*, 883 F.2d 1101 (1st Cir. 1989).

[176] *See generally W. Penn Allegheny Health Sys. v. UPMC*, 637 F.3d 85 (3d Cir. 2010) ("Broadly speaking, a firm engages in anticompetitive conduct when it attempts to 'exclude rivals on some basis other than efficiency,'... or when it competes 'on some other basis than the merits."); *Race Tires Am., Inc. v. Hoosier Racing Tire Corp.*, 614 F.3d 57 (3d Cir. 2010); *Cascade Health Solutions v. PeaceHealth*, 515 F.3d 883 (9th Cir. 2008) (explaining that predatory conduct is "behavior that tends to impair the opportunities of rivals and either does not further competition on the merits or does so in an unnecessarily restrictive way").

[177] *E.g., Brooke Group, Ltd. v. Brown & Williamson Tobacco Co.*, 509 U.S. 209 (1993); *see also R.J. Reynolds Tobacco Co. v. Cigarettes Cheaper!*, 462 F.3d 690 (7th Cir. 2006); *United States v. AMR Corp.*, 335 F.3d 1109 (10th Cir. 2003); *Stearns Airport Equip. Co. v. FMC Corp.*, 170 F.3d 518 (5th Cir. 1999).

[178] *Se. Mo. Hosp. v. C.R. Bard Co.*, 616 F.3d 888 (8th Cir. 2010).

[179] *See generally Aspen Skiing Co. v. Aspen Highlands Skiing Corp.*, 472 U.S. 585 (1986); *SmileCare Dental Group v. Delta Dental Plan*, 88 F.3d 780 (9th Cir. 1996).

[180] The classic discussion of the essential-facilities doctrine is in *MCI Communications Corp. v. Am. Tel. & Tel. Co.*, 708 F.2d 1081 (7th Cir. 1983). *See also Otter Tail Power Co. v. United States*, 410 U.S. 366 (1973); *Stein v. Pac. Bell*, 172 Fed. App'x. 192 (9th Cir. 2006); *Pittsburg County Rural Water Dist. No. 7 v. City of McAlester*, 346 F.3d 1260 (10th Cir. 2003). Significantly, the Supreme Court never has approved the doctrine. *See Verizon Commc'ns, Inc. v. Law Offices of Curtis V. Trinko, LLP*, 540 U.S. 398 (2004).

[181] *E.g., Dippin' Dots, Inc. v. Mosey*, 476 F.3d 1337 (Fed. Cir. 2007).

[182] *See, e.g. Prof'l Real Estate Invs., Inc. v. Columbia Pictures Indus., Inc.*, 508 U.S. 49 (1993); *Armstrong Surgical Ctr., Inc. v. Armstrong Mem'l Hosp.*, 195 F.3d 154 (3d Cir. 1999).

[183] *AD/SAT v. Associated Press*, 181 F.3d 216 (2d Cir. 1999) (*per curiam*); *Am. Airlines, Inc. v. United Airlines, Inc.*, 948 F.2d 536 (9th Cir. 1991); *Berkey Photo, Inc. v. Eastman Kodak Co.*, 603 F.2d 263 (2d Cir. 1979).

[184] For a fuller list, *see* 1 ABA Section of *Antitrust Law, Antitrust Law Developments*, 245–300 (6th ed. 2007).

competitors. The applicable principle is that even a firm with monopoly power has no general duty to deal with its competitors but that, in some narrow situations, it must have a rational business reason for refusing to do so if its refusal would have significant anticompetitive effects by permitting the firm to maintain its monopoly power.[185]

The mirror image of a monopolization claim is "monopsonization," where a buyer has substantial market power as a purchaser of a relevant product or service.[186] Presumably, a plaintiff seller would have to prove that the defendant has monoposony power and obtained or maintained that power by excluding other buyers from the market, such as through a predatory buying scheme.[187] It is not unlawful, however for a buyer with legitimately obtained monopsony power (*e.g.*, a health plan contracting with providers) to obtain the lowest price it can in purchasing its inputs.[188]

6.2.2.2 *Attempted Monopolization*

Section 2's attempted-monopolization provision prohibits firms with substantial market power from engaging in predatory conduct to achieve an actual monopoly.[189] A plaintiff must show that the defendant (1) had a "specific intent" to monopolize the relevant market, (2) engaged in predatory conduct to implement that intent, and (3) had a "dangerous probability" of acquiring monopoly power if the predatory conduct continued.[190]

By "specific intent to monopolize," the courts mean a "specific intent to destroy competition or build a monopoly."[191] Specific intent can be proved from the defendant's documents[192] or by inference from its predatory conduct.[193] The plaintiff also must prove that, if the predatory conduct were to continue, a dangerous probability exists that the defendant would obtain actual monopoly power. In general, to prove the "dangerous probability of monopolization" element, the plaintiff must show that the defendant has a large market share (typically, 40% or more), that entry barriers would prevent new entry, that firms already in the market lack the capacity to expand their output, and that the defendant's market share is likely to increase to a monopoly level (typically at least 65%).[194]

---

[185] *See generally Pac. Bell Tel. Co. v. linkLINE Commc'ns, Inc.*, 129 S.Ct. 1109 (2009); *Verizon Commc'ns Inc. v. Law Offices of Curtis V. Trinko, LLP*, 540 U.S. 398 (2004); *Aspen Skiing Co. v. Aspen Highlands Skiing Corp.*, 472 U.S. 585 (1986); *Four Corners Nephrology Assocs., P.C. v. Mercy Med. Ctr.*, 582 F.3d 1216 (10th Cir. 2009); *Covad Commc'ns Co. v. Bell Atl. Corp.*, 398 F.3d 666 (D.C. Cir. 2005).

[186] *See generally Powderly v. Blue Cross & Blue Shield*, 2008-2 Trade Cas. (CCH) ¶ 76,321 (W.D.N.C. 2008) (explaining that "it is beyond dispute that a *provider of health insurance* services is also a *buyer* of *health care services* capable of exercising monopoly power over the market for doctor's services"); *see also Campfield v. State Farm Mut. Auto. Ins. Co.*, 532 F.3d 1111 (10th Cir. 2008).

[187] *See, e.g., Weyerhaeuser Co. v. Ross-Simmons Hardwood Lumber Co.*, 549 U.S. 312 (2007).

[188] *E.g., W. Penn Allegheny Health Sys. v. UPMC*, 627 F.3d 85 (3d Cir. 2010) ("A firm that has substantial power in the buy side of the market (*i.e.*, monopsony power) is generally free to bargain aggressively when negotiating the prices it will pay for goods and services."); *Ocean State Physicians Health Plan v. Blue Cross & Blue Shield*, 883 F.3d 1101 (1st Cir. 1989).

[189] *See generally Ind. Grocery, Inc. v. Super Valu Stores*, 864 F.2d 1409 (7th Cir. 1988).

[190] *Spectrum Sports, Inc. v. McQuillan*, 506 U.S. 447 (1993); *W. Penn Allegheny Health Sys. v. UPMC*, 637 F.3d 85 (3d Cir. 2010); *E. Portland Imaging Ctr., P.C. v. Providence Health Sys.–Oregon*, 280 Fed. App'x 584 (9th Cir. 2008); *Gordon v. Lewistown Hosp.*, 423 F.3d 184 (3d Cir. 2005).

[191] *Times-Picayune Publ'g Co. v. United States*, 345 U.S. 594, 626 (1953).

[192] *E.g., Browning-Ferris Indus. v. Kelco Disposal, Inc.*, 845 F.2d 404 (2d Cir. 1988) (document stating that defendant wanted to "squish" plaintiff "like a bug").

[193] *E.g., Great W. Directories, Inc. v. Sw. Bell Tel. Co.*, 63 F.3d 1278 (5th Cir. 1995) ("Intent can be inferred by anticompetitive practices or proven by direct evidence.").

[194] *E. Portland Imaging Ctr., P.C. v. Providence Health Sys.–Oregon*, 280 Fed. App'x 584 (9th Cir. 2008); *Full Draw Productions v. Easton Sports, Inc.*, 182 F.3d 745 (10th Cir. 1999); *Rebel Oil Co. v. Atl. Richfield Co.*, 51 F.3d 1421 (9th Cir. 1995).

6.2.3 Section 7 of the Clayton Act

Section 7 of the Clayton Act prohibits all types of mergers and other forms of acquisitions that may lessen competition substantially. A first important issue, regardless of whether the transaction presents any competitive concern, is whether the parties must report the transaction to the Antitrust Division and the FTC under Section 7A of the Clayton Act,[195] the Hart-Scott-Rodino pre-merger notification provisions. It also is important to ensure that the parties will integrate sufficiently through the transaction so they constitute a single entity for antitrust purposes after the transaction.[196] If not, section 1 of the Sherman Act continues to apply to their actions after the transaction.[197] So, for example, if two physician practices "merge" but fail to totally integrate their operations, they may not constitute a single entity, and their negotiation of prices with health plans may constitute an unlawful horizontal price-fixing agreement.[198]

Mergers can be horizontal (between competitors), vertical (between buyers and sellers), or conglomerate. Only horizontal mergers are discussed here, because they raise the most antitrust concern.[199] In the last several years, the FTC, in particular, has become very active in investigating and challenging hospital mergers[200] and mergers between hospitals and other providers, including outpatient facilities[201] and physicians.[202] It has also filed high-profile cases challenging laboratory[203] and pharmaceutical mergers as well.[204]

In analyzing horizontal mergers in any industry, the single most important sources of guidance are the decided cases themselves and the Department of Justice and FTC *Horizontal Merger Guide-*

---

[195] 15 U.S.C. § 18a. Implementing regulations are at 16 C.F.R. §§ 801–803.

[196] *See generally HealthAmerica Pa., Inc. v. Susquehanna Health Sys.*, 278 F. Supp. 2d 423 (M.D. Pa. 2003) (holding that a hospital joint-operating agreement sufficiently integrated the hospitals so that they constituted a single entity for antitrust purposes). For discussion of this issue, *see* Mark J. Botti, Assistant Chief, Litigation I Section, Antitrust Division, "Virtual Mergers of Hospitals: When Does the *Per Se* Rule Apply?", and John J. Miles, "A Conceptual and Practical Approach to the Antitrust Analysis of Virtual Mergers," Prepared Remarks Before the American Health Lawyers Association Antitrust in the Healthcare Field seminar (Feb. 18, 2000); *see also* John J. Miles, *The Importance of Integration in Healthcare Antitrust Counseling*: Yakima *and* Susquehanna, Health Lawyers News, March 2004, at 16.

[197] For an example of this regarding a physician merger insufficient to result in a single medical practice, *see Surgical Specialists of Yakima, P.L.L.C.*, Dkt. No. C-4101 (FTC Nov. 14, 2003) (consent order), alleging that a physicians limited liability company was not sufficiently integrated so that its practices constituted a single entity.

[198] *E.g., Surgical Specialists of Yakima, P.L.L.C.*, 136 F.T.C. 840 (2003) (consent order) (FTC price-fixing enforcement action against allegedly "sham" entity negotiating contracts on behalf of competing medical practices).

[199] For discussions of the analysis of vertical mergers, *see Ford Motor Co. v. United States*, 405 U.S. 562 (1972); *HTI Health Servs., Inc. v. Quorum Health Group, Inc.*, 960 F. Supp. 1104 (S.D. Miss. 1997).

[200] *See* Admin. Compl., *Phoebe Putney Health Sys.*, Dkt. No. 9348 (FTC, filed Apr. 11, 2011) (FTC challenge to hospital merger in Albany, Georgia); *FTC v. ProMedica Health Sys.*, 2011-1 Trade Cas. (CCH) ¶ 77,395 (N.D. Ohio 2011) (granting preliminary injunction); *Allen B. Miller*, Dkt. No. C-4039 (FTC Apr. 19, 2011) (consent order) (requiring divestiture of psychiatric hospitals); *Inova Health Sys. Found.*, Dkt. No. 9326 (FTC June 17, 2008) (order dismissing case after parties abandoned transaction); *Evanston Nw. Health Care Corp.*, 2007-2 Trade Cas. (CCH) ¶ 75,814 (FTC 2007) (finding that hospital merger violated § 7).

[201] *Carilion Clinic*, Dkt. No. 9338 (FTC Oct. 7, 2009) (consent order) (requiring hospital to divest ambulatory surgery center and imaging center).

[202] *See Statement of Bureau of Competition Director Richard Feinstein on the Abandonment by Providence Health & Services of its Plan to Acquire Spokane Cardiology and Heart Clinics of the Northwest in Spokane*, Washington (Apr. 8, 2011).

[203] *FTC v. Lab. Corp. of Am.*, No. SACV 10-1873 AG MLGx (C.D. Cal. Feb. 22, 2011) (denying FTC motion for preliminary injunction).

[204] *FTC v. Lundbeck, Inc.*, 2011 WL 3810015 (D. Minn. Aug. 31, 2010) (finding pharmaceutical merger lawful).

lines.[205] The agencies issued new *Merger Guidelines* in August 2010 (replacing those issued in 1992), and these require close study by any attorney representing healthcare clients in planning and implementing a merger. The *Merger Guidelines* are not "the law," but courts have relied on them heavily in determining the antitrust ramifications of mergers.[206] They explain in some detail how the agencies analyze horizontal mergers, the factors that the agencies consider important in determining whether to challenge particular mergers, and the sources of evidence on which the agencies rely.[207]

The Merger Guidelines explain that "mergers should not be permitted to create, enhance, or entrench market power or to facilitate its exercise."[208] The twin potential antitrust concerns arising from horizontal mergers are that they might (1) permit one or both of the merging parties to exercise market power itself—so called "unilateral effects;"[209] or (2) result in a market sufficiently concentrated that firms will interact in a coordinated manner and raise prices, thus exercising market power jointly—so-called "coordinated effects."[210] In determining whether adverse unilateral effects are likely, the most important variables are the merging parties' post-merger market *share* and whether if one of the merging parties raised prices post-merger, a large number of its customers would switch to the other party rather than to some other competitor in the market. In determining whether coordinated effects are likely, the most important variable is the post-merger level of market *concentration*.

At present, antitrust merger analysis seem to be evolving in the sense that the principles and analysis of the new *Merger Guidelines* are not completely consistent with those applied by the federal courts. The courts, for example, tend to rely more heavily on market definition, market shares, and market concentration statistics in assessing mergers,[211] while the new *Merger Guidelines*, although considering these factors, emphasize a larger number of more "holistic" evidentiary factors, including actual effects in similar consummated mergers, the degree of overlap and "closeness" of the merging parties with respect to the services they offer and their geographical locations, economic performance in other markets with similar characteristics and market structures, and the results from econometric models that can be used to predict price increases from a merger, such as merger simulation. And although the case law includes market definition as an essential element in any merger challenge, the new *Guidelines* indicate that formal market definition is not always necessary. Because, however, the agencies do apply the new *Merger Guidelines*, a close reading and understanding of them is very important.

---

205 U.S. Dep't of Justice & Federal Trade Comm'n, *Horizontal Merger Guidelines* (2010) (hereinafter *Merger Guidelines*).

206 *See, e.g.*, *Chicago Bridge & Iron Co. v. FTC*, 515 F.3d 447 (5th Cir. 2008) (explaining that "the Merger Guidelines are not binding on the courts and the agency during adjudication but are only highly persuasive authorities as a 'benchmark of legality'").

207 *See Merger Guidelines* § 1 (explaining that the *Guidelines* "describe the principal analytical techniques and the main types of evidence on which the Agencies usually rely to predict whether a horizontal merger may substantially lessen competition").

208 *Id.*

209 *Id.* § 6. *See, e.g.*, *FTC v. Butterworth Health Corp.*, 946 F. Supp. 1285 (W.D. Mich. 1996), *aff'd per curiam without published opinion.*, 121 F.3d 708 (6th Cir. 1997); *FTC v. Staples, Inc.*, 970 F. Supp. 1066 (D.D.C. 1997).

210 *Merger Guidelines* § 7. *See, e.g.*, *Hosp. Corp. of Am. v. FTC*, 807 F.2d 1381 (7th Cir. 1986); *Chicago Bridge & Iron Co.*, Dkt. No. 9300 (FTC, Dec. 21, 2004) ("First, a merger may result in a single firm that so dominates a market that it is able to maintain prices above the level that would prevail if the market were competitive.... Second, a merger may result in only a few firms accounting for most of the sales of a product and thereby enable those firms to exercise market power by explicitly or tacitly coordinating their actions."), *petition for review denied*, 515 F.3d 447 (5th Cir. 2008).

211 For a recent example, *see FTC v. CCC Holdings, Inc.*, 605 F. Supp. 2d 26 (D.D.C. 2009).

Traditional antitrust merger analysis usually proceeds through the following steps.

6.2.3.1 *Definition of the Relevant Product Market*

Generally, as discussed before, the relevant product market includes the products or services sold by the merging firms and their reasonably interchangeable substitutes.[212] The agencies and some courts, however, hold that the relevant product market may not include all reasonably interchangeable substitutes, but only those sufficient to prevent a firm from exercising market power, *i.e.*, just those closest substitute products to which consumers would switch to prevent the firm from profitably raising price—not *all* substitutes to which consumers might switch.[213]

In hospital-merger cases, courts usually have found a relevant product market consisting of inpatient acute-care hospital services, excluding outpatient services.[214] In defining relevant product markets in physician-practice mergers or in analyzing other issues involving physician market power, a question that can arise is whether the relevant product market includes physicians in different specialties because both provide certain common services, or whether the product market is limited to services provided by a single medical specialty.[215] The answer is very fact-specific, depending primarily on whether health plans could substitute physicians in one specialty for those in the other in their networks.

6.2.3.2 *Definition of the Relevant Geographic Market*

As noted before, the relevant geographic market is the area of effective competition—the area in which the sellers in question operate and that to which their customers could turn to purchase the relevant product if those sellers attempted to raise prices.[216] The courts have emphasized the necessity for including in the relevant geographic market the more-distant sellers to whom customers could turn for services if sellers in closer proximity increased prices.[217] The relevant geographic market for most healthcare services is relatively local, and could encompass a city (or even only part of a large metropolitan area). As the services constituting the relevant product market become more complex and sophisticated (*e.g.*, organ transplants), the size of the relevant geographic market usually increases[218] because patients are willing to travel greater distances for them and health plans are willing to contract with more distant providers for their networks.

In the case of relevant geographic markets for hospitals, patient-discharge data showing where patients seek hospital services can provide significant insight into the relevant geographic market, but the agencies have warned that patient-discharge analysis is far from sufficient to define relevant geo-

---

212 *See generally HTI Health Servs., Inc. v. Quorum Health Group, Inc.*, 960 F. Supp. 1104 (S.D. Miss. 1997).

213 *Merger Guidelines* § 4.1.1.

214 *E.g., FTC v. Tenet Health Care Corp.*, 186 F.3d 1045 (8th Cir. 1999); *United States v. Mercy Health Servs.*, 902 F. Supp. 968 (N.D. Iowa 1995), *vacated and remanded with instructions to dismiss as moot*, 107 F.3d 632 (8th Cir. 1997).

215 *Cf.* Antitrust Division Business Review Letter to Allied Colon and Rectal Specialists (Jul. 1, 1996) (finding that general surgeons were substitutable for colon-rectal surgeons and thus part of the relevant product market), at www.usdoj.gov/atr/publicfbusrev/yavitz.htm.

216 *Brown Shoe Co. v. United States*, 370 U.S. 294 (1962).

217 *E.g., FTC v. Freeman Hosp.*, 69 F.3d 260 (8th Cir. 1995); *Cal. v. Sutter Health Sys.*, 130 F. Supp. 2d 1109 (N.D. Cal. 2001).

218 *Merger Guidelines*, § 1.2.

graphic markets.[219] The views of health plans regarding the substitutability of hospitals in particular areas for their networks is also quite important.

6.2.3.3 *Identification of Competitors in the Relevant Market*

The purpose for defining the relevant market is to identify competitors of the merging firms. Once the relevant product and geographic markets are delineated, competitors in those markets can be identified.

6.2.3.4 *Calculation of Each Competitor's Market Share*

The competitors' market shares should be calculated using several "universes." In hospital mergers, for example, applicable measures include licensed beds, staffed beds, admissions, inpatient days, and revenues. The *Merger Guidelines* provide that revenues is usually the appropriate measure.[220]

6.2.3.5 *Calculation of the Merging Firms' Post-Merger Market Share, the Level of Market Concentration, and the Increase in Market Concentration Resulting from the Merger*

The merging firms' post-merger market share provides an indication of whether they, together as a single firm, could exercise market power. As usual, no precise combined market share signals unlawfulness; nevertheless, concern generally begins to arise at a share of about 35%.

"Market concentration" refers to the number and relative sizes of competitors in a market—the fewer the sellers and the more disparate their market shares, the more concentrated the market.[221] Economic theory predicts an inverse relationship between the level of market concentration and market performance.[222] The more the merger increases the level of concentration, the greater the probability and degree of the likely anticompetitive effect because the more likely it becomes that firms in the market will establish their prices jointly or interdependently—*i.e.*, the market tends to become an oligopoly.

The preferred market-concentration measure is the Herfindahl-Hirschman Index (HHI). To calculate the *post-merger* HHI:

1. add the market shares of the *merging* firms;
2. square this share and the share of each competitor of other firm in the relevant market; and
3. sum the squares.

This results in a figure between zero (an infinite number of market participants) and 10,000 (one firm—a monopoly). To calculate the amount by which the merger would increase the HHI, multiply the market shares of the merging firms by each other, and multiply that product by two. Thus, if two

[219] *See generally* Federal Trade Comm'n & U.S. Dep't of Justice, *Improving Health Care: A Dose of Competition* Ch. 4 at 5–14 (2004).

[220] *Merger Guidelines* § 5.2.

[221] *See, e.g.*, Robert S. Pindyck & Daniel L. Rubinfeld, *Microeconomics* 358 (6th ed. 2005) ("When only a few firms account for most of the sales in a market, we say that the market is highly *concentrated*.").

[222] *See* generally F. M. Scherer & David Ross, *Industrial Market Structure and Economic Performance* 4–5, 277–79 (3d ed. 1990).

urology practices merge, one with a market share of 10% and the other with a share of 5%, the merger will increase the HHI by 100.

If the merging firms' post-merger market share or the level of market concentration and its increase are sufficiently high, then the merger is *prima facie* or rebuttably presumed unlawful. The burden of going forward then shifts to the merging parties to show that the market-share and concentration statistics are not an accurate indicator of the merger's likely effect on competition.[223]

According to the new *Merger Guidelines*, a post-merger HHI of 1,500 or less indicates an "unconcentrated" market, and the merger raises no issue regardless of the amount by which the merger would increase concentration. (The HHI for a market with six equal-size firms is about 1,500.) If, after the merger, the HHI is between 1,500 and 2,500, the market is "moderately concentrated," but no antitrust concern arises if the increase in the HHI does not exceed 100. If the increase is 100 or more, however, the merger "potentially raise[s] significant competitive concerns" depending on other factors, and further analysis may be warranted. If the post-merger HHI is above 2,500, the market is "highly concentrated." (The HHI for a market with four equal-size firms is 2,500.) Still, however, if the HHI increase is 100 or less, no problem should arise; if the increase is between 100 and 200, concern can arise depending on other factors, indicating that more in-depth analysis may be required; and if the increase in the HHI is more than 200, the merger "will be presumed to create or enhance market power," but this presumption can be rebutted.[224]

6.2.3.6 *Examination of Factors that Might Indicate that Post-Merger Market Share or Market Concentration Statistics are Misleading*

A number of factors can indicate that notwithstanding high concentration or a high post-merger market share, the merger would not likely lead to the exercise of single-firm market power ("unilateral effects) or market-wide market power resulting from interdependent business conduct ("coordinated effects")—or that, on balance, the merger would not be anticompetitive. In general, these factors can be grouped into four categories:

1. low entry barriers into the relevant market;[225]
2. market characteristics indicating that competitor tacit or explicit collusion, including interdependent competitive conduct among firms in the market, is not feasible or likely;[226]
3. the financial weakness of one of the merging firms;[227] and

[223] *E.g., United States v. General Dynamics Corp.*, 415 U.S. 486 (1974); *see also Chicago Bridge & Iron Co. v. FTC*, 515 F.3d 447 (5th Cir. 2008); *FTC v. CCC Holdings, Inc.*, 605 F. Supp. 2d 26 (D.D.C. 2009); *FTC v. Butterworth Health Corp.*, 946 F. Supp. 1285 (W.D. Mich. 1996), *aff'd per curiam without published opinion*, 121 F.3d 708 (6th Cir. 1997); *FTC v. Cardinal Health, Inc.*, 12 F. Supp. 2d 34 (D.D.C. 1998).

[224] *Merger Guidelines*, § 5.3.

[225] *Id.* § 9; *see generally United States v. Baker Hughes, Inc.*, 908 F.2d 981 (D.C. Cir. 1990).

[226] *Merger Guidelines*, § 7; *see generally FTC v. Elders Grain, Inc.*, 868 F.2d 901 (7th Cir. 1989).

[227] *E.g., Merger Guidelines* § 11; *see also Cal. v. Sutter Health Sys.*, 130 F. Supp. 2d 1109 (N.D. Cal. 2001) (explaining that the acquired hospital was failing firm, thus permitting the merger even if it had otherwise been unlawful); *FTC v. Univ. Health, Inc.*, 938 F.2d 1206 (11th Cir. 1991) (explaining that although the acquired hospital was not failing, a firm's weakness as a competitor is a factor in favor of the merger).

4. efficiencies generated by the merger.[228]

Federal and state antitrust enforcement agencies have filed numerous challenges to mergers in the healthcare sector. The largest number have involved hospital mergers[229] and pharmaceutical-manufacturer mergers.[230] For example, in 2007, the FTC held that Evanston Northwestern Healthcare's acquisition of Highland Park Hospital (both located in the north Chicago suburbs) in 2000 violated section 7.[231] The case involved a hospital merger that the FTC challenged four years after it was consummated. According to the FTC, the evidence showed that the merged hospital actually raised its prices significantly to health plans after the merger, a fact corroborated by the hospitals' own documents—a classic unilateral-effects case, as most hospital-merger cases are. The FTC defined a small relevant geographic market, which included only the merging hospitals themselves and indicated that when anticompetitive effects can be proven directly by actual evidence of price increases, it may not be necessary to define a relevant market. The FTC decision generated a subsequent private action seeking treble damages on behalf of purchasers of the system's hospital services.[232]

In another highly publicized hospital-merger matter, the FTC, in 2008, forced Inova Health System Foundation in northern Virginia to abandon its proposed acquisition of nearby Prince William Hospital.[233] Based in part on the results shown by an econometric merger-simulation model, the FTC believed that, post-merger, Inova would increase prices at both Prince William and at its own facilities. And several hospital-merger investigations are ongoing at this writing.

In addition to challenging hospital mergers, the agencies have challenged mergers in markets such as nursing homes,[234] outpatient dialysis facilities,[235] cardiac stents,[236] health plans,[237] and medical tests.[238] State attorneys general have challenged physician-practice mergers,[239] and the Antitrust Division, in business review letters, has threatened to do so.[240] The FTC has investigated several physician-practice mergers but has not challenged any thus far.

---

228 *Merger Guidelines*, § 10. For helpful discussions, *see* Debra A. Valentine, General Counsel, Federal Trade Commission, "Health Care Mergers: Will We Get Efficiencies Claims Right?," prepared remarks before the St. Louis University School of Law (Nov. 14, 1997); Thomas R. McCarthy, et al., "Efficiencies Analysis in Hospital Mergers," Prepared remarks before the ABA Antitrust law Section and Health Law Section Seminar, Oct. 15, 1998.

229 For a list of hospital merger cases, *see* 2 John J. Miles, *Health Care & Antitrust Law* § 12.1 at 12-5 n.8 (Supp. 2009).

230 *E.g.*, *Hospira, Inc.*, Dkt. No. C-4182 (FTC Jan. 18, 2007) (consent order); *Johnson & Johnson*, Dkt. No. C-4180 (FTC Jan. 16, 2007) (consent order); *Watson Pharms., Inc.*, Dkt. No. C-4172 (FTC Dec. 6, 2006) (consent order).

231 *Evanston Nw. Health Care Corp.*, 2007-2 Trade Cas. (CCH) ¶ 75,814 (FTC 2007).

232 *In re Evanston Nw. Healthcare*, 2008-1 Trade Cas. (CCH) ¶ 76,182 (N.D. Ill. 2008) (denying defendant's motion to dismiss based on the statute of limitations).

233 *Inova Health Sys. Found.*, Dkt. No. 9326 (FTC May 9, 2008 administrative complaint), (June 17, 2008 order dismissing complaint after abandonment of proposed merger).

234 *See, e.g.*, *United States v. Beverly Enters.*, 1984-1 Trade Cas. (CCH) ¶ 66,052 (M.D. Ga. 1984) (consent decree).

235 *Fresenius AG*, Dkt. No. C-4159 (FTC June 30, 2006) (consent order); *DaVita, Inc.*, Dkt. No. C-4152 (FTC Nov. 18, 2005) (consent order).

236 *Boston Scientific Corp.*, Dkt. No., C-4164 (FTC Jul. 25, 2006) (consent order).

237 *United States v. UnitedHealth Group, Inc.*, 2008-2 Trade Cas. (CCH) ¶ 76,318 (D.D.C. 2008) (consent order and competitive impact statement).

238 *Inverness Med. Instruments*, Dkt. No. C-4244 (FTC Jan. 23, 2009) (consent order).

239 *E.g.*, *Me. v. Me. Heart Surgical Assocs., P.A.*, 1996-2 Trade Cas. (CCH) ¶ 71,653 (Me. Sup. Ct. 1996) (consent decree).

240 *See* Antitrust Division Business Review Letter to Gastroenterology Assocs., Ltd. (Jul. 7, 1997), at http://www.usdoj.gov/atr/public/busrev/1174.pdf.

6.2.4 The Federal Trade Commission Act

Section 5(a)(1) of the FTC Act prohibits "[u]nfair methods of competition in or affecting commerce."[241] Only the FTC can enforce the Act; there is no private right of action.[242] Section 5 applies only to entities "organized to carry on business for [their] own profit or that of [their] members."[243] Sometimes referred to as the "nonprofits exemption," this provision means, in practical effect, that the FTC lacks authority to investigate and prosecute conduct that would violate section 5 when the action is implemented by nonprofit hospitals.[244]

Congress granted the FTC broad authority to determine those practices that constitute "unfair methods of competition." In general, the FTC may declare conduct that violates either the "letter" of any of the antitrust laws[245] or their "spirit"[246] to be an unfair method of competition.[247] The FTC has no authority to enforce the Sherman Act, but nevertheless can challenge conduct that violates the Sherman Act (plus other conduct) under section 5.[248] In determining whether a practice is an unfair method of competition, the FTC can consider values beyond those embedded in the letter or spirit of the antitrust laws.[249] Still, the antitrust laws and their goals serve as the guiding light in determining whether conduct is an unfair method of competition,[250] and the FTC must show that conduct challenged under section 5 has an anticompetitive effect.[251]

6.3 Exemptions, Immunities, and Scope of Coverage

A number of situations arise in which the antitrust laws are simply inapplicable to certain conduct or to certain parties or, while the antitrust laws are applicable, damages for violations cannot be recovered. Those exemptions most germane to healthcare industries are discussed below.

6.3.1 Nonprofit Entities

As a general rule, the antitrust laws apply to nonprofit entities as well as to for-profit entities.[252] A number of courts, however, have held that the antitrust laws do not apply to a nonprofit entity's "noncommercial" activities.[253]

---

241 15 U.S.C. § 45(a)(1).

242 *E.g., Am. Airlines, Inc. v. Christensen*, 967 F.2d 410 (10th Cir. 1992).

243 15 U.S.C. § 44.

244 Importantly, however, the "exemption" does not apply merely because the entity is established as a nonprofit entity. For discussions of the relevant analysis, *see Cal. Dental Ass'n v. FTC*, 526 U.S. 756 (1999); *Am. Med. Ass'n v. FTC*, 638 F.2d 443 (2d Cir. 1980), *aff'd by an equally divided court*, 455 U.S. 676 (1982).

245 *E.g., FTC v. Motion Picture Adver. Serv. Co.*, 344 U.S. 392 (1953).

246 *E.g., FTC v. Sperry & Hutchinson Co.*, 405 U.S. 233 (1972).

247 For a helpful discussion of the scope of section 5, *see Rambus, Inc.*, Dkt. No. 9302 (FTC Jul. 31, 2006) (Leibowitz, Comm'r, concurring), *rev'd on other grounds*, 522 F.3d 456 (D.C. Cir. 2008).

248 *E.g., FTC v. Superior Court Trial Lawyers Ass'n*, 493 U.S. 411 (1990).

249 *E.g., FTC v. Sperry & Hutchinson Co.*, 405 U.S. 233 (1972).

250 *FTC v. Ind. Fed'n of Dentists*, 476 U.S. 477 (1986); *see also E.I. Du Pont de Nemours & Co. v. FTC*, 729 F.2d 128 (2d Cir. 1984); *Boise Cascade Corp. v. FTC*, 637 F.2d 573 (9th Cir. 1980).

251 *See Rambus, Inc. v. FTC*, 522 F.3d 456 (D.C. Cir. 2008).

252 *Bd. of Regents v. NCAA*, 468 U.S. 85 (1984); *Am. Soc'y of Mech. Eng'rs v. Hydrolevel Corp.*, 456 U.S. 556 (1982).

253 *Bassett v. NCAA*, 528 F.3d 426 (6th Cir. 2008); *Big Bear Lodging Ass'n v. Snow Summit, Inc.*, 182 F.3d 1096 (9th Cir. 1999) ("A nonprofit organization that engages in commercial activity… is subject to federal antitrust laws."); *Smith v. NCAA*, 139 F.3d 180 (3d Cir. 1998); *Hamilton Chapter, Alpha Delta Phi, Inc. v. Hamilton Coll.*, 128 F.3d 59 (2d Cir. 1997); *United States v. Brown Univ.*, 5 F.3d 658 (3d Cir. 1993).

6.3.2 Federal Governmental Immunity

The antitrust laws do not apply to the conduct of the federal government, its agencies, or its individual agents.[254] For example, an antitrust suit against the Department of Health and Human Services, alleging that it monopsonizes the purchase of healthcare provider services would be futile.

6.3.3 State-Action Exemption

The state-action exemption is relevant when a conflict exists between a state regulatory scheme contemplating anticompetitive activity and the federal antitrust laws.[255] The standard for determining whether the state-action exemption applies to particular conduct depends in large part on the status of the party undertaking the action.[256] Anticompetitive conduct undertaken by a sovereign branch of the state—the legislature, the supreme court, and, presumably, the executive—is automatically exempt.[257] At the other end of the spectrum, the anticompetitive activities of private parties must, in the words of the Supreme Court, meet a two-pronged standard for the exemption to apply: "First, the challenged restraint must be one clearly articulated and affirmatively expressed as state policy; second, the policy must be 'actively supervised' by the state itself."[258] In the middle, subordinate state agencies and local governmental entities need only meet the first (*i.e.*, the "clearly-articulated") requirement; the state need not actively supervise their activities for the exemption to apply.[259]

To be "clearly-articulated" by the state, the state need not require or even explicitly authorize the challenged conduct. Rather, there need be evidence only that the state intended to replace competition with regulation, that the conduct was generally authorized by the state, and that its anticompetitive effects were foreseeable and reasonably contemplated by the state.[260] The "active-supervision" element requires that the state have ultimate control over the challenged conduct of private entities, and actually exercise the power to review and disapprove conduct not in accordance with state policy.[261] There must be actual supervision by the state, not merely the potential for active state supervision.[262]

---

[254] *E.g., United States Postal Serv. v. Flamingo Indus. (USA) Ltd.*, 540 U.S. 736 (2004); *McCarthy v. Middle Tenn. Elec. Corp.*, 466 F.3d 399 (6th Cir. 2006); *Home Health Licensing Specialists, Inc. v. Leavitt*, 2008-2 Trade Cas. (CCH) ¶ 76,448 (N.D. Tex. 2008); *Med. Ass'n v. Schweiker*, 554 F. Supp. 955 (M.D. Ala.), *aff'd per curiam sub nom., Med. Ass'n v. Heckler*, 714 F.2d 107 (11th Cir. 1983).

[255] *Parker v. Brown*, 317 U.S. 341 (1943).

[256] *S. C. State Bd. of Dentistry v. FTC*, 455 F.3d 436 (4th Cir. 2006).

[257] *Hoover v. Ronwin*, 466 U.S. 558 (1984); *see also Neo Gen Screening, Inc. v. New Eng. Newborn Screening Program*, 187 F.3d 24(1st Cir. 1999).

[258] *Cal. Retail Liquor Dealers Ass'n v. Midcal Aluminum, Inc.*, 445 U.S. 97, 105 (1980); *see also Shames v. Cal. Travel & Tourism Comm'n*, 607 F.3d 611 (9th Cir. 2010); *Brentwood Acad. v. Tenn. Secondary Sch. Athletic Ass'n*, 442 F.3d 410 (6th Cir. 2006).

[259] *Town of Hallie v. City of Eau Claire*, 471 U.S. 34 (1985); *see also City of Columbia v. Omni Outdoor Adver., Inc.*, 499 U.S. 365 (1991); *Stratienko v. Chattanooga-Hamilton Hosp. Auth.*, 402 Fed. App'x 990 (6th Cir. 2010); *Lafaro v. N.Y. Cardiothoracic Group, PLLC*, 570 F.3d 471 (2d Cir. 2009); *Surgical Ctr. v. Hospital Serv. Dist.*, 171 F.3d 231 (5th Cir. 1999) (*en banc*).

[260] *S. Motor Carriers Rate Conf v. United States*, 471 U.S. 48 (1985); *see also City of Columbia v. Omni Outdoor Adver., Inc.*, 499 U.S. 365 (1991); *Danner Constr. Co. v. Hillsborough County*, 608 F.3d 809 (11th Cir. 2010); *Jackson Hosp. Co. v. W. Tenn. Healthcare, Inc.*, 414 F.3d 608 (6th Cir. 2005).

[261] *Patrick v. Burget*, 486 U.S. 94 (1988).

[262] *FTC v. Ticor Title Ins. Co.*, 504 U.S. 621 (1992); *Ky. Household Goods Carrier Ass'n v. FTC*, 199 Fed. App'x 410 (6th Cir. 2006).

A state statute or regulatory scheme is preempted by the Supremacy Clause of the U.S. Constitution if it mandates conduct by private parties that constitutes a per se violation of the antitrust laws in every situation.[263] But even then, the defendants can escape liability if their conduct meets the requirements for state-action exemption protection.[264]

In healthcare, the state-action exemption arises in a number of contexts, including in staff-privilege antitrust cases where a governmental hospital has rejected or terminated a staff physician's privileges.[265] State-action exemption questions can also arise in the context of hospital mergers where the acquiring hospital is a local governmental entity.[266] Another important state-action exemption question, as yet unanswered, is whether state certificate-of-public-advantage laws, designed to sustain state-action-exemption protection for collaborative hospital activities, will do so.[267] The exemption also arises frequently in antitrust cases resulting from state certificate-of-need activities.[268] Although exemptions from the antitrust laws are generally disfavored and construed narrowly, the courts have applied the state-action exemption fairly liberally. The FTC, on the other had, has construed the exemption strictly.[269]

6.3.4 Solicitation of Governmental Action

The so-called "Noerr-Pennington" antitrust-immunity doctrine protects private parties when they individually or collectively solicit the government to take anticompetitive action.[270] This exemption is probably the broadest and most important of all the antitrust-exemption doctrines. Importantly, the Noerr-Pennington doctrine applies to non-antitrust federal and state claims, as well as to antitrust claims, because of its First Amendment underpinnings.[271] The type, branch, or level of government at

---

263 *E.g., 324 Liquor Corp. v. Duffy*, 479 U.S. 335 (1987); *Rice v. Norman Williams Co.*, 458 U.S. 260 (1986); *Flying J, Inc. v. Van Hollen*, 621 F.3d 658 (7th Cir. 2010).

264 *Freedom Holdings, Inc. v. Cuomo*, 624 F.3d 38 (2d Cir. 2010).

265 *Martin v. Mem'l Hosp.*, 86 F.3d 1391 (5th Cir. 1996), *subsequent decision*, 130 F.3d 1143 (5th Cir. 1997).

266 *See FTC v. Hosp. Bd. of Directors of Lee County*, 38 F.3d 1184 (11th Cir. 1994) (applying the state-action exemption to a hospital merger). The merging hospitals in the FTC's current challenge to the merger of Phoebe Putney Health System and Palmyra Park Hospital in Albany, Georgia, are expected the raise the state-action exemption because the acquiring hospital in owned by a state hospital authority special governmental district. *See* Admin. Compl., *Phoebe Putney Health Sys.*, Dkt. No. 9348 (FTC filed Apr. 19, 2011).

267 *See generally* Sarah S. Vance, *Immunity for State-Sanctioned Provider Collaboration After Ticor*, 62 Antitrust L.J. 409 (1994).

268 *E.g., Armstrong Surgical Ctr. v. Armstrong County Mem'l Hosp.*, 185 F.3d 154 (3d Cir. 1999). In general, the state-action exemption applies where there is a conflict between the federal antitrust laws and a state regulatory scheme replacing competition with regulation. Situations also arise presenting a conflict between the federal antitrust laws and a federal regulatory scheme. Where there is a clear repugnancy between the two, the antitrust laws are "impliedly repealed" to the extent necessary for the federal regulatory scheme to achieve its goals. *See Credit Suisse Secs. (USA) LLC v. Billing*, 551 U.S. 264 (2007); *Nat'l Gerimedical Hosp. & Gerontology Ctr. v. Blue Cross,* 452 U.S. 378 (1981).

269 *See N.C. State Board of Dental Examiners*, 2011-1 Trade Cas. (CCH) ¶ 77,331 (FTC 2011).

270 The doctrine takes its name from two of the Supreme Court decisions establishing the exemption. *UMW v. Pennington*, 381 U.S. 657 (1965); *E. R.R. Presidents Conf. v. Noerr Motor Freight*, 365 U.S. 127 (1961); *see Mercatus Group, LLC v. Lake Forest Hosp.*, 528 F. Supp. 2d 797 (N.D. Ill. 2007).

271 *See, e.g., BE&K Constr. Co. v. NLRB*, 536 U.S. 526 (2002); *Sosa v. DIRECTV, Inc.*, 437 F.3d 923 (9th Cir. 2006) (applying doctrine to federal RICO and state unfair-business statutes). *See also Andrx Pharms., Inc. v. Elan Corp.*, 421 F.3d 1227 (11th Cir. 2005); *Knology, Inc. v. Insight Commc'nss, L.P.*, 393 F.3d 656 (6th Cir. 2004) (explaining that the doctrine "allows businesses to combine and lobby to influence the legislative, executive, or judicial branches of government or administrative agencies without antitrust… liability, because the First Amendment's right to petition protects such activities").

which the petitioning is aimed is immaterial,[272] as is the petitioners' anticompetitive intent in soliciting the action[273] and whether they "conspired" with government officials to induce them to take the anticompetitive action.[274]

In determining whether the exemption applies to particular petitioning conduct, the key question is whether the challenged restraint on competition results directly from the action of the private parties (if so, the exemption does not apply) or from the governmental action they solicit (in which case the exemption does apply).[275] The exemption does not apply to coercive action by the petitioners against the government to force it to adopt their views[276]—such as an agreement among physicians not to participate in the Medicaid program unless the state increases the level of Medicaid reimbursement.

The doctrine does not protect "sham" petitioning.[277] In general, the sham exception to the Noerr-Pennington doctrine applies where "persons use the governmental *process*—as opposed to the *outcome* of that process—as an anticompetitive weapon."[278] For example, litigation (the filing of which normally is exempt under the doctrine) constitutes sham petitioning if it is objectively baseless in the sense that no reasonable person would expect it to succeed, and if the defendant's subjective intent is to interfere directly with the business relationships of a competitor, rather than to obtain the relief it sought from the court.[279]

6.3.5 Local Government Antitrust Act

Even if the state-action exemption does not provide a local governmental entity with protection from antitrust liability, the Local Government Antitrust Act provides it with absolute protection from damages in antitrust cases.[280] The term "local government" includes "special function governmental unit[s]," which include governmental hospital districts and authorities.[281]

The immunity from damages also applies to officials of local governments acting in their official capacities and to other persons, including private parties, engaged in official action directed by the local government. In general, individuals enjoy the immunity from damages if their actions were autho-

---

272 *E.g., Cal. Motor Transp. v. Trucking Unlimited*, 404 U.S. 508 (1972); *Freeman v. Lasky, Haas & Cohler*, 410 F.3d 1180 (9th Cir. 2005).

273 *E.g., Marian v. Fisher*, 338 F. 3d 189 (3d Cir. 2003) ("That immunity is so potent that it protects petitioning notwithstanding an improper purpose or motive."); *Sandy River Nursing Care v. Aetna Cas.*, 985 F.2d 1138 (1st Cir. 1993) (exemption applies even if defendants' motives were "entirely anticompetitive").

274 *E.g., City of Columbia v. Omni Outdoor Adver., Inc.*, 499 U.S. 365 (1991); *Tal v. Hogan*, 453 F.3d 1244 (10th Cir. 2006); *Boulware v. Nev.*, 960 F.2d 793 (9th Cir 1992).

275 *E.g., Allied Tube & Conduit Corp. v. Indian Head, Inc.*, 486 U.S. 492 (1988); *see also Armstrong Surgical Ctr., Inc. v. Armstrong County Mem'l Hosp.*, 185 F.3d 154 (3d Cir. 1999).

276 *Superior Court Trial Lawyers Ass'n v. FTC*, 493 U.S. 411 (1990).

277 *See generally Freeman v. Lasky, Haas & Cohler*, 410 F.3d 1180 (9th Cir. 2005); *Kottle v. Nw. Kidney Ctrs.*, 146 F.3d 1056 (9th Cir. 1998).

278 *City of Columbia v. Omni Outdoor Adver., Inc.*, 499 U.S. 365, 380 (1991) (emphasis in original).

279 *Prof'l Real Estate Invs., Inc. v. Columbia Pictures Indus.*, 508 U.S. 49 (1993); *Kaiser Found. Health Plan, Inc. v. Abbott Labs, Inc.*, 552 F.3d 1033 (9th Cir. 2009); *Andrx Pharms., Inc. v. Elan Corp.*, 421 F.3d 1227 (11th Cir. 2005); *Total Renal Care, Inc. v. W. Nephrology & Metabolic Bone Disease, P.C.*, 2009 U.S. Dist. LEXIS 80821 (D. Colo. Aug. 21, 2009). The FTC also opines that deliberate misrepresentations to government agencies in certain circumstances also negate the exemption. *Union Oil Co.*, Dkt. No. 9305 (FTC Jul. 6, 2004). Case law on this issue is not clear.

280 15 U.S.C. §§ 34–36.

281 *E.g., Bloom v. Hennepin County*, 783 F. Supp. 418 (D. Minn. 1992).

rized and supervised by the local governmental entity.[282] Their motives and those of the government are immaterial.[283] A plaintiff, however, still may obtain injunctive and declaratory relief if it proves a violation.[284]

6.3.6 Business of Insurance

The McCarran-Ferguson Act[285] provides the "business of insurance" with a limited exemption from the antitrust laws. For the Act's protection to apply, a defendant must prove three elements:

1. the challenged conduct constitutes the "business of insurance;"
2. the state regulates the business of insurance; and
3. the challenged conduct does not constitute "boycott, coercion, or intimidation."

In determining whether particular conduct constitutes the "business of insurance," courts examine three factors: whether the conduct (1) transfers or spreads policyholder risk, (2) is an integral part of the relationship between the insurer and its insureds, and (3) is limited to those within the insurance industry.[286] Based on these standards, provider agreements between health insurers and their participating providers do not constitute the business of insurance,[287] although contracts between insurers and their insureds do.[288]

The state must regulate the business of insurance for the Act's protection to apply. The courts have interpreted this requirement leniently, however, and it rarely raises an issue. Only the most general type of state-insurance regulation is required,[289] and even it need not be effective.[290]

Finally, the challenged conduct cannot constitute "boycott," "intimidation," or "coercion." Boycott, for purposes of the Act, refers to secondary boycotts—refusals to deal seeking an objective collateral to the main transaction[291] or "a refusal to deal in a collateral transaction as a means to coerce terms in a primary transaction."[292]

---

[282] *See generally Sandcrest Outpatient Servs., P.A. v. Cumberland County Hosp. Sys.*, 853 F.2d 1139 (4th Cir. 1988).

[283] *GF Gaming Corp. v. City of Blackhawk*, 405 F.3d 876 (10th Cir. 2005); *Cohn v. Bond*, 953 F.2d 154 (4th Cir. 1991).

[284] *Lancaster Cmty. Hosp. v. Antelope Valley Hosp. Dist.*, 940 F.2d 397 (9th Cir. 1991); *Swarz Ambulance Serv. v. Genesee County*, 666 F. Supp.2d 721 (E.D. Mich. 2009) (declaratory judgment).

[285] 15 U.S.C. §§ 1011–15.

[286] *E.g., Union Labor Life Ins. Co. v. Pireno*, 458 U.S. 119 (1982); *In re Ins. Brokerage Antitrust Litig.*, 618 F.3d 300 (3d Cir. 2010); *Arroyo-Melecio v. Puerto Rican Am. Ins. Co.*, 398 F.3d 56 (1st Cir. 2005).

[287] *Group Life & Health Ins. Co. v. Royal Drug Co.*, 440 U.S. 205 (1979); *Arroyo-Melecio v. Puerto Rican Am. Ins. Co.*, 398 F.3d 56 (1st Cir. 2005).

[288] *E.g., Health Care Equalization Comm'n v. Iowa Med. Soc'y*, 851 F.2d 1020 (8th Cir. 1988).

[289] *E.g., Klamath-Lake Pharm. Ass'n v. Klamath Med. Servs. Bureau*, 701 F.2d 1276 (9th Cir. 1983).

[290] *FTC v. Nat'l Cas. Co.*, 357 U.S. 560 (1958) (noting that there need not even be state enforcement).

[291] *Hartford Fire Ins. Co. v. Cal.*, 509 U.S. 764 (1993); *Arroyo-Melecio v. Puerto Rican Am. Ins. Co.*, 398 F.3d 56 (1st Cir. 2005); *Gilchrist v. State Farm Mut. Auto. Ins. Co.*, 390 F.3d 1327 (11th Cir. 2004); *Slagle v. ITT Hartford*, 102 F.3d 494 (11th Cir. 1996).

[292] *Uniforce Temporary Personnel, Inc. v. Nat'l Council on Compensation Ins., Inc.*, 87 F.3d 1296 (11th Cir. 1996).

6.3.7 Labor Unions

There is a *statutory* antitrust exemption for the conduct of labor unions flowing from sections 6[293] and 20[294] of the Clayton Act and sections 1,[295] 4,[296] 5,[297] and 13[298] of the Norris-LaGuardia Act. In addition, a "*nonstatutory*" labor exemption,[299] created by the courts, exists for agreements—primarily collective-bargaining agreements—between unions and employers that meet certain requirements.[300] The labor exemption, however is limited.

The major union-related antitrust issue to arise so far in healthcare focuses on the desire of some physicians to increase their bargaining strength with third-party payors by "unionizing." Some physicians have believed that forming or joining a physicians' union permits them to bargain collectively and thus jointly agree on prices in contracting with health plans, increasing their market power. For a group to constitute a *bona fide* union, however, an employee-employer relationship must exist between them and the party with which they bargain collectively. The exemption does not apply to collective bargaining between independent contractors and those who pay them.[301] Thus, the unionized physician-employees of a staff-model HMO or hospital enjoy the labor exemption when they bargain collectively with the HMO or hospital, but independent-contractor physicians bargaining collectively with health plans in which they are participating providers do not.[302] Indeed, the DOJ Antitrust Division has challenged the collective-bargaining activities of one physicians' union three times.[303]

Physicians and other providers have sought, without success thus far, federal legislation permitting them to bargain collectively with health plans. The most recent bill would permit providers to collectively bargain with health plans but would not permit "collective cessation of service to patients."[304]

6.3.8 Health Care Quality Improvement Act

The Health Care Quality Improvement Act[305] provides those engaging in the credentialing (or any "professional review action" by a "professional review body") of physicians with immunity from damages if the peer-review process meets certain requirements. The Act provides immunity only from

---

293 15 U.S.C. § 17.

294 *Id.* § 52.

295 29 U.S.C. § 101.

296 *Id.* § 104.

297 *Id.* § 105.

298 *Id.* § 113.

299 *See generally Brown v. Pro-Football, Inc.*, 518 U.S. 231 (1996) (discussing the nonstatutory labor exemption).

300 *See generally Cal. v. Safeway, Inc.*, 615 F.3d 1171 (9th Cir. 2010); *Clarett v. NFL*, 369 F.3d 124 (2d Cir. 2004); *Burlington N. Santa Fe Ry. v. Int'l Bhd. of Teamsters*, 203 F.3d 703 (9th Cir. 2000) (*en banc*); *Detroit Auto Dealers Ass'n v. FTC*, 955 F.2d 457 (6th Cir. 1992) (explaining that the nonstatutory exemption applies to agreements between unions and employers where the restraint affects primarily only the parties to a collective-bargaining agreement, the agreement concerns subjects of mandatory collective bargaining, and the agreement results from *bona fide* arm's-length bargaining).

301 *See generally Columbia River Packers Ass'n v. Hinton*, 315 U.S. 143 (1942).

302 For a helpful discussion of the physician-unionization issue, *see* Edward B. Hirschfeld, *Physicians, Unions, and Antitrust*, J. Health L. 43 (Winter 1999).

303 *United States v. Fedn' of Physicians and Dentists*, 2008-1 Trade Cas. (CCH) ¶ 76,062 (S.D. Ohio 2008) (consent decree and competitive impact statement) *United States v. Fed'n of Physicians and Dentists*, 2005-2 Trade Cas. (CCH) ¶ 75,006 (S.D. Ohio 2005) (consent decree and competitive impact statement); *United States v. Fed'n of Physicians and Dentists, Inc.*, 2002-2 Trade Cas. (CCH) ¶ 73,868 (D. Del. 2002) (consent decree).

304 Quality Health Care Coalition Act of 2011, H.R. 1409, 112th Cong., 1st Sess. (Apr. 7, 2011).

305 42 U.S.C. §§ 11101–52.

damages, not from injunctive relief.[306] It also provides that the defendants may recover their attorneys' fees if the plaintiff's suit challenging their professional-review action is frivolous.[307] The Act applies most frequently, but not exclusively, in staff-privilege antitrust cases when a hospital denies a physician's application for staff privileges or terminates or otherwise adversely affects those privileges.

For immunity from damages to attach, the professional review action must have been taken:

1. in the reasonable belief that it would improve quality healthcare;
2. after reasonable efforts to discover all the facts;
3. after adequate notice and hearing to the affected physician or after other fair procedures; and
4. with the reasonable belief that the action taken was warranted.[308]

The Act provides a presumption that the defendants' action met these requirements, which the plaintiff-physician may rebut by a preponderance of the evidence.[309] Thus, at the summary-judgment stage, the plaintiff, rather than the defendants, has the burden to adduce sufficient evidence to show that the defendant is not entitled to summary judgment on the question of whether the immunity applies.[310] An objective, rather than subjective, standard applies in determining whether the Act's requirements are met, so the reviewers' biases or motives are not relevant.[311] There is no private right of action for violation of the Act based on failure of the professional review action to meet the Act's requirements.[312]

6.4 Government Enforcement

The antitrust laws are enforced by the Antitrust Division of the U.S. Department of Justice, the FTC, and state attorneys general. As discussed in Section 6.5, private parties injured by antitrust violations may sue for damages and injunctive relief.

---

[306] *E.g., Islami v. Covenant Med. Ctr.*, 822 F. Supp. 1361 (N.D. Iowa 1992).

[307] 42 U.S.C. § 11113; *see generally Addis v. Holy Cross Health Sys. Corp.*, 88 F.3d 482 (6th Cir. 1996); *Gordon v. Lewistown Hosp.*, 2006-2 Trade Cas. (CCH) ¶ 75,454 (M.D. Pa. 2006).

[308] 42 U.S.C. § 11112(a).

[309] *Id.*; *see generally Moore v. Williamsburg Reg'l Hosp.*, 560 F.3d 166 (4th Cir. 2009); *Wahi v. Charleston Area Med. Ctr.*, 562 F.3d 599 (4th Cir. 2009); *Lee v. Trinity Lutheran Hosp.*, 408 F.3d 1064 (8th Cir. 2005); *Singh v. Blue Cross/Blue Shield*, 308 F.3d 25 (1st Cir. 2002); *Brader v. Allegheny Gen. Hosp.*, 167 F.3d 832 (3d Cir. 1999); *Mathews v. Lancaster Gen. Hosp.*, 87 F.3d 624 (3d Cir. 1996); *Bryan v. James E. Holmes Reg'l Med. Ctr.*, 33 F.3d 1318 (11th Cir. 1994).

[310] *See, e.g., Johnson v. Christus Spohn*, 334 Fed. App'x 673 (5th Cir. 2009); *Gordon v. Lewistown Hosp.*, 423 F.3d 184 (3d Cir. 2005) (noting that "this presumption of immunity creates an unusual standard for reviewing summary judgment orders, as the plaintiff bears the burden of proving that the professional review process was not reasonable and thus did not meet the standard for immunity.").

[311] *E.g., Poliner v. Tex. Health Sys.*, 537 F.3d 368 (5th Cir. 2008) (noting that the reviewers' good or bad faith in conducting the review is irrelevant).

[312] *E.g., Rowell v. Valleycare Health Sys.*, 2010-2 Trade Cas. (CCH) ¶ 77,214 (N.D. Cal. 2010); *MacArthur v. San Juan County*, 416 F. Supp. 2d 1098 (D. Utah 2005); *Jadali v. Alamance Reg'l Med. Ctr.*, 225 F.R.D. 181 (M.D.N.C. 2004), *aff'd*, 167 Fed. App'x 961 (4th Cir. 2006).

6.4.1 The Antitrust Division

The Antitrust Division primarily enforces sections 1 and 2 of the Sherman Act, and section 7 of the Clayton Act. The Sherman Act is both a civil and criminal statute, and the Antitrust Division has authority to investigate and prosecute both civil and criminal violations.[313] Almost all criminal prosecutions result from alleged violations of section 1. The Antitrust Division, however, limits its criminal prosecutions to hard-core *per se* violations—naked horizontal price-fixing, market-allocation, and bid-rigging agreements. Criminal prosecutions in the healthcare sector are rare, but not unheard of.[314] In its civil-enforcement actions, the Antitrust Division can obtain only injunctive relief, including disgorgement[315]—not damages or civil penalties. The overwhelming majority of all Antitrust Division enforcement actions are quickly settled by consent decrees, usually filed simultaneously with the complaint.

The Antitrust Division has a "Business Review Procedure" by which parties that intend to undertake specific activity can write the Division, explain their proposed conduct, and ask the Division to tell them whether, if they proceed, the Division will file suit.[316] Attorneys representing healthcare clients have used the process frequently,[317] especially for the review of joint contracting activities by provider-controlled contracting organizations, such as IPAs.[318]

6.4.2 The Federal Trade Commission

The FTC, an independent regulatory administrative agency, enforces primarily section 5 of the FTC Act and section 7 of the Clayton Act. The FTC has no authority to enforce the Sherman Act, but it can reach the same conduct under section 5 of the FTC Act. It cannot prosecute criminally; it sometimes does seek restitution or profit disgorgement[319] in addition to injunctive relief to stop the activity and prevent its recurrence. Most of its enforcement actions are settled by consent orders. The FTC's rules provide for two types of advisory opinions—formal commission advisory opinions and staff advisory opinions.[320] It has issued a large number of staff advisory positions dealing with healthcare antitrust issues.[321]

---

[313] Violation is a felony punishable by, in the case of a corporation, a fine not exceeding $100 million; and in the case of individuals, a fine not exceeding $1 million and imprisonment not exceeding 10 years.

[314] *See United States v. A. Lanoy Alston, D.M.D., P.C.*, 974 F.2d 1206 (9th Cir. 1992) (horizontal price fixing); *United States v. Country Lake Optometric Soc'y*, Cr. No. W9CR114 (W.D. Tex. Jul. 9, 1996) (same).

[315] *United States v. KeySpan Corp.*, 2011-1 Trade Cas. (CCH) ¶ 77,320 (S.D.N.Y. 2011).

[316] 28 C.F.R. § 50.6.

[317] *See* 3 John J. Miles, *Health Care & Antitrust Law* App. C (1992 and Supp.) (including full text of all healthcare business review letters).

[318] *See, e.g.*, Antitrust Business Review Letter to Michigan Hospital Group, Inc. (Apr. 3, 2002) (hospital contracting network), at www.usdoj.gov/atr/public/busrev/10933.pdf; Antitrust Division Business Review Letter to Rio Grande Eye Associates, P.A. (Aug. 29, 2001) (physician contracting network) at www.usdoj.gov/atr/public/busrev/18973.pdf.

[319] *See FTC v. Mylan Labs.*, 1999-2 Trade Cas. (CCH) ¶ 72,573 (D.D.C. 1999) (refusing to dismiss, for failure to state a claim, FTC's prayer that defendant disgorge $120 million in overcharges); *FTC v. Coll. of Physicians-Surgeons*, No. 97-2466 (D.P.R. Oct. 2, 1997) (consent decree) ($300,000 in restitution).

[320] For an excellent discussion of the FTC advisory opinion process, *see* Judith A. Moreland, Staff Attorney, Bureau of Competition, Federal Trade Commission, "Overview of the Advisory Opinion Process at the Federal Trade Commission," text of remarks before the National Health Lawyers Association *Antitrust in the Health Care Field* seminar (Feb. 13, 1997).

[321] *E.g.*, FTC Staff Advisory Opinion to Suburban Health Organization (Mar. 28, 2006), at http://www.ftc.gov/os/2006/03/suburbanhealthorganizationstaffadvisoryopinion03282006.pdf; FTC Staff Advisory Opinion to Medical Group Management Association (Nov. 3, 2003) (physician-fee survey) at www.ftc.govfbc/adops/mgmao31104.pdf; FTC Staff Advisory Opinion to Bay Area Preferred Physicians (Sept. 23, 2003) (messenger-model network) at www.ftc.govfbc/adopsfbapp/030923.htm. For a relatively complete listing of the FTC's healthcare-sector antitrust initiatives, *see* Markus Meier, Assistant Director, Bradley S. Albert, Deputy Assistant Director & Saralisa C. Brau, Deputy Assistant Director, Bureau of Competition, FTC, "Overview of FTC Actions in Health Care Services and Products (Sept. 2010) at http://www.ftc.gov/bc/0610hcupdate.pdf.

6.4.3 State Attorneys General

All states (except one) have their own state antitrust statutes,[322] most of which are patterned closely after the federal antitrust laws and are interpreted consistently with federal antitrust precedent. In addition to enforcing their own antitrust laws, states can enforce the federal antitrust laws in some circumstances. Under section 4C of the Clayton Act,[323] for example, states can file so-called *parens patriae* suits to recover damages on behalf of their citizens injured by violations of the federal antitrust laws.[324] States may file suit for damages as private parties under section 4(a) of the Clayton Act[325] when the state suffers damages from an antitrust violation—*e.g.*, as purchasers of goods or services from parties engaged in price fixing.[326] Several states have become quite active in investigating and prosecuting antitrust problems in the healthcare sector,[327] and states often conduct joint investigations and become co-plaintiffs with the federal enforcement agencies in bringing enforcement actions.[328]

6.5 Private Enforcement

Section 4(a) of the Clayton Act authorizes parties injured by antitrust violations to recover treble damages plus attorneys fees.[329] The statute of limitations for recovery of damages in antitrust cases is four years.[330] A plaintiff can sue for injunctive relief as well as damages and is entitled to its attorneys' fees if successful.[331] The statute of limitations does not apply to suits for injunctions. In general, to recover damages, a plaintiff must prove that:

1. it is a "person";
2. it was "injured";
3. the injury was to its "business or property";
4. the injury was "caused"by the antitrust violation;
5. the injury caused by the antitrust violation was "antitrust injury";
6. the plaintiff has "antitrust standing";
7. the plaintiff suffered damages as a result of the antitrust injury; and
8. the amount of its damages.

Several of these requirements are discussed here.

---

322 State antitrust statutes are collected at 6 Trade Reg. Rep. (CCH) ¶¶ 30,201 through 35,602.

323 15 U.S.C. § 15c.

324 For an example, *see Pa. v. Mid-Atl. Toyota Distribs.*, 704 F.2d 125 (4th Cir. 1983).

325 15 U.S.C. § 15(a).

326 *See, e.g., FTC v. Mylan Labs.*, 62 F. Supp. 2d 25 (D.D.C. 1999).

327 *See, e.g., Wis. v. Kenosha Hosp. & Med. Ctr.*, 1997-1 Trade Cas. (CCH) ¶ 71,669 (E.D. Wis. 1996) (consent decree permitting hospital merger to go forward under certain constraints).

328 *FTC v. Lundbeck, Inc.*, 2010 U.S. Dist. LEXIS 95365 (D. Minn. Aug. 31, 2010) (FTC and Minnesota attorney general joint action to rescind pharmaceutical merger).

329 15 U.S.C. § 15(a); *see, e.g., Gulfstream III Assocs., Inc. v. Gulfstream Aerospace Corp.*, 995 F.2d 414 (3d Cir. 1993).

330 15 U.S.C. § 15(b); *see generally Zenith Radio Corp. v. Hazeltine Research, Inc.*, 401 U.S. 321 (1971); *RX.com v. Medco Health Solutions, Inc.*, 322 Fed. App'x 394 (5th Cir. 2009); *Midwestern Mach. Co. v. Nw. Airlines, Inc.*, 392 F.3d 265 (8th Cir. 2004); *Xechem, Inc. v. Bristol-Myers Squibb Co.*, 372 F.3d 899 (7th Cir. 2004); *Varner v. Peterson Farms*, 371 F.3d 1011 (8th Cir. 2004).

331 15 U.S.C. § 26.

6.5.1 Causation

To prove causation, the plaintiff must prove that its injury resulted from the antitrust violation rather than from some other cause.[332] There must be some link between the violation and the plaintiff's injury. Although the antitrust violation need not be the sole cause of its injury, the violation must be a "material" or substantial cause of the injury in order for the plaintiff to recover.[333]

6.5.2 Antitrust Injury

In addition to causation, the plaintiff must show that its injury resulted from the anticompetitive effects of the violation. This "antitrust injury"—the type of injury the antitrust laws were meant to prevent—must flow from the effect that makes the conduct unlawful.[334] For a plaintiff to recover damages, its injury must have resulted from the competition-reducing effects of the violation.[335] Conduct that injures the plaintiff, but *not* competition, does not constitute antitrust injury[336]—*e.g.*, if the challenged conduct injures the plaintiff but increases competition. A plaintiff must prove antitrust injury in actions to both recover damages[337] and obtain injunctive relief.[338] And the plaintiff must prove antitrust injury even if the challenged conduct is *per se* unlawful under section 1 of the Sherman Act, where the adverse effect on competition is presumed.[339] It is entirely possible for defendants to engage in conduct that violates the antitrust law and for that conduct to injure the plaintiff, but the plaintiff not suffer antitrust injury because its injury results from some cause other than the competition-reducing effect of the violation.

6.5.3 Antitrust Standing

Antitrust standing requires determining whether the plaintiff is an appropriate party to enforce the antitrust laws. It is a narrower concept than "Article III" Constitutional standing, which requires merely that the plaintiff suffer some injury caused by the violation and have a redressable claim.[340]

---

332 *Simon v. Value Behavioral Health, Inc.*, 208 F.3d 1073 (9th Cir. 2000).

333 *E.g., J.B.D.L. Corp. v. Wyeth-Ayerst Labs., Inc.*, 485 F.3d 880 (6th Cir. 2007); *Gulf States Reorg. Group, Inc. v. Nucor Corp.*, 466 F.3d 961 (11th Cir. 2006). Some courts require the antitrust violation to be the "but-for" cause of the injury. *See SAS, Inc. v. Puerto Rico Tel. Co.*, 48 F.3d 39 (lst Cir. 1995).

334 *Brunswick Corp. v. Pueblo Bowl-O-Mat, Inc.*, 429 U.S. 477 (1977); *see also Eastman Kodak Co. v. Goodyear Tire & Rubber Co.*, 114 F.3d 1547 (Fed. Cir. 1997) (explaining that the purpose for the antitrust-injury requirement is to "ensure that the harm for which plaintiff seeks compensation corresponds to the rationale for finding a violation").

335 *E.g., Se. Mo. Hosp. v. C.R. Bard, Inc.*, 616 F.3d 888 (8th Cir. 2010); *Paycom Billing Servs., Inc. v. MasterCard Int'l, Inc.*, 467 F.3d 283 (2d Cir. 2006); *Cape & Sons v. PCC Constr. Co.*, 453 F.3d 396 (7th Cir. 2006) (agreeing with and affirming district-court holding that antitrust injury must involve a loss resulting from acts that reduce output or raise prices); *Johnson v. Univ. Health Servs.*, 161 F.3d 1334 (11th Cir. 1998); *McKenzie-Willamette Hosp. v. PeaceHealth*, 2004-2 Trade Cas. (CCH) ¶ 74,600 (D. Ore. 2004) (explaining that plaintiff must show that defendant's conduct injured it "and that the harm flowed from conduct that was antithetical to market-wide competition").

336 *E.g., Hodges v. WSM, Inc.*, 26 F.3d 36 (6th Cir. 1994); *Williams v. Univ. Med. Ctr.*, 688 F. Supp. 2d 1134 (D.Nev. 2010); *Veesom v. Atchison Hosp. Ass'n,* 2006 WL 2714265 (D. Kan. 2006) ("To show an antitrust injury, plaintiff would need to show that defendants' conduct 'affected the prices, quantity or quality of goods or services, not just his own welfare.'"); *Davies v. Genesis Med. Ctr.*, 994 F. Supp. 1078 (S.D. Iowa 1998).

337 *E.g., Brunswick Corp. v. Pueblo Bowl-O-Mat, Inc.*, 429 U.S. 477 (1977).

338 *E.g., Cargill Corp. v. Montfort of Colo., Inc.*, 479 U.S. 104 (1986); *Daniel v. Am. Bd. of Emergency Med.*, 428 F.3d 408 (2d Cir. 2005).

339 *E.g., Atl. Richfield Co. v. USA Petrol. Co.*, 495 U.S. 328 (1990).

340 *See generally Summers v. Earth Inst.*, 555 U.S. 488 (2009).

It is entirely possible for a plaintiff who is injured by the competition-reducing effect of an antitrust violation not to have antitrust standing to recover damages. The Supreme Court has explained that courts should examine and balance six factors in determining whether a plaintiff has antitrust standing:

1. the causal connection between the violation and any harm to the plaintiff;
2. whether the defendant intended to cause the harm to the plaintiff that occurred;
3. the nature of the plaintiff's injury, particularly whether the plaintiff was a customer or competitor in the relevant market allegedly affected by the violation;
4. the directness or indirectness of the injury, including whether other parties exist whose injury was more direct than the plaintiff's and who would likely sue;
5. whether the plaintiff's damages are highly speculative; and
6. the risk of duplicative recoveries and complex damage-apportionment problems if plaintiff is granted antitrust standing.[341]

Several courts synthesize these factors into a two-pronged test by examining whether the plaintiff (1) suffered antitrust injury and (2) is an "efficient enforcer" of the antitrust laws.[342] Antitrust injury is always a necessary, but not sufficient, condition for antitrust standing.[343]

A number of courts have held or suggested that, to have antitrust standing, a plaintiff must be either a customer or competitor in the relevant market adversely affected by the alleged violation.[344] The Supreme Court, however, has indicated that plaintiffs whose injuries are "inextricably intertwined" to the injury to competition in that market also have antitrust standing, even if they are not a participant in that market.[345]

Finally, so-called "indirect purchasers" cannot recover the overcharge they pay when they purchase from a "direct purchaser" from the alleged co-conspirators or monopolist. So, for example, if a price-fixing conspiracy results in supracompetitive prices to direct purchasers of the co-conspirators, and the direct purchasers resell the product to their "indirect purchaser" customers, passing on to them

---

[341] *Associated Gen. Contractors v. Cal. Council of Carpenters*, 459 U.S. 519 (1983); *see also Palmyra Park Hosp., Inc. v. Phoebe Putney Mem'l Hosp.*, 604 F.3d 1291 (11th Cir. 2010); *Stark v. Ear, Nose & Throat Specialists*, 185 Fed. App'x 120 (3d Cir. 2006); *Daniel v. Am. Bd. of Emergency Med.*, 428 F.3d 408 (2d Cir. 2005); *Am. Med. Ass'n v. UnitedHealthcare Corp.*, 588 F. Supp. 2d 432 (S.D.N.Y. 2008).

[342] *E.g.*, *Palmyra Park Hosp., Inc. v. Phoebe Putney Mem'l Hosp.*, 604 F.3d 1291 (11th Cir. 2010) ("We employ a two-prong test for antitrust standing…: first, the plaintiff must have alleged an antitrust injury, and second the plaintiff must be an efficient enforcer of the antitrust laws."); *Tal v. Hogan*, 453 F.3d 1244 (10th Cir. 2006); *Ertag v. Naples Cmty. Hosp.*, 121 F.3d 721 (11th Cir. 1997) (*per curiam unpublished opinion reprinted at* 1997-2 Trade Cas. (CCH) ¶ 71,966); *Todorov v. DCH Healthcare Auth.*, 921 F.2d 1438 (11th Cir. 1991); *Pierson v. Orlando Reg'l Health-Care Sys.*, 619 F. Supp. 2d 1260 (M.D. Fla. 2009).

[343] *Palmyra Park Hosp., Inc. v. Phoebe Putney Mem'l Hosp.*, 604 F.3d 1291 (11th Cir. 2010); *McCollough v. Zimmer, Inc.*, 382 Fed. App'x 225 (3d Cir. 2010); *Elliot Indus. Ltd. P'ship v. BP Am. Prod. Co.*, 407 F.2d 1091 (10th Cir. 2005); *Giampollo v. Somerset Hosp. Ctr. for Health*, 189 F.3d 464 (3d Cir. 1999) (*unpublished opinion reprinted at* 1999-2 Trade Cas. (CCH) ¶ 72,574) ("First we must determine whether a claimant suffered antitrust injury… Second, we must determine whether a claimant was the most efficient enforcer of the antitrust laws.").

[344] *E.g., W. Penn Allegheny Health Sys. v. UPMC*, 627 F.3d 85 (3d Cir. 2010) ("As a general matter, the class of plaintiffs capable of satisfying the antitrust injury reqirement is limited to consumers and competitors in the restrained market."); *McCollough v. Zimmer, Inc.*, 382 Fed. App'x 225 (3d Cir. 2010); *Norris v. The Hearst Trust*, 500 F.3d 454 (5th Cir. 2007).

[345] *Blue Shield v. McCready*, 457 U.S. 465, 484 (1982); *McCollough v. Zimmer, Inc.*, 382 Fed. App'x 225 (3d Cir. 2010); *Novell, Inc. v. Microsoft Corp.*, 505 F.3d 302 (4th Cir. 2007).

some of the overcharge paid by the direct purchaser, the direct purchaser can recover the entire overcharge, and the indirect purchasers cannot recover the portion of the overcharge passed on to them.[346] Many state antitrust laws, however, permit indirect purchasers to recover the damages they incur from the passed-on overcharge.

6.5.4 Damages

Once a plaintiff proves with reasonable certainty that the antitrust violation caused it damages,[347] the standard it must meet to prove the amount of damages it suffered is relaxed. That amount need not be proved with exactness, but rather can be reasonably estimated based on relevant data using several types of damage-measurement methodologies. Nevertheless, proof of the amount of damages cannot be based on conjecture, guesswork, or speculation.[348]

6.6 Conclusion

Antitrust laws apply fully to the healthcare sector.[349] The types of antitrust issues arising are almost endless, including hospital mergers,[350] physician-practice mergers,[351] exclusive contracts between hospitals and physicians as to particular services rendered at the hospital,[352] hospital decisions not to grant or to terminate the staff privileges of practitioners based on peer review,[353] hospital staff-privilege moratoriums,[354] squeezing physicians out after a hospital merger,[355] price-fixing by provider networks,[356] exclusion of providers from membership in provider networks,[357] different types of joint ventures,[358] hospital acquisitions of physician practices,[359] hospital acquisitions of individual

---

346 *See generally Illinois Brick Co. v. Illinois*, 431 U.S. 720 (1977); *Del. Valley Surgical Supply, Inc. v. Johnson & Johnson*, 523 F.3d 1116 (9th Cir. 2008); *Warren Gen. Hosp. v. Amgen, Inc.*, 2010-1 Trade Cas. (CCH) ¶ 77,043 (D.N.J. 2010) (not-for-publication opinion).

347 *See generally Amerinet, Inc. v. Xerox Corp.*, 972 F.2d 1483 (8th Cir. 1992).

348 *Zenith Radio Corp. v. Hazeltine Research, Inc.*, 395 U.S. 100 (1969); *Bigelow v. RKO Pictures, Inc.*, 327 U.S. 251 (1946); *see also Texaco, Inc. v. Hasbrouck*, 496 U.S. 543 (1990).

349 *See Boulware v. Nev.*, 960 F.2d 793 (9th Cir. 1991).

350 *United States v. Long lsland Jewish Med. Ctr.*, 983 F. Supp. 121 (E.D.N.Y. 1997).

351 Antitrust Division Business Review Letter to Gastroenterology Associates, Ltd. (Jul. 7, 1997), at www.usdoj.gov/atr/publicfbusrev/1174.htm.

352 *E.g.*, *Jefferson Parish Hosp. Dist. No. 2 v. Hyde*, 466 U.S. 2 (1984); *Lafaro v. N.Y. Cardiothoracic Group, PLLC*, 570 F.3d 471 (2d Cir. 2009); *Colonial Med. Group, Inc. v. Catholic Healthcare W.*, 2010-1 Trade Cas. (CCH) ¶ 77,039 (N.D. Cal. 2010); *Perinatal Med. Group, Inc. v. Childeren's Hosp.*, 2010-1 Trade Cas. (CCH) ¶ 77,078 (E.D. Cal. 2010).

353 *E.g.*, *Moore v. Williamsburg Reg'l Hosp.*, 560 F.3d 166 (4th Cir. 2009); *Four Corners Nephrology Assocs., P.C. v. Mercy Med. Ctr.*, 582 F.3d 1216 (10th Cir. 2009); *Benson v. St. Joseph's Reg'l Health Ctr.*, 575 F.3d 542 (5th Cir. 2009); *Vesom v. Atchison Hosp. Ass'n*, 279 Fed. App'x 624 (10th Cir. 2008).

354 *Allen v. Washington Hosp.*, 34 F. Supp. 2d 958 (W.D. Pa. 1999).

355 *Samuel v. Herrick Mem'l Hosp.*, 201 F.3d 830 (6th Cir. 2000).

356 *N. Tex. Specialty Physicians*, 2005-2 Trade Cas. (CCH) ¶ 75,032 (FTC 2005), *petition for review granted and part and remanded*, 528 F.3d 346 (5th Cir. 2008); *Roaring Fork Valley Physicians I.P.A., Inc.*, Dkt. No. C-4288 (FTC Apr. 5, 2010) (consent order); *Boulder Valley Individual Practice* Ass'n, Dkt. No. C-4285 (FTC Apr. 2, 2010) (consent order); *J. Allen Ramey, M.D., Inc. v. Pac. Found. for Med. Care*, 999 F. Supp. 1355 (S.D. Cal. 1998).

357 *Solla v. Aetna Health Plans*, 14 F. Supp. 2d 252 (E.D.N.Y. 1998), *aff'd*, 182 F.3d 901 (2d Cir. 1999) (Table).

358 *See New York v. St. Francis Hosp.*, 94 F. Supp. 2d 399 (S.D.N.Y. 2000).

359 *HTI Health Servs., Inc. v. Quorum Health Group, Inc.*, 960 F. Supp. 1104 (S.D. Miss. 1997).

physicians,[360] health plan mergers,[361] physician unionization,[362] certificate-of-need disputes,[363] payor refusals to contract with certain types of providers,[364] discriminatory prices granted by suppliers to nonprofit entities,[365] hospital tying arrangements with payers,[366] pharmaceutical price-fixing and price discrimination,[367] health-insurer use of most-favored-nations clauses,[368] provider standard-setting programs,[369] tobacco medical-cost suits,[370] hospital attempts to force managed-care plans not to contract with other hospitals,[371] exclusive contracts between payors and single groups of physicians,[372] provider fee-review programs,[373] provider-association advertising restraints,[374] pharmaceutical distributor mergers,[375] pharmaceutical manufacturer mergers,[376] pharmaceutical manufacturers "reverse payments" delaying entry of generic drugs,[377] "sham" patent-infringement litigation,[378] pharmacy boycotts of networks,[379] expulsion of physicians from their medical group,[380] hospital group purchasing of nursing services,[381] hospital price fixing of employed nurses' wages,[382] hospital price-fixing of prices paid for traveling nurses,[383] group purchasing organization exclusive vendor contracts,[384] provider price fixing to increase reimbursement from payers,[385] tying the purchase of third-party administration services

---

360 *Wichita Clinic, P.A. v. Columbia/HCA Healthcare Corp.*, 45 F. Supp. 2d 1164 (D. Kan. 1999).

361 *United States v. UnitedHealth Group, Inc.*, 2008-2 Trade Cas. (CCH) ¶ 76,318 (D.D.C. 2008) (consent decree and competitive impact statement); *United States v. UnitedHealth Group, Inc.*, 2006-1 Trade Cas. (CCH) ¶ 75,255 (D.D.C. 2005) (consent decree and competitive impact statement); *United States v. Aetna, Inc.*, 1999-2 Trade Cas. (CCH) ¶ 72,730 (N.D. Tex. 1999) (consent decree).

362 *United States v. Fed'n of Physicians and Dentists*, 2002-2 Trade Cas. (CCH) ¶ 73,868 (D. Del. 2002) (consent decree).

363 *Kottle v. Nw. Kidney Ctrs.*, 146 F.3d 1056 (9th Cir. 1998).

364 *Continental Orthopedic Appliances, Inc. v. Health Ins. Plan*, 40 F. Supp. 2d 109 (E.D.N.Y. 1999).

365 FTC Staff Advisory Opinion to Community CarePartners, Inc. (Jul. 2, 2010), at http://www.ftc.gov/os/2010/07100702carepartnersopinion.pdf.

366 *E.g.*, *Palmyra Park Hosp. v. Phoebe Putney Mem'l Hosp.*, 604 F.3d 1291 (11th Cir. 2010).

367 *In re Brand Name Prescription Drugs Antitrust Litig.*, 186 F.3d 781 (7th Cir. 1999).

368 *United States v. Blue Cross Blue Shield*, No. 2:10-cv-14155-DPH-MKM (E.D. Mich Oct. 18, 2010) (complaint); *United States v. Med. Mut.*, 1999-1 Trade Cas. (CCH) ¶ 72,465 (N.D. Ohio 1999) (consent decree and competitive-impact statement).

369 *DM Research, Inc. v. College of Am. Pathologists*, 170 F.3d 53 (lst Cir. 1999).

370 *Steamfitters Local Union No. 420 v. Philip Morris, Inc.*, 171 F.3d 912 (3d Cir. 1999).

371 *Surgical Ctr. v. Hospital Dist.*, 171 F.3d 231 (5th Cir. 1999) (*en banc*).

372 *Albani v. S. Ariz. Anesthesia Servs.*, P.C., 1997-2 Trade Cas. (CCH) ¶ 71,927 (D. Ariz. 1997).

373 *Mitchael v. Intracorp, Inc.*, 179 F.3d 847 (10th Cir. 1999).

374 *Cal. Dental Ass'n v. FTC*, 526 U.S. 756 (1999).

375 *FTC v. Cardinal Health, Inc.*, 12 F. Supp. 2d 34 (D.D.C. 1998).

376 *E.g.*, *Mylan Labs.*, Inc., Dkt. No. C-4200 (FTC Nov. 1, 2007); *Hospira, Inc.*, Dkt. No. C-4182 (FTC Jan. 18, 2007) (consent order).

377 *E.g.*, *In re Ciprofloxacin Hydrochloride Antitrust Litig.*, 544 F.3d 1323 (Fed. Cir. 2008); *Tamoxifen Citrate Antitrust Litig.*, 429 F.3d 370 (2d Cir. 2005).

378 *E.g.*, *Bristol-Myers Squibb Co.*, 135 F.T.C. 444 (2003) (consent order).

379 *Merck-Medco Managed Care, Inc. v. Rite Aid Corp.*, 22 F. Supp. 2d 447 (D. Md. 1998), *aff'd per curiam without published op.*, 201 F.3d 436 (4th Cir. 1999) (Table).

380 *Marshall v. Planz*, 13 F. Supp. 2d 1231 (M.D. Ala. 1998).

381 *All Care Nursing Serv., Inc. v. High Tech Staffing Servs., Inc.*, 135 F.3d 740 (11th Cir. 1998).

382 *Fleischman v. Albany Med. Ctr.*, 728 F. Supp. 2d 130 (N.D.N.Y. 2010).

383 *Doe v. Ariz. Hosp. & Healthcare Ass'n*, 2009-2 Trade Cas. (CCH) ¶ 76,591 (D. Ariz. 2009); *United States v. Ariz. Hosp. & Health Ass'n*, 2007-2 Trade Cas. (CCH) ¶ 75,869 (D. Ariz. 2007) (consent decree and competitive impact statement).

384 *E.g.*, *Se. Mo. Hosp. v. C.R. Bard, Inc.*, 616 F.3d 888 (8th Cir. 2010); *Allied Orthopedic Appliances, Inc. v. Tyco Health Group, LP*, 592 F.3d 991 (9th Cir. 2010).

385 *Untied States v. Idaho Orthopaedic Soc'y*, 2010-2 Trade Cas. (CCH) ¶ 77,142 (D. Idaho 2010) (consent decree and competitive impact statement).

and participation in a network,[386] use of bundled discounts in contracts between hospitals and payers[387] and between group purchasing organizations and vendors,[388] physician efforts to destroy allied-practitioner competitors,[389] boycotts of practitioners by specialty boards,[390] competition from the state in providing medical air-transport services,[391] hospital efforts to stifle competition from members of the medical staff establishing physician-owned specialty hospitals and outpatient facilities,[392] pharmaceutical-purchaser price-fixing agreements facilitated by pharmacy benefit management companies,[393] and challenges to anticompetitive state healthcare regulatory board decisions.[394]

As even this incomplete list shows, antitrust is an integral part of health law today.

6.7 References

A number of websites and publications provide particular assistance in researching issues relating to healthcare antitrust law and antitrust economics. The following is a partial list of helpful resources.

- American Health Lawyers Association (Health Lawyers) Antitrust Practice Group: http://www.healthlawyers.org/Template.cfm?Section=Resources2
- Health Lawyers antitrust books and papers: http://www.lexisnexis.com/ahla/
- 1–6 John J. Miles, *Health Care & Antitrust Law* (1992 and Supp. 2011) (Thomson/West Group)
- ABA Section of Antitrust Law, *Antitrust Law Developments* (6th ed. 2007)
- ABA Section of Antitrust Law, *Antitrust Health Care Handbook* (4th ed. 2010)
- ABA Section of Antitrust Law, *Health Care Mergers and Acquisitions Handbook* (2003)
- ABA Section of Antitrust Law, *State Enforcement Handbook* (2003) (Chapter on state antitrust enforcement in healthcare)
- 1–14 Phillip Areeda & Herbert Hovenkamp, *Antitrust Law* (various dates)
- Phillip E. Areeda & Herbert Hovenkamp, *Fundamentals of Antitrust Law* (2003 and Supp. 2009)
- Herbert Hovenkamp, *Federal Antitrust Policy* (3d ed. 2005)
- John H. Shenefield, *The Antitrust Laws: A Primer* (4th ed. 2001)
- Lawrence A. Sullivan & Warren S. Grimes, *The Law of Antitrust: An Integrated Handbook* (2d ed. 2006)
- Richard A. Posner, *Antitrust Law* (2d ed. 2001)

---

386 *Brokerage Concepts, Inc. v. U.S. Healthcare, Inc.*, 140 F.3d 494 (3d Cir. 1998).

387 *Cascade Health Solutions v. PeaceHealth*, 515 F.3d 883 (9th Cir. 2008).

388 *E.g.*, *Warren Gen. Hosp. v. Amgen, Inc.*, 2010-1 Trade Cas. (CCH) ¶77,043 (D.N.J. 2010) (not-for-publication opinion).

389 *Minn. Ass'n of Nurse Anesthetists v. Unity Hosp.*, 208 F.3d 655 (8th Cir. 2000).

390 *Ezekwo v. Am. Bd. of Internal Med.*, 18 F. Supp. 2d 271 (S.D.N.Y. 1998).

391 *Evac, LLC v. Pataki*, 89 F. Supp. 2d 250 (N.D.N.Y. 2000).

392 *Little Rock Cardiology Clinic, PA v. Baptist Hosp.*, 591 F.3d 591 (8th Cir. 2009); *Peoria Day Surgery Ctr. v. OSF Healthcare Sys.*, 2010-1 Trade Cas. (CCH) ¶ 76,870 (C.D. Ill. 2009); *Tex. v. Mem'l Hermann Healthcare* Sys., 2009-1 Trade Cas. (CCH) ¶ 76,479 (Tex. Dist. Ct., Jan. 26, 2009) (consent decree); *Heartland Surgical Specialty Hosp., LLC v. Midwest Div.*, 527 F. Supp. 2d 1257 (D.Kan. 2007); Surgical *Care Ctr. v. Hospital Serv. Dist. No. 1*, 2001-1 Trade Cas. (CCH) ¶ 73,215 (E.D. La. 2001), *aff'd*, 309 F.3d 936 (5th Cir. 2002).

393 *Bellvue Drug Co. v. Advance PCS*, 2004-1 Trade Cas. (CCH) ¶ 74,329 (E.D. Pa. 2004).

394 *S.C. State Board of Dentistry*, Dkt. No. 9311 (FTC Sept. 6, 2007) (consent order).

- Federal Trade Commission & U.S. Department of Justice, *Improving Health Care: A Dose of Competition* (Jul. 2004)
- Roger D. Blair & David L. Kaserman, *Antitrust Economics* (2d ed. 2009)
- Paul J. Feldstein, *Health Care Economics* (6th ed. 2005)
- Dennis W. Carlton & Jeffrey M. Perloff, *Modern Industrial Organization* (4th ed. 2005)
- F.M. Scherer & David Ross, *Industrial Market Structure and Economic Performance* (3d ed. 1990)
- Robert S. Pindyck & Daniel L. Rubinfeld, *Microeconomics* (6th ed. 2005)
- Federal Trade Commission: http://www.ftc.gov
- National Association of Attorneys General/Antitrust: http://www.naag.org/antitrust.php
- U.S. Department of Justice, Antitrust Division: http://www.justice.gov/atr/index.htm

7

The Source of Payment: The State and Federal Regulation of Private Healthcare Plans

Daniel J. Schwartz, Esquire*
Greensfelder, Hemker, & Gale PC

This Chapter will discuss the nature and extent of state and federal regulation of employer sponsored private healthcare plans,[1] in light of the historic rights granted to the states to regulate insurance and the sweeping changes made by the federal government through the Patient Protection and Affordable Care Act.[2]

7.1 The Basis of Regulation

7.1.1 The State Regulation of the Business of Insurance

The McCarran-Ferguson Act of 1945 endows states with the primary authority to regulate the "business of insurance."[3] State regulation of the insurance industry, however, did not commence with the passage of the McCarran-Ferguson Act. To the contrary, as early as 1851, states began enacting laws to regulate what was then becoming a burgeoning insurance industry.[4] Not everyone was enamored with the state regulation of insurance. Not surprisingly, the insurance industry was particularly concerned with the burdens of complying with multiple state regulatory schemes and, as a result, often chose to ignore the laws of other states. The first United States Supreme Court case to consider the right of the states to regulate insurance arose in this context.[5]

* The author wishes to thank Matthew F. Pearson for his assistance in preparing this Chapter.

1 Generally, for purposes of this Chapter, an employer sponsored healthcare plan is a non-governmental entity or organization that provides indemnity against certain medical expense, or otherwise provides for or arranges for the provision of, and pays for, certain covered healthcare services. A detailed description of those organizations that operate health plans, as well as those organizations that are an integral part of many health plans, is discussed in Section 7.2. For a discussion of governmental sponsored health programs (*e.g.*, Medicare), *see* Chapter 3. Keep in mind, however, that sometimes a governmental program (*e.g.*, the Medicaid+Choice Program or the Federal Employees Health Benefits Program), will contract with a private health plan to obtain coverage for the beneficiaries of the governmental plan.

2 P.L. 111-148, hereinafter referred to as the Patient Protection and Affordable Care Act (PPACA).

3 15 U.S.C. §§ 1011–1015.

4 *See* Susan Randall, *Insurance Regulation in the United States: Regulatory Federalism and the National Association of Insurance Commissioners*, 26 Fla. St. U. L. Rev. 625, 630 (1999) (hereafter Randall).

5 *See Paul v. Virginia*, 75 U.S. (8 Wall.) 168 (1869). *See also* Randall, at 630–36.

In *Paul v. Virginia,* the Court was asked to overturn Samuel Paul's conviction in the state of Virginia for the unauthorized business of insurance. Mr. Paul was an insurance agent for New York-licensed insurers. Although he applied for an agent's license in Virginia, he refused to deposit the necessary bond and was denied a license. He nonetheless acted as an insurance agent in Virginia, and was ultimately convicted of acting as an agent without a license.[6]

On appeal, Mr. Paul argued that the power to regulate insurance resided in the federal government under the Commerce Clause of the United States Constitution. The Court held that the issuance of an insurance policy was "not the transaction of commerce," thus leaving the regulation of insurance to the states.[7] The Court reaffirmed its *Paul* decision in 1913,[8] and the *Paul* case remained good law until 1944, when the Court reversed itself in *United States v. South-Eastern Underwriters Association.*[9] In reversing its earlier decision, the Court held that insurance contracts do affect interstate commerce and, therefore, are subject to federal regulation under the Commerce Clause.[10]

In the nearly 100 years that passed between the enactment of the first state insurance law and the Supreme Court's ruling that insurance contracts are subject to federal regulation, many states had developed comprehensive regulatory schemes.[11] Therefore, it is not surprising that, in response to the *South-Eastern Underwriters Association* case, an organization comprised of state insurance regulators[12] proposed a bill that would squarely place the primary authority to regulate insurance back with the states. This bill, which would become known as the McCarran-Ferguson Act, became law in 1945.[13]

Specifically, the McCarran-Ferguson Act exempts the business of insurance from federal antitrust regulation to the extent that it is regulated by the states.[14] More importantly for purposes of this Chapter, the McCarran-Ferguson Act provides that states have the express authority to regulate the business of insurance, and that no federal law or regulation shall preempt that authority unless the federal law specifically relates to the business of insurance.[15]

Though the McCarran-Ferguson Act provides for state regulation of the business of insurance, it does not itself define what constitutes the "business of insurance." Interestingly, many states do not fill this void by including such a definition in their state regulatory schemes. Other states provide statutory definitions that lack clarity or provide multiple conflicting definitions that vary depending upon the activity that is the subject of the particular statutory provision.[16] Those states that do provide a statutory

---

6 *Paul*, at 169.

7 *Id.*

8 *See New York Life Ins. Co. v. Deer Lodge County*, 231 U.S. 495 (1913).

9 *United States v. South-Eastern Underwriters Ass'n*, 322 U.S. 533 (1944). *See also* Randall, *supra*, at 633.

10 *United States v. South-Eastern Underwriters Ass'n.*, at 510.

11 Randall, at 632.

12 Randall, at 633. This organization would become known as the National Association of Insurance Commissioners (NAIC). The nature and role of NAIC is discussed in Section 7.2.1.

13 Randall, at 633. For general discussion of the McCarran-Ferguson Act, *see* Charles D. Weiller, *The McCarran-Ferguson Act's Antitrust Exemption for Insurance: History and Policy*, 1978 Duke L.J. 587 (1978).

14 15 U.S.C. § 1012.

15 *Id.*

16 Stephen K. Phillips & Daniel K. Settlelmayer, *Provider Risk Sharing and Provider Sponsored Organizations* 5 (Health Lawyers 1998).

definition, however, generally define the business of insurance as involving a contract under which one party undertakes, on behalf of another party, to indemnify against certain expenses, or directly pay certain costs, upon the occurrence of certain contingencies.[17]

Though not all states statutorily define the business of insurance, state-court decisions have produced a fairly consistent common-law definition which includes as its essential components the shifting of risk, for the payment of a fee, from an insured to an insurer who is able to assume that risk by pooling together the payments received from all individuals, thereby spreading the risk among a defined population.

Of course, some level of risk is present in almost every arrangement whereby one person pays another person for something of value. For instance, in the case of a restaurant that operates an "all you can eat" buffet for a set price, the restaurant owner has assumed the risk that the set price charged for the buffet per person, when added together with all the revenues received from all other diners, will not only cover the owner's cost but will, in fact, produce a profit. More specifically, the owner assumes that some people will eat a lot, and some people will eat a little, but by spreading the cost of the food and service among all diners on an equal basis (regardless of the amount they actually consume), the restaurant can bear the risk of those large-capacity eaters.

One certainly could argue that, analyzed in those terms, the "all you can eat" buffet represents an insurance arrangement, because it meets all of these five common-law elements. Under that example, however, the strict application of the five elements produces an absurd result. For this reason, in applying the five essential elements cited, state courts have recognized a distinction between "business risk" and "insurance risk."[18] Specifically, state courts distinguish between situations in which the key objective is the provision of a service (*e.g.*, an all-you-can-eat buffet) and situations in which the key objective is the provision of indemnity (*i.e.*, financial reimbursement for the cost of a particular loss).[19]

The case of *Transportation Guaranty Co., Ltd. v. Jellins* illustrates this distinction.[20] The *Jellins* case involved a plaintiff truck-maintenance corporation that agreed, in exchange for a set monthly fee, to maintain specified trucks owned by the defendant in "mechanical repair [and] to garage and fuel said" trucks.[21] The defendant breached these contracts, and the plaintiff sued for damages. In response, the defendant alleged that the maintenance contracts were void and unenforceable because the plaintiff was engaged in the unlicensed business of insurance. In finding in favor of the plaintiff, the Supreme Court of California ruled that this arrangement did not constitute an insurance contract, because the plaintiff corporation merely agreed to provide its service and labor but never agreed to indemnify the

---

[17] *See, e.g.,* Colo. Rev. Stat. § 10-1-102(7); Fla. Stat. Ann. § 624.02; N.C. Gen. Stat. § 58-1-10. *See generally* Nat'l Ass'n of Ins. Comm'rs, *The Regulation of Risk Bearing Entities*, app. at A-IV-4(V) (1997) (hereafter NAIC White Paper); Allison Overbay & Mark Hall, *Insurance Regulation of Providers That Bear Risk*, 22 Am. J.L. & Med. 361 (1996).

[18] *See generally* Ericka L. Rutenberg, *Managed Care and the Business of Insurance: When is a Provider Group Considered to be at Risk?,* 1 DePaul J. Health Care L. 267, 272–80 (1996).

[19] *Id. See also* Douglas J. Witten, *Regulation of "Downstream" and Direct Risk Contracting by Health Care Providers: The Quest for Consumer Protection and a Level Playing Field*, 23 Am. J.L. & Med. 449, 458–62 (1997).

[20] *Transp. Guar. Co. v. Jellins*, 174 P.2d 625 (Cal. 1946). Other cases make this distinction as well. *See, e.g., Griffin Sys., Inc. v. Ohio Dep't of Ins.*, 575 N.E.2d 803 (Ohio 1991); *Prof'l Lens Plan v. Dep't of Ins.*, 387 So.2d 548 (Fla. 1980); *Cal. Physicians' Serv. v. Garrison*, 172 P.2d 4 (Cal. 1946); *Nat'l Auto Serv. Corp. v. State*, 55 S.W.2d 209 (Tex. Civ. App. 1932).

[21] 174 P.2d at 626.

purchaser of the arrangement against a risk of loss.[22] In so holding, the court explained that "every business arrangement entails some assumption of risk, some gambling."[23] Therefore, the assumption of risk is not controlling. Rather, one must look at the arrangement, as a whole, to determine whether the principle objective is service or indemnity.

Historically, courts have made similar distinctions in cases involving healthcare-related arrangements.[24] *Jordan v. Group Health Association* is the seminal case in this area.[25] The *Jordan* case explored the nature of the arrangement between a nonprofit corporation, Group Health Association (GHA), and its members. Specifically, GHA members would pay fixed monthly-membership dues to GHA, depending on whether the individual purchased a family or individual membership. In exchange for the payment of these monthly dues, GHA arranged for its members to receive medical and surgical services, subject to certain limitations, from specified providers.[26]

In order to provide these services, GHA paid a fixed annual fee to its physician providers (payable in monthly installments) for providing covered services. This fixed payment did not vary with the volume of services that the physicians rendered. Although GHA accepted the membership dues, and used these dues to enter into prepaid arrangements with physician providers, the GHA bylaws made it clear that GHA's only obligation was to enter into these provider contracts. GHA expressly disclaimed any guaranty that these providers would perform their obligations, and further disclaimed any liability for any such failure to perform or for the negligent performance of those obligations.[27]

Given those facts, the court ruled that GHA was really a "consumer cooperative" and not an insurer.[28] As a consumer cooperative, its main purpose was to arrange for its members to receive a service at a reasonable price through the pooling of purchasing power and other economies of scale. GHA's primary purpose was not to provide financial protection against loss caused by a specified occurrence.[29] Acknowledging that GHA's arrangement may include some element of risk-distribution or assumption, the court stated that a focus only on the element of risk, rather than looking at the contract as a whole, would result in insurance statutes "engulf[ing] practically all contracts."[30]

Interestingly, with the advent of managed care, the distinction between the provision of healthcare (the "service") and the financing of healthcare (the "indemnity") has become blurred. As the line between service and indemnity has become less clear, state regulators have become less willing to apply this "service vs. indemnity" analysis to determine whether an arrangement constitutes the business of insurance. As a result, some states have enacted regulatory schemes or espoused policy positions

---

22 *Id.* at 631.
23 *Id.* at 629.
24 *See, e.g., Mich. Podiatric Med. Ass'n v. Nat'l Foot Care Program, Inc.*, 438 N.W.2d 350 (Mich. 1989); *Prof'l Lens Plan v. Dep't of Ins.*, 387 So.2d 548 (Fla. 1980); *New Mexico Life Ins. Guar. Ass'n v. Moore*, 596 P.2d 260 (N.M. 1979); *Cal. Physicians' Serv. v. Garrison*, 172 P.2d 4 (Cal. 1946); *State v. Cmty. Health Serv., Inc.*, 30 A.2d 44 (N.J. 1943); State *ex. rel Fishback v. Universal Serv. Agency*, 87 Wash. 413 (1915).
25 *Jordan v. Group Health Ass'n*, 107 F.2d 239 (D.C. Cir. 1939).
26 *Id.* at 242.
27 *Id.* at 241–44.
28 *Id.* at 247.
29 *Id.*
30 *Id.* at 248.

that would provide for some level of regulation over an activity that, under the analysis of these court cases, probably involves the provision of a service.

The United States Supreme Court has had myriad opportunities to define the business of insurance. These opportunities have arisen in connection with the application of the McCarran-Ferguson Act and ERISA. The Supreme Court first explored the definition of the "business of insurance" in the context of the McCarran-Ferguson Act in the case of *Group Life and Health Insurance Co. v. Royal Drug Co.*[31] The *Royal Drug* case involved an antitrust challenge by a group of pharmacies to a participating pharmacy agreement entered into between Blue Shield of Texas and certain pharmacies. The Supreme Court did not consider the merits of the antitrust challenge. Rather, the sole issue before the Court was whether Blue Shield's participating pharmacy program—in particular, its contractual arrangement with participating pharmacists—constituted the "business of insurance" so as to render those contracts exempt from federal antitrust laws under the McCarran-Ferguson Act.[32]

The specific practice under review in *Royal Drug* was an arrangement under which Blue Shield insureds were entitled to get their prescriptions filled at participating pharmacies for $2.00. Insureds also could get their prescriptions filled at non-participating pharmacies. If the insured exercised that option, however, the insured would only receive reimbursement equal to 75% of the difference of the amount paid for the drugs and $2.00. In order to offer this benefit, Blue Shield entered into agreements with participating pharmacies. Under these agreements, the participating pharmacy would agree to accept, as payment in full for services rendered, the $2.00 received from the insured plus an additional reimbursement from Blue Shield equal to the pharmacy's cost of acquiring the drugs.[33]

In the *Royal Drug* case, the Supreme Court found that the participating-pharmacy agreements between Blue Shield and its participating pharmacists did not constitute the business of insurance. After acknowledging that the McCarran-Ferguson Act did not define the business of insurance, the Court looked to the legislative history of the McCarran-Ferguson Act in order to determine what Congress meant by the "business of insurance." In this regard, the Court found that "Congress understood the business of insurance to be the underwriting and spreading of risk."[34] Having made that determination, the Court then shifted its focus to whether the arrangement between Blue Shield and its participating pharmacists involved the transfer and spreading of risk. Relying heavily on the *Jordan* case discussed earlier, the Court found that the arrangement between Blue Shield and its participating pharmacists involved only an agreement that Blue Shield purchase goods at a set price.[35] Therefore, the arrangement between Blue Shield and its participating pharmacies did not constitute the business of insurance, because it did not involve a true underwriting of risk.

Subsequently, in *Union Labor Life Insurance Co. v. Pireno,*[36] the United States Supreme Court considered whether an insurer's use of a peer-review committee to decide the reasonableness and necessity of services provided by chiropractors involved the business of insurance so as to exempt the

[31] *Group Life and Health Insurance Co. v. Royal Drug Co.,* 440 U.S. 205 (1979).
[32] *Id.* at 209.
[33] *Id.* at 205.
[34] *Id.* at 220–21 (citing legislative history contained in House reports).
[35] *Id.* at 229.
[36] 458 U.S. 119 (1982).

insurers from an antitrust challenge by chiropractors with respect to this practice.[37] In holding that the peer-review committee did not involve the business of insurance, the Court articulated the following three elements as relevant to the determination of whether the activity involved the business of insurance:

1. whether the practice involved the transfer or spreading of risk of policyholders;
2. whether the practice was an integral part of the policy relationship between the insurer and the insured; and
3. whether the practice is limited to entities within the insurance industry.[38]

Later United States Supreme Court cases have consistently reaffirmed these criteria, which frequently are referred to as the "McCarran-Ferguson factors."[39]

The McCarran-Ferguson Act continues to serve as the foundation of the state's authority to regulate insurance. In accordance with the requirements of the McCarran-Ferguson Act, however, subsequent federal laws (*e.g.,* ERISA,[40] the Consolidated Omnibus Reconciliation Act of 1985 (COBRA), the Health Insurance Portability and Accountability Act of 1996 (HIPAA),[41] and the PPACA) have placed limits on this state power through express regulation of certain aspects of the business of insurance.

7.1.2 Federal Regulation and the Pre-Emption of State Laws

Although motivated (through the development and passage of ERISA) to prevent mismanagement of employee-benefit funds, Congress did not want to thwart the continued growth of employer-sponsored programs. The preemption provision of ERISA was a way to balance these interests. On the one hand, ERISA preemption provided for uniform federal regulation of benefit programs that ensured ERISA protections to all plan beneficiaries across the country. At the same time, however, the preemption provision released employers from the burdens of complying with "conflicting or inconsistent state and local regulation of employee benefit plans,"[42] thereby reducing the cost of plan administration.

Intuitively, courts and lawyers have struggled with the ERISA preemption statute since its inception. Indeed, the statute has been notorious for producing divergent results in virtually identical fact patterns. In *Rush Prudential HMO, Inc. v. Moran*, U.S. Supreme Court Justice David Souter observed that "[t]he unhelpful drafting of these antiphonal clauses... occupies a substantial share of this Court's time..."[43]

---

[37] *Id.* at 122.
[38] *Id.* at 126.
[39] *See, e.g., Pilot Life Ins. Co. v. Dedeaux*, 481 U.S. 41 (1987); *Metropolitan Life Ins. Co. v. Massachusetts*, 471 U.S. 724 (1985). *See also Unum Life Ins. Co. of Am. v. Ward*, 526 U.S. 358 (1999).
[40] 29 U.S.C. §§ 1001–1461.
[41] Health Insurance Portability And Accountability Act of 1996, Pub. L. No. 104-191, 110 Stat. 1936 (1996).
[42] *See* 120 Cong. Rec., 29,933 (1974) (Statement of Senator Williams). *See also Shaw v. Delta Airlines, Inc.*, 463 U.S. 85, 105 (1983).
[43] *Rush Prudential HMO, Inc. v. Moran*, 536 U.S. 355, 122 S.Ct. 2151, 2153 (2002).

The ERISA preemption provision is not absolute. The limitations imposed on federal preemption are best understood by analyzing the three separate clauses that together comprise ERISA's preemption provision:

1. the "preemption clause;"[44]
2. the "saving clause;"[45] and
3. the "deemer clause."[46]

Under the preemption clause, ERISA supersedes any and all state laws that "relate to" an employee-benefit plan subject to ERISA.[47] The saving clause "saves" from the preemption clause certain state laws regulating the business of insurance. Specifically, ERISA does not preempt state laws that regulate insurance, even if those laws otherwise "relate to" an ERISA plan.[48] Finally, the deemer clause creates an exception to the savings clause by providing that no employee-benefit plan, or trust established under such a plan, may be deemed to be "an insurance company or other insurer… for purposes of any state law purporting to regulate insurance companies [or] insurance contracts."[49] Synthesizing these three components of ERISA's preemption provision has produced two clear concepts.

First, states can continue to regulate the business of insurance, even if the state laws that regulate the business of insurance sometimes impact ERISA plans. For instance, states may enact laws applicable to health-insurance companies, even though health-insurance companies sometimes contract to provide group health coverage to beneficiaries of a plan subject to ERISA. As a result, when an employer purchases insurance to provide benefits for plan beneficiaries under the terms of the insurer's policy, that insurer is subject to state insurance regulation.

Second, states may not impose insurance regulation on self-insured ERISA benefit plans even if those plans are otherwise engaged in the "business of insurance" by state definition. In other words, if an employer bears all or most of the risk for medical claims, then states may not regulate the benefit-plan activities of the employer by calling it "insurance."

Unfortunately, however, as will be discussed more fully, the application of these two "clear" concepts in the context of specific arrangements is often anything but clear. First, it is not always clear when a state law constitutes the regulation of insurance, thus "saving" the law from preemption even if the law in question relates to an ERISA benefit plan. A state's mere inclusion of a law within its insurance code does not automatically make that law an insurance regulation. Second, determining when ERISA preempts a state law that does not constitute the regulation of insurance because that state law "relates to" an ERISA plan is similarly challenging. As stated, if a state law does not constitute the regulation of insurance, but also does not "relate to" an ERISA plan, then ERISA preemption does not occur. Finally, analyzing the interplay between the saving clause and the deemer clause against the backdrop of contemporary healthcare financing and reimbursement arrangements poses special ques-

[44] 29 U.S.C. § 1144(a).
[45] 29 U.S.C. § 1144(b)(i).
[46] 29 U.S.C. § 1144(b)(ii).
[47] 29 U.S.C. § 1144(a).
[48] 29 U.S.C. § 1144(b)(i).
[49] 29 U.S.C. § 1144(b)(ii).

tions. Specifically, the line between when an ERISA plan is self-funded and when it is insured may be hard to determine. For this reason, analyzing certain state laws for purposes of determining whether they are preempted by ERISA can seem more like an art than a science.

Nevertheless, a growing body of case law, particularly recent United States Supreme Court decisions, does provide useful guidance. While many questions remain unanswered, these cases form the basis of the current ERISA-preemption analytical framework.

Under early case law, it seemed as though almost every state law that did not directly relate to the regulation of the business of insurance was within the reach of ERISA's preemption provision. This is because early cases, including early Supreme Court decisions, interpreted the "relate to" phrase literally. For instance, in its 1983 decision in *Shaw v. Delta Airlines, Inc.,* the United States Supreme Court stated that a "state law 'relates to' an employee benefit plan, in the normal sense of the phrase, if it has a connection with or reference to such plan."[50] Later Supreme Court decisions continued to apply this expansive reading of the "relate to" language.[51] In 1995, however, the Supreme Court, in *New York State Conference of Blue Cross & Blue Shield Plans v. Travelers Insurance Co.*,[52] retreated from this broad, literal interpretation that liberally found the necessary connection between a state law and an ERISA plan, and moved towards a more narrow interpretation that attempts to define parameters for what laws "relate to" a benefit plan through analysis of ERISA's objectives.

In the *Travelers* decision, the Court was asked to consider whether ERISA preempted a New York law requiring hospitals to collect surcharges from certain HMOs, as well as from patients whose commercial-insurance coverage was purchased by an employee-healthcare plan.[53] Several commercial insurers and their trade association filed actions against New York state officials, claiming that ERISA preempted the New York surcharge law on the basis that the surcharge law relates to an employee-benefit plan. The Court ruled that ERISA did not preempt this New York state law.[54] In so holding, the Court observed that "if 'relate to' were taken to extend to the furthest stretch of its indeterminacy, then for all practical purposes preemption would never run its course, for really, universally, relations stop nowhere."[55] In making this observation, the Court acknowledged that its prior attempts to construe the phrase "relate to" do not give much help drawing an appropriate line.[56]

The Court then stated that, in order to draw that line and determine whether a law has a connection with an ERISA plan, it must look to the objectives of the ERISA statute "as a guide to the scope of the state law that Congress" intended to preempt.[57] The Court noted that the objective of ERISA was to

---

50 *Shaw v. Delta Airlines, Inc.*, 463 U.S. 85, 96–97 (1983).

51 *See, e.g., FMC Corp. v. Holliday*, 498 U.S. 52 (1990); *Ingersoll-Rand Co. v. McClendon*, 498 U.S. 133 (1990); *Pilot Life Ins. Co. v. Dedeaux*, 481 U.S. 41 (1987).

52 *New York State Conference of Blue Cross & Blue Shield Plans v. Travelers Ins. Co.*, 514 U.S. 645 (1995).

53 *Id.*

54 *Id.* at 661.

55 *Id.* at 655 (quoting H. James, Roderick Hudson (New York ed., World's Classics 1980)).

56 *Id.*

57 *Id.* at 656. Citing *Shaw v. Delta Airlines, Inc.*, 463 U.S. 85, 96–97 (1983), the Court noted that a law relates to an ERISA plan if it either has a connection with or makes reference to such a plan. *Id.* at 656. The Court went on to explain that the law in question clearly did not make a "reference" to an ERISA plan because the surcharges are imposed on patients and HMOs, regardless of whether the coverage is ultimately secured by an ERISA plan. *Id.* The real question for the Court, therefore, was whether the surcharge law otherwise had a "connection" with an ERISA plan. *Id.*

eliminate the threat of conflicting and inconsistent state and local regulation—in other words, to avoid a multiplicity of regulation in order to permit a nationally uniform administration of employee-benefit plans.[58] Therefore, the intent of the preemption language was to preempt those state laws that would affect the ability of plan administrators to implement nationally uniform benefit levels.

In the case under review, the New York statute did not in any way impact or preclude a uniform administrative practice or the provision of a uniform interstate benefit package. Rather, it merely impacted the cost of providing those benefits in one state (New York) versus another. The Court concluded by saying that cost uniformity was not an objective of ERISA. Accordingly, a state statute that affects the *cost* of providing a benefit, but not the *administration* of the benefit, does not bear the requisite "connection with" an ERISA plan so as to trigger the preemption.[59]

The Court's holding, however, was not without limitation. Specifically, the Court acknowledged that, in some cases, a state law might produce such acute economic effects so as to force an ERISA plan to adopt certain substantive provisions, or otherwise effectively restrict its choice of insurers, and that such a state law might be preempted under ERISA. In the present case, however, the Court found that the New York surcharges did not fall within that category.[60]

Though reaching different results in terms of whether the state law in question was preempted, later Supreme Court decisions have continued to apply the *Travelers* "ERISA objectives" analysis when determining whether ERISA preempted the specific state laws under review.[61] Specifically, when the Supreme Court determines that a state law operates to "frustrate [the] objectives" of ERISA, it continues to find that ERISA preempts the state law in question.[62] On the other hand, when a state law merely imposes an increased cost upon an ERISA plan but does not dictate the choices available to the plan, the Court has found that ERISA does not preempt the state law.[63]

As noted, whether a state law involves the regulation of insurance is one aspect of ERISA preemption analysis. ERISA does not preempt state laws that regulate insurance, even when such laws relate to an ERISA benefit plan. The only exception to this broad saving clause is that states may not impose insurance regulation on ERISA self-funded benefit programs.

---

58 *Id.* at 657.

59 *Id.* at 662.

60 *Id.* at 668.

61 *See, e.g.*, *Rush Prudential HMO, Inc. v. Moran*, 536 U.S. 355, 122 S.Ct. 2151 (2002); *Boggs v. Boggs*, 520 U.S. 833 (1997); *Cal. Div. of Labor Standards Enforcement v. Dillingham Constr. Co.*, 519 U.S. 316 (1997); *DeBuono v. NYSA-ILA Med. & Clinical Servs. Fund*, 520 U.S. 806 (1997). The Travelers decision and its progeny are consistent with general federal "field" and "conflict" preemption analysis. Specifically, the case law dealing with issues of federal preemption indicates that federal preemption includes three categories: (1) express preemption, where Congress specifies preemption in the text of an act; (2) "field" preemption, where federal regulation of a particular field is so pervasive that one may reasonably infer that Congress intended to dominate the field and preclude state laws; and (3) "conflict" preemption, where there is a direct conflict in state and federal law such that a private party could not possibly comply with both laws. *See, e.g.*, *Cal. Div. of Labor Standards Enforcement v. Dillingham Constr. Co.*, 519 U.S. 316 (1997); *Dalton v. Little Rock Family Planning Servs.*, 516 U.S. 474 (1996); *Lorincie v. Southeastern Pa. Transp. Auth.*, 34 F. Supp.2d 929 (1998). For a discussion of the Court's movement towards traditional field and conflict preemption in the context of ERISA, *see* the concurring opinion of Justice Scalia in *Dillingham*. 519 U.S. at 334.

62 *Boggs v. Boggs*, 520 U.S. 833 (1997).

63 *Cal. Div. of Labor Standards Enforcement v. Dillingham Constr. Co.*, 519 U.S. 316 (1997); *DeBuono v. NYSA-ILA Med. & Clinical Servs. Fund*, 520 U.S. 806 (1997).

The Supreme Court has provided guidance with respect to what constitutes the business of insurance. As stated in Section 7.1.1, the Court initially interpreted what constitutes the "business of insurance" in the context of the McCarran-Ferguson Act antitrust exemption. Under that exemption, if a particular practice constituted the business of insurance, then it was immune from federal antitrust scrutiny to the extent regulated by state law. In this context, the Court developed the three-part McCarran-Ferguson factors referenced earlier.

In *Metropolitan Life Insurance Co. v. Massachusetts*, the Supreme Court first applied this three-part test to determine whether a state law involved the regulation of insurance so as to save that law from ERISA preemption.[64] In applying the three McCarran-Ferguson factors developed under the McCarran-Ferguson Act, the Court explained that the "business of insurance" must be defined consistently for purposes of ERISA and the McCarran-Ferguson Act.

Thus, in *Metropolitan Life*, a Massachusetts statute that required specified minimum mental-healthcare benefits for persons covered under an insurance policy was saved from preemption. In so holding, the Court explained that determining whether a law is saved from ERISA preemption as the regulation of insurance requires the application of a two-part analysis. First, from a "common-sense standpoint," does the statute in question constitute insurance regulation? Second, applying the three McCarran-Ferguson factors, does the statute regulate the business of insurance?

Having determined that the mandated benefit law satisfied the common-sense test, the Court, applying the three McCarran-Ferguson factors, found that the mandated benefit law in question constituted the regulation of insurance, because the law met all three McCarran-Ferguson factors. Specifically, the law mandating coverage for certain mental-health benefits did the following:

1. spread policyholder risk by spreading the risk of mental healthcare;
2. regulated an integral part of the relationship between the insurer and the policyholder by limiting the type of insurance that an insurer may sell to the policyholder; and
3. applied only to entities within the insurance industry.[65]

Having found that the mandated benefit law met all three of the McCarran-Ferguson factors, the Court held that the law was saved from preemption.

After *Metropolitan Life,* lower courts were uncertain as to the specific importance of the three McCarran-Ferguson factors, which created a split among the circuits. Specifically, the lower courts did not agree whether, under Supreme Court precedent, a practice had to meet all three McCarran-Ferguson factors in order to be saved from preemption. Some courts held that a law had to regulate a practice that met all three McCarran-Ferguson factors for the saving clause to apply.[66] Other courts held that each of the three factors were "relevant," but that none was dispositive in determining whether a law constituted insurance regulation. Under this view, a state statute may be saved from preemption as the regulation of insurance even if it does not satisfy all three McCarran-Ferguson factors.[67]

---

64 *Metro. Life Ins. Co. v. Massachusetts*, 471 U.S. 724 (1985).

65 *Id.* at 743.

66 *See, e.g., Tex. Pharmacy Ass'n v. Prudential Ins. Co. of Am.*, 105 F.3d 1035 (5th Cir. 1997).

67 *See, e.g., Cmty. Health Partners, Inc. v. Kentucky*, 230 F.3d 1357, 2000 U.S. App. LEXIS 30754 (2000).

In 1999, the Supreme Court addressed this question in the case of *Unum Life Insurance Co. of America v. Ward*.[68] The *Unum* case involved an ERISA preemption challenge to California's notice-prejudice rule. Under this law, California insurers could not deny benefits to a plan beneficiary solely on the basis of a late claim submission unless the insurer could establish prejudice. In this case, the Court clearly held that, although the three McCarran-Ferguson factors are all "relevant" factors to consider, none is individually dispositive. In so holding, the Court explained that "*Metropolitan Life* asked first whether the law therein questioned fit a common-sense understanding of insurance regulation… and then looked to the McCarran-Ferguson factors as checking points or guideposts, not separate essential elements that must each be satisfied." Accordingly, a law relating to a practice that does not satisfy all three McCarran-Ferguson factors may still regulate the business of insurance and, therefore, be saved from ERISA preemption. In specific reference to the California notice-prejudice rule, the Court found that it constituted the regulation of insurance, even though it did not clearly satisfy the second McCarran-Ferguson factor. Taken as a whole, using the McCarran-Ferguson factors as guideposts, the notice-prejudice rule constituted insurance regulation.

In *Kentucky Association of Health Plans, Inc. v. Miller*, the Supreme Court revamped its approach regarding the savings-clause analysis. In *Kentucky Association of Health Plans, Inc.*, the Court addressed the issue of whether ERISA preempted two broad Kentucky "any willing provider" statutes.[69] The two statutes (one directed to providers in general, and one directed to chiropractic care) prohibited a health insurer from discriminating against any provider who was willing to meet the terms and conditions for participation established by the insurer.

The Court adopted the Sixth Circuit's assumption that the Kentucky laws related to employee-benefits plans, and instead devoted its analysis to the question of whether the laws regulated insurance. In departing from the McCarran-Ferguson Act analysis that had pervaded most previous circuit-court opinions, Chief Justice Anton Scalia reasoned that ERISA's savings clause is not concerned (as is the McCarran-Ferguson Act) with how to characterize conduct undertaken by private actions, but rather with how to characterize state laws in regard to what they "regulate." Kentucky's laws "regulate" insurance by imposing conditions on the right to engage in the business of insurance. To come within ERISA's savings clause, those conditions must also substantially affect the risk- pooling arrangement between insurer and insured.

The Court concluded:

> Today we make a clean break from the McCarran-Ferguson factors and hold that for a state law to be deemed a "law… which regulates insurance" under Section 1144(b)(2)(A), it must satisfy two requirements. First, the state law must be specifically directed towards entities engaged in insurance… second… the state law must substantially affect the risk pooling arrangement between the insurer and the insured.

As discussed, ERISA saved from preemption those state laws that regulate the business of insurance. Congress, however, created an exception to this broad "saving clause" that prohibits states from

[68] *Unum Life Ins. Co. of Am. v. Ward*, 526 U.S. 358 (1999).
[69] *Kentucky Association of Health Plans, Inc. v. Miller*, 538 U.S. 329 (2003).

regulating self-funded ERISA plans by calling them "insurance." In short, as courts have observed, just as states cannot regulate an employee-benefit plan by labeling it insurance, neither can an insurance program avoid state regulation by calling itself an employee-benefit plan.[70]

Although the exact application of the "deemer" clause remains elusive, understanding the distinction between a self-funded program and an insured program creates a beginning framework for understanding the interplay between the "saving clause" and the "deemer clause."

The court cases point to the following common elements of an ERISA self-funded program that distinguish a self-funded program from an insured program:

1. An ERISA-qualified employer promises to provide to employees a benefit defined in the plan.
2. The employer retains ultimate liability for the "losses" covered under the plan. This employer specifically retains this liability even if the employer transfers some financial risk to another party. In short, the employer remains responsible to perform if such other party fails to honor its obligations.
3. No direct contract is made between the employee and any person other than the employer relative to the securing of covered benefits. In other words, there is no privity of contract between the employee and any third party who may have agreed, on behalf of an employer, to assume certain risk of loss.
4. The benefit program is not marketed to the general public.[71]

For example, the Fourth Circuit has held that ERISA preempted a Maryland state law seeking to regulate stop-loss coverage purchased by an ERISA employer as health insurance, because the ERISA employer maintained a self-funded plan that the state could not deem to be an insurer. The court found that the employer's plan was self-funded, even though the employer purchased stop-loss coverage to protect against some of the losses covered under the plan. Specifically, the employer remained responsible for coverage if the stop-loss carrier failed to perform, and no relationship existed between the stop-loss carrier and the employees. The stop-loss carrier's only obligation was to provide the employer with stop-loss coverage when the employer's claims experience reached the attachment point of the policy.[72] Likewise, a Kansas District Court has found that a purported employee-benefit plan was really insurance, because it was provided by a third party, there was a direct relationship between that party and the employees, and the employer was not even made aware when the employee elected to purchase the plan.[73]

Again, it is clear that states may regulate the business of insurance, even when such regulation impacts an ERISA plan. Mandated benefit laws applicable to health-insurance companies, such as the law in question in *Metropolitan Life*, provide a clear example of this point. In other cases, however,

---

[70] *See Bell v. Employee Sec. Ben. Ass'n*, 437 F. Supp. 382 (D. Kan. 1977).

[71] *See, e.g., American Med. Sec., Inc. v. Bartlett*, 111 F.3d 358 (4th Cir. 1997); *Bell v. Employee Sec. Ben. Ass'n*, 437 F. Supp. 381 (D. Kansas 1977).

[72] *American Medical Security, Inc. v. Bartlett*, 111 F.2d 358, 364 (4th Cir. 1997).

[73] *Bell, supra*, at 392.

the practical application of the *Travelers* "relates to" test or the analysis of McCarran-Ferguson factors is not so clear.

In two Supreme Court cases, the Court analyzed ERISA's interrelationship with state laws affecting the operation of HMOs. In both cases (perhaps constituting a trend), the Court allowed state laws to stand in the face of an ERISA challenge. In *Rush Prudential HMO, Inc. v. Moran*,[74] the United States Supreme Court, continuing its *Traveler's* analysis, held that ERISA did not preempt an Illinois law establishing an independent medical-review process. Under the law, an HMO is obligated to provide services in the event that a reviewing physician determines that the services are medically necessary. The plaintiff, Deborah Moran, sought treatment for numbness and pain in her right shoulder. Defendant Rush Prudential HMO (Rush), which provided the coverage, denied Moran's request to have surgery by an unaffiliated specialist on the ground that the procedure was not medically necessary. Ms. Moran pursued her right under the Illinois law. However, Rush refused Ms. Moran's demand, and Ms. Moran sued in state court. The court ordered the review, which found the treatment necessary, but Rush again denied the claim. While the suit was pending, Ms. Moran had the surgery and amended her complaint to seek reimbursement, at which time the case was removed to federal court. The district court treated Ms. Moran's claim as a suit under ERISA, and denied it on the ground that ERISA preempted the Illinois statute. The Seventh Circuit reversed, concluding that the state act was not preempted as a state law that relates to an employee-benefit plan because the state act also regulates insurance under ERISA's savings clause. In a five-to-four decision, with Justice Souter delivering the opinion, the Court agreed with the Seventh Circuit's findings.

The analysis turned on the view that the Illinois law fell within the "savings clause" of ERISA because it "regulates insurance." In deciding whether a law regulates insurance, the court considered a common-sense view of the matter looking in part at whether the law was specifically directed toward the insurance industry. Because HMO organizations are simultaneously providers of healthcare and entities that assume risk, the HMO was considered to be undertaking the traditional functions of an insurance company. Moreover, because states typically have regulated HMO activity through state insurance departments, common sense dictated that the law was regulating insurance. The court reviewed the McCarran-Ferguson factors to confirm its common-sense view of the savings clause. The court recognized that, although a state law does not have to satisfy all three factors to survive preemption, the Illinois law clearly satisfied two—the factor that a provision regulate an integral part of the relationship between the insurer and the insured, and the factor that the law be aimed at a practice limited to entities within the insurance industry.

The court dismissed the argument that "conflict preemption" nullified the savings-clause approach. That doctrine provides that, where a conflict exists, the congressional policy of exclusive federal remedies overrides the state's regulation of insurance. The court held that the doctrine did not apply, because the state statute did not enlarge the claim process beyond the benefits that were available under ERISA, and it did not interfere with the congressional policy to provide a uniform federal system of rights and obligations under ERISA.

---

[74] *Rush Prudential HMO, Inc. v. Moran*, 536 U.S. 355, 122 S.Ct. 2151 (2002).

Although not a preemption case, in *Pegram v. Herdrich*,[75] the Court further addressed the interrelationship between HMOs and ERISA. In *Pegram*, the Court held that physicians were not ERISA fiduciaries when making mixed eligibility/treatment decisions. In this case, the medical plan and its related management company functioned as an HMO organized for profit, with the physicians who provided prepaid medical services to the participants serving as its owners. A Carle physician, defendant Lori Pegram, examined a covered participant, plaintiff Cynthia Herdrich, who was experiencing pain in the midline area of her groin. Six days later, Dr. Pegram discovered an inflamed mass in Ms. Herdrich's abdomen. Dr. Pegram did not order an ultrasound, but decided that Herdrich would have to wait eight more days for a diagnosis. In the interim, Herdrich's appendix ruptured, causing peritonitis. Herdrich sued the HMO in state court for fraud (among other violations); Carle responding that ERISA preempted the claim. The district court granted Carle's summary judgment on one count, but granted Herdrich's leave to amend the other. Her amended count alleged that the provision of medical services was a breach of an ERISA fiduciary duty because the structured arrangement with the physicians rewarded limited medical treatment. The district court granted Carle's motion to dismiss, on the ground that Carle was not acting as an ERISA fiduciary. On appeal, however, the Seventh Circuit reversed the dismissal.

The Supreme Court, in an opinion written by Justice Souter, held that mixed treatment and eligibility decisions by HMO physicians are not fiduciary decisions under ERISA. In its unanimous opinion, the Court held that the question of whether Carle was a fiduciary when acting through its physician owners did not depend on the ownership status of the physicians, but rather on the background of the facts and laws about HMO organizations, medical-benefit plans, and fiduciary obligations. The Court concluded that the traditional guideposts of determining fiduciary status should be used. Ms. Herdrich's claim that Carle became a fiduciary acting through its physicians when it created the arrangement, and that it then then breached that duty by making decisions affecting medical treatment while influenced by a self-serving reimbursement plan, was not persuasive. The Court recognized that the claim encompassed decisions related to eligibility and treatment, and that Congress did not intend that an HMO be treated as a fiduciary to the extent that it makes such mixed decisions acting through its physicians. Finally, the Court recognized that, while ERISA might provide a convenient avenue for relief, there was no reason to federalize state-malpractice claims.

Rush and *Pegram* both suggest that the states may have a far broader reach in regulating managed-care entities than originally thought. In fact, states establishing statutory causes of action against these entities may now find that their statutes survive preemption.[76]

"Any willing provider" laws come in various shapes and sizes. Generally speaking, however, they have one common element: These laws require that any "insurer" that maintains a panel of preferred providers allow any provider willing to accept the insurer's contract terms to participate in the preferred panel. Supporters of these laws contend that they increase patient access to providers of choice, and prevent HMOs and insurers from arbitrarily excluding competent providers. Opponents contend

[75] *Pegram v. Hendrich*, 530 U.S. 211 (2000).

[76] *See* § 3428 of the California Civil Code, requiring healthcare service plans and managed-care entities to operate under a duty of ordinary care; *see also* § 88.002 of the Texas Civil Practices and Remedies Code.

that they increase costs by denying the HMO or insurer the ability to deliver a high volume of patients to selected providers in exchange for reduced rates.

Although it was generally accepted that any-willing-provider laws "relate to" ERISA plans, the issue was whether the statute was "saved" from preemption as the regulation of insurance. Prior to the Supreme Court's decision in *Miller*, the circuits were split on this issue, with the Fourth and Sixth Circuits holding that the state statute was saved from preemption and the Eighth and Fifth Circuits holding that it was not.[77]

In *Kentucky Association of Health Plans, Inc. v. Miller,*[78] the United States Supreme Court resolved the division among the circuits, and held that Kentucky's any-willing-provider statutes were not preempted by ERISA. In so holding, Chief Justice Scalia discarded the McCarran-Ferguson factors that had been used as guideposts in previous cases in favor of a two-pronged test. The court held that, for a state law to be deemed a "law… which regulates insurance," it must:

- be specifically directed towards entities engaged in insurance; and
- substantially affect the risk-pooling arrangement between the insurer and the insured.

The court found that the Kentucky statute was specifically directed toward the insurance industry. The court held that the statutes, by their terms, imposed prohibitions on "health insurers" and "health benefit plans that include chiropractic benefits." The fact that other non-insurance entities (*e.g.*, providers) may have been affected by the law was not persuasive to the court, because regulations directed toward certain entities will almost always disable other entities from certain activity.

Secondly, the court found that the Kentucky law had a substantial affect on the risk-pooling arrangement between the insurer and the insured. The court reasoned that, by expanding the number of providers from whom an insured may receive health services, any-willing-provider laws alter the scope of permissible bargains between insurers and insureds in a manner similar to the mandated benefit laws.

Kentucky fits squarely within the trend established by *Rush* and *Pegram*. In all three cases, state laws regulating an important aspect of an HMO's operation were held to survive challenges. Moreover, ERISA (which was designed to establish national uniformity with respect to the operation of healthcare plans) seems to have "taken a back seat" to the concept of the state regulation of insurance. At a minimum, it is clear that ERISA's statutory structure enacted in the 1970s is ill-equipped to regulate the delivery systems which have evolved.

---

[77] *See Kentucky Association of Health Plans, Inc. v. Commissioner of Kentucky Dept. of Insurance*, 227 F.3d 352 (6th Cir. 2000), *cert. granted*, U.S. (June 28, 2002); *Stewart Circle Hosp. Corp. v. Aetna Health Management*, 995 F.2d 500 (4th Cir. 1993); *Prudential Ins. Co. of Am. v. Nat'l Park Med. Ctr.*, 154 F.3d 812 (8th Cir. 1998); *Tex. Pharmacy Ass'n v. Prudential Ins. Co. of Am.*, 105 F.3d 1035 (5th Cir. 1997), *cert. denied*, 118 S.Ct. 75 (1997); *Cigna Health Plan v. Louisiana*, 82 F.3d 642 (5th Cir. 1996), *cert. denied*, 117 S.Ct. 387 (1996).

[78] *Kentucky Association of Health Plans, Inc. v. Miller,* 538 U.S. 329 (2003).

7.2 The State Regulation of Private Healthcare Plans

In order to adequately understand the scope of state regulation of private health plans, it is important to first identify the key players that form the basis of the healthcare-financing system. In some cases, these players are themselves health plans. In other cases, these players represent an integral part of a health plan's operations or the health plan's delivery of benefits to its insureds. The nature and extent of state regulation of health plans varies as the core functions of these players shift from pure indemnity on the one hand to comprehensive delivery systems (which integrate the financing and healthcare-delivery functions) on the other.

These key players include the following entities or organizations: indemnity insurers, preferred provider organizations (PPOs), health maintenance organizations (HMOs), point-of-service programs (POS), third party administrators (TPAs), provider-sponsored networks (PSNs), and Blue Cross and Blue Shield plans. A description of these entities and the regulatory schemes under which they operate follows.

7.2.1 Indemnity Insurers

An indemnity health insurer is a company that provides an insured with "indemnity" against a specified medical expense in exchange for the payment of a premium. Coverage is typically catastrophic in nature. This means that the insured has coverage for expenses arising from illness or accident, but not for preventative care. This form of health coverage is primarily a financing system as opposed to a healthcare delivery system. In other words, when the insured (the patient) incurs a specified loss (a healthcare-related expense), the insurer reimburses, or indemnifies, the patient for that loss up to a specified limit. Under a pure indemnity contract, absent an assignment of benefits, the insurer makes payment directly to the insured (and not the healthcare provider) upon the submission of a claim. Indemnity policies typically include deductibles (costs that the insured must incur and bear before becoming eligible for coverage). They also include coinsurance, which requires the insured to pay a certain portion of covered expenses.[79]

As healthcare expenses began to spiral in the 1980s, many "indemnity insurers" began to incorporate "managed care" concepts into their policies. For example, many insurers added a "medical necessity" requirement into their coverage documents.[80] Specifically, the insurer would not pay for certain services listed in the benefits schedule unless the delivery of that service was medically necessary. The definition of medical necessity is discussed in Section 7.2.3.1 below.

Similarly, insurers began to impose second-opinion and pre-certification requirements upon their insureds. Under second-opinion programs, the insured is required to obtain a second opinion from a qualified practitioner supporting the need for certain procedures. Some second-opinion requirements apply to all surgical procedures, and others apply only to certain surgical procedures (*e.g.*, hysterectomies) that insurers believe are subject to abuse. Under pre-certification requirements, the insured is required to obtain a certification from the insurer that a proposed hospitalization is "medically neces-

[79] *See generally* Paul J. Routh & Ronald A. Kladder, *Welfare Benefits Guide 1999*, at 183–85 (West 1999).
[80] *Id.* at 271–72, 294–95.

sary" prior to admission. Typically, the insurer "pre-certifies" a specified number of inpatient days based on established criteria. If the patient stay is going to extend beyond the days initially certified, then the insured is required to obtain certification for those additional days.

States regulate indemnity insurers through their departments of insurance. Due to the financing focus of the health coverage provided by an indemnity insurer, state laws regulating health insurers traditionally focused on financial regulation by prescribing capital and financial reserve requirements, as well as requiring insurers to submit to annual financial examinations. In fact, most of the NAIC core model laws required for accreditation relate to financial matters.[81]

States also generally provide certain consumer protections and filing requirements. From a consumer-protection standpoint, states prohibit insurers from engaging in unfair claims practices, and they require certain disclosures. They may also include mandated benefits that require the insurer to provide coverage for certain services, and may prohibit the insurer from discriminating against certain classes of providers in providing such coverage.

From a filing-requirement standpoint, states generally require insurers to file, and obtain insurance department approval of, insurance contracts and marketing materials. Some states also regulate rate-setting endeavors, requiring insurers to submit rates for approval before use. Finally, states subject insurers to periodic market-conduct reviews by the department of insurance, which are designed to ensure that insurers have complied with all applicable laws.

As indemnity insurers have begun to impose certain managed-care requirements upon insureds, states have begun enacting laws that impose requirements on those administrative functions performed by the insurer that play a role in determining (through coverage decisions) whether, where, and under what circumstances a medical service is provided. For instance, many states have enacted laws regulating the insured's performance of the utilization-review function through which the insurer makes its medical necessity determinations. These statutes often address who may make such decisions (*e.g.*, only a qualified physician licensed in that state), how quickly they must be made, and the types of appeal processes that the insurer must maintain relative to coverage denials.[82]

7.2.2 Preferred Provider Organization

As the name implies, a PPO is an organization that creates a panel of "preferred" providers from which beneficiaries may obtain care as part of their health-benefits program. Beneficiaries generally are rewarded for obtaining services from these preferred providers in two ways. First, they receive increased coverage when they obtain services from a preferred provider. This increased coverage is usually in the form of lower deductibles or decrease of other out-of-pocket expenses. For instance, the insurer may reduce a $500 deductible to $200 if the insured obtains services from a preferred provider.

[81] *See generally* Nat'l Ass'n of Ins. Comm'rs, *Nat'l Ass'n of Ins. Comm'rs Model Laws Regulations and Guidelines* (1997). In addition to its model laws, the NAIC, through its Health Organizations Risk-Based Capital Working Group, has been working on the development of a risk-based capital formula for health organizations. The purpose of this formula is to measure the risk profile of particular organizations based on the level of risk assumed, and to then establish capital standards consistent with this risk profile.

[82] *See, e.g.*, Mo. Rev. Stat. §§ 376.1350 to .1399, which imposes requirements on the utilization review activities of all "health carriers" including insurers and HMOs.

A second way that beneficiaries are encouraged to obtain services from a provider who is part of the PPO network is through the reduction of paperwork. Specifically, due to their contractual arrangement with the health plan, the preferred provider will submit claims directly to the health plan for payment. As a result, the beneficiary has no responsibility for submitting claims.

A PPO may be part of an insured health-benefits program. In other words, a traditional indemnity insurer often will offer its insureds a preferred-provider option. Under this option, insureds may obtain care from preferred providers in order to obtain higher levels of coverage, but the insureds remain free to obtain covered services from a provider of their choosing.

TPAs also can operate a PPO. Such an administrator develops, through contractual arrangements, a network of preferred providers. The TPA then "rents" that network to insurance companies or self-funded benefit plans. In those situations, the TPA is not, generally speaking, financially at risk.[83] The providers look to the applicable payor (*e.g.*, the insurance company or the self-funded plan) for payment.

Contracts between PPOs and their participating providers generally reflect the following reimbursement methodologies.[84]

1. *Discounted fee-for-service reimbursement methodologies*, under which the provider receives, as compensation for the services the provider renders, a percentage of the provider's usual, reasonable, and customary charge for these services or a discounted fee based on the payor's fee schedule.
2. *Case rate payments,* under which the provider receives a set case rate as compensation for a defined course of treatment. An example of this is a surgical case rate under which a surgeon receives a fixed case rate for performing the surgery, and for providing specified pre-operative and post-operative care.
3. *Per-diem rates,* under which a hospital or other facility receives a set payment for all services provided during a single day, regardless of the actual intensity of service provided.
4. *Payments based on diagnosis-related groups* (DRGs), under which hospitals receive a set payment that covers all services provided by the hospital to patients admitted with a particular diagnosis, regardless of their length of stay or intensity of care.

Given their nature, PPOs generally do not compensate preferred providers on a "risk" basis. In other words, PPOs do not transfer to providers any financial risk for the cost of health services. This is true for two reasons. First, as stated, PPOs themselves often are not at financial risk. Second, because beneficiaries are given a choice of obtaining care from preferred providers or from their selected provider, it is difficult to predict how many enrollees will receive care from participating providers; further, of those who seek services from participating providers, it is difficult to predict the specific

[83] Though uncommon due to the nature of a PPO, some PPOs do accept some form of financial risk even when providing services on an administrative basis. The American Managed Care Review Association conducted a survey in October 1994, which found that of the respondents only 4% of PPOs were at risk. This survey also found that, of the respondents, 16% of PPOs placed hospitals at some financial risk and 7% of PPOs placed physicians at some financial risk. *See* AMCRA Foundation, 1994–95 Managed Health care Overview 20 (1995).

[84] *See* Rutenburg, *supra*, at 287.

participating provider from whom they will obtain services. Being able to create a defined population is critical in establishing risk arrangements. Specifically, from an actuarial perspective, it is difficult to accurately predict the cost of care provided by preferred providers without knowing, without any degree of certainty, the number of plan beneficiaries who will obtain treatment from the preferred providers. (Risk arrangements are more fully described in Section 7.2.3.1.)

PPOs operated by an insurance company as part of an insurance product are regulated by the insurance statutes of the state(s) in which they operate. Those that operate as an independent administrative function (*i.e.*, that create a network and rent the network to others), however, may not be subject to state regulation. Only about one-half of the states have adopted some form of PPO statute or regulation. Of those states, about six have adopted the NAIC model act.[85]

Of those states that have adopted some form of PPO regulation, the most frequent areas of regulation include:

- mandatory provider-contract provisions;
- prohibitions against certain restrictions in provider participation;
- patient access-to-care requirements; and
- restrictions on provider incentives; and requirements relative to the PPO's utilization-review program.[86]

In some cases, these laws include broad "any willing provider" provisions that require the PPO to include, in its provider panel, any provider willing to accept the contract terms (including the financial terms) offered by the PPO to participating providers. Many state laws, similar to the NAIC's model act, specifically exempt self-funded ERISA benefit plans from the requirements of the law.[87] Although the state still would require a PPO providing services on behalf of a self-funded ERISA health-benefit program to obtain state certification or registration, the PPO would not be subject to the requirements of the law (*e.g.*, access-to-care provisions, any-willing-provider requirements) when serving as a third-party administrator of an ERISA health-benefit program.

7.2.3 Health Maintenance Organizations

7.2.3.1 Description

It is difficult to describe with any precision exactly what an HMO is, because HMOs have evolved over time and are continuing to undergo dramatic change in response to market dynamics, technological developments, and liability exposure. Historically, HMOs organized as nonprofit corporations that operated as "pre-paid" plans. This meant that HMOs would contract with select providers on a

---

85 *See* Nat'l Ass'n of Ins. Comm'rs., *Model Regulation Service* (Oct. 1997).

86 *Id. See generally* Group Health Ass'n of Am. & Am. Managed Care and Review Ass'n, *Guide to State PPO Laws and Regulations* (1995).

87 Interestingly, merely making reference to an "ERISA plan" in a statute by expressly excluding ERISA plans from the application of the law may in and of itself result in preemption. *See Prudential Ins. Co. of Am. v. Nat'l Park Med. Ctr.*, 154 F.3d 812 (8th Cir. 1998); *CIGNA Healthplan of La., Inc v. State of Louisiana*, 82 F.3d 642 (5th Cir. 1996). *See also District of Columbia v. Greater Wash. Bd. of Trade*, 506 U.S. 125 (1992).

pre-paid (risk) basis to provide care to the HMO's enrollees. In other words, the HMO would pay the provider a fixed periodic payment to provide all medical services to enrollees, without regard to the actual volume or value of services rendered. The arrangement between GHA, its members, and its participating providers as described in the *Jordan* case (*see* Section 7.1.1) is a good example of an early HMO in terms of the role of an HMO and the financial relationship between an HMO, its enrollees, and participating providers.

Today, HMOs are more complex and, in many respects, look and act a lot like insurance companies. Specifically, HMOs are organized on both a nonprofit and for-profit basis, and often reimburse their providers on a fee-for-service basis in addition to, or in lieu of, a prepaid-reimbursement risk-based methodology.

Some key distinctions between HMOs and indemnity plans remain, however. First, unlike traditional indemnity insurers, HMOs are responsible for providing, or arranging for the provision of, certain basic healthcare services for their enrollees. The "M" in HMO stands for "maintenance;" these basic healthcare services focus on preventative care—not just coverage for services connected with illness and injury. Therefore, HMOs must provide or arrange, and pay, for a broad array of preventative-health services.

Second, as stated, HMOs are required to "provide or arrange" for these basic health services. In order to do this, HMOs must create a comprehensive healthcare-delivery network covering the full spectrum of covered health services (*e.g.*, physician services, hospital services, ancillary services) through contractual arrangements with providers. In turn, enrollees must obtain care from the HMO's participating providers except in cases of emergency. In other words, except in the case of emergency services, HMO enrollees do not have coverage for the services provided by non-participating providers. An exception to this rule exists for those enrollees participating in an HMO that offers a "point of service" option. (A discussion of this option can be found in Section 7.2.4 below.)

Third, HMOs generally require their enrollees to select a primary care physician (PCP) responsible for maintaining the enrollee's health and coordinating the overall healthcare provided to the enrollee. This means that the PCP is responsible for making referrals, as appropriate, to other providers and ensuring that the enrollee receives all appropriate medical services. HMO coverage documents typically provide that enrollees do not have coverage for health services unless provided or arranged for by their selected PCP. For this reason, the PCP is sometimes referred to as the "gatekeeper." Generally, PCPs include general practitioners, family practitioners, internists, and pediatricians, although gynecologists may also serve as a PCP in some plans. Under certain "open access" options, enrollees often are not required to select a PCP.

Fourth, HMOs provide coverage only for "medically necessary" services. There is not one set definition of medical necessity. Generally speaking, however, a medical treatment or procedure is "medically necessary" if, given the nature of the patient's condition and/or illness, the proposed treatment or procedure is: (i) likely to produce therapeutic benefits; (ii) provided in the lowest-cost setting and level, and for the shortest length, likely to produce the best outcome that can reasonably be expected; and (iii) not provided in a manner based on provider or patient convenience. For instance, if a provider can effectively and safely provide a patient with treatment for a specific condition on an outpatient basis, then inpatient services for the treatment of that condition are not medically necessary. HMOs take a proactive role in encouraging the provision of medically necessary services through a variety of administrative functions including provider credentialing, medical management, and provider contracting.

From a credentialing standpoint, an HMO may monitor the performance of its participating providers, and may continue to contract with only those providers who meet both quality and medical-management criteria. This is sometimes known as "economic credentialing."

From a medical-management standpoint, HMOs may employ a variety of techniques. Originally, medical management (which was then often called utilization review) focused primarily on pre-certification, concurrent review, and discharge planning. Today, medical management is much broader and includes techniques (*e.g.,* case management or disease management) under which the HMO closely monitors the care provided to patients with complex medical conditions or specific diseases in order to ensure that the enrollee receives cost-effective quality care. Under these programs, the HMO may establish practice guidelines for particular conditions. These guidelines provide recommended treatment protocols for those conditions. HMOs may also assume an active role in the overall coordination of the enrollee's care. For instance, the HMO will try to ensure that the enrollee receives the appropriate tests and treatment at the appropriate time, that the enrollee does not receive duplicative tests or treatment, and that the enrollee has the appropriate social support in order to enable the enrollee to adhere to the treatment plan.

Today's medical management also may include data-driven processes and systems. Under such systems, the HMO collects data regarding the items and services provided to its enrollees, and uses this data to conduct outcome studies or create provider profiles. These profiles may include data regarding a physician's utilization of healthcare resources against established norms, or data comparing the outcomes achieved by the patients of specific providers to the outcomes of other plan providers or providers nationally. The HMO may then use this data to develop "best practices" (*e.g.*, treatment protocols), educate providers, or educate their "consumers" regarding which providers render the most cost-effective care consistent with quality outcomes.

From a contracting perspective, HMOs will contractually require participating providers to participate in, and cooperate with, the HMOs' medical-management and other programs. These contracts often contain provisions designed to align the economic incentive of the provider with the economic incentive of the HMO by placing the provider at whole, or partial, financial risk for services provided. (A more detailed discussion of various risk arrangements is described later in the Chapter.)

Finally, unlike indemnity carriers (which impose deductible and coinsurance requirements), HMOs usually require enrollees to pay only nominal copayments for each service the patient receives. These are usually stated as a specific dollar amount, but may sometimes be stated as a percentage of the cost of the service.

As a result of these characteristics, HMOs promote a high degree of integration between the financing element of healthcare delivery and the actual delivery of care. This high level of integration has given rise to liability exposure, which is not common elsewhere in the insurance industry. For instance, HMOs are often sued on a vicarious-liability basis for the negligent performance of their participating providers.[88] Such suits typically allege an ostensible agency relationship between the HMO and the provider.[89] In addition, HMOs also are sued on a direct-liability basis for their own corporate negligence. Such actions include allegations that the HMO: (i) negligently performed its credentialing functions;[90] (ii) negligently performed medical management;[91] (iii) created inappropriate financial incentives;[92] or (iv) negligently provided care (when the HMO is seen to have evolved into a healthcare provider).[93]

HMOs create a delivery system of participating providers through five different models, each of which will be described in turn: the Staff Model HMO; the Group Model HMO; the Network Model HMO; the Independent Practice Association (IPA) Model HMO; and the Direct Contract Model HMO.[94] Keep in mind, however, that most HMOs do not operate in accordance with these rigid classifications. Instead, HMOs often create their networks of participating providers through a combination of two or more of these models.

1. **Staff Model HMOs.** A Staff Model HMO is one that actually employs a variety of providers (including physicians), and provides care through clinics it owns and operates. Some Staff Model HMOs employ only physicians, physician-support personnel, and allied health professionals; other Staff Model HMOs have actually owned and operated hospitals. The providers under these models are salaried employees of the HMO, and do not practice outside the HMO's clinics. Though Staff Model HMOs were once prevalent out of necessity, HMOs have moved away from this model as other forms of providing, or arranging for, care on a cost-effective basis (*e.g.,* risk-contracting with independent providers on a group and individual basis), have become possible.
2. **Group Model HMOs.** Although very similar to a Staff Model HMO, the key distinction is that a Group Model HMO does not directly employ its own providers. Instead, the HMO contracts with a single independent medical group (which, in turn, employs its own providers) to provide care to the HMO's enrollees. These groups are typically closely affiliated with the HMO, and generally have exclusive contracts with the HMO that prevent the group from providing care to patients other than the HMO's enrollees.
3. **Network Model HMO.** In a Network Model HMO, the HMO contracts with not just one medical group, but rather with several different medical groups in order to provide care to its

88 *See, e.g.*, *Petrovich v. Share Health Plan of Ill., Inc.*, 719 N.E.2d 756 (Ill. 1999).
89 *Id.*
90 *See, e.g.*, *Harrell v. Total Health Care*, No. W.D. 39809, slip op., 1989 WL 153066 (Mo. Ct. App. 1989), *rev'd. on other grounds*, 781 S.W.2d 58 (Mo. 1989).
91 *See, e.g.*, *Ardary v. Aetna Health Plans of Cal., Inc.*, 98 F.3d 496 (9th Cir. 1996).
92 *See, e.g.*, *Pegram v. Herdrich*, 530 U.S. 211 (2000).
93 *See, e.g.*, *In re U.S. Healthcare, Inc.*, 193 F.3d 151 (3d Cir. 1999).
94 The IRS has recognized four of these models (the Staff Model, Group Model, IPA Model, and Network Model). *See* Gen. Couns. Mem., 39,829 (Aug. 30, 1990). In addition, four of these models (the Staff Model, Group Model, IPA Model, and Direct Contract Model) are recognized in the Federal Health Maintenance Organization Act of 1973 and its accompanying regulations. 42 U.S.C. §§ 300 *et seq.* and 42 C.F.R. § 417. For a general discussion of these models, *see Rutenberg*, *supra*, at 284–86.

enrollees. These groups are usually, but not always, less closely affiliated with the HMO than the group that contracts with the Group Model HMO.

4. **IPA Model HMO.** Under an IPA Model HMO, the HMO contracts with one or more IPAs comprised of independent physicians. Specifically, the HMO holds a contract with the IPA, which in turn contracts with independent participating providers who agree to provide services to the HMO's enrollees.
5. **Direct Contract Model HMO.** In a Direct Contract Model HMO, the HMO directly contracts with individual physicians and other providers.

Because enrollees of HMOs are required to obtain care from participating providers—and, in most instances, enrollees are required to select a primary care physician—it is easy to create defined populations comprised of either the entire HMO enrollment base or particular subsets of the HMO enrollment base (*i.e.*, all enrollees who have selected particular primary care physicians). As a result, it is possible for HMOs to contract with providers in a manner that transfers some degree of financial risk to the provider for services rendered. Moreover, as indicated, HMOs traditionally operated prepaid plans that involved fixed payments to providers.

Risk arrangements vary and, often, HMOs and their providers combine several forms of risk sharing into a single agreement. Nevertheless, risk arrangements entered into between HMOs and their participating providers can be separated into the five risk models, which are described as follows.

1. Withhold Arrangements
   - A withhold arrangement is any arrangement under which the HMO retains a portion of the provider's compensation for services rendered. For instance, the HMO may retain 20% of the compensation otherwise payable to the physician.
   - Withhold arrangements can be used in connection with both fee-for-service arrangements and prepaid arrangements such as capitation. (Capitation arrangements are described later in the Chapter.)
   - The HMO will return to the provider the aggregate amount of the withhold after a specified period of time, depending on the provider's performance against established goals. These goals may be either financial (*e.g.*, actual healthcare expenditures are lower than projections) or clinical (*e.g.*, the provider's adherence to preventative health guidelines, documentation guidelines) in nature. Sometimes, an HMO will include both financial and quality goals in its contract.
2. Bonus Arrangements
   - A bonus arrangement is an arrangement under which an HMO pays a provider an additional "bonus" tied to performance. Similar to the withhold model described, payment of the bonus is tied to the provider's achievement of the specified goals.
   - As with a withhold arrangement, bonus arrangements can be tied to financial performance, clinical performance, or both. A bonus arrangement can work in conjunction with both fee-for-service and prepaid arrangements. In practice, little distinction usually is made between a withhold arrangement and a bonus arrangement. In order to create a

bonus arrangement in lieu of a withhold, the HMO may opt merely to reduce the amount of its reimbursement to providers.

- It is not unusual for agreements to include both a withhold component and a bonus component. These separate components may be tied to separate factors, or may be tied to achievement of the same factors.

3. Capitation Arrangements
   - A capitation arrangement is any prepayment mechanism under which the HMO pays a provider a specified dollar amount for each "assigned member" for each month in return for providing a specified scope of services. This is known as a "per member per month" (PM/PM) payment. This PM/PM payment does not vary based on the volume or value of services rendered by the provider or the amount of payment that the HMO receives in premium. The agreement will define those enrollees that are considered "assigned" under the agreement. Usually, "assigned members" will be all enrollees who have selected particular physicians as their primary care physicians. In other situations, the assigned members may be all members enrolled in a particular product offered by the HMO.
   - The capitation payment may cover only services provided by the at-risk provider. For instance, HMOs frequently pay their primary care physicians on a capitated basis for the services they provide to their assigned enrollees. Other times, a capitation payment may also cover services provided by other providers. For example, a physician may sometimes accept risk for certain services, such as referral services or inpatient care, provided by others.
   - In addition to traditional capitation, some HMOs will pay specialty providers on a "contact" capitation basis. Under contact capitation, an HMO may pay its specialists a set payment for each "contact" that specialist has with the enrollee. Generally, each visit with the specialist does not constitute a contact. Rather, the contact is defined as all of the services provided by that specialist to the enrollee for the condition for which the enrollee was referred to that specialist.
   - A plan may have capitation rates that are adjusted based on the age or gender of the enrollee, may have different capitation rates for different benefit plans or programs, or may have one or more "blended" rates.
   - A capitation arrangement can include a withhold or bonus feature (or both).
   - Capitation arrangements can also be used in conjunction with pool/fund arrangements. (See the discussion of pool/fund arrangements later in this Chapter.)

4. Percent-of-Premium Arrangements
   - A percent-of-premium arrangement is any prepaid arrangement under which an HMO pays a provider a specified portion (x percent) of the premium revenue received by the HMO for providing a specified scope of services on a monthly basis with respect to all "assigned" members. The scope of service may be broad (covering all plan benefits), or may be more narrow (covering only a subset of plan benefits).

- Similar to a capitation arrangement, the percent-of-premium arrangement will not vary based on the volume or value of services that the provider renders or the assigned members receive. The payment will vary, however, depending upon the rate charged to the contract holder.
- Again similar to capitation arrangements, the percent of premium received by a particular provider may be designed to cover only the services provided by that provider, or they may be designed to cover the services of other providers, thereby placing the provider at risk for referral services.
- Percent-of-premium arrangements do not typically have a "withhold" in the classic sense, though they often are operated in conjunction with, or administered through, pool/fund arrangements. (*See* following discussion of pool/fund arrangements.)

5. Pool/Fund Arrangements
    - Pool/Fund arrangements are often used as a mechanism to administer withhold/bonus arrangements or prepaid arrangements, such as capitation and percent-of-premium arrangements.
    - A pool or fund arrangement is any arrangement under which an HMO sets up a financial budget relative to the cost of providing specified covered services. Generally, the HMO establishes the budget by crediting the "pool" with a specified PM/PM payment. The HMO retains control over the pool. This PM/PM payment may be a capitation payment, or may be a specified percent of premium. The HMO then "debits" from the pool amounts it has paid on behalf of assigned members for covered healthcare services.
    - If, after a specified period of time (usually one year), the amount of the total debits for claims paid by the HMO is less than the amount of the credits, then the pool is in a "surplus" position. The provider typically receives all or some defined portion of the "surplus." The provider, may, however, also be liable for all, or a portion, of the deficits.
    - The plan may have one overall pool or may have a series of separate pools (*e.g.,* a professional-services fund, institutional fund, and pharmacy fund) covering different types of service.

Under some of these arrangements, the HMO may delegate some of its administrative functions (*e.g.,* claims payment or medical management) to the provider. In many cases, however, the HMO continues to perform these functions.

Of course, as stated, today it is not uncommon for HMOs to compensate providers on a non-risk basis. Such compensation mechanisms include the discounted fee-for-service, case rates, *per diem* arrangements, and DRG-based reimbursement.

Sometimes, however, HMOs will incorporate a risk component into even these reimbursement models. For instance, an HMO might take a typical case-rate arrangement, under which the physician provides a specific course of treatment in exchange for a fixed case-rate fee and add a risk component by including, within the case rate, reimbursement for the services provided by others. An illustration of this is an agreement between an HMO and an orthopedic surgeon under which the surgeon receives a fixed case-rate payment for the orthopedist's own services in connection with total hip-replacement surgery, as well as for the related inpatient services and physical therapy. Such an arrangement places the orthopedist at risk for not only the cost of the professional orthopedic services, but also for the cost of the related hospital and physical-therapy services. If a particular patient requires more hospitalization or therapy than anticipated, then the surgeon is nonetheless responsible for that cost.

7.2.3.2 *Scope of State Regulation*

Initially, HMOs were not regulated as part of the business of insurance. Given their pre-paid nature, they were often viewed as providing a predominantly service-related function, rather than a predominantly indemnity-related function. As HMOs began to evolve over time and to perform functions that looked indemnity-like (*e.g.,* compensating providers on a fee-for-service basis), however, states began enacting distinct regulatory schemes with laws and regulations tailored to an HMO's unique integration of the financing and delivery of healthcare. As a result, in addition to the detailed financial regulation to which HMOs are subject, HMOs also are subject to regulation relating to the delivery of care.[95] Likewise, although states generally regulate HMOs through their departments of insurance, many states also regulate HMOs through a department of health or similar regulatory body that the state considers better able to provide regulatory oversight of an HMO's healthcare-delivery function.

Financial regulation of HMOs generally covers net-worth and reserve requirements, as well as solvency protections. Similar to insurers, HMOs are generally required to submit, on an annual basis, audited financial statements. HMOs are also subject to market conduct surveys.

7.2.3.3 *Typical Areas of Regulation*

As stated, however, given the unique attributes of HMOs, states also have regulatory schemes (which are often complex) designed to address the pre-paid nature of HMOs, as well as the role they play in the delivery of healthcare. A sampling of these types of regulations is provided. This is an evolving list. In recent years, states have enacted sweeping managed-care reforms as a response to quality-of-care concerns expressed by physicians and patients. For this reason, the scope of HMO regulation has been increasing, and may continue to increase in the future.

(a) Member Hold-Harmless Provisions. Under these laws, HMOs are required to include in their provider contracts language under which the provider agrees not to seek payment from the HMO enrollee (or anyone acting on the enrollee's behalf) for covered services under *any* circumstances—including the event of the HMO's non-payment, insolvency, or breach of the provider's agreement.

(b) Continuity of Care. These laws require HMOs to include language in their provider contracts that requires providers to continue to provide care after the termination of their provider agreement with the health plan in certain circumstances. At a minimum, these laws tend to require the provision of continued care to enrollees who are hospital inpatients on the date of contract termination.

[95] Although HMOs are subject to financial regulation, HMOs are often subject to less-stringent financial regulation than traditional indemnity insurers for several reasons. HMOs maintain a closed panel of providers, many of whom are compensated on a risk basis, and all of whom are subject to statutory hold-harmless provisions under which the providers are prohibited from seeking payment from the HMO's enrollees in the event of HMO nonpayment for any reason including insolvency.

Some continuation-of-care laws, however, require continuation of care for a specified period of time to all enrollees under active treatment (not just inpatients), as well as enrollees with certain chronic conditions.[96]

(c) Insolvency Protection. These laws require HMOs to include special hold-harmless and continuity-of-care requirements in their provider contracts that apply in the event that the provider terminates the contract due to the HMO's insolvency. Typically, the provider is required to continue to provide care to all enrollees (regardless of health status) for the duration of time for which premiums were paid to the HMO. The provider is required to hold the enrollee harmless for the cost of any care provided during this continuation period.

(d) Quality Assurance. Under these provisions, HMOs are required to operate quality-assurance programs that stress health outcomes and provide review by physicians and other healthcare professionals of the processes followed in the provision of care that meet certain requirements. HMOs often are required to submit summaries of the activities that they conduct through their quality-assurance program to the state regulatory body that provides oversight of quality-of-care functions. In some states, HMOs are deemed to meet the requirements of these laws if they maintain accreditation in good standing with a nationally recognized accreditation body, such as the National Committee for Quality Assurance.

(e) Mandated Benefits/Coverage Requirements. HMOs are required to provide coverage for specific services. At a minimum, this includes coverage for "basic healthcare" services. With some limitations, basic healthcare services generally include the full scope of medical and hospital services necessary for the diagnosis and treatment of illness or injury, as well as preventative care such as physicals and related testing (*e.g.*, mammography) designed to maintain good health.[97] In most states, basic healthcare services do not include services such as pharmaceuticals, durable medical equipment (DME), or dental care, although states allow HMOs to offer these benefits on a "supplemental" basis.

In addition to basic healthcare services, common-coverage mandates include coverage for specific hospital lengths of stay following childbirth, coverage for reconstructive breast surgery following a mastectomy, and coverage for one "well-woman" exam by a gynecologist per year without the necessity of a referral from a primary care provider.[98] Finally, states generally prohibit HMOs from imposing deductibles relative to basic healthcare services, and strictly regulate the nature and extent of any enrollee copayment that HMOs may impose.

(f) Women's Health. In addition to mandates regarding one well-woman exam per year with a gynecologist, some states require that women be allowed to designate an obstetrician/gynecologist (OB/GYN) as their primary care physicians.[99]

---

[96] *See* National Conference of State Legislatures, *Health Policy Tracking Service Issue Brief, Finance: Continuity of Care* (Oct. 1, 1999).

[97] Note, however, that many states have adopted limited health services legislation under which "HMO-like" organizations that provide or arrange for, and pay for, a single, specialty service (such as vision or dental services) may obtain limited licensure to provide those benefits without offering a broader scope of basic healthcare services.

[98] *See* National Conference of State Legislatures, *Health Policy Tracking Service Issue Brief, Finance: Mandated Benefits* (Sept. 28, 1999).

[99] *Id.*

(g) Emergency Services/Prudent-Layperson Standard. In most states, HMOs must provide coverage for emergency services without authorization in the event that a "prudent layperson" possessing average knowledge of medicine would have believed that her symptoms or conditions required emergency treatment, regardless of whether the actual diagnosis confirmed the existence of an emergency.[100]

(h) Network Adequacy. These laws require HMOs to ensure that they meet specific network-adequacy standards. These requirements are designed to ensure that an HMO's provider network is adequate to appropriately care for the needs of the HMO's members. For instance, state law may require HMOs to maintain certain enrollee-to-provider ratios, as well as meet certain standards for geographic coverage (*e.g.*, drive time to certain providers) and wait times for appointments.

(i) Access to Specialists. These laws require HMOs to issue a "standing" referral to a specialist for an entire course of treatment, and allow enrollees with chronic conditions to designate specific specialists as the enrollee's primary care physician. Some states allow enrollee access to non-contracted specialists when the HMO's network does not contain a specialist "qualified" to provide treatment for the enrollee's condition.[101]

(j) Anti-Gag Clause Rules. A large number of states have enacted laws that prohibit HMOs from including clauses in their contracts with participating providers that prohibit providers from communicating with their patients regarding the provider's treatment recommendations. These laws often specifically provide that providers must be free to communicate all treatment alternatives to their patients, regardless of whether those treatments are covered under the patient's plan. They further provide that the HMO cannot take action against a provider for serving as a patient advocate.

(k) Regulation of Certain Financial Incentives. Increasingly, states are enacting provisions that prohibit HMOs from paying incentives to providers to reduce or limit medically necessary services to any specific enrollee.[102] Unfortunately, states often have failed to provide meaningful guidance (*e.g.*, through promulgation of regulations) regarding the types of arrangements that would be prohibited under these laws. When states do provide guidance, they sometimes adopt very restrictive views regarding, and impose significant restrictions on, the level of risk that is permissible.[103]

(l) Enrollee Grievances and Appeals. These laws require HMOs to maintain specific enrollee-grievance and appeal processes, including expedited appeal processes in the case of urgently needed care. In more than one-half of the states, these provisions allow (after the enrollee's exhaustion of the

---

100 *See* National Conference of State Legislatures, *Health Policy Tracking Service Issue Brief, Finance: Emergency Care* (Nov. 12, 1999).

101 *See* National Conference of State Legislatures, *Health Policy Tracking Service Issue Brief, Finance: Direct Access* (Oct. 1, 1999).

102 About one-half of all states have adopted statutes or regulations prohibiting financial incentives that seek to limit medically necessary care. *See* D. Pimley, *States Tell Health Plans that Incentives May Not Limit Medically Necessary Care*, 7 Health L. Rep. (BNA) No. 40, at 1581 (Oct. 8, 1998).

103 *See, e.g.*, Consent Order between Commission of the Texas State Department of Insurance and Methodist Health Plan, Inc. (Aug. 19, 1998). Though not applicable to private health plans unless they contract with CMS as a Medicare+Choice organization, CMS has promulgated regulations imposing restrictions regarding the type and level of risk, which physicians and physician groups may assume. *See* 42 C.F.R. § 417.

HMO's internal appeal mechanisms) for an appeal to an independent external-review body.[104] States often require HMOs to maintain detailed logs of enrollee's grievances, documenting the nature of the grievance and the resolution thereof.

At least one court has held that mandating external reviews is preempted by ERISA. This court reasoned that such a law did not constitute insurance regulation, because it did not meet the third McCarran-Ferguson factor.[105]

(m) Provider Selection and Deselection. These laws require HMOs to provide certain providers with a minimum amount of notice prior to termination of the provider's HMO-participation contract without cause. In addition, they often give providers certain appeal rights, and prohibit HMOs from taking action against providers for advocating on behalf of their patients. Finally, most states require HMOs to maintain written credentialing criteria; some states require HMOs to disseminate a copy of the HMO's credentialing criteria to providers upon request.

(n) Indemnification Provisions. Nearly half the states have enacted laws prohibiting HMOs from including clauses in their provider contracts requiring the provider to indemnify the HMO for the losses arising out of the HMO's coverage determinations.[106]

(o) Utilization-Management Laws. HMOs are required to maintain written medical-management policies that meet certain requirements in connection with the operation of these utilization or medical-management programs. For instance, HMO laws often require HMOs to make and communicate utilization-management decisions within specific timeframes, depending on whether the recommended treatment is emergent, urgent, or routine. HMO laws also may require that any person who makes medical-management decisions meet certain qualifications (*e.g.,* licensure as a physician under the laws of that state). Finally, HMOs may be prohibited from retroactively denying coverage for a treatment that the HMO preauthorized through its utilization-review process. In other words, if a provider or an enrollee obtains preauthorization from an HMO before providing or obtaining a service, then that HMO cannot later deny coverage for the authorized service. Exceptions apply in cases of fraud or a loss of health-plan coverage.[107]

Though not yet typical, a handful of states have enacted laws that specifically allow enrollees to sue HMOs for medical malpractice, or that remove barriers which would have prohibited enrollees from suing.[108] The only court to consider an ERISA-preemption challenge to this type of legislation

---

[104] As of July 2008, 44 states and D.C. had adopted managed-care reform legislation that includes a provision for external reviews. *See* American Association of Health Plans, *State External Review Laws and Regulations* (July 20, 1999) (Available from AAHP). *See* also National Conference of State Legislatures, *Health Policy Tracking Service Issue Brief, Finance: Consumer Grievance Procedures: Internal and Independent Appeals* (Oct. 1, 1999).

[105] *See*, *Corporate Health Ins. Co. v. Tex. Dept. of Ins.*, 215 F.3d 526 (5th Cir. 2000).

[106] National Conference of State Legislatures, *Health Policy Tracking Service Issue Brief, Finance* (Oct. 1, 1999).

[107] Though not directly related to insurance regulation, it is important to note a trend in the case law for courts to find that utilization management constitutes the practice of medicine. *See, e.g.*, *Murphy v. Bd. of Med. Examiners*, 949 P.2d 530 (Ariz. App. 1997); *Morris v. D. C. Bd. of Med.*, 701 A.2d 364 (D.C. Ct. App. 1997). *But see* Ohio Op. Att'y. Gen. 99-044 (1999), wherein Ohio's attorney general opined that, under existing Ohio statutory law, utilization-review activities do not constitute the practice of medicine. Applying state practice-of-medicine requirements on health plans could have significant impact on plan operations.

[108] *See, e.g.*, S.B. 386, 75th Leg. Tex. § 1 (1997). *See generally* National Conference of State Legislatures, *Health Policy Tracking Service* (Oct. 1, 1999).

held that this provision was not preempted because it did not "relate to" an ERISA plan under the ERISA objectives analysis annunciated in the *Travelers*' decision.[109] Specifically, quality control of benefits is a field traditionally regulated by the states. Shifting from the traditional state regulation of the quality of healthcare received to the federal government was not an objective of ERISA.

As discussed, ERISA may sometimes preempt state "insurance" laws (regardless of whether the law is included within the state's insurance code or HMO act) if the law in question does not constitute insurance regulation based on the application of the McCarran-Ferguson factors. In addition to ERISA preemption, under the Balance Budget Act of 1997 (the BBA), Congress provided for federal preemption of certain state-insurance laws when applied to organizations that contract with the Centers for Medicare & Medicaid Services (CMS) to provide benefits to Medicare+Choice beneficiaries (M+C).

Specifically, the BBA provides that the federal laws governing M+C organizations preempt state laws relating to the inclusion or treatment of providers.[110] As a result, at least with respect to their enrollment, M+C organizations are not subject to state "any willing provider" laws that would otherwise apply to a state-licensed HMO. Due to federal M+C preemption, M+C organizations also may be exempt from other state laws governing the relationship between the M+C organization and its providers (*e.g.*, laws restricting or prohibiting financial-incentive arrangements). Similarly, the scope of coverage and duration of benefits under the M+C program preempts conflicting state law.[111] Finally, the BBA's implementing regulations provide that M+C standards and contract requirements supersede any conflicting state laws and regulations.[112]

7.2.4 Point-of-Service Programs

Though similar in underlying concept to preferred provider programs, POS programs actually are the "mirror image" of preferred-provider programs. As indicated under Section 7.2.2, under a preferred-provider program, the insured is offered a certain level of benefits for all medical services. If the insured obtains care from a preferred provider, however, then the insured is typically rewarded with lower out-of-pocket expenses. In other words, a PPO product is an adjunct to a program under which the beneficiary may obtain care from any provider.

A POS program, on the other hand, is usually an adjunct to an HMO product under which the enrollee is *required* to obtain services only from participating providers. Under a POS program, the enrollee has an option to "leak out" of the HMO's provider network and obtain services from non-participating providers. Such "leaking out" has a price. Enrollees have standard HMO coverage for in-network services. This means that the enrollee has no deductible or coinsurance. If enrollees obtain services outside the network, however, they are often subject to indemnity-type benefits, including deductibles and coinsurance. POS programs can be broad in scope, allowing enrollees to obtain access to non-participating providers for the full array of covered health services. Under other POS programs,

---

109 *Corporate Health Ins. Co. v. Tex. Dept. of Ins.*, 215 F.3d 526 (5th Cir. 2000).
110 42 U.S.C. § 1856(b).
111 42 U.S.C. § 1856.
112 42 C.F.R. § 422.402.

however, the enrollee may only be permitted to obtain services from non-participating providers for certain services.

POS programs are sometimes confused with "open access" programs. These programs, however, are fundamentally different. Again, under a POS program, an enrollee *may* obtain certain services from non-participating providers. Under an open-access program, on the other hand, the enrollee typically does not have the option of obtaining services from non-participating providers; rather, the enrollee has "open access" to all of the HMO's participating providers without referral. In other words, the enrollee may obtain covered services from any participating provider without first obtaining a referral from a primary care physician or the HMO.

As indicated, POS programs are generally HMO products. Accordingly, they are regulated under the same regulations that regulate HMOs. In some states, HMOs may offer a POS option, which is in essence an indemnity option, under their HMO license (with certain restrictions) through a supplemental-benefits rider. Of those states, some allow the HMO itself to underwrite the benefits, while others require the HMO to enter into an underwriting agreement with an insurance company. In other states, however, HMOs may not provide any indemnity benefits. In those states, POS programs are offered as a dual option: An HMO offers the HMO product, and a licensed insurance company provides the POS benefits.

7.2.5 Third-Party Administrators

A TPA is any independent third party that provides certain administrative services incident to the operation of a health-benefits program by another party. TPAs contract to provide services on behalf of licensed insurers, as well as self-funded benefit programs. Services available on a third-party basis include claims-adjudication services, provider-network development and access (*see* discussion of PPOs in Section 7.2.2), and utilization and medical-management services. These medical-management services may include traditional utilization review, case or disease-management services, or both.

Given the nature of TPAs, their services typically are not provided on a risk basis. In other words, the TPA provides administrative services—but it is in no way *financially* responsible for the cost of care. In certain circumstances, however, the TPA may be eligible for incentive payments for meeting certain performance standards. In addition, a TPA providing utilization-management services may receive a portion of the "savings" achieved through the TPA's utilization-review activities.

More than half the states have laws or regulations governing the activities of TPAs that perform the claims-adjudication function. Of those states, about 23 have adopted the NAIC model legislation or similar legislation.[113] Similarly, a majority of states have enacted statutes or regulations governing utilization review agents. Of those states, however, only about seven states have adopted the NAIC model act or similar legislation.[114]

In the utilization-review context, these laws often regulate: how quickly the TPA must make and communicate utilization-review decisions; who is qualified to make specific utilization-review deci-

[113] *See* National Assoc. of Ins. Comm'rs, *Model Regulation Service* (July 1999).
[114] *Id.*

sions (particularly adverse-coverage determinations); and the enrollee-appeal processes that must be in place. Furthermore, in some cases, these laws may specifically prohibit a utilization-review agent from accepting compensation on the basis of the savings achieved.[115] In many cases, these laws specifically provide an exemption for activities provided by, or on behalf of, self-funded ERISA plans.[116] In fact, the NAIC's "Third Party Administrator Statute" specifically provides for such an exception.[117] Most courts that have reviewed the issue of preemption in the context of TPAs have found that these statutes are preempted by ERISA as they relate to services provided on behalf of ERISA self-funded benefits programs.[118] Some courts, however, have reached contrary decisions.[119]

States do not require licensed entities (*e.g.,* HMOs or insurers) to obtain separate licensure under these laws to the extent that they are providing services on behalf of their own enrollees. If, however, they provide services on behalf of another party (*e.g.,* a self-funded benefit program), then they must obtain separate licensure. Likewise, if an HMO delegates any of these functions, such as when an HMO delegates medical management to a provider group as part of a risk agreement, then state laws often require the delegate to obtain and maintain licensure or registration under these TPA laws.

7.2.6 Provider-Sponsored Networks

Generally speaking, a PSN is an organization comprised of healthcare providers who have formed together to create a provider network capable of contracting with health plans to provide specific services. Sometimes these networks will be broad (covering the full spectrum of the healthcare-delivery system); in other cases, they may narrowly cover a particular specialty.

PSNs will enter into a contract with a health plan to provide, or arrange for the provision of, services to the beneficiaries of the plan. Sometimes that health plan is the payor itself (*e.g.*, an insurance company or an HMO); at other times, that health plan is a TPA that is merely contracting with a PSN to obtain access to its network of providers on behalf of a payor. The PSN will provide or arrange for the contracted services through its contracts with participating providers.

The nature of the reimbursement arrangement between the PSN and its participating providers usually depends on the nature of the reimbursement agreed to between the health plan and the PSN. For instance, if the health plan and the PSN have entered into a discounted-fee arrangement, then the "downstream" payment to the PSN-participating provider will be on a discounted fee-for-service basis. If, on the other hand, the health plan and the PSN have entered into some type of risk arrangement, then the downstream reimbursement arrangement between the PSN and the participating provider may range from a discounted fee-for-service arrangement to any or all of the types of risk arrangements discussed in Section 7.2.3.1.[120]

---

[115] *See, e.g.*, Mo. Rev. Stat. § 376.1361.9.

[116] *See, e.g.*, Mo. Rev. Stat. § 376.500.6(d).

[117] *See* Nat'l Ass'n of Ins. Comm'rs, *Model Regulation Service* (July 1999).

[118] *See, e.g.*, *Self-Insurance Inst. of Am. v. Gallagher*, 11 Employee Benefits Cas. (BNA) 2162 (N.D. Fla. 1989), *aff'd*, 909 F.2d 1491 (11th Cir. 1990). When a law expressly excludes an ERISA plan from its scope, however, that law may make a "reference to" an ERISA plan which subjects the law to ERISA preemption.

[119] *See Benefax Corp. v. Wright*, 757 F. Supp. 800 (W.D. Ky. 1990).

[120] Although outside the scope of this Chapter, antitrust laws impact the nature of the compensation arrangements entered into between the PSN and the health plan, as well as the downstream arrangements between the PSN and its participating providers in those situations in which the PSN is comprised of independent competing providers.

PSNs come in a variety of forms. These include, for instance, physician/hospital organizations (PHOs) and IPAs. PHOs and IPAs are generally comprised of independent competing providers who have formed together to create a network for managed-care contracting. PHOs and IPAs are substantially similar. As the name implies, PHOs include a hospital participant that usually plays some role in the governance structure of the organization. IPAs, on the other hand, typically include physicians or other providers, but do not include (at least at the governance level) a hospital partner. Many IPAs, however, subcontract with hospitals in order to arrange for hospital services for which they have assumed financial risk.

Fully integrated medical groups, in which physicians share in the profits and losses of the practice, can also operate as a PSN. Medical-group model PSNs sometimes will contract only to provide or arrange for services that are within the scope of practice of the medical group. Medical-group PSNs also may contract to arrange, and be at financial risk, for the services provided by others. In those situations, that medical-group PSN often will subcontract with other providers to access those services. In addition, medical groups will sometimes operate a "wrap-around" IPA. Specifically, the medical group will contract on behalf of its own employed physicians, as well as certain individual physicians who have agreed to participate in that medical group's contracting network.

In addition to contracting to provide or arrange for specific services, PSNs often agree to perform certain administrative services. This is particularly common in the context of risk agreements. These administrative services may include claims-payment or medical-management services. In the claims-payment context, HMOs may pay a PSN a specified capitation or percent of premium for specified services, and then require the PSN to pay all claims related to such services. Given concerns over PSN solvency, however, HMOs are becoming less willing to delegate claims payment. Instead, they often will administer capitation or percent-of-premium arrangements through pool/fund arrangements under which the HMO retains the claims-adjudication function.

The scope of state regulation of PSNs as relates to their health-plan contracting activities depends on the nature and extent of the services that the PSN provides (*i.e.*, medical care only or also certain administrative functions), the nature of the compensation arrangement between the health plan and the PSN, and whether the health plan is a licensed entity or an ERISA self-funded benefits program.

State regulation of PSNs has received the most attention in the context of PSN risk-contracting activities. From a purely regulatory perspective, state insurance regulators seek to achieve three primary objectives: protect consumers, regulate risk-bearing entities that perform similar functions similarly (*i.e.*, regulation by function), and adapt to the evolving health insurance market. Through the enactment of laws or the issuance of insurance bulletins, states have adopted different positions on the issue of the regulation of risk-bearing PSNs. These positions vary depending on how the applicable state generally defines the business of insurance and, when the PSN is contracting with a self-insured ERISA plan, how the state interprets the interplay between ERISA's saving clause and deemer clause.

(a) State Approaches to Regulation. The majority of states take the position that, when a PSN contracts on a "full risk" basis directly with an unregulated entity (an entity not regulated by the department of insurance, *e.g.*, an ERISA self-funded benefit plan), that PSN is engaged in the unlicensed business of insurance unless it obtains a license as a HMO or insurer.[121] A PSN accepts "full risk" when it is paid on a pre-paid and capitated basis for all covered medical services.[122] Similarly, most states permit PSNs to accept "downstream" risk, even on a full-risk basis, from a licensed entity such as an HMO or indemnity insurer.

In other words, if the PSN has entered into a full-risk agreement with an HMO, then the PSN is not engaged in the unlicensed business of insurance. When that same PSN, however, enters into the same arrangement with a self-funded ERISA plan, it is engaged in the unauthorized business of insurance.

Interestingly, though this position addresses the consumer-protection objective of insurance regulation described earlier, it does not necessarily achieve the objective of treating like risk-bearing entities performing like services in the same manner. Nor is it necessarily consistent with a "business of insurance" analysis. Specifically, if a PSN that contracts with an ERISA self-funded plan is engaged in the unauthorized business of insurance, then it is not clear why that same entity is *not* engaged in the unauthorized business of insurance when it contracts with a *licensed* entity. Neither the definition of the business of insurance based on the McCarran-Ferguson factors nor the common-law definition of insurance seem to support that distinction.

From a regulatory perspective, the distinction between these situations is clear. When a PSN contracts with a licensed entity such as an HMO, the licensed entity (which is ultimately responsible for the cost of care if the PSN fails to perform) is subject to comprehensive state regulatory oversight, including solvency regulation. In addition, the state can impose regulations on the licensed entity that set forth certain PSN contracting requirements designed to provide consumer protections. For instance, the state may enact laws or regulations prohibiting or restricting certain risk arrangements, or requiring the regulated entity to only contract with PSNs that meet certain requirements. Regardless of the merits of this position from a public-policy perspective, it is not entirely clear that this position is consonant with principles of ERISA preemption. ERISA preemption in this context is discussed further in later sections of this Chapter.

Interestingly, although a majority of the states clearly take the position that an unlicensed PSN may not accept full risk from an unregulated entity, a few states have taken the position that PSNs are *not* subject to state regulation when: (i) the full-risk arrangement involves the transfer of risk from an ERISA qualified self-funded plan to a provider; and (ii) the employer ultimately remains at risk for healthcare costs should the PSN fail to perform.[123] These states reason that, when the employer retains ultimate responsibility for the financial risk if the PSN fails to perform, and when no direct contractual arrangement exists between the beneficiaries and the PSN, the PSN is not engaged in the business of insurance. Only when the PSN has a direct contractual relationship with the beneficiary and assumes

---

[121] *See* Group Health Ass'n of Am., *Fifty States' Survey of Regulator's Attitudes Toward PHO Licensure* (1995) (the GHAA Survey).

[122] *See* GHAA Survey.

[123] *See* Illinois Department of Insurance, Insurance Bulletin, *Provider-Based Market Systems—When to Regulate* (Apr. 1996).

ultimate risk is the PSN engaged in the business of insurance. At least one group of employers publicly has taken the position that ERISA preempts such regulation.[124]

Less consistency exists among the states on the issue of whether a PSN can accept some type of partial risk from a self-funded benefit plan without being deemed to be engaged in the unauthorized business of insurance.[125] Some states have adopted a very strict view, taking the position that any acceptance of risk by a PSN from an unregulated entity constitutes the unauthorized business of insurance unless the PSN is appropriately licensed.[126] For instance, in response to a question regarding whether some "degree" of risk assumption may be assumed by a provider (for instance if a provider accepted a capitation payment only for services that provider could personally render) without being engaged in the unauthorized business of insurance, the deputy director of the Ohio Department of Insurance responded that there is no degree of risk assumption that would be considered *de minimis*: "It's like being a little bit pregnant."[127]

Although this position may address regulatory concerns about PSN solvency (and therefore achieve consumer-protection objectives), it appears inconsistent with case-law precedent, including the Supreme Court's *Royal Drug* opinion, which recognizes a service vs. indemnity distinction in what constitutes the business of insurance. Other states have taken a more pragmatic view, indicating that whether a partial-risk arrangement involves assumption of insurance risk by the provider would depend on the nature and extent of the risk arrangement.[128]

Just as some states diverge from the majority view that risk-bearing PSNs that contract with ERISA self-funded plans must obtain appropriate state licensure to assume that risk, some states diverge from the majority view that risk-bearing PSNs may freely contract with regulated entities (*e.g.*, insurers and HMOs). For instance, at least two states require even those entities that accept downstream risk from a licensed carrier to obtain some degree of licensure.[129]

In addition, several states, though allowing risk-bearing PSNs to engage in downstream contracting with HMOs without licensure, impose special requirements upon HMOs with respect to their downstream risk arrangements. For instance, some states require HMOs to include mandatory provisions in their contracts with risk-based providers. Other states regulate the type of entity that may accept risk, as well as the type of risk that the PSN may assume.[130]

---

124 *See Witten*, *supra*, at 481–84.

125 *See* GHAA Survey, *supra*.

126 *See* Memo from David J. Randall, Deputy Director, Ohio Department of Insurance, to John E. Callender, Senior Vice President, Ohio Hospital Association (July 28, 1994).

127 *Id.*

128 *See* GHAA Survey, *supra*.

129 *See* GHAA Survey, *supra*. Most notable is California's Knox-Keene Act, under which physicians can accept risk for services which they personally provide but cannot accept any risk for other services, such as hospital services. *See also Rutenberg*, *supra*, at 300–04.

130 For instance, statutes in both Florida and Pennsylvania have contracting requirements that impact the arrangement between the licensed HMO and the PSN. In addition, under Texas law, only an approved nonprofit health corporation may accept full risk from a licensed carrier. *See* Kathrin E. Kudner, *Risk Regulation—Fifty State Survey*, paper presented at the National Health Lawyers Association Managed Care Institute (Dec. 11–13, 1996). *See generally Rutenberg*, *supra*.

Finally, although most states have taken the position that PSNs may not accept direct risk from an unlicensed entity, a few states have developed special regulatory schemes under which PSNs may obtain a license to contract directly with employers. If a state does not permit PSNs to engage in direct risk-contracting with unlicensed entities and has not adopted a special regulatory scheme, then PSNs operating in that state must be licensed as an HMO or insurer. States that have adopted special regulatory schemes include Iowa, Minnesota, and Texas.[131]

As will be discussed more fully, NAIC does not favor the creation of special insurance laws applicable to PSNs. Instead, NAIC supports the creation of a uniform licensing scheme that applies to all risk-bearing entities equally, regardless of the "form" of the risk bearer. Of course, even NAIC would recognize an exception for downstream risk arrangements from regulated entities. Though NAIC has not yet produced any model legislation in this area to date, at least one state (Ohio) has adopted a managed- care uniform-licensure act that clearly requires all risk-bearing "health insuring corporations" to obtain licensure.[132] Under this uniform act, all risk-bearing entities would need to obtain a certificate of authority under the application of the same rules, regardless of whether the health-insuring corporation was a PSN or an HMO. The uniform act does not, however, require licensure for entities only accepting downstream risk.

(b) Legal Analysis. No clear judicial pronouncement has been made to date in this area relative to the issue of ERISA preemption. Nor is there general agreement among commentators regarding whether ERISA preempts state attempts to regulate risk-contracting by PSNs with ERISA self-funded employers.[133] One could certainly argue that, because a self-funded insurer cannot be "deemed" to be engaged in the business of insurance, ERISA preempts any state attempt to regulate risk-bearing PSNs that contract with ERISA plans when the ERISA plan retains the ultimate responsibility for payment if the PSN fails to perform. Specifically, the risk-bearing arrangement with the PSN does not convert the employer's self-funded plan into an insured plan because of the following elements: (1) the employer remains ultimately at risk for the specified loss; (2) no direct contractual arrangement exists between the PSN and the plan beneficiaries; and (3) neither the employer nor the PSN markets the plan to the general public. Under similar facts, courts have held that ERISA's deemer clause results in the preemption of certain insurance laws applicable to entities to whom the employer has shifted some degree of risk.[134]

Moreover, to the extent that a PSN accepts only partial risk from a self-funded ERISA employer in the form of a capitation payment for services personally provided by the PSN's providers, it could be argued that such a PSN is not engaged in the business of insurance on the basis of the "service objective" versus "indemnity objective" distinction made by many courts in defining whether an organization is engaged in the business of insurance.[135] Therefore, ERISA would preempt state attempts to regulate such arrangements to the extent that they relate to an ERISA benefit plan.[136]

131 *Id.*
132 Ohio Rev. Code Ann. § 1751.
133 Some commentators argue that ERISA would clearly preempt this type of regulation, while others are equally as adamant that ERISA would not preempt such regulation.
134 *Id.*
135 *See Group Life and Health Ins. Co. v. Royal Drug Co.*, 440 U.S. 205 (1979).
136 *See* discussion regarding the "relate to" test as established by the Travelers' case and its progeny in Section 7.1.2.

On the other hand, as was discussed in Section 7.1.2, the exact interplay between the deemer clause and saving clause remains elusive. Moreover, the practical application of the McCarran-Ferguson factors against the backdrop of specific practices is not always clear. It is certainly possible to argue that, focusing solely on the activities of the PSN, full-risk arrangements meet more than one (if not all) of the McCarran-Ferguson factors. If risk-contracting by a PSN constitutes the business of insurance, then regulation of risk-bearing PSNs is saved from preemption. With compelling arguments on both sides, it is very difficult to reconcile ERISA's saving clause and deemer clause in the context of risk-bearing PSNs.

(c) NAIC View. Although the correct application of ERISA preemption in this context may not be entirely clear, NAIC released in 1995 a memorandum from its Health Plan Accountability Working Group of the Regulatory Framework Task Force (HPAWG), in which NAIC took the position that PSNs can accept either full or partial downstream risk from entities licensed by an insurance department.[137] When a PSN, however, assumes full or partial financial risk for the delivery of healthcare services from an unlicensed entity, including an ERISA employer, that PSN is engaged in the unauthorized business of insurance.[138] In reaching this conclusion, NAIC pointed to what has, in essence, become the accepted common-law definition of insurance. In applying the common law definition, however, the NAIC made no reference to the business vs. indemnity distinction often made by the courts.

This memorandum was issued as part of NAIC's Consolidated Licensure of Entities Assuming Risk (CLEAR) initiative. Pursuant to the CLEAR initiative the HPAWG was charged with considering the development of a single model healthcare-licensing act for all "health carriers" (the CLEAR Model Act). The purpose of this CLEAR Model Act is to foster the creation of a uniform-licensing scheme that would apply to all risk-bearing entities equally, regardless of the "form" of the risk-bearer. According to NAIC, this would promote a "more competitive market place by ensuring that entities that perform the same or similar functions are subject to a level regulatory playing field." In 1997, in anticipation that the states would adopt the CLEAR Model Act, NAIC issued its white paper on the regulation of risk-bearing entities in order to provide guidance to the states regarding the analysis of this issue. NAIC has yet to release its CLEAR Model Act.[139]

(d) PSOs that Contract as M+C Organizations. Although the issue of ERISA preemption with respect to state regulation of PSNs is not clear, Congress has created a limited exception from state licensure requirements under certain circumstances for provider-sponsored organizations or (PSOs) contracting with CMS under the M+C program. Specifically, under the BBA, PSOs may contract to become M+C organizations. Although such organizations are required to be licensed to accept risk under applicable state law, the BBA provided a special exception for PSOs; a PSO seeking to become a M+C organization can apply to the Secretary of the Department of Health and Human Services (DHHS) for a waiver of the state licensing requirements.[140] In order to obtain such a waiver, the

---

[137] *See* Memorandum from Kenney Shipley, Chair, NAIC Health Plan Accountability Working Group, to the Insurance Commissioners, Directors and Superintendents (Aug. 10, 1995) (NAIC Memorandum).

[138] *Id.*

[139] The NAIC did issue its White Paper, however, to provide guidance to the states regarding the analysis of this issue in anticipation that the states would adopt the CLEAR Model Act.

[140] *See* Balanced Budget Act of 1997, Pub. L. No. 105-33, 111 Stat. 312, § 1855(a) (1997).

PSO must have applied no later than November 1, 2002. The DHHS Secretary may grant a waiver if it determines that any of the following criteria are met:

1. The state failed to complete action on a PSO's licensing action within 90 days;
2. The state denied the PSO licensure based on discriminatory treatment; or
3. The state denied the PSO's licensing application on the basis of the organization's failure to meet the state's solvency requirements (assuming that they are different from the M+C solvency requirements).

Waivers are issued for non-renewable 36-month periods.[141] As a result of the BBA, a PSN that otherwise meets the qualifications of a PSO may contract with the M+C program on a risk basis, even if not licensed under state law, if it obtains a wavier.

7.2.7 Blue Cross and Blue Shield (BC/BS) Plans

What we think of today as BC/BS Plans actually have their roots as separate organizations. Blue Cross was originally formed as a prepaid hospital plan. Blue Cross traces its origins to 1929, when Justin Ford Kimball, then working for Baylor University, designed a plan to provide schoolteachers with coverage for a specified number of hospital days at a set price.[142] This concept began to flourish, and other Blue Cross plans emerged. Eventually, these independent prepaid hospital plans formed a national organization that became known as the Blue Cross Association. Plans that met certain guidelines were allowed to use the Blue Cross symbol.

At around the same time, prepaid medical plans began to surface. These early plans were usually designed by employers (typically in the lumber and mining industries) who provided medical services for their employees by entering into prepaid arrangements with physicians who agreed to provide the employees with specified medical service for a fixed fee.[143] From these roots, the first modern-day Blue Shield plan emerged when California Physicians' Service, touted as the nation's first medical-service prepayment plan, was incorporated in 1939. This plan enrolled low-income subscribers who paid a fixed monthly fee in exchange for coverage of physician office visits.[144] A group of independent Blue Shield plans formed what eventually became known as the National Association of Blue Shield Plans in 1948. Like the system adopted by Blue Cross plans, those prepaid medical plans that met certain conditions were allowed to use the Blue Shield symbol.

Though Blue Cross plans and Blue Shield plans have separate origins, they have a common core: Both were developed as nonprofit local organizations, and both were largely formed in order to provide an alternative to government- and commercial- based indemnity health insurance, particularly for the less-affluent members of society. Even with this common core, the Blue Cross Association and the National Association of Blue Shield Plans remained independent for many years. It was not until 1982 that the two organizations formally merged, forming the Blue Cross and Blue Shield Association.

---

141 *Id.*

142 *See* Blue Cross and Blue Shield Association, *Who We Are*, available at www.bluecares.com/whoweare/index.html.

143 *Id.*

144 *Id. See also* Robert Cunningham, III & Robert Cunningham, Jr., *The Blues: A History of the Blue Cross and Blue Shield System* 45–46 (Northern Univ. Press 1997).

Today, the Blue Cross and Blue Shield Association licenses its trademarks and names to independent plans that meet and maintain specified standards. One of the most notable of these standards, that plans maintain nonprofit status, was dropped in 1994.[145]

Like early HMO regulation, state laws regulating BC/BS plans reflected their unique character as local, nonprofit prepaid plans that directly furnish or provide reimbursement for certain medical services to "members." Though the laws governing these plans are highly state-specific, most have special legislative schemes that limit licensure to nonprofit corporations, and provide for exemption from certain taxes (*e.g.*, state premium tax) in recognition of their nonprofit, service-oriented, status. Like insurers and HMOs, however, BC/BS plans are subject to financial regulation in the form of capital and reserve requirements, and are also subject to financial filings and examinations.

As indicated, the traditional regulation of BC/BS plans involves a regulatory scheme tailored to the business of a local, nonprofit prepaid plan. Nevertheless, given the changes in the healthcare market over the last fifteen years and in order to remain competitive, most BC/BS plans today operate a variety of products and programs, many of which involve activities beyond those authorized under these traditional licensure statutes. These products include indemnity products, PPO programs, and HMO products, as well as administrative-services arrangements whereby the BC/BS plan serves as a TPA for a licensed insurer or self-funded ERISA employer. When offering these products, BC/BS plans operate under the licensure scheme applicable to the product being offered. For this reason, most BC/BS plans hold multiple licenses (*e.g.,* an HMO license, an insurance license, and a license as a health-services corporation) either directly or through one or more affiliates.

7.3 The Federal Regulation of Private Healthcare Plans

7.3.1 Background

Congress enacted ERISA in 1974[146] in response to growing concerns that employer sponsors of welfare and pension programs were not managing plan assets appropriately, thereby threatening the availability of those assets for plan beneficiaries when needed.[147] At the same time, however, Congress wanted to preserve the voluntary growth of employer-sponsored benefit plans.[148] In order to provide the beneficiaries of these employer-sponsored programs with the desired protection, while simultaneously continuing to motivate employers to voluntarily offer benefit programs, ERISA created a federal

---

[145] Rosemary A. Stevens, Foreword to Cunningham & Cunningham. The topic of nonprofit conversion is outside the scope of this Chapter. It is important to note, however, that as the market began to change, many BC/BS plans began to "convert" from nonprofit to for-profit organizations. Although the term "convert" has no precise definition, a conversion from nonprofit to for-profit status is generally considered to have occurred when the nonprofit, through one or more transactions, transfers all, or a substantial portion of, its assets to a for-profit entity. A variety of factors are cited as encouraging this trend. The most commonly cited factor is the need to raise capital in order to build the infrastructure necessary to maintain a competitive managed-care product. Given the exemption from state premium tax generally enjoyed by BC/BS plans, states often challenge these conversions under cy pres doctrine, and on the basis that these conversions were not carried out in accordance with applicable statutory authority.

[146] 29 U.S.C. §§ 1001–1461.

[147] 29 U.S.C. § 1001(a). *See also Shaw v. Delta Airlines, Inc.*, 463 U.S. 85 (1983). *See generally* Margaret G. Farrell, *ERISA Preemption and Regulation of Managed Healthcare: The Case for Managed Federalism*, 23 Am. J.L. & Med. 251 (1997); Brummond, *Federal Preemption of State Insurance Regulation Under ERISA*, 62 Iowa L. Rev. 57 (1976).

[148] Farrell, *supra*, at 251.

statutory scheme with a broad federal preemption provision, applicable to all employers (except certain governmental employers and church plans) offering welfare and pension plans.

This statutory scheme established standards of conduct, including reporting and disclosure mandates,[149] and imposed fiduciary responsibilities on plan administrators.[150] It also created participation and vesting requirements,[151] as well as funding standards.[152] Finally, it created criminal sanctions for certain violations, and established a comprehensive civil-enforcement scheme.[153]

At the outset, ERISA did not require that plan sponsors offer specific benefits, nor did it dictate the substance of any benefit plan.[154] It simply provided a structure regarding how such plans operate, providing guidance on such matters as claims procedures and fiduciary responsibility. However, Congress steadily and with greater boldness increased its imprint on the substantive operation of private healthcare plans. The march toward federal regulation reached its high water mark with the 2010 enactment of the Patient Protection and Affordable Care Act (PPACA). As explained below, while PPACA represents a radical escalation of the federal regulation of private healthcare, in the broader view it can be seen as a continuation of a process begun with the enactment of ERISA.

7.3.2 ERISA

7.3.2.1 COBRA

Signed into law by President Reagan on April 7, 1986, COBRA amended ERISA, the Internal Revenue Code, and the Public Health Service Act (PHSA). This act requires that, under certain conditions, a group health plan must provide former participants and qualified beneficiaries the opportunity to elect and pay for extended health-insurance coverage after separation from employment.[155] The purpose of COBRA is to make group healthcare available on a continuation-coverage basis to employees and their dependents who would otherwise lose healthcare coverage. COBRA applies to group health plans provided by public and private employers other than: (1) churches; (2) governmental entities of the United States; (3) state and local government agencies not receiving funds from the Public Health Service Act; and (4) employers whose total number of employees is fewer than 20 on a "typical business day" in the prior calendar year.[156]

Under COBRA, an employee or qualified beneficiary who would otherwise lose her coverage must be allowed to elect continuation coverage for a certain period of time upon the occurrence of

[149] 29 U.S.C. §§ 1002–1031.
[150] 29 U.S.C. §§ 1101–1114.
[151] 29 U.S.C. §§ 1051–1061.
[152] 29 U.S.C. §§ 1081–1086.
[153] 29 U.S.C. §§ 1131–1145.
[154] *Shaw v. Delta Airlines, Inc.*, 463 U.S. 85, 91 (1983).
[155] 29 U.S.C. § 1161(a); John K. DiMugno & Paul E.B. Glad, *Group Health, Disability and Life Insurance*, Cal. Law Ins. Handbook § 36.05. COBRA provisions are contained in the Internal Revenue Code and ERISA. For simplicity, citations to ERISA will be used.
[156] 29 U.S.C. § 1161(b).

a qualifying event.[157] A qualified beneficiary is any individual covered by a group health plan on the day before a qualifying event, which often includes the employee's spouse and dependent children.[158]

The type of qualifying event determines the requisite length of the extended-coverage period. If the qualifying event is the covered employee's termination or reduction in hours, then the required extended coverage period is eighteen months from the event.[159] In most other instances, the extended coverage period is 36 months.[160] COBRA coverage may be terminated before the otherwise applicable coverage period if:

- the employer terminates any group health coverage to any employee;
- coverage ceases because of a failure to make a timely health-insurance premium payment;
- the qualified beneficiary obtains group health insurance (as long as the new health plan does not exclude or limit coverage on the basis of any preexisting condition of the beneficiary); or
- a beneficiary becomes eligible for Medicare; or legal separation between the spouse and employee terminates the coverage.[161]

Plan-provided continuation coverage must be identical to the plan's coverage for similarly situated beneficiaries who have not experienced a qualifying event.[162] The employee or beneficiary may be required to pay a premium not exceeding 102% of the otherwise-applicable plan premium.[163] At the end of the 18- or 36-month period, the employer must offer conversion to an individual policy if the group plan includes a conversion privilege.[164]

Qualifying events for an employee include:

- voluntary termination;
- involuntary termination (except for gross misconduct);
- reduction in hours rendering the employee ineligible under the insurance plan;
- a covered employee's entitlement to benefits under Title XVIII of the Social Security Act; or
- a proceeding in a case under Title XVI of that act beginning on or after July 1, 1986, with respect to the employer from whose employment the covered employee retired at any time.[165]

The principal qualifying events that allow a qualified *beneficiary* to elect continuation coverage are: (1) a covered employee's death; (2) a covered employee's termination (other than for gross mis-

157 29 U.S.C. § 1161(a).

158 29 U.S.C. § 1162. In certain circumstances, a retired employee, retired employee's spouse, and dependent children may also be included as qualified beneficiaries. *See* Health Benefits Under COBRA—The Consolidated Omnibus Budget Reconciliation Act of 1986, available online at www.cobrainsurance.net/COBRA_Law.htm.

159 29 U.S.C. § 1162(2)(A).

160 29 U.S.C. § 1162(2)(A)(ii)–(iv).

161 29 U.S.C. § 1162(2)(C)(D).

162 29 U.S.C. § 1162(1).

163 29 U.S.C. § 1162(3)(A). The beneficiary may choose to pay the premiums in monthly installments. 29 U.S.C. § 1162(3)(B).

164 29 U.S.C. § 1162(5); Employee Benefit Research Institute, *Fundamentals of Employee Benefit Programs* 218 (1997).

165 29 U.S.C. § 1163.

conduct), or reduction in hours; (3) divorce or legal separation from a covered employee; (4) a covered employee's becoming entitled to Social Security benefits; or (5) a dependent child's ceasing to be a dependent under the plan.[166] Upon the occurrence of a qualifying event, the plan must give the qualifying beneficiary at least 60 days in which to elect continuation coverage.[167]

COBRA requires that employees and qualified beneficiaries be provided with two notices.[168] The first notice must be sent to employees and their spouses when COBRA coverage first becomes effective, or when new employees and their spouses first become eligible to participate in the plan.[169] The second notice must be sent upon the occurrence of a qualifying event.[170] In the event of death, termination of employment, or entitlement to benefits under the Social Security Act, the employer must notify the plan administrator within 30 days of the date of such event.[171] In case of a divorce or legal separation from a covered employee, or the reaching of independent status of a covered employee's child, the employee or qualified beneficiary must notify the plan administrator within 60 days.[172] At that time, the plan administrator must, within fourteen days, inform the employee and each qualified beneficiary of his or her right to elect continuation coverage.[173] The plan administrator must provide notification, regardless of whether the employee is aware of her rights to continuation coverage under COBRA.

COBRA governs employer-sponsored medical expense plans, HMO options, dental plans, vision-care plans, prescription-drug plans, and often includes employee assistance plans.[174] In the event of the failure of a state, political subdivision, or agency to comply with the COBRA requirements, an individual may enforce her COBRA rights through ERISA.[175]

7.3.2.2 Mental Health Parity Act

Although equality between mental-health coverage and other types of medical coverage had long been the subject of much discussion, the concept of parity in insurance plans did not become nationally significant until the 1990s.[176] On September 26, 1996, President Clinton signed into law the Mental Health Parity Act (MHPA).[177] The MHPA requires that, when group health plans subject to ERISA offer coverage for both physical and mental illnesses, the annual or lifetime dollar limits on coverage

---

166 *Id.*
167 29 U.S.C. § 1165.
168 29 U.S.C. § 1166.
169 29 U.S.C. § 1166(a)(1).
170 29 U.S.C. § 1166.
171 29 U.S.C. § 1166(a)(2).
172 29 U.S.C. § 1166(a)(3).
173 29 U.S.C. § 1166(c).
174 29 U.S.C. § 1161.
175 29 U.S.C. § 1132.
176 Christopher Aaron Jones, *Special Project: Current Issues in Mental Health Care: Legislative "Subterfuge"?: Failing to Insure Persons with Mental Illness Under the Mental Health Parity Act and the Americans With Disabilities Act*, 50 VAND. L. REV. 753, 754 (1997).
177 *Id.* at 757; Vickie Yates Brown and Barbara Reid Hartung, *Managed Care at the Crossroads: Can Managed Care Organizations Survive Government Regulation?*, 7 ANN. HEALTH L. 25, 34 (1998). The Mental Health Parity Act of 1996 amended the Public Health Service Act (PHSA) and ERISA. *See* Center for Mental Health Services, CMHS Programs: Organization and Financing: Mental Health Parity Act Summary, available online at www.mentalhealth.org/cmhs/ManagedCare/Parity/Summary.asp (CMHS Programs).

must be the same, unless the employer demonstrates financial hardship.[178] MHPA provisions for group health plans became effective on January 1, 1998.[179] Because the MHPA includes a "sunset provision," the MHPA requirements will no longer apply to benefits for services furnished after December 31, 2003.[180]

Due to concerns regarding the increased cost of this mandate, the MHPA only applies to plans sponsored by employers with more than 50 employees that provide both medical and surgical benefits and mental health benefits, as well as to insurers offering coverage for such plans.[181] This mandate exempts small employers with an average of two or more, but fewer than 50, employees, as well as plans in which the cost of compliance would exceed 1%.[182] Additionally, the mental-health parity requirements do not apply to benefits for substance abuse or chemical dependency, nor do they apply for policies sold in the individual market.[183]

The MHPA does not obligate any plan to alter its coverage to include mental-health benefits.[184] In addition, the act has no effect on the amount, duration, or scope of mental-health benefits (including cost-sharing, limits on visits, or days of coverage) beyond the mandated financial parity.[185]

The MHPA applies regardless of whether plans administer their mental-health benefits along with or separately from their medical and surgical benefits. For this reason, a plan cannot avoid mental-health parity by offering separate coverage for both benefits.[186] If a group health plan offers two or more benefit package options under the plan, however, the requirements of the MHPA apply separately to each option.[187]

Many states have adopted their own parity laws requiring more-favorable treatment of mental-health benefits under health-insurance coverage offered by issuers. Such state laws are not preempted by the MHPA provisions. This is due to the fact that, although group health plans must comply with the federal parity requirements, *issuers* are subject to state law.

---

178 29 U.S.C. § 1185a; Linda C. Fentiman, *Symposium on Health Care Policy: What Lessons Have We Learned from the AIDS Pandemic: Article: AIDS as a Chronic Illness: A Cautionary Tale for the End of the Twentieth Century*, 61 ALB. L. REV. 989, 993 (1998); Jack A. Rovner, *Federal Regulation Comes to Private Health Care Financing: The Group Health Insurance Provisions of the Health Insurance Portability and Accountability Act of 1996*, 7 ANN. HEALTH L. 183, 203 (1998).

179 29 U.S.C. § 1185a(c).

180 29 U.S.C. § 1185a(f), amended by Job Creation and Worker Assistance Act of 2002, Pub. L. No. 107-147, § 610, 116 Stat. 60 (2002).

181 29 U.S.C. § 1185a(c).

182 *Id.* As to the exemption for plans where the application of the act results in an increase in the cost under the plan of at least 1%, the MHPA does not discuss what costs must be considered, or how the exemption is to be administered.

183 29 U.S.C. § 1185a(e)(4); Center for Mental Health Services, CMHS Programs: Organization and Financing: Employer Questions and Answers on the Mental Health Parity Act, available online at www.mentalhealth.org/cmhs/ManagedCare/Parity/Employer.asp (CMHS Questions).

184 29 U.S.C. § 1185a(b)(1).

185 29 U.S.C. § 1185a(b)(2).

186 *Id.*; 29 C.F.R. § 2590.712(d)(1).

187 29 U.S.C. § 1185a(d). For instance, if a plan offers employees a choice between indemnity insurance and an HMO, then mental-health benefits within each option need match only the medical and surgical benefits of that same option. *Id.*

7.3.2.3 HIPAA's Pre-Existing Condition Rule

One of the most comprehensive changes to ERISA occurred with the passage of the HIPAA, signed into law on August 21, 1996.[188] Regulations issued under HIPAA by the Department of Labor (DOL), the Department of Treasury, and DHHS extended the scope of ERISA to include preexisting conditions, an area previously regulated only by state insurance laws.[189] The act's requirements apply to local governments through the Public Health Services Act, and generally apply for plan years beginning after June 30, 1997.[190] Additionally, HIPAA applies to insured as well as self-insured health plans, except where self-funded non-federal plans elect to exempt themselves from specific HIPAA requirements. One purpose of HIPAA is to increase the portability of health coverage by requiring group health plans to limit preexisting-condition exclusions.

A "preexisting condition exclusion" is defined as a limitation or exclusion placed on the benefits a plan will provide for costs with respect to a participant or beneficiary's physical or mental condition that existed before the date of enrollment in the plan by the participant or beneficiary, regardless of whether the participant or beneficiary received any medical advice, diagnosis, care, or treatment before the enrollment date. Group health plans may apply preexisting condition clauses if the HIPAA requirements are met, the exclusions apply uniformly to all similarly situated individuals, and they are not directed at individual participants and beneficiaries.

Under HIPAA, a group health plan may only impose a preexisting-condition exclusion if:

- the exclusion concerns a physical or mental condition, regardless of its cause, for which medical advice, diagnosis, care, or treatment has been suggested and received within the six-month period ending on the enrollment date;
- the exclusion applies for no longer than 12 months after the enrollment date (or 18 months, in the case of a late enrollee);
- and the period of any exclusion is reduced by the aggregate periods of creditable coverage applicable to the participant or beneficiary as of the date of enrollment.[191]

If, for example, a patient has had diagnosed scoliosis for 30 years, but has not sought treatment in the six months prior to enrolling in a group health plan, then the plan cannot exclude coverage for scoliosis treatment.[192] Furthermore, even in situations where the preexisting-condition exclusion is applied, payment cannot be denied for conditions unrelated to the preexisting condition. Continuing with the previous example, even in the event that the patient diagnosed with scoliosis had received treatment in the six months preceding enrollment (and therefore scoliosis was an excludable preexist-

---

[188] Alexander Hamilton Institute, Acknowledgment of Receipt of COBRA Notice, available online at www.benefitsalert.com/basics/forms/hipaanotice.rtf.

[189] Michael J. Canan & David Rhett Baker, *Health Insurance Portability Requirements*, 1 Qual. Retirement Plans § 2.8 (2002); Alexander Hamilton Institute, *supra*.

[190] James P. McElligott, HIPAA and Local Government Health Plans, available online at www.mcguirewoods.com/news-resources/publications/taxation/article032.asp.

[191] 29 U.S.C. § 1181(a), (c).

[192] Clifford C. Dacso, What in the World is a Preexisting Condition?, available online at www.hipaadvisory.com/views/archives/HIPAAconnection5.htm.

ing condition), a myocardial infarction she experiences on the first day of her new plan's coverage may not be excluded, because it is unrelated to the scoliosis.

As stated, plans must reduce any preexisting-condition exclusion period by the length of prior continuous coverage.[193] This is known as "creditable coverage."[194] If no break in coverage occurs, an insurer may not refuse to provide coverage to a person with a preexisting condition. Waiting periods required by plans prior to commencing coverage do not qualify as breaks in coverage. If there is a break in coverage of 63 days or more, however, then a health plan may exclude a preexisting condition.[195] Employers or plan sponsors must provide certification of prior coverage when (1) an individual loses coverage or becomes covered under COBRA, (2) COBRA coverage ends, or (3) an individual requests such certification (provided the request is made no more than 24 months after coverage ceases).[196] The effect of the creditable-coverage requirement is that individuals with existing medical conditions may now change jobs without fear that they will lose their insurance coverage.

Group plans also cannot exclude from coverage newborns or adopted children under the age of 18, as long as the child is enrolled within 30 days after birth, adoption, or placement for adoption.[197] This exception does not apply to an individual after the end of the first 63-day period, during all of which the individual was not covered under any creditable coverage.[198] In addition, HIPAA prohibits the imposition of a preexisting-condition exclusion based on pregnancy. [199] This prohibition applies regardless of the period of creditable coverage.[200]

7.3.2.4 HIPAA's Privacy Rules

HIPAA required, in the event that Congress failed to enact a privacy law within 36 months of its effective date, that DHHS promulgate regulations to serve as minimum privacy standards.[201] As Congress did not enact a privacy law, DHHS carried out its assignment with the publication of proposed privacy standards on November 3, 1999,[202] and final privacy standards on December 28, 2001.[203]

The final regulations set forth an extensive and highly complex set of rules that will be difficult for healthcare plans to follow. In essence, these rules provide that individually identifiable health data shall be held in confidence unless a specific exemption applies. Incident to the basic premise, handlers of individually identifiable health data are subject to strict behavioral guidelines governing the confidential treatment of data. Also, individuals have certain rights to access their medical records.

---

193 29 U.S.C. § 1181(c); Auxillium West, The Health Insurance Portability and Accountability Act (HIPAA) of 1996, available online at www.auxillium.com/hipaa.shtml.

194 29 U.S.C. § 1181(c); Anne Maltz, *Insurance Law: Understanding the ABCs*, 673 P.L.I. Litig. 359, 376 (2002).

195 29 U.S.C. § 1181(c).

196 29 U.S.C. § 1181(e).

197 29 U.S.C. § 1181(d)(1)–(2).

198 29 U.S.C. § 1181(d)(4); Hugh Alexander and Steve Fitzsimmons, Kennedy-Kassebaum Advisory, available online at www.aescon.com/slba/advis07.htm.

199 29 U.S.C. § 1181(d)(3).

200 29 U.S.C. § 1181(d)(4).

201 Health Insurance Portability and Accountability Act, Pub. L. No. 104-191, 821 1996.

202 64 Fed. Reg. 59,917.

203 45 C.F.R. 160, as amended by 65 Fed. Reg. 82,461 (2000); 45 C.F.R. 164; 65 Fed. Reg. 82,461 (2000).

As general principle, group health plans, along with other Covered Entities under HIPAA (*e.g.*, healthcare clearinghouses and healthcare providers) may not use or disclose protected health information without first receiving the consent of the identified individual.[204] The regulations provide for several exceptions to the rule, which in large part are designed to accommodate the public-policy goals of law enforcement, public safety, emergency needs, and patient care.[205]

7.3.2.5 Qualified Medical Child Support Orders

In order to help children of divorced parents receive healthcare coverage, medical child support was established under Part D, Title IV of the Social Security Act.[206] This provision requires state agencies administering child support to include medical coverage as part of a child-support order whenever healthcare coverage is reasonably available to the noncustodial parent.[207] When such support is granted, the notice given to the applicable health plan must conform to the Qualified Medical Child Support Order (QMCSO) requirements of ERISA.[208] If a state court's notice conforms to QMCSO, then the group health plan is required to provide health benefits to the participant's child (assuming benefits are generally available to children).[209] In addition, the QMCSO is excepted from the ERISA supersedure clause; as a result, the state may bring a civil action to enforce compliance with the QMCSO.[210]

A QMCSO recognizes the right for a group health-plan participant's child to receive benefits for which the participant is eligible.[211] To qualify as a QMCSO, an order must meet the following requirements:

1. it must be a judgment, decree, or order made by a court of competent jurisdiction or issued through an administrative process, which (i) provides for health benefit coverage of a child, pursuant to a state domestic-relations law, and relates to benefits under such plans or (ii) is pursuant to a law that relates to the medical child support in section 1908 of the Social Security Act;[212]
2. it must clearly specify the name and last mailing address of the participant and of each alternate recipient;[213]
3. it must describe the type of coverage (or how such coverage will be determined) for each alternate recipient;[214]
4. it must define the period to which the order applies;[215] and

---

[204] 45 C.F.R. § 164.500.
[205] 45 C.F.R. §§ 506 *et seq.*
[206] 42 U.S.C. § 652(f).
[207] *Id.*
[208] 29 U.S.C. § 1169.
[209] 29 U.S.C. § 1144(a); 29 U.S.C. § 1144(8) (exception granted to QMCSOs).
[210] 29 U.S.C. § 1132(a)(7).
[211] 29 U.S.C. § 1169(a)(2)(A) and (C).
[212] 29 U.S.C. § 1169(a)(2)(B).
[213] 29 U.S.C. § 1169(a)(3)(A) (under some circumstances, the name and mailing address of an official of a state may be substituted for that of each alternate recipient). An alternate recipient is a child of a participant who is recognized as having a right to enrollment in a group health plan under a QMCSO. *Id.*
[214] 29 U.S.C. § 1169(a)(3)(B).
[215] 29 U.S.C. § 1169(a)(3)(C).

5. it must not require the plan to provide any options or benefits that the plan does not normally provide, unless otherwise required by law.[216]

When a group benefit's plan administrator receives a child support order, she is supposed to notify the participant and the alternate recipients that such notice has been received.[217] The plan administrator then shall follow the plan's established procedures for determining whether the order is a QMCSO.[218] After the administrator has made a determination, she must notify the participant and each alternate recipient of his determination.[219] When determining whether the alternate recipient is eligible for coverage under the group health plan, the administrator must not consider whether the child is eligible for state medical assistance (*e.g.*, Medicaid).[220]

The Child Support Performance and Incentive Act of 1998 (CSPIA) provided for the promulgation of a National Medical Support Notice to be issued by states enabling them to enforce the health coverage provisions of child support orders.[221] Under the direction of CSPIA, the Secretary of DHHS and the Secretary of Labor jointly issued regulations providing for National Medical Support Notice.[222] Once such notice has been received by a group health plan and has been determined to be a QMCSO, the plan administrator must, within 40 business days, notify the state agency that issued the QMCSO as to whether the child is covered by the plan and (if the child is) the effective date of such coverage.[223] During this same timeframe, the plan administrator must notify the custodial parent of coverage availability, in addition to any additional steps that must be taken for coverage to be effectuated.[224]

When coverage is effectuated, any payment of benefits or medical reimbursements under the plan must be distributed to the alternate recipient, the custodial parent, or legal guardian of such alternate recipient.[225] This payment provision is intended to ensure that the party paying for the medical expenses receives the benefit of the group plan coverage, thus alleviating the problem of a custodial parent having to request reimbursement from their former spouse, or of a legal guardian having to request reimbursement from the child's natural parents.

---

216 29 U.S.C. § 1169(a)(4). The order may require the plan to provide benefits or options it would not otherwise provide to the extent required to meet the guidelines relating to medical child support in § 1908 of the Social Security Act. *See id. See also* 42 U.S.C. § 1369g-1.

217 29 U.S.C. § 1169(a)(5)(A).

218 29 U.S.C. § 1169(a)(5)(A)(ii) and (B). The group health plans' procedures for determining whether a medical child-support order qualifies as a QMCSO must meet the following requirements: (i) it must be in writing; (ii) it must provide for the notification of each person the order grants benefits; and (iii) it must permit an alternate recipient to designate a representative. 29 U.S.C. § 1169(a)(5)(B)(i)–(iii).

219 29 U.S.C. § 1169(a)(5)(A)(ii).

220 29 U.S.C. § 1169(b)(2).

221 29 U.S.C. § 1169(a)(5)(C), as added by the Child Support Performance and Incentive Act of 1998, Pub. L. No. 105-200 § 401(b).

222 29 U.S.C. § 1169(a)(5)(C)(i), as added by as added by the Child Support Performance and Incentive Act of 1998, Pub. L. No. 105-200 § 401(b)(5). *See also* 29 C.F.R. 2590.609-2. National Medical Support Notice forms can be found at www.dol.gov/dol/pwba.

223 29 U.S.C. § 1169(a)(5)(C)(ii).

224 *Id.* There may be additional forms that the custodial parent will have to fill out for the child to receive coverage under the group health plan. A QMCSO, however, does not require the group health plan to offer benefits or eligibility under the plan that are generally not provided under the plan. *See* 29 U.S.C. § 1169(a)(5)(C)(iii).

225 29 U.S.C. § 1169(a)(8). Payment to a state official whose name has been substituted for that of the alternate participant's will satisfy the required payment. *See* 29 U.S.C. § 1169(a)(9). Such payment for benefits must be made in accordance with any assignment of rights made on behalf of the participant, or beneficiary of such participant, in accordance with a state plan for medical assistance under title XIX of the Social Security Act. 29 U.S.C. § 1169(b)(1). In this manner, the state may acquire the right of payment with respect to such participant. 29 U.S.C. § 1169(b)(3).

7.3.2.6 Coverage for Adopted Children

If a group health plan provides coverage for the dependant children of its participants or beneficiaries, then it must also provide benefits for children placed for adoption with such participants or beneficiaries.[226] These benefits must be granted on the same terms as any natural child of the participant or beneficiary.[227] In addition, the benefits granted on behalf of an adopted child must not be restricted on the basis of a preexisting condition.[228]

7.3.2.7 Coverage for Pediatric Vaccines

Section 609(e) of ERISA requires that group health plans provide the same level of coverage for the cost of pediatric vaccines as was provided as of May 1, 1993.[229] The COBRA continuation-coverage excise-tax penalty applies in the event that a group health plan fails to follow the pediatric-vaccine coverage requirement.[230]

7.3.2.8 Maternity Protection

On September 26, 1996, Congress enacted the Newborns' and Mothers' Health Protection Act of 1996 (NMHPA).[231] The NMHPA amended ERISA and the Public Health Service Act. This act imposes certain requirements on health plans with respect to coverage of newborns and mothers.[232] The NMHPA mandates that all health plans be designed to include payment for in-hospital coverage for at least 48 hours following a normal vaginal delivery, and 96 hours following a delivery by caesarian section.[233] Discharge from the hospital is permitted sooner *only* when the decision is made by an attending provider, in consultation with the mother.[234] This law applies to persons enrolled in group health plans and to persons who have individual healthcare coverage alike.[235]

The NMHPA allows plans to impose copayments and deductibles for hospital stays in connection with childbirth.[236] Despite this, a group health plan may not provide incentives to mothers to stay less than the required minimum time, nor may they deny or restrict plan coverage or benefits of any por-

---

226 29 U.S.C. § 1169(c)(1). To qualify, the child must be younger than 18 on the date of adoption or placement for adoption. 29 U.S.C. § 1169(c)(3). A "placement for adoption" occurs when the person with whom the child is being placed assumes and retains the legal obligation for total or partial support of the child in anticipation of adoption. *See id.*

227 *See id.*

228 29 U.S.C. § 1169(c)(2).

229 29 U.S.C. § 1169(e).

230 Internal Revenue Code § 4980B(f).

231 Utah Law Review Society, *Insurance Law Amendments*, 2000 Utah L. Rev. 964, 968 (2000) (ULRS).

232 Michael J. Canan & William D. Mitchell, *Other Laws Concerning Health Benefits, Employee Fringe and Welfare Benefit Plans* § 10.4 (West).

233 29 U.S.C. § 1185; Ann H. Nevers, *ERISA Right to Sue: An Rx for Health Care that Places Forum Over Substantive Consumer Rights*, 31 New Mexico L. Rev. 493, 495 (2001). These regulations specify that a hospital stay begins at the time of delivery if the delivery occurred in a hospital, or at the time of admission if the mother or newborn was admitted after a delivery occurring outside the hospital.

234 29 U.S.C. § 1185(a)(2). An attending provider is "an individual, licensed under State law, who is directly responsible for providing maternity or pediatric care" to the mother or newborn child. "In addition to physicians, an individual such as a nurse midwife, physician assistant, or nurse practitioner may be an attending provider. A plan, hospital, insurance company, or HMO would not be an attending provider." Centers for Medicare & Medicaid Services, The Newborns' and Mothers' Protection Act, available online at cms.hhs.gov/hipaa/hipaa1/content/nmhpa.asp (CMS Protection Act).

235 29 U.S.C. § 1185(a)(1).

236 29 U.S.C. § 1185(c)(3).

tion of the required minimum hospital stay as an inducement to circumvent the act's requirements.[237] Furthermore, the act does not require a mother to give birth in a hospital, or to stay in the hospital for a fixed period of time following the birth of her child.[238] The act, however, does not limit an insurance company from intervening after the 48-hour minimum stay.

The NMHPA provisions are effective with respect to plan years beginning on or after January 1, 1998. In addition, the NMHPA requirements are preempted with respect to health insurance coverage if: (1) state law which requires a 48-hour hospital stay after normal delivery, and a 96-hour stay after caesarian section; (2) a state law requires maternity and pediatric care coverage in accordance with guidelines established by the American College of Obstetricians and Gynecologists, the American Academy of Pediatrics, or other established professional medical associations; or (3) a state law requires that the hospital length of stay for maternity care is left to the decision of the attending provider, in consultation with the mother.[239]

DHHS, the DOL, and the Department of the Treasury are responsible for implementation and enforcement of the NMHPA. On October 27, 1998, these departments developed a Joint Interim Rule. This rule applies to plans and issuers in the group and individual markets for plan years or health-insurance coverage beginning on or after January 1, 1999. The interim rule provides guidance on how the NMHPA will be implemented and enforced, and explains the jurisdiction of each department.

7.3.2.9 Minimum Cancer Treatment

As Congressional awareness of the problems women face in the context of managed care began to rise by the end of the 105th Congress, Democrats and Republicans together focused on passing legislation addressing women's health concerns.[240] The Women's Health and Cancer Rights Act of 1998 (WHCRA), signed into law on October 21, 1998, is one such piece of legislation.[241] This act amended ERISA and the Public Health Service Act, and is administered by the DOL and DHHS.[242]

The WHCRA applies to women covered by insured and self-insured plans, as well as HMOs provided by private and governmental employees.[243] The WHCRA mandates that these health plans notify women about the coverage it requires upon enrollment for insurance, and thereafter on a yearly basis.[244] It requires health plans already providing coverage for mastectomies to provide reimbursement

---

237 29 U.S.C. § 1185(b).

238 29 U.S.C. § 1185(c).

239 42 U.S.C. § 300gg-4(f).

240 Tiffany F. Theodos, *The Patients' Bill of Rights: Women's Rights Under Managed Care and ERISA Preemption*, 26 Am. J.L. and Med. 89, 102 (2000).

241 29 U.S.C. § 1185b; Dennis K. Schaeffer, *Insuring the Protection of ERISA Plan Participants: ERISA Preemption and the Federal Government's Duty to Regulate Self-Insured Health Plans*, 47 Buffalo L. Rev. 1085, 1130 (1999). The WHCRA passed as part of the omnibus appropriations bill. *Id.* at 102–03.

242 Public Welfare Benefits Administration, The Women's Health and Cancer Rights Act of 1998: Questions and Answers, available online at www.dol.gov/pwba/pubs/womhlth.htm (last updated November 1998) (PWBA Cancer Rights Act).

243 29 U.S.C. § 1185b(a); Mary Anne Bobinski and Phyllis Griffin Epps, *Women, Poverty, Access to Health Care, and the Perils of Symbolic Reform*, 5 J. Gender Race & Just. 233, 255 (2002).

244 29 U.S.C. § 1185b(a); American Cancer Society, Women's Health and Cancer Rights Act, available online at www.cancer.org/eprise/main/docroot/MIT/content/MIT_3_2x (ACS Cancer Rights Act). These health-insurance carriers were also required to notify individuals of coverage directly after the enactment of the WHCRA. *See* PWBA Cancer Rights Act, *supra*.

for breast reconstructive surgery and surgery to achieve breast symmetry, prostheses, and treatment for physical complications, as needed, following mastectomy.[245] Coverage for reconstructive surgery may not be denied or reduced on the grounds that it is cosmetic in nature, or that it otherwise does not meet the coverage definition of "medically necessary."[246] The act's requirements apply to group health plans for plan years beginning on or after October 21, 1998.[247] In addition, these requirements also apply to individual health-insurance policies offered, sold, issued, renewed, in effect, or operated on or after October 21, 1998.[248]

Because the WHCRA applies to all types of group health plans and individual health plans, this regulation benefits most women. At the same time, however, the act only mandates coverage of reconstructive services where mastectomy benefits are already provided; it does not require health plans or issuers to pay for mastectomies.

At the time this law was enacted, several states already had in effect regulations requiring health plans covering mastectomies to provide coverage for breast reconstructive surgery following a mastectomy.[249] This act does not preempt any such state laws.[250] Thus, the WHCRA covers those plans not currently covered by state law, and sets a minimum standard securing this service for all women in all states.[251]

7.3.3 The Patient Protection and Affordable Care Act

The federal regulation of healthcare began in earnest in 1965 with the enactment of the Social Security Act of 1965 which created two revolutionary programs: Medicare and Medicaid. Nine years later, federal effort to regulate healthcare took another forward leap with the enactment of ERISA. Although ERISA's primary focus was designed to secure the promise of qualified plans, owing largely to the failed promise of certain multi-employer pension plans, welfare plans were also regulated. Further federal regulation of healthcare plans occurred through the enactment of COBRA continuation coverage in 1986 and the enactment of HIPAA in 1996.

Serious efforts at overhauling the healthcare system, at the federal level, were undertaken by President Clinton. On March 26, 1997, President Clinton appointed the Advisory Commission on Consumer Protection and Quality in the Health Care Industry to "advise the President on changes occurring in the healthcare system and recommend measures as may be necessary to promote and ensure healthcare quality and value, and protect consumers and workers in the health care system." As part of its work, the President asked the Commission to draft a "Consumer Bill of Rights and Responsibilities," and in November 1997, the Commission produced its recommended Consumer Bill of Rights consistent with its charge. However, as a result of, among other things, crushing lobbying pressures, the legislative effort stalled and comprehensive healthcare reform under the Clinton administration never materialized.

---

245 29 U.S.C. § 1185b(a).
246 29 U.S.C. § 1185b(c).
247 PWBA Cancer Rights Act, *supra*.
248 *Id.*
249 ACS Cancer Rights Act, *supra*.
250 29 U.S.C. § 1185b(e).
251 *Id.*

Further efforts at overhaul occurred in 2003. On December 8, 2003, President George W. Bush ensured that there would be sweeping changes to the Medicare system by enacting the Medicare Prescription Drug, Improvement, and Modernization Act (Medicare Modernization Act or MMA) into federal law. The MMA allowed for the establishment of new Medicare Advantage Plans, which offered great advantages over Medicare+Choice plans for insurers. These new plans, among other things, allowed enrollees to sign on to the plan for an entire year, restricted care to a network of providers, allowed the use of formularies to restrict prescription drug choices, created the possibility for prescription drug coverage to be deferred to the patient or a prescription plan, restricted care other than emergency care to a particular region, and allowed for the adjustment of federal reimbursement according to the health risk of particular enrollees. While the MMA was great for insurers, it also offered advantages to Medicare recipients, particularly for the elderly and disabled. Among its most important changes was the introduction of an entitlement benefit for prescription drugs, which would be funded through tax breaks and subsidies.

Throughout the 2004 presidential election, healthcare proposals were offered and defended by both President Bush and Senator John Kerry. The Bush and Kerry plans were on different ends of the spectrum when it came to affordability, coverage, and methodology.[252] President Bush took a modest approach to the issue, while Senator Kerry offered a much more comprehensive plan.[253] During President Bush's second term, he set a goal of doubling the number of patients served, primarily through increased support for community health clinics.[254] Large-scale healthcare reform would eventually happen, but its proponents would have to wait until the next election.

The issue of healthcare was critical to the 2008 presidential election. Senator John McCain proposed a system of open-market competition based on tax credits for individuals and families without health insurance.[255] Senator Barack Obama, on the other hand, advocated universal healthcare, under which every citizen or resident was to have access to healthcare regardless of income level or employment status. The focus of Senator McCain's plan was to make health insurance more affordable, while the purpose of Senator Obama's plan was to allow for more people to have health insurance.

President Obama was inaugurated, and shortly thereafter announced that he would begin working with Congress to carry out his plan for healthcare reform. In July 2009, committees of the House of Representatives approved a series of healthcare reform bills that would go on to become the Affordable Health Care for America Act (H.R. 3962).[256] This Act aimed to increase consumers' choices when it comes to plans, increase competition based on quality and price, improve the quality of care for every American, ensure that responsibility for a quality healthcare system is fairly apportioned, reduce fraud and abuse, reduce the overall deficit, as well as ensure the solvency of Medicare and Medicaid.[257] The House of Representatives passed the Affordable Health Care for America Act on November 7, 2009, and forwarded it to the senate for its approval.

---

252 Robin Toner, *The 2004 Campaign: Political Memo; Biggest Divide? Maybe It's Health Care*, NY Times, May 14, 2004.

253 *Bush Plan: Covers Less Uninsured, Tax Credits, Consumer-Driven Healthcare; Kerry Plan: Cover All Uninsured Children and Most Adults, Subsidies in Exchange for Premium Reductions, Extremely Expensive*, *Id.*

254 *Editorial: Mr. Bush's Health Care Legacy*, NY Times, Jan. 2, 2009.

255 Scott Anderson, Tax Credits at Heart of McCain's Health Care Proposal, CNN, April 29, 2008, available at http://articles.cnn.com/2008-04-29/politics/mccain.healthcare_1_health-care-mccain-health-insurance?_s=PM:POLITICS.

256 Nu Online News Service, The Battle of the Giant Health Bills, Life and Health Insurance News, Nov. 8, 2009, available at http://www.lifeandhealthinsurancenews.com/News/2009/11/Pages/House-Passes-HR-3962-Focus-Shifts-To-Senate.aspx.

257 *Id.*

Instead of considering the Affordable Health Care for America Act (H.R. 3962), the Senate instead reviewed H.R. 3590, which was a bill granting housing tax breaks to service members.[258] The Senate completely revised H.R. 3590, amending the content to become their proposal for a healthcare bill, and called it the Patient Protection and Affordable Care Act (PPACA). After overcoming a filibuster threat, the Senate voted to end debate on the bill and eventually passed the bill on December 24, 2009.[259]

The Congressional proponents of healthcare reform decided that their best course of action was to scrap the House of Representatives' Affordable Health Care for America Act, and instead pass the Senate's PPACA.[260] Congress would then be able to pass amendments to the PPACA with a different bill that allows the Senate to pass the amendments through the reconciliation process.[261] The House of Representatives eventually passed the PPACA on March 21, 2010[262] and, on March 23, 2010, President Obama signed the PPACA into federal law.[263]

Congress immediately exercised its reconciliation powers and enacted the Health Care and Education Reconciliation Act (H.R. 4872) in order to make its desired changes to the PPACA. The House of Representatives passed the Act on March 21, 2010, and then the Senate also passed the act on March 25, 2010. President Obama signed the Health Care and Education Reconciliation Act into law on March 30, 2010, one week after PPACA.[264] The goal of the Health Care and Education Reconciliation Act is to "ensure that all Americans have access to quality, affordable health insurance…."[265]

Paired together with the PPACA, the Health Care and Education Reconciliation Act makes great strides toward a complete healthcare overhaul. The Act contains provisions that aim to, among other things, reduce premiums for seniors and fill the Medicare prescription drug "donut hole," extend reforms to grandfathered plans, enhance premium tax credits to make coverage more affordable, strengthen provisions attacking waste and fraud in Medicare and Medicaid, increase funding for community health centers, make improvements to Medicaid, improve shared responsibility between individuals and employers, and make fees more reasonable.[266]

---

258 Rick Maze, *House Oks Tax Breaks for Military Homeowners*, Air Force Times, Oct. 8, 2009, available at http://www.airforcetimes.com/news/2009/10/military_homeownerhelp_taxfree_100809w/.

259 Patient Protection and Affordable Care Act: Vote on H.R. 3590 Before the Senate, 11th Cong., Dec. 24, 2009, available at http://www.senate.gov/legislative/LIS/roll_call_lists/roll_call_vote_cfm.cfm?congress=111&session=1&vote=00396.

260 Sheryl Stolberg and Robert Pear, *Obama Calls for 'Up or Down Vote' on Health Care Bill*, NY Times, Mar. 3, 2010, available at http://www.nytimes.com/2010/03/04/health/policy/04health.html?hp.

261 *Id.* "Reconciliation" is a legislative process of the United States Senate intended to allow consideration of a contentious budget bill with debate limited to 20 hours under Senate Rules.

262 Reconciliation Act of 2010: Vote on H.R. 4872 Before the House of Representatives, 111th Cong., Mar. 21, 2010, available at http://clerk.house.gov/evs/2010/roll167.xml.

263 Sheryl Stolberg and Robert Pear, *Obama Signs Health Care Overhaul Bill, With a Flourish*, NY Times, Mar. 23, 2010, available at http://www.nytimes.com/2010/03/24/health/policy/24health.html.

264 William Branigin, *Obama Signs Higher-Education Measure Into Law*, Washington Post, March 30, 2010, available at http://voices.washingtonpost.com/44/2010/03/obama-signs-higher-education-m.html?hpid=topnews.

265 Staff of H. Comms. on Ways and Means, Energy and Commerce, and Education and Labor, 111th Cong., Report on Affordable Health Care for America (Comm. Print Mar. 18, 2010), available at http://docs.house.gov/energycommerce/SUMMARY.pdf.

266 *Id.*

Since PPACA was enacted into law, the act has faced several challenges to its Constitutionality.[267] The challenges center around PPACA's "individual mandate," which requires individuals to purchase health insurance or pay a penalty for failing to maintain coverage. The argument against the Constitutionality of PPACA is that requiring an individual to purchase insurance is beyond the scope of the Commerce Clause.

As of the date of this writing, three district courts have ruled to uphold the PPACA, while two district courts have ruled that the act is unconstitutional as written. Importantly, one of the courts ruling that the mandate is unconstitutional invalidated all of PPACA's provisions under the theory that the mandate requirement could not be severed from the balance of PPACA's provisions.

7.3.3.1 No Lifetime or Annual Coverage Limits

Prior to the March 23, 2010, enactment of the PPACA, group health plans were permitted to set lifetime and annual dollar limits on the benefits received by the covered individuals. In fact, over half of individuals who received employer-provided benefits in 2009 had policies containing lifetime limits of $1 million or $2 million.[268] On the other hand, annual dollar limits are much less common, and are utilized by only 8% of large employer plans, 14% of small employer plans, and 19% of individual market plans.[269]

Effective September 23, 2010, group health plans are no longer allowed to set lifetime dollar limits on essential benefits, such as hospitalization, doctor's office visits, and prescriptions.[270] The use of annual limits will also be restricted, and eventually eliminated altogether, contingent on an exception for pre-2014 annual limits.[271] Group health plans may enforce a restricted annual limit for all plans issued before January 1, 2014, on the value of benefits received by a covered group or individual for "essential health benefits," which are defined by the Secretary of Health and Human Services.[272] The Secretary's responsibility is to make sure that insurance premiums are not significantly raised due to the provision of necessary services.[273] Importantly, group health plans will still be free to impose a lifetime or annual dollar limit on spending for healthcare benefits that are not considered "essential."[274]

---

[267] *State of Florida v. United States Department of Health and Human Services* (C.A. No.: 3:10-cv-91-RV/EMT) (N.D. FLA); *Commonwealth of Virginia v. Kathleen Sebelius* (C.A. No.: 3:10-cv-00188-HEH) (E.D. VA); *Liberty University, Inc. v. Timothy Geithner* (C.A. No.: 6:10-cv-00015-nkm-mfu) W.D. VA); *Thomas More Law Center v. Barack Hussein Obama* (C.A. No.: 2:10-cv-11156-GCS-RSW) (E.D. MI); *Mead v. Holder* (C.A. No.: 1:10-cv-00950-GK) (D.C.).

[268] The Impact of Lifetime Limits, Prepared for the National Hemophilia Foundation on behalf of the Raise the Caps Coalition (PriceWaterhouseCoopers), Mar. 2009, available at http://hemophilia.org/docs/lifetimelimitsreport.pdf.

[269] Fact Sheet: The Affordable Care Act's New Patient's Bill of Rights, healthreform.gov, June 22, 2010, available at http://www.healthreform.gov/newsroom/new_patients_bill_of_rights.html.

[270] *Id.*

[271] PPACA § 1001(5) as amended by ACA § 10101(a) adding PHSA § 2711(a)(1).

[272] ACA ¶ 205.

[273] PPACA § 1001(5) as amended by ACA § 10101(a) adding PHSA § 2711(b).

[274] Fact Sheet: The Affordable Care Act's New Patient's Bill of Rights, healthcarereform.gov, June 22, 2010, available at http://www.healthreform.gov/newsroom/new_patients_bill_of_rights.html.

7.3.3.2 Prohibition on Rescission

Prior to the passage of the PPACA, group health plans were free to rescind an enrollee's coverage for a multitude of reasons and group health plans and insurers often took advantage of this right.

Upon the passage of the PPACA, the guaranteed renewability provisions of the PHSA were expanded to prohibit group health plans and health insurance issuers from rescinding coverage except in cases of fraud or misrepresentation of a material fact.[275] If an insurer plans to rescind coverage, at least 30 days advanced notice must be provided to afford covered parties an opportunity to appeal.[276]

7.3.3.3 The Appeals Process

PPACA imposes several requirements for "internal" claims or appeals, including:

- The definition of "adverse benefit determination" has been expanded to include a rescission of coverage, even if that rescission does not have an adverse effect on benefits (for example, coverage is rescinded but the participant had not actually incurred any claims that could be affected by that rescission).
- In situations in which a participant requires urgent care, a plan administrator must notify the participant of its coverage decision as soon as possible, but in any event within 24 hours of receiving the initial claim for urgent care benefits.
- A participant must be allowed to continue coverage while his or her appeal is pending, except in cases where there is an appeal of a rescission of coverage.
- Notifications of benefit determinations must be provided in a culturally and linguistically appropriate manner.[277]

Adherence to the internal requirements—both the existing requirements under ERISA *and* the new PPACA mandates—will be *strictly* required under joint regulations issued by the IRS, DOL and HHS. A plan's failure to closely follow these rules will mean that participants will automatically be deemed to have exhausted the internal process and can proceed to an external review of their claims or even proceed directly to litigation. Even minor or "de minimis" violations of these requirements by the plan will result in a deemed exhaustion.

PPACA, in a dramatic new approach, now requires that participants may take advantage of an "external" review process. For many insured plans, state law may already require an external review process, and procedures are already in place for complying with these requirements. For self-funded plans, however, this requirement alone may make maintaining grandfathered status a particularly important issue. More specifically, the external appeals requirements provide that:

- If a plan (such as a fully insured plan or a church plan) is subject to state law and that state has a process for external appeals which satisfies minimum standards set forth in the Regulations

---

275 *Id.*

276 *Id.*

277 Model notices of adverse benefit determinations are available at www.dol.gov/ebsa.

(based on the National Association of Insurance Commissioners Uniform Model), the plan must comply with that state process.

- If a plan (such as a self-funded plan) is *not* subject to state law (or if a plan is subject to a state process that does not satisfy the minimum federal standards), the plan must comply with federal requirements. In general, the federal requirements follow the National Association of Insurance Commissioners Uniform Model.[278]

In general, the new appeals rules take effect for plan years beginning on or after September 23, 2010. For calendar year plans, this means compliance generally began January 1, 2011. Other non-calendar year plans may already be required to comply with the new appeals rules.

However, there is a limited "safe harbor" for some plans. Until additional guidance is released with respect to the external appeals process, the IRS and DOL will not take enforcement action against non-grandfathered, self-funded plans subject to the federal process if the plans comply either with procedures based on the National Association of Insurance Commissioners Uniform Model or with the relevant state process, even if that state process would not otherwise apply to the plan. Similarly, HHS will not take enforcement action against health insurance issuers (insurance companies) if the issuer uses either a state process or a temporary process established by HHS.

7.3.3.4 Coverage of Preventative Health Services

PPACA requires all group health plans and health insurance issuers to provide coverage for preventative services, effective for plan years beginning on or after September 23, 2010.[279] These services must be provided without any cost sharing and at a minimum must include certain services supported by the U.S. Preventative Task Force and the Health Resources and Services Administration.

7.3.3.5 Extension of Dependent Coverage

PPACA requires all group health plans covering dependent children to provide health coverage until the dependent attains age 26. Many group health plans that currently offer coverage to children require the child to satisfy certain criteria, such as maintaining full-time student status after the child has attained age 19. With respect to dependents who have not attained age 26, a plan may not define the term "dependent" for purposes of eligibility for coverage other than in terms of a relationship between the parent and child. The result of this change is that a plan may no longer require an adult child to be a full-time student or live with parents to remain eligible for group health coverage.[280]

Grandfathered plans are not exempt from extending dependent health coverage to children until they have reached age 26. However, for plan years beginning before January 1, 2014, a grandfathered plan may continue to exclude from coverage adult children who have not attained age 26 if the child is eligible to enroll in another employer-sponsored health plan.

---

[278] The National Association of Insurance Commissioners Uniform Model may be found at www.dol.gov/ebsa/pdf/externalreviewmodelact.pdf. Additional guidance is expected soon to provide additional details regarding the external review processes.

[279] PHSA § 2713.

[280] PHSA § 2714.

For a child whose health coverage ended, or who was denied coverage because the plan's coverage availability ended before the child attained age 26, a plan is required to provide the participant with written notice of the opportunity and to enroll the child. The enrollment opportunity (including the written notice) must be provided no later than the first day of the first plan year beginning on or after September 23, 2010. Any child enrolling in group health plan coverage under the transitional rule must be treated as a "special enrollee" under HIPAA. Therefore, the child must be offered all the benefit packages available to, and the child cannot be required to pay more for coverage than similarly situated individuals who did not lose coverage by reason of cessation of dependent status.[281]

7.3.3.6 *Standardization of Coverage Documents*

In an effort to provide a more meaningful explanation of healthcare benefits, the Secretary of Health and Human Services is required to develop standards for group health plans and insurers regarding benefit summaries and coverage explanations. The new document is limited to four pages, must be culturally and linguistically appropriate, and must use terminology that is understandable by the average participant. A fine of up to $1,000 is imposed for each willful failure.[282]

7.3.3.7 *Information Regarding Transparency*

A group health plan or health insurer seeking to become a provider under the newly created exchanges must provide claims and enrollment information to the relevant state insurance commission, Secretary of Health and Human Services and the exchange authorities.[283]

7.3.3.8 *Prohibition of Discrimination in Favor of Highly Compensated Individuals*

Self-insured healthcare plans have been and are currently prohibited from discriminating in favor of highly compensated employees, both as to benefits and eligibility under § 105(h) of the Internal Revenue Code. Under PPACA, insured plans must now comply with the same non discrimination requirements.[284] Insured grandfathered plans are exempt from this requirement until 2014.

7.3.3.9 *Reporting; Quality of Care*

By March 23, 2012, the Secretary of Health and Human Services is required to develop quality reporting requirement standards in connection with coverage and reimbursement arrangements for group health plans and insurers. Group health plans and insurers will be required to annually report to the federal government and to enrollees as to whether the coverage:

- improves health outcomes;
- includes activities to prevent hospital readmissions; and
- includes activities to improve patient safety.[285]

---

281 Model language appears on the DOL website at http://www.dol.gov/ebsa/dependentsmodelnotice.doc.
282 PHSA § 2715, as amended by PPACA § 10101(b).
283 PHSA § 2715A, as added by PPACA § 10101(c).
284 Section 2716(a) of the PHSA as added by § 1001(5) of the PPACA.
285 PHSA § 2717, as added by PPACA § 1001(5).

7.3.3.10 Essential Benefits Coverage

Effective for 2014 and years following, qualified health benefit plans offered by private insurers are intended to be made available through a state-operated market place know as an Exchange. In order to be offered through the Exchange, the qualified health benefit plan must offer coverage which provides for "minimum essential benefits," limits on cost-sharing, and provides either bronze, silver, gold, or platinum levels of coverage. The "minimum essential benefits" must include: (a) ambulatory patient services; (b) emergency services; (c) hospitalization; (d) maternity and newborn care; (e) mental health and substance abuse services, including behavioral health treatment; (f) prescription drugs; (g) rehabilitation and habilitative devices; (h) laboratory services; (i) preventative and wellness services and chronic disease management; and (j) pediatric services, including oral and vision care.[286]

7.3.3.11 Prohibition on Excessive Waiting Period

For plan years beginning on or after January 1, 2014, group health plans may not require an individual to experience a waiting period of greater than 90 days.[287] A waiting period is the time that a potential participant or beneficiary must wait to become covered by a healthcare plan.

7.3.3.12 Prohibition of Pre-Existing Condition Based on Health Status

Effective for plan years beginning on or after January 1, 2014, group health plans and insurers may not impose a pre-existing condition exclusion as a design element of the plan.[288]

7.3.3.13 Prohibition of Discrimination Against Individual Participants and Beneficiaries Based on Health Status

For plan years beginning on or after January 1, 2014, group health plans and health insurance issuers are prohibited from imposing conditions for eligibility on an individual or dependent of an individual based on the following factors: Health status, medical condition (physical or mental), claims experience, receipt of healthcare, medical history, genetic information, evidence of insurability, disability, or any other factor deemed appropriate by the Secretary of Health and Human Services.[289] Group health plans and health insurers are not permitted to use these factors in order to require any individual to pay a larger premium or contribution than that paid by a similarly situated individual or dependant of that individual enrolled in the same plan.[290] Similarly, group health plans and health insurance issuers are not allowed to request or require that an individual undergo genetic testing for underwriting purposes, or as a condition for eligibility for participation in the plan.[291] "Wellness programs," or programs offered by employers that are designed to promote health or prevent disease, will not violate the nondiscrimination rule as long as all similarly situated individuals are given the option

---

286 PPACA § 1302.

287 Section 1201(4) PPACA, adding § 2708 of the PHSA.

288 PHSA § 2704(a).

289 PHSA § 2705(a), as added by the PPACA § 1201(4).

290 PHSA § 2702 and PHSA § 2705, as amended by the PPACA § 1201(4).

291 *Id.* PHSA § 2705 states that "genetic information" includes the information of any fetus of an individual or family member of an individual who is pregnant. "Genetic information" also extends to include information of any embryo legally held by an individual or family member utilizing an assisted reproductive technology.

to participate, and conditions for securing a premium discount, rebate, or other reward are not based on satisfying a standard related to the above-listed health status factors.[292]

Even if securing a premium discount, rebate, or other reward for participation in a wellness program is in fact conditioned on an individual satisfying a standard related to a health status factor, such a program may still be permissible. A wellness program of this sort will not violate the nondiscrimination rules as long as: The reward for the program, along with rewards for other programs that consider particular health status factors, does not exceed 30% of the cost of employee-only coverage under the plan; the program is reasonably designed to promote health or prevent disease; individuals eligible for the program are afforded the opportunity to qualify for the reward under the program at least once each year; all similarly situated individuals have access to the full reward under the program; and there is a reasonable alternative standard which is disclosed in all plan materials that describe the terms of the program.[293]

Along those same lines, some wellness programs that appear to violate the nondiscrimination rules will not do so as long as conditions for obtaining premium discounts, rebates, or other rewards under the program are not based on satisfying a standard that is related to a health status factor, and participation in the plan offering the program is offered to all similarly situated individuals. Such permissible wellness programs include: a program that reimburses all or part of the cost for memberships in a fitness center; a diagnostic testing program that provides a reward for participation and does not base the reward on outcomes; a program that encourages preventative care related to a health condition through the waiver of the copayment or deductible requirement under the group health plan for the costs of certain items or services related to a health condition; a program that reimburses individuals for the costs of smoking cessation programs without regard to whether the individual quits smoking; and a program that provides a reward to individuals for attending a periodic health education seminar.[294]

The Secretary of Health and Human Services, together with the Secretaries of Labor and the Treasury, are mandated to implement a 10-State demonstration project by July 1, 2014.[295] Further, within three years of the date of enactment of the PPACA, the Secretaries are required to consult and submit a status report to the appropriate Congressional Committees detailing the impact and effectiveness of the demonstration project.[296]

7.3.3.14 Tax Credit for Small Business

If an eligible small employer makes nonelective contributions that pay for at least 50% of the cost of health insurance premiums for the coverage of its participating employees, then that employer may claim a tax credit in tax years beginning after 2009.[297] The amount of such a tax credit in tax years beginning in 2010 through 2013 is equal to 35% of the lesser of either the sum of nonelective employer contributions or the sum of nonelective contributions which the employer would have made if each

---

292 PHSA § 2705(j), as added by the PPACA § 1201(4).
293 PHSA § 2705(j)(3), as added by the PPACA § 1201(4).
294 PHSA § 2705(j)(2), as added by the PPACA § 1201(4).
295 PHSA § 2705(l)(1), as added by the PPACA § 1201(4).
296 PHSA § 2705(m)(1), as added by the PPACA § 1201(4).
297 Internal Revenue Code § 45R, as amended by the PPACA.

employee had enrolled in a qualified health plan.[298] This limitation serves to prevent an employer from claiming the tax credit on the portion of employer paid premiums that exceeds the average premium charges in the State's small group market.[299]

An eligible small employer may also claim a health insurance credit for any tax year beginning after 2013, with the credit period being the two-consecutive-tax year period beginning with the first tax year in which the employer offers a qualified health plan to its employees through an Exchange.[300] The amount of such a tax credit for a tax year beginning after 2013 is equal to 50% of the lesser of either the sum of nonelective employer contributions or the sum of nonelective contributions that would have been made during that taxable year if each employee had enrolled in a qualified health plan.[301]

In order to receive the tax credit, employers must make nonelective contributions through an "arrangement."[302] For tax years beginning in 2010 through 2013, the arrangement must consist of the employer making nonelective contributions on behalf of each enrolled employee that equal a uniform percentage that is greater than 50% of the premium cost of the qualified health plan.[303] In order for an employer contribution to be considered "nonelective," it simply must be something other than a contribution pursuant to a salary reduction agreement.[304] In the instance of a tax year beginning after 2013, the arrangement must offer the insurance through an Exchange as discussed above, while the use of an Exchange is optional for tax years earlier than 2013.[305]

Only an "eligible" employer may take advantage of the tax credit. To be considered an eligible small employer it must have no more than 25 full-time employees for that taxable year, its employees' average annual wages must not exceed twice the applicable dollar amount for that tax year, and it must have a qualified healthcare arrangement in effect.[306]

There are special rules for an eligible small employer that also has tax-exempt status. For tax years beginning in 2010 through 2013, the credit percentage for an eligible small employer with tax-exempt status is 25%.[307] For tax years beginning after 2013, the credit percentage goes up to 35%.[308] In order for a small employer to qualify under these special rules, that employer must be "eligible," as described above, and it also must be an Internal Revenue Code § 501(c) organization that is exempt from the tax code under Internal Revenue Code § 501(a).[309] If the amount of the tax credit is greater

[298] Internal Revenue Code § 45R(b) and (g), as amended by the PPACA.

[299] U.S. Congress, The Staff of the Joint Committee on Taxation, Technical Explanation of the Revenue Provisions of the Reconciliation Act of 2010, as Amended, in Combination with the Patient Protection and Affordable Care Act (JCX-18-10), text from Committee Reports, available at http://www.jct.gov/publications.html?func=startdown&id=3673.

[300] Internal Revenue Code § 45R(a) and (e)(2), as added by the PPACA; PPACA § 3011 states that "exchanges" are to be established by each state no later than January 1, 2014, using money to be awarded by the Federal Government no later than March 23, 2011. An "exchange" must be operated as a government agency or a non-profit organization, and health insurance offered through "exchanges" is subject to specific requirements.

[301] Internal Revenue Code. § 45R(b), as added by the PPACA.

[302] Internal Revenue Code § 45R(d)(4) and (g)(3), as added by the PPACA.

[303] *Id.*

[304] Internal Revenue Code § 45R(e)(3), as added by the PPACA.

[305] Internal Revenue Code § 45R(d)(4) and (g)(3), as added by the PPACA.

[306] Internal Revenue Code § 45R(d)(1), as added by the PPACA.

[307] Internal Revenue Code § 45R(b) and (g)(2)(A), as added by the PPACA.

[308] *Id.*

[309] Internal Revenue Code § 45R(f)(2), as added by the PPACA.

than the amount of payroll taxes paid by the employer during a particular taxable year, then the credit amount is capped by the amount paid in payroll taxes.[310]

7.3.3.15 Automatic Enrollment for Employees of Large Employers

Effective March 23, 2010, an employer (other than one that sponsors a grandfathered plan) employing more than 200 full-time employees that sponsors a healthcare plan is required to automatically enroll new full-time employees in one of the plans offered by the employer. In conjunction with this requirement, an employer must provide adequate opt-out notices sufficient to inform the employee of his or her right to opt-out.[311]

7.3.3.16 Employer Requirement to Inform Employees of Coverage Options

Effective after March 1, 2013, employers must provide to each employee at the time of hiring a written notice:

- informing the employee of the existence of an exchange, a description of the services provided by the exchange and the manner in which to contact the exchange;
- if the employer plan's share of total allowed costs of benefits is less than 60%, that the employee may be entitled to certain tax and cost-sharing benefits, if benefits are purchased through an exchange; and
- if the employee purchases a benefit through an exchange and the employer does not offer a free choice voucher, the employee may lose the employer contribution to any health benefit plan and that all or a portion of the contribution may be excludable from income.[312]

7.3.3.17 Shared Responsibility

Generally, effective for months beginning after December 31, 2013, employers who employ an average of at least 50 full-time employees per calendar year and who have at least one full-time employee enrolled in a state-exchange plan will be required to provide a health plan with minimum essential coverage or pay a penalty tax. Generally, the penalty tax equals 1/12 of $2,000 for any month in which there is no coverage, multiplied by the number of full-time employees employed by the employer.[313] Even if an employer offers a health plan with minimum essential coverage, the employer will be penalized with respect to each employee choosing a state-exchange option. The monthly penalty tax is equal to 1/12 multiplied by $3,000 multiplied by the number of full-time employees choosing the state-exchange plan.[314]

[310] Internal Revenue Code § 45R(f)(1), as added by the PPACA; "Payroll taxes" are calculated pursuant to Internal Revenue Code § 45R(f)(3)(A), as added by the PPACA.
[311] PPACA § 1511.
[312] PPACA § 1512, adding § 18B of the Fair Labor Standards Act.
[313] PPACA § 1513.
[314] *Id.*

7.3.3.18 *Reporting of employer Health Insurance Coverage*

Employers who on average employ at least 50 employees and certain other employers who offer minimum essential coverage will, effective in 2014, be required to file a report with the Secretary of Treasury. The report will essentially describe the scope and extent of coverage afforded to full time employees. In addition, the report must also be provided to each full-time employee who is covered under the plan.[315]

7.3.3.19 *Cafeteria Plan Changes*

Effective for tax years beginning after December 31, 2012, a health flexible spending account will be limited to a maximum of $2,500 per year.[316] Further, effective December 31, 2013, employees will not be able to utilize an employer's cafeteria plan to pay for healthcare benefits purchased through an exchange. Certain small employers electing to offer benefits through an exchange are exempted from this rule.[317]

7.4 Conclusion

After nearly a century of state regulation of private healthcare plans, the enactment of ERISA and PPACA has brought about a sweeping era of federal regulation. Practitioners representing employers, health plans, or providers must become familiar with the unique regulatory scheme impacting health plans, as well as their subsidiary arrangements, in the states in which they practice. Such practitioners must watch closely for relevant legislative or policy changes. Practitioners also must stay abreast of potential changes at the federal level through newly enacted legislation, newly promulgated regulation, and a developing body of case law. The one certainty in this area is that, as long as managed care is under scrutiny and healthcare reform is part of the legislative agenda, the landscape of regulating healthcare insurance will continue to change.

315 PPACA § 1514, amending Internal Revenue Code § 6056.
316 PPACA §§ 9005 and 10902.
317 PPACA § 1515.

8

Regulation of Hospitals

Sandra M. DiVarco, Esquire
Kerrin B. Slattery, Esquire
McDermott Will & Emery LLP

8.1 Introduction

The operation of hospitals has never been more complex than it is today. The concept of a "hospital" includes many different types of institutions, though each has the common feature of providing diagnostic and therapeutic services to inpatients. The United States has approximately 5,800 general acute care hospitals. Almost 3,000 hospitals are organized as charitable, nonprofit, tax-exempt corporations. Approximately 1,000 hospitals are owned and operated as for-profit enterprises (*i.e.*, with public company ownership). Some hospitals are single, freestanding, and unaffiliated organizations, while others are part of regional systems or nationwide chains. Over 1,100 hospitals are owned by state or local municipalities (*e.g.*, hospital districts or authorities), or are city or county-owned hospitals. Still others are owned and operated by the federal government (*e.g.*, Department of Veterans' Affairs (VA) hospitals).

Hospitals serve diverse communities, from rural areas to densely populated metropolitan regions, and collectively form the backbone of the healthcare delivery system in the United States. Hospitals are also a vital part of the economic system, and are often one of the largest employers in the communities they serve. As a result, state and local governments have an interest in regulating the operation of hospitals in order to protect the public. Further, because of the significant cost involved in providing care in hospitals, almost all hospitals participate in governmental funding programs. As a result, hospitals are also subject to regulation by the federal government, which focuses on the protection of federal healthcare program beneficiaries' health and welfare in addition to the fiscal integrity of federal healthcare programs.

In addition, passage of the Patient Protection and Accountable Care Act of 2010 (PPACA) contemplates sweeping nationwide healthcare reforms and places a new emphasis on quality and data reporting, requiring hospitals around the country to develop and enhance processes to comply with new requirements in order to obtain reimbursement for care. Further, healthcare reform is driving continued consolidation of hospitals and healthcare systems, which events trigger the need to comply with various state and federal requirements pertaining to mergers and acquisitions.

Given the variety of hospitals, this Chapter will primarily focus on regulation of general, acute care hospitals, and will not address all the particular requirements for specialty or single-service hospitals (*e.g.,* children's hospitals, heart hospitals, psychiatric hospitals or long-term acute care hospitals) or VA/federal facilities. Further, the discussion will apply to for-profit, non-profit and governmental hospitals alike, rather than the unique issues arising from particular types of ownership.

This Chapter highlights in summary fashion the breadth and nature of the regulation of hospitals by federal and state governments, as well as by accrediting organizations. In order to get a full picture of the regulatory landscape within which hospitals operate, the authors suggest that all readers explore the Chapters in this book that address in greater detail the complex regulations with which general acute care hospitals must comply.

8.2 State and Local Regulations

8.2.1 Licensure

All states regulate the operation of hospitals to one degree or another, based on the premise that the public good demands careful oversight of healthcare provided to state residents. State regulation generally takes the form of licensure laws and regulations. Obtaining a license to operate a hospital typically requires the filing of a detailed application by the proposed operator with the appropriate state authority (most often a department of public health (DPH)). The application usually requires a description of the intended operations at the hospital and detailed information regarding ownership of the facility. Not all general acute care hospitals provide all medical services to their patients, but generally there are minimum requirements for hospital operation which vary by state (*e.g.*, emergency department, laboratory, etc.). Many hospitals specialize in particular services, and even more hospitals limit their scope of services for financial or other practical reasons. In many states, specialty hospitals are licensed separately from acute care hospitals, and the delivery of inpatient mental healthcare and skilled nursing care may be separately licensed within an already-licensed facility.

Many states regulate the types of hospital services provided in their jurisdiction. Some states take these steps as part of Certificate of Need (CON) laws (as further discussed in Section 8.2.5), and others do so merely to maintain an inventory of available health resources. All states regulate the standards used for building construction, including the construction of hospitals, which standards are largely directed at enhancing patient safety (*i.e.,* earthquake protection requirements in California) and fire safety. Increasingly, DPHs also require or recommend the reporting of errors in hospitals.

In addition, numerous other licenses and permits are required to operate a hospital in compliance with state and local regulations. Examples of permits required by state and local regulation that impact hospitals range from licensure of pharmacy and laboratory, to building permits (*e.g.*, boiler, elevator), to heliport, radioactive materials, food service, and gift shop licenses.

8.2.2 Patient Safety and Patient Rights

A number of state regulations governing hospitals focus on patient rights and patient safety issues, such as regulations regarding mandatory dissemination of patient rights information and specific rights and restrictions related to patient restraint and seclusion, the ability to make a complaint or grievance regarding care and imposition of mandatory staffing ratios. State agencies target these areas in an attempt to inform individuals of their rights as patients and to protect them from harm in the course of receiving hospital care. Although the scope of this Chapter does not permit a detailed exploration of all such regulations, the following discussion is illustrative of the type of such regulations.

The use of restraint or seclusion of patients in healthcare facilities has long been a focus of patient safety regulations. A patient might need to be restrained while in a hospital bed for protective reasons; for example, if the patient has a psychiatric condition, then the patient might need to be physically restrained or chemically restrained through the use of medication to prevent them from harming themselves or others (*e.g.*, staff or other patients). However, the use of restraints can carry significant risk of patient injury. Over the years, patients have been killed or injured due to the type of restraint used, the manner in which a restraint was imposed, the duration of the use of the restraint, and/or the failure to appropriately monitor the patient while the restraint was in use. Because of this potential for patient harm, use of restraints has become a highly regulated activity.

A second realm of patient rights emphasized in recent years is the requirement for hospitals to have in place a patient grievance process to investigate and respond to patient complaints about their care in the hospital. Hospitals can be penalized for failing to establish, maintain, and monitor such a program.

Finally, the statutory imposition of nurse-to-patient staffing ratios is yet another example of state-level regulation intended to protect the health and safety of patients within the hospital. In states with such staffing regulations, hospitals are charged with staffing patient care units in compliance with law rather than based on patient acuity. Mandatory staffing ratios are viewed by some as the most efficient way to address the potential association between nurse workload and patient mortality and morbidity. However, studies on the efficacy of such programs in improving morbidity and mortality vary widely, and the American Hospital Association and other groups have opposed laws mandating specific nurse-to-patient staffing ratios due to the impact on hospital scheduling and staffing flexibility in the face of continual nursing shortages. Bolstered by the support of nurse associations and nurse unions, mandatory staffing legislation has been enacted in California and is presently under consideration in a number of other states.

When states enact or amend regulations or standards, hospitals must review patient care policies and procedures and adapt them to fit the new regulatory environment. Moreover, hospital administrators must hold educational sessions with hospital employees and hospital medical staff to ensure that the new standards are understood and adhered to on a continuous and consistent basis within the hospital. In addition to training staff, hospitals must implement ongoing internal auditing mechanisms to ensure continued compliance. Thus, for example, even in the case of a hospital that has never experienced a patient injury from the use of a restraint, the hospital would still need to be aware of and comply with the state's regulations. Failure to do so could be used as compelling evidence of malpractice in a lawsuit alleging the provision of substandard care by the hospital, in addition to the potential loss of licensure for failure to comply with state law.

8.2.3 Regulations Impacting Medical Staff

Beyond issues pertaining to patient safety, state regulations also govern how hospitals relate to physicians and other health professionals who practice within the hospital. The reasons for these regulations are multifaceted. On one level, by regulating who can practice within a hospital, a state can foster the careers of particular medical practitioners, or impede the ability of other medical practitioners to practice their chosen profession. Thus, in many states, only persons licensed as particular types of medical practitioners are allowed to be members of a medical staff, while other individuals who provide healthcare services may be prohibited from joining a medical staff. For example, a chiropractic physician may be licensed by the state to provide services while being prohibited under state law from being a full member of the hospital medical staff.

Regulation of a hospital's relationships with its medical staff also relates to the idea that many medical staff practitioners need a hospital in which to practice their professions. Accordingly, it is in the interest of the public, as well as those practitioners, to enforce rules pertaining to how a hospital relates to practitioners that use the hospital, or how a hospital may limit particular practitioners in the practice of their profession. The theory underlying these regulations is that the power of the state must be used to protect the individual medical practitioner against the perceived market power of a local hospital, which may be an essential part of the practitioner's professional activities. In this way, regulations often relate to whether a hospital provides practitioners with all available opportunities to argue their case for medical staff membership and/or clinical privileges; the question of whether "due process" was followed by a hospital is a major part of many of these regulations.

8.2.4 Regulation of Patient Health Information

In addition to federal laws regarding privacy of health information (as described in Section 8.3.1), another area of state regulatory oversight is the protection of the privacy of patient health information. Public concern continues to rise about persons playing no role in an individual's medical care obtaining access to the individual's medical record. A particular concern exists that employers will use medical information in an adverse action against the employee or that members of the general public would discriminate against individuals if people knew of their medical conditions. In order to avoid those problems—or the mere perception of such problems—state regulators have proposed a myriad of standards for the processing and handling of medical records. Hospitals are required to adhere to these regulations, in addition to ensuring that members of a hospital medical staff and employees comply.

For privacy reasons, many states have recognized specific statutory protections for certain patient conditions. Hospitals therefore are required to process patient records and deal with patients in ways that minimize the possibility of misusing health information and medical records. Examples of this type of specific regulation of medical records and patterns of practice are the laws pertaining to the confidentiality of "highly confidential" information, such as that related to psychiatric treatment, substance abuse treatment or treatment of sexually transmitted diseases. Thus, although a hospital licensing statute in a particular state is normally the primary source of regulations of hospitals in that state, practitioners are well served to determine whether particular statutes governing records or treatment of particular illnesses or conditions also impose requirements on the operations of hospitals.

8.2.5 Construction of Facilities

Many states regulate development of hospital facilities and services through CON laws and regulations. Such regulatory frameworks, originally outgrowths of federal health planning initiatives that have long since expired, still continue in effect in approximately half of the states.

CON laws generally prohibit construction of new hospitals, addition of new hospital beds, establishment of major hospital services, acquisition of expensive medical equipment, or sale or transfer of ownership or control of a hospital without obtaining the prior approval of the state agency. Such laws also usually prohibit the cessation of services or the closure of a hospital without prior approval. CON laws and regulations are intended to protect the public from an oversupply of hospital services or unanticipated withdrawal of services that would unnecessarily escalate the cost of hospital care, as well as the entry of unqualified or financially unstable operators owning essential healthcare facilities within the state. CON regulations are extraordinarily complex and prescriptive. The process of administrative review and appeal often subjects these highly competitive projects to lengthy administrative and (on appeal) judicial proceedings. Any hospital in a state where CON laws still exist must be intimately familiar with the intricacies the system in their state before undertaking significant projects and those in the ordinary course of operations.

8.3 Federal Regulation

Federal regulation of general acute care hospitals was relatively limited until the federal Medicare program was established in 1966.[1] The program was established in order to promote the provision of nondiscriminatory, cost-effective, and cost-efficient services to Medicare and Medicaid beneficiaries. The Centers for Medicare & Medicaid Services (CMS), the agency responsible for Medicare and Medicaid regulation, oversight, survey and certification, has developed an incredibly complex series of regulations affecting almost every aspect of hospital operations.

In order to be eligible to bill the federal government for care provided to a Medicare or Medicaid program beneficiary, a hospital must first qualify as a provider in the program. As a program provider, a hospital must comply with the statutory Medicare Conditions of Participation for Hospitals (CoPs),[2] along with subsidiary and ancillary regulations of the Medicare and Medicaid programs. Although such participation in Medicare and Medicaid is voluntary, most hospitals realistically cannot exist without being providers under one or both of the programs, due to the number of patients who are beneficiaries of those programs.

---

1 42 U.S.C. § 1395.

2 42 C.F.R. Part 482.

Federal oversight of a hospital's compliance with the CoPs is exercised by state DPH surveyors or CMS Regional Office (RO) survey teams, either on a periodic basis or resulting from complaints made by patients or others. Surveyors will survey a hospital by reviewing medical records, conducting staff interviews and facility tours, etc., which will ultimately result in a report to the hospital of the state or CMS surveyor's findings (Statement of Deficiencies). Hospitals have certain regulatory timeframes in which to respond to the Statement of Deficiencies, depending in large part upon the severity of the findings, and must file a corrective action plan with the state and/or CMS (Plan of Correction). The Plan of Correction must address in detail the steps taken to come into compliance with the CoPs in order to avoid the ultimate penalty of termination of the hospital's provider agreement with CMS. In cases where surveyors identify an immediate threat to patient health and safety, also known as "immediate jeopardy," this termination can occur as soon as 23 days after the survey. In other cases, a longer 90-day termination track is imposed. Failure to timely submit an acceptable Plan of Correction, or failure to carry through on corrective actions set forth therein, could ultimately result in termination of the hospital's provider agreement that permits it to participate in Medicare.[3] As one could easily imagine, termination would have significant financial impact on the operations of almost any hospital.

The PPACA contemplates the establishment and ongoing maintenance of quality-related initiatives and metrics in almost every aspect of healthcare, and requires health plans and insurers, insurance exchanges, hospitals and other healthcare facilities, as well as physicians, to compile, report and receive payment adjustments related to quality metrics. While the parameters of these new processes are still being developed, it is expected that significant additional regulation will result from the PPACA as the 2014 implementation date draws closer.

8.3.1 HIPAA

The Health Insurance Portability and Accountability Act of 1996 (HIPAA)[4] established significant requirements governing the delivery and payment of healthcare and the protection of information concerning patients and their care. To implement HIPAA, the Department of Health and Human Services (DHHS) issued national standards or rules governing (1) the privacy of personal health information; (2) the security of personal health information; (3) electronic transactions and code sets; and (4) unique health identifiers for electronic transactions. HIPAA and these implementing regulations apply to all Covered Entities, which are defined as health plans, healthcare clearinghouses or healthcare providers, including hospitals, that transmit health information in connection with certain electronic transactions, such as claims and payment.[5]

One area of healthcare reform established by HIPAA is that of privacy of personal health information. On December 28, 2000, DHHS published its final HIPAA Privacy Rule[6] to provide the first comprehensive federal privacy protection for the privacy of health information by defining the circumstances and parameters under which Covered Entities may use or disclose personal health information.

---

3 Additional remedies short of termination are also provided for, and state law may also provide for the imposition of fines or other penalties where certain deficiencies are identified on survey.

4 Health Insurance Portability and Accountability Act of 1996, Pub.L. 104-191 (1996).

5 45 C.F.R. § 160.103.

6 45 C.F.R. §§ 160 and 164.

It covers all medical records and other individually identifiable health information used, maintained, or disclosed by a Covered Entity, without regard as to whether such dissemination is communicated electronically, on paper, or orally. In addition, the Privacy Rule establishes certain rights an individual has with respect to his or her personal health information.

The Privacy Rule met with a great deal of controversy (including the filing of a number of lawsuits challenging the validity and constitutionality of the Privacy Rule) and much public comment. Despite a number of healthcare, business, and charitable groups asking the Secretary of DHHS to delay implementation of the Privacy Rule and consider several key revisions, the rule became effective on April 14, 2001. Guidance[7] regarding the Privacy Rule was published by DHHS in July 2001, and final modifications to the Privacy Rule were published in August 2002.[8] Most Covered Entities were required to be in compliance with the Privacy Rule, as modified, as of April 14, 2003.

DHHS prepared a separate set of regulations governing the security of electronically transmitted healthcare data (Security Standards).[9] The final version of these Security Standards was published on February 20, 2003. The Security Standards require hospitals to undertake a wide range of activities designed to enhance the security of automated information. These measures include implementing physical security measures (*e.g.*, locked facilities) as well as software-security measures (*e.g.*, user authentication) and data-transmission protections (*e.g.*, encryption). Most hospitals were required to be in compliance with the Security Standards by April 21, 2005.

In 2009, the Privacy Rule and Security Standards were expanded by the Health Information Technology for Economic and Clinical Health Act (HITECH),[10] which was passed as part of the American Recovery and Reinvestment Act. Under HITECH, Covered Entities are required to notify patients when unsecured personal health information is the subject of a security breach. For larger-scale breaches involving 500 or more individuals, a Covered Entity must also notify the media. HITECH grants individuals expanded rights with respect to their personal health information and imposes additional restriction on the use and disclosure of personal health information.

A third set of HIPAA regulations, known as the Transaction and Code Set Standards,[11] pertains to the use of uniform electronic-data transmission standards for certain electronic administrative transactions, such as health plan enrollment or disenrollment, patient eligibility determinations, healthcare claims and payment transactions. These provisions were intended to reduce administrative costs by encouraging electronic communication in the healthcare industry. As of October 16, 2003, every healthcare provider was required to follow these standards when transmitting health information over electronic data interchanges (EDI). Most healthcare providers, health plans, and certain clearinghouses of healthcare information—including all hospitals, as Covered Entities under HIPAA—had to make significant changes to hardware, software, and operations to comply with the Transactions and Code Sets Rule.

---

[7] Available online at www.hhs.gov/ocr/hipaa/news2001.html.

[8] 67 Fed. Reg. 53182 (Aug. 14, 2002).

[9] 68 Fed. Reg. 8334 (Feb. 20, 2003).

[10] H.R. 1, S.1, American Recovery and Reinvestment Act of 2009, Health Information Technology for Economic and Clinical Act, §§ 13001 *et seq.* (Feb. 17, 2009) (codified at 42 U.S.C. § 3001(b)).

[11] 74 Fed. Reg. 3296 (Jan. 16, 2000).

In July 2003, CMS released guidance[12] on compliance with the Transactions and Code Sets Rule whereby CMS indicated that it would focus on obtaining voluntary compliance with the Rule, and use a complaint-driven approach for enforcement. CMS further indicated that Covered Entities would be given an opportunity to demonstrate compliance, and that CMS would consider Covered Entities' good-faith efforts to comply. Further, recognizing that Covered Entities would need their own contingency plans, CMS posted guidelines for such contingency plans for Covered Entities.

On January 16, 2009, DHHS announced that most Covered Entities would be required to implement an updated version of the transaction standards, known as HIPAA Version 5010, by January 1, 2012.[13] According to CMS, Version 5010 was created to address business needs surfaced by users and better address the data needed, collected and transmitted for electronic transactions. DHHS also announced that Covered Entities need to begin using updated diagnosis and procedure code sets, known as ICD-10, by October 1, 2013.[14] According to CMS, the new ICD-10 code sets improve on the prior code sets, by, for example, allowing new procedures and diagnoses to be more easily incorporated as new codes. If a hospital is unable to successfully implement these changes, then reimbursement of insurance claims could be disrupted. Any such disruption in reimbursement could have a material adverse effect on the financial condition of the hospital.

Finally, on January 23, 2004, CMS published the final regulations for the "Standard Unique Health Identifier for Health Care Providers."[15] This final rule amends the rule adopted in 2002,[16] and generally requires employers to use their tax-identification numbers as their identifiers. The final rule also establishes a national provider identifier (NPI) which is a unique 10-digit identification number that Covered Entities must use in certain standard administrative and financial transactions, such as healthcare claims. As of May 23, 2008, all Covered Entities must use an NPI for these standard transactions.

8.3.2 Treatment of Medical Emergencies

In 1986, Congress passed the Emergency Medical Treatment and Labor Act (EMTALA).[17] At its most basic, EMTALA requires Medicare-participating hospitals to medically screen all persons who present to the hospital for emergency care without delay, and to stabilize those with emergent conditions, regardless of the individual's ability to pay. EMTALA provides that, if an individual comes to the emergency department of a hospital and the individual requests (or a request is made on that individual's behalf) examination or treatment of a medical condition, then the hospital must provide an appropriate medical screening examination within the capabilities of the hospital. If the hospital determines that the individual has an emergency medical condition, then the hospital is further obligated to provide either necessary stabilizing treatment or an appropriate transfer.

[12] DHHS Office of Civil Rights, Medical Privacy—National Standards to Protect the Privacy of Personal Health Information, available online at www.hhs.gov/ocr/hipaa/index.html.

[13] 74 Fed. Reg. 3296 (Jan. 16, 2009).

[14] 74 Fed. Reg. 3328 (Jan. 16, 2009).

[15] 69 Fed. Reg. 3434 (Jan. 23, 2004).

[16] 67 Fed. Reg. 38009 (May 31, 2002).

[17] 42 U.S.C. § 1395dd; 42 C.F.R. § 489.24.

CMS has defined "hospital with an emergency department" to include only those departments that are operated as "dedicated emergency departments."[18] A dedicated emergency department refers to a specially equipped and staffed area of the hospital that is used a significant portion of the time for the initial evaluation and treatment of outpatients for emergency medical conditions. It can be located on the main hospital campus or off the main hospital campus. Examples of dedicated emergency departments include an emergency department, a labor and delivery department, an outpatient psychiatric department that provides drop-in evaluations, and off-campus urgent-care sites. Other off-campus departments of hospitals, however, are not obligated to comply with EMTALA obligations unless the location meets the definition of a dedicated emergency department.

Although EMTALA was enacted in response to concerns that indigent patients were being denied emergency care because of their inability to pay, violation of the statute does not require proof that a hospital refused treatment for economic reasons. EMTALA's purpose is to ensure that all patients receive medical care as soon as possible. Therefore, all hospital actions in the emergency room, even routine questions pertaining to financial information in the patient registration process, must be undertaken in a manner that is in full compliance with EMTALA and its implementing regulations.

EMTALA obligations are satisfied with respect to an individual who presented at a hospital for emergency services, was determined to have an emergency medical condition, and whose condition is stabilized as documented by relevant clinical data in the individual's medical record, even if the individual's medical condition later declines. Moreover, a hospital has no responsibility under EMTALA to an inpatient who is admitted for elective (nonemergency) diagnosis or treatment, even if such individual has an abrupt deterioration of her medical condition after admission. Rather, the general Medicare CoPs exist to protect inpatients.

In addition to a hospital's obligation to screen and stabilize individuals, EMTALA governs the emergent transfer of patients from one hospital to another. When a hospital emergently transfers a patient to another institution for care, it is required to document notification of the other institution prior to the transfer, obtain the signature of the transferring physician on a form attesting to the condition of the patient and the need for the transfer, among other details. Even in the event that a patient does not complain about a transfer or the receiving institution does not complain about a transfer, if the paperwork surrounding the patient's transfer is not accurately completed, and such deficiency is discovered upon a subsequent survey of the institution, that incomplete paperwork can be the basis for an allegation of a violation of the statute.

Other requirements under EMTALA include adoption and enforcement of written policies and procedures to ensure compliance with the statute, reporting obligations, posting of EMTALA-explanatory signage, record-keeping, and maintaining a central log and a list of on-call physicians.

With regard to maintaining a list of on-call physicians, on-call lists need to include, by name, the physician on call for a particular specialty. Every hospital must establish rules on how quickly a physician must respond to a page for emergency services and how quickly he or she must come to the emergency department if it is determined that the doctor's presence is necessary for the patient's screening

[18] 42 C.F.R. § 489.24(b).

or stabilizing treatment. Each hospital has the discretion to maintain the on-call list in a manner to best meet community needs. Physicians, including specialists and subspecialists, are not required to be on-call at all times; hospitals, therefore, must have policies and procedures to be followed when a particular specialty is not available or when the on-call physician is unable to come to the hospital.

8.3.3 Conditions of Participation and Compliance Programs

All healthcare facilities that participate in the federal Medicare program are required to comply with the regulations adopted by CMS to implement the program, including, for hospitals, the CoPs. As noted previously, hospitals that are determined to be operating outside of the CoPs, which may be determined through a state DPH or CMS survey, risk termination of their provider agreement with CMS.

During the 1980s, CMS became concerned that many hospitals and physicians were not complying fully with the CoPs. As a result, the government started to implement a program for healthcare that was similar to one which had been implemented in the defense industry: individual hospitals were required to have a compliance policy, a senior level committee responsible for compliance issues, and an individual who would be designated as the compliance officer. The intent of this initiative was to establish within a hospital a hierarchy of individuals whose primary purpose was to ensure that the organization fully complied with the CoPs and other federal laws.

This effort was augmented by the adoption of the Federal Sentencing Guidelines in 1991.[19] The Federal Sentencing Guidelines require a federal court to impose severe economic sanctions on an entity convicted of a criminal violation. The purpose of removing judicial discretion was to provide just punishment, adequate deterrence, and incentives for organizations to maintain internal mechanisms for preventing, detecting, and reporting criminal conduct. The Federal Sentencing Guidelines require the sentence to be based on the seriousness of the offense and the culpability of the defendant organization, as measured by significant factors such as whether high level personnel participated in or condoned the criminal behavior. A mitigating circumstance, however, is the presence within the defendant organization of an effective program designed to detect violations of law. In addition, if the defendant self reported the violation and cooperated in the investigation, then its "culpability score" is once again reduced. Reductions in a culpability score significantly reduce the amount of fines that can be assessed against the defendant organization.

Even though many hospital administrators considered their institutions to be attempting to comply with the federal rules, the Federal Sentencing Guidelines have led almost all hospitals to adopt compliance programs in accordance with guidelines for hospital compliance programs published by the Office of the Inspector General (OIG) of DHHS (Compliance Program Guidance for Hospitals).[20] Following the Compliance Program Guidance for Hospitals is not mandatory; despite this, however, most hospitals attempt to follow it as closely as possible. The presumption is that a fully functioning compliance program will minimize the possibility that the organization will violate federal law, and that, if such a violation were to occur, a fully functioning compliance program will mitigate the imposition of penalties. Moreover, private enforcement of healthcare fraud received a significant en-

[19] Available online at www.ussc.gov/2006guid/TABCON06.htm.
[20] 63 Fed. Reg. 8987 (Feb. 23, 1998), as revised 70 Fed. Reg. 4858 (Jan 31, 2005).

hancement through the 1986 amendments to the Civil False Claims Act,[21] which empowers private individuals to sue on behalf of the government through *qui tam* or "whistleblower" suits and receive a percentage of any recovery of monies by the federal government.

Implementation of an effective compliance program has become one of the more important regulatory realities for the hospital industry. All hospital executives must pay as much attention to compliance regulations as they dedicate to hospital licensing standards and complying with standards promulgated by accrediting bodies such as The Joint Commission. It is a simple reality that, if a hospital violates federal law, the OIG or a private whistleblower likely will cause the violation to be reported and/or discovered; further, if a conviction results, then subsequent penalties are likely to be imposed, which will be much more severe and restricting than they would have been if an effective compliance program had been in place.

8.3.4 Regulation of Medical Staff Disciplinary Procedures and Excluded Provider Verification

The Health Care Quality Improvement Act of 1996 (HCQIA)[22] was passed by Congress with the intent to offer healthcare institutions, including hospitals, a limited form of immunity if the institution performed credentialing actions regarding its medical staff in accordance with minimum due process procedures as set forth in statute and its implementing regulations.[23] As a result of HCQIA, hospitals include in their medical staff bylaws a process to permit medical staff members the appropriate period of time required by HCQIA (*i.e.,* 30 days) within which to respond to notices of adverse actions, to provide for the use of attorneys at disciplinary hearings, and to adopt other minimum standards for evidentiary decisions.

Another component of HCQIA was the establishment of a national repository for practitioner information, the National Practitioner Data Bank (NPDB). The NPDB was designed to afford hospitals and other entities associated with medical practitioners a means to find out information about the issues of patient care or professional competence such practitioners might have experienced at other institutions. The obvious intent was to make it difficult for poor quality practitioners to move from one institution to another without anyone knowing about their practice history. Because of the perceived negative impact on a healthcare practitioner as a result of a report filed in the NPDB, the ability to discipline a medical staff practitioner has moved from a somewhat collegial activity to one where the medical practitioner believes his or her career may be at stake—an escalation often resulting in heightened degree of activity among lawyers for the individual and the institution alike.

Hospitals are required to file a report with the NPDB in certain instances, for example, if there has been a "professional review action" (as defined by HCQIA) that is based on matters related to the professional competence or conduct of a medical practitioner which has adversely affected clinical privileges for a period longer than 30 days. In addition, if the practitioner voluntarily surrenders or agrees to a restriction of his or her clinical privileges while under investigation or in order to avoid an

---

21 31 U.S.C. § 3729.

22 Title IV of Public Law 99-660, 42 U.S.C. § 11101.

23 45 C.F.R. Part 60.

adverse professional review action, then the hospital also must report that action to the NPDB. Malpractice judgments and settlements are also reportable to the NPDB.

Hospitals are charged with reviewing the listing of individuals who have been sanctioned by the Medicare programs so that the hospital does not do business with nay individual who has previously been removed as a Medicare provider. Federal law authorizes the imposition of civil monetary penalties against healthcare providers and entities that employ or enter into contracts with excluded individuals or entities to provide items or services to federal healthcare program beneficiaries.[24] The basis of this restriction is the theory that an individual or entity found to have violated Medicare rules would be more likely to commit that action in the future. CMS has established a website listing the names of all such sanctioned individuals.[25] A Hospital is advised to check the listing each time it enters into a contract with an individual, begins an employment relationship, or grants medical staff privileges and annually thereafter. If the hospital allows a sanctioned individual to join or remain on its medical staff, to perform as its employee, or to serve as one of its contractors, the hospital can be subject to civil monetary penalties and/or removal from the Medicare program. Because of the seriousness of these penalties, hospitals have made it a part of their normal routine to verify the status of all individuals or entities as qualified providers under the Medicare program.

8.3.5 Regulation of Hospitals as Employers

In many communities, the largest employer is the local hospital and its related healthcare operations. As employers, hospitals are regulated much the same as any other business with employees. However, the specific laws and regulations that govern healthcare add an additional layer of complexity to hospital operations.

State law impacts how physicians and other licensed healthcare professionals are employed. In many states, the corporate practice of medicine (or, in some cases, other professions) doctrine limits the ability of corporations to directly employ licensed professionals. Exceptions are commonly provided for by law, for example, statutes explicitly permitting hospitals to employ physicians or other professionals as part of the hospital's purpose of providing healthcare, so long as the healthcare professionals are permitted to use independent medical judgment in providing care.

Moreover, and as described in greater detail below, hospitals may have a partially or completely unionized workforce, which brings special challenges. Hospitals have also been accused of anti-competitive behavior, and recently dozens of hospitals and healthcare systems were put on the defensive in wage and hour litigation brought by nurses who accused hospitals of colluding to set wages.

---

[24] Publication of the OIG Special Advisory Bulletin on the Effect of Exclusion From Participation in Federal Health Care Programs, 64 Fed. Reg. 52791 (Sept. 30, 1999).

[25] This website can be accessed by visiting www.npdb-hipdb.com/query.html.

8.3.6 Regulation of Unionization of Nurses and Doctors

Physicians are increasingly becoming employed by hospitals and hospital-affiliated medical groups, and those who are employed in this manner are eligible under the National Labor Relations Act (NLRA) to engage in collective-bargaining activities,[26] and physicians are increasingly becoming employed by hospitals and hospital-affiliated medical groups. Currently, most physicians who are represented by unions are interns, residents, or doctors employed by state or federal governments. However, with the increasing pressures on physician incomes, many physicians employed by private hospitals, medical schools, universities, ambulatory-care centers and other providers may be more receptive in the future to organizing efforts by various collective-bargaining organizations. During 1999, the American Medical Association voted to establish a collective-bargaining unit, and many state medical societies have established collective-bargaining units.

However, due to federal antitrust laws, self-employed physicians are not eligible to engage in collective bargaining with entities such as commercial health plans. Self-employed physicians are considered to be competitors of each other, and are not considered to be "employees" as defined under the NLRA. In addition, even among employed physicians, many individual physicians will not be eligible to join unions because they would be categorized as "supervisors" under the National Labor Relations Board (NLRB) rules. A supervisor is a person who can make hiring and other personnel decisions concerning other employees and who is entitled to use independent judgment in making those decisions. Other persons also will be deemed to be managerial employees (and thus also ineligible to join a union) if they participate in the formulation of the policies of the employing entity and if their status within the entity establishes an element of conflict of interest between employees of the entity and the employing entity.

If physicians were to organize on a general basis, then presumably they would seek to acquire some enhanced degree of control over their employment situations. Many physicians have indicated, however, that they would not seek to develop a union for the purpose of having the right to strike (and, therefore, refuse to deliver patient care services). However, any union of physicians would undoubtedly enjoy the legal right to strike, even if publicly the union indicated it would not.

Nurses and other categories of healthcare workers have been members of unions for quite some time. Their organizing efforts have not been without difficulty, however. In 2001, the U.S. Supreme Court held that registered nurses (RNs) are supervisors under Section 2(11) of the NLRA because their duties were conducted in the interests of the employer and used independent judgment in their job duties, even though the judgment involved the use of technical or professional judgment. In 2006, the NLRB decided three cases in which it redefined its test for determining supervisory status (creating new definitions for the terms "assign," "responsibly direct" and "independent judgment"), making it easier for an employer to demonstrate supervisory status of RNs.[27] Nevertheless, the issue is not entirely resolved, legislation to limit a finding of supervisory status has been proposed but not enacted, and the contest of this issue will continue.

---

[26] 29 U.S.C. § 151.

[27] *Oakwood Healthcare, Inc.*, 348 NLRB No. 27 (Sept. 29, 2006); *Golden Crest Healthcare Center*, 348 NLRB No. 39 (Sept. 29, 2006); and *Croft Metals, Inc.*, 348 NLRB No, 38 (Sept. 29, 2006).

Another issue that could affect organizing efforts among physicians and other healthcare professionals is the growing trend within the industry of outsourcing workers and "right-sizing" through the engaging of part-time or temporary workers. Anyone employed by an entity and then "leased" by that entity to another company is not an employee of the second company. Thus, persons with whom workers have day-to-day contact may not in fact be their fellow workers, which would make it difficult to establish organizing efforts.

Private healthcare institutions are subject to the NLRA, but most public healthcare facilities are excluded from such coverage. The NLRA imposes upon healthcare providers the obligation to bargain with their employees and with union organizers in good faith. In order to avoid a proliferation of bargaining units in hospitals, the NLRB has developed criteria pertaining to appropriate bargaining units in a hospital. There are eight such groups, made up of separate units for nurses, physicians, professionals other than nurses and physicians, technical employees, skilled maintenance employees, business office clerical employees, guards, and all nonprofessional employees (other than technical employees, skilled maintenance employees, and guards). These eight units are the only permitted bargaining units within a hospital. These units may, however, be combined in certain circumstances, including circumstances in which fewer than five employees are represented within a particular unit. These rules apply to hospitals whose average length of stay is less than 30 days, including general acute care facilities.

In addition to the NLRA, the federal Labor Management Relations Act[28] limits certain union efforts in connection with strikes and picketing. In particular, unions are required under this law to give a minimum of 10 days' written notice of an intention to strike or picket, because healthcare organizations need an adequate amount of time to make alternative arrangements for patients who might be adversely affected by a work stoppage.

8.4 Accreditation; Survey Activity

The Medicare program requires, as a basic premise, that all participating hospitals be organized and operated in a manner beneficial to their patients. This premise is sound, as CMS has a vested interest in paying only for an appropriate level of quality care for federal healthcare program beneficiaries. Hospitals demonstrate their compliance with the CoPs through the survey and certification process, either through state agency jurisdiction (where a state DPH surveys and maintains oversight of a facility on behalf of CMS) or through accreditation by an accrediting body with the ability to confer "deemed status"—in other words, that compliance with accreditation requirements is proxy for satisfying the CoPs.

Virtually all hospitals seek accreditation by an accrediting body CMS has recognized as having sufficient standards, policies, and personnel to perform an inspection of the hospitals and facilities and confer deemed status upon the hospital. The three accrediting bodies currently authorized by CMS to confer "deemed status" upon hospitals are The Joint Commission, the Healthcare Facilities Accreditation Program (HFAP, first formed to accredit osteopathic hospitals) and Det Norske Veritas (DNV). Compliance with the accreditation standards of The Joint Commission, in its *Comprehensive Accreditation Manual for Hospitals, The Official Handbook* (CAMH), or as set forth in the manuals

[28] 29 U.S.C. § 193.

of HFAP or DNV, as verified by survey, is the path to "deemed status." In addition, compliance with the standards of The Joint Commission, HFAP or DNV has become an accepted measure of quality within the industry and is typically included as one of the requirements of financing instruments used by hospitals to obtain necessary capital financing. Of entities that have deeming authority, The Joint Commission has been in existence the longest and continues to accredit a majority of the market, and as such is the focus of our discussion in this area.

The CAMH (and the manuals of HFAP and DNV) consists of thousands of individual standards describing virtually every aspect of hospital operations, from governance to the environment of care. Given the broad scope of accreditation, each hospital seeking to obtain or maintain accreditation typically assigns individuals to be responsible for maintaining compliance with the standards within their respective areas of responsibility. Most hospitals, by necessity, look upon compliance with the standards as an integral part of ongoing operations. Joint Commission accreditation expires no later than three years from the date of the last survey of the hospital, which is commonly referred to as the triennial survey.

The Joint Commission surveys hospitals on an unannounced basis to ensure that the hospital integrates standards compliance into daily operations, not only when a survey is expected. Pursuant to a policy change in 2010, hospitals are accredited in accordance with their CMS certification number (CCN, formerly known as the provider number). Specifically, related hospitals with separate CCNs will be surveyed and accredited separately; similarly, two or more hospitals that share a CCN that were accredited separately in the past are required to be surveyed and accredited as a single organization. Related entities and service providers may be surveyed as part of a hospital if there are Joint Commission standards applicable to such entity and there is organizational and functional integration between the related entity and the hospital.[29] Physician practices are also included where the practice is reported on the hospital's cost report as a provider-based practice and/or the physician is employed by that hospital and the practice is held out to the public as part of the hospital.[30] The Joint Commission communicates with accredited facilities primarily through a proprietary "extranet" site available to each accredited facility.

Triennial surveys by The Joint Commission are conducted in person, on-site at the hospital over the course of a week or more. Additional surveys may be triggered by complaints made to The Joint Commission by patients or healthcare providers. The Joint Commission utilizes a "tracer" methodology that follows care delivered to patients from admission to discharge as a means of reviewing all aspects of hospital operations and ensuring quality and compliance with standards at every step. Each survey also includes interaction with hospital leadership, a review of provider credentialing and privileging, reviews of the environment of care and Life Safety Code compliance, and additional interactions with hospital staff as the surveyors request. The results of the survey are compiled and scored by The Joint Commission, and shared with the hospital via the extranet site. If recommendations for improvement (RFIs) with standards compliance are made, hospitals must demonstrate and provide evidence of standards compliance (ESCs) for each RFI. The ESCs, which are to be submitted 45 to

[29] *See* 2010 Comprehensive Accreditation Manual for Hospitals (CAMH) at ACC-3.

[30] *See* CAMH at ACC-8.

60 days after the survey report is issued based on the severity of the RFIs, must specify in detail how the hospital came into compliance with the elements of the standard and measured its success with compliance.

Upon acceptance of the ESCs by The Joint Commission, the hospital will receive a decision of "Accredited", indicating that the hospital is fully accredited by The Joint Commission, allowing it to have deemed status. If the RFIs are not acceptable, there is a range of levels of accreditation below the "Accredited" level which provide the opportunity to come into compliance with additional action.[31] These levels may also be imposed where an accredited hospital is found to have ongoing or significant standards compliance issues via a complaint survey.[32] Mechanisms of review and appeal are provided through and until there is a determination of Denial of Accreditation.

Ongoing periodic performance review is an integral part of the triennial Joint Commission accreditation process, inasmuch as it focuses on assisting accredited facilities in remaining compliant with accreditation standards on a day-to-day basis. Further day-to-day monitoring of standards compliance is inherent in other Joint Commission guidelines, such as the reporting of sentinel events,[33] the performance of related root cause analyses,[34] and compliance with Joint Commission-established National Patient Safety Goals.[35]

In addition to visits from The Joint Commission, accredited hospitals also can anticipate unannounced visits by CMS Regional Office or state DPH surveyors (acting on behalf of CMS) to track compliance with the CoPs and to investigate complaints that a hospital may have violated the CoPs. If the CMS RO or state DPH identifies noncompliance with CoPs, an accredited hospital's deemed status is removed pending resolution, placing the hospital under the jurisdiction of the state agency on behalf of CMS rather than The Joint Commission. As with the RFI process, hospitals must clearly set forth and provide evidence of steps taken to come into compliance and to facilitate ongoing compliance in the post-survey period (as described in Section 8.3).

Once the Plan of Correction is accepted, accredited hospitals may be resurveyed on all CoPs and required to prepare additional Plans of Correction to address any additional deficiencies identified by the surveyors. Upon successful completion of the survey cycle, the hospital is returned by CMS to deemed status as conferred by The Joint Commission. The Joint Commission may elect to make a separate inquiry into resolution of the matter before deemed status is reinstated.

In summary, although this Chapter has only touched the surface of the regulations applicable to hospitals, each practitioner should be aware of the incredibly diverse and in-depth scope of federal and state regulation that may apply to such facilities. A full examination of all such regulations is simply beyond the intent of this Chapter.

---

[31] *See* CAMH at ACC-65-67.

[32] *See* CAMH at ACC-66.

[33] Defined by The Joint Commission as "an unexpected occurrence involving death or serious physical or psychological injury, or the risk thereof." *See* CAMH at GL-29.

[34] Which analyses are focused on identification of causative factors in any unusual occurrence, including sentinel events. *See* CAMH at GL-28.

[35] The National Patient Safety Goals provide standards and specific steps for hospitals to reduce errors and enhance patient safety at all stages of care. *See* CAMH.

9

Representing Physicians

Michael F. Schaff, Esquire*
Wilentz, Goldman & Spitzer PA

9.1 Introduction

As with other clients, it is important for attorneys who represent physicians to recognize characteristics attributable to most physicians. Generally, physicians are intelligent over-achievers who are extremely dedicated to their profession. The vast majority of physicians, however, do not think about or analyze business issues in the same way that business people traditionally do. Physicians have spent significant time in school studying to earn their degrees and, during that time, are usually isolated from the business world. This makes representing physicians different than representing most other individuals who own and operate small businesses. Additionally, the dynamics of a physician group are unique; one physician normally takes the lead in business decisions, and the other physicians are more interested in practicing medicine than running the practice's business. An attorney should take a *proactive* approach in representing physicians: recognizing the role of physicians as healthcare providers, counsel should be prepared to expend extra time to explain to their physician clients the ramifications of each scenario in order to effectively guide the physicians' practices and the resultant effect on their professional careers.

This Chapter is written for attorneys who do not have extensive experience representing physicians. The basic issues and concepts are laid out to give practical insight into the dynamics of physicians and physician groups. Attorneys with extensive experience in representing physicians may be better served by other Health Lawyers publications. Because the vast majority of physicians are currently employed in the private practice of medicine—and not in academia, research, or hospital employment—this Chapter focuses on representing physicians in the private practice of medicine.

9.2 Life Cycle of Physician-Practice Association

Most physicians in the private practice of medicine tend to follow a similar path through their career development. This path generally begins with association or employment with a practice, followed by ownership, and (hopefully) ends with retirement. Although this process appears to be simple, many issues arise in each phase that can trigger the need for the physician to retain an attorney.

---

* The author gives a special thanks to Glenn P. Prives, Esquire, an associate with his firm, who assisted with the update of this Chapter.

9.2.1 Overview

9.2.1.1 *Who is Your Client?*

Of key importance to the attorney representing physicians and physician practices is the question of "Who is your client?" The answer to this question will indicate the approach to take in creating and negotiating employment contracts for physicians. Attorneys who have recently commenced their practices are more likely to initially represent employed physicians individually, rather than the group itself. In this regard, this Chapter is geared to raising issues necessary for an attorney to advise an individual or employed physician.

9.2.1.2 *Who Can Employ a Physician?*

Unlike the situation inherent in the employment of unlicensed individuals, states regulate who can employ a physician. In some states, employment is regulated through the "Corporate Practice of Medicine Doctrine." The Corporate Practice of Medicine Doctrine varies from state to state, requiring physicians and their attorneys to review all relevant local laws and regulations governing the specific physician. Often, prohibitions regarding the Corporate Practice of Medicine Doctrine are set forth in the applicable licensure regulations for physicians (*see* Section 9.3.1). Some states strictly enforce the Corporate Practice of Medicine Doctrine, while others practically have abandoned it; the scope of the doctrine truly varies from state to state.

The Corporate Practice of Medicine Doctrine generally prohibits unlicensed individuals or entities from "practicing medicine." "Practicing medicine" may include the employment of certain healthcare professionals; the ownership of professional practices; and the provision of medical diagnoses, fee splitting, and/or the treatment or care of patients. These prohibitions can extend to, for example, the prohibition of ownership of diagnostic testing facilities by anyone other than a plenary licensed physician, and even may extend to the broad concept of "excessive influence" over physicians and their clinical judgment.

Historically, the Corporate Practice of Medicine Doctrine arose out of fear that laypersons and general corporations, driven to increase "bottom line" profits, would unduly influence physicians and their medical decisions, with the provision of possibly unnecessary healthcare (or too little care) as a result. The concern was that a business interest in profit would conflict with a physician's commitments to serve patients and provide the best treatment available. Thus, some jurisdictions prohibit physicians from splitting fees from professional services with unlicensed individuals or entities. Other jurisdictions may simply treat such activity as evidence that a professional is enabling an unlicensed person or entity to practice medicine.

Under the current law of many states, physicians cannot be employed by unlicensed entities, general business corporations, or general business limited liability companies (LLCs). Many states, however, allow a physician to form a professional corporation or LLC, which allows physicians to enjoy the limited liability protection of a corporation or LLC, except for limitation of a liability for their malpractice.

Regarding the restriction on employment of physicians, most states that follow the Corporate Practice of Medicine Doctrine provide exceptions that allow physicians to be employed by health maintenance organizations (HMOs) and other licensed facilities. In addition, licensed entities (*e.g.*, hospitals, fraternal organizations, and other state-licensed entities) may often employ physicians and other healthcare practitioners in limited roles. Physicians involved in nontraditional practices should be aware of any state law governing their particular entity's structure. In addition, states may differentiate between employment of physicians and employment of other healthcare practitioners of more limited license. Again, these exceptions, and the question of whether a Corporate Practice of Medicine Doctrine is effective in the state in which the physician will be employed, are state-specific and require individual research.

Although the Corporate Practice of Medicine Doctrine is often honored in its breach, violation of existing state law can result in the exclusion of a physician from the Medicare/Medicaid programs and other insurance programs. Therefore, even if the respective state does not strictly enforce or adhere to its Corporate Practice of Medicine rules or regulations, physicians should be careful to comply with any existing laws.[1]

9.2.2 Employment Contracts

Although employment agreements vary in complexity, certain general topics make up the substance of most physician-employment agreements. Attorneys representing physicians should look for the following items to be incorporated in any physician-employment agreement.

9.2.2.1 *Duties and Responsibilities*

It is important to understand what duties and responsibilities an employed physician will be required to perform for the employer. The employment agreement should delineate the work schedule (including night and weekend on-call duties); the requirement for staff privileges at certain hospitals or facilities; the location of the physician's employment; and specific responsibilities regarding supervision of nurses, clerical staff, and other physicians. The physician may be required to perform administrative functions. Under all circumstances, a physician's duties should be consistent with and commensurate with the position as a physician.

9.2.2.2 *Compensation*

Compensation of employed physicians varies widely depending on the area of specialty, years of practice, and geographic region. The employment agreement should specify both the amount and timing of compensation. Many employment agreements contain either a base compensation or a formula compensation based on productivity measures. In addition, many employment agreements provide for bonuses to employed physicians on the occurrence of certain events. It is important to ensure that these events are attainable, so physician clients can perform a proper analysis of the total compensation

---

[1] See *Patient Care and Professional Responsibility: Impact of the Corporate Practice of Medicine Doctrine and Related Rules and Regulations* (American Health Lawyers Association 1997), available online at http://www.healthlawyers.org/Template.cfm?Section=Home&Template=/ContentManagement/ContentDisplay.cfm&ContentFileID=3692.

package offered. Compensation formulas sometimes are very complicated; in practice, some may not work. In this regard, the agreement should include an example regarding the respective formula using expected numbers in order to avoid any confusion as to future interpretation.

9.2.2.3 *Benefits and Perquisites*

A significant portion of a total compensation package includes the perquisites (more often called perks) or fringe benefits that are granted to the employed physician. By structuring certain "perks" and fringe benefits separately from compensation, the employed physician may be able to save a significant amount of money in taxes, due to the fact that these benefits are generally not taxable if paid by the employer, but may be taxable income if the employer included them in compensation and the employee purchased these benefits separately. Key benefits include: continuing medical education reimbursement; payments for periodicals and subscriptions; beeper, car, or cellular telephone fees; automobile allowance; and health, life, disability, and malpractice insurance. Other benefits can include reimbursement of moving expenses, retirement plans, vacation, and disability/sick/maternity leave.

It is important to understand the distinction between "occurrence" and "claims made" malpractice insurance. Occurrence malpractice insurance covers the physician if she had insurance on the date the malpractice occurred, regardless of whether she has insurance on the date the claim is made. "Claims made" insurance covers the physician only if she has insurance on the date the claim is made. It is important to note that a physician who has claims made insurance will need to purchase a "tail" insurance policy to protect the physician and the practice from malpractice actions that occurred while employed and whose claim is made after the claims made policy lapsed. Tail insurance involves a significant cost, and it is important to spell out whether it is the employer's or employee's obligation to maintain such insurance upon termination.

While advising physicians of the total compensation package, attorneys should ask their clients questions to ascertain which benefits are most important to them. Making a list of types of benefits, and reviewing the agreement to see if those benefits are included, should be of great help. Be proactive; suggest types of benefits that may be of interest to the client, and ask the opposing counsel why a particular benefit has not been included. In many cases, employers may include that benefit without changing the employed physician's salary and/or bonus formula. Attorneys may also request that the employer pay for legal fees associated with review of the proposed agreement (an attempt that works about 20% of the time).

9.2.2.4 *Ownership Opportunities*

In assessing the merits of an employment offer, physicians generally consider the long-term relationship that will develop while associating with a specific practice. It is in the physician-employee's best interest to work out (in advance) the terms and conditions of any ownership opportunities in the practice. This includes not only the time at which the physician-employee becomes eligible for "partnership," but also the economic ramifications associated with becoming an owner, including any buy-in amounts, compensation, and buy-out obligations (*see* Section 9.2.3). The structure of a buy-in has unique tax consequences, and physicians should consult with their tax advisors regarding tax issues.

Many employers are reluctant to guarantee future ownership opportunities in an initial employment agreement. The physician client's interests can be protected by adding a simple paragraph that lays out the terms of ownership, indicates that these terms are only the current intentions of the parties, and emphasizes that neither party is bound by these provisions. Even if nonbinding, such a provision is important; most physicians tend to honor these written current intentions when "partnership" opportunities arise, due to the fact that a relationship usually develops between the employed physician and the employer over the course of employment.

It is also advantageous to build in a review process where the employer periodically reviews and advises the employed physician on whether the employed physician is on "partnership track." For further discussion of the specific terms associated with ownership, *see* Section 9.2.3.

9.2.2.5 *Term/Termination*

The employment agreement should have defined commencement and expiration dates. Whether a long- or short-term agreement is desirable depends upon the client's particular circumstances. Many agreements provide for an "evergreen clause," a provision allowing the contract to continually renew from year to year. This type of clause is generally advantageous from the employed physician's perspective; if an evergreen clause is inserted, however, the compensation section should provide for periodic increases or review of compensation.

In the absence of a specific provision in the agreement, employment is generally "at will" and can be terminated by either party without notice for any reason. In representing the employed physician, it is preferable to limit the employer's ability to terminate to specific causes. The agreement should include a notice provision, as well as the ability to cure any alleged default, breach, or cause in a reasonable period of time. The definition of "cause" is normally hotly negotiated, and its operational definition with respect to the agreement should be carefully reviewed to ensure that the client understands each of the reasons for termination for cause (*see* Section 9.2.3.3).

9.2.2.6 *Post-Termination Restrictive Covenant*

Employers generally incorporate a post-termination restrictive covenant in their employment agreements. These covenants generally include both noncompetition and nonsolicitation elements. They are designed to prevent the employed physician from competing with the employer in a particular geographic area for a specific period of time, and may also include a prohibition on soliciting patients, referral sources, and employees of the former employer.

To be legally enforceable, restrictive covenants in any form must be reasonable in scope and duration, must not be injurious to the public at large, and should not prohibit the employed physician from pursuing activities not engaged in by the employer. These provisions should be discussed at length and in a detailed manner with a physician client to ensure that, upon termination, the physician will retain the ability to practice medicine without major disruption.

In some instances, the employment agreement includes a pre-termination restrictive covenant prohibiting the employed physician from "moonlighting" or having other employment. This may not be important to a client, but it should be specifically addressed. Attorneys should also note that, in some states, a post-termination restrictive covenant is not enforceable, so applicable state law should also be reviewed.

9.2.2.7 *Other Issues*

Employment agreements also contain provisions dealing with recordkeeping, legal compliance, dispute resolution, assignability, notice, and many others that are not unique to physician-employment agreements. Although such items are not addressed here due to limitation of space, counsel should take care to account for these and similar measures.

9.2.3 Ownership

Most employed physicians strive to become owners in the medical practices where they work. Becoming an owner, in their eyes, means that they have "arrived." Similar to becoming a partner in a law firm, becoming an owner in a medical practice instills maturity and a sense of stewardship in physicians' careers. Depending on the specific medical practice, ownership has many meanings. Ownership can include the ability to assist with or make decisions, share in the profits or losses of the practice, and grant the physician equity and appreciation in the value of the practice.

9.2.3.1 *Buy-In*

As a physician becomes an owner of a practice, a significant number of documents may be used to evidence the buy-in. Documents may be labeled differently depending upon whether the practice is a corporation, an LLC, a partnership, or a sole proprietorship. Although the names of these documents will differ and the types of ownership that will be acquired have different names, they essentially have similar characteristics. These documents can include: (1) a purchase agreement for the ownership interest that takes the form of a stock, partnership, or LLC member interest (hereinafter referred to as a Purchase Agreement); (2) an ownership agreement (*e.g.*, a stockholders' agreement and bylaws for a corporation, a partnership agreement in a partnership, and an operating agreement for an LLC); (3) new employment agreements commensurate with being an owner; (4) termination pay agreements; and (5) other documents, depending on the business structure.

Of initial importance is the Purchase Agreement, whereby the physician employee becomes an owner in the practice. That document should specifically set forth the individual's ownership percentage, the purchase price, and the payment terms. Purchase Agreements generally provide significant representations and warranties by the seller and the practice, which disclose important information about the practice.

Typical representations and warranties may include disclosure of the assets owned and liabilities owed by the practice; whether the practice is in good standing in the state; that the practice has filed all required tax returns and paid all taxes; that entering into the Purchase Agreement does not and will not violate any agreements under which the practice may be obligated; and that the books, records, and tax returns of the practice reflect its business history.

Of particular importance to an employed physician buying into the practice will be a representation and warranty of the seller and the practice setting forth all transactions where the existing owners of the practice, their family, or friends are involved. For example, it is possible that the other owners of the practice (or their families or friends) own the facility where the practice is located and lease the space to the practice. In these instances, the rental value should be based on fair-market rent, not an inflated rent whereby the existing owners are funneling practice money into their (or their families' or friends') pockets. In addition, a representation and warranty should be included that all billing has been done in accordance with law.[2]

9.2.3.2 *Ownership Agreements*

Upon buying into a medical practice, the owners usually set forth rights and obligations as owners in an ownership agreement. Ownership agreements generally deal with two major issues: (1) control and management; and (2) transferability of ownership interests. The first major issue will be discussed in this section, and the second is discussed in Section 9.2.4.

Depending on the practice size and dynamics, control and management issues have a varying degree of importance. From a legal point of view, a group practice is managed by its officers, board of directors, or managers (depending on the legal structure of the practice). In reality, the management titles usually have no real importance (they often are based on seniority), and the functions and the responsibilities for each physician owner often are delegated based upon their ability. The legal significance of these positions, however, is important. Should a dispute arise between the owners of the practice, the managing positions assigned to the physician-client could have an impact as to what legal rights and recourse exist. For instance, specific rights inherent to the position of "president" will allow the president to hire or fire employees, absent any provisions or agreements to the contrary.

Typically, a practice will allow each owner to have an equal vote in the management of the practice. Nevertheless, voting may be based instead upon factors such as seniority, stock ownership, productivity, compensation, or any other factor the practice may deem relevant. It is important to ensure that clients understand the voting rights they obtain upon their buy-in, as well as the voting rights of the other owners.

In large practices, it is common to have an executive or management committee that is responsible for the day-to-day operations of the practice. In these circumstances, the executive or management committee may have the legal authority to make decisions on certain issues without receiving the input or consent of all of the practice's owners. The practice's documentation should set forth the powers of any executive or management committee. The executive and management committees typically have the ability to negotiate and execute managed-care contracts on behalf of the practice, physician hiring and discipline, check signing, determination of compensation, and other major administrative issues.

If physician-clients are concerned that the practice may make decisions and take certain actions without their consent, then minority-owner protection issues should be addressed. In these circumstances, certain actions should be delineated that require a supermajority (*i.e.,* above 51%, such as

[2] *See* Chapter 4.

75% or greater) or unanimous vote before they are taken. Examples of such actions might include purchasing equipment over an agreed-upon dollar amount, hiring new physicians or terminating employed physicians, obtaining loans on behalf of the practice, entering into related-party transactions, selling all or part of the practice, issuing ownership interests to new or existing owners, amending the practice's organization documents, or making a capital call (asking owners for more money).

Too often, and despite their clear importance, control and management issues are not discussed or set forth in ownership documents. In those instances, a majority vote controls. Once signed, these documents usually are "put in a drawer" and are not looked at again unless a problem develops. At that time, the client will be glad that her rights are spelled out and protected.

9.2.3.3 *Employment and Compensation*

Employment agreements for physician owners are similar to the employment agreements for associate physicians set forth in Section 9.2.2, but they differ in at least three major areas.

One difference between a physician owner's employment agreement and an associate's employment agreement comes in the area of compensation and fringe benefits. As an owner, the physician client should have a larger risk in the profits and/or losses of the practice, resulting in a base salary that is proportionally lower than total compensation; normally, the remaining amount is paid as funds become available via a bonus mechanism. Nonetheless, spelling out the ways in which compensation is determined and any bonus is calculated remains very important.

A second difference between employee agreements applicable to physician owners and those for physician employees is how each may be terminated by the practice. Generally, employment agreements for physician owners limit termination by the practice only for cause, while practices reserve the right to terminate non-owners without cause. Some physician-owner employment agreements, however, permit termination by the practice without cause by a vote of a supermajority vote of the shareholders (usually 75% or greater). This is an important distinction, because the applicability of a post-termination restrictive covenant may depend on the reason the employment is terminated; if employment is terminated without cause by the practice, then the restrictive covenant may not be germane.

Termination for cause can have either a broad or a narrow definition. The physician-owner will be wearing two "hats" in determining whether the definition should be construed broadly or narrowly. When wearing the "owner" hat, the physician owner may want a broad definition that would give the practice the ability to terminate other physician owners if required. When wearing the "employee" hat, the physician-employee may want a narrow definition that would limit the practice's discretion on termination. Because this inherent conflict does not permit both approaches, it is important to advise physician clients of this duality and the need to use a consistent approach. A new physician-owner should also review the existing physician owners' employment agreements to ensure that they are comparable to the employment agreement being signed. Termination "for cause" provisions include, but are not limited to, the following: termination for loss of license; regulatory violations (including federal, state, hospital, medical society); insubordination (or failure to comply with direction); criminal activities (embezzlement, drug possession, or use); damage to reputation of the entity (or moral turpitude); bankruptcy; inability to maintain malpractice insurance at standard rates; low productivity or hours; and/or the ineffective or incompetent practice of medicine.

A third difference may be in the definition of disability. Practices tend to compensate a physician-owner during disability for a longer period of time than an employed physician, and they allow physician-owners a greater period of time to recover prior to terminating their employment. These different standards for disability between owners and non-owners are prevalent in the medical community. The physician-client should analyze any differences to determine the impact of these changes on disability-insurance policies (*see* Section 9.2.4.3).

9.2.4 Retirement/Sale of Ownership Interest

The physician's life cycle of association ceases upon the occurrence of certain triggering events. These triggering events generally include death, disability, retirement, or termination of employment (whether with or without cause). Ownership agreements generally prohibit or restrict transferability of ownership interests. Thus, any attempt at voluntary termination will normally be deemed a breach of contract, as well as trigger an automatic offer to the remaining owners to purchase the offered ownership interests. Each triggering event has different ramifications with respect to buy out obligations, as well as any post-termination restrictions.

9.2.4.1 Valuation of Ownership Interests

A medical-practice valuation is comprised of three basic elements: (i) hard (tangible) asset valuation, which incorporates all the physical assets of the practice, including desks, chairs, medical equipment, computers, and other such items; (ii) accounts receivable, including the billings for services rendered that have not been collected by the practice (which are generally worth significantly less than their face value, because managed care has led to significant discounts from billed amounts); and (iii) "goodwill value," a nebulous term that basically reflects the going concern value of a practice, or the value of continuing the business. Depending upon the triggering event, different valuation approaches may be applicable.

Owners should discuss the value of the ownership interest, and they may wish to annually arrive at and confirm an "agreed value" for their ownership interest. This alleviates any argument as to the value of the interest when an owner leaves, but it may create other problems. The most typical problem arises when many years pass without any change in the established agreed value. To combat this, most ownership agreements provide that if the valuation is stale (*e.g.*, over 12 to 18 months old), then either party can reject the price. In those instances, an alternate valuation approach is generally laid out in the form of a formula value, which could either be a specific formula or an adjustment to the agreed price based on the change in the value of the assets since the date of the last valuation. These valuation approaches should be delineated to avoid any confusion or argument. It might be advantageous from a tax perspective for both the practice and the remaining owners to limit the valuation of the ownership interest to the net "book value" of the practice (the value of the hard assets, as set forth earlier), with the accounts receivable and the goodwill value incorporated in either a severance package or a termination pay or severance agreement. The tax analysis associated with these issues is beyond the scope of this Chapter; in this event, consultation with a tax attorney or accountant is recommended.

9.2.4.2 *Payment Terms and Collateral*

In any buy-out, the practice and remaining physician-owners would experience undue hardship if they were forced to pay a lump sum to the departing owner. Because of this hardship, most buy-out agreements provide for an extended payout with reasonable interest. Typically, these extended payouts are anywhere from two to 10 years, depending on the triggering event. If insurance funding has been obtained (*see* Section 9.2.4.3), then the insurance proceeds are paid up front, with the remaining amount (if any) payable over a period of 12 to 24 months, depending on the amount remaining. Any termination or severance payment that is deferred is generally represented by a promissory note, which may be guaranteed by the practice or the remaining owners. In general, promissory notes will include provisions concerning interest rate, payment terms, and default. Normally, a reasonable cure period regarding any default is included so that the outstanding principal does not accelerate upon default. The goal should be to represent this as an obligation and not as a "bank."

To create collateral for the promissory note and the future payment obligations, the typical buy-out includes a pledge of the ownership interest that was purchased, as well as the guarantees of the other owners or the practice, depending on who the purchaser is. In some instances, a security interest is granted on the assets of the company, which will act as additional collateral. In those instances, it should be noted that granting a security interest in the accounts and assets of the practice might have a negative effect on the practice's credit availability with other lenders. In these instances, a subordination agreement will be appropriate.

9.2.4.3 *Funding Buy-Outs with Insurance*

In some cases, it may be appropriate for the practice and the remaining owners to purchase life or disability buy-out insurance on each owner to fund a death or disability buyout. Any purchase of life insurance or disability buy-out insurance should be coordinated with the particular valuation approach chosen. The benefit of purchasing insurance is that the funds will be readily available on the occurrence of a triggering event, and neither the practice nor its remaining owner(s) will be burdened by an unexpected payout. Having insurance proceeds available also will ease the burden on any spouse of a deceased owner, because funds will be immediately available to pay a significant portion of the purchase price, and no negotiations in price will be necessary. Many types of insurance exist; some are quite complicated, so consultation with a reputable insurance agent is recommended.

One major issue regarding insurance is determining who bears the costs of the insurance policy: Determining whether the practice or the individual owners hold the policy, and who pays the premiums associated therewith, can have different tax consequences. Again, this issue should be analyzed with a tax expert to ensure that clients' economic interests are properly protected.

Many physicians become confused about the difference between disability-income insurance and disability buy-out insurance. Simply put, disability-income insurance is used to supplement the loss of base salary on account of disability. Usually, the insurance policy will not begin to pay lost salary for 30 to 90 days. If the physician pays the premiums with after-tax dollars, then the disability payments received by the disabled physician are generally tax-free. If these premiums are deducted by the practice, then generally the payments under the disability policy are taxable income when received by the disabled physician. Conversely, disability buy-out insurance provides a lump sum or periodic payment to fund the buyout of a physician's ownership interest in the practice upon the occurrence of the physician's permanent disability. It is important to review the definitions in the policies (and the ownership agreement) in order to maintain appropriate coverage.

9.2.4.4 Post-Termination Restrictive Covenant

Ownership agreements generally provide for a post-termination restrictive covenant similar to the restrictive covenant that an employed physician signs (*see* Section 9.2.2). The major difference in the buy-out situation is that the practice or the remaining owners are paying the departing owner for the value of her interest in the practice, which may include an amount for goodwill. Whenever a goodwill payment is made, it is reasonable to require the departing owner(s) to restrict their practice so that the remaining owners and the practice actually receive the value paid on account of the goodwill. In these instances, it is typical for the duration of the restrictive covenant to be expanded by a few years, or be parallel to the payout term under the buyout. In many cases, if there is a breach of the restrictive covenant, then the buy-out payments cease, and monies paid under the buyout must be returned. Post-termination restrictive covenants generally have longer durations, and greater restrictive areas, than restrictive covenants for employed physicians. Sometimes the departing physician-owner may waive out of a restrictive covenant by paying an agreed-upon amount or giving up a portion of the total buy-out amount. This issue is often hotly negotiated.

9.2.4.5 Breaking Up/Dissolution

Many ownership agreements provide that if the owners are not getting along, the practice will dissolve or "break up." The following three issues are of key importance in any dissolution or break up: (i) the future use of the office location; (ii) the use of the telephone number; and (iii) possession of patient charts. In many cases, the most senior owner retains the right to use the office location and telephone number without having to pay for them, because the senior owner is often the "founder" of the practice, and it could be inequitable for the younger owners to receive the benefit of the established locale and phone number. In many cases, however, the telephone can be answered by a "phone intercept." A typical phone intercept is a service (*i.e.,* voicemail) that either directs callers to a new phone number for the physicians or directly connects the caller to an individual physician's office. For example, the phone intercept message might be, "If you would like Dr. Jones, please press 1; for Dr. Smith, please press 2; for Dr. Green, please press 3."

Phone intercepts help avoid potential future conflict as to whether a caller was given the appropriate locale or telephone number of the departed physician(s). Typically, patient charts follow the physician who will continue to perform services for the patients.

In many instances, the assets of the practice are divided based upon their value and the ownership percentages of each owner. It is important that the practice is represented by an accountant who is trusted by each of the physicians to coordinate the economics of the dissolution. Each physician also may wish to obtain individual representation by attorneys and/or accountants to ensure that her individual interest is represented.

9.3 Licensure and Credentialing

Although matters surrounding employment and ownership of physician practices are important, a more basic and crucial area to consider when representing physicians is licensure and credentialing. Every physician must be licensed in order to practice medicine in every state in which the physician renders medical care. In addition, most physicians maintain specialty and sometime subspecialty certifications conferred by private accrediting boards, and are required by regulation to do so in order to promote themselves as specialists. Certification in a relevant specialty is also often required in order for the physician to maintain admitting privileges at hospitals or other facilities. This section will discuss these and related issues.

9.3.1 State Licensure Law

Every state has standards governing the licensure of healthcare professionals that create a minimum competency level for each healthcare practitioner in the state. The licensure laws ostensibly ensure quality of care in the medical profession. Healthcare practitioners can be penalized for practicing in states in which they are not licensed, or for practicing outside the scope of their respective licenses. Medical doctors and doctors of osteopathy generally have "plenary" licenses, which enable them to perform services in virtually any field of medicine in the states in which they are licensed. Because licensure is state-specific, attorneys representing physicians must be careful to check the laws and regulations of the states in which their clients are practicing medicine.

The laws of several states do have some universal features, however, such as the creation of boards or agencies to oversee medical professionals (*e.g.*, a Board of Medical Examiners, Board of Chiropractic Examiners), a definition of "practicing medicine," educational and professional training pre-requisites and examination requirements for becoming licensed to practice medicine and continuing education requirements to maintain licensure, and delineation of behavior that can result in the imposition of sanctions, such as loss or suspension of a license. States usually have standards governing the admission of physicians who have been trained in foreign countries.[3]

Many states' laws restrict the business structure of physician practices by explicit regulation or under the "corporate practice" doctrine, which generally holds that when a business entity (such as a corporation or limited liability company) that does not hold a professional license employs or otherwise engages a licensed physician or other licensed professional to perform professional services on its behalf, the *entity* is engaged in the unlicensed practice of the profession. In states where the "corporate practice" doctrine is applied, only certain types of entities, such as professional corporations or partnerships owned only by licensed professionals, and hospitals or other types of licensed healthcare facilities, may employ or otherwise engage professionals to perform professional services.

State-by-state physician licensing requirements sometime conflict with recent developments in technology and the medical economics—such as the advent of telemedicine,[4] the national standard

---

[3] For a more in-depth discussion of licensure, *see* Scott Becker, *Health Care Law: A Practical Guide*, Chapter 17 (Mathew Bender 2d ed. 2001).

[4] *See* Section 9.5. For a more in-depth discussion of telemedicine, *see* Tara Kepler, *Telemedicine*, Chapter 3 in *Representing Physicians*, Second Edition (American Health Lawyers Association 2009).

of care now applied to physicians, and the trend toward larger group practices—creating barriers to practicing medicine in an increasingly managed care oriented and technological world. For instance, telemedicine may be construed as "practicing medicine across state lines." This raises the question of whether physicians can be said to practice medicine in states in which they are not physically present. Many states allow interstate consultations without licensure in the particular state, especially for highly specialized areas of medicine, but individual state laws vary on this point. In addition, large physician groups are becoming more common as physicians realize that they have increased bargaining power in greater numbers. In areas such as the tri-state area of New York, New Jersey, and Connecticut, for example, it is not unusual for patients to cross state lines for care; the next logical step is that group practices likewise will cross state lines. Under the current status of licensure, each of the physicians in the group may need to be licensed in each state in which the group practices or advertises its services. Attorneys representing physicians in multi-state practices must be familiar with the licensure laws in each state to adequately protect their physician clients.

9.3.2 Reports to the National Practitioner Data Bank

The National Practitioner Data Bank (NPDB) is a centralized system that was established by the Health Care Quality Improvement Act of 1986 (HCQIA).[5] Originally, only certain actions taken against physicians were to be reported to the NPDB, including revocation or suspension of a license by a state medical board (including censure, reprimand, or surrender of a license due to reasons related to professional conduct or competence), medical-malpractice claims paid by malpractice-insurance companies, peer-review actions that result in suspension of at least 30 days, and resignation during a peer-review action that is related to the peer-review action. Failure to report such actions may result in sanctions.[6]

Nonetheless, in addition to the NPDB, the secretary of the Department of Health and Human Services (DHHS) also maintained the Healthcare Integrity and Protection Data Bank (HIPDB) to which federal and state government agencies and health plans were required to report the following final adverse actions to the HIPDB:

- civil judgments in federal or state court against a healthcare provider, supplier, or practitioner related to delivery of healthcare;
- criminal convictions against a healthcare provider, supplier, or practitioner related to delivery of healthcare;
- actions by agencies responsible for licensure and certification of healthcare providers, suppliers, or practitioners;
- exclusion from a federal- or state-funded healthcare program; and
- anything else the secretary of DHHS establishes by regulation relating to final adverse actions taken against healthcare practitioners, providers, and suppliers.[7]

---

5 *See* 42 U.S.C. §§ 11101 *et seq.*; NPDB Fact Sheet, available online at http://www.npdb-hipdb.com/factsheet.html.
6 42 U.S.C. §§ 11131, 11132, 11133.
7 42 U.S.C. §§ 1301 *et seq.*

Recognizing that there was some overlap between the NPDB and the HIPDB, two developments occurred in 2010 that drastically affect the maintenance of the two databases. The first of these took effect on March 1, 2010. As of that date, all licensure actions taken by state licensure authorities that were a result of a formal proceeding against all healthcare practitioners—not just physicians and dentists—and all healthcare entities must now be reported to the NPDB. Additionally, peer review organizations and private accreditation entities (if they have due process mechanisms) will report certain "negative actions or findings" to the NPDB, if taken as the result of a formal proceeding against a healthcare practitioner, physician, dentist, hospital or other healthcare entity.[8] Peer review organizations are groups of organizations staffed by local practicing physicians that were established by the Tax Equity and Fiscal Responsibility Act of 1982 to evaluate the quality, necessity, cost, and adherence to professional standards of medical care provided to Medicare patients as a prerequisite for payment of the medical services by Medicare. A private accreditation entity is an entity or organization that:

- evaluates and seeks to improve the quality of healthcare provided by a healthcare entity;
- measures a healthcare entity's performance based on a set of standards and assigns a level of accreditation;
- conducts ongoing assessments and periodic reviews of the quality of healthcare provided by a healthcare entity; and
- has due process mechanisms available to healthcare entities.

A "negative action or finding" includes:

- a final determination of denial or termination of an accreditation status from a Private Accreditation Entity that indicates a risk to patients' safety or quality of healthcare services;
- a recommendation by a Peer Review Organization to sanction a healthcare practitioner, physician or dentist; or
- a negative action or finding that under the state's law is publicly available information and rendered by a licensing or certification authority, including, but not limited to, limitations on the scope of practice as well as "liquidations, injunctions, and forfeitures."

Entities that have access to the NPDB have always included licensing boards, hospitals, and HMOs that have, or may have, a relationship with the physician. Additionally, effective March 1, 2010, several government agencies, including those administering federal and state healthcare programs, federal and state law enforcement officials and agencies, and state Medicaid Fraud Control Units now have access to the NPDB.[9] Hospitals may now self-query themselves as well.

The second major development affecting the NPDB occurred due to the passing of the Patient Protection and Affordable Care Act (PPACA) on March 23, 2010. Pursuant to Section 6403 of the PPACA, the HIPDB will be terminated and all of the data in the HIPDB will be transferred to the NPDB. Further, the DHHS will now maintain a national healthcare fraud and abuse data collection

[8] *See* National Practitioner Data Bank for Adverse Information on Physicians and Other Health Care Practitioners: Reporting on Adverse and Negative Actions, 75 Fed. Reg. 4,656 (Jan. 28, 2010) (amending 45 C.F.R. Pt. 60).
[9] *See* National Practitioner Data Bank, 75 Fed. Reg. 4,656.

program for reporting certain adverse actions taken against healthcare providers, suppliers, and practitioners, These actions will also be reported to the NPDB.[10] Regulations implementing these changes have not been proposed as of the date of this publication.

Patients do not have access to the NPDB, but it is presumed that hospitals have checked the NPDB when they have admitted doctors to the medical staff. In limited circumstances, however, an attorney for an injured patient (or a patient representing herself) may obtain information from the NPDB and use this information to show that a hospital was negligent in granting privileges to a physician who was involved in the patient's care.

Once a physician has been reported to the NPDB, the physician can find it very difficult to obtain employment elsewhere. A letter, censure, or reprimand in a peer-review action thus may be preferable to disciplinary action, because such reprimands are not reported to the NPDB. Physicians often challenge reports to the NPDB, and a formal process exists for disputing reports.[11]

9.3.3 Exclusion from Medicare/Medicaid

Physicians who receive reimbursement for their professional services from Medicare and/or Medicaid must comply with the federal laws and regulations regarding submission of claims and prohibitions against fraud and abuse.[12] Violation of these laws can lead to exclusion from the Medicare and Medicaid programs, as well as other federally funded programs. As a result, no federal healthcare program payments will be made for any items or services (i) furnished, whether directly or indirectly, by the excluded person or entity or (ii) directed or prescribed by an excluded physician when the person furnishing the item or service knew or had reason to know of the exclusion.[13]

The Office of the Inspector General (OIG) of DHHS released a Special Advisory Bulletin on September 28, 1999, stating that healthcare providers will be held responsible for excluded employees or contractors and that they must determine whether potential and current employees and independent contractors have been excluded from Medicare and/or Medicaid.[14] The general rule is that no federal funds can be used to pay an excluded individual or entity in any way, regardless of whether the funds pay salary, expenses, perquisites, or other benefits, or whether the excluded individual or entity provides direct patient care. Thus, an employer who employs or contracts with an excluded entity or individual must ensure that all payments derive solely from nonfederal funding, and that all services performed are for nonfederal program patients.

---

[10] *Id.*

[11] *See* 45 C.F.R. § 60.14 regarding disputing reports.

[12] *See* Chapters 3 and 4.

[13] 42 C.F.R. § 1001.1901.

[14] *See* DHHS OIG Special Advisory Bulletin, *The Effect of Exclusion from Participation in Federal Health Care Programs*, Sept. 28, 1999, available online at http://www.oig.hhs.gov/fraud/docs/alertsandbulletins/effected.htm. The OIG was established as a part of DHHS to identify and eliminate fraud and abuse in DHHS programs, which the OIG does by auditing, inspecting, and investigating healthcare providers. The OIG is responsible for periodically issuing special advisory bulletins, in addition to advisory opinions (which are in response to specific queries) to provide guidance about fraud and abuse issues to the healthcare industry. These advisories are designed to help prevent fraud and abuse and to promote ethical use of the federal funding systems.

In addition to the ability to exclude individuals and entities from federal-program payment, the OIG's power also extends to imposition of civil monetary penalties (CMPs) against excluded individuals or entities that seek reimbursement, including entities that employ or contract with the excluded individuals or entities for provision of services under federal programs after being excluded.[15] Penalties can run as high as $10,000 for each item or service provided by an excluded entity or individual; further, the responsible party can be held accountable for treble the amount claimed. Thus, physicians and physician groups must be very aware of the employees and independent contractors they hire, and be cautious when merging with other physician group practices.

The OIG's exclusion power and authority to impose CMPs on providers was greatly expanded by the PPACA.[16] Although the specific expanded circumstances in which the OIG may wield this power is beyond the scope of this Chapter, it is important how expansive and devastating to the bottom line exclusion can be. Further, states, as the administrators of Medicaid, now have limited exclusion authority as well. Section 6501 of the PPACA requires states to terminate providers or individuals from Medicaid upon their termination from Medicare or another state's Medicaid program, with certain exceptions.[17] Also, Section 6502 requires state Medicaid agencies to exclude providers or individuals from participation in Medicaid for a period of time if they own, control or manage an entity that: (i) has failed to repay overpayments; (ii) has been suspended, terminated or excluded from any Medicaid program; or (iii) is affiliated with an entity or individual that has been suspended, terminated, or excluded.[18]

9.3.4 Medical Staff Privileges—Credentialing and Other Concerns

Either by employment contract or by necessity, physicians are generally required to be members of the medical staffs of hospitals or other healthcare facilities (*e.g.*, ambulatory surgery centers or nursing homes). The medical staff is a group of physicians who are permitted to treat patients in, and admit patients to, a particular hospital or healthcare facility. Not every physician can become a member of a particular facility's medical staff; the physician must first apply to become a member and undergo a review process. The medical staff, acting as a body in accordance with its own bylaws and regulations, has responsibilities with regard to care provided to patients at the facility, including making recommendations to the facility concerning granting, revoking, and restricting medical staff memberships and clinical privileges.

The term that comes up most often when discussing medical staffs is "credentialing." Medical staff credentialing is used to refer to both the initial review of an application to obtain medical-staff privileges and the ongoing review of the ethical and professional conduct of the members of the medical staff. Medical staff credentialing is thus a form of licensure in that it creates parameters that must be met in order for physicians to function within a particular facility.

---

[15] The OIG website contains a List of Excluded Individuals/Entities for healthcare providers to query in order to avoid potential liability. *See* http://oig.hhs.gov/fraud/exclusions/listofexcluded.html.

[16] *See* Pub. L. No. 111-148 §§ 6402, 6406(c), and 6408(a).

[17] *Id.* at § 6501.

[18] *Id.* at § 6502.

Medical staff credentialing is a sensitive area that often leads to litigation, as it can prevent physicians from accessing hospitals and other essential healthcare facilities; further, it can lead to malpractice suits for hospitals (and for physicians, if physicians are not appropriately credentialed). Thus, courts will review denial of access to medical staffs, but the courts are split on what degree of review is appropriate. One view is that courts should only review the procedural aspect of the medical staff's bylaws to ensure that the procedure was followed.[19] The other view, however, will review both the procedural aspect of the denial of privileges and the substantive aspect (*i.e.*, whether it was fair to deny privileges).[20] The case law in this area varies from state to state; attorneys representing physicians in credentialing actions must be aware of the standard for review in their respective states.

If a denial or revocation of medical-staff privileges does not follow the proper procedures set forth in the medical staff's bylaws, then courts will require the facility to follow its own bylaws, even if the entity is private. It is important to note, however, that courts are deferential to the medical judgment exercised in peer review, and that patient care is considered the realm of the healthcare facility and the members of the medical staff, rather than that of the courts.

Employment contracts often spell out the medical staff privileges that a physician-employee is expected to maintain, and termination of employment can sometimes be based upon loss of medical staff privileges. Therefore, it is important for physicians and their attorneys to have an understanding of the bylaws at the hospitals and other healthcare facilities in which the physicians have staff privileges. In that way, in the event credentialing issues arise, attorneys and their clients are properly prepared to challenge any action that could realistically affect the rest of the physicians' careers.

9.4 Reimbursement Issues

The term "reimbursement" is used to denote payment to physicians or other healthcare providers in exchange for their services, equipment or supplies. Reimbursement comes from a variety of payors: (i) patients may pay privately; (ii) private insurance companies may pay on a traditional fee-for-service basis; (iii) managed care companies may pay capitated rates to physicians each month; or (iv) federal programs such as Medicare and Medicaid may reimburse physicians for their services based on a complex calculation called a resource based relative value scale (RBRVS) fee schedule.[21] In common jargon, reimbursement is often specifically associated with payments from Medicare and Medicaid. Chapter 3 of this book discusses Medicare and Medicaid in more detail; this Chapter addresses basic reimbursement issues facing physicians.

9.4.1 Problems in Reimbursement

Historically, patients either paid privately for physicians' services or they obtained fee-for-service insurance that paid physicians a discounted rate for any services rendered to a member of the insurance plan. The advent of HMOs and managed care contracting has changed the way physicians are paid for their services. Instead of payment per patient visit, certain physicians (*e.g.,* general practitioners) are

---

19 *See generally Mahmoodian v. United Hosp. Ctr., Inc.,* 404 S.E.2d 750 (W.Va. 1991).

20 *See generally Nanavati v. Burdette Tomlin Mem. Hosp.*, 107 N.J. 240, 526 A.2d 697 (N.J. 1987).

21 *See* Chapters 3 and 4 for further information on federal reimbursement issues.

paid on a capitated basis, which usually means that they receive a flat fee each month based upon the number of patients that he or she treats in a particular health plan (regardless of the actual number of patient visits). Thus, physicians have been forced to bear the risk in managed care contracting, whereas in traditional fee-for-service insurance, the insurance companies bear the risk of patients' illness and cost.[22]

The result is that physicians have been forced to find ways to service the large number of patients that managed care organizations (MCOs) send to them, while still earning enough money to remain in the profession. In furtherance of that, physicians have been finding ways to collaborate in order to negotiate with MCOs and reduce the bargaining power held by the MCOs. One method for cooperation is called horizontal integration, in which groups of physicians have formed service organizations. Another method, called vertical integration, also has occurred, in which hospitals and physicians work together in order to improve efficiency and create more complete packages to MCOs. An examination of the variations of such arrangements is too complex to explore in this discussion, so this section will only address two of the most common horizontal-integration relationships.

Many states have laws regarding payment by traditional insurers and MCOs that delineate the amount of time payors may take to reimburse physicians for their services. Each state's laws differ, so attorneys representing physicians must be aware of the laws and regulations in their jurisdictions so that they know how to answer the inevitable question of "When do I get paid?"

9.4.2 Independent Practice Associations

An independent practice association (IPA, also sometimes called an independent provider association or independent physician association) is an entity that is created and owned by physicians and/or physician groups practicing independently. The primary purpose of an IPA is to contract with MCOs. IPAs differ from group practices in that the physicians in the IPA do not combine their practices and do not necessarily contract solely through the IPA. IPAs may negotiate the terms and conditions of MCO contracts, as well as other third-party payor contracts, on behalf of the members of an IPA and process the claims for services performed by members of the IPA.

IPAs can have different structures and levels of commitment by the physicians and physician groups involved. Many IPAs are "messenger model" IPAs, which means that the IPA acts as a messenger system to broker contracts for the members of the IPA; each physician in the IPA then independently decides if the terms of the contract are acceptable. The messenger cannot coordinate the responses of the IPA physicians, communicate their decisions to other physicians in the IPA, or enable the providers to collude in entering into contracts. Such actions will raise serious antitrust concerns.[23]

There are also disadvantages to joining an IPA. Attorneys representing physicians must help their clients to also consider the ramifications of being part of an IPA before joining one. The fact that an IPA itself contracts with a payor for Medicare and/or Medicaid reimbursement can affect a physician's

---

22 *See* Chapter 7 for more information on insurance and related issues.

23 *See* U.S. Department of Justice and Federal Trade Commission, Statements of Antitrust Enforcement Policy in Health Care (Aug. 1996). Additionally, *see generally* David Marx Jr. and James H. Sneed, *Antitrust and Healthcare: Meeting the Challenge*, Second Edition (American Health Lawyers Association 1998).

individual status with Medicare and Medicaid. For instance, a physician's individual levels of reimbursement from Medicare and Medicaid can be affected by membership in an IPA. In addition, IPAs are often less efficient than group practices in terms of overhead costs and other administrative issues, which can lead to the failure of the IPA if the physicians involved are unable to see the long-term benefits. Also, if physicians render more services to the patients of an IPA than to their own patients, then they may be considered employees (as opposed to independent contractors) of the IPA by the Internal Revenue Service.[24] IPAs can run into antitrust problems if a large number of physicians from a geographic location participate in the IPA.[25] Attorneys should also be alert to "most favored nation" clauses, which require providers in the IPA to accept as full reimbursement the lowest amount paid by any patient of the provider. Such clauses are now frowned upon by federal agencies because they raise antitrust concerns; these clauses are seen as restraints on natural price competition. Although IPAs may assist physicians in building or maintaining a patient base, these and other issues must be raised so that physician-clients understand the issues associated with joining an IPA.

With the passage of the PPACA and associated statutes and regulations, IPAs may have new life breathed into them as they may become integral components of Accountable Care Organizations, as discussed further in Section 9.7.

9.4.3 Unionization

The predominance of managed care in the medical industry has created a renewed interest in physician unions and the potential bargaining power they promise. It is important to understand that only employed physicians (meaning physicians employed by hospitals or other healthcare entities) can consider unionization; self-employed physicians may not unionize, as it is considered a violation of the antitrust laws. Thus, the same physicians who lack bargaining power and/or protection from MCOs are the ones who cannot unionize or bargain collectively with healthcare plans. The American Medical Association's policy is to seek changes in the law to expand physicians' ability to negotiate collectively with payors.[26]

Some states are beginning to pass laws that allow physicians to collectively bargain with insurance companies. For example, New Jersey passed legislation permitting physicians to bargain collectively with payors under limited circumstances.[27] Movements have begun to alter federal law in order to allow unionization and/or collective bargaining by physicians with MCOs and other healthcare plans.

---

[24] *See generally* Bruce John Shih, *Healthcare Transactions: A Guide to Mergers, Acquisitions and Integration* (American Health Lawyers Association 1998).

[25] For more information on antitrust issues in healthcare, *see Statements of Antitrust Enforcement Policy in Health Care*, U.S. Department of Justice and the Federal Trade Commission, issued Aug. 1996.

[26] *See* American Medical Association (AMA) Policy, H-385.973, H-385.976. The AMA does not advocate withholding patient care in order to gain bargaining leverage. *See id.* at H-405.998.

[27] N.J. Stat. Ann. §§ 52:17B-196 *et seq.*

9.5 Telemedicine

Telemedicine is a broad term that has no universal definition. The Institute of Medicine has defined it as the use of electronic information and communications technologies to provide and support healthcare when distance separates participants. This can include electronic transmission of medical images, video conferencing, and dispatching information to a distant—often otherwise unreachable—location. The Centers for Medicare and Medicaid Services (CMS) defines telemedicine as "multimedia communications equipment that includes, at a minimum, audio and video equipment permitted two-way, real-time interactive communication between the patient and distant site physician or practitioner. Telephones, facsimile machines, and electronic mail systems do not meet the definition of an interactive telecommunications system."[28]

As mentioned earlier, the use of telemedicine may be considered to be practicing medicine across state lines. An attorney representing a physician practicing via telemedicine should review interstate licensure laws and regulations associated with telemedicine and the practice of medicine across state lines. Many states allow interstate consultations, especially for highly specialized areas of medicine, but individual state laws must be consulted.

Malpractice is a concern with respect to the use of telemedicine. Many related interstate issues remain largely unresolved, including whether a physician/patient relationship exists, the standard of care to be applied to telemedicine relationships, and which state's law would apply in the event of a malpractice suit. These issues are compounded by the undefined nature of telemedicine, and that a simple telephone call across state lines could violate licensure regulations. A related sub-issue is whether malpractice insurance would cover physicians practicing medicine in state A to reach a patient in state B (or in another country) via telemedicine. These issues are worthy of consideration for a client who practices telemedicine.

Additionally, questions arise as to whether medical practitioners will be reimbursed; if they will be reimbursed, a related question is whether they will be able to bill payors for services that the physicians provide via telemedicine. Telemedicine seems to qualify as a consultation; with evolving technology, however, it could also involve readings of diagnostic tests and even more-direct patient treatment. Insurance companies do not encourage experimental procedures; telemedicine could easily be rejected for that reason, or as being simply too expensive to cover. Generally, Medicare covers consultations, office and other outpatient visits, individual psychotherapy, pharmacological management, psychiatric diagnostic interview examinations, and end stage renal disease services delivered via telecommunications systems.[29] Such coverage is subject to strict requirements before payment may be made.[30]

The confidentiality of health information involved in the practice of telemedicine is also at issue. Physicians must be familiar with the HIPAA Privacy Regulations, the HIPAA Security Regulations, other relevant federal privacy requirements, and the privacy requirements of the states in which the services are being delivered *and* received.

---

[28] 42 C.F.R. § 410.78(a)(3).

[29] For a more in-depth discussion of telemedicine, *see* Thomas Wm. Mayo, Esquire et al., *Telemedicine: Survey and Analysis of Federal and State Laws*, (Health Lawyers Expert Series, American Health Lawyers Association 2007).

[30] *Id.*

Of particular note, some fraud and abuse issues arise in telemedicine. In an important Advisory Opinion,[31] the OIG found that, based on the facts presented, no prohibited remuneration was taking place because the use of the telemedicine equipment was not intended to induce referrals.[32] Two anti-kickback safe harbors are relevant to telemedicine. The safe harbors apply when a physician receives free electronic prescribing items or services or free electronic health records items or services.[33] Similar exceptions to the Stark law are also applicable to telemedicine.[34]

Generally, the provision of equipment and/or loans for telemedical equipment can create a concern about kickbacks and other fraud and abuse issues that should be addressed specifically. Any leasing or subleasing of equipment for telemedicine should meet the elements for the OIG's equipment-rental "safe harbor." In addition, federal and state self-referral prohibitions, along with state laws and regulations regarding fee-splitting, could be sources of concern. For further information on fraud and abuse issues, *see* Chapter 4.

9.6 Physician/Patient Relationships

Generally, a physician/patient relationship[35] is initiated when both parties manifest consent to the relationship; the physician functions as a healthcare professional, and the patient relies on the advice or diagnosis given.[36] Physicians are not generally obligated to enter into a physician/patient relationship and treat individuals requesting treatment in accordance with the professional standard of care, except situations where there has been an affirmative undertaking by the physician, or an existing contractual obligation to the patient or a health plan or undertaking to provide physician coverage for a hospital's emergency department.[37] Once a physician/patient relationship exists, however, only certain procedures will end the relationship.

Although the law on termination of physician/patient relationships varies from state to state, some basic tenets apply. The physician/patient relationship will continue until: (1) the patient has no further need for medical care; (2) the patient affirmatively terminates the relationship; or (3) the physician terminates the relationship after giving the patient reasonable notice and affords the patient an opportunity to obtain alternate care. If, however, the patient is unable to obtain care with another qualified physician, then the treating physician who wishes to terminate the physician/patient relationship may have an obligation to continue care, or the physician may be liable for patient abandonment and open to malpractice liability.[38]

---

[31] *See* OIG Advisory Opinion 98-18.

[32] The OIG made this conclusion due to the facts that (1) the optometrist with the consultative telemedicine equipment did not intend to advertise the equipment, (2) neither the optometrist nor the ophthalmologist intended to bill Medicare or another insurer for the consultations, and (3) patients were free to choose any ophthalmologist for follow-up care. These elements should be considered in any telemedicine consultative arrangement.

[33] 42 C.F.R. § 1001.952(x) and (y).

[34] *Id.*. § 411.357(v) and (w).

[35] Chapter 2 discusses patient issues, so this Chapter will only briefly touch on physicians' obligations to patients in terms of terminating patient relationships.

[36] *See* Becker at § 13.03.

[37] *See O'Neill v. Montefiore Hosp.*, 11 A.D.2d 132, 202 N.Y.S.2d 436 (N.Y. App. Div. 1960).

[38] *See, e.g., Groce v. Myers*, 224 N.C. 165, 29 S.E.2d 553 (1944). The case law in this area is well established, dating back to the late 1800s.

In addition, some state regulations require physicians who participate in a managed care plan to continue to treat certain patients after the physician's agreement to participate in the plan terminates. For example pregnant women and patients who have begun a course of care with the physician would be entitled to continued care by the physician throughout the pregnancy or the course of care, and the physician would be required to accept payment in accordance with the otherwise terminated agreement between the physician and the plan. Physicians are not, otherwise, generally not bound to continue relationships with patients who are not under continuing care at the time the contract's termination.

The law in this area may vary from state to state, so it is very important for an attorney representing physicians to consult local laws and regulations. The governing regulations applicable to physicians in a given state may not be under the aegis of one agency; for example, they may be the result of a combination of regulations promulgated by a board of medical examiners, the department of health, and the department of insurance. Thus, a thorough search is necessary in order to advise a physician who plans to terminate patient relationships.

9.7 Accountable Care Organizations

One of the most prominent components of healthcare reform is the encouragement of the development of Medicare Accountable Care Organizations (ACO). While certainly not new, ACOs have existed in relative obscurity until now, but by January 1, 2012, Section 3022 of the PPACA requires DHHS to develop a Medicare shared savings program through an ACO.[39] The program will encourage accountability for a specified patient population, coordinate items and services under Medicare Parts A and B and invest in processes for high quality, but cost-efficient, delivery of care. Groups of providers, including physicians, will work with suppliers to manage and coordinate care for Medicare fee-for-service beneficiaries, such groups forming ACOs. To be eligible, an ACO must fulfill the following requirements:

- include a number of primary care professionals sufficient for the minimum number of Medicare fee-for-service beneficiaries, which is 5,000;
- have a mechanism for shared governance;
- have a formal legal structure that allows for the ACO to receive and distribute payments for shared savings to participating providers and suppliers;
- be accountable for the quality, costs and overall care of the Medicare fee-for-service beneficiaries who are assigned to the ACO;
- provide information regarding the member providers as the Secretary of DHHS determines is necessary;
- define processes to promote evidence-based medicine in patient engagement, report on quality and cost measures, and coordinate care, such as the use of telemedicine, remote patient monitoring, and other such enabling technologies;
- enter into an agreement to participate in the Medicare Shared Savings Program for a minimum of three years;

[39] Pub. L. No. 111-148 § 3022.

- develop a leadership and management structure that includes clinical and administrative systems; and
- demonstrate that it meets patient-centeredness criteria specified by the Secretary of DHHS such as the use of patient and care giver assessments or individualized care plans.[40]

The expected explosion of ACOs presents the opportunity for most physicians to use a new delivery model for care. Nonetheless, until final regulations are issued by the Centers for Medicare and Medicaid Services (CMS), several legal and regulatory questions remain unresolved. Specifically, the relationships contemplated by ACOs raise questions under the Stark law, the Anti-Kickback Statute, the Civil Monetary Penalty Statute, anti-trust laws, the Internal Revenue Code, and state laws. CMS published proposed regulations in the April 7, 2011 issue of the *Federal Register*. Additionally, on April 7, 2011, CMS and the OIG jointly issued a notice with comment period regarding possible waiver of the Stark law, the Anti-Kickback Statute, and the Civil Monetary Penalty Statute. As of the time of this writing, CMS is expected to publish final regulations in August 2011 along with final waiver provisions in conjunction with the OIG.

9.8 Conclusion

Representing physicians requires an extensive knowledge of many areas. Hopefully, this Chapter has laid a framework of some of the physician-representation issues that healthcare attorneys will encounter. Health Lawyers' Physician Organizations Practice Group, which the author currently chairs, has also recently published a second edition of the *Representing Physicians* Handbook which delves into greater detail on many of the issues discussed in the Chapter and discusses other advanced issues.

[40] *Id.*

10

Post-Acute Providers and Suppliers

Carol Colborn Loepere, Esquire*
Reed Smith, LLP

10.1 Introduction

Home care providers, such as home medical equipment (HME) suppliers, home health agencies (HHAs), and hospices, are subject to extensive regulation at the state and federal levels. Similarly, long-term care facilities must abide by state and federal laws and regulations. These healthcare entities in particular are under increased scrutiny for compliance with quality-of-care, billing and resident-rights requirements. This Chapter sets forth a summary of the state licensure, certificate of need (CON), and Medicare and Medicaid regulatory requirements for these providers, as well as key legal issues to be considered with respect to fraud and abuse concerns and compliance programs.

10.2 Home Medical Equipment Suppliers

HME suppliers (sometimes known as durable medical equipment (DME) suppliers) are providers of medical equipment and supplies to patients for use in the home. Examples of home medical equipment include wheelchairs, walkers, oxygen and oxygen equipment, and hospital beds.

10.2.1 State Licensure

HME suppliers are licensed under state law in about 20 states. For example, Illinois requires suppliers of "home medical equipment and services" to be licensed.[1] Similarly, Florida requires licensure of any person or entity that holds itself out as providing HME.[2] HME is broadly defined by the Florida statute to include: (1) any product defined under the Federal Drug Administration's Drugs, Devices and Cosmetics Act; (2) any product reimbursed by Medicare Part B; or (3) any product reimbursed by the Florida Medicaid programs, with the exception of: prosthetics and orthotics; splints, braces, or aids custom fabricated by a licensed healthcare practitioner; motorized scooters; personal transfer systems; and medically-necessary specialty beds.[3] The scope of some state licensure statutes is limited, however, to those devices, apparatuses, machines, or similar articles that *must be prescribed* by a

* The author wishes to thank Debra McCurdy, Senior Health Policy Analyst, and Elizabeth O'Brien, Associate, at Reed Smith LLP, who provided invaluable assistance to the completion of this Chapter.

1 *See* 225 Ill. Comp. Stat. 51/15.

2 Fla. Stat. § 400.93(1).

3 *Id.* § 400.925(6).

physician for use in the home. When consulting state law to determine whether HME suppliers must be licensed, it is important to review the scope of the licensure because some types of HME may not be covered by the statute.[4]

State licensure may also be a condition of participation in state Medicaid programs, and is a requirement for Medicare participation.[5] Suppliers who provide drugs must be licensed under state pharmacy statutes. This situation arises because the DME benefit under Medicare includes drugs integral to the use of a piece of covered equipment (*e.g.*, the albuterol sulfate in a nebulizer). Under new Medicare supplier standards effective September 27, 2010, suppliers are prohibited from contracting with another individual to perform licensed services, with certain exceptions (such as if such contracting is allowed in the state where licensed services are being performed). Medicare DME suppliers also are required to obtain oxygen from a state-licensed oxygen supplier (as applicable in the state).[6]

10.2.2 Medicare

10.2.2.1 Coverage

Medicare covers DME under a specific coverage category of the Social Security Act (SSA). In addition, HME suppliers often provide other categories of products (including prosthetics, orthotics, and supplies) which are covered under separate provisions of the SSA. These products collectively are known as DME, prosthetics, orthotics, and supplies (DMEPOS).

10.2.2.1.1 Categories of Coverage

The SSA sets forth broad statutory areas under which the component elements of DMEPOS are covered.[7] These general categories are further defined by federal statute as follows:

(A) *Durable medical equipment* means equipment, furnished by a supplier or a home health agency that—

  (1) Can withstand repeated use;

  (2) Is primarily and customarily used to serve a medical purpose;

  (3) Generally is not useful to an individual in the absence of an illness or injury; and

  (4) Is appropriate for use in the home.

(B) *Prosthetic and orthotic devices* means—

  (1) Devices that replace all or part of an internal body organ, including ostomy bags and supplies directly related to ostomy care, and replacement of such devices and supplies;

---

[4] The National Supplier Clearinghouse (NSC) has compiled a DMEPOS State Licensure Directory at http://www.palmettogba.com/palmetto/statelicensure.nsf. This is a useful guide; however, it is advisable to consult the specific state law.

[5] *See* 42 U.S.C. § 1395m(j); 42 C.F.R. § 424.57(c)(1).

[6] *See* 42 C.F.R. § 424.57(c)(2) and (27). *See also* Section 10.2.2.2.

[7] *See generally* 42 U.S.C. § 1395x.

(2) One pair of conventional eyeglasses or contact lenses furnished subsequent to each cataract surgery with insertion of an intraocular lens; and

(3) Leg, arm, back, and neck braces, and artificial legs, arms, and eyes, including replacements if required because of a change in the beneficiary's physical condition.[8]

Supplies and drugs prescribed for the effective use of DME, a prosthetic, or an orthotic also are covered. This can include such items as the albuterol sulfate used in nebulizers, the oxygen in an oxygen concentrator, or the batteries in a pacemaker.

Coverage for products is limited to certain indications and circumstances, as set forth in national and local medical review policies. For example, oxygen is covered only for patients with designated blood gas-oxygen levels who meet other specified conditions. A Foley catheter is considered a prosthetic device and is covered only when prescribed for a patient with permanent urinary incontinence because it replaces the function of a permanently inoperative internal body organ. Catheters are not otherwise covered as prosthetic devices.[9]

In addition, the following specific categories of items commonly are supplied by HME suppliers, reimbursed through the regional Medicare carriers, and covered under Medicare through separate statutory benefits:

- home dialysis equipment and supplies;
- immunosuppressive drugs;
- therapeutic shoes for diabetics; and
- surgical dressings.

10.2.2.1.2 Statutory Exclusion

The SSA enunciates a general rule under which products, procedures, or services may be *excluded* from coverage: "[N]o payment may be made under Part A or Part B… for any expenses incurred for items or services… which are not *reasonable and necessary* for the diagnosis or treatment of any illness or injury or to improve the functioning of a malformed body member."[10] If a patient fails to meet the coverage criteria for an item of DMEPOS, coverage will be denied on the grounds that the item is not "reasonable and necessary."

10.2.2.1.3 National Coverage Policies

In enforcement of this statutory limitation of "reasonable and necessary," the Centers for Medicare & Medicaid Services (CMS) makes national coverage policies through its central office in Baltimore, Maryland. National coverage policies, known as National Coverage Determinations (NCDs), are binding on all Medicare contractors. Congress has statutorily restricted the judicial review of NCDs, and

[8] 42 C.F.R. § 414.202.

[9] *See* 42 C.F.R. § 414.202; *see also Medicare Benefit Policy Manual* (CMS Pub. 100-02), Chapter 15 § 120(A).

[10] 42 U.S.C. § 1395y(a)(1)(A) (emphasis added).

provided that the determinations cannot be challenged on the grounds that CMS failed to abide by the Administrative Procedure Act.[11]

10.2.2.1.4 DME MAC Coverage Policies

Suppliers submit claims to one of four special regional Medicare contractors known as Durable Medical Equipment Medicare Administrative Contractors (DME MACs, formerly known as Durable Medical Equipment Regional Carriers, or DMERCs). Each region also has an affiliated Program Safeguard Contractor (PSC)[12] to perform selected Medicare program integrity functions, including fraud investigations, prepay and post-pay medical review of claims, and data analysis. Although regional contractors must defer to national policy, in the absence of a national policy on a given issue, the contractors may make a local coverage policy. Local coverage policies are more likely to be based upon issues of overuse and abuse, while NCDs are generally focused on the clinical safety and efficacy of a product. DME MACs can review procedures, devices, and services to develop coverage policies that are effective only in the contractor's geographic area. Generally, however, the regions are expected to have consistent coverage policies.[13] For some items of DMEPOS, certificates of medical necessity or other specific medical necessity documentation are required for coverage. These coverage requirements are set forth in the regional Supplier Manuals.[14]

10.2.2.1.5 Coding

DMEPOS generally are identified using the Healthcare Common Procedure Coding System (HCPCS), also known as Level II Common Procedure Terminology (Level II CPT) codes. Suppliers and manufacturers may petition CMS to establish HCPCS codes for new products or for products that are inadequately described by the current codes. The Pricing Data Analysis and Coding Contractor (PDAC) (formerly known as the Statistical Administrative Durable Medical Equipment Contractor, or SADMERC) is the Medicare contractor designated by CMS to make coding verifications and determine appropriate HCPCS coding regarding a DMEPOS item for Medicare purposes. Some products, such as certain orthotics, can only be billed to Medicare under specified codes if the item has been submitted to the PDAC for coding verification.[15]

---

11 5 U.S.C. § 553. *See* 42 U.S.C. § 1395ff(c)(3)(B).

12 PSCs are transitioning to zone program integrity contractors (ZPICs). *See Medicare Program Integrity Manual* (CMS Pub. 100-08), Chapter 4 § 4.1.

13 *See* 42 C.F.R. § 400.202; additionally, *see Medicare Program Integrity Manual* (CMS Pub. 100-08), Chapter 13.

14 The supplier manuals are available directly from the DME MACs and through various legal publishers. They also are available on the websites for each of the DME MACs:

Region A: http://www.medicarenhic.com/dme/;
Region B: http://www.ngsmedicare.com/portal.aspx?CatID=3;
Region C: http://www.cignagovernmentservices.com/jc/index.html; and
Region D: https://www.noridianmedicare.com/dme/index.html.

15 *See* www.dmepdac.com.

10.2.2.2 Requirements of Participation

HME/DME suppliers under Medicare must meet the following statutory requirements:

- comply with all applicable [s]tate and [f]ederal licensure and regulatory requirements;
- maintain a physical facility on an appropriate site;
- have proof of appropriate liability insurance; and
- meet such other requirements as the Secretary of the Department of Health and Human Services (DHHS) may specify.[16]

The primary regulatory requirement for a supplier is compliance with the Medicare supplier standards.[17] These 30 standards, which were updated and expanded in August 2010,[18] both implement the requirements in the SSA and set forth additional criteria for qualification as a Medicare supplier. Such criteria include, for example: (1) responsibility for delivery of covered items to beneficiaries; (2) honoring all warranties both express and implied; (3) the direct or contractual maintenance and repair of items rented to beneficiaries; (4) maintaining a complaint resolution process; and (5) documentation criteria, including providing a copy of the supplier standards to all Medicare beneficiaries. The 2010 update to the standards generally prohibits suppliers from sharing a practice location with any other Medicare supplier or provider (with certain exceptions); imposes new physical facility requirements on suppliers, including square footage, accessibility, signage, and storage requirements; clarifies the prohibition on the direct solicitation of Medicare beneficiaries; prohibits suppliers from contracting with another individual to perform licensed services, with certain exceptions; requires the use of a primary business telephone; establishes minimum hours of operation (with certain exceptions); and makes other clarifications to the supplier standards.[19] The new standards became effective September 27, 2010, although suppliers with existing leases have an extended timeframe for complying with the physical facility standards. The NSC engages inspectors to conduct site surveys to verify compliance with the supplier standards. If a DMEPOS supplier is found to be out of compliance, the supplier's Medicare Part B supplier number will be deactivated until the supplier demonstrates compliance with all standards.

In addition, the Medicare Prescription Drug, Improvement, and Modernization Act of 2003 (MMA)[20] requires all suppliers to be accredited as meeting quality standards established by CMS. On August 15, 2006, CMS released final supplier quality standards, setting forth general business standards and product-specific requirements; these standards were updated in October 2008.[21] All suppliers must comply with the supplier standards in order to furnish any Medicare Part B DMEPOS item or service and to receive and retain a supplier billing number. Under the timeline established by the Medicare Improvements for Patients and Providers Act (MIPPA), all DMEPOS suppliers were required to be accredited by September 30, 2009 (although CMS had established earlier accreditation

[16] 42 U.S.C. § 1395m(j).

[17] *See* 42 C.F.R. § 424.57.

[18] *See* 75 Fed. Reg. 52,629 (Aug. 27, 2010).

[19] *Id.*

[20] Pub. L. No. 108-173, 117 Stat. 2003.

[21] *See* http://www.cms.gov/MedicareProviderSupEnroll/Downloads/DMEPOSAccreditationStandardsCMB.pdf.

deadlines for some suppliers).[22] MIPPA also exempted certain health professionals from the accreditation requirement. In addition, the Patient Protection and Affordable Care Act (PPACA),[23] as amended by the Health Care and Education Reconciliation Act of 2010[24] (collectively known as the Affordable Care Act or ACA) exempted pharmacies from accreditation if they meet certain criteria.[25] The MMA also requires the DHHS Secretary to establish Medicare clinical standards as a condition of payment for "power mobility devices," including a face-to-face examination requirement and restrictions on who can prescribe such equipment.[26]

In addition to complying with the supplier standards, CMS published a rule on January 2, 2009 requiring most Medicare-enrolled DMEPOS suppliers to submit a surety bond, with certain limited exceptions. Specifically, suppliers are required to post a $50,000 surety bond from an authorized surety, unless (1) the supplier is a high-risk supplier (*e.g.*, has had a supplier number revoked, a license suspended, felony conviction, or health program exclusion within 10 years), in which case the bond amount will be increased or (2) the supplier qualifies for an exemption from the surety bond requirement (*e.g.*, certain physicians and nonphysician practitioners, certain state-licensed orthotic and prosthetic personnel, and government-operated suppliers if bonded under state law).[27] More recently, the ACA requires the Secretary to consider a supplier's billing volume in determining the amount of the surety bond.[28]

10.2.2.3 Payment

Medicare payment for DMEPOS is based on the statutory category into which the equipment is classified. Payments are updated annually according to statutory formula. Special payment provisions apply in competitive bidding areas and in certain special circumstances.

10.2.2.3.1 Payment Categories

DMEPOS payment categories include the following:

1. capped rental;
2. inexpensive or routinely purchased items;
3. customized items;
4. orthotics and prosthetics;
5. oxygen equipment and supplies; and
6. medical supplies.

Payment generally is made at the lesser of the supplier's actual charge or a fee schedule amount (which varies by state), as reduced by applicable deductible and coinsurance requirements. There are complex payment rules associated with the various DMEPOS payment categories. Major provisions are highlighted below.

---

22 Pub. L. No. 110-275, 122 Stat. 2494.
23 Pub. L. No. 111-148, 124 Stat. 119 (2010).
24 Pub. L. No. 111-152, 124 Stat. 1029 (2010).
25 PPACA § 3109.
26 *See* 71 Fed. Reg. 17,021 (Apr. 5, 2006).
27 *See* 74 Fed. Reg. 165 (Jan. 2, 2009).
28 PPACA § 6402(g).

Capped Rental & Oxygen Payment

Items classified as capped rental are paid at the lesser of (1) the actual charge for the equipment or (2) a fee-schedule amount determined according to a statutory payment formula. Under the DME payment formula, monthly rental payments are initially made at 10% of the "national limited payment amount" of the equipment. After three months, the rental payment percentage changes to 7.5%. The rental payments continue for the period during which a medical need exists for the equipment, but historically have been limited to 15 continuous months. If the period of medical need extended for a period beyond 15 months, no payment would be made for the next six months. Until recently, for each succeeding period of six months, however, a maintenance and servicing payment could be made (for parts and labor not covered by the seller's or manufacturer's warranty) during the first month of each such six-month period.[29] Notably, no actual repair or servicing was required to receive payment, but the patient must have had a continuing medical need for the product. Under longstanding rules, capped rental items used for 10 consecutive months were required to be offered for purchase, and power-driven wheelchairs would be required to be offered for purchase in addition to rental when the item is first furnished by the supplier.

The Deficit Reduction Act of 2005 (DRA)[30] modified this longstanding DME rental policy. Specifically, the DRA eliminated the 15-month rental option for capped rental DME. Instead, suppliers are required to transfer the title of capped rental DME to the beneficiary after 13 months. The option for beneficiaries to purchase power-driven wheelchairs when initially furnished was retained, although the ACA subsequently eliminated the purchase option for power-driven wheelchairs other than complex, rehabilitative power wheelchairs. The ACA also modifies the rental payment framework for power-driven wheelchairs. Effective for items furnished on or after July 1, 2011, payment is set at 15% (rather than 10%) of the purchase price for the first three months, changing to 6% (rather than 7.5%) of the purchase price for each of the remaining 10 months (with special rules for items furnished pursuant to the competitive bidding program, which is discussed below).

The DRA also eliminated automatic maintenance and servicing payments; such payments will be made only if reasonable and necessary, and will cover parts and labor not otherwise covered by the supplier's or manufacturer's warranty. These provisions are effective for items for which the first rental month is on or after January 1, 2006.

Moreover, the DRA limits the rental period for oxygen equipment to 36 months, after which the title transfers to the beneficiary (although rental payments for oxygen contents still will be available). Maintenance and servicing payments will be made if determined by the Secretary to be reasonable and necessary and not otherwise covered by the supplier's or manufacturer's warranty. This provision became effective January 1, 2006 (although for individuals receiving oxygen equipment as of December 31, 2005, the 36-month period began January 1, 2006).

[29] 42 U.S.C. § 1395m(a)(7).

[30] Pub. L. No. 109-171, 120 Stat. 2005.

Inexpensive or Routinely Purchased Items

For inexpensive or routinely purchased items of DME ("routinely purchased" in this context means purchased more than 75% of the time), CMS has a fee schedule that is based upon historical charges for each product. The state payment levels, however, are subject to payment limitations. The national floor is 85% of the median of all the state fees, and the ceiling is the median of all the state fees. Alaska, Hawaii, and Puerto Rico are excluded from these payment limitations. Payment is made on a lump-sum basis at the time of purchase.

Customized Items

Customized items (*e.g.*, certain custom wheelchairs) are defined as items that must be uniquely constructed or substantially modified for a specific beneficiary, according to the description and orders of a physician, and thereby are made to be so different from another item used for the same purpose that the two cannot be grouped together for the purpose of pricing. Payment is made on a lump-sum basis, with the amount determined by the carrier's individual consideration and judgment of a reasonable payment amount for each customized item.[31]

Prosthetic and Orthotic Devices

For prosthetics and orthotics that do not require custom fitting and adjustment, Medicare uses 10 regional fee schedules. As with the fee schedule for inexpensive and routinely purchased DME, the fee schedule for prosthetics and orthotics is subject to payment limitations. The national floor is 90% of the average of all the regional fees, and the ceiling is 120% of thc average. Payments are increased annually with an update for inflation, subject to periodic statutory limitations.

Under BIPA, Congress directed the DHHS Secretary to use negotiated rulemaking to establish standards for those suppliers billing Medicare for orthotics and certain custom-fabricated orthotics. While a negotiated rulemaking committee was convened, it was unable to reach a consensus. The final rule has not been issued to date.

Drugs Administered Through DME

Certain drugs administered through DME (including inhalation and infusion drugs administered through DME) are covered under the Medicare Part B program, despite longstanding limitations on Medicare coverage of self-administered drugs prior to the establishment of the Medicare Part D outpatient drug benefit in 2006. Under a new reimbursement policy implemented in 2004, inhalation drugs administered through DME generally are reimbursed at 85% of the average wholesale price (AWP) as of April 1, 2003, although certain respiratory products (*e.g.*, albuterol) that the OIG and the General Accountability Office (GAO) previously have reported to be overpaid are reimbursed at even lower levels. Moreover, the MMA freezes Medicare payment for infusion drugs provided in connection with DME at 95% of the April 1, 2003 AWP rate.

---

[31] 42 C.F.R. § 414.224.

10.2.2.3.2 Payment Updates

Payment amounts are updated annually by the consumer price index for urban consumers (CPI-U), subject to certain adjustments mandated by Congress. For instance, payment levels were frozen by the BBA for a period of five years, beginning in 1998. The Balanced Budget Refinement Act of 1999 (BBRA) restored a portion of the increases for 2000 and 2001.[32] Moreover, BIPA further modified payments for DME (other than oxygen and oxygen equipment) by including a full inflation update for DME provided in 2001. The MMA again imposed a freeze on Medicare payment amounts for DME (other than Class III medical devices) for the years 2004 through 2008; thereafter, rates were scheduled to increase by the percentage increase in the CPI-U. The MMA also required the DHHS Secretary to reduce the payment amounts in 2005 for specific items of DME if the HCPCS code for the item or supply is identified by the DHHS Office of Inspector General (OIG) as being excessive compared to payments under other government programs.[33]

Most recently, the PPACA also eliminates the full inflation update to the DME fee schedule for 2011 through 2014. Instead, beginning in 2011, DMEPOS rates will be increased annually by the rate of increase in the CPI minus a "productivity adjustment"[34] designed to reflect productivity gains in delivering healthcare services and to encourage more efficient care.

10.2.2.3.3 Competitive Bidding

The MMA requires the Secretary of DHHS to implement competitive acquisition programs for DME whereby suppliers will go through a bidding process and meet certain program standards in order to supply covered items within the competitive acquisition area. Items to be included in competitive acquisition are: (1) DME (including DME used with infusion and drugs, other than inhalation drugs) and supplies used in conjunction with DME; (2) enteral nutrients, equipment, and supplies; and (3) off-the-shelf orthotics. This requirement builds on earlier CMS demonstration projects in Polk County, Florida and in the San Antonio, Texas area that used competitive bidding to significantly reduce Medicare payment for certain DMEPOS items.

Excluded from competitive acquisition are: inhalation drugs; parenteral nutrients, equipment, and supplies; and Class III devices under the federal Food, Drug, and Cosmetic Act (FDCA). The Secretary of DHHS may exempt certain rural areas as well as areas with low population density in urban areas. Competitive acquisition areas may differ for different items and services. The MMA required the program to be phased in, applying to 10 of the largest metropolitan statistical areas (MSAs) in 2007, 80 such areas in 2009, and additional areas thereafter, although this timeframe subsequently was modified. Only successful bidders meeting all program standards may supply the covered items in the acquisition area, and they will be reimbursed based on bid amounts.

---

[32] *See* 42 U.S.C. § 1395m(a).

[33] This provision applied to oxygen and oxygen equipment, standard wheelchairs, nebulizers, lancets and testing strips used for management of diabetes, hospital beds, and air mattresses. For these items, the payment amount was reduced by the percentage difference between the Medicare payment in 2002 and the median Federal Employees Health Benefit Program (FEHBP) price for the same item as identified by the OIG.

[34] The productivity adjustment equals the percentage change in the 10-year moving average of changes in annual economy-wide private nonfarm business multi-factor productivity, as reported by the Bureau of Labor Statistics.

On April 10, 2007, CMS published its final rule establishing the Medicare DMEPOS competitive bidding program.[35] The rule requires suppliers to meet a number of program requirements (including being accredited). To participate, suppliers must bid on all specified codes within the designated product category, and reimbursement will be set at the median of the winning suppliers' bids for the bid items.

In 2007, CMS conducted the first round of bidding in the following 10 competitive bidding areas (CBAs): Charlotte-Gastonia-Concord (NC-SC); Cincinnati-Middletown (OH-KY-IN); Cleveland-Elyria-Mentor (OH); Dallas-Fort Worth-Arlington (TX); Kansas City (MO-KS); Miami-Fort Lauderdale-Miami Beach (FL); Orlando-Kissimmee (FL); Pittsburgh (PA); Riverside-San Bernardino-Ontario (CA); and San Juan-Caguas-Guaynabo (PR). CMS selected the following product categories for the first round of bidding: (1) Oxygen Supplies and Equipment; (2) Standard Power Wheelchairs, Scooters, and Related Accessories; (3) Complex Rehabilitative Power Wheelchairs and Related Accessories; (4) Mail-Order Diabetic Supplies; (5) Enteral Nutrients, Equipment, and Supplies; (6) Continuous Positive Airway Pressure Devices, (7) Respiratory Assist Devices, and Related Supplies and Accessories; (8) Hospital Beds and Related Accessories; (9) Negative Pressure Wound Therapy Pumps and Related Supplies and Accessories; (10) Walkers and Related Accessories; and (11) Support Surfaces (Group 2 and 3 mattresses and overlays) in Miami-Fort Lauderdale-Miami Beach, FL and San Juan-Caguas-Guaynabo, PR only. The contract term for all product categories except mail order diabetes supplies was three years.

CMS offered contracts to 23% of bidding suppliers, with prices averaging 26% below Medicare fee schedule amounts. The program briefly went into effect July 1, 2008, but significant concerns about the program implementation resulted in Congress taking the rare step of terminating round one contracts through enactment of MIPPA. MIPPA directed CMS to conduct a new round one rebid in nine geographic areas in 2009, and conduct a second phase of bidding in 2011 in an additional 70 of the largest MSAs. MIPPA also added a series of beneficiary safeguards and made certain procedural improvements to the bidding process. The delay in bidding was financed by cutting fee schedule payments for items included in round one by 9.5% nationwide beginning January 1, 2009, followed by a 2% increase in 2014 (although that increase subsequently was repealed by the ACA).

CMS conducted the round one rebid in 2009. On July 2, 2010, CMS announced that payment amounts under the round one rebid will average 32% below the Medicare DMEPOS fee schedule amounts. Contract prices are scheduled to go into effect January 1, 2011.[36]

The ACA further expands competitive bidding requiring the Secretary to include a total of 100 of the largest MSAs in the second round of bidding. In addition, the ACA requires the Secretary to use competitive bidding payment information to adjust DMEPOS fees in areas outside of competitive bidding areas beginning in 2016.[37]

---

[35] 72 Fed. Reg. 17,992 (Apr. 10, 2007) (to be codified at 42 C.F.R. pts. 411 and 414).

[36] CMS announcements regarding implementation of the program are available at http://www.cms.gov/DMEPOSCompetitiveBid/01_overview.asp. In addition, the competitive bidding implementation contractor (CBIC) has posted bid instructions and a variety of other guidance documents at http://www.dmecompetitivebid.com/palmetto/cbic.nsf/DocsCat/Home.

[37] PPACA § 6410.

10.2.2.3.4 *Inherent Reasonableness*

As discussed, payment for most DMEPOS is on the basis of a fee schedule, which are based upon historical reasonable charges for products. GAO, CMS, and the OIG have observed in several reports that fee schedule payments commonly are much higher than both marketplace charges and charges to other governmental health programs (*e.g.*, the Veterans' Administration). The Medicare statute, as amended by the BBA, allows CMS or the DMERCs (now called DME MACs) to impose payment adjustments on items of DMEPOS of up to 15% by providing limited notice and without consulting suppliers. Reductions in excess of 15% can be made by CMS if notice and comment is provided in the *Federal Register* and if CMS meets other legislative criteria such as considering the impact of such reductions on suppliers.[38]

The criteria for making "inherent reasonableness" (IR) adjustments is whether the fee-schedule amounts for the products are not inherently reasonable because they are grossly excessive or grossly deficient. Use of this authority is significant for DMEPOS, because payment changes traditionally have occurred slowly over time. IR authority provides CMS with the ability to make significant changes in payment relatively quickly.

The Secretary issued a January 7, 1998 interim final regulation to implement this authority.[39] Moreover, on August 13, 1999, HCFA published a notice of proposed IR reduction for six items of DMEPOS (certain types of folding walkers, commode chairs, transcutaneous electrical nerve stimulators, and vacuum erection systems).[40] The proposed reductions in payment for these items ranged from 22 to 57%.

Due to the concerns regarding prior use of the IR authority, the BBRA provided that the DHHS Secretary may not use, or permit fiscal intermediaries or carriers to use, the IR authority until after the GAO released a report on this policy and the Secretary issues a final rule responding to the GAO report. The GAO's report, issued in July 2000, generally found that HCFA acted properly in issuing an interim final rule to implement the BBA's IR provisions. Furthermore, in GAO's opinion, it clearly was within HCFA's authority to delegate partial responsibility for adjusting payment rates to carriers, including the DMERCs.

On December 13, 2002, CMS issued its long-awaited interim final rule with comment period establishing a process for adjusting payments for Medicare Part B services (other than physician services) when existing payment amounts are determined to be either grossly excessive or deficient.[41] The interim final rule describes the factors CMS or its contractors will consider in making such determinations, as well as the procedures (including notice and comment period) that will be followed in establishing new payment amounts, effective February 11, 2003. Notably, CMS decided not to apply IR adjustments unless the difference between the current and proposed payment amounts are at least 15% (although CMS does not preclude adjustments of less than 15% in a given year once it is determined

---

[38] *See also* 63 Fed. Reg. 687 (1998) (codified at 42 C.F.R. pt. 405).
[39] *See* § 223 of the Consolidated Appropriations Act for FY 2000 (incorporating the BBRA).
[40] 64 Fed. Reg. 44,227 (1999).
[41] 67 Fed. Reg. 76,684 (Dec. 13, 2002) (codified at 42 C.F.R. § 405.502).

that an overall adjustment of 15% or more is justified). Nevertheless, the rule establishes a process that could have a significant impact on Medicare payments for DME and other Part B services.

10.2.2.4 Medicare Upgrade Provisions/Advance Beneficiary Notices

The BBA provided that Medicare beneficiaries purchasing or renting items of DME can choose an upgraded item in place of a standard item, effective upon publication of implementing regulations. Under this provision, suppliers receive payment from the Medicare program as if the item were a standard item, and the Medicare beneficiary was to pay the difference between the standard item and the upgraded item.

In 2002, CMS implemented a process by which suppliers may bill on an assignment basis for upgraded DME using Advance Beneficiary Notices (ABNs).[42] The ABNs, based on section 1879 of the SSA, inform beneficiaries that they may be responsible for payment for items, given the fact that the supplier expects Medicare payment for these items to be denied. Under the ABN process, the supplier is permitted to bill on an assigned or unassigned basis for the item that would be covered by Medicare. The supplier then bills the beneficiary for the difference between Medicare's allowed amount and the cost of the upgraded feature.

10.2.2.5 Consolidated Billing for DMEPOS Furnished in Skilled Nursing Facilities and to Patients of Home Health Agencies

10.2.2.5.1 Skilled Nursing Facilities

Section 4432 of the BBA required the establishment of a prospective payment system (PPS) for Part A skilled nursing facility (SNF) services for cost-reporting periods beginning on or after July 1, 1998. The SNF PPS consists of *per diem* rates, which vary based on the intensity of resources required by each resident. With a few exceptions, the PPS rate covers all routine, ancillary, and capital costs of services furnished to patients during a covered Part A stay.[43] This means that for patients in a covered Part A stay, suppliers generally do not receive separate reimbursement for items and services; rather, they must look to the SNF for payment.

In conjunction with the PPS for Part A services, the BBA also established "consolidated billing" for SNFs with respect to most Part B services (including supplies) furnished to patients who are no longer eligible for Part A coverage.[44] Under this provision, SNFs were to be responsible for billing, and payment was to be made, to SNFs for all covered services, regardless of whether those services were furnished by facility employees or by an outside contract service provider. Outside suppliers were expected look to SNFs for payment for their services.

---

[42] 67 Fed. Reg. 21,617 (May 1, 2002). Also see 42 C.F.R. § 411.404(b) and (c). Copies of the ABNs, as well as additional details about the ABN requirements, are available on the CMS website at http://www.cms.gov/BNI/01_overview.asp.

[43] *See* 42 U.S.C. § 1395yy(e).

[44] While Part B coverage is not available for most DME furnished in a SNF setting because a SNF is not considered a patient's "home," a limited number of items including enteral nutrients and supplies, urologicals, and surgical dressings may be furnished under Part B in the nursing home setting in stays that are not covered under Part A.

Subsequently, however, federal legislation (in BIPA) limited the consolidated-billing requirements to services and items furnished to SNF residents in a Medicare Part A covered stay, and to therapy services furnished in Part A and Part B covered stays. As a result, for residents not covered under a Part A stay, SNFs may choose to bill for nontherapy Part B services and supplies, or they may elect to have suppliers continue to bill Medicare directly for these services. The BBA also specified that the amount of payment to the SNF for Part B services is the applicable Part B fee-schedule amount.[45]

10.2.2.5.2 *Home Health Agencies*

The BBA also mandated establishment of a PPS for HHAs, effective October 1, 2000. As part of this payment system, payment for home health items and services is made only to the HHA that establishes the beneficiary's home health plan of care, regardless of whether the item or service was furnished by the agency, by others under arrangement, or under any other contracting or consulting arrangement.[46]

The BBRA excluded DME and oxygen and oxygen supplies (but not medical supplies) from the consolidated-billing requirement. In other words, DME and oxygen suppliers may bill the Medicare program directly for items and services provided under the home health benefit, rather than be dependent on an HHA for payment.

10.2.3 Medicaid

In general, HME is covered under most state Medicaid benefits. Consult state law for specific determination of HME benefits. In order to receive payment, Medicaid HME suppliers must enroll as state Medicaid providers, after meeting state standards and conditions of participation. Many state Medicaid programs require prior authorization before paying for DMEPOS.

10.2.4 Fraud and Abuse

While the healthcare industry as a whole has long been subject to scrutiny by law-enforcement officials, in recent years the HME industry has been one of the main targets of government fraud and abuse efforts. HME has been singled out for certain abusive billing practices, problems with the proper documentation of medical necessity, kickbacks for referrals, and improper marketing. The OIG also has noted that "low barriers to entry and weak oversight and enforcement of enrollment standards make DMEPOS a compelling target for fraudulent suppliers," while excessive Medicare reimbursement levels "makes DMEPOS fraud particularly lucrative, further attracting bad actors to the system."[47]

Such concerns have prompted a number of focused enforcement efforts, such as a two-year DHHS pilot project announced June 28, 2007 designed to prevent Medicare DME fraud in Southern California and Southern Florida. This pilot project requires DMEPOS suppliers in the demonstration locales to reenroll in Medicare, expands the reasons for revoking Medicare billing privileges, and subjects

[45] *See* 42 U.S.C. §§ 1395u(b)(6), 1395yy(e)(9).

[46] *See id.* § 1395fff.

[47] Testimony of Daniel R. Levinson, Inspector General, DHHS, House Committee on Energy and Commerce, Subcommittee on Health Hearing on "Medicare's Competitive Bidding Program for Durable Medical Equipment: Implications for Quality, Cost and Access," Sept. 15, 2010.

suppliers to an enhanced fraud review, including site visits. Likewise, in September 2003, CMS and the OIG launched "Operation Wheeler Dealer" to combat improper Medicare payments for power wheelchairs.

Since 2007, DHHS also has teamed with the Department of Justice (DOJ) to use "Strike Forces" to target fraudulent Medicare billing, including fraud involving DMEPOS suppliers, in selected geographic areas. According to the OIG, in the first year of Strike Force activity in Miami, Medicare billing for DMEPOS decreased by $1.7 billion or 63%, compared to the previous year's billing.[48] As of July 2010, Medicare Fraud Strike Forces have obtained indictments of more than 810 individuals and organizations that have billed Medicare for more than $1.85 billion.[49] Likewise, in May 2009, DOJ and DHHS launched a new interagency effort called the Health Care Fraud Prevention and Enforcement Action Team (HEAT), to target Medicare fraud using new resources and data analysis techniques.

Because of significant fraud and abuse concerns related to the Medicare DMEPOS benefit, the OIG released a comprehensive set of compliance guidelines for the entire industry. These guidelines, called the "OIG's Compliance Program Guidance for the DMEPOS Industry," address "suspect practices" which could trigger scrutiny by regulators, and outline the specific elements that each DMEPOS supplier should consider when developing and implementing an effective compliance program.[50] The guidance is an excellent summary of rules and requirements applicable to HME suppliers.

The ACA also includes a number of program integrity provisions aimed at DMEPOS suppliers. Among other things, the ACA: requires physicians to document a face-to-face encounter with a beneficiary during the six-month period preceding a written order for any DME; allows the Secretary to disenroll for up to one year a Medicare supplier that fails to maintain and provide access to written orders for DME; authorizes the DHHS Secretary to hold Medicare claims for up to 90 days for certain new DME suppliers if the Secretary determines that there is a significant fraud risk; and mandates a variety of new screening procedures for Medicare and Medicaid providers. On September 23, 2010, CMS published a proposed rule that would implement the ACA provider/supplier screening requirements.[51] Notably, the proposed rule would classify new DMEPOS suppliers and HHAs (unless publicly-traded) as "high risk" entities subject to the most stringent screening requirements, including background checks and fingerprinting. Among many other things, the rule also would authorize CMS and the states to impose moratoria on the enrollment of new providers when deemed necessary to protect against a high risk of fraud; authorize the suspension of payments pending an investigation of a credible allegation of fraud; and solicit comments on new compliance program requirements. The rule has not been finalized as of this writing.

---

[48] *Id.*

[49] U.S. Department of Justice Press Release, "Medicare Fraud Strike Force Charges 94 Doctors, Health Care Company Owners, Executives and Others for More Than $251 Million in Alleged False Billing," July 16, 2010, available at http://www.justice.gov/opa/pr/2010/July/10-ag-821.html.

[50] 64 Fed. Reg. 36,368 (1999). The guidance also is available on the OIG website at oig.hhs.gov/fraud/complianceguidance.html.

[51] 75 Fed. Reg. 58,204, available at http://edocket.access.gpo.gov/2010/pdf/2010-23579.pdf.

10.3 Home Healthcare

10.3.1 State Licensure and Certificate of Need

HHAs and private duty nursing companies are home care providers that bring nurses and other practitioners to the patient's home. HHAs generally provide skilled nursing, therapy, or social services to patients in their homes, in addition to certain medical supplies and equipment. HHAs may be either freestanding or hospital-based in organization. HHAs are generally subject to state licensure requirements. In some states, licensure is only required if the entity provides skilled nursing and at least one type of therapy service. In others, the provision of skilled nursing services alone (*e.g.,* through a private-duty nursing agency or a home infusion-therapy company) may trigger licensure. Consult state law and regulations. Some states (*e.g.,* New York) require a CON to operate an HHA.[52] In other states, only institutional providers are subject to CON. Consult state law.

10.3.2 Medicare

10.3.2.1 Coverage

In order to qualify for Medicare coverage of HHA services, a Medicare beneficiary must be:

- confined to the home;
- under the care of a physician;
- receiving services under a plan of care established and periodically reviewed by a physician; and
- in need of intermittent skilled nursing care, physical therapy, or speech-language pathology, or have a continuing need for occupational therapy.

"Intermittent" is defined as skilled nursing care that is either provided or needed on fewer than seven days per week, or less than eight hours per day for periods of 21 days or less (with extensions in exceptional circumstances when the need for care is finite and predictable).[53]

In recent years, concerns have arisen among providers and Medicare beneficiaries that the Medicare definition of "confined to the home" or "homebound" has been applied too restrictively by CMS and the regional home health intermediaries (RHHIs) that process claims for home health services. In essence, the Medicare program required the patient literally to be confined to the home. If the patient left the home for nonmedical purposes, these absences would have to be for short periods of time in duration or occur only infrequently.

In 2000, Congress expanded the homebound definition to allow patients to attend adult daycare programs or religious services.[54] Further, on July 26, 2002, CMS issued changes to its *Home Health*

[52] *See, e.g.*, N.Y. PUB. HEALTH § 3606.

[53] *See Medicare Home Health Agency Manual* (CMS Pub. 11), §§ 204, 205.1.C., available on the CMS website at http://www.cms.hhs.gov/Manuals/PBM/itemdetail.asp?filterType=none&filterByDID=-99&sortByDID=1&sortOrder=ascending&itemID=CMS021914&intNumPerPage=10.

[54] Consolidated Appropriations Act, 2001, Pub. L. 106-554, § 507(a) (amending 42 U.S.C. §§ 1395f(a) and 1395n(a)).

Agency Manual to require Medicare contractors to be more flexible in determining if a severely disabled individual is qualified as homebound for purposes of the Medicare home-health benefit. According to CMS, some HHAs and contractors have interpreted this policy to require that home-health benefits be terminated if a beneficiary attends a special event, even though the beneficiary otherwise continues to qualify as homebound. CMS's current policy makes clear that chronically disabled individuals who otherwise qualify as homebound should not lose home health services because they leave their homes infrequently for short periods of time for special occasions, such as family reunions, graduations, or funerals. Specifically, the program manual accomplishes the following:

- expands the list of examples used to illustrate occasional absences from the home, and notes that the list is still not all-inclusive;
- adds the late stages of amyotrophic lateral sclerosis (ALS, also known as Lou Gerhig's Disease) or other neurodegenerative disabilities to the list of examples of conditions that may indicate that the patient cannot leave her home; and
- makes it clear that the determination as to whether a person is homebound is one that must be made over a period of time, not on a daily or weekly basis—in effect, that a few special trips outside the home would not be used to disqualify a patient who has a normal inability to leave the home.[55]

10.3.2.2 Conditions of Participation

Medicare-certified HHAs are subject to relatively detailed federal standards.[56] These standards, called "conditions of participation," govern issues such as the qualifications of personnel, furnishing services, developing plans of care, and the like.[57] A hospital or SNF is not considered to be the patient's home for purposes of HHA coverage;[58] an assisted living facility, however, may be the patient's home for coverage of HHA services. HHAs are subject to a variety of penalties—including civil monetary penalties (CMPs) of up to $10,000 per day—if they do not comply with these standards.[59]

An additional condition of participation, recently elaborated on by program transmittal, requires HHAs to provide advance beneficiary notices (HHABNs) if an HHA believes that services may not be covered or that are an extension of the add-on for rural payments.[60] These requirements apply, for example, where a beneficiary faces potential liability for care that has been received but may be reduced or terminated, where the HHA has reason to believe a service that is generally covered may be found not to be reasonable or necessary in a given situation, or where the HHA decides for its own reasons no longer to provide some or all of its care.[61]

---

55 A copy of the transmittal is available on the Internet at https://www.cms.gov/transmittals/downloads/R302HHA.pdf.

56 42 U.S.C. § 1395m.

57 *See* 42 C.F.R. §§ 484.1 *et seq.*

58 42 C.F.R. § 409.42.

59 *See* 42 U.S.C. § 1395bbb(e)–(f).

60 *See* Transmittal 1025 regarding revised HHABNs (Aug. 11, 2006), available at http://www.cms.hhs.gov/BNI/03_HHABN.asp.

61 The standard form is available at http://www.cms.gov/BNI/03_HHABN.asp. Per an August 26, 2009 note on this webpage, HHABN Form CMS-R-296 is currently undergoing the final stages of the Office of Management and Budget (OMB) review in accordance with the Paperwork Reduction Act, and HHAs should continue to use the existing HHABN until the revised HHABN receives final OMB approval and is posted to the website.

As part of CMS's November 10, 2009 final prospective payment system (PPS) home health rule for 2010, CMS adopted a provision stating that if the owner of an HHA sells (including asset sales or stock transfers), transfers or relinquishes ownership of the HHA within 36 months after the effective date of the HHA's enrollment in Medicare, the provider agreement and Medicare billing privileges do not convey to the new owner.[62] CMS states that the purpose of this new rule is to ensure that HHAs that are sold remain in compliance with Medicare's conditions of participation. CMS also asserts that this change was needed to avoid individuals buying HHAs solely for resale with no intention of operating the business. CMS states that the rule "will help to ensure that individuals establishing an HHA are doing so with the long-term view of furnishing services, rather than establishing a business for the purposes of selling it a short time later."[63]

HHAs use a standardized evaluation instrument known as the Outcomes and Assessment Information Set (OASIS) to document the care needs and services for every patient admitted for services. The OASIS is also used to categorize patients for payment purposes under the Medicare prospective payment system for HHAs. *See* discussion in the following section.

10.3.2.3 Payment

Historically, HHA services were reimbursed on a reasonable cost basis. The BBA imposed strict per-beneficiary and per-visit caps, known as the interim payment system (IPS), which was an interim system until a prospective system for HHAs was implemented. HHAs submit claims and cost reports to the designated RHHIs.

The BBA directed the Secretary of DHHS to establish a PPS for home health services beginning October 1, 1999, although actual implementation was delayed until 2000. Under the BBA, all services covered and paid on a reasonable-cost basis at the time of enactment (including medical supplies) are to be paid under the PPS. Services reimbursed on the basis of a fee schedule, including DME and orthotics and prosthetics, are not to be included in the PPS rate. Congress directed the DHHS Secretary to determine an appropriate unit of service, along with the number, type, and duration of visits provided within the unit; their costs; and a "general system design that provides for continued access to quality services."[64] No particular type of unit (*e.g.,* per visit or per episode) was specified.

Payment amounts initially were based on the most current audited cost-report data available to the HHS Secretary, and total payment amounts for fiscal year (FY) 2000 must equal the amount that would have been made if the PPS system had not been in effect, except that this amount is to reflect a 15% reduction in cost limits and per-beneficiary limits that were in effect on September 30, 1999. Actual payments are to be adjusted to reflect case mix, area wages, and inflation. Additional outlier payments or adjustments may be made, but they may not exceed 5% of the total PPS payments estimated to be made in that year.

The BBA also required consolidated billing by the HHA for home health items and services furnished to an individual who (at the time the item or service is furnished) "is under a plan of care of a

[62] 42 C.F.R. § 424.550(b)(1).

[63] Medicare Program; Home Health Prospective Payment System, 74 Fed. Reg. 58,078, 58,118 (Nov. 10, 2009).

[64] *See* BBA, Pub. L. No. 105-33, 111 Stat. 273, § 4603(a) (amending 42 U.S.C. § 1395u).

home health agency," without regard to whether or not the item or service was furnished by the agency, by others under arrangement with the agency, due to any other contracting or consulting arrangement, or otherwise.[65] In other words, if a beneficiary is receiving care under an HHA plan of care, most items and services must be billed by the HHA, rather than the supplier.

On October 28, 1999, HCFA issued a proposed rule to implement the home health PPS;[66] on July 3, 2000, HCFA issued the final rule.[67] Certain key elements of the home health PPS are as follows:

- *The unit of service is a 60-day episode of care.* There are no limits to the number of episodes a beneficiary who is eligible for the home health benefit can receive. HHAs receive half of the payment up front, and the balance after the 60-day period (unless there is an applicable adjustment).
- *Case-mix adjusted payment.* Based on the OASIS resident-assessment instrument, patients are classified into one of 153 home health resource groups (HHRGs) by clinical severity, patient functional status, and service intensity. Payment thus is intended to reflect the care needs of the patient.
- *Payment rates are subject* to wage indices to account for geographical variations in labor costs.
- *Low Utilization Payment Adjustment (LUPA).* Payments are adjusted when the patient needs four or fewer visits. The LUPA essentially converts the PPS to a fee-for-service payment for these types of patients.[68]
- *Partial Episode Payment Adjustment (PEP).* Payments are adjusted when a patient changes HHAs during the 60-day period, or is discharged and readmitted to the same HHA during the 60-day period. The "old" period begins when the last visit occurs, and the "new" episode begins as for the first visit. Payment is pro-rated based on the number of days the patient is under the care of the agency. The PEP does not apply when a beneficiary transfers to an HHA that has common ownership.
- *Outlier Payments.* Payments are adjusted for patients where the costs of care exceeds the fixed payment rate under the HHRG greater than the outlier threshold. The outlier payment is the difference between the cost of the episode and the outlier threshold. HHAs are paid at 80% of the costs above the outlier threshold (known as the loss-sharing ratio). Notably, the outlier adjustment does not make up for all of the costs exceeding the HHRG payment. Rather, as the name implies, it is a way for the HHA to make up some, but not all, of its costs. Effective January 1, 2010, outlier payments may compromise no more than 10% of an HHA's total home health PPS payments for the year.

[65] BBA, Pub. L. No. 105-33, 111 Stat. 273, § 4603(c) (amending 42 U.S.C. § 1395fff(b)(2)).

[66] Medicare Program; Prospective Payment System for Home Health Agencies, 64 Fed. Reg. 58,134 (Oct. 28, 1999).

[67] Medicare Program; Prospective Payment System for Home Health Agencies, 65 Fed. Reg. 41,128 (2000).

[68] Originally the HHA PPS had a Significant Change in Condition Payment Adjustment for when the patient's condition changed during the 60-day episode. This was eliminated effective January 1, 2008. *See* 72 Fed Reg 49,762, 49,850 (2007).

- *Consolidated Billing.* HHAs must bill for all home health items and services provided to the patient as set forth in the plan of care except DME, including oxygen and oxygen supplies. Notably, however, most medical supplies still are subject to the consolidated billing requirement.[69]

The DRA made numerous changes to HHA payments.[70] The DRA eliminated the update to Medicare home health PPS rates for fiscal year 2006, freezing rates at 2005 levels. The law did, however, provide for a one-year, 5% rural add-on for rural HHAs for 2006. Beginning in 2007, the DRA ties home health rate increases to the submission of quality data. Specifically, HHAs are required to submit quality data that the Secretary of HHS determines to be appropriate for measuring healthcare quality. The data must be submitted in a form and manner and at a time specified by the Secretary. The Secretary must establish a process for making the data available to the public (although the HHA must have an opportunity to review the data before it is released to the public). HHAs that report the quality data receive the full market basket update; HHAs that do not report the quality data receive the market basket update minus 2 percentage points (the update will not be taken into account in determining payments in subsequent years).

To implement this statutory requirement, CMS utilized the current OASIS as the reporting instrument. Therefore, as a practical matter, since most HHAs were already reporting OASIS data, most received the full market basket update in 2007. The results of the quality measures from the OASIS reports are now reported on CMS's Home Health Compare website.[71] This information, and how an HHA compares to state and national averages, is publicly available.

On November 9, 2006 CMS published its final calendar year 2007 Medicare home health PPS update. Under the rule, HHAs that submit the required quality data as mandated by the DRA receive payments based on the full proposed home health market basket update of 3.1%. If an HHA does not submit quality data, the home health market basket percentage increase is reduced by 2 percentage points to 1.1%, as mandated by the DRA.[72]

The DRA also directs the Medicare Payment Advisory Commission (MedPAC) to submit a report to Congress no later than June 1, 2007 on a value-based purchasing program for home health services. The report must include recommendations on the structure of the program, the determination of thresholds, the size of value-based payments, sources of funds, and the relationship of payments for improvements in healthcare quality. In June 2007 MedPAC included its assessment of value-based purchasing for home care in its report to Congress. In the report, MedPAC concludes that financial incentives for quality is one tool to be used to enhance quality, along with other payment reforms (such as improving the accuracy of payment amounts) and other incentives to promote quality, such

[69] Information and links regarding HHA billing are available at https://www.cms.gov/center/hha.asp.

[70] DRA, Pub. L. No. 109-171, 120 Stat. 4, § 5201 (amending 42 U.S.C. § 1395fff).

[71] The Home Health Compare website is available at http://www.medicare.gov/HHCompare.

[72] Medicare Program; Home Health Prospective Payment System Rate Update for Calendar Year 2007 and Deficit Reduction Act of 2005 Changes to Medicare Payment for Oxygen Equipment and Capped Rental Durable Medical Equipment, 71 Fed. Reg. 65,884 (Nov. 9, 2006) (to be codified at 42 C.F.R. pts. 414 and 484).

as public reporting.[73] In its March 2010 report, MedPAC concludes that home health payments must be reduced.[74]

CMS has made a number of refinements to the home health PPS over the years.[75] Recently, in CMS's 2010 home health PPS final rule published November 10, 2009,[76] Medicare spending was expected to be reduced due to a 2.0% HHA MBI increase ($350 million), offset by the effects of an updated wage index (-$10 million), and a 2.75% decrease resulting from the third year of a four-year phase-in of adjustments to rates to account for case-mix changes (-$480 million). Additionally, CMS adopted various provisions designed to "mitigate possible billing vulnerabilities associated with excessive outlier payments," such as capping per-agency outlier payments at 10% for 2010. This final rule also included various payment safeguards for HHAs. In the proposed rule, CMS had proposed to deny Medicare billing privileges to a prospective HHA if the HHA is determined to be sharing its practice location or base of operations with another Medicare-enrolled HHA or supplier. Although CMS expressed its concerns with this type of arrangement, CMS declined to adopt this broad prohibition.

In July 2010, CMS published its proposed rule updating home health PPS rates for 2011, which includes a decrease by an estimated $900 million for CY 2011 in Medicare payments to HHAs and implements certain ACA provisions.[77]

The ACA also makes changes to the Medicare HHA payment methodology. For instance, the ACA imposes an HHA market basket reduction of 1 percentage point in 2011 through 2013 and a productivity adjustment on HHAs beginning in CY 2015.[78] Other ACA changes to the Medicare HHA reimbursement scheme include a 10 percent cap on the amount of outlier payments that each HHA can receive, 3% add-on payment for rural home health providers, and a requirement that the Secretary submit a plan to Congress by October 1, 2011 to include HHAs as part of a Medicare value-based purchasing program.

The ACA also directs the DHHS Secretary to submit a plan to Congress by FY 2012 outlining how to effectively move HHAs into a value-based purchasing payment system.[79]

---

[73] MedPAC, Report to the Congress, Promoting Greater Efficiency in Medicare, Chapter 4 (June 2007), available at http://www.medpac.gov/documents/Jun07_EntireReport.pdf.

[74] MedPAC, Report to the Congress: Medicare Payment Policy, available at http://www.medpac.gov/documents/Mar10_EntireReport.pdf.

[75] *See, e.g.*, 72 Fed. Reg. 25,358 (May 4, 2007) (to be codified at 42 C.F.R. pt. 484); Medicare Program; Home Health Prospective Payment System Rate Updated for Calendar Year 2010; Final Rule, 74 Fed. Reg. 58,078 (Nov. 10, 2009) (to be codified at 42 C.F.R. pts. 409, 424, 484).

[76] Medicare Program; Home Health Prospective Payment System Rate Updated for Calendar Year 2010; Final Rule, 74 Fed. Reg. 58,078 (Nov. 10, 2009) (to be codified at 42 C.F.R. pts. 409, 424, 484).

[77] Medicare Program; Home Health Prospective Payment System Rate Update for Calendar Year 2011; Changes in Certification Requirements for Home Health Agencies and Hospices, 75 Fed. Reg. 43,236 (Jul. 23, 2010), available at http://edocket.access.gpo.gov/2010/pdf/2010-17753.pdf.

[78] *See* PPACA § 3401.

[79] PPACA § 3006.

10.3.3 Medicaid HHAs

10.3.3.1 *Coverage*

The provision of home health services is an optional requirement for state Medicaid programs, but most states provide such benefits.[80] States also may provide payment for private-duty nursing.[81] Most state Medicaid programs follow Medicare coverage rules for HHAs. Some offer programs that cover other types of home care services (*e.g.*, personal care services).[82]

10.3.3.2 *Qualifications*

Most states follow the Medicare HHA conditions of participation, as well as state licensure.

10.3.3.3 *Payment*

Payment is determined by each state Medicaid program, and methodologies differ among the states. Some states apply a flat rate per visit, where actual cost is not a factor. Others use cost reports to set a prospective rate, subject to applicable caps. Still others use a retrospective cost reimbursement system, subject to applicable caps. Consult state law.

10.3.3.4 *Fraud and Abuse*

HHAs continue to be the subject of DOJ, OIG, and RHHI audits and investigations. Key concerns have included submission of false cost reports, providing care to patients not homebound,[83] billing for services not rendered, kickbacks for referrals, and improper marketing. In light of these concerns, in August 1998, the OIG issued an HHA Compliance Program Guidance identifying specific elements HHAs should consider when developing and implementing an effective compliance program and "risk areas" to be addressed.[84] The guidance is a useful summary of rules and regulations applicable to HHAs. Since then, HHAs have been subject to the federal government's efforts to combat fraudulent Medicare practices.

Pursuant to its 2010 Work Plan, the OIG will examine Part B payments for home health beneficiaries; Medicare claims submitted by HHAs to determine the extent to which HHRG billing codes are accurate and supported by documentation in the medical record; incidence of Medicare home health services outlier payments for insulin injections; CMS's methodology for calculating outlier payments to HHAs to determine whether the methodology reimburses HHAs as intended for high cost episodes; PPS controls; HHA profitability; Medicare home health payments for diabetes self-management training services; oversight of OASIS.[85]

---

80 42 U.S.C. §§ 1396a(10)(A), 1396d(a)(7).

81 *Id.* § 1396d(a)(8).

82 *Id.* § 1396d(a)(24).

83 *See* Section 10.3.2.1.

84 Publication of the OIG Compliance Program Guidelines for Home Health Agencies, 63 Fed. Reg. 42,410 (Aug. 7. 1998), available at http://oig.hhs.gov/authorities/docs/cpghome.pdf.

85 *See* OIG Work Plan, Fiscal Year 2010, available at http://oig.hhs.gov/publications/docs/workplan/2010/Work_Plan_FY_2010.pdf.

10.3.3.5 Audits

RHHIs perform sample audits of the medical necessity of home health services provided to Medicare beneficiaries, and sometimes extrapolate sample results to the entire "universe" of patient claims for the relevant period. HHAs therefore need to perform routine internal audits to make sure documentation supports the care provided, that the plan of care is appropriately updated, and that patients who do not qualify for the Medicare home health benefit are discharged.

10.3.3.6 Hospital Discharge Planning

The Medicare hospital conditions of participation require hospitals to evaluate patients for post-acute hospital services and the availability of those services.[86] The Medicare statute and implementing regulations specifically require hospitals to consider a patient's home health, hospice and post-hospital extended care service needs.[87] In response to concerns about hospitals steering patients to specific HHAs, including those in which they had a financial interest, Congress enacted legislation requiring hospitals to provide Medicare beneficiaries in need of home health services with a list of all Medicare-certified HHAs in the area that have requested to be listed by the hospital. The list must also indicate the HHAs that are enrolled in managed care organizations. Hospitals must inform patients of their freedom of choice of home-health providers, and cannot limit or restrict qualified HHAs that may wish to care for patients following discharge.[88] Hospitals must document in the patient record that the list was presented to the patient or person acting on behalf of the patient.[89] The discharge plan must also identify any HHA to which the patient is referred in which the hospital has a disclosable financial interest.[90] HHAs cannot undertake discharge-planning functions required of the hospital, but can undertake an evaluation of the patient once a referral to the HHA has been made.

10.4 Hospice Care

10.4.1 Introduction

The hospice benefit is available to eligible Medicare and Medicaid beneficiaries who are terminally ill.[91] By electing hospice care, the beneficiary decides to forgo curative medical intervention in favor of palliative care to ease the final stages of the beneficiary's life. Hospice care is provided under an established plan of care by an interdisciplinary team of professionals and volunteers who administer to the physical, social, and spiritual needs of the patient.

---

86 42 C.F.R. § 482.43(a) and (b).

87 *See* 42 U.S.C. § 1395x(ee)(2); 42 C.F.R. § 482.43.

88 *See* 42 U.S.C. § 1395x(ee)(2); 42 C.F.R. § 482.43(c).

89 42 C.F.R. § 482.43(c)(6).

90 *Id.* § 482.43(c)(5), (6).

91 *See* 42 U.S.C. § 1395d, f, x(dd), § 1396.

10.4.2 State Licensure and Certificate of Need

A hospice provider may be a public agency or private organization that is certified to participate in the Medicare program.[92] In addition to compliance with federal laws and regulations, a hospice provider must comply with applicable state and local licensure laws as a condition of participation in the Medicare program.[93] Most states license hospices. Many state licensure laws closely track the federal Medicare conditions of participation.[94] Others impose additional or more specific requirements.[95] All hospice employees also must be properly licensed in accordance with applicable federal, state, and local laws. Finally, certain states require hospices to obtain a CON prior to establishing the hospice program.[96] Consult individual state's laws and regulations regarding licensure and CON requirements.

10.4.3 Qualifications for Medicare Coverage

Generally, to qualify for Medicare coverage of hospice care, the beneficiary must be diagnosed with a terminal illness, which is defined as a life expectancy of six months or less if the illness runs its normal course.[97] The beneficiary's terminal prognosis must be certified by both the hospice's medical director and the patient's attending physician (if any).[98] The beneficiary must consent to receive only palliative care to manage discomfort and relieve the symptoms of the illness, thereby waiving Medicare benefits for curative medical treatments.[99] The hospice care must be furnished under a plan of care established by the attending physician, the hospice's medical director, and the interdisciplinary group.[100] The hospice must maintain complete and accurate documentation for each patient in a clinical record.[101]

10.4.4 Conditions of Participation

As with other types of Medicare providers, hospices are subject to specific federal standards.[102] These standards, called "conditions of participation," govern issues such as the qualifications of personnel, furnishing services, developing plans of care, and the like.[103] The Medicare State Operations Manual (SOM) provides further guidance on how CMS and state survey agencies interpret these regulations.[104]

---

92 *See* 42 C.F.R. § 418.3.
93 *See id.* § 418.72.
94 *See, e.g.*, Fla. Stat. Ann. § 400.6085.
95 *See, e.g.*, Wis. Admin. Code § HHS 131.21 (establishing detailed patient and family bill of rights).
96 *See, e.g.*, Fla. Stat. Ann. §§ 400.606(5), 408.031–408.045.
97 *See* 42 C.F.R. § 418.3; *see also* Section 10.4.6.
98 *Id.* § 418.22(c).
99 *See id.* § 418.24(b), (d).
100 *See id.* § 418.58(a).
101 *See id.* § 418.74.
102 42 U.S.C. § 1395m.
103 *See generally* 42 C.F.R. §§ 418.1 *et seq.*
104 *See Medicare State Operations Manual* (CMS Pub. 107), Appendix M (available on the CMS website at http://www.cms.hhs.gov/manuals/downloads/som107_Appendicestoc.pdf.

10.4.4.1 New Conditions of Participation

On November 22, 2005, CMS issued revised hospice rules to update and amend different sections of the regulations.[105] The rule expands the hospice benefit periods, clarifies and enhances documentation requirements to support certification and recertification of terminal illness, provides guidance on hospice admission procedures, clarifies hospice discharge procedures to allow discharges from hospice for cause under very limited circumstances, updates coverage and payment requirements, and addresses the changing needs of beneficiaries, suppliers, and the Medicare program. These revisions reflect the statutory changes required by the BBA, the BBRA, and BIPA, as well as updated policy.

More recently, on June 5, 2008, CMS published a final rule making extensive revisions to the conditions of participation that hospices must meet to participate in the Medicare and Medicaid programs. Most notably, the rule requires hospices to implement "an effective, ongoing, hospice-wide data-driven quality assessment and performance improvement (QAPI) program." Rather than establishing detailed requirements for such assessments, the rule states that "each hospice is free to decide how to implement the QAPI requirement in a manner that reflects its own unique needs and goals." The rule also revises conditions of participation provisions related to patients' rights; patient assessments; and interdisciplinary group (IDG), care planning, and coordination of services. In addition, the rule modifies a number of staffing policies, such as by requiring the physician member of the IDG and the medical director to be an employee of or under contract with the hospice, and permitting nurse practitioners to provide services to beneficiaries receiving hospice care if state law permits. Moreover, the rule clarifies a hospice's responsibility for care provided to hospice patients residing in a nursing facility.[106] The new conditions of participation became effective on December 2, 2008.

10.4.4.2 Types of Hospice Care

A hospice provider may furnish care to beneficiaries in a variety of settings, including a freestanding hospice facility, a SNF, a hospital, or in the beneficiary's home. Hospice care falls into four basic categories:

- *Routine home care* is the typical level of care provided to a hospice patient, and is furnished in the patient's home or in a facility that is the patient's residence.
- *Continuous home care* is provided for eight to 24 hours per day for brief periods while a hospice patient is in crisis but can be maintained at home. If a hospice provides this level of care, 51% of the care must be provided by a licensed RN.
- *Inpatient respite care* is provided when the hospice patient's family or caregiver requires a temporary reprieve, which is not related to the patient's physical decline. This level of care can be provided in a facility for up to five days and, after five days, the hospice patient must be converted to another level of care. An RN must be available to provide direct patient care 24 hours a day.

---

105 70 Fed. Reg. 70,532 (2005); 42 C.F.R. 418.

106 73 Fed. Reg. 32,088 (June 5, 2008).

- *General inpatient care* is provided when a hospice patient requires admission to an inpatient facility for pain control, or for acute or chronic symptom management that cannot be accomplished in another setting.[107]

Inpatient hospice care for pain control, symptom management, or respite purposes may be provided in inpatient hospice facility, hospital, or SNF.[108] A hospice facility that provides inpatient hospice care directly must meet certain requirements concerning physical plant, room-like décor, and extended visiting hours.[109] All the hospice inpatient facilities must provide: (1) 24-hour nursing services that are sufficient to meet the patient's needs; (2) a registered nurse on each shift who provides direct patient care; and (3) patient area requirements to meet the comfort and privacy of patients and their families.[110]

A hospice that contracts with a hospital or SNF to provide inpatient care must ensure that:

- the agreement specifies the inpatient services to be furnished;
- the hospice will furnish a copy of the patient's plan of care;
- the inpatient provider's policies are consistent with the hospice;
- the inpatient provider will abide by the hospice's patient-care protocols;
- the medical record will include all inpatient services furnished; and
- the hospice retains responsibility for hospice care training for all personnel involved in providing care pursuant to the agreement.[111]

As noted, hospice services may be provided in long-term care facilities and assisted-living facilities where that is the patient's home. In May 2002, CMS released a memorandum to its regional offices and state survey agencies outlining "promising practices" for the successful implementation of the Medicare hospice benefit for nursing home residents.[112] The practices described in the memorandum are not regulatory requirements; nevertheless, according to CMS, they are consistent with federal requirements if properly implemented. They are intended to assist hospices and nursing homes to structure a collaborative relationship when providing care to common patients and their families at the end of life.

10.4.4.3 Hospice Services

The hospice provides and supervises services through an interdisciplinary group comprised of at least the following individuals, who (except for the physician)[113] must be employees of the hospice:

- a doctor of medicine or osteopathy;
- a registered nurse;

107 *See* 42 C.F.R. § 418.302. *See also Medicare Benefit Policy Manual* (CMS Pub. 100-02), Chapter 9.
108 *See id.* § 418.98.
109 *See id.* § 418.100(c); (e); (f).
110 *See id.* §§ 418.98(a)(2); (b)(2); 418.100(a), (e).
111 *See id.* § 418.56(e).
112 The memorandum is available on CMS's website at http://www.cms.gov/SurveyCertificationGenInfo/downloads/SCLetter02-29.pdf.
113 *See* 42 U.S.C. § 1395xdd(2) (providing that the hospice physician may be an independent contractor or employee).

- a social worker; and
- a pastoral or other counselor.[114]

This interdisciplinary group is responsible for establishing, periodically reviewing, and updating the hospice patient's plan of care, as well as establishing policies governing the daily provision of hospice care.[115]

The hospice must provide certain "core" covered services, which include physician services, nursing services, medical social services, and counseling services.[116] Except during periods of peak patient load or under extraordinary circumstances, core services must be provided by hospice employees. If the hospice provides any services under arrangements with contracted staff, then "the hospice must maintain professional, financial, and administrative responsibility for the services."[117]

The hospice physician is responsible for the palliation and management of the patient's terminal illness and related conditions, as well as any general medical needs that are not being met by the patient's attending physician.[118] Nursing services must be provided by, or under the supervision of, a registered nurse in accordance with recognized standards of practice.[119] Medical social services must be provided to a hospice patient "by a qualified social worker, under the direction of a physician."[120]

Several types of counseling services must be available to the hospice patient and the patient's family. Bereavement counseling must be provided through an organized program under the supervision of a qualified professional. The hospice must establish a plan of care for bereavement services that adequately reflects the needs of the patient's family.[121] The hospice also must provide dietary counseling by a qualified individual, as needed, for the hospice patient.[122] In addition, the hospice must make spiritual counseling available to the hospice patient and the patient's family.[123]

In addition to these core services, the hospice must provide physical therapy, occupational therapy, and speech-language pathology services either through employees or under arrangements.[124] Home health-aides and homemaker services also must be available and be provided under the supervision of a registered nurse.[125] The hospice is required to use volunteers, as well, who must provide administrative or direct patient care equal to at least "5% of the total patient care hours of all paid hospice employees and contract staff."[126]

---

114 *See* 42 C.F.R. § 418.68(a).
115 *See id.* § 418.68(b).
116 *See id.* § 418.202.
117 *Id.* § 418.80.
118 *See id.* § 418.86.
119 *See id.* § 418.82.
120 *Id.* § 418.84.
121 *See id.* § 418.88(a).
122 *See id.* § 418.88(b).
123 *See id.* § 418.88(c).
124 *See* 42 C.F.R. § 418.92.
125 *See id.* § 418.94.
126 *Id.* § 418.70.

10.4.5 Election of Hospice Benefit

An individual who is entitled to Medicare Part A benefits and is certified as terminally ill is eligible to elect the hospice benefit.[127] An eligible individual may elect the hospice benefit for an initial 90-day period, followed by a second 90-day period, and then unlimited subsequent 60-day periods for the beneficiary's lifetime.[128]

If the beneficiary is mentally or physically incapacitated at the beginning of the initial or a subsequent hospice election period, then the individual must be certified as incapacitated to make healthcare decisions pursuant to applicable state law. Many states require at least one physician (and some require two physicians) to certify that the patient is incapacitated to make healthcare decisions. A healthcare guardian or representative then must be appointed, pursuant to state law, to make healthcare decisions for the incapacitated individual.

A Medicare beneficiary who elects hospice care must file with the designated hospice an election statement that (1) identifies the designated hospice, (2) specifies the effective date of the election, and (3) is signed by the beneficiary or the beneficiary's representative.[129] The election statement also must acknowledge the beneficiary's or representative's informed consent to the palliative (rather than curative) nature of hospice care.[130] In addition, the election statement must include an acknowledgment of the beneficiary's or representative's waiver of other Medicare and Medicaid benefits for the treatment of the terminal illness (except services furnished by the attending physician), and waiver of benefits for services rendered by another hospice, unless those services are provided under arrangements with the designated hospice.[131]

An individual or representative may revoke the hospice election at any time by filing a signed statement revoking the hospice election for the remainder of that period. The individual then will resume the Medicare benefits previously waived through the election of hospice care.[132]

10.4.6 Issues in Physician Certification

Both the hospice's medical director (or physician member of the hospice interdisciplinary group) and the individual's attending physician (if any) must provide the initial certification that an individual is terminally ill. For subsequent benefit periods, only the hospice's medical director or physician member of the interdisciplinary group is required to recertify the individual for hospice care.[133] The hospice facility must have a written physician certification or recertification for each benefit period.[134] If the hospice cannot obtain a written certification at the beginning of a benefit period, then the hospice may accept an oral certification, but must obtain the written physician certification within two calendar

[127] *See id.* § 418.20.
[128] *See* 42 U.S.C. § 1395d(d); 42 C.F.R. § 418.21.
[129] *See* 42 C.F.R. § 418.24(a), (b).
[130] *See id.* § 418.24(a)(2).
[131] *See id.* §§ 418.24(a)(3), (d).
[132] *See id.* § 418.28.
[133] *See id.* § 418.22(c).
[134] *See id.* § 418.22(a)(1).

days and before it submits a claim for payment.[135] The written certifications must be filed in the hospice patient's clinical record.[136]

Effective October 1, 2009, physicians must include a brief narrative explanation of the clinical findings that supports a life expectancy of six months or less as part of the certification and recertification forms, or as an addendum to the certification and recertification forms.[137] Likewise, the ACA requires a hospice physician or nurse practitioner to: (1) have a face-to-face encounter with each hospice patient prior to the 180th-day recertification and each subsequent recertification to determine continued eligibility for hospice care, and (2) attest that such visit took place, effective January 1, 2011.[138]

An issue that arises often in hospice care is the attending physician's uncertainty regarding when a patient has reached the terminal stage of an illness and qualifies for the hospice benefit. In many cases, attending physicians also may be uncertain of what constitutes a terminal illness (*e.g.*, the end stages of Alzheimer's disease, which now is recognized as a terminal illness). The result is that patients often have been referred for hospice care when the patient has far less than six months to live and cannot utilize the full benefits of hospice care.

In response to concerns regarding the chilling effect on physicians and hospices concerning patient eligibility for hospice care, Congress amended the Medicare statute in 2000 to provide that the certification by the physician of the patient's terminal illness must be based on the physician's or medical director's "clinical judgment" regarding the normal course of the individual's illness."[139] The purpose of this amendment was to make clear that the six-month certification requirement was not a "hard and fast" rule, but rather one based on the physician's clinical judgment. Likewise, in May 2002, CMS Administrator Thomas A. Scully issued a letter to physicians acknowledging the difficulty in making end-of-life care prognoses and, in particular, making accurate or exact prognoses. He noted that making these determinations is not an exact science and that the impact of a hospice's services may initially improve a patient's condition. Thus, Medicare regulations use the terms "expectancy" and "if the terminal illness runs its normal course" to indicate that it is possible for hospice services to be needed for more than a six-month period. He also noted the statutory requirement, coupled with the recognition of the difficulty in making exact predictions, as evidence that physicians certifying Medicare patients for hospice care are expected only to use their best "clinical judgment regarding the normal course of the individual's illness."[140] Such initiatives have resulted in an increase in hospice lengths of stay in recent years. According to MedPAC, the average hospice length of stay rose from 54 days in 2000 to 83 days in 2008.[141] In response to the trend towards longer-stay patients, the ACA requires the Secretary to establish procedures for medical review of patients whose stays exceed 180 days in hospices with high levels of long-stay patients.[142]

---

135 *See id.* § 418.22(a)(3).
136 *See id.* § 418.22(d).
137 74 Fed. Reg. 39,384 (Aug. 6, 2009).
138 PPACA § 3132.
139 BIPA § 322 amending § 1814(a) of the Social Security Act, 42 U.S.C. § 1395f(a).
140 A copy of this letter is available online at www.nhpco.org/files/public/scully-2.pdf or from the National Hospice and Palliative Care Organization (NHPCO).
141 MedPAC Report to the Congress: Medicare Payment Policy, at 150 (Mar. 2010).
142 PPACA § 3132.

10.4.7 Reimbursement

10.4.7.1 *Medicare*

Medicare reimburses providers under Part A for covered hospice services rendered to eligible beneficiaries. Medicare Part A pays a separate *per diem* rate for routine, continuous, inpatient-respite, and general inpatient hospice-care services.[143] The Part A payment also covers the general supervisory services furnished by the hospice medical director, as well as services rendered by other hospice-employed physicians.[144] Medicare limits the total payment to the hospice per beneficiary to the cap amount set by the program for the cap period.[145] The Medicare program also sets a cap on the total amount of reimbursement to the hospice for inpatient care days for Medicare patients.[146] The cap amount is adjusted each year for inflation or deflation.[147] Payment for the hospice's total number of inpatient care days (general or respite) may not exceed 20% of the total number of days for which Medicare patients received hospice care.[148]

Medicare Part B reimburses for services furnished by the patient's attending physician not employed by the hospice, and for services rendered by other physicians for care that is not related to the patient's terminal illness.[149]

Effective January 1, 2007, hospices must include site-of-service codes on their claims. Specifically, hospices must report a HCPCS code along with each revenue code to identify the type of service location where that level of care was provided.[150]

In addition, as of January 1, 2010, hospices must report visits in 15-minute intervals by discipline (nursing, hospice aide, medical social work, physical therapy, occupational therapy, or speech language therapy) provided each day at each site of service.[151] Visits for patients receiving general inpatient care are summed and reported by week (Sunday through Saturday); hospices are not required to report the length of general inpatient visits. Physician visits are to be reported daily, at a procedure code level and are subject to the correct coding policy requirements.[152]

Note that Medicare hospice payment is still based upon the *per diem* amounts, regardless of actual services rendered, but CMS is requiring additional reporting of the time spent on various patient care-related activities. All visits up to 15 minutes are reported as one 15-minute increment, regardless of the length of the visit. Visits longer than 15 minutes are rounded to the nearest 15-minute increment (up or down). For example: a five-minute visit is counted as one 15-minute increment, a 20-minute visit

---

143 *See* 42 C.F.R. § 418.306.
144 *See id.* § 418.304(a), (b).
145 *See id.* § 418.308.
146 *See id.* § 418.302(f).
147 *See id.* § 418.309.
148 *See id.* §§ 418.98(c), 418.302(f)(1).
149 *See id.* § 418.304(c).
150 *See* Change Request 5245 (July 28, 2006) available at http://www.cms.hhs.gov/transmittals/downloads/R1011CP.pdf; *see also* http://www.cms.hhs.gov/mlnmattersarticles/downloads/MM5345.pdf.
151 *See* Change Request 6440 (Apr. 24, 2009), as revised, available at https://www.cms.gov/transmittals/downloads/R1738CP.pdf.
152 *See Medicare Claims Processing Manual* (CMS Pub. 100-04), Chapter 12, § 30.

is counted as one increment, and a 25-minute visit is counted as two increments. Hospices may report social worker telephone calls for providing or coordinating care or counseling the patient's family as long as they are described in the plan of care and documented in the patient's clinical record. Also, each reportable call should be reported on the claim as a billable visit. Travel time and time in IDG meetings do not count as a visit because these are not patient care activities. Where multiple healthcare providers are providing care at the same time, each interaction counts as a visit as long as the visits (1) are required for the palliation and management of the terminal illness and related conditions as described in the plan of correction and (2) are not listed for the purposes of increasing the number of visits. For example, a nurse teaching another nurse to perform a procedure would not comprise two visits. A nurse and an aide turning a difficult patient would constitute one visit each (although there would likely be other tasks performed as part of those visits).

Effective April 29, 2010, hospices must also report a separate service line for each level of care each time the level of care changes. For example, if the level of care starts at routine home care, then becomes continuous home care, followed by another period of routine home care, the claim should report two lines for routine home care and one line for each day of continuous home care. The line item date of service for each of the level of care lines should reflect the first day at that level of care.[153]

The ACA includes a number of changes in Medicare hospice reimbursement policy. The inflation update for hospice services will be subject to a productivity adjustment based on changes in productivity in the nation's overall economy, beginning in FY 2013. Further, hospice payments will be subject to a market basket reduction of 0.3% for FYs 2013 to 2019 (although the reductions in FYs 2014 through 2019 will be waived if a designated threshold for reductions in the uninsured population is not achieved).[154] In addition, the ACA provides that for hospices that do not submit data on quality measures as specified by the Secretary, their annual update will be reduced by 2 percentage points.[155] Hospices must begin reporting the quality measures by FY 2014, and the reported hospice quality data must be made available to the public. The ACA also requires the Secretary to develop broader reforms to the Medicare hospice payment framework. These reforms, which can be instituted no earlier than FY 2013, could include adjustments to per diem payments reflecting changes in resource intensity in providing hospice services over the entire episode of hospice care. Any payment revisions must be budget-neutral.[156] The ACA also requires the Secretary to conduct a Medicare pilot program to test value-based purchasing programs for certain types of Medicare providers, including hospice programs, by January 1, 2016.[157] A separate ACA demonstration would allow hospice-eligible patients to receive all other Medicare-covered services while receiving hospice care, using funds that otherwise would be paid to hospice programs.[158]

---

153 *See* Change Request 6791 (January 29, 2010), available at https://www.cms.gov/transmittals/downloads/R1897CP.pdf; *see also* https://146.123.140.205/MLNMattersArticles/downloads/MM6791.pdf.

154 PPACA § 3401(g) as amended by § 10319(f).

155 PPACA § 3004(c).

156 PPACA § 3132.

157 PPACA § 10326.

158 PPACA § 3140.

10.4.7.2 Medicaid

Hospice is an optional state benefit.[159] If a state provides a hospice benefit, then the coverage must be equivalent in scope and payment to the Medicare benefit.

When a Medicaid-eligible nursing home resident elects the hospice benefit, the state is required to pay an amount, referred to as the "unified rate," that is equal to 95% of the Medicaid *per diem* rate for nursing-home room and board. The state pays the room and board rate in addition to the Medicaid *per diem* rate paid to cover hospice care, if applicable. Both the room-and-board and hospice *per diem* rates are paid to the hospice which, in turn, pays the nursing facility for the hospice patient's room and board.[160]

10.4.8 Fraud and Abuse Issues

Like other healthcare providers, hospice providers continue to be the subject of audits and investigations by DOJ and the OIG in their focus on fraudulent and abusive practices within the healthcare industry. Particular areas of concern for hospice include ineligibility of individuals for hospice care, improper physician certification, lack of informed consent in electing the hospice benefit, falsified medical records and plans of care, improper billing practices, and improper patient solicitation activities, including incentives offered to actual or potential referral sources.

The government is especially wary of hospice arrangements with nursing facilities, which may be particularly vulnerable to fraud and abuse. On March 25, 1998, the OIG released a Special Fraud Alert on "Fraud and Abuse in Nursing Home Arrangements with Hospices."[161] In the Special Fraud Alert, the OIG cited instances of hospices offering free goods, goods at prices below fair market value, and inflated payments to nursing homes for room and board and "additional" services as potential kickbacks to influence the referral of patients to hospices. The OIG continues to examine such arrangements, including a 2007 review that concluded that Medicare beneficiaries in nursing facilities typically spend more time in hospice care and are associated with higher Medicare hospice care reimbursement than beneficiaries in other settings.[162] A separate 2009 OIG report also found that 82% of hospice claims for beneficiaries in nursing facilities did not meet at least one Medicare coverage requirement.[163] The OIG also has focused attention recently on hospice billing for physician services. In a 2010 report, the OIG noted that Medicare paid nearly $566,000 in 2009 to physicians for hospice care that the OIG characterized as "questionable" because the physician was paid for the service both under Part A and Part B.[164]

---

[159] *See* 42 U.S.C. § 1396d(a)(18), (o).

[160] *See id.* §§ 1396a(a)(13)(B), 1396d(o)(3).

[161] *See* 64 Fed. Reg. 54,031 (1999). This guidance is also available online at http://oig.hhs.gov/authorities/docs/hospicx.pdf.

[162] OIG Report, "Medicare Hospice Care: A Comparison of Beneficiaries in Nursing Facilities and Beneficiaries in Other Settings" (2007).

[163] OIG Report, "Medicare Hospice Care for Beneficiaries in Nursing Facilities: Compliance With Medicare Coverage Requirements" (2009).

[164] OIG Report, "Questionable Billing for Physician Services for Hospice Beneficiaries" (2010).

The government has used the federal False Claims Act (FCA)[165] as a basis for filing actions against hospice providers, alleging that fraudulent practices result in the submission of false claims for Medicare and/or Medicaid reimbursement. One example of the government's efforts in this area is the Odyssey settlement agreement. Odyssey Healthcare, Inc., a Dallas, Texas-based hospice provider, agreed to pay the United States $12.9 million to settle allegations that the company billed the Medicare program for services provided to hospice patients who were not terminally ill and hence were ineligible for the Medicare hospice benefit. Odyssey Healthcare also entered into a Corporate Integrity Agreement (CIA) with the OIG, effective July 6, 2006.[166] The CIA is in effect for a period of five years and requires Odyssey, among other procedures, to establish a compliance committee and appoint a compliance officer, to develop, implement a Code of Conduct and Policies and Procedures for compliance, issue various notices and reports to government agencies, retain an independent verification organization, and implement a disclosure program.[167]

10.4.9 Compliance Guidance for Hospices

On September 30, 1999, the OIG issued its final version of Compliance Program Guidance for Hospices.[168] The OIG's hospice compliance guidelines, like other compliance guidelines, outlines the elements for inclusion in any hospice compliance program, and identifies the "risk areas" to be addressed in policies and procedures. Generally, a hospice compliance program should demonstrate clearly the hospice's commitment to compliance with all applicable federal, state, and private insurance standards, and should emphasize the prevention of fraud and abuse. The OIG's Compliance Program Guidance for Hospices is a useful summary of areas the OIG believes may present compliance risks for hospices. For example, thc OIG urges caution in the areas of physician certification, informed consent to elect the hospice benefit, patient solicitation activities, medical records, and billing procedures.

10.5 Long Term Care

10.5.1 State Licensure

All states require licensure or its equivalent to operate a nursing home. The majority of states require licensure to operate an assisted-living facility or residential-care facility. A licensed facility is subject to certain requirements pertaining to staffing, provision of services, and physical plant, as set forth in the applicable licensure statute and regulations. Consult state law.

---

165 31 U.S.C. § 3729.

166 *See* "The Department of Health and Human Services and The Department of Justice Health Care Fraud and Abuse Control Program Annual Report for FY 2006" at 22, available at http://oig.hhs.gov/publications/docs/hcfac/hcfacreport2006.pdf.

167 The Corporate Integrity Agreement is available at http://oig.hhs.gov/fraud/cia/agreements/odyssey_healthcare_inc_07072006.pdf.

168 Available at http://oig.hhs.gov/fraud/complianceguidance.asp.

10.5.2 State Certificate of Need

Approximately two-thirds of states require a CON or its equivalent to develop or construct a new healthcare facility (such as a nursing home), incur a capital expenditure by or on behalf of a healthcare facility above a specified expenditure threshold, add beds/services to an existing healthcare facility, change the location of a facility, and, in some cases, acquire or change a majority of ownership of an existing healthcare facility. Consult state law and regulations governing the projects subject to review, any exemptions, any expedited review process, or the standard review process, if applicable. Some states have placed moratoria on new construction; others impose requirements on new healthcare facilities (*e.g.*, participation in the state Medicaid program). A few states (*e.g.*, New Jersey) subject assisted-living facilities to CON review.[169]

10.5.3 Medicare Skilled Nursing Facilities

Nursing homes participating in the Medicare program are known as skilled nursing facilities (SNFs). A nursing home may have one wing or floor that is a Medicare-certified SNF, or the whole facility may be certified by Medicare. Current Medicare payment rules provide fewer advantages to partial certification than had been granted under the previous cost-based reimbursement system. Some states require facilities to certify the whole facility for Medicare participation. The services offered by SNFs generally include: nursing care; room and board; physical, occupational, and speech therapy; social services; and other necessary services, supplies, and equipment.[170]

10.5.3.1 Coverage

Medicare SNF coverage applies for Medicare beneficiaries who have been in a hospital for at least three days and enter a SNF within 30 days of discharge. The benefit only extends for 100 days per spell of illness; Medicare pays 100% for the first 20 days, and beneficiaries are responsible for a daily deductible for the next 80 days.[171] Residents must also require a skilled level of care.[172]

10.5.3.2 SNF Qualifications

Under the Omnibus Budget Reconciliation Act of 1987 (OBRA '87),[173] SNFs must meet extensive quality standards set forth in requirements for participation, and are subject to strict enforcement remedies for failure to comply with applicable standards. SNFs are required to provide the care and necessary services "to attain or maintain the highest practicable physical, mental, and psychosocial well-being of each resident."[174]

Among the specific quality requirements SNFs must meet are: minimum nurse staffing standards; required training of nurse's aides; the obligation to provide, or arrange for, all of the resident's care

---

169 *See* N.J. Admin. Code § 8:36-2.1.
170 *See* 42 U.S.C. § 1395x(h) (describing the various extended care services that may be furnished to SNF residents).
171 *See id.* §§ 1395d(a)(2), 1395e(a)(3).
172 *See* 42 C.F.R. § 409.30; *Medicare Benefit Policy Manual* (CMS Pub. 100-02), Chapter 8 § 30.
173 Omnibus Budget Reconciliation Act of 1987, Pub. L. No. 100-203, 101 Stat. 1330.
174 42 U.S.C. § 1395i-3(b)(2).

needs; and residents' rights requirements.[175] CMS has elaborated upon the requirements SNFs must meet in interpretive guidelines to the regulations in SOM Appendices. Key areas with additional requirements pertain to medical director services, pharmacy and consulting pharmacist services, psychosocial severity guide, and pain assessments.[176]

Failure to adhere to these standards, as determined by an onsite survey conducted by the state survey agency, can result in a wide range of remedies: appointment of temporary management, denial of Medicare payment for new admissions, directed plans of correction, closure of facilities, termination of Medicare participation, and CMPs up to $10,000 per day or per instance. Penalties can be increased for repeat deficiencies and repeat findings of substandard quality of care (defined as deficiencies in the areas of resident behavior and facility practices, quality of life, or quality of care that are widespread with actual harm or potential for more than minimal harm, or that constitute immediate jeopardy).[177] Remedies are subject to an informal dispute resolution process (by state) and administrative appeal.[178]

10.5.3.3 Reimbursement

Historically, the Medicare program reimbursed SNFs for the "reasonable costs" of providing covered Part A services, subject to certain limits.[179] SNFs were responsible for providing or arranging for the provision of covered Part A services, and billed for their costs of providing these services. In cases where the SNF did not provide ancillary services through its own employees and, instead, opted to outsource these services to an outside ancillary service provider, the SNF would report the ancillary service provider's charge on its Medicare cost report.

At the same time, Medicare recognized that, once a patient's eligibility for benefits under Medicare Part A was exhausted, a patient could still be eligible for coverage of certain ancillary services (*e.g.*, therapy services) under Medicare Part B, Medicaid, or other third-party payment programs. Under these circumstances, as well as where certain Part A services were not furnished by the facility,[180] the outside ancillary service provider would bill Medicare Part B, Medicaid, or other third-party payors directly for services furnished to patients. The Medicare program then would pay the outside supplier based on the applicable Part B or other payment methodology.

Section 4432 of the BBA required the Secretary of HHS to establish, for cost-reporting periods beginning on or after July 1, 1998, a PPS for Part A SNF services consisting of *per diem* rates that vary based on the intensity of resources required by each resident. With a few exceptions, the PPS rate covers all routine, ancillary, and capital costs of services furnished to patients during a covered Part A stay.[181] Residents are placed in a particular resource utilization group (RUG) based upon clinical and other information collected in the minimum data set (MDS) assessment tool. Payment is based on 53 RUGs that are intended to reflect the resources needed to care for the resident. Currently, CMS

---

175 *See id.* § 1395i-3(b)–(d); 42 C.F.R. § 483.1.

176 The SOM, including the Appendices, is available at http://www.cms.hhs.gov/Manuals/IOM/list.asp.

177 42 C.F.R. §§ 488.404, 488.414.

178 *Id.* §§ 488.331, 498.5(b).

179 *See* 42 C.F.R. Part 413.

180 *See, e.g., Medicare Carriers Manual*, CMS Pub. 14, § 2255.

181 *See* 42 U.S.C. § 1395yy(e).

reimburses under the RUG-III classification system. In 2005, CMS initiated a national study, the Staff Time and Resource Intensity Verification (STRIVE) Project, intended to collect data to update the Medicare payment systems.[182]

In the final rule updating SNF PPS payment for FY 2010, CMS announced that a revised case-mix classification methodology (RUG-IV) would be implemented for FY 2011 starting on October 1, 2010.[183] Under § 10325 of the ACA, this implementation is delayed until FY 2012; however, certain components of RUG-IV (concurrent therapy and look-back revisions) will be applied in FY 2011. The FY 2010 SNF payment rule also required that version 3.0 of the MDS (MDS 3.0) go into effect on October 1, 2010 for FY 2011.

The BBA, as amended by BBRA and BIPA, also imposed "consolidated billing" under which the SNF must submit Medicare claims to the Part A Medicare fiscal intermediary for all services that its residents receive (except for certain specifically excluded services)[184] in a Part A stay, and for all Part B therapy services (*e.g.*, physical, occupational, and speech therapy) provided in the SNF. In other words, where previously a third-party provider may have furnished certain services to a SNF resident and billed the program directly, these services must now *only* be billed to the Medicare program by the SNF. The SNF must furnish the services either directly or under an arrangement with an outside provider, and the SNF must bill Medicare. In addition, the BBA requires that Part B services furnished to SNF residents and outpatients (*i.e.*, nonresidents receiving care at the facility) be reimbursed according to the otherwise-applicable fee schedule (or actual charge, if it is less than the applicable fee amount).[185]

The SSA requires CMS to establish a SNF market basket index, which is intended to reflect pricing changes of an appropriate mix of goods and services included in SNF services.[186] Under the ACA, the SNF market basket update will be subject to a full productivity adjustment beginning in FY 2012.[187]

The PPS and consolidated-billing requirements established by the BBA create powerful incentives for SNFs to seek out cost-effective methods of delivering ancillary services. Some SNFs have responded to these challenges by bringing certain activities "in-house." Others have sought to enter into new contracting arrangements with ancillary suppliers, which provide incentives for controlling costs or which share the risk of increased costs. These arrangements may include discounts, *per diem* rates, "risk corridor" arrangements, or similar approaches. In some cases, discounts may apply only to Part A patients; in others, the arrangement may cover all of the patients at a particular facility. The OIG has warned that providing deep discounts on Medicare Part A items and services in return for the

---

[182] CMS, Time Study (STRIVE) http://www.cms.gov/SNFPPS/10_TimeStudy.asp#TopOfPage.

[183] *See* Medicare Program; Prospective Payment System and Consolidated Billing for Skilled Nursing Facilities for FY 2010, 74 Fed. Reg. 40,288, 40,294 (Aug. 11, 2009).

[184] *See* http://www.cms.gov/SNFPPS/05_ConsolidatedBilling.asp#TopOfPage. Currently excluded services for Part A patients in a covered stay include: physician's professional services; certain dialysis-related services; certain ambulance services; Erythropoietin for certain dialysis patients; hospice care; chemotherapy; chemotherapy administration services; radioisotope services; magnetic resonance imaging; cardiac catherization; hospital outpatient radiation therapy; hospital outpatient angiography; lymphatic and venous procedures; and customized prosthetic devices.

[185] *See* 42 U.S.C. §§ 1395u(b)(6), 1395yy(e)(9).

[186] 42 U.S.C. § 1395yy(e).

[187] *See* PPACA § 3401.

referral of Part B business that the vendor bills at standard rates could be found to constitute an illegal kickback under the federal Anti-Kickback Statute and could subject the vendor to exclusion for billing Medicare "substantially in excess" of other payors.[188]

10.5.3.4 *Transparency and Accountability Requirements*

The ACA implemented various requirements for improved SNF transparency. For example, both SNFs and Medicaid nursing facilities are required to have an operational compliance and ethics program within 36 months of enactment.[189] Additionally, the ACA requires the establishment of a quality assurance and performance improvement program for facilities by December 31, 2011 for which regulations will be forthcoming. Additionally, the ACA expands the SNF ownership disclosure requirements already found in the SSA.[190]

10.5.4 Medicaid Nursing Facilities

Nursing homes participating in a state Medicaid program are known as nursing facilities (NFs). A nursing home may have one wing or floor that is a Medicaid-certified NF, or the whole facility may be certified. Many states require facilities to certify the whole facility for Medicaid participation. Under OBRA '87, less of a distinction is made between SNFs and NFs, as both are generally required to provide the same level of care. As with SNFs, the services offered by NFs generally include: nursing care; room and board; physical, occupational, and speech therapy; social services; and other necessary services, supplies, and equipment. The amount and degree varies based upon each particular state's Medicaid-program requirements.

10.5.4.1 *Coverage*

State Medicaid programs are required by federal law to provide coverage for NF services.[191] The amount and scope is based upon the state's Medicaid state plan, subject to federal Medicaid requirements. Consult state law.

10.5.4.2 *Qualifications*

Under OBRA '87, NFs must meet the same extensive quality standards as Medicare SNFs, and are subject to similar enforcement remedies for failure to comply with applicable standards.[192] NFs are required to provide the care and necessary services "to attain or maintain the highest practicable physical, mental, and psychosocial well-being of each resident."[193] Among the specific quality requirements NFs must meet are: minimum nurse-staffing standards; required training of nurse's aides; the obligation to provide, or arrange for, all of the resident's care needs; and residents' rights requirements.[194] Failure to adhere to these standards, as determined by survey, can result in a wide range of remedies,

---

188 *See* OIG Advisory Opinion 99-2 (Mar. 1999).
189 PPACA § 6102.
190 *See* PPACA § 6101.
191 42 U.S.C. §§ 1396a(a)(10), 1396d(a)(4)(A).
192 *Id.* § 1396a(28).
193 *Id.* § 1396r(b)(2).
194 *See* 42 U.S.C. § 1396r(b)–(d); 42 C.F.R. § 483.1.

including: appointment of temporary management; denial of Medicaid payment for new admissions; directed plans of correction; closure of facilities; termination of Medicaid participation; and CMPs up to $10,000 per day or per instance. Significantly, if Medicare terminates a facility from program participation, then the state Medicaid program also is required to terminate the facility from the Medicaid program.[195]

10.5.4.3 Reimbursement

Historically, the federal Medicaid statute and regulations contained several specific limitations on payments for NFs. As a general matter, facilities were required to be reimbursed at a rate that was "reasonable and adequate to meet the costs that must be incurred by efficiently and economically operated facilities in order to provide care and services in conformity with applicable State and Federal laws, regulations, and quality and safety standards."[196] This standard commonly is referred to as the Boren Amendment. Under a separate provision, a state's institutional reimbursement rates could not, in the aggregate, result in greater payments than can reasonably be estimated to be made for comparable services under Medicare payment principles.[197] This provision is generally known as the "Medicare upper limit."

The BBA repealed the Boren Amendment, thus granting states considerable flexibility in establishing Medicaid rates for NFs. The Boren Amendment has been replaced with a "notice and public process" procedure under which states must "publish" and provide "justifications" for rates.[198] State Medicaid plans must comply with various requirements for establishing payment rates.[199]

States employ a variety of rate-setting methodologies to establish NF rates. A rate-setting methodology may be either retrospective or prospective. Under a retrospective methodology, Medicaid makes interim cost-based payments throughout the year, and reconciles the interim payments with the provider's actual reported costs at the end of the year. Under a prospective system, the state establishes a rate in advance of the year by "trending forward" previous years' costs through an inflation factor. Facilities that keep their costs within the prospectively set rate keep the difference; those with costs greater than that rate suffer a loss.

In addition to the retrospective/prospective distinction, states' Medicaid rates can be established on either a class or individual basis. In a class-based system, a state groups similar facilities together for rate-setting purposes, and each of the facilities within the class receives the same rate. In an individual-facility rating system, a facility's rate will be set on the basis of its costs.

State rate-setting methods also may take into account the level of services to be provided to the individual through the use of level of care distinctions, diagnosis-related groups, or case-mix indices (similar to the RUGs system now used for Medicare SNFs). Under these systems, the state generally

---

195 42 C.F.R. § 488.456.

196 This language previously appeared at 42 U.S.C. § 1396a(a)(13) and was replaced by language from BBA, Pub. L. No. § 4711(a)(1).

197 42 C.F.R. § 447.272.

198 42 U.S.C. § 1396a(a)(13)(A).

199 42 C.F.R. §§ 447.201 *et seq.* and 447.250 *et seq.*

pays higher rates for residents with greater care needs. Finally, some states pay supplemental amounts for "administratively necessary" days (*i.e.*, days in which the patient is in the facility awaiting placement in the community) and "reserved bed days" (*e.g.*, days in which a nursing-facility patient is in the hospital).[200]

10.5.4.4 Transparency and Accountability Requirements

The ACA implemented various requirements for improved NF transparency. Both SNFs and Medicaid nursing facilities are required to have an operational compliance and ethics program within 36 months of enactment.[201] Additionally, the ACA requires the establishment of a quality assurance and performance improvement program for facilities by December 31, 2011 and expands the nursing facility ownership disclosure requirements already found in the SSA disclosure of ownership information.[202]

10.5.5 Quality of Care

10.5.5.1 Resident Assessment Instruments (RAIs)

CMS requires long-term care facilities to conduct comprehensive, accurate, standardized, reproducible assessments of each resident's functional capacity and to transmit this information to CMS using a standard form known as the minimum data set (MDS) assessment instrument. The information from the MDS is compiled into an electronic data system. The instrument includes information about the patient and the patient's health status.[203] States must use either the federally established resident assessment instrument; or an alternate instrument designed by state and approved by CMS. The assessment is intended to help CMS and state surveyors better identify nursing homes for immediate onsite inspections, detect and correct systemic problems early, and ultimately help nursing homes improve quality. Beginning July 1, 2002, a shorter version of the MDS—the Medicare PPS Assessment Form (MPAF)—became available for use to satisfy Medicare assessment requirements. CMS estimates that the MPAF roughly half the time to complete as the original MDS.[204]

The most recent iteration of this assessment tool is the MDS 3.0. The MDS 3.0 was developed to improve the reliability, accuracy, and usefulness of the MDS, after some expressed concern that the MDS 2.0 failed to obtain critical information since it did not include items that relied on direct resident interviews. Some also expressed concern regarding the reliability, validity, and relevance of MDS 2.0.[205] Consequently, MDS 3.0 was developed to improve the reliability, accuracy, and usefulness of the MDS. This new version included resident assessment and other standard protocols used in

---

200 For a general summary of state Medicaid payment methodologies, *see* CCH Medicare & Medicaid Guide Explanations and Annotations ¶ 14,724.

201 PPACA § 6102.

202 PPACA § 6101.

203 Medicare and Medicaid; Resident Assessment in Long Term Care Facilities, 62 Fed. Reg. 67,174 (Dec. 23, 1997) (codified at 42 C.F.R. part 483).

204 Medicare Program; Notice of Modification of Beneficiary Assessment Requirements for Skilled Nursing Facilities, 67 Fed. Reg. 38,128 (May 31, 2002).

205 CMS, MDS 3.0 for Nursing Homes and Swing Bed Providers, https://www.cms.gov/NursingHomeQualityInits/25_NHQIMDS30.asp#TopOfPage.

other settings. The FY 2010 SNF payment rule also required that version 3.0 of the MDS (MDS 3.0) go into effect October 1, 2010 for FY 2011.

10.5.5.2 Collection and Publication of Quality Information

Increasing focus on nursing home quality information has resulted in CMS publication of Quality Measures (QMs) for facilities in all states, the District of Columbia and some U.S. territories. The purpose of the QMs is to make people aware of the performance of individual nursing homes. The information can be used by Medicare beneficiaries and families to make placement decisions and for nursing homes to improve the quality of care.

In January 2004, CMS began reporting an enhanced set of QMs endorsed by the National Quality Forum (a voluntary standard setting, consensus-building organization representing providers, consumers, and researchers), which makes it easier for consumers to compare nursing home quality, deficiency, and staffing information. The 14 enhanced QMs build on the original 10 measures and are publicly posted on the Nursing Home Compare website.[206]

In 2005, CMS and several industry groups adopted an initiative called Advancing Excellence in America's Nursing Homes to focus on eight areas for quality improvement: reducing high-risk pressure ulcers; reducing use of physical restraints; pain management for short- and long-term residents; setting specific targets for quality improvement; assessing resident and family satisfaction; increasing staff retention; and making staffing assignments more consistent. Facilities are asked to focus on three of eight areas.

Additional information is collected by surveyors as "Quality Indicators" (QIs). Unlike access to QMs, which are for the use of consumers and the public, access to QIs is restricted. QIs measure 24 indicators relating to chronic populations. There are some QMs that overlap with the QIs.

10.5.5.3 Quality Improvement Organizations (QIOs)

QIOs are organizations staffed by doctors and other healthcare professionals who are trained to review medical care and help beneficiaries with quality of care complaints, and improvements in quality of care. CMS contracts with one QIO contractor in each state as well as D.C., Puerto Rico, and the U.S. Virgin Islands. CMS has created the MedQIC website at www.medqic.org to support QIOs and Medicare service providers in finding, using, and sharing quality improvement resources.

The MMA directs the Institute of Medicine (IOM) to study the work of the QIO community, as well as CMS's oversight of the QIO program, and report to Congress in June 2006. In June 2004, CMS delivered presentations to the IOM covering virtually every aspect of the QIO program, including its history, current activities, and future plans. The IOM issued its report in March 2006, and CMS issued a responsive report that includes QIO improvement actions such as better assessments of the impact of the QIO program, stronger financial oversight, and other actions aimed at improving quality of care.[207]

---

[206] Medicare, Nursing Home Compare, www.medicare.gov/NHcompare.

[207] Report to Congress: Improving the Medicare Quality Improvement Organization Program–Response to the Institute of Medicine Study, available at https://www.cms.gov/QualityImprovementOrgs/downloads/QIO_Improvement_RTC_fnl.pdf.

As part of the QIO initiatives, CMS launched the Care Transitions Project. In August 2008, CMS awarded contracts for the QIO Program's 9th Statement of Work. A major theme of this publication is Care Transitions, which aims to improve the quality of care for Medicare beneficiaries transitioning among care settings with an aim to reduce hospital readmissions.[208] One key tool to achieve these goals is a standardized assessment instrument called Continuing Assessment Record and Evaluation (CARE), which allows healthcare providers to measure and compare Medicare beneficiaries' health status across care settings over time. CMS hopes that this project will help CMS to move forward in developing a single, uniform data set to compare quality and cost across provider settings.

10.5.5.4 Mandated Staffing

Federally-certified nursing facilities must post staffing information in a clearly visible location. Legislation has been introduced in Congress to impose daily nursing home staffing minimums—most recently the Nursing Home Transparency and Quality of Care Improvement Act of 2008 included provisions regarding the reporting of staffing information—but such efforts have not moved beyond committee in either the House or Senate. Efforts to address nursing home staffing will likely continue. Several states have mandated nursing staffing levels. Consult state law.

CMS is in the process of developing staffing quality measures. Phase I of this effort, which occurred between September 2003 and July 2005, included a stakeholder meeting in March 2004 which considered the aspects of nursing home staffing most important to the stakeholders and constituencies; how to improve the measures of staffing information currently presented on Nursing Home Compare; and how to present staffing measures to the public (for example: as staffing levels, percentiles, ranks, thresholds, rating systems, or other). According to the CMS 2007 Action Plan for Further Improvement of Nursing Home Quality, the Long Term Task Force is continuing to study the issue.[209] The agency is also in the process of developing data reporting requirements for the submission of payroll data to calculate measures of staffing and producing draft outcome quality measures based on this data as part of Phase II of the process. As of the CMS 2008 Action Plan, CMS is continuing to work on these issues.[210]

Most recently, the ACA imposed staffing requirements: within two years of enactment of the ACA, facilities must electronically submit direct staffing information based on payroll, as well as other verifiable and auditable data, in a uniform format.[211]

---

[208] *See* CMS, Office of Clinical Standards and Quality, Fact Sheet: Update: Use of CARE Instrument in the QIO Program 9th Statement of Work (June 25, 2009), available at https://www.cms.gov/QualityImprovementOrgs/downloads/CAREFSUpdate062509.pdf.

[209] CMS 2007 Action Plan for (Further Improvement of) Nursing Home Quality is available at http://www.cms.hhs.gov/SurveyCertificationGenInfo/downloads/2007ActionPlan.pdf.

[210] *Id.*; CMS 2008 Action Plan for (Further Improvement of) Nursing Home Quality is available at http://www.cms.gov/CertificationandComplianc/Downloads/2008NHActionPlan.pdf.

[211] PPACA § 6106.

10.5.5.5 Nursing Home Value-Based Purchasing Demonstration

Since 2009, CMS has been operating a demonstration project in three states aimed at improving the quality and efficiency of care furnished to Medicare beneficiaries.[212] CMS intends to assess the following four domains of each participating nursing home: staffing, appropriate hospitalizations, MDS outcomes, and survey deficiencies. CMS will award the nursing homes certain points based on the nursing home's performance on each of those measures. A nursing home's score will determine whether the home is eligible for a share of the state's savings pool.

The ACA directs the Secretary to submit a plan to Congress no later than FY 2012 showing how to move SNFs into a value-based purchasing payment system.

10.5.6 Survey, Certification, and Enforcement for Long Term Care Facilities

10.5.6.1 Survey Policies and Procedures

Survey Protocol and Interpretive Guidelines are contained in the SOM. There have been many changes to the SOM over the years. The following highlights significant revisions. Consult Appendices P and PP in the SOM.[213]

The data-driven survey system and reporting tool includes Quality Indicators (QIs), as discussed above. Standard surveys should be completed on consecutive workdays, whenever possible, and may be conducted at any time during the day, including weekends. The SOM also includes criteria for ensuring that surveys are unannounced. Civil Monetary Penalties (CMPs) may be issued per instance or per day for violations.

Individual nursing home survey results and violation records are posted on the Internet to increase accountability and flag repeat offenders for families and the public. The Nursing Home Compare website provides detailed information about the past performance of every Medicare and Medicaid certified nursing home in the country. It is one of the most popular tools on www.medicare.gov. The ACA requires certain information to be included on the Nursing Home Compare website, such as staffing data for facilities, links to state websites with information on state surveys, certifications, and inspection reports, information on substantiated complaints, and the number of adjudicated instances of a SNF's criminal violations.[214]

In 2005, CMS launched a demonstration project in five states called the Quality Indicator Survey (QIS) project to use customized software to guide surveyors through the survey. The goal was to improve consistency and accuracy of quality of care and quality of life problems. Unlike the standard survey that uses the QM/QI indicator report (discussed below), surveyors use MDS data and the QIS Data Collection Tool software to identify a larger sample of residents to review prior to their onsite inspection. Surveyors then use onsite observations and data to identify care issues. According to the

---

212 For information on this demonstration program, *see* the CMS resources available at http://www.cms.gov/DemoProjectsEvalRpts/MD/itemdetail.asp?filterType=dual,%20keyword&filterValue=value&filterByDID=0&sortByDID=3&sortOrder=descending&itemID=CMS1198946&intNumPerPage=10.

213 The SOM is available on the Internet at http://www.cms.hhs.gov/Manuals/IOM/list.asp.

214 PPACA § 6103.

Final Report issued in 2007, the results of the study were mixed and did not lead to any firm conclusions regarding the effectiveness of the QIS.[215]

10.5.6.2 Stronger Enforcement Actions

CMS continues to actively enforce the nursing home safety and quality regulations, including the following:

- increasing citations for conditions alleged to present "serious and immediate jeopardy" to residents;
- nursing homes with a second offense for violations resulting in the harm of residents may have sanctions imposed and will not receive a "grace period" that allows them to correct problems and avoid penalties;
- nursing home inspections are being conducted more frequently ("just in the neighborhood") for repeat offenders with serious violations (so-called "special focus facilities") for two facilities per state;
- nursing home inspection times are being staggered, with a set amount to be performed on weekends and evenings;
- CMS altered its revisit policy so that states must conduct an onsite revisit for any deficiency greater than substantial compliance (more serious than an "A," "B," or "C" deficiency) if there is a "G" or higher deficiency at any time in the survey cycle; and
- CMS has directed states to identify special-focus facilities in their states to focus their enforcement efforts on nursing homes with a record of noncompliance with federal rules; these facilities are being terminated from Medicare program participation if they are unable to achieve substantial compliance with program requests.

10.5.6.3 Stronger Federal Oversight of State Inspections

To target states with weak inspection systems, CMS has:

- provided additional training and other assistance to surveyors in states that are not adequately protecting residents;
- enhanced federal review of the surveys conducted by the states, including implementation of standard evaluation protocols in every state; and
- monitored state surveyors' enforcement of CMS's policy to sanction nursing homes with serious violations, and required that sanctions cannot be lifted until after an onsite visit has verified compliance.

[215] Evaluation of the Quality Indicator Survey (QIS), Final Report (Dec. 2007), available at http://www.cms.gov/CertificationandComplianc/Downloads/QISExecSummary.pdf.

10.5.6.4 Preventing Pressure Ulcers, Dehydration, and Malnutrition

CMS has stepped up its review of nursing homes' ability to prevent pressure ulcers, dehydration, and malnutrition. Nursing homes with patterns of serious violations will be sanctioned. CMS is also working with a variety of entities (including the Administration on Aging, the American Dietetics Association, clinicians, consumers, and nursing homes) to develop a repository of "best-practice" guidelines for residents at risk of weight loss and dehydration.

10.5.6.5 Combating Resident Abuse

State inspectors will review each nursing home's system to prevent, identify, and stop physical or verbal abuse, neglect, and misappropriation of resident property. A description of each nursing home's abuse-prevention plan will be shared with residents and families. CMS and the OIG also have directed nursing homes to enquire about criminal convictions when interviewing potential personnel.

Additionally, the ACA requires each individual owner, operator, employee, manager, agent, or contractor of a long-term care facility that receives at least $10,000 in federal funds annually to report to the Secretary of DHHS and one or more local law enforcement entities, any "reasonable suspicion" of a crime against anyone who is a resident of, or is receiving care from, the facility. Steep penalties can be imposed on individuals for failure to report within specified timeframes. The law also contains whistleblower protections for facility employees and provides for additional penalties for retaliation. In addition, each facility must post conspicuously in an appropriate location a sign, in a form to be specified by the Secretary, specifying the rights of employees under the law. Such signs shall include a statement that an employee may file a complaint with the Secretary against a facility that violates the law, and information regarding how to file such a complaint. Terms such as "abuse," "elder justice," "exploitation" and "neglect," among others, are specifically defined in the ACA.[216] Finally, the law requires facilities to include as part of initial nurse aide training and competency evaluation programs patient-abuse prevention training.[217]

10.5.6.6 Prosecution of Egregious Violations

CMS is working with the OIG and DOJ to ensure that state-survey agencies and others refer appropriate cases to DOJ for prosecution under federal civil and criminal statutes, particularly cases that result in harm to individual patients. The OIG also will work with CMS to conduct training for, and provide technical assistance to, federal survey and certification staff and CMS contractors on how to make appropriate referrals to the OIG.[218]

---

216 PPACA § 6703 (adding new § 1150B of the SSA).

217 PPACA § 6121.

218 Individual nursing home survey results and violation records now are posted on the Internet at www.medicare.gov/NHCompare/Home.asp. This is intended to increase accountability and flag repeat offenders for families and the public.

10.5.6.7 OIG and GAO Reports

The OIG and the GAO have issued several reports on long-term care, including Medicare payment for and utilization of rehabilitation therapy services, effectiveness of state ombudsman programs, abuse and neglect reporting, and weaknesses of the survey system. These reports are critical because they often signal areas for CMS and OIG enforcement and new legislation or regulations. A few recent GAO reports have focused on the Special Focus Facility Program, a program that CMS established to monitor poorly performing nursing homes.[219]

10.5.6.8 Federal False Claims Actions Based on Quality of Care

The government has used the federal False Claims Act (FCA), 31 U.S.C. §§ 3729 *et seq.*, as a basis for filing actions against providers, alleging that fraudulent practices resulted in the submission of false claims for Medicare and/or Medicaid reimbursement. These include so-called quality of care cases and more traditional payment related cases. In the quality of care cases, the government has applied two principal theories:

- *implied certification theory:* provider certified that it met the Medicare/Medicaid requirements for participation but did not, and
- *worthless services theory:* the care was so deficient as to be the equivalent of providing no services at all.

Pennsylvania and Maryland are two jurisdictions in which U.S. Attorneys have made extensive use of these theories, but many other jurisdictions have followed suit. The OIG has made so-called quality of care FCA cases a top enforcement priority.

10.5.6.9 Fraud and Abuse, Compliance Program Guidance and the OIG 2007 Work Plan

Nursing homes, like others in the healthcare industry, continue to be subject to investigations and enforcement actions by the HHS OIG, DOJ, and State Medicaid Fraud Control Units (MFUCs). In 2000, the OIG issued its Compliance Program Guidance (CPG) for Nursing Facilities.[220] The guidance outlines the elements to be included in an effective compliance program and the "risk areas" to be addressed. The guidance is also a useful summary of rules and regulations applicable to nursing homes. In 2008, the OIG published supplemental CPG addressing issues that have arise since the original CPG was published, including quality of care issues, billing issues, and kickback concerns.[221]

The OIG's Work Plan for Fiscal Year 2010 (Work Plan) summarizes the major projects the OIG intends to pursue in the coming year in each of HHS' major operating areas, including CMS. [222] The

---

[219] *See, e.g.*, GAO, Poorly Performing Nursing Homes: Special Focus Facilities are Often Improving, but CMS's Program Could Be Strengthened (Mar. 2010), available at http://www.gao.gov/cgi-bin/getrpt?GAO-10-197.

[220] Publication of the OIG Compliance Program Guidance for Nursing Facilities, 65 Fed. Reg. 14,289 (Mar. 16, 2000), available at http://oig.hhs.gov/authorities/docs/cpgnf.pdf.

[221] OIG Supplemental Compliance Program Guidance for Nursing Facilities, 73 Fed. Reg. 56,832 (Sept. 30, 2008), available at http://edocket.access.gpo.gov/2008/pdf/E8-22796.pdf.

[222] *See* OIG Work Plan, Fiscal Year 2010, available at http://oig.hhs.gov/publications/docs/workplan/2010/Work_Plan_FY_2010.pdf.

OIG's priorities for SNFs include reviewing Medicare Part B payments for psychotherapy services provided to nursing home residents during noncovered Medicare Part A stays; assessing how SNFs have addressed certain federal requirements related to quality of care; reviewing SNF claims for Medicare reimbursement to determine the accuracy of RUG coding; reviewing nursing home emergency plans and preparedness; determining whether and the extent to which nursing facilities have employed individuals with criminal convictions; reviewing CMS's and states' use of enforcement measures to determine their impact on improving quality of care in poorly-performing nursing homes; reviewing extent of Part B services provided to nursing home residents whose stays are not paid under Part A; and reviewing the extent to which nursing home residents aged 65 or older received certain antipsychotic drugs.

10.6 Home and Community-Based Services

10.6.1 Introduction

The ACA includes a provision that expresses the Sense of the Senate that Congress should address long-term services and support services for the elderly and disabled so that they are guaranteed the necessary care both in the community and in institutions.[223] A growing trend in caring for elderly and disabled individuals is the provision of home and community-based services (HCBS). In fact, the ACA creates financial incentives for states to shift Medicaid beneficiaries out of nursing homes and into HCBS.[224]

HCBS include a range of health services provided to individuals in their homes and the community, including residents of ALFs, to promote functional independence and individuals at whatever age to be able to live outside institutions in the setting that is as integrated as possible into the community. Some of the most common home and community services are:

- *Adult Day Service (ADS) programs*, designed to meet the needs of adults with cognitive or functional impairments, as well as adults needing social interaction and a place to go when their family caregivers are at work. They provide a variety of health, social, and other support services in a protective setting during part of the day. Adult day centers typically operate programs during normal business hours five days a week; some have evening and weekend hours. These programs do not provide 24-hour care.
- *Case managers/geriatric care managers* are healthcare professionals (typically nurses or social workers) who specialize in assisting patients with long-term care needs. This includes but is not limited to assisting, coordinating, and managing long-term care services; developing a plan of care; and monitoring long-term care needs over extended periods of time. These are often provided through managed care programs or demonstration projects.
- *Emergency response systems*, which provide an automatic response to a medical or other emergency via electronic monitors.

[223] PPACA § 2406. The ACA also provides $10 million funding to state Aging and Disability Resource Centers for FYs 2010 to 2014. *Id.*, § 2405.

[224] *See* PPACA Reconciliation Act, § 10202 (describing financial incentives, including, subject to certain conditions, increases in FMAP matching funds to states seeking to rebalance their total HCBS expenditures).

- *Friendly visitor/companion services*, which are typically staffed by volunteers who regularly pay short visits (under two hours) to someone who is frail or living alone.
- *Home healthcare/home care* (discussed above).
- *Homemaker/chore services* provide general household activities such as meal preparation, routine household care, and heavy household chores such as washing floors, windows, or shoveling snow.
- *Meals programs*, which include both home-delivered meals (*e.g.*, Meals-on-Wheels) or congregate meals, which are provided in a variety of community settings.
- *Respite Care*, which gives families temporary relief from the responsibility of caring for family members who are unable to care for themselves. Respite care is provided in a variety of settings including in the home, at an adult day center, or in a nursing home.
- *Senior Centers*, which provide a variety of services including nutrition, recreation, social and educational services, and comprehensive information and referral to help people find the care and services they might need; and
- *Transportation services* to help patients get to and from medical appointments, shopping centers and access a variety of community services and resources.

Payment has traditionally been private pay, community block grants, or some Medicaid funding. The Home and Community Based Services Waiver Provision of the SSA gives the Secretary of the HHS authority to waive certain Medicaid provisions in order to allow long-term care services to be delivered in community settings.[225] This program is the Medicaid alternative to providing comprehensive long-term services in institutional settings. While initially used sporadically, many states now have various § 1915(c) waiver programs reflecting an increasing trend toward seeking Medicaid funding for non-institutional long-term care.

States desiring an alternative to waivers now have another option under the ACA. The ACA directs the Secretary to issue regulations to give states options to provide HCBS through a state plan amendment to individuals with higher levels of need. Additionally, the ACA gives states the option to extend full Medicaid benefits to individuals receiving HCBS under a state plan amendment.[226]

10.6.2 Related Legal Developments

In 1999, the Supreme Court issued what has come to be known as the "integration mandate" in *Olmstead v. L.C.*[227] The Court ruled that states are required to administer services, programs, and activities "in the most integrated setting appropriate to the needs of qualified individuals with disabilities." The Olmstead decision interpreted Title II of the Americans with Disabilities Act (ADA), which gives civil rights and protections to individuals with disabilities and guarantees equal opportunity for individuals with disabilities in public accommodations, employment, transportation, state and local government services, and telecommunications. Patient advocates have used this law to advocate for more funding for community-based services.

[225] 42 U.S.C. § 1396n(d).
[226] PPACA § 2402.
[227] 527 U.S. 581 (1999).

The New Freedom Initiative (NFI) was announced by President Bush on February 1, 2001, followed up by the Executive Order 13217 on June 18, 2001. The initiative is a nationwide effort to remove barriers to community living for people of all ages with disabilities and long-term illnesses and to support states' efforts to comply with the *Olmstead* decision.

The DRA includes a provision to allow states to add HCBS to their permanent array of benefits without having to go through a waiver program. The DRA also includes the Money Follows the Person (MFP) "rebalancing" initiative to provide grants to states to encourage the use of HCBS.[228] Currently, 29 states and the District of Columbia have implemented MFP Demonstration Programs, and in July 2010, CMS issued a new MFP grant solicitation to encourage states not yet involved to apply for grant funds.

Under the DRA, these grants are to design programs with four major objectives:

- increase the use of home and community-based, rather than institutional, long-term care services;
- eliminate barriers or mechanisms that prevent Medicaid-eligible individuals from receiving support for appropriate and necessary long-term services in the settings of their choice;
- increase the ability of the state Medicaid program to assure continued provision of home and community based long-term care services to eligible individuals who choose to move from an institutional to a community setting; and
- ensure that procedures are in place to provide quality assurance for individuals receiving Medicaid home and community-based long-term care services and to provide for continuous quality improvement in such services.

Through the ACA, the MFP Rebalancing Demonstration Project has been extended through September 30, 2016. Additionally, the ACA changed the eligibility requirements for individuals participating in the project from six months to 90 consecutive days and excludes short-term rehabilitation stays.[229]

10.6.3 Medicaid Quality Assurance/Quality Improvement and Oversight

CMS has taken action to implement an HCBS Quality Framework to ensure that states are measuring and working toward seven desired outcomes. These outcomes include participant access, sufficient provider capacity and capabilities, participant rights and satisfaction, and system performance.[230] The CMS website includes a series of Quality Letters and HCBS Promising Practices reports summaries which provide guidance on the direction in which quality measurement for these programs is headed. Consult individual state program websites for more information on implementation of this guidance in oversight programs.

---

228 For information on the MFP initiatives, *see* CMS, Money Follows the Person Community Services and Long Term Supports, http://www.cms.gov/CommunityServices/20_MFP.asp.

229 PPACA § 2403.

230 Links to information regarding the HCBS quality initiatives are available at http://www1.cms.gov/CommunityServices/.

11

Healthcare Transactions and Contracting

Anthea R. Daniels, Esquire
Calfee, Halter & Griswold, LLP

11.1 Introduction

Healthcare mergers and acquisitions are alive and well.[1] Many hospital systems consolidated in the mid 1980s until the end of the past century. For example, various healthcare providers (including hospitals, physician groups, and nursing homes) and ancillary healthcare providers (including ambulatory surgery centers (ASCs), durable medical equipment (DME) suppliers, and home healthcare (HHC) and hospice providers) joined together with other healthcare providers or healthcare payors (including traditional indemnity-insurance companies, health maintenance organizations (HMOs), and preferred provider organizations (PPOs)) to form integrated delivery systems and enter into joint ventures and affiliations.[2] These integrated entities were formed for various reasons, including: (i) providers, such as physicians, wanted to be able to offer a complete array of healthcare services to their patients; (ii) providers wanted to improve and enhance their access to capital; (iii) providers wanted to negotiate and obtain favorable managed-care contracts or better commercial insurance rates; (iv) certain providers wanted to eliminate their business and administrative responsibilities; and (v) certain providers had the option of going out of business or joining forces. Many providers and payors in the healthcare marketplace believed that "bigger" would be "better" and that it was necessary to provide a full array of services in order to capture patients.

---

[1] In the first decade of the 21st Century, there were 597 announced hospital mergers and acquisitions. Richard Pizzi, *600 Hospital Mergers in Last Decade*, Healthcare Finance News, May 11, 2010, available at http://www.healthcarefinancenews.com/news/600-hospital-mergers-last-decade. The second half of the decade saw a 140% increase in total capital committed to fund these deals over the first half. *Hospital Pricing Indicators Rose in 2009, Despite Reduced M&A Activity, According to New Irving Levin Five-Year Hospital M&A Report*, Business Wire, June 22, 2010, available at http://www.businesswire.com/portal/site/home/permalink/?ndmViewId=news_view&newsId=20100622005708&newsLang=en.

[2] For example, in 1999, HealthSouth Corp., a publicly traded integrated delivery system based in Birmingham, Alabama, had more than 1,900 facilities (primarily outpatient surgery and rehabilitation facilities) in every state and in Puerto Rico, the United Kingdom, and Australia. 29 Modern Healthcare (Aug. 30, 1999). In 2010, HealthSouth had over 150 facilities in the United States, with hospitals in 27 states. *See* HealthSouth's website, http://www.healthsouth.com/where_we_are/national_map.asp. In 2000, there were approximately 850 integrated healthcare delivery systems in the United States. Bonnie Boone, *Integrated Health Care Delivery Systems Challenges*, IRMI.com (June 2000). In 2008, Hospitals Corporation of America (HCA) was the largest private hospital system in the United States, with 163 hospitals, 105 freestanding surgery centers, and revenues exceeding $28 billion. *See* HCA Fact Sheet, available at http://www.hcahealthcare.com/CPM/CurrentFactSheet1.pdf.

On account of all of these acquisitions, mergers, joint ventures, and affiliations, the healthcare marketplace has undergone significant consolidation, leaving far fewer choices in acute care healthcare providers today in certain regions. For example, while a major metropolitan city may have had eight independent hospitals in the past, today that same region may have only three hospital systems that operate those same eight hospitals. Many of these providers are healthcare powerhouses that offer a wide range of services encompassing a complete continuum of care, from outpatient services to tertiary care, nursing home services, and even HMOs. As a result of these transactions, a myriad of contractual arrangements were and continue to be established between the providers (*e.g.*, hospitals and physicians) and other providers and payors.

Notwithstanding that a significant amount of consolidation occurred in the last two decades, healthcare providers and payors continue to enter into joint ventures, mergers, acquisitions and affiliations in order to further their business or charitable purposes.[3] Additionally, the Federal Trade Commission and the Department of Justice have recently reviewed several hospital mergers and have requested the unraveling or renegotiation of those relationships.[4] Further, many in the industry are predicting that healthcare reform, PPACA,[5] also known as National Health Reform, will cause more integration of healthcare providers, as discussed herein.[6] Therefore, this Chapter will explore various types of healthcare transactions and contractual arrangements, and will provide an overview of certain current legal issues that will need to be reviewed when structuring, drafting, and negotiating healthcare transactions and contracts.

---

[3] In June 2010, 11 hospital and health system mergers and acquisitions occurred. *See* Rachel Fields, *Hospital and Health System Mergers and Acquisitions–June 2010*, Becker's Hospital Review, July 7, 2010, http://www.beckershospitalreview.com/hospital-transactions-and-valuation-issues/hospital-and-health-system-mergers-a-acquisitions-june-2010.html.

[4] For example, in February 2004, the FTC issued an Administrative Complaint against a three-hospital system in a suburb north of Chicago, alleging that the system, created in 2000, substantially impaired competition. *See Evanston Nw. Healthcare Corp.*, FTC Docket No. 9315, at *1 (Oct. 20, 2005), available at http://www.ftc.gov/os/adjpro/d9315/051021idtextversion.pdf. The Administrative Law Judge, ruling that the merger violated Section 7 of the Clayton Act, ordered one of the hospitals be divested from the system. *Id.* at 205. The hospital system appealed, but the FTC unanimously upheld the decision that the merger illegally eliminated pre-merger price competition. *See Evanston Nw. Healthcare Corp.*, FTC Docket No. 9315, (slip op.) at *88–89 (Aug. 6, 2007), available at www.ftc.gov/os/adjpro/d9315/070806opinion.pdf. However, the full Commission reversed the divesture, instead opting to require the hospital system to use two separate, independent negotiating teams for payor contracts. *Id.* at 90. The Commission feared that divesture would have a substantial, negative effect on one of the hospital's cardiac units and implementation of a state-of-the-art medical record system. *Id.* at 89. The Commission noted that divesture is still the preferred remedy for consummated hospital mergers. *Id.* at 90–91. In 2009, the FTC challenged another post-acquisition hospital transaction, alleging that Carilion Clinic's purchase of two outpatient clinics decreased competition while increasing prices by as much as 800%. Press Release, Fed. Trade Comm'n, Commission Order Restores Competition Eliminated by Carilion's Clinic's Acquisition of Two Outpatient Clinics (Oct. 7, 2009), available at http://www.ftc.gov/opa/2009/10/carilion.shtm. Carilion settled the claim by agreeing to sell both clinics within three months. *Id.*

[5] Patient Protection and Affordable Care Act, Pub. L. No. 111-148, 124 Stat. 119.

[6] *See, e.g.*, Jennifer Rossa, *One Impact of Health-Care Reform: Expect More Hospital Deals*, Wall Street Journal Private Equity Beat, (June 23, 2010), http://blogs.wsj.com/privateequity/2010/06/23/one-impact-of-health-care-reform-expect-more-hospital-deals/; Caralyn Davis, *Investors Expect Healthcare M&A Uptick Through 2Q 1011*, Fierce Health Finance, July 21, 2010, http://www.fiercehealthfinance.com/story/investors-expect-healthcare-m-uptick-through-2q-2011/2010-07-21 ("government healthcare reform initiatives will be the biggest driver of M&A activity); Jenny Gold, *Hospitals Hope to Improve Outlook by Turning for-Profit*, Kaiser Health News, Jul. 13, 2010, http://www.kaiserhealthnews.org/Stories/2010/July/13/hospital-mergers.aspx (suggesting an increase in merger and acquisition activity as urban hospitals become more profitable as more of their patients become insured); Scott Graham, *The Need for Cash, Health Reform Could Fuel Md. Hospital Mergers*, Baltimore Business Journal, June 11, 2010; Milt Capps, *Hospital M&A Not Expected to be a "Tidal Wave," but Deep Capital Shortage Means Surge*, Financial Times, May 21, 2010, http://www.ft.com/cms/s/2/aab536aa-64f1-11df-aa4d-00144feab49a.html (hospital M&A will "intensify" in order to help hospitals cope with increase of new patients due to the healthcare reform).

11.2 Structure of Healthcare Transactions

There are various ways in which a transaction among providers and/or payors can be structured depending on the goals of the parties involved. Often, an arrangement is structured based on the amount of integration and autonomy that a healthcare provider or payor desires. This section of the Chapter will address several types of transactional structures, from the most integrated model to the least integrated model.

11.2.1 Acquisitions and Mergers

11.2.1.1 Stock Transactions and Member Substitutions

In general, an acquisition is where one entity (the Buyer) acquires another entity (the Seller or the Target Company). There are three basic forms of acquisitions: the stock transaction, the asset transaction, and the merger. In a stock transaction, the Buyer purchases certain or all of the stock of the Seller, and the sale proceeds from the sale of the stock, after liabilities are extinguished, are distributed to the selling shareholders of the Seller. If the Seller is a nonprofit entity rather than a for-profit entity, then under nonprofit state laws, it has members, rather than shareholders. A nonprofit "stock" deal is sometimes referred to as a member substitution arrangement.[7] Unlike shareholders, the members do not "own" the healthcare entity; instead, the members protect the nonprofit entity and its charitable assets on behalf of the community. Thus, if the members sell the "membership" of the healthcare entity to a Buyer, the members are not entitled to divide the purchase price among themselves, as a for-profit entity would amongst its shareholders. Instead, any monies received, after all liabilities are extinguished, would have to be donated to another nonprofit tax-exempt entity pursuant to specific provisions on distribution of assets upon sale as set forth in the selling organization's organizational documents.

In this type of arrangement, whether it be a stock sale or a member substitution, the Buyer becomes the new member or the shareholder of the Target Company (*See* Figure 1). Thus, the Buyer, XYZ Company, now controls and has become the shareholder or member of ABC Healthcare entity. As the sole shareholder or sole member of ABC Healthcare entity, XYZ Company has the ability to appoint all of ABC's board of trustees or directors, who in turn elects all of the officers of ABC Healthcare, who control the day-to-day operations of the ABC Healthcare entity. Often a transaction will be structured as a stock deal or a member substitution because either the Buyer wants to make sure it is buying all of the assets and business of the Seller or the Seller wants to sell the entire business, including eliminating all of its liabilities and obligations regarding the business. However, a Buyer may not want to acquire all of the liabilities of the business, and would rather only purchase certain assets that it chooses and leaving certain of the liabilities with the Seller. Obviously, this is one of the initial deal points that is negotiated between the parties and obviously can become a deal breaker.

---

[7] Gerald R. Peters, *Healthcare Integration: A Legal Manual for Constructing Integrated Organizations* 68 (1995). *See also* Bruce John Shih, *Healthcare Transactions: A Guide to Mergers, Acquisitions & Integration* (1998).

Figure 1

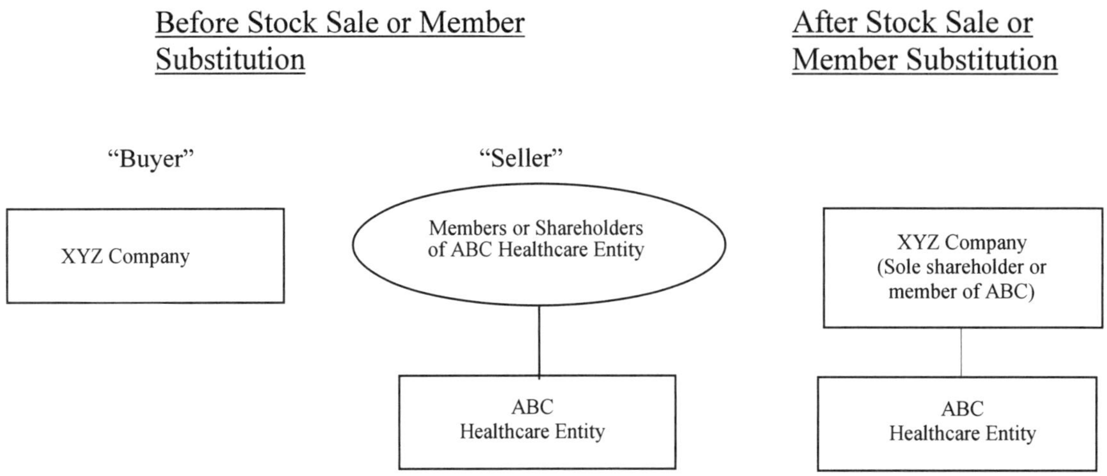

This transaction could also be accomplished by a merger wherein ABC Healthcare entity is merged into XYZ Company (or vice versa), where either XYZ Company or ABC Healthcare is the surviving entity. Unlike a stock or member substitution where there are still two entities after the closing of the transaction (the parent corporation and a subsidiary), with a merger there is only one entity remaining after the merger. (*See* Figure 2).

Figure 2

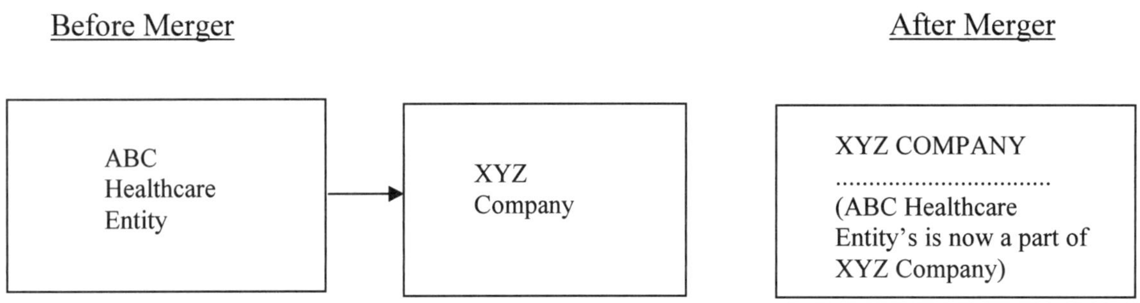

11.2.1.2 Asset Transactions

In asset transactions, some or all of the assets of the Seller are acquired by the Buyer. Transactions are often structured as asset deals because: (1) the Buyer does not want to purchase all of the Seller's assets; (2) the Seller only wants to sell a portion of its assets; or (3) the Buyer does not want to assume the Seller's liabilities. Specifically, many healthcare transactions are structured as asset deals because the Buyer does not want to assume the Seller's Medicare and Medicaid billing agreements and provider numbers and wants to avoid the potential liabilities for the prior billing errors that may have been made by the Seller and would become the Buyer's assumed liabilities if the agreements are acquired. Notwithstanding these considerations, certain courts have held that, even in asset transactions the Buyer may still be responsible for the Seller's prior billing liabilities, even in the event that the provider agreements and numbers were not acquired.[8] The flexibility to purchase certain assets and assume certain liabilities is the main difference between an asset transaction and a stock transaction/ member substitution transaction.

Notwithstanding the specific structure of the transaction, the Buyer should conduct extensive due diligence of the Seller's business and assets prior to consummating the transaction. Due diligence is a comprehensive review of the Seller's business, assets, and known and contingent liabilities. It is typically conducted by the Buyer and its attorneys, accountants, billing experts, and its employees and agents who review the Seller's corporate books and records, tax records, financial, audit and cost reporting statements, contracts, deeds, title searches, environmental concerns, billing records, litigation, physical plant, labor and employee-benefit issues, intellectual property, medical staff and physician issues, in addition to many more documents. The purpose of the Buyer's due diligence is to ensure that the Buyer is aware of the condition of the assets or business it is acquiring and any potential liabilities associated with those assets. Given the scope of all of the liabilities assumed in a stock transaction, due diligence will often be more thorough and exhaustive, since it must cover every aspect of the entity being acquired. Thus, due diligence covers a myriad of topics. In healthcare transactions, certain key due-diligence areas include Medicare and Medicaid billing and cost-reporting issues, federal and state government investigations, healthcare accreditation and licensure, Health Insurance Portability and Accountability Act of 1996 (HIPAA) compliance, contracts with providers and payors, tax-exempt issues, and contractual relationships and joint ventures with physicians. All of these considerations are in addition to the more typical corporate due-diligence issues, which include employee benefits, tax issues, environmental matters, labor issues, governance issues, intellectual property, and real estate. Due diligence is also an important process because the results will affect the terms of the agreement, including the purchase price, post-closing conditions and the nature and scope of the representations and warranties the Seller will make to the Buyer in the definitive agreement (discussed below in Section 11.6.4). A Seller may also conduct due diligence of the Buyer but it is typically limited to certain concerns that the Seller may have. For example, if the Seller is taking a note in the transaction, the Seller may want to ensure that the Buyer has the appropriate finances to enter into the deal. If the Seller is a nonprofit tax-exempt entity, it may want to conduct due diligence to ensure that the Buyer is also a tax-exempt entity and is not operating in such as manner as to potentially jeopardize its charitable status.

---

[8] *See, e.g.*, *United States v. Vernon Home Health Care*, 21 F.3d 693 (5th Cir. Tex. 1994); *Delta Health Group, Inc. v. U.S. Dep't of Health & Human Servs*., 459 F.Supp.2d 1207, 1210 (N.D.Fla. 2006) (denying Delta Health Group's claim to recover $250,000 in civil monetary fines assessed against it for violations incurred by a corporation whose provider agreement and number Delta had acquired). In *Vernon*, the court held Vernon Home Health Care was liable for the Medicare overpayments to a corporation whose assets Vernon purchased. *Id.* at 694. Because Vernon had acquired the corporation's Medicare agreement and provider number, it was jointly and severable for the debts created under the agreement, even though the purchase agreement provided that Vernon had purchased assets and assumed no liabilities. *Id.* at 696. The court noted that the government had conceded the case would have been different if Vernon had not assumed the provider number. *Id.* The Eighth Circuit has cited *Vernon* for the proposition that applying for a new provider agreement prevents a new operator from liabilities incurred under the old agreement. *See Deerbrook Pavilion, LLC v. Shalala*, 235 F.3d 1100, 1105 (8th Cir. 2000).

11.2.2 Joint Ventures

Sometimes healthcare entities may want to collaborate with another provider but may not want to merge or be acquired. In this instance, the parties may enter into a joint venture. A joint venture is an arrangement whereby the parties agree to collaborate for a specific purpose. According to the Internal Revenue Service (IRS), "[a] joint venture is created when two or more persons enter into an arrangement to invest in a project and the parties share the control, benefits, and risks of the project."[9] The joint venture may establish collaboration on anything from a single service to a variety of services. Unrelated hospitals and hospitals and physicians have entered into joint ventures for various projects.

Some hospitals enter into joint ventures for the creation of ancillary healthcare services. For example, the joint venture may provide specialty services by acquiring equipment (*e.g.*, a lithotripter). A joint venture is often appropriate when neither party has enough patients that will need the service, there is a need for capital, or location of a service. Thus, the parties enter into a joint venture to decrease each of their capital and operating costs (and potentially to lower the cost of the service to patients) while increasing utilization.

Unlike an acquisition or a merger, the parties to a joint venture remain independent entities. The joint venture is created by a contract or by creating a new entity that would be jointly owned by the parties offering a specific service or set of services (*See* Figure 3). Often, a joint venture may be the first step toward further integration of the parties. Many healthcare joint ventures have recently been structured as limited liability companies (LLCs). An LLC member does not have personal liability for the debts of the LLC in excess of the amount paid for the members' units and an LLC can be treated for tax purposes as a pass-through entity and thus avoid double-level taxation. The LLC does not pay any income taxes or have to file tax returns if it shares an employer identification number with its parent/ member. Instead, the individual members of the LLC are taxed on their distributions. LLCs and similar corporate organizational structures are governed by state rather than federal laws.

Figure 3

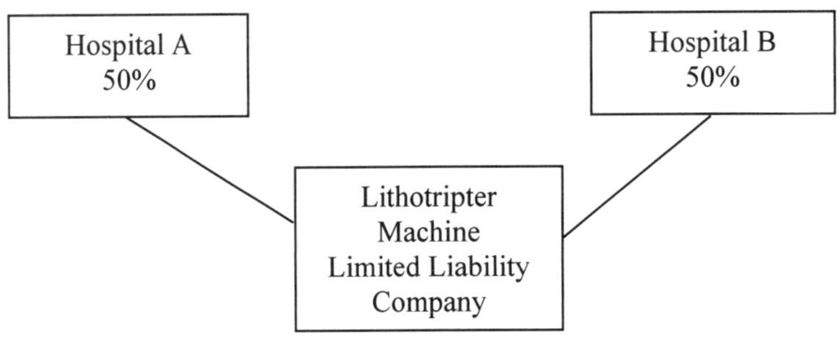

Physicians and hospitals have established joint ventures to jointly own or operate ancillary services providers (*i.e.*, ASCs), medical office buildings, clinics, medical imaging centers, hospitals, and

[9] *Whole Hospital Joint Ventures*, Fiscal 1999 CPE Text for Exempt Organizations 2. "The Tax Court has defined a joint venture as a special combination of two or more persons where in some specific venture a profit is jointly sought without any actual partnership or corporate designation." *Sierra Club v. Commissioner*, 103 T.C. 307, 322, 86 F.3d 1526 (9th Cir. 1996).

physician hospital organizations (PHOs), described in Section 11.3.2. The Anti-Kickback Statute[10] and the Stark laws[11] make the formation of such joint ventures challenging when trying to structure these arrangements. Certain providers have formed joint ventures and have obtained an Advisory Opinion from the Office of the Inspector General (OIG) of the Department of Health and Human Services (DHHS) to guarantee that the arrangement does not violate the Anti-Kickback Statute or is not the type of arrangement that would be investigated by the federal government as being deemed a violation of the Anti-Kickback Statute.[12]

There are many reasons providers are entering into joint ventures. One reason is that one party may bring resources to the joint venture, while the other party brings expertise. For example, two hospitals may form a joint venture to construct and operate an ASC where the one hospital will finance a majority of the project and the other hospital has management expertise in operating ASCs. Alternatively, perhaps these parties decide to joint venture the ASC because the community only needs one ASC; in this case, rather than each hospital operating its own ASC, the parties will collaborate and avoid duplicate facilities. Additionally, parties may pursue a joint venture on a risky project in order to spread the risk among a larger group of participants. Another joint-venture example is a surgeon owned and operated ASC where all of the surgeon investors provide services at the facility. In this scenario, the joint venture's success relies upon obtaining many active referring investors so that the facility will be used. Many physicians want to provide ancillary services, whether by joint venture or not, because they are looking for additional revenue sources and it often is a convenience to their patients to offer the service in the office. Alternatively, hospitals want to joint venture with physicians in order to enhance the physician's loyalty to the facility, which in turn means the physician may utilize that hospital for its patients.

Unlike acquisitions and mergers, joint ventures may be either limited in duration to a specific amount of time (as set forth in a joint-venture agreement) or perpetual. Most joint ventures are perpetual. Thus, a joint venture may only be in effect for a three-year period of time, and may incorporate provisions that permit one party to terminate the joint venture if certain incidences occur (*e.g.*, breach by the other party of the terms in the joint-venture agreement). In this situation, the parties may or may not have created a separate corporate entity that holds the asset (*i.e.,* the lithotripter as set forth in the example in Figure 3). If a separate corporate entity is not established, then the parties agree, via a contractual arrangement, to share the expenses and profits of the lithotripter. Hence, the joint venture is established by a contract rather than through a separate corporate entity controlled by the joint-venture participants. Either way, a definitive purchase agreement sets forth the relationship of the parties and the obligations of each.

---

10 42 U.S.C. § 1320-7b(b).

11 *Id.* § 1395nn.

12 In one Advisory Opinion, a hospital and a group of radiologists created a joint venture of a medical imaging center. The OIG stated that, although the arrangement does not fit within a safe harbor, the activity does not violate the Anti-Kickback Statute because radiologists do not refer patients to the facility or the hospital, but rather merely provide radiology services to patients who are referred by other physicians. OIG Advisory Opinion 97-5 (Oct. 6, 1997).

11.2.3 Affiliations

In the world of corporate transactions, affiliation arrangements require the least amount of integration of the parties involved. No specific definition has been established as to what constitutes an affiliation as does with a merger or acquisition; no singular clearly identifiable type of affiliation arrangement is common to all affiliation arrangements. Rather, an affiliation can be created between two or more parties to accomplish anything that the parties desire. Typically, an affiliation arrangement will be memorialized in an agreement executed by the parties to the affiliation. One common use for affiliation agreements is when parties contract for a specific purpose. Unlike a joint venture, the activities may be more informal. Healthcare entities have entered into affiliations with other healthcare entities or providers for various reasons, including to create loose networks of similar types of entities that would potentially explore further integration in the future. Entities may enter into an affiliation arrangement because they are not mentally or fiscally prepared to merge, sell, or buy. Thus, a party may enter into an affiliation arrangement in order to explore the possibilities of further integration in the future.

Many hospitals have entered into affiliation agreements with other hospitals in order to create arrangements that could evolve into a merger or an acquisition if the parties became more comfortable with the other party and its operations. Another common type of affiliation agreement is between a hospital or an integrated delivery system (IDS) and an educational institution (*i.e.,* a medical, nursing, or physical therapy school). These educational institutions enter into affiliation agreements with hospitals so that their students can receive training from the hospitals. Typically, these agreements do not involve any compensation provisions. Instead, the key sections of the contract are the insurance, indemnification, and description of the responsibilities of the parties. (Section 11.6.5 discusses the structure of affiliation agreements.)

11.3 Healthcare Corporate Structures

11.3.1 Integrated Delivery Systems

IDSs started to be formed in the 1980s and 1990s and continue to evolve in the 21st century, with some continuing to grow and others shrink. Some are shrinking because the health system perhaps expanded into an area that was not profitable, was beyond its core services, or did not fully understand how to operate (*e.g.*, health maintenance organizations, long-term care facilities). IDSs are a variety of healthcare providers that are integrated as part of one corporate structure or system. There is no one specific corporate organizational model for IDSs. Thus, one IDS may have four hospitals, three physician groups, and a DME company all in one corporation; another IDS may have one hospital, one nursing home, a physician group, an HMO, and a management services organization, all in separate corporate entities with a parent holding company. The structure will primarily be dictated by tax, liability, and other business concerns (*See* Figure 4).

Figure 4

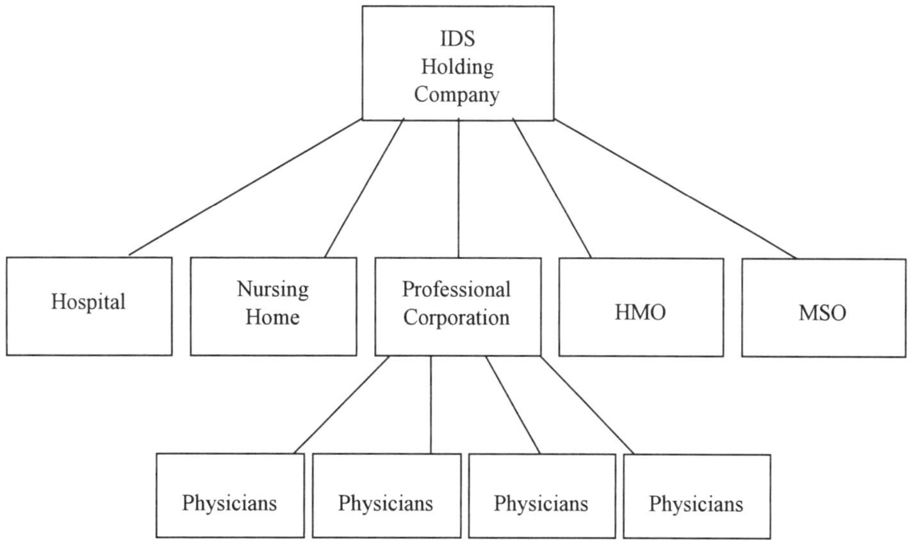

IDSs were formed by healthcare providers for many reasons. Many systems wanted to create an entity that would be a full-service provider of healthcare services that a patient may need. For example, an IDS would have physician employees who may refer patients to the IDS's hospital and other providers. Once discharged, the patient would receive at-home services from the IDS's HHC, and might purchase a wheelchair from the IDS's DME company. If the patient needed further sub-acute care, then the patient could be referred to the IDS's step-down facility or assisted-living facility. Hence with the IDS, the patient has "one-stop shopping," and does not need to look for healthcare services outside of the IDS. In turn, the IDS can coordinate care for a patient among all of its entities, and perhaps provide better care to its patients because of the anticipated coordination between all of the providers in the IDS and the sharing of one medical record. In addition, if all of the providers of the IDS have access to the same electronic medical record, then time efficiencies and improved quality of care are reasonable expectations.

Another reason for the wave of creating IDSs was to create a structure that would have sufficient leverage and power to negotiate favorable contracts with managed-care payors. An IDS that negotiates on behalf of four hospitals and 1,000 physicians most probably would be able to obtain more favorable rates and contractual terms than an individual hospital. An IDS will also have larger amounts of capital available to withstand decreases in revenues and/or increased competition. For whatever reason, the healthcare industry has consolidated, and the individual hospital entity is almost extinct in urban areas as the IDS has become the norm.

Many legal issues need to be analyzed when structuring and operating an IDS. In fact, several books are completely dedicated to addressing this issue.[13] This Chapter will provide a brief overview of certain of the legal issues surrounding an IDS.

---

[13] *See supra*, note 7.

11.3.1.1 Antitrust

When entities integrate to form an IDS, various antitrust laws need to be reviewed to ensure that a proposed IDS is in compliance with federal and state antitrust laws. Specifically, a proposed IDS needs to be reviewed under Section 2 of the Sherman Act to ensure that the IDS would not be deemed to constitute a monopoly if it has significant market share (and thus makes it prohibitive for others to enter the marketplace). Monopolizations apply to a single entity that has significant market power and prevents other participants from competing in that industry.[14]

In addition to monopoly and market-power issues, when healthcare entities decide to merge or integrate, the entities may need to provide premerger notification. The premerger-notification report is referred to as a Hart-Scott-Rodino premerger notification (Hart-Scott filing), and must be made to the Federal Trade Commission (FTC), as required by Section 7 of the Clayton Act, and to the Department of Justice (DOJ). After the filing is made, an applicable waiting period must expire before the parties are permitted to close their transaction.[15] The necessity of a Hart-Scott filing depends on the size of the Buyer and the Seller. A Hart-Scott filing will be necessary if the value of the assets or voting securities to be acquired meet or exceed certain standards. Typically, very few physician-acquisition transactions or small hospital acquisitions will require a Hart-Scott filing; by contrast, many hospital-acquisition transactions may require a Hart-Scott filing depending on the specific revenues and assets of the parties involved.

11.3.1.2 Fraud and Abuse

Fraud and abuse issues also need to be reviewed when structuring an IDS to ensure that the proposed structure does not create a potential for an anti-kickback violation.[16] When structuring an IDS, the parties want to be particularly careful if the IDS includes physicians or physician groups. Because

---

[14] A monopoly is defined by having "the power to control prices or exclude competition." *United States v. E.I. DuPont de Nemours*, 351 U.S. 377, 391 (1957). *See* Chapter 6 for further discussion on monopolies and the Sherman Act.

[15] 15 U.S.C. § 18a (the waiting period will "end on the thirtieth day" after receipt of the appropriate documentation, or on the fifteenth day "in the case of a cash tender offer," unless the FTC or Attorney General extends the deadline by requesting additional relevant information).

[16] Social Security Act § 1128B(b); 42 U.S.C. § 1320a-7b(b).

> Sec. 1128B(a) Whoever—
>
> (b)(1)Whoever knowingly and willfully solicits or receives any remuneration (including any kickback, bribe, or rebate) directly or indirectly, overtly or covertly, in cash or in kind—
>
> (A) in return for referring an individual to a person for the furnishing or arranging for the furnishing of any item or service for which payment may be made in whole or in part under a Federal health care program, or
>
> (B) in return for purchasing, leasing, ordering, or arranging for or recommending purchasing, leasing, or ordering any good, facility, service, or item for which payment may be made in whole or in part under a Federal health care program,
>
> shall be guilty of a felony and upon conviction thereof, shall be fined not more than $25,000 or imprisoned for not more than five years, or both.
>
> (2) Whoever knowingly and willfully offers or pays any remuneration (including any kickback, bribe, or rebate) directly or indirectly, overtly or covertly, in cash or in kind to any person to induce such person—
>
> (A) to refer an individual to a person for the furnishing or arranging for the furnishing of any item or service for which payment may be made in whole or in part under a Federal health care program, or
>
> (B) to purchase, lease, order, or arrange for or recommend purchasing, leasing, or ordering any good, facility, service, or item for which payment may be made in whole or in part under a Federal health care program,
>
> shall be guilty of a felony and upon conviction thereof shall be fined not more than $25,000 or imprisoned for not more than five years, or both.
>
> *See* Chapter 4 for a complete discussion of the Anti-Kickback Statute.

the Anti-Kickback Statute generally prohibits any type of payment to a person (including a physician) in exchange for a referral of a government-sponsored patient, which includes Medicare and Medicaid recipients in addition to recipients under other government-sponsored programs, any arrangement with physicians needs to be scrutinized to ensure that any payments to the physicians are not deemed to be a kickback.[17] The parties should also review the safe harbors to the Anti-Kickback Statute[18] to determine whether the proposed structure for the IDS fits within one of the applicable safe harbors.

Typically when forming an IDS, the safe harbors that may be applicable are the investment interests safe harbors,[19] which includes a safe harbor for publicly traded companies and another for entities owned by either active or passive investors. If the arrangement is a joint venture to create an ASC, then the ASC safe harbor should be reviewed.[20] Also potentially applicable when structuring such a transaction are the safe harbors for employment arrangements, agreements with independent contractors, and leases for real and personal property. Because the safe harbors are narrowly written, very few transactions satisfy all of a particular safe harbor's criteria. Notwithstanding this dilemma, it is important to remember that the mere fact that an arrangement does not fit within a safe harbor does not make the transaction illegal; instead, the transaction is subject to review by the government and may be a violation of the law.

11.3.1.3 Stark Law

The Ethics in Patient Referrals Act of 1989 (Stark Law)[21] also needs to be reviewed to ensure that the IDS does not violate this act. In general, the Stark Law prohibits a physician (and certain family members of physicians) from having a financial relationship, including ownership and compensation arrangements, with an entity that provides designated health services (DHS), as well as from referring Medicare or Medicaid patients to such entity for a DHS[22] unless a Stark exception is satisfied. Thus, if the IDS has a financial arrangement with a physician, then the arrangement must satisfy a Stark exception. If the arrangement does *not* satisfy an exception, then the physician would be precluded from referring any Medicare or Medicaid patients to the IDS for a DHS. Because the list of DHSs is very complete, most compensation/investment arrangements with physicians must satisfy a Stark exception. PPACA made several changes to the Stark Law, and some of the PPACA Stark changes impact

[17] The Patient Protection and Affordable Care Act (PPACA) has clarified the meaning of "knowingly and willingly" within the meaning of the Anti-Kickback statute by stating that a violator need not have specific knowledge the action violates the Anti-Kickback statute or specific intent to violate the law. Patient Protection and Affordable Care Act § 6402(f); PPACA also makes False Claims Act violations easier to prove, by making the establishment of a violation of the anti-kickback rules the establishment of the filing of a false claim. Patient Protection and Affordable Care Act § 6402(f); the False Claims Act makes anyone who knowingly makes false claims to the government liable for up to three times the amount of the claim plus mandatory penalties. 31 U.S.C. § 3729(a).

[18] 56 Fed. Reg. 35,932 (July 29, 1991); 59 Fed. Reg. 37,202 (July 21, 1994); 61 Fed Reg. 2,122 (Jan. 25, 1996); proposed safe harbors 58 Fed. Reg. 49,008 (Sept. 21, 1993); 64 Fed. Reg. 63,504 (Nov. 19, 1999); 64 Fed. Reg. 63,518 (Nov. 19, 1999).

[19] 42 C.F.R. § 952(a).

[20] 42 C.F.R. § 1001.952(r).

[21] Social Security Act 1877; 42 U.S.C. § 1395nn.

[22] The 11 designated health services set forth in the Stark Law are: clinical lab services; physical therapy services; occupational therapy services; radiology services (including magnetic resonance imaging, computerized axial tomography scans, and ultrasound services); radiation therapy services and supplies; durable medical equipment and supplies; parenteral and enteral nutrients, equipment and supplies; prosthetics, orthotics, and prosthetic devices and supplies; home health services; outpatient prescription drugs; and inpatient and outpatient hospital services. 42 U.S.C. § 1395nn(h)(6).

integration.[23] For example, PPACA has put a freeze on the creation of physician owned hospitals after 2010.[24] Additionally, those in operation will be severely limited in expanding their facilities unless they can show need in the community.[25]

11.3.1.4 Tax

Various tax laws will need to be reviewed when structuring an IDS. For example, if a tax-exempt hospital is acquiring entities to create an IDS,[26] then the hospital needs to be cautious if creating an IDS with for-profit entities, which would include physicians and physician groups, proprietary health systems, etc. The tax-exempt hospital needs to ensure that it will not be jeopardizing its tax-exempt status by engaging in private inurement or private benefit, and expose the facility to intermediate sanctions, by forming the IDS.[27] Such a situation could arise if the hospital offered a physician a purchase price for the physician's practice that exceeds the practice's fair market value. The excess amount paid to the physician could be deemed a benefit to a private individual, and could expose certain parties to penalties under the intermediate sanctions that are available to the IRS in the event that the physician is deemed to be a disqualified person.[28] Other tax issues to review are unrelated business income tax issues, as well as reviewing each transaction in light of the tax-exempt mission and applicable IRS determination letter to ensure ongoing recognition by the IRS as a tax-exempt entity.

11.3.1.5 Other Legal Issues

Various other legal issues affect the structuring of an IDS. For example, certain states have corporation practice of medicine statutes that prohibit a corporation whose shareholders are not physicians from employing physicians.[29] Hence, if the IDS wants to employ physicians directly, then the IDS's counsel should review the applicable state(s) statutes to see whether any prohibition is made on such employment, or whether the state allows employment in all cases or in certain circumstances. Vari-

23 Patient Protection and Affordable Care Act § 6001. *See* Sean A. Timmons, *Fraud and Abuse Provisions in the PPACA*, May 20, 2010, available at http://healthlaw.ncbar.org/newsletters/prognosis-may-2010/fraud-and-abuse-provisions-in-the-ppaca-.aspx.

24 *See* PPACA § 6001. *See also* Timmons, *supra* (noting that two of the Stark law exceptions, codified at 42 U.S.C. § 1395nn(d)(2) and (3)—the rural provider exception and the hospital owner exception—will not apply to physician owned hospitals created after Dec. 31, 2010).

25 *See id.* (suggesting that the number of physician owned hospitals will significantly decrease after Dec. 31, 2010).

26 Section 501(c)(3) of the Internal Revenue Code holds that

> Corporations… organized and operated exclusively for religious, charitable, scientific, testing for public safety, literacy, or educational purposes… no part of the net earnings of which inures to the benefit of any private shareholder or individual, no substantial part of the activities of which is carrying on propaganda, or otherwise attempting, to influence legislation… and which does not participate in, or intervene in… any political campaign on behalf of (or in opposition to) any candidate for public office.

27 I.R.C. § 4958.

28 *Id.* § 4958.

29 The prohibition on corporate medicine is against any person or entity other than a licensed physician/dentist/optometrist holding herself out as a provider of diagnoses, treatment or care of patients, billing in the name of such non-licensed entity for such diagnoses, treatment or care of patients, and/or ownership or other control of professional medical, dental, or optometric delivery systems by non-licensed persons or entities. *Patient Care and Professional Responsibility: Impact of the Corporate Practice of Medicine Doctrine and Related Laws and Regulations*," NHLA/AAHA (1997). *See also* Mary Michal et al., *Corporate Practice of Medicine Doctrine: 50 State Survey Summary*, available at http://www.nhpco.org/files/public/palliativecare/corporate-practice-of-medicine-50-state-summary.pdf (briefly stating the law in each state as of 2006 along with a short summary of legal guidance).

ous states have corporate practice of medicine statutes that prohibit even a *hospital* from employing a physician.[30]

Reimbursement issues also need to be addressed when structuring an IDS. Applicable Medicare and Medicaid regulations should be reviewed prior to any transactions to see if the amount of government reimbursement will be affected, limited, or prohibited by the proposed structure of the IDS. For example, when physician practices are acquired by a hospital and become part of an IDS, depending upon the circumstances, the physician services may be billed as either hospital-based services or freestanding services (which are rendered in a physician's office).[31] If the service is billed as hospital-based to Medicare, then typically two bills are generated to the Medicare program: one for the technical component of the service (*i.e.*, office overhead, non-professional assistance, supplies) and the other for the professional component of the service (the physician's service). If the service is billed as freestanding, then one professional bill is sent to the Medicare carrier, which incorporates an overhead component. In order for the IDS to determine how it should bill, the Medicare regulations and other advisory information should be reviewed, including the Medicare provider based rules. Additionally, the "incident to" rules[32] under Medicare will often affect the structuring of physician entities within an IDS, as well as the successor-liability issues with acquiring provider agreements/numbers.

State certificate of need (CON) issues may also need to be reviewed if the IDS operates in a state that has CON laws that affect the transaction.[33] State laws typically require a state health department's approval prior to a healthcare entity providing certain types of activities within the state. For example, a CON may be necessary for the acquisition of healthcare facilities, construction or renovation of facilities, or the acquisition of specialized healthcare equipment (*e.g.,* lithotripter or magnetic resonance imagining equipment). CON laws were initially enacted to discourage overbuilding of healthcare entities (*i.e.*, an ASC on every corner, a hospital on every major street), as well as to ensure that facilities that provide highly technical services, such as organ transplant procedures and open-heart surgery, can provide a sufficient volume of those services in order to obtain proficiency. Thus, the CON laws limit the number of facilities constructed within the state, as well as the types of procedures that can be performed. State law should be reviewed to determine whether a CON law exists, and what impact the CON law would have on the proposed transaction.

In summary, each IDS formation and transaction is unique. Thus, a myriad of legal issues may influence how the IDS is structured in order to comply with all applicable federal and state laws. All of these laws (and others, depending on the specifics) should be reviewed during the structuring phase of the transaction.

---

30 *E.g.,* Ohio Revised Code § 1701.3(D) (prohibiting a corporation formed for the combination of professional services from controlling the professional judgment of doctors and other healthcare providers); *see also* Col. Rev. Stat. Ann. 25-3-103.7(3); *Conrad v. Medical Bd. of California*, 48 Cal. App. 4th 1038, 1050 (hospitals may not employ physicians but may use them as independent contractors); *Grupta v. Idaho Tumor Inst., Inc.*, 140 S.W. 3d 747, 752 (Tex. App. 2004) (illegal for a corporation comprised of lay persons to hire physicians to treat patients); Iowa Op. Att'y Gen. 91-7-1 (July 12, 1991) (the legality of employment of physicians is determined on an individual basis and depends on degree of control exercised).

31 42 C.F.R. § 413.65, 65 Fed. Reg. 18,538 (Apr. 7, 2000).

32 *See Medicare Carriers Manual* § 2050. Billable incident services are those that are: (1) "an integral, although incidental, part of the physician's professional service," § 2050.1; (2) "commonly rendered without charge or included in the physician's bill," § 2050.1A; (3) "of a type that are commonly furnished in physician's offices or clinics," § 2050.1A; and (4) "furnished by the physician or by auxiliary personnel under the physician's direct supervision," § 2050.1B.

33 *See, e.g.*, Ala. Code § 22-21-260; Cal. Health & Safety Code § 127170; Ohio Rev. Code Ann. § 3702.51.

11.3.2 Physician/Hospital Organizations

Physician/hospital organizations (PHOs) were created in the early 1990s by hospitals that were interested in establishing a bond with physicians in order to offer an attractive full-service provider product to managed-care payors and employers. A PHO can be structured in various ways, but it is typically structured by creating a new entity that is jointly owned by physicians and a hospital. Customarily a PHO is established either as a for-profit corporation, a partnership or a limited liability company. (*See* Figure 5.)

Figure 5

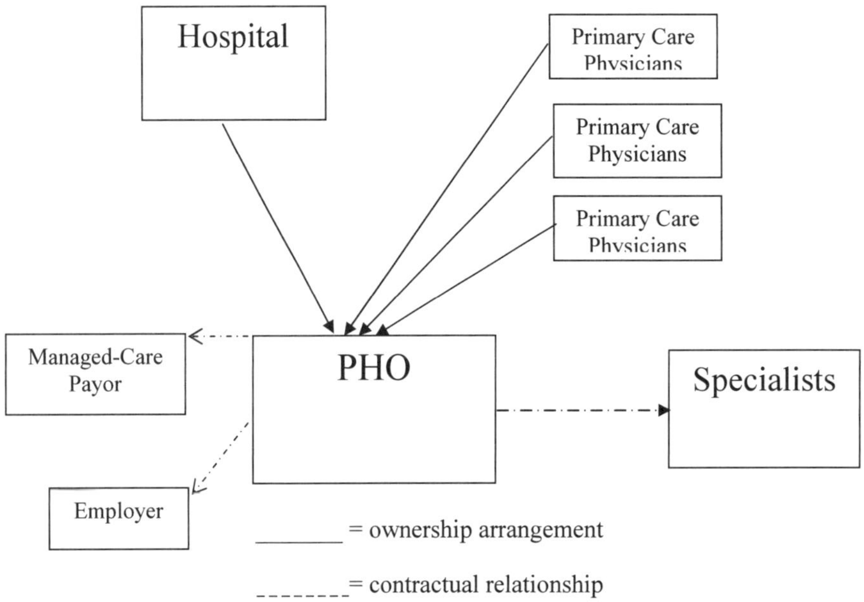

Typically the specialty physicians (*e.g.*, cardiologists, surgeons, anesthesiologists, radiologists) would not be offered ownership in the PHO; rather, the PHO would contract with such physicians to provide those type of specialty medical services to the PHO's patients. Specialty physicians are typically not offered ownership opportunities in the PHO because, unlike primary care physicians, a specialist usually does not manage care in the same way a primary care physician does. Specialists typically do not have regular appointments with a patient, and thus do not monitor a patient's care in a general fashion. Specialty physicians are not gatekeepers, as primary care physicians are in managed care. For example, a primary care physician sees a patient and determines whether the patient should be sent to a gastroenterologist. The primary care physician has the opportunity to try to keep the patient well so that she will not have to be referred to a specialist; the physician's goal is to eliminate an unnecessary referral to a specialist when it is not medically necessary. This is one of the basic premises concerning the economics of managed care: if primary care physicians properly manage the care of their patients and keep their patients healthy, then patients should need less services from specialty physicians and ancillary providers, as well as fewer hospital inpatient and emergency room visits.

Once formed, the PHO would then contract directly with managed-care plans, which would now have a "one-stop-shopping" type of arrangement with the PHO: In one contract, the managed-care plan simultaneously arranges for the PHO provision of hospital tertiary-care services, primary-care services, and specialty-physician services. The managed care organization (MCO) would no longer need to enter into several agreements with individual physicians and specialists; instead, the MCO would have an agreement for the entire scope of services from the PHO. Some PHOs also contract with other types of ancillary providers who would, like the specialists, be contract providers to the PHO and not owners of the PHO. Those providers might include nursing homes, HHC providers, and DME suppliers.

As with all healthcare transactions, a wide variety of legal issues influence the formation of a PHO. One of the most fundamental legal issues to review is tax concerns. If the hospital is an entity that is deemed to be tax-exempt under federal law (a § 501(c)(3) organization under the Internal Revenue Code), and if the hospital is going to enter into a joint venture with physicians or any other entity to create the PHO, then the tax-exempt hospital must receive a commercially appropriate percentage of the joint-venture vehicle in exchange for its investment in order not to be subject to tax penalties or loss of tax-exempt status.

For example, if the hospital provides 50% of the capital to establish the PHO, it should receive 50% of the partnership or the stock of the PHO, depending on its corporate structure. If it does not receive its fair share of the PHO for its investment, then the IRS may view this as the hospital engaging in private inurement or private benefit by offering the physicians a greater investment portion of the PHO in relation to the physicians' investments. A hospital may be tempted to do this because the physicians may not have the necessary capital, the physicians do not want to borrow funds, or the physicians selected are ones who use the hospital's services and refer a lot of patients to the hospital. Such a transaction, if reviewed by the IRS, could jeopardize the tax-exempt status of the hospital because it would be deemed to have wasted its charitable assets on a private individual or for the benefit of private persons. In such instance, the IRS has the ability to revoke the hospital's tax-exempt status or, pursuant to regulations, the IRS could impose financial sanctions on the hospital[34] for entering into excess-benefit transactions with the physicians. (*See* Chapter 5 for more discussion on private inurement, private benefit, and intermediate sanctions.)

In addition to the necessary tax analysis, the structure of a PHO has to be reviewed to ensure compliance with the Stark laws and the Anti-Kickback Statute. A Stark exception may have to be satisfied if the PHO will provide designated health services (DHS), and if the physicians will refer Medicare and Medicaid patients to the PHO for such DHS. Often a PHO does not directly provide any healthcare services, but rather is an entity that is created for managed-care contracting purposes and not as a provider of services. Instead, the PHO contracts with providers who will render the DHS or other services. Thus, the Stark laws would probably not apply.

If the PHO provides DHS and a Stark exception is not satisfied, then the physician would be precluded from referring government-sponsored patients for DHS to the PHO. Eleven DHS categories have been established, encompassing a vast array of healthcare services such as clinical laboratory services, radiology services, and hospital inpatient and outpatient services. The Stark Law sets forth

[34] I.R.C. § 4958.

various exceptions, including for ownership arrangements, compensation arrangements, and ownership and compensation arrangements. Because a proposed PHO would involve an ownership arrangement between the hospital and the physicians, and because the physicians would have an ownership interest in the PHO, an ownership exception would need to be satisfied.

Under the Anti-Kickback Statute, the PHO arrangement would be reviewed to determine whether referrals are made between the parties. The analysis will change depending on whether the PHO is also a provider. Nevertheless, the PHO's advisors should review the arrangement and comply with the Anti-Kickback Statute, given that most probably the physicians will refer patients to the hospital. Thus, the arrangement should not be deemed to offer the physicians a kickback in exchange for their referrals. An example of a gross violation would be if the PHO's distributions (profits) were allocated based on referrals to the hospital, or if a physician received a PHO percentage distribution disproportionate to her capital investment in the PHO. Therefore, the structure of the PHO should be reviewed, in addition to any other contracts with parties who are referral sources and, thus, implicate the fraud and abuse laws.

Additionally, depending on the structure of the PHO, there may be antitrust implications if there is not sufficient integration of the parties and sharing of risk. The Federal Trade Commission and the Department of Justice look at these factors (in addition to others) to ensure appropriate integration of the PHO. The goal of the PHO is to allow the parties to the PHO, who are competitors, the ability to negotiate jointly reimbursement fees with the MCOs for professional services rendered by the PHO's providers.

Certain PHOs have been formed in part to contract directly with an employer so that the PHO may provide services directly to an employer's employees without the involvement of an insurance company. Many large employers have contracted with PHOs in order to obtain better rates by eliminating the MCO, as well as to establish more control over who are the employer's healthcare providers. In these arrangements, the employer does not have to be limited to the MCO's providers; instead, the employer can select its own providers. Depending on the employer's expertise, the employer may contract with a third-party administrator (TPA) who would pay the providers' claims, administer the healthcare plan on behalf of the employer, credential the providers, and provide utilization review services for cost and quality-control measures. This arrangement between an employer and providers is often referred to as direct contracting. When direct contracting is a possibility, employers and PHOs should review their state insurance laws to determine whether the PHO would be deemed to be an insurance entity as a result of having taken on the business of insurance. This analysis usually turns on whether the party has assumed "insurance risk" rather than "business risk", as defined in the particular state's laws. Therefore, the state insurance laws and regulations should be reviewed. Other legal issues that could arise include corporate practice of medicine issues (because of the possible employment by the PHO of physicians), as well as billing and collection issues.

11.3.3 Independent Practice Associations

Similar to a PHO, an Independent Practice Association (IPA) is typically a group of unaffiliated physicians who join together to create an organization for managed-care contracting and administrative-efficiency purposes. (It is important to note that an IPA commonly also will refer to an independent physician association or independent professional association.) IPAs come in many sizes, from several doctors to several hundred doctors. An IPA can be organized in several ways, including as a corporation or a partnership or limited liability company. Figure 6 reflects a physician or a physician group who purchases an equity interest in the IPA. This example also illustrates the IPA's entering into a contract with payors to provide physician services to the payor's beneficiaries.

Figure 6

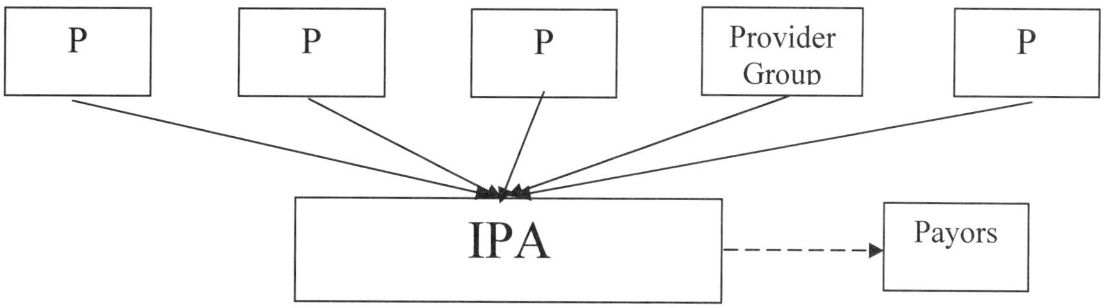

The IPA's participating providers (which either can be limited to owner-physicians of the IPA or expanded to include other healthcare providers who have contracted with the IPA) agree to provide services to the MCO's beneficiaries. As noted in the earlier discussion of PHO structures, MCOs find contracting with IPAs beneficial because a potentially large group of physicians can serve a large number of the MCO's enrollees as a result. Rather than requiring the MCO to contract with 100 individual doctors, it can enter into *one* contract with the IPA. One downside from the MCO's perspective is that the MCO may now be negotiating this contract with a large entity that has greater bargaining power because of its number of providers. Thus, the IPA may be able to negotiate better terms (*e.g.*, higher reimbursement, definition of what constitutes a covered service) in the managed-care agreements than the individual physician who does not have sufficient bargaining power and often has to sign a form agreement.

Aside from managed-care contracting, some IPAs are also formed to offer administrative services to its provider members. For example, the IPA may provide marketing services, billing and collection services, or supplies and equipment to the IPA's members. An IPA will provide these services hoping to achieve some "economies of scale," as the IPA is able to purchase items or services in larger quantities and then distribute them to its members. (*See* Figure 7.)

Figure 7

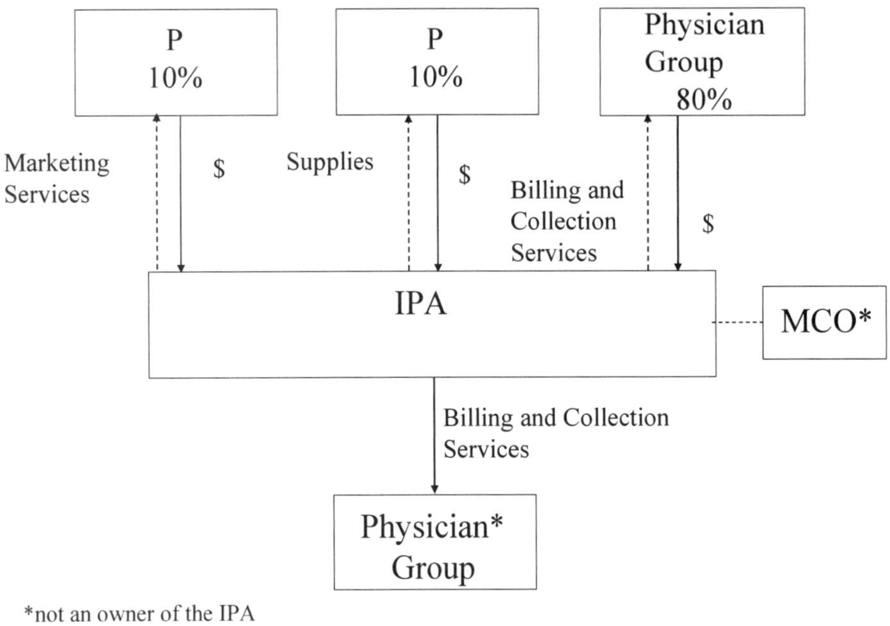

In Figure 7, physician-investors contract with the IPA to provide various services. Additionally, the IPA provides billing and collection services for noninvesting physician groups or individual physicians via contracts in which the physician group pays the IPA for billing and collection services.

Many physicians also participate in IPAs because they want to have the benefits of affiliation (*e.g.*, greater bargaining power in managed-care contracts) without total integration. Thus, with an IPA, the physicians typically still own their separate medical practices, and they continue to provide their professional services in their own practices. The IPA merely provides a vehicle in which unaffiliated parties can unite and enter into a joint venture for specific purposes (*e.g.*, managed-care contracting and group purchasing).

The paramount legal issue that needs to be reviewed when structuring an IPA is the antitrust laws because the potential exists for price fixing whenever unaffiliated parties that are deemed to be competitors join together to negotiate prices amongst themselves in order to offer a fee schedule or payment terms to an MCO. In general terms, however, the antitrust laws allow competitors to share and discuss pricing information if an appropriate level of shared risk and integration exists.[35] If this is the case, then the arrangement may be deemed to be pro-competitive rather than anti-competitive, and may not be deemed to be a violation of the antitrust laws. Hence, when structuring an IPA, a thorough review of the antitrust laws and applicable guidelines must be made. Specifically, the joint FTC and DOJ Antitrust Guidelines for Collaboration Among Competitors should be reviewed.[36]

35 *See* Statement 8 (Physician Network Joint Ventures) of the Department of Justice and Federal Trade Commission Statement of Antitrust Enforcement Policy in Health Care.

36 Federal Trade Commission and the U.S. Department of Justice, *Antitrust Guidelines for Collaboration Among Competitors* (2000).

11.3.4 Professional Corporations

A Professional Corporation (P.C.) is usually a corporation recognized by state statute, allowing professionals of the same or different specialties to join together and form a corporation to provide professional services. If physicians want to integrate more fully than in an IPA model and operate as a single physician practice, then the next step would be for the physicians to create a P.C. In such an arrangement, each physician could be a shareholder of the P.C., in addition to providing professional services on behalf of the P.C. as an employee. Some state statutes prohibit nonprofessionals from directly holding shares in a professional corporation.[37]

Very few sophisticated legal issues affect the structuring of a P.C. Unlike an IPA, for the most part a P.C. does not implicate antitrust issues because the physicians have integrated into one organization; thus, it cannot conspire with itself to set fees. However, a P.C. may pose antitrust concerns if it has so many physician shareholders in the community that it could be considered a monopoly. Additionally, P.C.s in states with corporate practice of medicine statutes should ensure that all of its shareholders are permitted under state law to be shareholders.

The distribution of profits and salaries among the physicians should also be analyzed under the Stark Law and the Anti-Kickback Statute. For example, there could be an anti-kickback problem if one physician in the P.C., is paid a salary that takes into account referrals to other persons in the P.C.[38] Additionally, under this hypothetical, if the P.C. provides DHS (*e.g.*, clinical lab service), then the Stark exception for in-office ancillary services would probably not be satisfied due to the fact that the P.C. probably does not satisfy the Stark definition of a group practice, as compensation is based on referrals.[39] Thus, this arrangement would also create a Stark problem. Lastly, many states have created their own statutory versions of the Stark and Anti-Kickback Laws.[40] Therefore, counsel for such practitioners should review the applicable state statutes with respect to any state limitations regarding payments to physicians and other providers.

11.3.5 Management-Services Organizations

A management-services organization (MSO) is an entity that provides various types of administrative and management services to providers in their practices. The types of services offered by MSOs traditionally include billing and collection; credentialing; marketing; insurance; provision of staff support, supplies, and equipment; office space; utilization review; HIPAA compliance; managed care; and other contracting. Many hospitals and IDSs have organized MSOs as part of their system to provide services to its physicians or its medical staff. Hospitals and IDSs constantly are in search of ways to create a closer bond with these physicians. Many such physicians have not been interested in

---

37 *See* OH. REV. CODE ANN. § 1785 for an example of state corporate-practice-of-medicine statutes.

38 The federal government may not deem payments among members in a group practice to violate the Anti-Kickback Statute if the organization satisfies the definition of a group practice in section 1877(h)(4) of the Social Security Act and the implementing regulations, which is the Stark Law. 42 C.F.R. § 1001.952(p); 64 Fed. Reg. 63,518, 63,555 (1999).

39 In the Stark Law regulations and requirement of a group practice, the definition requires "no physician who is a member of the group directly or indirectly receives compensation based on the volume or value of referrals by the physician." § 1395nn(A)(iv).

40 *See, e.g.*, Kathryn Leaman, Note, *State Anti-kickback Statutes: Where the Action Is*, 9 J. HEALTH CARE COMPLIANCE 23 (2007).

selling their practices to and becoming employees of the IDS. Some physicians have sold practices to the IDSs, only to have the practices sold back to the physicians after the arrangement failed. Many of these physicians wanted to retain their autonomy, and did not desire or trust an employment relationship with the IDS. In other situations, the integration proved to be financially impossible, and the practices were sold back to the physicians. In light of current economic and compliance trends, however, physicians have sought assistance from MSOs and other administrative providers, desiring to purchase various services from an MSO in order to relieve various administrative burdens and for the providers to concentrate on practicing medicine.

From the IDS's viewpoint, this creates a contractual relationship between the physician and the IDS, and perhaps will foster some loyalty of the physician to the IDS and the services it provides. These MSO services can also be offered to other hospitals, clinics, ASCs, nursing homes, and other providers and facilities. Additionally, some providers may choose to purchase one service, while others purchase a wider range of services. In some instances, this contractual arrangement has been a precursor to further integration between the parties. This contractual arrangement thus affords the parties the opportunity to get to know each other and become acquainted with one another's operations before committing to an employment or independent-contractor relationship. Additionally, some MSOs are now also becoming providers of healthcare services.

As with all other potential arrangements between a hospital or IDS and a physician, the Stark and Anti-Kickback Laws need to be reviewed. For example, the Anti-Kickback Laws established a safe harbor for personal services and management contracts between parties that have a potential referral relationship. In order for an MSO contractual arrangement to fit within the safe harbor, it would have to satisfy all of the criteria of that specific safe harbor.[41] Again, however, even if the MSO contract does not satisfy all seven parts of the safe harbor, it does not mean that the arrangement is illegal; rather, the contract would be subject to scrutiny and might be deemed a violation.

With regard to the formation of the MSO, typically these entities are wholly owned by the IDS, a hospital, or a group of physicians. If the MSO is owned by a combination of these participants, then Stark and anti-kickback issues would need to be analyzed to ensure that the ownership investments are proportional to the specific amount invested by each investor, as discussed earlier in this Chapter. For example, if a physician invests only 10% of the capital but gets 50% ownership of the MSO, then the arrangement likely will lead to an anti-kickback problem, a Stark violation, and/or potential tax problems (if a charitable entity is involved). Specifically, an anti-kickback problem might result because the government could argue that the physician received a 50% ownership interest, rather than a 10% ownership interest, because the other owners of the MSO offered this extra 40% investment interest to the physician in order to encourage him or her to refer government-sponsored patients to the IDS's facilities.

[41] The requirements of the personal services and management contracts safe harbor are as follows: (i) the agreement must be in writing and signed by the parties; (ii) the agreement specifies all of the services provided and covers all of the services provided by the agent; (iii) if the services are sporadic, the agreement has a schedule for such services and the resulting charges; (iv) the term of the agreement is for at least one year; (v) the aggregate service charge is set in advance and based on arm's-length negotiations, and does not take into account any referrals of government sponsored patients; (vi) the services under the agreement do not promote or involve a business activity that violates any state or federal law; and (vii) the aggregate services contracted for do not exceed those that are reasonably necessary to accomplish the commercially reasonable business purposes of the services. 42 C.F.R. § 1001.952(d).

Similarly, a Stark violation would follow from physician-investor referral of Medicare and Medicaid patients to the MSO for DHS if a Stark ownership exception is not satisfied.

There would also be a tax problem if the IDS is a tax-exempt entity. In such case, the IRS might deem the physician to be an "insider" of the IDS for tax purposes, and *any* amount of benefit given to the physician (*e.g.*, the excess 40% ownership interest) would be deemed to be private inurement, which could either jeopardize the tax-exempt status of the IDS and its facilities or allow the IRS to impose intermediate sanctions, the latter of which could include financial penalties on both the physician and the IDS and its managers.

11.4 Key Issues in Structuring Transactions

11.4.1 Purpose of the Venture

Before the parties (and their lawyers, accountants, and consultants) start structuring the transaction and drafting documents to reflect such structure, the parties should make sure that they have reviewed the purposes for the venture. If the parties do not understand what the goals of the venture are and whether they can be satisfied, then perhaps the parties should not enter into the transaction. Some element of risk is always present with a new venture, and it may be impossible to ascertain the possibility or probability of reaching the goals of the venture. In such an instance, perhaps the parties should discuss, earlier rather than later, what will happen if the goals are not satisfied. These issues are discussed more fully in Section 11.5.

11.4.2 Operational Issues

As important as it is to be aware of the purpose of the transaction that is being contemplated, it is just as important to understand the operational issues of the client. For example, if one party wants to ensure that the billing of Medicare services after the closing of the transaction will be handled in a certain manner, then it is important when structuring the transaction to make sure that the operational billing issues of that party are satisfied, or that the party is fully aware of the potential problems or complications. Another example may be that a client wants to employ the physicians as part of the transaction. Therefore, the deal may have to be structured so as not to violate a state prohibition on the corporate practice of medicine or a Medicare billing limitation. Thus, it is important to devote significant time to discussing the key operational issues or goals that the parties hope to resolve or accomplish by entering into the transaction, and flush out any legal concerns or challenges at an early stage.

11.4.3 Legal Issues

As was discussed earlier in this Chapter, a myriad of legal issues affect the types of transactions that are available to the parties, and many of these same issues impact structuring the specifics of the transaction. In many instances, healthcare providers may want to engage in some form of transaction that will not be possible due to legal constraints. For example, many hospitals and physicians want to create a joint venture to share imaging centers or clinical labs. Many such arrangements are impossible to structure, however, without violating the Stark laws and the Anti-Kickback Statute. In general, hospitals have wanted to enter joint ventures with physicians to create a stronger relationship between the parties, but it is clear that the Stark, fraud and abuse, and tax-exemption laws sometimes make such a transaction illegal, or otherwise create a risky arrangement that could be challenged by governmental authorities. Instead, the parties may have to choose another structure or forego the entire proposed transaction because of the legal prohibitions.

Because of the varied regulatory issues that affect healthcare transactions, the parties should be aware of the legal issues when initially contemplating the structure of a transaction, so that the parties do not have to change the structure or unwind the transaction due to a violation of applicable laws and regulations. Sometimes providers will structure a transaction and agree on the specifics of the deal only to find out, at a later date, that the transaction is illegal and impossible to restructure in order to comply with existing federal and state laws and regulations. Therefore, it is best to include the legal team in the initial discussions and negotiations of the structure, so that the proposed transaction or arrangement complies with applicable federal and state laws.

11.5 Unwinding Transactions

At a stage when the parties are structuring a deal and entering into a new venture, no one wants to focus on issues that may arise if the transaction is unsuccessful. The parties to a transaction are typically optimistic, and do not want to contemplate what should happen if the transaction does not materialize as the parties intended. Because not all transactions are successful, however, the following issues should be discussed and addressed in the transactional documents.

11.5.1 Termination Provisions

If the venture does not roll out as one or both parties intended, then the parties may want to make sure legal means are available to terminate the arrangement. This is typically not an issue if all of the parties mutually consent to terminate the agreement. In the event that only one party wants to terminate, however, this could be a big problem if no termination provisions are included in the governing documents. Transactions involving the acquisition of an entity (either through a merger, stock transaction, or asset transaction) usually cannot be reversed after the transaction closes, and will only be unwound under extraordinary circumstances. In a non-acquisition arrangement (*i.e.,* an affiliation, joint venture, or service agreement), however, the arrangement can easily be terminated if the governing document allows for termination in various circumstances. (*See* Section 11.7 for further discussion on termination provisions.) Even if the agreement provides for termination, the parties may not want to terminate the arrangement without receipt of the assets that they sold or contributed to the venture. Thus, certain agreements contain a repurchase right for the terminating party under certain circumstances and in accordance with specific terms in the agreement.

11.5.2 Rights to Repurchase; Repurchase Obligations

In certain transactions, the parties may want to include a provision in the governing documents that sets forth a repurchase right in the event that certain circumstances occur, or if the parties mutually agree to terminate the relationship. The repurchase right may be a compulsory obligation imposed on the party that sold or contributed the asset at the time of termination. The repurchase clause could also be a discretionary right that is given to a terminating party who contributed or sold assets to the venture. In either case, it is best if the governing agreement sets forth the particulars of a buy-back, specifying whether it is a compulsory obligation or discretionary right, the latter of which can be exercised if elected by the former owner of the assets.

The agreement may also delineate the type of event that must occur in order for the repurchase rights or obligations to be triggered. The agreement would also set forth the terms of the repurchase (*e.g.*, purchase price or valuation methodology, timing of transaction, post-transactional issues). If the agreement does not contain a repurchase provision and only one party wants to terminate the contractual relationship, then (notwithstanding a breach, which might allow one party to terminate the agreement and buy back the assets) the other party would not be legally required to sell the assets back to the original seller.

11.5.3 Bankruptcy

In a typical contractual service arrangement, a party is able to terminate the relationship if the other party files for receivership or bankruptcy. This situation might also trigger a contractual right on one party to buy back the business or assets that were originally sold to the purchaser. For example, a P.C. that purchased the assets of a physician's practice and later files for bankruptcy might afford the physician (via her employment agreement with the P.C.) the opportunity to terminate the agreement and repurchase the assets from the P.C. If the terms of the contractual relationship do not afford the other party the right to terminate in such instances, then the parties may be mired in a relationship with a party who is in receivership or in bankruptcy proceedings.

11.6 Types of Healthcare Contracts

Written contracts serve to memorialize the understanding and formal agreement between the parties, setting forth all of the details of the arrangement. The written agreement not only clearly defines the terms of the arrangement, but also addresses how to resolve disputes if they arise in the future. The document should address how to resolve such issues based on the agreed-upon terms in the agreement. Parties should be very cautious when using form agreements or documents from a prior transaction because each agreement and arrangement is unique to the specific facts of each situation. Therefore, if a form is used, it may not include, for example, indemnification provisions or other terms that are crucial to one of the parties. Thus, when using a form document, each party should review each term in the agreement to ensure that it is appropriate for the specific deal at hand.

Parties will often spend hours, days, weeks, and months negotiating the agreement. Often, however, certain points that have been agreed to may not be memorialized in the agreement, perhaps due to oversight. Thus, each party should review the agreement carefully to ensure that all agreed-upon points have been incorporated into the agreement in a clear and unambiguous manner.

11.6.1 Employment and Independent Contractor Agreements

In structuring various types of transactions, the arrangement may include the employment of a professional or some other type of contractual relationship. For example, if an IDS has purchased the assets of a physician's practice, then the IDS will usually employ or enter into an independent-contractor relationship with the physician, unless the physician is retiring or moving to another community. The main theoretical difference between employing a physician and merely contracting with the physician as an independent contractor is the amount of control that can be exercised by the employer over the physician. In an employment relationship, the employer is expected to exert control over its employees; in an independent contractor arrangement, on the other hand, the independent contractor performs the services under her own direction with very little supervision.

One key contractual element to be aware of in these types of agreements is the section of the agreement that addresses the status of the parties. It should be clearly stated in the agreement whether the parties have entered into an employment or independent-contractor relationship. This is extremely important for tax reasons. Specifically, if the status of the parties is unclear, or the IDS exercises too much control over the physician, then the IRS may deem the relationship to be an employment arrangement. In this case, the perceived "employer" would be penalized by the IRS for not withholding taxes, as well as being held responsible for paying all related employment taxes on behalf of the employee. Even if the agreement sets forth that the parties are independent contractors, in the event that the IDS possesses too much control over the physician, the IRS can still find an employment relationship and penalize the "employing" party. The IRS has released guidance on whether someone should be deemed an employee or an independent contractor.[42] Some agreements may incorporate a provision that, in the event of a determination by the IRS that one party is deemed to be an employee, the independent contractor will indemnify the other party for all taxes, interest, and penalties imposed by the IRS on the "employer."

---

[42] Rev. Rul. 87-41, 1987-1 C.B. 296. In this tax ruling, the IRS reviewed 20 primary factors used by the IRS to determine whether a worker is an employee. These questions are as follows:

1. To what degree does the recipient direct the worker?
2. Does the employer provide training?
3. Is the worker distinguished from the employer's regular employees?
4. Is the work performed characterized by personal service?
5. Are assistants subject to control by the employer?
6. Does the worker provide continuing services for the employer?
7. Are work hours set by the employer?
8. Does the worker devote full time to one employer?
9. Is the work performed at the employer's place of business?
10. Does the employer designate the order or sequence of work to be performed?
11. Is the worker required to submit regular reports?
12. Is the worker paid per time intervals?
13. Does the employer of the services pay business and traveling expenses?
14. Are tools furnished by the employer?
15. Has the worker made significant investments in his or her business?
16. Is the worker exposed to normal profit and loss risks associated with operating a business?
17. Does the worker provide services to more than one employer?
18. Does the worker provide service to the general public?
19. Under what conditions can the worker be fired?
20. Is the worker subject to a breach of contract charge if he or she prematurely terminates the working relationship?

Another key provision is the "noncompete" clause or restrictive covenant. This term customarily prohibits a physician or other type of healthcare provider from providing services for a specific period of time, and within a defined geographical area, during the agreement's term and after the termination or expiration of the agreement. Typically, the geographical area covered by the noncompete clause will surround the location in which the physician or provider rendered services during the term of the agreement.[43] Although legal in some jurisdictions, these provisions are unenforceable in others or are only enforceable if the person agreed to the noncompete as part of a sale of assets or stock.[44] Those jurisdictions that enforce covenants not to compete consider whether the non-compete provision is (i) reasonably limited in time or geographic scope and (ii) serves the purpose of protecting the former employer from unfair competition without being harmful to the public or unduly burdensome to the former employee. (*See* Section 11.7.3 for a further discussion on noncompete clauses.)

Compensation terms also are often heavily negotiated. When physicians are employed by hospitals and offered a fixed salary, the physician may lose her entrepreneurial spirit and not work as hard for the employer as when she was self-employed. Thus, hospitals and IDS have tried to incorporate financial incentives in order to encourage the physicians to treat a certain volume of patients, comply with protocols, and watch overhead expenses.[45] Notwithstanding these attempts, hospitals have terminated relationships with physicians on account of a lack of productivity and financial viability.

In addition to key provisions of an employment or agency agreement, it is also important to be aware of the key legal issues that affect these agreements. For example, in states prohibiting the corporate practice of medicine, a physician cannot be employed by corporations other than professional corporations or other specified entities. Thus, it is important to check the applicable state statutes and determine which entities are legally permitted to employ physicians and other ancillary healthcare professionals.

Liability concerns may be another reason for structuring an arrangement as either an employment or agency relationship. In an employment relationship, the employer is liable for the acts of its employees. Thus, the employer will purchase and maintain malpractice and general-liability insurance on behalf of its employees. In an independent-contractor arrangement, independent contractors will purchase their own malpractice insurance. In a healthcare transaction agreement, however, one party may impose an amount and type of insurance that must be acquired and maintained by an independent contractor. Notwithstanding the foregoing, cases abound in which one party may be held liable for the acts of its independent contractors because of a presumed employment arrangement. This liability,

---

43 *See, e.g.*, *Prairie Eye Center, Ltd. v. Butler*, 768 N.E. 2d 414, 329 Ill. App. 3d 293 (April 16, 2002).

44 Cal. Bus. & Prof. Code §§ 16600, 16601; *see also Edwards v. Arthur Anderson LLP*, 44 Cal 4th 937, 950 (Cal. 2008) (noncompete contracts are invalid per se unless needed to protect trade secrets).

45 "Physician employment with incentives is the model most often used.... 79% of systems used that arrangement to increase their physician integration." Deanna Bellandi, *Making Money But Struggling*, Modern Healthcare, Aug. 30, 1999, at 58. A 2009 survey found that "seventy percent of physicians employers have incentive based compensation." SullivanCotter Releases Results of 17th Annual Physician Compensation and Productivity survey, Marketwire, May 5, 2010, available at http://www.marketwire.com/press-release/Physician-Compensation-Survey-Reveals-Shrinking-Income-Gap-Between-Primary-Care-Specialty-1160289.htm. Fifty-four percent of organizations used measured based on quality or patient satisfaction. *Id.*

which is imposed on one party, is referred to as "respondent superior."[46] A specific example is when a hospital is held liable for the acts of its independently contracted emergency room physicians.[47]

Other legal issues that need to be reviewed include the Stark laws and the Anti-Kickback Statute. The compensation paid to the physician needs to be reviewed to ensure that a Stark exception is satisfied, given that the physician probably will refer patients to the employer for DHS. If no referrals are made, then Stark will not apply. Similarly, the Anti-Kickback Statute needs to be reviewed to ensure that the compensation paid to the provider is not deemed to be a kickback to encourage the physician to refer patients to the employer.[48] Stark laws and the Anti-Kickback Statute alike feature exceptions and safe harbors for employment and agency relationships.[49]

11.6.2 Physician Recruitment Agreements

One common type of healthcare arrangement is a physician recruitment agreement. A physician recruitment contract is usually between a physician and an IDS, a hospital, or physician practice group. The recruitment agreement provides for a physician to be recruited, to relocate, or to remain in a certain community after completing a residency in exchange for certain financial benefits, which either are delineated in the recruitment agreement or offered to a practicing physician that may be relocating. These agreements are usually made between the physician in question and a hospital, rather than other forms of healthcare providers, because community hospitals often need to recruit primary-care physicians or certain specialists in order to provide a full range of healthcare services to the community, as well as the fact that they have the funds to offer recruitment and relocation incentives.

A hospital may enter into a recruitment agreement with an oncologist, for example, if a demonstrable need exists for an oncologist in the hospital's community. Typically, these agreements will offer the physician certain financial perks for accepting the agreement. For example, if the physician relocates and practices in the community for a specific number of years, she may be offered a signing bonus, relocation expenses, malpractice insurance, or a guaranteed amount of compensation for

---

[46] "Generally, employer or principal is vicariously liable for torts of its employees or agents under doctrine of respondeat superior, but not for negligence of independent contractor over whom it retained no right to control mode and manner of doing contracted-for work." *Clark v. Southview Hosp. & Family Health Ctr.*, 68 Ohio St. 3d 435, 438, 628 N.E.3d 46, 48 (1994).

[47] In *Clark*, the court reviewed various factors in making its determination that the hospital is liable for the acts of its independent contractors. *Id.* at 54. Two factors that the court reviewed in making its determination were that the hospital held itself out as a provider of a full range of medical services, and that no evidence was present that the patient was informed or knew that the emergency care was being rendered by an independent contractor who merely used the site to provide services and was not an employee. *Id.* at 53.

[48] For example, in 2010, the Health Alliance, and one of its former members, Christ Hospital, settled an Anti-Kickback suit brought by a whistleblower and joined by the Justice Department, for $108 million. Mary Vanac, *Cincinnati Health Alliance, Christ Hospital Settle Suit for $108M*, MedCity News, May 21, 2010. The suit alleged that the hospital violated the Anti-Kickback Statute by remunerating doctors for referring cardiac patients to the hospital in a "pay-to-play" scheme. The suit further alleged that the scheme violated the False Claims Act because any claim filed to Medicare or Medicaid as a result of an illegal kickback constitutes a violation of that act. Because Christ Hospital refused to enter into a Corporate Integrity Agreement in conjunction with the settlement, the U.S. Department of Health and Human Services was considering dropping Christ Hospital from Medicare and Medicaid reimbursement. *See Christ Hospital Could Lose Medicare, Medicaid Reimbursement*, Business Courier of Cincinnati, May 28, 2010. The Corporate Integrity Agreement would have permitted additional government oversight of the hospital. *Id.*

[49] Under the Stark laws, *see* Social Security Act, § 1877(e)(2) and (3). For fraud and abuse topics, *see* 42 C.F.R. § 1001.952(d) and (i).

a specific time period. Often these agreements contain provisions that obligate the physician to repay some of these financial incentives in the event that the physician leaves the community before the time frame set forth in the agreement. It is important to note, however, that these agreements are neither employment arrangements nor service agreements where the physician provides services to the other contracting party. Instead, these agreements set forth some minimum qualifications that the physician must satisfy in order to be entitled to such recruitment incentives.

Various legal issues need to be reviewed before entering into a recruitment agreement. The Stark laws and their implementing regulations need to be reviewed to ensure that a compensation exception is satisfied, due to the fact that the physician will most likely make referrals of patients to the contracting party (*i.e.*, the hospital or IDS). The fraud and abuse laws also should be reviewed to make sure that there is no requirement to refer patients in exchange for the benefits, and that the physician has been legitimately recruited. There is a practitioner-recruitment safe harbor, but it is limited to practitioners who are recruited to work in a "health professional shortage area."[50] Thus, if the physician is being recruited to work in an area that is not recognized as a health professional shortage area, then this safe harbor does not lend any specific protection.

Additionally, if the recruiting party is federally recognized as a tax-exempt entity, then the remuneration offered to the physician must be reviewed to make sure that it is not deemed to be a private inurement or an arrangement that constitutes an excess benefit, which is subject to IRS intermediate sanctions. In general, the remuneration offered to the physician under all of these federal laws (Stark, fraud and abuse, and tax) require that the compensation be reasonable and independent of any referrals by the physician to the other party. Additionally, the benefits should represent fair market value for the value of relocating the physician to the community (or, alternatively, for the benefit to be gained by the physician relocating to the area). Because there may not be any services provided by the physician in a recruitment agreement, the value of the physician moving to the community and staying for an amount of time agreed upon by the parties should be valued to determine whether the payment is appropriate and not a violation of these laws.

11.6.3 Management and Service Agreements

Due to the integration and consolidation of healthcare providers, a myriad of management and service agreements have developed. For example, if a hospital purchases a physician's practice but does not employ the physician, then the hospital may enter into a service agreement with the physician to provide professional medical services to the hospital's practice. Alternatively, if the hospital

[50] This safe harbor only applies to practitioners working in their specialties for less than one year or relocating their practices. Additionally, the practitioner must be relocating to a health professional shortage area (HPSA). There are nine standards to the safe harbor: (1) the agreement must be in writing and signed by the parties; (2) 75% of the revenues of the new practice must be generated from new patients; (3) benefits can only be offered for a maximum of three years, and the terms of the agreement cannot be renegotiated during the term of the agreement; (4) there can be no requirement to refer, and the recruiting entity can require the physician to maintain privileges at its facility; (5) the entity cannot restrict the practitioner from obtaining privileges elsewhere; (6) the benefits offered to the physician do not vary based on volume or value of referrals; (7) there is an agreement to treat all federal healthcare beneficiaries in a nondiscriminatory manner; (8) at least 75% of revenues of the new practice must be generated from persons residing in a HPSA or medically underserved area or be part of a medically underserved population; and (9) the payment can only be to a practitioner and not to any other person or entity in position to make or influence referrals to recruiting entity. 42 C.F.R. § 1001.952(n).

was not able to purchase the physician's practice (perhaps because the physician did not want to sell the practice or because the hospital did not want to own the physician's practice), then the hospital might offer management services to the physician's practice, either directly or through a subsidiary organization. In any of these situations, the hospital and the physician must enter into some form of a services agreement.

Many physicians prefer these arrangements because they allow physicians to dedicate their time to the practice of medicine while a third party provides the administrative services. Some management-service agreements may provide the physician with all nonprofessional administrative services. Thus, the physician has what is commonly referred to as a "turnkey" operation: the physician merely enters the premises and provides her professional services; meanwhile, the management company provides all of the other services as the physician's independent contractor. For example, the management company provides office space and personnel, billing and collection services, medical-records maintenance, compliance with laws including HIPAA, supplies, malpractice insurance, contracting, and all other services.

In other arrangements, the physician might contract with the entity for one or two specific services. Often physicians will contract with a third party to provide billing and collection services because many companies specialize in physician coding and billing. Additionally, many hospitals have contracted with third parties to outsource various services that the hospitals had traditionally provided in-house. Some of these services include billing and collection, food services, laundry, housekeeping, cafeteria, pharmacy, plant operations, equipment maintenance, credentialing of physicians, and the like.[51] Many hospitals also are interested in outsourcing maintenance services.[52] Because of the different types of relationships, there are many different types of service and management arrangements among healthcare providers and healthcare-service entities.

The key terms in a service or management contract are contained in the section that delineates all of the services to be provided and what the payment is for such services. Other important provisions include hold-harmless provisions, in which one party agrees to hold the other party harmless for its acts and the acts of its employees. Thus, it is important to have a clear delineation of what services each party provides so that a hold-harmless provision is meaningful. For example, if the third party provides billing and collection services, then the billing company may agree in the contract to hold the physician practice harmless for its billing errors if the activity was that of the third party. Other key provisions include malpractice-insurance requirements and ownership of medical records, especially if a third party is hired to maintain them.

Several legal issues will need to be reviewed when structuring management and service agreements. Depending on the parties to the contract and the services being contracted for, the following laws should be reviewed. Antitrust laws may be implicated if the entities will provide managed-care

---

[51] Hospital outsourcing contracts increased from 10,009 contracts in 1997 to 10,915 contracts in 1998. Christine Ngeo, *Outsourcing Keeps Growing,* Modern Healthcare, Aug. 30, 1999, at 42. A 2008 survey found that outsourcing increased in 16 of the top 20 categories in the healthcare industry. Sean Rhea, *Wanted: A New COO*, Modern Healthcare, Oct. 6, 2008; *but see* Joe Carlson, *Outsourcing Focus on Information Technology Niche*, Modern Healthcare, Sept. 29, 2009 (pointing out that a 2009 survey of the same respondents found a slowdown in outsourcing).

[52] Ngeo, *supra.*

contracting services. If such services are provided for in the contract, then the contract may be prohibited if not structured properly because the parties may not be appropriately integrated and may be deemed competitors. Therefore, a thorough review of the antitrust laws (and especially the antitrust guidelines for the healthcare industry) must be undertaken. Stark and fraud and abuse implications will also need to be reviewed (in addition to tax laws, if at least one of the entities is tax-exempt). Additionally, certain Medicare and Medicaid rules and regulations may affect the contractual arrangement depending on the structure of the contract. For example, certain regulations must be satisfied in order for a physician to be able to reassign her right to a third party to bill the Medicare program for her services.[53]

11.6.4 Merger and Acquisition Agreements

In acquisition and merger agreements, various terms are essential to the arrangement. In a merger agreement, in which one entity will be subsumed by the other, one essential provision is determining which entity will be the surviving corporation. The merger agreement generally will set forth the surviving corporation, along with which governance documents apply and who will be the officers of the surviving corporation. Even though one corporation is chosen as the surviving corporation, however, that in itself does not mean that all of that corporation's operations will stay intact. For example, the parties may still negotiate and incorporate into the merger agreement the identities of the officers of the newly merged company, especially because mergers usually result in redundancies in officers (*e.g.*, two chief executive officers, two chief financial officers, etc.). All of these issues, in addition to any other major post-merger operational issues, should be addressed specifically in the merger agreement.

In acquisition documents, the parties should clearly set forth in the agreement whether the Buyer is purchasing the stock or assets of the target company. As was discussed in Section 11.2.1, if the target company is a nonprofit entity, then members of the corporation rather than shareholders, are the "owners;" further, if the Buyer is purchasing the entire business of the nonprofit target company, then the transaction is often referred to as a member substitution transaction (*See* Figure 1). Because no stock purchase is involved, the acquisition document will reflect that the Buyer is becoming the sole member of the target company. Thus, the previous members of the target company cease to exist as members and are replaced by the Buyer.

Naturally, the amount of the purchase price and how it will be paid are also important terms in acquisition agreements. Many entities will obtain an independent appraisal of the assets being acquired from a qualified independent appraiser, which serves to establish and reflect the fair market value of the business being purchased.[54] With regard to the payment terms, some agreements may have the

---

[53] This Medicare regulation permits a physician the right to reassign to a third party his or her right to bill and collect from the Medicare program for services rendered by the physician. Some of the permittable assignees include the employer of the physician, the hospital, or other facility where the services are provided in which there is a contractual arrangement between the physician and facility that allows the facility to submit such bills, and to an entity that provides coverage of the services under a health benefits plan. 42 U.S.C. § 1395u(b)(6).

[54] The Office of the Inspector General (OIG) has expressed concern with hospitals acquiring physician practices if the amount of the purchase price exceeds the value of the acquired stock or assets. The OIG believes that such excess amount could be paid to the physician in order to encourage the physician to refer patients to the hospital after the closing is com-

Buyer withhold a portion of the purchase price for a period of time after the closing of the transaction. For example, the Buyer may withhold a portion of the purchase price to cover some potential anticipated liabilities of the target company. After a certain amount of time following the closing, the Buyer would remit that amount to the Seller if those liabilities did not materialize and/or become a debt of the Buyer. If the transaction is an acquisition of assets, then the Buyer wants to be precise concerning what assets and liabilities it is assuming. This is also an important issue for the target company because liabilities that are not assumed by the Buyer will remain the responsibility of the Seller. Thus, it is important to clearly delineate which liabilities will remain the legal responsibility of the Seller.

Another key provision may be the acquisition of the Seller's Medicare billing provider agreement and billing number. If the Buyer assumes such number, then it is also assuming the liability for all prior inappropriate or false claims made by the Seller in its billing activities.[55] For these reasons, many deals are structured so as not to assume the Medicare billing agreement and number, instead choosing to either use the Buyer's existing number or have the Buyer apply for a new Medicare number. One problem with trying to obtain a new Medicare billing number is that it can take several months before Medicare issues the number. This may lead to financial constraints on the Buyer, due to the fact that it likely would be rendering services already and would be unable to bill for them until receipt of the Medicare number. Additionally, often a provider is precluded from billing for services which were rendered prior to survey and certification. All of this is dependent upon the type of provider number being requested. Therefore, it is necessary to check the specific terms required for a Medicare provider agreements and numbers.

Other important terms in an acquisition agreement are the representations and warranties. Representations are descriptions by each of the parties about their company, assets, employees, filings, etc. These representations are usually made by both parties; however, the Seller usually gives more exhaustive representations than the Buyer because the majority of the representations address the Seller's knowledge regarding its business, in addition to the condition of its assets and potential liabilities. For example, the Seller will represent to the Buyer that the assets are in good condition, no environmental problems exist regarding the property, no liens have been made on the property or the assets, no unions or threats of unionization exist, and no litigation is pending. Parties will usually give such representations with a caveat that the representations are true except as set forth on a schedule to the agreement, or are given pursuant to a "best effort" or "good-faith" basis. Any such schedule(s) would then delineate, for example, all of the threatened or pending litigation claims against the Seller.

---

plete. According to a December 22, 1992, letter from D. McCarty Thornton, DHHS General Counsel's Office, to T.J. Sullivan, IRS:

> Merely because another buyer may be willing to pay a particular price is not sufficient to render the price paid to be fair market value. The fact that a buyer, in a position to benefit from referrals, is willing to pay a particular price may only be a reflection of the value of the referral shown that is likely to result from the purchase.

Letter from D. McCarty Thornton, Health and Human Services General Counsel's office, to T.J. Sullivan, Technical Assistant, the Internal Revenue Services regarding Hospital Acquisition of Physician Practices, Dec. 22, 1992, available at http://oig.hhs.gov/fraud/docs/safeharborregulations/acquisition122292.htm.

[55] In *Vernon*, *supra*, the acquiring entity was held liable for the billing activities of the predecessor company because the billing number was one of the assets acquired. *United States v. Vernon Home Health Care*, 21 F.3d 693 (5th Cir. Tex. 1994). *See also Deerbrook Pavilion, LLC v. Shalala*, 235 F.3d 1100 (8th Cir. Mo. 2000) (finding successor nursing home liable for civil monetary penalties incurred by predecessor under the same Medicare provider agreement).

In the event that one of the representations is untrue and the Buyer finds this out after the closing of the transaction, then the Buyer would be able to seek damages as permitted in the indemnification provisions, which are discussed further in Section 11.8. According to a declaration of the American Bar Association's Business Law Section:

> Bare representations, if false, may support claims in tort and for federal securities act violations [if applicable] and also claims for breach of an implied warranty, breach of an implied promise that a representation is true, or breach of an express warranty if the description is basic to the bargain.[56]

In addition to the myriad of contractual terms that make up an acquisition agreement, several legal terms affect mergers and acquisitions. Antitrust laws must be reviewed in both merger and acquisition transactions, as was discussed earlier in this Chapter. Some states have premerger notice or approval requirements that mandate that an entity not merge or be acquired without state notice or approval.[57] Additionally, depending on the specifics of the transaction, securities laws, tax issues, fraud and abuse, Stark laws, and Medicare reimbursement laws and regulations may be applicable to the transaction (among other potentially applicable laws). Acquisitions and mergers are very fact-specific situations and, depending on the specific structure, could require the review of various laws at the federal and state level.

11.6.5 Affiliation Agreements

This type of agreement is used to create an affiliation between parties. As stated earlier in this Chapter, many hospitals enter into affiliation agreements with other hospitals or physician groups because they are not prepared to merge, sell, or be acquired. Thus, the parties enter into an affiliation agreement as an intermediate transitional step. Because most of these affiliation agreements have no specific clauses that trigger further integration (*e.g.*, there is no clause which requires a merger or acquisition at a specific future date), these agreements often are ignored. For certain entities, these agreements nevertheless provide an opportunity for parties to affiliate and discuss potential future integration options.

Because most affiliation agreements are unique, no standard terms or forms exist. Nevertheless, all affiliation agreements should set forth the purpose for the affiliation. Additionally, an expiration date should be specified for the affiliation. Perhaps such an expiration (*i.e.,* the affiliation exists only for a two-year period) will encourage the parties to commence merger, acquisition, or next-step negotiations.

---

[56] American Bar Association, Business Law Section, *Model Stock Purchase Agreement* 47 (1995).

[57] *See, e.g.*, Ohio law, which requires Ohio Attorney General approval if a for-profit entity acquires a nonprofit hospital or HMO. OH. REV. CODE. ANN. § 109.34(B). The non-profit must provide the Attorney General with certain information, including the names of the parties and the terms of the transactions. *Id.* Different notification rules apply when both parties to the transaction are tax-exempt nonprofits. 109.34(G). Certain states may also have Certificate of Need laws, which require state approval before acquisitions can be completed. *See Certificate of Need: State Health Laws and Programs*, NATIONAL CONFERENCE OF STATE LEGISLATIONS (Apr. 30, 2009), http://www.ncsl.org/default.aspx?tabid=14373 (providing an overview of which states have Certificate of Need laws).

Depending on the specifics of the affiliation, various legal issues may be implicated. For example, if the parties are affiliating to negotiate managed-care contracts with managed-care payors, then such affiliation needs to be reviewed under the antitrust laws to ensure that the affiliation arrangement is not deemed to be a conspiracy between competitors, which would make it illegal for such persons to share pricing information and negotiate fees jointly. Other laws may apply to the affiliation arrangement based on the specific terms of the affiliation.

11.6.6 Confidentiality Agreements

The most important term in a confidentiality agreement is that one or both of the parties agree to keep certain information confidential. For example, in merger negotiations, the parties may enter into a confidentiality agreement prior to any discussions between the parties taking place.[58] This is done so that neither party is able to disclose the information that it learns about the other party during the negotiation and due diligence process. The key provision in a confidentiality agreement is the term that sets forth what information will be maintained as confidential, and for how long. With the enactment of the HIPAA privacy regulations, many confidentiality agreements will specifically refer to compliance with these regulations. Usually, the parties are required to maintain the confidentiality of the information indefinitely. There may also be a provision that one party has to notify the other in the event of receiving a subpoena to disclose the confidential information covered by the agreement. Additionally, if this agreement is used as a precursor to negotiations of a merger or acquisition, then customarily a "no-shop" provision will be included in the agreement. A no-shop provision precludes typically a Seller from entering into any negotiations with any other party regarding the merger or sale under discussion for a certain length of time. This often may be a benefit to the Buyer if the Buyer fears that the Seller may be "shopping" the business or assets to multiple potential Buyers.

There are not many legal issues to review in these types of agreements; usually the necessary terms can be memorialized in a very short document.[59] State confidentiality laws should be reviewed, however, to ensure that the provisions in the confidentiality agreement are enforceable under state law. Traditionally, no payment terms are specified in a confidentiality agreement; as a result, the typical healthcare legal issues do not apply.

11.7 Termination of Agreements

Parties often exclusively focus on entering into an agreement and/or closing the merger or acquisition. Parties rarely focus on the potential termination of the transaction or what to do if the deal fails and one party wants to terminate the relationship or unwind the transaction.[60] Termination, exit, repay-

[58] "The Confidentiality Agreement is usually the first document in the acquisition process, signed by the prospective Buyer before the Company provides any confidential material." *Model Stock Purchase Agreement,* at 327.

[59] "The Confidentiality Agreement is often in letter form from the Company to Buyer…." *Id.*

[60] Unfortunately, termination occurs. For example, the Health Alliance, which began in 1995 with four hospitals, had only one by mid 2010. Health Alliance had been struggling since shortly after its inception, losing $88 million in 1997–1998. *See* Tim Bonfield, *Money Woes Threaten Health Alliance Future*, CIN. ENQUIRER, Oct 19, 1999. The loss triggered an exit clause in the operating agreement, allowing any member to leave. *Id.* The clause allowed termination "upon the occurrence of an event of default, by any non-defaulting party after notice from the non-defaulting party to the defaulting party and any non-defaulting party and a failure to cure by the defaulting party as described in section 16.4." *Health Alliance of Greater Cincinnati v. The Christ Hosp.*, No. C-070426, 2008 Ohio App. LEXIS 4191 (Ohio. App. 1 Dist. 2008).

ment, and post-termination provisions are key aspects of all acquisition agreements. It is important for the parties to discuss these issues relating to the termination of the transaction when structuring deals. By requiring the parties to focus some of their time and attention on defining the parties' responsibilities if the transaction is terminated, the parties may be able to avoid disputes and potential litigation in the future. In some situations (*i.e.*, a merger), there are no longer two corporations. Hence, it may be virtually impossible to undo the transaction. With respect to a member substitution, on the other hand, the parties could enter into an agreement to undo what the "member substitution" transaction had accomplished earlier. Thus, the acquiring member could decide to end its membership, and the corporation put in place a new member. In the case of a hospital acquisition of a physician's practice, the hospital could resell the assets or stock back to the physician and/or terminate the professional service arrangement between the two parties.

Some parties commit the fatal flaw of not including a way—or enough ways—in which a party can terminate an agreement. For example, the agreement may only permit termination by a party in the event of bankruptcy, loss of license or accreditation, death, or permanent disability. The physician in the situation, however, may want to have the right to terminate the agreement immediately on account of nonpayment of the physician's salary. Thus, the parties should try to anticipate what types of complications may occur in the future, and draft appropriate termination and post-termination provisions. For example, in an acquisition document, the parties may want to set forth the purchase price in the event of a repurchase of the assets by the Seller.

Various other terms in an agreement become important after the termination or expiration of the agreement. A sound agreement addresses not only issues during the term, but also for certain actions after the agreement has expired or terminated. This section presents a brief discussion of some of those terms.

The following are some terms that only become important after the closing of a transaction.

11.7.1 Indemnification Provisions

Indemnification clauses are traditionally part of a stock or asset transaction. An indemnification provision provides that, if one of the representations and warranties made by a Seller is false, then the Buyer who relied on such representation or warranty can seek indemnification for the resultant damages incurred by the Buyer. This indemnification is sought from the party who made the false

Health Alliance stayed intact until 2006, when Health Alliance filed for a declaratory judgment in 2006 after failing to gain the consent of the member hospitals for a major change to the operating agreement. *Id.* at *1. Health Alliance asked the court to find that Christ Hospital had no basis to leave. *Id.* at *2. The court, however, ruled that Christ Hospital had a proper basis to leave because its board had made a good faith determination that continued membership would impede its charitable mission. *Id.* The court also found that St. Luke Hospitals could leave on the basis of uncured events of default involving Christ Hospital. *Id.* St. Luke Hospital, located in Northern Kentucky, also thus left the Health Alliance, reaching an undisclosed settlement in September 2008. *See Health Alliance, Christ Hospital Reach Deal*, CIN. ENQUIRER, Jan. 12, 2009. Health Alliance further split apart in early 2010 as one of the two remaining hospitals of the group decided to merge with an unaffiliated hospital. Mary Vanac, *Health Alliance of Greater Cincinnati Members Agree on Dissolution*, MEDCITY NEWS, March 1, 2010. The Ohio Attorney General had asked the potential merger be placed on hold until a Cleveland lawyer could mediate the dispute between the Health Alliance members. *Id.* The mediation resulted in a memorandum that provided for an "orderly departure," hopefully preventing litigation. *Id.* The dispute may show the problems faced by hospitals that share operations but not governance. *Id.* When one member leaves, it takes assets, but not necessarily proportionate liabilities, leaving the remaining group with a worse ratio of assets to liabilities. *Id.*

statement. For example, in an asset acquisition, a physician may buy assets from another physician. One of the assets could include real property. Typically, in transactions with real property, the Buyer will conduct an investigation of the property regarding title and environmental issues. In addition, the Buyer may also want the Seller to give a real estate representation. This representation may set forth that, to the best of the Seller's knowledge, there are no defects in the title or any claims made by a third party against the property (including liens), and that the property does not contain any environmental hazards or toxic substances. If, after the closing, the Buyer discovers underground leaking storage tanks that must be removed, then the Buyer will seek to recover its costs from the Seller for cleaning the property pursuant to the indemnification provisions in the acquisition agreement. The Buyer will have a right to recover its costs for cleaning the property from the Seller because the Seller breached the real estate representation contained in the acquisition agreement by failing to disclose the presence of leaking underground storage tanks to the Buyer. Notwithstanding the existence of indemnification clauses, disputes may arise concerning which party is actually responsible for the acts or omissions that resulted in the damages.

Indemnification clauses are written in various ways. Typically, however, they contain a survival clause or a time limit. Thus, a party may be able to seek indemnification for a period of three years after the closing date. Hence, in our hypothetical, if the physician becomes aware of the tanks four years after the closing date, then the Seller is not contractually obligated to indemnify the Buyer. Additionally, the parties may agree to limit the amount of indemnification that one party can seek to recover from the other party. For example, the amount of indemnification may be capped at the amount of the purchase price of the assets. Some indemnification clauses incorporate minimum thresholds (*i.e.*, floor) that must be reached before one party can bring a claim for indemnification against the other party. This requirement eliminates one party seeking indemnification for an immaterial matter.

In a member substitution or a merger, the Seller either ceases to exist or becomes part of the Buyer; no corporate entity "Seller" remains from which a Buyer may seek indemnification. In certain situations where a charitable Seller was involved, the purchase price may be paid to a foundation that is established by the former members of the entity merged out of existence.[61] In exchange for the purchase price, the former members may guarantee the representations and warranties contained in the acquisition agreement and indemnify the Buyer. For example, in a transaction where a for-profit hospital chain has acquired a nonprofit hospital, the nonprofit hospital converts to a for-profit hospital and becomes part of the for-profit hospital chain. It would be meaningless for the nonprofit hospital to indemnify the for-profit chain due to the fact that, once the closing occurs, the nonprofit hospital is *part* of the for-profit chain. If the for-profit hospital paid the purchase price to a foundation or other third party, however, and such entity also provided the representations to the Buyer, then the foundation or third party may agree to indemnify the Buyer for any breach of the representations and warranties contained in the acquisition agreement.

---

[61] *See, e.g.*, Andrew Wineke, *Memorial Sale Could Create Heavy-Hitting Health Charity*, THE GAZETTE, June 17, 2010, available at http://www.gazette.com/articles/health-100369-mean-few.html (reporting that the Colorado Attorney General stated that the proceeds of the sale of a city-owned hospital would have to be used for charitable purposes in accordance with the state's Hospital Transfer Act). These foundations may also be given a right of first refusal if the for-profit hospital wishes to sell the formerly non-profit hospital or a substantial part of the hospital. *See, e.g.*, *Foundation for Seacoast Health v. HCA Health Services of New Hampshire*, 157 N.H. 487, 489 (2008) (discussing the foundation's right to first refusal created by acquisition agreement).

11.7.2 Confidentiality and Ownership of Records

These provisions usually codify that certain parties are obligated to maintain the confidentiality of all records, which may include business and medical records. Additionally, ownership of the records after the termination or expiration needs to be addressed in the agreement.

Confidentiality provisions are important, especially in professional service contractual arrangements. For example, a clinic may employ a physician for a five-year period to provide professional medical services to the clinic. When the five-year period expires, the physician leaves the clinic. At this time, a dispute may arise between the parties concerning ownership or access to the medical records. Thus, it is important in this type of arrangement (where medical records are created and maintained during the contract) to incorporate an explicit provision in the agreement that sets forth who owns the medical records after the termination or expiration of the agreement. Additionally, if the clinic maintains the records, then the physician or the physician's counsel may want to ensure that the clinic (and its employees, agents, and the like) maintain the confidentiality of those records and to provide the physician with access to such records to defend herself for audits, etc. It is necessary to review state law to determine whether a statutory requirement exists for certain parties to maintain the confidentiality of the medical records, in addition to the HIPAA federal privacy restrictions.

Problems could arise if a clinic maintains the records without a confidentiality requirement, and if state law does not require such entity to maintain the confidentiality of such records. The clinic might then disclose the medical record information to third parties. Because a privileged relationship exists between the patient and the physician (and not necessarily between the patient and the clinic) in many states, the physician may be subject to liability claims brought by the patient claiming that the physician owed the patient the duty to maintain the confidentiality of the medical records. Notwithstanding these state laws, the federal HIPAA regulations require all types of healthcare providers to maintain the confidentiality of all patient records.

Notwithstanding the HIPAA regulations, it is advisable to incorporate a contractual clause that requires all parties, at all times, to maintain the confidentiality of the medical records, limit disclosure of such information, and perhaps even incorporate a provision to protect other *business* information of the parties that is disclosed during the relationship. If a clinic was contractually obligated to maintain the confidentiality of the records, and if the clinic disclosed the records to a third party, then the physician would have recourse against the clinic for breach of contract for violating the confidentiality provision. Parties are currently addressing confidentiality by having a provision which requires the parties to comply with HIPAA.

11.7.3 Noncompete and Non-Interference Clauses

These clauses are very important in professional agreements and acquisition transactions. A noncompete provision or a restrictive covenant usually prohibits a person (for the term of the agreement and for a certain period of time after the termination or expiration of the agreement) from providing similar services as those set forth in the agreement. Usually, these provisions have a geographic and time limitation, as well as a specific limitation with respect to the certain services provided. For example, a hospital who employs a physician may include a noncompete provision in the employment agreement so that, for a period of one year after the termination or expiration of the agreement, the physician cannot provide professional medical services within the same city, county, or within a 10-mile radius of the employer hospital. Further, certain services may be excluded from the covenant because the party had been providing such service prior to entering into the agreement that contains the restrictive covenant. For example, an emergency room physician may have an exclusive arrangement with Hospital A, and has agreed to a covenant not to compete with Hospital A, but with a caveat that allows such physician to provide services to Hospital B in recognition of the fact that the physician rendered services to Hospital B prior to entering into the agreement which contained the restrictive covenant.

Although some states have upheld the legality of noncompete clauses for physicians and other medical professionals,[62] other states find such provisions to be illegal and unenforceable.[63] In a Massachusetts case, the physician employment contract did not contain a noncompete provision, but a specific dollar penalty was imposed if the physician were to practice in a certain area after the expiration of the agreement.[64] The court found this provision to be unenforceable and likening it to a noncompete provision, which would be prohibited in that jurisdiction.[65] The court noted that the state favors the public interest in allowing patients to choose their physicians over the benefit to the medical profession in upholding covenants not to compete.[66]

Noncompete clauses are also common in transactions where an entire business is purchased and the Buyer wants to prohibit the Seller from practicing or operating a similar business in the same marketplace for a specific period of time after the closing of the transaction.

Non-diversion and non-solicitation clauses, on the other hand, basically prohibit a party from contacting the other party's employees, agents, customers, and patients after the expiration or termination of the agreement. As with restrictive covenants, these provisions usually have a specific timeframe as to when the non-diversion and non-solicitation applies. These provisions typically are not as controversial or litigated as a covenant not to compete. These provisions nevertheless are customary and necessary in certain industries. For example, in managed-care contracting, MCOs often include a non-diversion provision so that their providers cannot solicit the MCOs' beneficiaries after the expiration of the agreement. Often the physician will want to send a notice to his or her patients to alert them that the physician participates in other managed care plans or provide similar notifications. Perhaps some of these patients would be willing to switch health plans in order to be treated by the same physician. Customarily, however, a non-diversion and non-solicitation clause would prohibit the physician from sending such letters.

---

62 *See, e.g.*, *Prairie Eye Center, Ltd. v. Butler*, 329 Ill. App.3d 293 (Ill. App. 4 Dist. 2002); *Bollengier v. Gulati*, 650 N.Y.S.2d 56 (233 A.D. 2d 721 (1996)).

63 According to California state statute (Cal. Bus. & Prof. Code § 16600), contract provisions that prevent anyone from engaging in a lawful profession, trade, or business are void; also review the laws of the state of Colorado (*i.e.*, Colo. Rev. Stat. § 8-2-113(3)).

64 *Falmouth Ob-Gyn Assocs., Inc. v. Abisla*, 417 Mass. 176, 629 N.E.2d 291 (1994).

65 *Id.* at 179.

66 *Id.* at 180.

These post-termination provisions are only a sampling but represent some of the more important post-termination issues that may be incorporated into an agreement. Depending on the specific situation, facts, parties, and their goals, however, other post-termination provisions are also important, including billing and collection post-closing, arbitration, and final payment issues.

11.8 Current Climate of Healthcare Transactions and Contracting

As was discussed in the introduction to this Chapter, since the late 1980s, healthcare organizations and providers have been in a merger and acquisition "mania" to create IDSs. This integration currently continues as healthcare providers evolve and face new challenges. Additionally, many transactions have not been successful for various reasons, and so the parties have unwound these transactions, whether through bankruptcy, repurchase arrangements, or sales to third parties, which creates a whole new opportunity for corporate transactional work.[67] Nevertheless, hospitals and other institutional providers continue to seek ways in which to affiliate with physicians or other types of healthcare providers or suppliers in joint ventures and service arrangements, and to create meaningful alliances. Many healthcare providers have entered into transactions in order to be a part of a bigger healthcare system so that they will survive by having enough physicians on staff, capital for improvements and acquisitions, and a full complement of services so that loyal patients do not stray to a competitor for other services. Many physicians merely want to practice medicine and not bother themselves with the ever-growing regulatory nightmare of Medicare, Medicaid, and PPACA. What we have seen in the last 30 years is that healthcare providers have entered into these arrangements, have divested such arrangements and then, years later, once again entered into similar types of arrangements in the constant battle of physician integration. The climate continues to be ripe for integration and affiliation, and it appears that these collaborations will continue in the future, especially in light of the unknown impact of federal healthcare reform.

[67] A 1999 poll of 129 healthcare systems found that 36% of health systems acknowledged that they have considered or recently experienced some form of disintegration. Of this 36%, 39% concerned a health plan, 33% a physician group, 28% a home health group, and 15% divested a hospital. *Making Money But Struggling*, *supra*, at 56. The recent Health Alliance scenario, *supra*, where three of four major hospitals divested within a two-year period, shows some of the results of disintegration. Failed mergers also cause long-term problems. In 2002, Tufts-New England Medical Center amicably split from the Lifespan system. *Lifespan and Tufts-New England Medical Center Announce plans to Restructure*, BUSINESS WIRE, Aug. 28, 2002. Although Tufts-New England had unconditionally pledged to pay $1.83 million to Lifespan at the end of 2005, Tufts refused to pay. Jeffrey Krasner, *Hospital Breakup Spills into Court*, BOSTON GLOBE, Jun. 21, 2007. The breakdown of settlement discussions prompted litigation. *Lifespan Corp. v. New England Medical Center*, NO. 06-CV-421-JNL, 731 F. Supp. 2d 232, 2010 U.S. Dist. LEXIS 74659 at *1 (D.R.I. July 20, 2010) (granting motion for summary judgment in part but determining balance of dispute would need be resolved at trial). In 1999, a merger between hospitals owned by Stanford and the University of California at San Francisco dissolved, costing the two intuitions $176 million. Sabin Russell, *$176 Million Tab on Failed Hospital Merger*, SAN FRAN. CHRON., Dec. 14, 2000.

12

Bioethics

Thomas Wm. Mayo, Esquire
Director, Maguire Center for Ethics and Public Responsibility
Associate Professor, SMU/Dedman School of Law
Adjunct Associate Professor, University of Texas–Southwestern Medical School
Of Council, Haynes and Boone, LLP

Bioethics is a growing area of concern for health lawyers, no matter who their clients may be. This Chapter addresses major legal developments in three fields: human reproduction (abortion and surrogacy); organ transplantation; and genetics. Treatment issues in connection with dying patients and human research issues are discussed in Chapter 2.

12.1 Human Reproduction

12.1.1 Abortion

12.1.1.1 *Roe v. Wade*

Few issues in the past 30 years have been more politically controversial or have focused more attention on the unique role of the United States Supreme Court in the federal judicial system. Nevertheless, the law of abortion has been relatively stable, at least in broad outline, since the Court's decision in *Roe v. Wade*[1] in 1973. At issue in *Roe* was the constitutionality of Texas's abortion laws—similar to those of a majority of states at the time—which made it a crime to "procure an abortion" except "by medical advice for the purpose of saving the life of the mother."

One of the bedrock issues fueling the abortion debate concerns the moral status of the fetus: is it a "person" with the attributes and rights associated with that status? Or is the fetus an inchoate being of another sort, more than a clump of cells but not yet possessed of "personhood"? The rhetoric of abortion policy and politics is grounded on this question, but it is a question the Court chose not to answer. Instead, it concluded that, for purposes of the Fourteenth Amendment (which confers its protections upon "persons"), a fetus is not a "person." Once the Court ruled that a fetus has no constitutionally protectable interests, the *Roe* opinion turned to the rights of the pregnant woman, creating an analysis of the state's interests in limiting those rights.

---

1 *Roe v. Wade,* 410 U.S. 113 (1973).

The *Roe* Court was built primarily upon its 1965 decision in *Griswold v. Connecticut*,[2] which struck down a Connecticut law that made it a crime for any person to use "any drug, medicinal article or instrument for the purpose of preventing conception," as well as to "counsel" or "assist" a person to violate the prohibition of the use of contraception. The Court held that a "zone of privacy" is created by "specific guarantees in the Bill of Rights [that] have penumbras, formed by emanations from those guarantees that help give them life and substance",[3] and that this zone of privacy is broad enough to protect "an intimate relation of husband and wife and their physician's role in one aspect of that relation."[4]

Although various justices in *Griswold* offered a number of possible sources for this constitutional right of privacy, the Court did not coalesce around one answer until *Roe v. Wade*. Despite the checkered history of the constitutional doctrine of "substantive due process," a majority of the justices nonetheless anchored the Court's privacy doctrine "in the Fourteenth Amendment's concept of personal liberty and restrictions upon state action."[5] Recognizing that the right of privacy is "fundamental" but not absolute, the Court balanced the pregnant woman's interest in deciding whether to continue or to terminate her pregnancy against the state's interests in the promotion of maternal health and the protection of fetal life. In perhaps its most controversial move (in an opinion that had many of them), the Court ruled that the interests of the state, and the weight that should be accorded to those interests, changed in each of the trimesters of the pregnancy:

> A state criminal abortion statute of the current Texas type, that excepts from criminality only a life-saving procedure on behalf of the mother, without regard to pregnancy stage and without recognition of thc other interests involved, is violative of the Due Process Clause of the Fourteenth Amendment. (a) For the stage prior to approximately the end of the first trimester, the abortion decision and its effectuation must be left to the medical judgment of the pregnant woman's attending physician. (b) For the stage subsequent to approximately the end of the first trimester, the State, in promoting its interest in the health of the mother, may, if it chooses, regulate the abortion procedure in ways that are reasonably related to maternal health. (c) For the stage subsequent to viability, the State in promoting its interest in the potentiality of human life may, if it chooses, regulate, and even proscribe, abortion except where it is necessary, in appropriate medical judgment, for the preservation of the life or health of the mother.[6]

12.1.1.2 Post-Roe Developments

Using the trimester approach outlined in *Roe*, the Court subsequently ruled on the constitutionality of a number of state abortion regulations. The Court struck down state laws: (i) that required abortions to be performed in a hospital accredited by a private accrediting organization, that required the procedure to be approved by the hospital staff abortion committee, and that required two physicians

---

2 *Griswold v. Connecticut*, 381 U.S. 479 (1965).
3 *Id.* at 484.
4 *Id.* at 482.
5 410 U.S. at 153.
6 *Id.* at 164–65.

in addition to the patient's attending physician concur in the procedure;[7] (ii) that imposed a spousal-consent requirement, a parental-consent requirement, and an obligation on the attending physician to exercise all care and diligence to preserve the life and health of the fetus without regard to the stage of viability;[8] (iii) that required all abortions after the first trimester to be performed in a hospital;[9] (iv) that imposed a variety of detailed informed-consent requirements deemed by the Court to be intended to discourage abortion, rather than to help inform the pregnant woman's choice;[10] and (v) that required a 24-hour waiting period after the woman had given her informed consent to the procedure.[11]

On the other hand, the Court held that *Roe*'s trimester approach permitted states to require: (i) that an abortion be based upon the physician's "best clinical judgment that an abortion was necessary;"[12] (ii) that abortions be performed either in a hospital or a licensed outpatient clinic (if licensing standards are consistent with accepted medical practice);[13] (iii) that tissue removed during clinic abortions be submitted to pathologic testing, and that a second physician be present during post-viability abortions to assist in saving the life of the fetus;[14] and (iv) that either one parent or both parents be notified of a minor's intent to obtain an abortion, as long as a judicial-bypass mechanism was available.[15] The Court also ruled that the privacy doctrine in *Roe* did not require either Congress or the states to provide public funding for abortions.[16] That reasoning also extended to a state's prohibition against the use of public facilities, employees, and resources for abortions (unless necessary to save the life of the mother).[17]

12.1.1.3 The Transformation of Roe

Roe's trimester approach to the right to privacy lasted 19 years. During this time the Court considered and rejected a number of invitations to overrule *Roe*. Many litigants and commentators (and at least some justices) believed that the ruling (1) was constitutionally illegitimate, (2) had plunged the Court into matters that were reserved by the Constitution to the states, (3) invited the Court to make political and policy judgments rather than legal ones, and (4) led to unpredictable results based upon increasingly labored distinctions that threatened to undermine public confidence in the Court. Against this onslaught, *Roe*'s "days were numbered," and its number finally came up in *Planned Parenthood of Southeastern Pennsylvania v. Casey*.[18]

Although the Court in *Casey* invalidated Pennsylvania's spousal-notification requirement, it upheld the state's detailed informed-consent requirements, its mandated 24-hour waiting period, a requirement that minors obtain the consent of at least one parent (subject to a judicial bypass procedure),

7 *Doe v. Bolton*, 410 U.S. 179 (1973).
8 *Planned Parenthood v. Danforth*, 428 U.S. 52 (1976).
9 *City of Akron v. Akron Ctr. for Reproductive Health*, 462 U.S. 416 (1983).
10 *Id.*; *see also Thornburgh v. American College of Obstetricians & Gynecologists*, 476 U.S. 747 (1986).
11 *Akron Ctr. for Reproductive Health.*
12 *Doe v. Bolton.*
13 *Simopolous v. Virginia*, 462 U.S. 506 (1983).
14 *Planned Parenthood Ass'n v. Ashcroft*, 462 U.S. 476 (1983).
15 *Ohio v. Akron Ctr. for Reproductive Health*, 497 U.S. 502 (1990); *Hodgson v. Minnesota*, 497 U.S. 417 (1990).
16 *Harris v. McRae*, 448 U.S. 297 (1980); *Poelker v. Doe*, 432 U.S. 519 (1977); *Maher v. Roe*, 432 U.S. 464 (1977); *Beal v. Doe*, 432 U.S. 438 (1977).
17 *Webster v. Reproductive Health Servs.*, 462 U.S. 416 (1983).
18 *Planned Parenthood of Southeastern Pennsylvania v. Casey,* 505 U.S. 833 (1992).

and extensive reporting requirements on abortion facilities. Most of these provisions would probably not have survived the strict scrutiny required by *Roe*, but a three-justice plurality (consisting of Justices O'Connor, Kennedy, and Souter) abandoned *Roe*'s trimester approach as too rigid and not necessary to carry out the "essential holding" of *Roe*. In an opinion that mentioned neither "fundamental right" nor "strict scrutiny," the three justices wrote:

> *Roe*'s essential holding, the holding we reaffirm, has three parts. First is a recognition of the right of the woman to choose to have an abortion before viability and to obtain it without undue interference from the State. Before viability, the State's interests are not strong enough to support a prohibition of abortion or the imposition of a substantial obstacle to the woman's effective right to elect the procedure. Second is a confirmation of the State's power to restrict abortions after fetal viability, if the law contains exceptions for pregnancies which endanger the woman's life or health. And third is the principle that the State has legitimate interests from the outset of the pregnancy in protecting the health of the woman and the life of the fetus that may become a child.[19]

Since 1992, lower courts have struggled to apply the *Casey* Court's "undue burden" test largely without additional guidance from the Court itself.[20]

In *Carhart v. Stenberg*,[21] the Court considered a major abortion issue—whether states may prohibit late-term abortions (called "partial-birth abortions" by opponents of the procedure). Late-term abortion involves the extraction of a fetus, legs first, through the birth canal. Because the procedure is performed up to approximately the 24th week of gestation, the size of the skull usually requires that the skull be cut, its contents drained, and the skull itself reduced in size in order for delivery to be completed.

Carhart affirmed the U.S. Court of Appeals for the Eighth Circuit's decision to strike down a Nebraska statute prohibiting late-term abortion. Justice Breyer deemed the Nebraska statute unconstitutional for two reasons. First, it did not contain an exception for situations in which a late-term abortion might be necessary to save the life of the pregnant woman. Second, as the Eighth Circuit had noted, the statute's definition of the procedure was overbroad, and could include not only the late-term abortion procedure (dilation and extraction) but also the much more commonly performed dilation and evacuation procedure, which is usually performed early in the second trimester. The Supreme Court held that the potential restriction of dilation-and-evacuation procedures unconstitutionally limited a woman's right to choose abortion.

---

19 *Id.* at 846.

20 *See, e.g., Fargo Women's Health Org. v. Schafer*, 18 F.3d 526 (8th Cir. 1994) (informed-consent and 24-hour waiting period requirements not unconstitutional, in part because counseling may be done by telephone and therefore two trips to the clinic are not required); *Planned Parenthood, Sioux Falls Clinic v. Miller*, 63 F.3d 1452 (8th Cir. 1995) (a parental notification provision that does not include judicial bypass option except for abused or neglected minors is unconstitutional on its face), *cert. denied sub nom.*, 517 U.S. 1174 (1996); *Barnes v. Mississippi*, 992 F.2d 1335 (5th Cir.) (upholding two-parent consent requirement with constitutionally adequate judicial bypass option), *cert. denied*, 510 U.S. 976 (1993). The Supreme Court has not been totally silent. In addition to the late-term abortion cases discussed in the text, the Court decided *Lambert v. Wicklund*, 520 U.S. 292 (1997), *rev'g*, 93 F.3d 567 (9th Cir. 1996)), which upheld the judicial-bypass provision of a Montana statute that allowed waiver of notice requirement if notification of parent or guardian was not in minor's best interest.

21 530 U.S. 914 (2000).

After the Court handed down its decision in *Stenberg*, Congress passed the Partial Birth Abortion Act of 2003,[22] which is nearly identical to the Nebraska statute struck down in *Stenberg*. The Act makes it a crime (punishable by a fine or up to two years' imprisonment or both) for a physician to perform a dilation and extraction procedure, except if it is necessary to save the life of the mother. After three district courts and three courts of appeals—all relying principally upon the Court's opinion in *Carhart*—struck down the federal law, many observers were surprised when the Supreme Court upheld the Act in *Gonzales v. Carhart*.[23] Opponents of the law claimed that it had the same defects as the Nebraska law: the procedure was described in terms that could make it illegal to perform second-trimester dilation-and-extraction procedures, and the law lacked an exception for the protection of a woman's *health*.

The Court held that the Act was neither void for vagueness nor an undue burden on a woman's right to abortion based on its overbreadth or lack of a health exception. The Court distinguished the Act from the Nebraska statute in *Stenberg*, holding that it could not reasonably be read to prohibit the standard dilation-and-evacuation procedure. The Court also upheld the act's failure to provide for an exception to protect the pregnant woman's health, based upon Congress' detailed (and controversial) findings that dilation and extraction is never needed to protect a woman's health. In dissent, Justice Ginsburg called the decision "alarming" and noted that little had changed in the years since it handed down *Stenberg* other than the Court's membership. Ginsburg wrote, "[the majority decision] tolerates, indeed applauds, federal intervention to ban nationwide a procedure found necessary and proper in certain cases by the American College of Obstetricians and Gynecologists," adding that "the Court's defense [of the ban] cannot be understood as anything other than an effort to chip away at a right declared again and again by this Court."

12.1.1.4 *Medical and Emergency Abortion*

Other methods of abortion remain controversial. Medical (*i.e.*, drug-induced, as opposed to surgical) abortion, though legal in other countries for years, was banned in the United States until 1993.[24] On September 28, 2000, the Food and Drug Administration (FDA) approved mifepristone, the so-called "abortion pill," also known as RU-486 or Mifeprex. Taken in combination with a prostaglandin, this drug causes uterine contractions and bleeding, terminating over 95% of pregnancies of fewer than seven weeks' gestation. The FDA approved the drug solely for the termination of early pregnancy, defined as 49 days or fewer as measured from the beginning of the woman's last menstrual period.[25] It warned that the drug should not be used for women with certain medical conditions (*e.g.*, ectopic pregnancy or bleeding disorders), and that complications, including severe bleeding, may occur that would require surgical intervention.

On August 24, 2006, the FDA approved the emergency contraceptive drug levonorgestrel, also know as "Plan B" or the "morning-after pill," as an over-the-counter option for women aged 18 and

22 *See, e.g.*, 18 U.S.C. § 1531.

23 127 S. Ct. 1610, 550 U.S. 124 (2007).

24 The first President Bush banned the importation of mifepristone, but the ban was lifted by President Clinton in his first term.

25 United States Department of Health and Human Services, HHS News P00-19, *FDA Approves Mifepristone for the Termination of Early Pregnancy* (Sept. 28, 2000).

older.[26] Levonorgestrel works like a birth-control pill to prevent pregnancy mainly by stopping the release of an egg from the ovary, or possibly by preventing fertilization of the egg, or by preventing a fertilized egg from attaching to the uterus. Plan B does not work if pregnancy has already occurred.

On August 13, 2010, the Food and Drug Administration approved a new form of emergency contraception that can prevent pregnancy as many as five days after sex.[27] The prescription-only product, ulipristal acetate (called ella™), can prevent pregnancy if taken within 120 hours after contraceptive failure or unprotected sex.[28]

The FDA's approval of ella™ has reopened the heated abortion debate. Ella is a progesterone agonist/antagonist that works by blocking progesterone's activity and therefore delaying ovulation.[29] Critics claim that ella™'s chemical similarities to RU-486, which also blocks progesterone, make it another "abortion drug."[30] They also worry that ella™'s classification as an emergency contraceptive, instead of an abortion pill, will make it eligible to receive federal subsidies which are not available for RU-486.[31] Because it is only available by prescription, ella™ will also likely contribute to the ongoing debates about conscience clauses as applied to both doctors who refuse to write prescriptions and pharmacists who refuse to fill them.

Proponents point out that there is no evidence that ella™ works as anything other than a contraceptive and that it has only been tested within five days of unprotected sex.[32] "According to the product's labeling, women with known or suspected pregnancy and women who are breastfeeding should not use ella. A patient package insert also will be provided to ensure that women are fully informed of the benefits and risks involved in the use of ella."[33] Officials from HRA Pharma of Paris, which makes ella™, claim that there are no plans to test it as an abortion drug and that it did not appear to cause any problems for the handful of women who became pregnant after taking the drug.[34]

Ella was approved in Europe last year and is available in at least 22 European countries.[35] It became available in the United States in December 2010.[36]

Following upon the FDA's approvals in this field, at least 21 states have statutes related to emergency contraception.[37] Nine states have programs designed for increased access to emergency contra-

---

26 Plan B will remain available as a prescription-only product for women age 17 and younger.

27 Press Release, U.S. Food & Drug Administration, FDA Approves ella™ Tablets for Emergency Contraception (August 13, 2010) (available at http://www.fda.gov/NewsEvents/Newsroom/PressAnnouncements/ucm222428.htm).

28 *Id.*

29 *Id.*

30 Rob Stein, *FDA Approves ella as 5-Day-After Emergency Contraceptive*, Wash. Post, Aug. 13, 2010, at A01.

31 *Id.*

32 *Id.*

33 Press Release, U.S. Food & Drug Administration, *supra.*

34 Stein, *supra.*

35 *Id.*

36 *See* Press Release, Watson Pharmaceuticals, Watson Launches ella® (ulipristal acetate) Emergency Contraceptive (Dec. 1, 2010), available at http://ir.watson.com/phoenix.zhtml?c=65778&p=irol-newsArticle&ID=1501974.

37 *See, e.g.,* Cal. Ins. Code § 10604.1; 410 Ill. Comp. Stat. § 70/2.2; Mass. Ann. Laws ch. 41 § 97B; N.J. Stat. Ann. § C.26:2H-12.6; N.Y. Pub. Health Law § 2805; 28 Pa. Code §§ 117.53, .55, .57; Tex. Health & Safety Code Ann. § 323.005. For a full list of these states, *see* The National Conference of State Legislatures, http://www.ncsl.org/default.aspx?tabid=14420.

ception through direct pharmacy access programs.[38] Nine states now provide Medicaid coverage of over-the-counter emergency contraception.[39]

These state laws have prompted the latest debate over reproductive rights.[40] One of the major issues involves pharmacists refusing to dispense birth control or emergency contraception.[41] In some states, legislators are pushing laws that would grant pharmacists the right to refuse to dispense drugs related to contraception or abortion on moral grounds.[42] Other states require pharmacists to fill any legal prescription for birth control.[43] Still others have enacted laws to make the morning-after pill more accessible by requiring hospitals to offer it to rape victims or allowing certain pharmacists to sell it without a prescription.[44]

Abortion rights advocates contend that the emergency contraception pill is not an abortion drug because it does not destroy an embryo, but instead it prevents ovulation or fertilization or blocks a fertilized egg from becoming implanted in the uterus. Advocates of the drug say it is crucial for pharmacists to stock the morning-after pill because women have only a small window of time after sex in which to obtain and use it, and the pill would lead to fewer abortions. Opponents argue that the emergency contraception pill has the same effect of an abortion drug destroying life because it can prevent an already fertilized egg from implanting in the uterus.

12.1.1.5 Access to Abortion Facilities

The ongoing controversy over abortion has generated not only public debate but also violence against women who choose to undergo or perform abortions. Congress passed the Freedom of Access to Clinic Entrances (FACE) Act of 1994[45] to protect and promote the public safety and health. The act established federal criminal penalties and civil remedies for violent, threatening, obstructive, and de-

---

38 Alaska, California, Hawaii, Maine, Massachusetts, New Hampshire, New Mexico, Washington and Vermont allow pharmacists to initiate emergency contraception drug therapy after they have completed a training program in emergency contraception.

39 Pro–ChoiceAmerica, http://www.prochoiceamerica.org/what-is-choice/fast-facts/emergency_contraception.html (Hawaii, Illinois, Maryland, New Jersey, New Mexico, New York, Oklahoma, Oregon, and Washington).

40 *See* Nat'l Women's Law Ctr., Pharmacy Refusals 101, at 3 (Nov. 28, 2006), available at http://www.nwlc.org/pdf/PharmacyRefusals101_11.28.06.pdf (discussing the legislative and administrative responses to pharmacist refusals).

41 *See, e.g.*, Lora Cicconi, *Pharmacist Refusals and Third-Party Interests: A Proposed Judicial Approach to Pharmacist Conscience Clause*, 54 UCLA L. Rev. 709 (2007).

42 These are the "conscience clause bills" which that allow pharmacists to refuse to dispense contraceptives if they have moral or religious objections. Four states already have pharmacist-refusal statutes in place. *See* Ark. Code Ann. § 20-16-304; Ga. Comp. R. & Regs. 480-5-.03; Miss. Code Ann. § 41-107-5; S.D. Cod. Laws § 36-11-70. Illinois, Colorado, Florida, Maine, Tennessee, and Washington have broad refusal clauses that do not specifically mention pharmacists. *See* 745 Ill. Comp. Stat. Ann. § 70/1-17/14; Colo. Rev. Stat.§ 25-6-102(9); Fla. Stat. Ann. § 381.0051; Me. Rev. Stat. Ann. tit. 22 § 1903(4); Tenn. Code Ann. § 68-34-104; Wash. Rev. Code Ann. § 48.43.065. Several other states have statutes protecting government employees who refuse to provide family planning services. *See, e.g.*, Colo. Rev. Stat. § 25-6-207; Ga. Code Ann. § 49-7-6; Or. Rev. Stat. § 435.225; W.Va. Code § 16-2B-4; Wyo. Stat. Ann. § 42-5-101.

43 Seven states—California, Illinois, Maine, Massachusetts, Nevada, New Jersey, and Washington—explicitly require pharmacists to ensure legal prescriptions are filled. In Illinois, then-Governor Rod Blagojevich issued emergency rules that required pharmacists to provide the morning after pill. *See* Ill. Adm. Code § 1330.91(j). Seven state pharmacy boards—Alabama, Delaware, New York, North Carolina, Oregon, Pennsylvania, and Texas—have issued policy statements that prohibit pharmacists from obstructing patient access to medication or from refusing to transfer prescriptions to another pharmacy. *See* http://www.nwlc.org/sites/default/files/pdfs/AppendixA-update.pdf.

44 *See, e.g.,* Mass. Gen. Laws Ann. ch. 111 § 70E(o).

45 18 U.S.C. §§ 1961–68.

structive conduct intended to injure, intimidate, or interfere with persons seeking to obtain or provide reproductive health services. In 1994, the National Organization for Women, Inc. (NOW), a nonprofit organization that supports legal availability of abortions and abortion clinics, brought a class action suit against individuals and organizations that oppose legal abortions, alleging that they violated the Racketeer Influenced and Corrupt Organizations Act[46] (RICO) by engaging in a nationwide conspiracy to shut down abortion clinics through racketeering and extortion. After 12 years of litigation, the Supreme Court held that threatening or committing violent acts unrelated to robbery or extortion falls outside the Hobbs Act,[47] therefore the Pro-Life Action Network (PLAN) was not liable for conspiracy.

12.1.1.6 Informed-Consent Laws Redux

Another disputed issue involves attempts to regulate professional communications between healthcare providers and their patients. Under the first Bush administration, the Department of Health and Human Services (DHHS) took steps to distance taxpayer dollars from abortion services. DHHS implemented regulations prohibiting clinics receiving federal funds under Title X of the Public Health Service Act[48] from engaging in abortion counseling, referral, and activities advocating abortion as a method of family planning. Physicians who supervised Title X funds questioned the constitutionality of these new regulations in *Rust v. Sullivan*.[49] The Supreme Court declared the regulations permissible:

> The regulations do not violate the First Amendment free speech rights… by impermissibly imposing viewpoint-discriminatory conditions on Government subsidies. There is no question but that § 1008's prohibition is constitutional, since the Government may make a value judgment favoring childbirth over abortion and implement that judgment by the allocation of public funds. In so doing, the Government has not discriminated on the basis of viewpoint; it has merely chosen to fund one activity to the exclusion of another.[50]

The dissent argued that the Court was impinging upon free speech by manipulating the doctor/patient dialogue, in an effort "to deter a woman from making a decision that, with her physician, is hers to make."[51] It also asserted that the Court's actions were "nearly as noxious as overruling *Roe* directly, for if a right is found to be unenforceable, even against flagrant attempts by government to circumvent it, then it ceases to be a right at all."[52]

In 2005, South Dakota amended its informed-consent law to add a number of specific required disclosures that must be made by a physician or the physician's agent before an abortion procedure is performed. The new disclosures, which must be provided in writing at least two hours before the procedure, include:

1. That the abortion will terminate the life of a whole, separate, unique, living human being;

---

46 *National Organization for Women v. Scheidler*, 510 U.S. 249 (1994).
47 *Scheidler v. National Organization for Women*, 547 U.S. 9 (2006).
48 Public Health Service Act, § 1008, as amended, 42 U.S.C. §§ 300a, 300a-6.
49 500 U.S. 173 (1991).
50 *Id.* at 174 (citations omitted).
51 *Id.* at 219 (quoting *Thornburgh v. American College of Obstetricians & Gynecologists*, 476 U.S. 747, 759 (1986)).
52 *Id.* at 220 (Blackmun, J., dissenting).

2. That the pregnant woman has an existing relationship with that unborn human being and that the relationship enjoys protection under the United States Constitution and under the laws of South Dakota; [and]
3. that by having an abortion, her existing relationship and her existing constitutional rights with regards to that relationship will be terminated....[53]

A district court preliminarily enjoined the enforcement of these three disclosure requirements in 2005,[54] and the U.S. Court of Appeals for the Eighth Circuit affirmed.[55] The court of appeals concluded that the compelled statements were ideological speech, rather than medical facts or disclosures based upon science. The court distinguished South Dakota's requirements from the Pennsylvania informed-consent disclosure upheld by the *Casey* Court as truthful, nonmisleading factual information.[56]

12.1.2 Commercial Surrogacy

Surrogacy—the practice by which a woman bears a child for a woman who cannot conceive or cannot carry a fetus to term—has biblical roots.[57] Commercial surrogacy, by contrast, appears to be a modern invention. As the term implies, commercial surrogacy involves the payment of a fee to the surrogate mother. Commercial surrogacy is usually facilitated by a broker who matches infertile couples with a woman who agrees to become pregnant, carry the fetus to term, and turn the newborn over to the couple, who assume the role of "social parent." Commercial surrogacy has increased the supply of potential surrogate mothers, and has moved surrogate parenting outside the traditional circle of family and friends. In so doing, it has brought strangers together in ways strangers have seldom interacted before, which has created new legal issues that have not yet been completely resolved.

Prior to the development of reliable *in vitro* fertilization techniques, conception with a surrogate mother occurred through either coitus or artificial insemination; as a result, the surrogate mother was both the genetic parent and the gestational parent of the offspring so conceived. *In vitro* fertilization eventually became an option that permitted couples to contribute their own genetic material to an embryo that was created in a fertility laboratory and subsequently transplanted into the womb of the surrogate. As a result, it has become possible for a second type of surrogacy, a purely "gestational surrogacy," to occur, in which the surrogate mother contributes her womb for nine months, but not her gametes. Although other combinations of genetic, gestational, and social parents can be imagined,[58] traditional and gestational surrogacy are by far the two most common types of surrogacy arrangement.

---

[53] S.D. Codified Laws § 34-23A-10.1(1)(b)–(d).

[54] *Planned Parenthood Minnesota v. Rounds*, 375 F. Supp. 2d 881 (S.D.S.D. 2005).

[55] *Planned Parenthood Minnesota v. Rounds*, 467 F.3d 716 (8th Cir. 2006).

[56] *Id.* at 722. On January 6, 2007, the Eighth Circuit vacated the panel's opinion and granted rehearing en banc, and oral argument was held on April 11, 2007. http://www.ca8.uscourts.gov/tmp/053093.html. Litigation is still ongoing. *See* 530 F.3d 724 (2008) (vacating injunction and remanding the case); 650 F. Supp. 2d 972 (2009) (cross motions for summary judgment).

[57] *See Genesis* 16:1–6, 30:1–13.

[58] *See* Alexander M. Capron, *Alternative Birth Technologies: Legislative Challenges*, 20 U.C. Davis L. Rev. 679, 682 (1987) (describing eight surrogacy scenarios, including the "Brave New World" surrogacy arrangement: five different, unrelated persons contribute the male and female gametes, gestation, and social parents of the child).

The ethical and public-policy issues surrounding surrogacy have been intensely debated. Critics argue that the practice constitutes an undesirable "commodification" of life, is indistinguishable from the universally prohibited practice of baby-selling, reduces surrogate mothers to "baby machines" and "fetal containers," is a form of prostitution or slavery, is unfair to the child and its siblings, and exploits surrogate mothers whose life situations may make them particularly vulnerable to the allure of a fee of $25,000 or more. Defenders of the practice note that reproductive decisions are generally given the highest degree of constitutional protection[59] and argue that the autonomous reproductive decisions of competent adults are entitled to respect, that laws "protecting" women from their bargains are unnecessarily paternalistic, and that the human desire for offspring that are related to one or more of the intended (social) parents should be accorded respect.

The legal issues created by surrogate parenting generally fall into two categories. First, what should the state's policy be with respect to the practice itself? The options range from outright prohibition to detailed judicial supervision of every aspect of the practice. Second, in the event that the surrogate agreement is violated, when and on what basis should the state provide a remedy? In particular, how should courts rule when the surrogate mother refuses to relinquish her parental rights (which is a rare, but dramatic, occurrence)?

12.1.2.1 *Prohibition and Regulation*

A surrogacy arrangement is a daunting legal task even in instances when a pregnancy is uneventful—the child is born in good health, and all individuals involved behave exactly as they have agreed (assuming no state-law obstacles to the practice). In most jurisdictions it will involve a relinquishment of parental rights by the surrogate mother (and probably by her spouse, if she is married), as well as an adoption by one or both of the social parents. It may also involve the execution of collateral documents intended to overcome various common-law and statutory presumptions of parentage that were not developed with surrogate parenting in mind.[60] An additional element of uncertainty results when state laws provide (as most states do) that the relinquishment of parental rights, the consent to adoption, and the adoption decree itself do not become final and irrevocable until some time after the birth of the child. The Uniform Status of Children of Assisted Conception Act (USCACA) provides alternative approaches for adopting states, which can either declare surrogacy arrangements to be void or provide for a type of preconception adoption proceeding.[61] So far only two states have adopted the

---

[59] *Cf. Skinner v. Oklahoma*, 316 U.S. 535 (1942) (procreation deemed a fundamental right); *Eisenstadt v. Baird*, 405 U.S. 438, 453–54 (1972) (procreative decisions fall within the right of privacy).

[60] For example, under the Uniform Parentage Act (UPA) of 2000, if a married woman, with the consent of her husband, has been artificially inseminated with semen donated by someone other than her husband, then the husband is deemed to be the natural father of the child so conceived. Uniform Parentage Act § 705. In a surrogacy arrangement that is subject to this law, therefore, the surrogate's husband typically must execute a statement that he does not consent to the artificial insemination of his wife in order to avoid the creation of a legislative presumption that he, rather than the donor of the sperm, is the natural father of the child.

[61] The pre-birth adoption decree solves one vexing problem that faces hospitals in which a surrogate mother delivers a child. Hospital policies routinely call for newborns to be sent home with their birth mothers. With a surrogacy arrangement, that is not the parents' usual intention, but on what basis should a hospital release the newborn to someone who is not the birth mother, and may not be the genetic mother either? A court order upon which the hospital presumably may rely would clear the matter up considerably.

USCACA;[62] Virginia chose the regulatory option, while North Dakota refuses to enforce all surrogacy arrangements.[63]

At least 26 states have enacted laws that specifically address surrogate parenting. Some states regard all surrogacy contracts to be void,[64] while others refuse to enforce commercial surrogacy arrangements,[65] and a third group specifically declare surrogacy arrangements to be lawful and enforceable.[66] States in this last group typically provide for judicial approval of the agreement, as well as continuing jurisdiction to resolve disputes under the agreement as they arise.[67] At least Florida and Texas explicitly require "pure gestational" surrogacy (*i.e.*, surrogacy contracts must provide for the use of an egg other than one from the surrogate's body).[68]

12.1.2.2 *Custody Disputes*

Although the vast majority of surrogacy arrangements are uneventful, a small number have resulted in dramatic litigation that occasionally has commanded national attention. Three of these cases mark the evolution of custody law as it applies to three distinct surrogate relationships. The most famous of these is *In re Baby M*,[69] in which the surrogate mother (that is, the genetic and gestational mother) renounced her obligations under the surrogacy contract and refused to relinquish custody of the child to the intended parents. The parents sued to enforce their rights under the surrogacy contract, which the New Jersey Supreme Court ruled was void and unenforceable on public-policy grounds. Applying the traditional "best interests of the child" standard, the court concluded that the intended parents should be awarded custody and that the surrogate was entitled to visitation rights on a basis to be determined on remand to the trial court.

The surrogate mother fared less well in *Johnson v. Calvert*.[70] This case involved a gestational surrogacy arrangement, a deteriorating relationship between the surrogate and the intended parents

---

62 *See* N.D. Cent. Code § 14-18 (surrogacy contracts are void); Va. Code Ann §§ 20-156 to -165 (surrogacy contracts subject to regulation and judicial supervision).

63 The UPA was revised in 2000 and amended in 2002 to reflect technological changes, such as exact genetic identification for paternity tests. The National Conference of Commissioners on Uniform State Laws addressed modern developments through additional uniform laws: the Uniform Putative and Unknown Fathers Act (UPUFA) (1989) and the USCACA (1989). As already noted in the main text, only two states adopted the USCACA, and the UPUFA was not adopted anywhere. The revision to the UPA "attempts to integrate the best of [the three uniform acts]." *See* "Prefatory Note," Uniform Parentage Act (2000). The conference also withdrew all previous versions of the UPA, as well as the USCACA and UPUFA. *Id.*

64 *See, e.g.*, Ky. Rev. Stat. Ann. § 199.590; La. Rev. Stat. Ann. § 9:2713; Mich. Comp. Laws Ann. § 722.855; N.Y. Dom. Rel. Law § 22:122.

65 *See, e.g.*, Wash. Rev. Code Ann. § 26.26.230.

66 *See, e.g.*, Fla. Stat. Ann. § 742.15; Tex. Fam. Code ch. 160.574; Va. Code Ann. §§ 20-159, 20-160(b)(4). All require that the intended mother must be infertile. Additionally, Virginia requires advance judicial approval of the surrogacy agreement, as well as limits who may act as a surrogate.

67 One type of dispute that might arise involves the surrogate mother's promise to avoid unhealthy or dangerous practices (smoking, drinking, ingesting controlled substances, skydiving), to seek regular medical care, and to follow all recommendations of her obstetrician. These promises create difficult issues when the intended parents seek enforcement through injunctive decrees or rescission on grounds of a material breach. *See* Thomas Wm. Mayo, *Medical Decision Making During a Surrogate Pregnancy*, 25 Hous. L. Rev. 599 (1988).

68 Fla. Stat. Ann. §§ 742.13–.15; Tex. Family Code § 160.754(c).

69 *In re Baby M*, 537 A.2d 1227 (N.J. 1988).

70 *Johnson v. Calvert*, 851 P.2d 776 (Cal. 1993), *cert. denied*, 510 U.S. 874 (1993).

throughout the pregnancy, and competing lawsuits in which the surrogate and the intended parents each sought a declaration of parentage. The California Supreme Court held that California law permitted only one person to be a "mother," and that person should be the intended (and genetic) mother, not the gestational surrogate.[71]

A third surrogacy case, *In re Buzzanca*, was noteworthy for two reasons: the baby was not genetically related to either intended social parent; and the genetic and surrogate parents (as well as one of the intended social parents) did not want custody.[72] According to a surrogacy contract, the Buzzancas, a married couple, both wished to initiate the process of having a baby. They created an embryo, using genetic material that was not theirs, and implanted the embryo into a surrogate mother. The couple separated before the baby was born, and Mr. Buzzanca tried to disclaim any parental responsibility. Mrs. Buzzanca asked the court to declare that she and Mr. Buzzanca were the legal parents.

The Buzzanca child could have had any of six possible legal parents: either of the genetic parents; the gestational mother or her spouse; or Mr. or Mrs. Buzzanca. However, a trial court declared the baby a legal orphan. The California Court of Appeals for the Fourth District reversed, declaring that the legislature had declared a "preference for assigning individual responsibility for the care and maintenance of children, not leaving the task to taxpayers."[73] The court designated the Buzzancas the legal parents, reasoning by analogy to artificial insemination; section 7613 of the California Family Code states that, when a husband gives permission for his wife to be artificially inseminated by another man, the husband is treated in law as the natural father.[74] The court also stated that, even if Mrs. Buzzanca had promised to shoulder all parental responsibilities, as Mr. Buzzanca argued, this promise was void and unenforceable.

Surrogacy contracts remain difficult legal ground; the court in *Buzzanca* was careful to note that it was not ruling on the enforceability of the surrogacy contract, but rather on "the consequences of those agreements as *acts* which *caused the birth* of the child."[75] The court called on the legislature to clarify parental rights and responsibilities in the legal area of artificial reproduction.[76]

---

[71] Justice Kennard vigorously challenged this conclusion in his dissenting opinion, in which he identified "three discrete aspects of motherhood: genetic, gestational, and social," *id.* at 791 (Kennard, J., dissenting), not one of which provided a solid basis for a judicial decree of parentage. Justice Kennard concluded that the best interests of the child, not the genetic bond or the intent of the parties, should control. In the most recent commercial surrogacy case, *In re Roberto*, 399 Md. 267, 923 A.2d 115, 2007 Md. LEXIS 269 (Md. Ct. App. 2007), the Court of Appeals of Maryland granted certiorari to hear a father, whose sperm was used to fertilize donor's eggs and implanted into a gestational carrier, petition the court to issue a birth certificate that did not list the carrier as the mother. The court held that the best-interest-of-the-child standard did not apply; the carrier was not required to be listed as the mother on birth certificates; and under the Equal Rights Amendment both males and females can challenge their parental status based on their genetic connection.

[72] *In re Buzzanca*, 61 Cal. App. 4th 1410 (Cal. App. 4th Dist. 1998).

[73] *Id.* at 1411.

[74] One court even decided that this law should apply to the partner of an artificially inseminated lesbian woman, where the couple had obtained a marriage license. *Karin T. v. Michael T.*, 484 N.Y.S.2d 780 (N.Y. Fam. Ct. 1985).

[75] *Id.* at 1423.

[76] *Id.* at 1428.

12.2 Organ Transplantation

The framework for organ procurement, allocation, and transplantation is provided by the National Organ Transplant Act (NOTA),[77] which authorizes DHHS to contract with a private entity to establish and operate the Organ Procurement and Transplantation Network (OPTN).[78] The only contractor in the history of the OPTN has been the United Network for Organ Sharing (UNOS), a nonprofit corporation whose bylaws and policies have been the cornerstone of federal organ-transplant policy.[79]

NOTA prohibits the purchase or sale of organs in interstate commerce,[80] as does the Uniform Anatomical Gift Act (UAGA).[81] Consequently, the United States relies on an entirely voluntary system for organ donation. Federal law currently requires Medicare- and Medicaid-eligible hospitals to inform families of potential organ donors of the option to donate (and their right to decline) and to notify their local organ procurement organization (OPO) of potential organ donors.[82]

12.2.1 Strategies to Increase the Supply of Organs

The number of organs produced by the voluntary-donation system falls woefully short of the demand for transplantable organs. As a result, many attempts have been made to increase the supply, not all of them successful.

The UAGA provides that an anatomical gift takes effect upon or after the death of the donor. The determination of death is a matter of state law; although a majority of states still follow cardio-respiratory criteria for determining death,[83] all states have adopted the whole-brain-death criterion, as well.[84] Under the "brain death" criterion, death occurs when all brain functions—those of the brain stem as well as the cerebral hemispheres—ease.[85] The brain-death criterion has been useful for transplant purposes; it allows a determination of death to be made even while an individual's cardiac and respiratory functions are being artificially maintained, thus precluding a determination of death according to cardio-respiratory criteria.

---

[77] 42 U.S.C. §§ 273–274g.

[78] *Id.* § 274(a).

[79] Hospitals in which transplants are performed must, as a condition of participation in the Medicare and Medicaid programs, be members of UNOS and comply with its policies and rules. *Id.* § 1320b-8(a)(1)(B). UNOS policies may be found at www.unos.org/policiesandbylaws/policies.asp?resources=true, and bylaws are posted at www.unos.org/policiesandbylaws/bylaws.asp?resources=true.

[80] 42 U.S.C. § 274e(a). Federal law, however, does permit "the reasonable payments associated with the removal, transportation, implantation, processing, preservation, quality control, and storage of a human organ in connection with donation of the organ." *Id.* at § 274e(c)(2).

[81] Uniform Anatomical Gift Act (UAGA) § 10 (1987). All 50 U.S. states adopted the 1968 version of the UAGA, which was silent on the subject of organ sales; 27 states subsequently repealed the 1968 UAGA and enacted the 1987 UAGA (which departs significantly from the Uniform Act's language in some instances). *See* "General Notes," *id.* (2003). Thus, approximately 20 states still do not prohibit the purchase or sale of human organs, although the point is largely moot as long as federal law prohibits the practice. *See* Comment, *Organ Donation, Procurement and Transplantation: The Process, The Problems, The Law*, 65 UMKC L. Rev. 201, 218 (1996).

[82] 42 U.S.C. § 1320b-8(a)(1)(A)(i) and (iii).

[83] Cardio-respiratory criteria usually provide that death occurs upon the irreversible cessation of spontaneous cardiac and respiratory functions. *See, e.g.,* Dan W. Brock, *Death and Dying*, in *Medical Ethics* 363, 364 (Robert M. Veatch ed., 2d ed. 1997).

[84] *See* Alan Meisel & Kathy L. Cerminara, *The Right to Die* § 6.04[A] (3rd ed. 2004).

[85] *See* Bernard Lo, *Resolving Ethical Dilemmas: A Guide for Clinicians* 177–78 (2d ed. 2000).

Occasionally, however, waiting for the brain-death criteria to be satisfied will result in the loss of transplantable organs. This has led to occasional attempts to get around the brain-death criteria and declare death on some other basis. For example, in *In re T.A.C.P.*,[86] parents of an anencephalic newborn petitioned for a declaration that their child was "dead" for purposes of organ donation. Because an anencephaly denotes the absence of the cerebral hemispheres but the presence of some or all of the brain stem, the Florida Supreme Court ruled that an anencephalic newborn could not be declared dead, and therefore could not be an organ donor until her brainstem ceased to function or she satisfied the cardio-respiratory criterion for death, even though that meant the organs of most anencephalic infants would not be transplantable.

Similarly, patients in a persistent (or permanent) vegetative state (PVS) have suffered the irreversible loss of higher-brain functions, but some or all of their brain-stem functions are intact. The wait for death according to brain-death criteria may mean the loss of transplantable organs in PVS situations, especially when the PVS results from sudden trauma and cardio-pulmonary functioning has been restored before the organs have suffered from lack of oxygen. This loss could be avoided in many such cases if the states were to adopt a "neocortical" or "higher-brain" criterion for determining death, rather than the "whole-brain" criterion that is now universally recognized. Although the "higher-brain" proposal has been eloquently defended,[87] it has not gained much support.[88]

With the strong encouragement of UNOS and the Joint Commission and the support of the Institute of Medicine,[89] some hospitals are returning to cardio-respiratory criteria to determine death in at least some circumstances. These donors are referred to as "non-heart-beating cadaver donors," and their deaths are declared in the operating room, rather than the intensive care unit, after the removal of artificial life support and two to five minutes[90] of either pulselessness or fibrillation (ineffectual "quivering" action of the heart muscle fibers).[91] Drugs usually are administered at this point to dilate the patient's blood vessels and to impede the clotting process, both in an attempt to maintain maximum blood flow to the organs. Several criticisms have been raised against the use of non-heart-beating cadaver donors,[92] and it is not yet clear whether societal intuitions concerning the death will embrace or

---

[86] *In re T.A.C.P.*, 609 So. 2d 588 (Fla. 1992).

[87] *See, e.g.*, Robert M. Veatch, *The Impending Collapse of the Whole-Brain Definition of Death*, 23 Hastings Center Rep't 18 (July–Aug. 1993).

[88] The principal objections are (i) the higher-brain criterion confuses "loss of personhood," which arguably occurs with PVS and anencephaly, with "death" and (ii) no reliable tests are available to date to establish that higher-brain-death has occurred, and the symbolism of burying or cremating a person who still has a pulse and is still breathing offends deep-seated intuitions about the nature of death. *See* Bernard Lo, at 178–79.

[89] *See* Robert Steinbrook, *Organ Donation after Cardiac Death*, 357 New Eng. J. Med. 209 (2007).

[90] Early protocols called for a two-minute loss of cardio-pulmonary function and, despite a recommendation by the Institute of Medicine to increase the period to five minutes, most organ procurement protocols have retained the two-minute standard. *See* Stuart J. Youngner, Robert M. Arnold & Michael A. DeVita, *When is "Dead"?*, 29 Hastings Ctr. Rep't 14 (Nov.–Dec. 1999).

[91] Gina Kolata, *Organ Shortage Leads to Nontraditional Transplants, and Ethical Concerns*, N.Y. Times, June 2, 1993, at A15, col. 1.

[92] The concerns include the following: (i) whether donors truly satisfy the cardio-respiratory criteria for the determination of death (in theory or in practice); (ii) the extent to which terminal care of patients may be compromised; (iii) the potentially undignified manner by which a patient/donor will die if he continues to breathe or have a pulse for "too long," and is returned to the intensive-care unit; and (iv) the possibility that death might occur not from the removal of life-support but from the organ-retrieval process itself, thus stepping over the line between "letting die" and "killing." *See* Bernard Lo, at 330. These concerns are rigorously analyzed in John A. Robertson, *Policy Issues in a Non-Heart-Beating Donor Protocol*, 3 Kennedy Instit. of Ethics J. 241 (1993).

reject this approach to increasing the supply of cadaveric organs, although it appears to be gaining in acceptance.[93]

Finally, In 2007 the Department of Justice determined that paired organ exchanges among couples who do not match within their own family but do match someone else on the waiting list do not violate NOTA's prohibition against organ sales.[94] Congress subsequently amended NOTA to express its agreement with Justice that a paired organ exchange does not constitute "valuable consideration" within the meaning of the law.[95]

Other proposals have been suggested but not implemented in this country. These include repealing the federal ban on organ sales[96] and creating a "presumed consent" rule, the latter having been adopted by a number of European countries. At the present time, however, little support exists for either option.

12.2.2 Allocation Policies

Because of the extreme shortage of organs for transplant, a great deal of attention has focused on the development of allocation rules for organs. UNOS has dominated the issue pursuant to a Congressional mandate to set national policy; until 1999, DHHS largely deferred to UNOS's lead.

Organs are allocated through a two-step process. First, a potential recipient has to be placed on the UNOS list for an organ, a decision that is guided by UNOS policies and, ultimately, left up to the patient's physician. Although the policies are specific as to the criteria to be used in deciding whether to put a patient on the list, their execution seems to have varied in the following ways: considerable variation has appeared among hospitals and regions; transplant centers adopted different approaches to liver and intestinal organs, on the one hand, and thoracic organs on the other; and some centers "gamed" the system by prematurely admitting a patient to the ICU and listing patients on multiple regional lists.[97]

The second step in the process involves matching patients on the UNOS waiting list to a particular organ. Historically, UNOS' policies provided for a match to be made first locally (within the OPO's service area); if no match is possible locally, then the search moved to regional lists and, absent a match at that level, the national list. This system was designed to avoid (to the extent possible) the detriment that transportation causes to fragile organs; moreover, a potential donor often is encouraged by the knowledge that her organs would be given to someone from her area. Such a largely geography-driven system, however, resulted in two types of disparity. First, significant differences were seen in waiting times for patients on the UNOS list, seemingly a function of widely different local levels of supply and demand. This led to a second feature of the system: when organs were matched locally or

---

93 *See* Robert Steinbrook, *Organ Donation After Cardiac Death*, 357 N. Eng. J. Med. 209 (July 19, 2007).

94 *See* U.S. Dep't of Justice, *Memorandum Opinion for the General Counsel, Department of Health and Human Services: Legality of Alternative Organ Donation Practices under 42 U.S.C. § 274e* (2007).

95 Pub. L. No. 110-144, § 2, 121 Stat. 1813 (2007).

96 *See, e.g.*, Lloyd R. Cohen, *Increasing the Supply of Transplant Organs: The Virtues of a Futures Market*, 58 Geo. Wash. L. Rev. 1 (1989).

97 *See Developments in the Law—Medical Technology and Law*, 103 Harv. L. Rev. 1614 (1990).

regionally, patients on the national list who were far sicker and medically needier often had to continue to wait for an organ that survived the system's preference for local-then-regional matches.[98]

On October 20, 1999, DHHS published a final rule that attempted to address these disparities.[99] The rule directs the OPTN to develop allocation policies that will distribute cadaver organs to the maximum extent feasible on the basis of medical need, without regard to geographic location.[100] Thoracic organs—because of their relative fragility outside the body—continue to be allocated on a geographical basis, and "zero-antigen-mismatch" kidneys are matched anywhere in the country that such a match can be made, in recognition of the increased prospect of a successful graft. The rule also brings the OPTN squarely within the regulatory orbit of DHHS, which was technically but not factually the case before 1999.

12.3 The New Genetics

As a result of the Human Genome Project, a greater understanding of the genetic basis of many diseases and conditions promises as great a revolution in healthcare as the germ theory of disease produced 150 years ago. In the areas of genetic testing, counseling, and therapy, new techniques are developed almost daily for detecting an individual's genetic predisposition to particular illnesses. This information, however, creates new and challenging ethical and legal dilemmas. Congress addressed this when it appropriated funds for the Human Genome Project by simultaneously earmarking 3% (later increased to 5%) of the total budget for the study of ethical, legal, and social issues.[101] Areas of major concern include confidentiality of genetic information, nondiscrimination, and the use of embryonic and fetal tissue cells in research.

12.3.1 Confidentiality

All states require that medical information and medical records be kept confidential. In addition to these generic requirements, however, many states have statutes that specifically protect the confidentiality of genetic information or prohibit genetic discrimination by employers and insurers,[102] and bills on this topic have been introduced in Congress for at least the last 10 years.[103] The rationale for these

[98] These disparities are documented and analyzed in *Institute of Medicine, Organ Procurement and Transplantation* (1999).

[99] *Organ Procurement and Transplantation Network*, 64 Fed. Reg. 56,650 (Oct. 20, 1999), codified at 42 C.F.R. Part 121.

[100] This description is vastly oversimplified, but accurate as far as it goes. In addition to the separate policies noted in the text for thoracic organs and "zero-antigen-mismatch" kidneys, UNOS has separate allocation rules for pediatric patients. *See, e.g.,* UNOS Rules 3.5.11.5, 3.6, 3.6.4.2, 3.6.4.3, and 3.7.4. http://www.unos.org/policiesandbylaws/policies.asp?resources=true.

[101] Much of the work in this area is described at the Human Genome Project's "Ethical, Legal and Social Issues" website at www.ornl.gov/sci/techresources/Human_Genome/elsi/elsi.shtml.

[102] *See,e.g.,* 410 Ill. Comp. Stat. § 513/15; Tex. Ins. Code Ann. § 546.102; Va. Code. Ann. § 38.2-508.4. Many of these state laws are analyzed in Karen H. Rothenberg, *Genetic Information and Health Insurance: State Legislative Approaches*, 23 J. Law, Med. & Ethics 312 (1995) (discussing statutes enacted by Alabama, California, Colorado, Florida, Georgia, Maryland, Minnesota, New Hampshire, North Carolina, Ohio, Oregon, Virginia, and Wisconsin). *See* Deborah Hellman, *What Makes Genetic Discrimination Exceptional?*, 29 Am. J. L. & Med. 77 (2003); Sharon Hoffman, *Legislation and Genetic Discrimination*, 16 J.L. & Health 47 (2001); National Conference of State Legislatures, State Genetic Privacy Laws, http://www.ncsl.org/programs/health/genetics/prt.htm.

[103] *See* H.R. 493 and S. 358, Cong. 110 (2007) (Genetic Information Nondiscrimination Act of 2007); S. 306, Cong. 109 (2005) (Genetic Information and Nondiscrimination Act of 2005); H.R. 3636 IH, Cong. 108 (2003) (Genetic Privacy and

statutes is that the unauthorized release of genetic information has the potential for creating a unique mixture of injuries—not only to the privacy and autonomy interests of the individual tested, but also the privacy interests of that person's extended family, as well as to his or her economic interests (*i.e.,* employment opportunities, and the cost and availability of insurance) and social and psychological well-being.[104]

In addition to any genetic privacy law that may emerge from Congress in the future, DHHS' final privacy rule[105] enforcing that portion of the Health Insurance Portability and Accountability Act (HIPAA) is already in place. It places significant restrictions on the communication of health information without at least notification to the patient; for some uses, the patient's affirmative consent is needed. HIPAA also contains hefty penalties for its violation. The rule preempts contrary state laws that are less protective of individually identifiable health information; thus, the state laws discussed earlier, and the state cases that will be discussed, need to be reconsidered in light of this new federal standard for privacy protection.

Confidentiality is not an absolute value; as a practical matter, the storage and dissemination of genetic information is relatively easy and has potential benefits. Accordingly, difficult issues arise concerning when and under what circumstances *may* genetic information be disclosed without a person's consent, and whether a *duty to disclose* such information exists at any point. At least two courts have considered whether a treating physician may have a duty to inform close family members that the patient has a disease for which the family members may be at risk due to the heritability of the gene that is linked to the disease. In *Pate v. Threlkel,*[106] the Florida Supreme Court accepted, for purposes of reviewing a dismissal for failure to state a claim, the allegation that the prevailing standard of care required a physician to warn a patient of the genetically transferable nature of her disease, and ruled that such a duty would run to the benefit of third parties, such as the patient's children. The court stopped short of imposing a duty to warn third parties directly, however:

> If there is a duty to warn, to whom must the physician convey the warning? Our holding should not be read to require the physician to warn the patient's children of the disease. In most instances the physician is prohibited from disclosing the patient's medical condition to others except with the patient's permission.... Moreover, the patient ordinarily can be expected to pass on the warning. To require the physician to seek out and warn various members of the patient's family would often be difficult or impractical and would place too heavy a burden upon the physician. Thus, we emphasize that in any circumstances in which the phy-

---

Nondiscrimination Act of 2003); H.R. 602, Cong. 107 (2001) (Genetic Nondiscrimination in Health Insurance and Employment Act); H.R. 1057 & S. 573, Cong. 106 (1999) (Medical Information Privacy and Security Act); H.R. 2878, Cong. 106 (1999) (Medical Information Privacy and Security Act); H.R. 5612, Cong. 101 (1990) (Human Genome Privacy Act). These culminate with the passage of the Genetic Information Nondiscrimination Act of 2008 (GINA), Pub. L. No. 110-233, 122 Stat. 881.

104 *See* Lawrence O. Gostin, *Genetic Privacy*, 23 J. Law, Med. & Ethics 320, 322 (1995).

105 The Health Information Portability and Accountability Act (HIPAA) privacy rule has a long and tortuous history, the explication of which is beyond the scope of this Chapter. Much of it is recounted in the preambles to the final rule and its various corrections and amendments. *See Standards for Privacy of Individually Identifiable Health Information*, 65 Fed. Reg. 82,462 (Dec. 28, 2000) (original final rule); 65 Fed. Reg. 82,944 (Dec. 29, 2000) (technical corrections); 66 Fed. Reg. 12,434 (Feb. 26, 2001) (correction of effective and compliance dates); 67 Fed. Reg. 53,182 (Aug. 14, 2002) (substantial modifications to final rule).

106 *Pate v. Threlkel*, 661 So. 2d 278 (Fla. 1995).

sician has a duty to warn of a genetically transferable disease, that duty will be satisfied by warning the patient.[107]

A New Jersey appellate court rejected the Florida Supreme Court's resolution of the issue in *Safer v. Pack*,[108] in which an adult daughter sued the estate of her father's physician on the ground that the physician failed to warn her that her father's diagnosis put her at increased genetic risk of contracting cancer. The court ruled that (i) "the duty to warn of avertable risk from genetic causes, by definition a matter of familiar concern, is sufficiently narrow to serve the interests of justice,"[109] and (ii) it would not rule that disclosure of the familial risk to the patient satisfied the physician's duty to warn. The court did not "resolve a conflict between the physician's broader duty to warn and his fidelity to an expressed preference of the patient that nothing be said to family members about the details of the disease,"[110] because the case had not yet been tried and there was not yet a factual record that would require the court to rule on the question.

12.3.2 Nondiscrimination

State legislatures have focused primarily upon genetic discrimination in the insurance and employment contexts, recognizing the reality that businesses have a strong economic incentive to find out about an individual's genetic predisposition for certain expensive medical conditions, and to act on that information. Before addressing state requirements and prohibitions, however, a recent federal enactment must be considered.

In 2008 the Federal government passed the Genetic Information Nondiscrimination Act (GINA), which also focuses on discrimination in the context of insurance and employment. It prohibits discrimination in health insurance coverage and employment based on genetic information.[111] GINA provides a minimum level of protection on a nation-wide basis. Thus, "all entities that are subject to [it] must, at a minimum, comply with all applicable GINA requirements, and may also need to comply with more protective state laws."[112]

The statute defines "genetic information" as

> information about an individual's genetic tests, genetic tests of the individual's family members, genetic tests of any fetus of an individual or family member who is a pregnant woman, and genetic tests of any embryo legally held by an individual or family member using assisted reproductive technology, the manifestation of a disease or disorder in family members, any request for, or receipt of, genetic services or participation in clinical research that includes genetic services by an individual or family member."

[107] *Id.* at 282.
[108] *Safer v. Pack*, 677 A.2d 1188 (N.J. Super. A.D.), *cert. denied,* 683 A.2d 1163 (N.J. 1996).
[109] *Id.* at 1192.
[110] *Id.* at 1192–93.
[111] *See* The Genetic Information Nondiscrimination Act of 2008, Pub. L. No. 110-233 122 Stat 881.
[112] *See* Health and Human Services Information for Researchers and Healthcare Professionals (Apr. 6, 2009) available at http://www.genome.gov/Pages/PolicyEthics/GeneticDiscrimination/GINAInfoDoc.pdf.

"Genetic test" is defined as "analysis of human DNA, RNA, chromosomes, proteins, or metabolites that detects genotypes, mutations, or chromosomal changes." This definition does not include "analyses of proteins or metabolites that are directly related to a manifested disease, disorder, or pathological condition that could reasonable be detected by a health care professional with appropriate training and expertise in the field of medicine involved."[113]

Title I of GINA, in conjunction with HIPAA,[114] "generally prohibits health insurers or health plan administrators from requesting or requiring genetic information of an individual or the individual's family members, or using it for decisions regarding coverage, rates, or preexisting conditions." It will be enforced by the Department of Labor, the Department of Treasury, and the Department of Health and Human Services, and "remedies for violations include corrective action and monetary penalties."[115]

Title II of GINA "prohibits most employers from using genetic information for hiring, firing, or promotional decisions, and for any decisions regarding terms of employment" and will be enforced by the Equal Employment Opportunity Commission (EEOC).[116] As with Title I, the remedies for violation under Title II include corrective action and monetary penalties, although Title II also provides a "right to pursue private litigation."[117]

GINA provides a "research exception" to its application. Health plans are permitted to request, but not require, that a plan participant or beneficiary undergo a genetic test for "research purposes" if the following conditions are met:

(a) The request is made in writing and complies with relevant state and federal laws;

(b) The plan or issuer clearly indicates

   i. Compliance is voluntary; and

   ii. Non-compliance will have no effect on enrollment status or premiums

(c) None of the information collected shall be used for underwriting purposes

(d) The plan or issuer notifies the Secretary in writing that activities will be conducted pursuant to the exception.[118]

Additionally, "GINA does not extend to life insurance, disability insurance and long-term care insurance, "does not mandate coverage for any particular test or treatment," and "does not prohibit health insurers or health plan administrators from obtaining and using genetic test results in making

[113] *Id.*

[114] In passing HIPAA, Congress limited the ability of group health plans to exclude subscribers on the basis of a preexisting condition. *See* 42 U.S.C. § 300gg. "Genetic information" is not a "condition" for which an insurer may impose a preexisting-condition exclusion "in the absence of a diagnosis of the condition related to such information." *See* 42 U.S.C. § 300gg. This limitation does not extend to rating policies or establishing premiums on the basis of genetic information, and provides no protection to applicants or insureds in individual policies.

[115] *Id.*

[116] *Id.*

[117] *Id.*

[118] *See* Pub. L. No. 110-233, 122 Stat 881, Title I § 101.

health insurance payment determinations."[119] The employment provisions "generally do not apply to employers with fewer than 15 employees."[120]

12.3.2.1 Insurance

With respect to insurers, the several states have pursued a number of different strategies. Several states have prohibited an insurer from denying coverage because of genetic information.[121] Several states prohibit insurers from limiting coverage, or determining rates or premiums, based on genetic information.[122] Several states also prohibit insurers from canceling or refusing to renew policies on the basis of such information.[123] Florida, Louisiana, and Tennessee prohibit an insurer from considering whether the applicant made a request for a genetic test.[124] Oregon and Texas have laws that prohibit an insurer from using favorable genetic tests as an inducement for coverage,[125] while Indiana and Illinois allow insurers to consider the results of a genetic test if the results are voluntarily submitted and favorable to the applicant or insured.[126] Several states forbid insurers from seeking information about a person's genetic characteristics for any nontherapeutic purpose.[127] Georgia has declared that genetic information is the unique property of the individual tested.[128]

12.3.2.2 Employment

As is the case with insurers, employers have an economic interest in screening job applicants or employees for genetic conditions that may lead to a higher rate of health-insurance claims, as well as a higher incidence of absenteeism and disability claims.[129] Title I of the federal Americans with Disabilities Act (ADA) provides that "no covered entity shall discriminate against a qualified individual with a *disability* because of the disability of such an individual in regard to job application procedures, the hiring, advancement, or discharge of employees, employee compensation, job training, and other terms, conditions, and privileges of employment."[130] A "disability" within the meaning of the ADA includes a condition that is regarded by others to be a disability, regardless of the actual impact of the condition upon a major life activity.

---

[119] *Id.*

[120] *Id.*

[121] *See, e.g.*, CAL. INS. CODE § 10140(b); D.C. CODE § 2-1402.11; FLA. STAT. ANN. § 627.4301(2)(a); GA. CODE ANN. § 33-54-1; 410 ILL. COMP. STAT. § 513/20; MASS. ANN. LAWS ch. 175 § 108H; N.J. STAT. ANN. § 17B:30-12; N.Y. INS. LAW ANN. § 3221(q)(1)(F); TEX. INS. CODE § 546.052; VA. CODE ANN. § 38.2-508.4.

[122] *See, e.g.*, CAL. INS. CODE § 10143; FLA. STAT. ANN. § 627.4301; MASS. ANN. LAWS. ch. 175 § 108H; N.J. STAT. ANN. § 17B:30-12; OHIO REV. CODE ANN. § 3901.49; TEX. INS. CODE ANN. § 546.052; VA. CODE ANN. § 38.2-508.4.

[123] *See, e.g.*, CAL. INS. CODE § 10140(b); FLA. STAT. ANN. § 627.4301(2)(a); MASS. ANN. LAWS. ch. 175 § 108H; N.J. STAT. ANN. § 17B:30-12; TEX. INS. CODE § 546.052; VA. CODE ANN. § 38.2-508.4.

[124] *See* FLA. ST. ANN. § 627.4301(2)(b); LA. REV. STAT. ANN. § 22:213.7; NEV. REV. STAT. § 689A.417;TENN. CODE ANN. § 56-7-2703.

[125] *See* OR. REV. STAT. § 746.135(2); TEX. INS. CODE ANN. § 546.051(c).

[126] *See* IND. CODE ANN. § 27-8-26-9; 410 ILL. COMP. STAT. § 513/20(b).

[127] *See* CAL. INS. CODE § 10140(c); GA. CODE ANN. § 33-54-4; IND. CODE ANN. § 27-8-26-5; MO. ANN. STAT. § 375.1303.

[128] *See* GA. CODE ANN. § 33-54-1.

[129] *See* Mark Rothstein, *Genetic Discrimination in Employment and the Americans with Disabilities Act*, 29 HOUS. L. REV. 23, 27 (1992).

[130] 42 U.S.C. § 12112(a) (emphasis added).

The Equal Employment Opportunity Commission (EEOC) has the responsibility to develop standards and guidelines to implement the ADA. In its first formally published statement on the subject, the EEOC concluded that genetic discrimination fell within the scope of the ADA.[131] The EEOC's compliance manual now includes a short statement that addresses the "regarded as having a disability" prong of the ADA's disability test. The statement provides that the ADA "[a]pplies to individuals who are subjected to discrimination on the basis of genetic information relating to illness, disease, or other disorders."[132]

President Clinton issued an Executive Order on February 8, 2000[133] prohibiting discrimination in federal employment based on genetic information. In general, the order protects information about an individual's genetic tests, or the genetic test of an individual's family member, and information about the occurrence of disease, medical condition, or disorder in family members of the individual.

Employment discrimination appears not to have attracted as much state legislative attention as insurance discrimination. In 1981, New Jersey was the first to enact legislation addressing employment discrimination based on genetic testing. This law prohibited "employment discrimination based on an individual's atypical hereditary cellular or blood trait."[134] In 1996, New Jersey revised this law to ban discrimination based on "genetic information," including information "that may derive from an individual or family member."[135]

Iowa, New Hampshire, Texas, and Wisconsin provide virtually identical statutory provisions. They prohibit an employer, labor organization, employment agency, or licensing agency from: (1) directly or indirectly soliciting, requiring, or administering genetic testing as a condition of employment, labor organization membership, or licensure; (2) affecting the terms, conditions, or privileges of employment, labor organization membership, or licensure of any individual based on genetic testing; or (3) terminating the employment, labor organization membership, or licensure of any individual based on genetic testing.[136]

12.3.3 Genetic Engineering

In some ways, the topic of genetic engineering brings this Chapter "full circle:" from decisions about reproduction (terminating a pregnancy, aiding a pregnancy) to scenarios similar to that in the novel *Brave New World* for reproducing human life in the laboratory. Predictably, the political and public-policy thicket of abortion, with which this Chapter began, also marks the developments (or the lack thereof) in this field.

---

131 Melinda B. Kaufman, *Genetic Discrimination in the Workplace: An Overview of Existing Protections*, 30 Loy. U. Chi. L.J. 393 (1999).

132 EEOC Compliance Manual (BNA) § 902.8(a) (1995).

133 www.opm.gov/pressrel/2000/genetic_eo.htm.

134 *See* Mark A. Rothstein, *The Law of Medical and Genetic Privacy in the Workplace*, in *Genetic Secrets: Protecting Privacy and Confidentiality in the Genetic Era* 281, 291 (Mark Rothstein, ed., 1997) (citing N.J. Stat. Ann. § 10:5-5(x), which states that "[a] typical hereditary cellular or blood trait" means sickle cell trait, hemoglobin C trait, thalassemia trait, Tay Sachs trait, or cystic fibrosis trait.").

135 *Id.*

136 *See* Iowa Code Ann. § 729.6; N.H. Rev. Stat. Ann. § 141-H:3; Tex. Labor Code §§ 21.401–.405; Tex. Ins. Code § 557.051; Wis. Stat. Ann. § 111.372.

12.3.3.1 Embryonic and Fetal-Cell Research

Genetic therapies that use fetal cells have long been thought to hold promise for curing or ameliorating the symptoms of many diseases; the potential for medical advances based upon embryonic cells—especially stem cells[137]—is regarded as one of the most significant scientific achievements of the past decade.[138] Most federally sponsored research using embryonic and fetal cells, however, stopped when Congress enacted a ban in 1985 on most fetal research,[139] followed by a ban in 1997 on the use of federal funds "for the creation of a human embryo or embryos for research purposes… or research in which a human embryo or embryos are destroyed, discarded or knowingly subjected to risk of injury or death."[140] The National Institutes of Health (NIH) tested the limits of this federal ban by proposing "Draft Guidelines for Research Involving Human Pluripotent Stem Cells."[141] The guidelines were based upon an opinion issued by the general counsel of DHHS that pluripotent stem cells are not "embryos" within the meaning of the federal research ban, and therefore NIH could legally fund stem-cell research.[142] Under the guidelines, federally sponsored researchers could not derive stem cells from embryos, but they were permitted to conduct research on stem cells that were so derived by private (nonfederally funded) researchers.

In August 2001, President Bush announced that federal funds may be awarded for research using human embryonic stem-cell lines that meet certain criteria, such as "where the life and death decision has already been made."[143] According to the president, approximately 60 cell lines met the specifications: their derivation process began before 9:00 pm E.D.T. on August 9, 2001; they were derived from an embryo created for reproductive purposes; and informed consent was obtained from the embryo donor, without financial inducement. Some have criticized the president's decision, accusing him of unnecessarily and arbitrarily restricting scientific progress. Others, however, have praised the decision as an appropriate restriction on potentially unethical and dangerous research. NIH has implemented the president's decision by creating a Human Embryonic Stem Cell Registry, which lists the human embryonic stem cells that meet the eligibility criteria.[144]

In March 2009, President Obama issued an Executive Order (Removing Barriers to Responsible Scientific Research Involving Human Stem Cells) that revoked President Bush's Executive Order of August 9, 2001.[145] The order provides that, "[t]he Secretary of Health and Human Services, through

---

137 Stem cells have the ability to divide for indefinite periods in culture and to give rise to specialized cells. "Pluripotent" stem cells can give rise to many types of cells, and could help to identify the factors involved in the cellular decision-making process that results in cell specification. National Institutes of Health, *Stem Cells: A Primer* (May 2000), available online at www.nih.gov/news/stemcell/primer.htm.

138 *See* Stephen S. Hall, *The Recycled Generation*, N.Y. Times Mag., Jan. 30, 2000, at 30.

139 Pub. L. No. 99-158, 99 Stat 820, § 498 (1985), *codified at* 42 U.S.C. § 289g. The law makes an exception for research that will not result in harm to the fetus, but that exception is of no real use to fetal-cell researchers.

140 Pub. Law No. 105-78, 111 Stat. 1467, § 513 (Nov. 13, 1997). The prohibition was re-enacted in Pub. L. No. 105-277, 112 Stat. 2681, § 511 (Oct. 21, 1998); and Pub. L. No. 106-113, 113 Stat. 1501, § 510 (Nov. 29, 1999).

141 Draft National Institutes of Health Guidelines for Research Involving Human Pluripotent Stem Cells, 64 Fed. Reg. 67,576 (Dec. 2, 1999).

142 *See* "Guidelines for Research Using Human Pluripotent Stem Cells," 65 Fed. Reg. 51,975 (2000). The opinion also stated that stem cells derived from human fetal tissue falls within the definition of human fetal tissue and would continue to be subject to the federal prohibition.

143 White House Press Release, Fact Sheet, *Embryonic Stem Cell Research,* Aug. 9, 2001.

144 *See* www.nih.gov.

145 Exec. Order No. 13,505, 74 Fed. Reg. 10667 (Mar. 11, 2009).

the director of NIH, may support and conduct responsible scientifically worthy human stem cell research, including human embryonic stem cell research, to the extent permitted by law."[146] The intended effect of this order was to allow for federal funding of research on many more stem cell lines that the 21 lines in existence when President Bush issued his order in 2001. The order directed NIH to "review existing NIH guidance and other widely recognized guidelines on human stem cell research" and "issue new NIH guidance on such research that is consistent with this order."[147]

In response to the order, NIH published draft guidelines entitled "Draft Guidelines for Human Stem Cell Research Notice" in April 2009.[148] The Draft Guidelines allowed "funding for research using human embryonic stem cells that were derived from human embryos created by *in vitro* fertilization (IVF) for reproductive purposes and were no longer needed for that purpose."[149] The final Guidelines, published on July 7, 2009, set forth eligibility requirements to determine which embryonic stem cell lines could be used in research funded by NIH.[150]

Under these guidelines, applicant institutions proposing research on human embryonic stem cells (hESCs) derived from embryos donated in the U.S. on or after the effective date of the NIH guidelines must use hESCs that are posted on the NIH registry, or establish eligibility for NIH funding by submitting a certificate of compliance with Section II(A) of the NIH guidelines.[151] Section II(A) requires that research involves only ESCs that were derived from human embryos that "were created using *in vitro* fertilization for reproductive purposes and were no longer needed for this purpose" and "were donated by the individuals who sought reproductive treatment… and who gave voluntary written consent for the human embryos to be used for research purposes."[152] Section II(A) further requires documentation of the following:

a. All options available in the healthcare facility where treatment was sought pertaining to the embryos no longer needed for reproductive purposes were explained to the individual(s) who sought reproductive treatment.
b. No payments… were offered for the donated embryos.
c. Polices and/or procedures were in place at the healthcare facility where the embryos were donated that neither consenting nor refusing to donate embryos for research would affect the quality of care provided to potential donor(s).
d. There was a clear separation between the prospective donor(s)'s decision to create human embryos for reproductive purposes and the prospective donor(s)'s decision to donate human embryos for research purposes.[153]

146 *Id.*
147 *Id.*
148 National Institutes of Health, *Draft Guidelines for Human Stem Cell Research Notice*, 74 Fed. Reg. 18,578 (Apr. 23, 2009).
149 *Id.*
150 National Institutes of Health, *Guidelines for Human Stem Cell Research*, 74 Fed. Reg. 32,170 (July 7, 2009).
151 *See id.* at 32,174.
152 *Id.*
153 *Id.*

In order to comply with the congressional ban on funding for research in which an embryo is destroyed, section V(A) of the Guidelines provides, "NIH funding of the derivation of stem cells from human embryos is prohibited by the annual appropriations ban on funding of human embryo research…, otherwise known as the Dickey Amendment."[154]

On August 23, 2010, United States District Court for the District of Columbia issued a preliminary injunction that blocked federal funding of stem cell research pursuant to the Guidelines.[155] The court held that

> [i]f one step or "piece of research" of an ESC research project results in the destruction of an embryo, the entire project is precluded from receiving federal funding by the Dickey-Wicker Amendment. Because ESC research requires the derivation of ESCs, ESC research is research in which an embryo is destroyed.[156]

Therefore, "by allowing federal funding of ESC research, the [NIH] Guidelines are in violation of the Dickey-Wicker Amendment."[157] The court concluded that the language of the Dickey-Wicker Amendment is clear, unambiguous, and intended to "encompass *all* 'research in which' an embryo is destroyed, not just the 'piece of research' in which the embryo was destroyed."[158] As of this writing, the litigation continues.

12.3.3.2 Cloning

When the news first broke in 1996 that a laboratory in Scotland had successfully cloned a sheep,[159] the worldwide reaction was not primarily concerned with the implications for animal husbandry and herd control. Instead, political and opinion leaders immediately asked, "are human beings next?" and "should they be?" Although the answer to the first question was "probably not,"[160] the answer to the second question was a resounding "no!".

The legal response has been swift and negative. At least 10 states have enacted laws prohibiting the cloning of human cells,[161] and bills to punish or deny public funds for human cloning have been drafted in more than 20 state legislatures.[162] At the federal level, then-President Clinton concluded that the federal ban on embryo research might not be fully effective in stopping cloning research, and issued a memorandum to all executive-department and agency heads in 1997 "direct[ing] that no Fed-

154 *Id.* at 32,175.
155 *Sherley v. Sebelius*, 704 F. Supp. 2d 63 (D.D.C. 2010).
156 *Id.* at 71–72.
157 *Id.* at 72.
158 *Id.* at 71 (emphasis added).
159 *See* K.H.S. Campbell *et al.*, *Sheep Cloned by Nuclear Transfer from a Cultured Cell Line*, 380 Nature 64–66 (Mar. 7, 1996).
160 *See* Lee M. Silver, *Remaking Eden: Cloning and Beyond in a Brave New World* 102–05 (1997) (arguing that safety issues strongly counsel cloning experiments with other mammals first).
161 *See, e.g.*, Cal. Bus. & Prof Code § 2260.5; Mich. Comp. Laws Ann. § 333.16274; Va. Code Ann. § 32.1-162.22.
162 *E.g.*, 2004 Ala. H.B. 282; 2004 Az. H.B. 2685; 2004 Conn. H.B. 5536; 2004 Fla. H.B. 559; 2004 Ill. H.B. 6693; 2003 Ind. H.B. 1984; 2004 Ky. H.B. 171; 2004 Md. H.B. 1021; 2003 Mass. S.B. 2400; 2004 Miss. H.B. 727; 2003 Neb. L.B. 602; 2004 N.J. A.B. 2388; 2003 N.Y. S.B. 7524; 2003 Ok. S.B. 1607; 2003 Or. H.B. 2538; 2003 S.C. H.B. 3819; 2003 Tenn. H.B. 1075; 2003 Tex. S.B. 156; 2003 Vt. H.B. 326; 2003 Wash. H.B. 2336; 2004 W. Va. H.B. 4887. *See* http://www.ncsl.org/default.aspx?tabid=14284 for a list of all state legislation on human cloning as of January 2008.

eral funds shall be allocated for cloning of human beings."[163] President Clinton also requested the National Bioethics Advisory Commission to review the ethical and legal issues raised by human cloning, and to make recommendations for federal policy. That commission's report, issued in June 1997, concluded that "it is morally unacceptable for anyone in the public or private sector, whether in a research or clinical setting, to attempt to create a child using somatic cell nuclear transfer cloning."[164] The commission also recommended a continuation of the moratorium announced by President Clinton, as well as enactment of federal legislation "to prohibit anyone from attempting, whether in a research or clinical setting, to create a child through somatic cell nuclear transfer cloning."[165] Although bills were introduced in the 106th House of Representatives,[166] Congress *did not* enact legislation adopting the commission's recommendation.

President Bush has stated that, although two types of human cloning have been distinguished in public debate, he "believe(s) all human cloning is wrong, and both forms of cloning ought to be banned."[167] He endorsed a proposed bill in 2001 that would ban all human cloning in the United States, including the cloning of embryos for research. The "Human Cloning Prohibition Act of 2003" passed in the House of Representatives,[168] but failed in the Senate.

The first report of the President's Council on Bioethics[169] recommended (by a 9-7 vote, with one member abstaining) in July 2002 that "cloning-to-produce-children" be banned and that Congress should enact a four-year moratorium on "cloning-for-biomedical-research."[170]

12.4 Conclusion

The challenging topic of bioethics is perhaps a fitting way to end a volume that attempts to present the fundamentals of health law. From the earliest stirring of human existence, through the disposition of human tissue and organs after death, bioethics represents the struggle to forge public policy in the face of technological advances and ethical uncertainty. The entire field of health law faces a similar challenge: to eke out a legal response to the constantly moving target of enlightened health policy. At any moment, the picture that emerges is at best a work in progress, as complex as the needs and strivings of our large and diverse population.

---

163 William J. Clinton, *Memorandum for the Heads of Executive Departments and Agencies Re: Prohibition on Federal Funding for Cloning of Human Beings*, Mar. 4, 1997.

164 Nat'l Bioethics Advisory Comm'n, *Cloning Human Beings* iii (1997).

165 *Id.* at iii–iv.

166 H.R. 571 and H.R. 2326, 106th Cong (1999).

167 White House Press Release, *President Bush Calls on Senate to Back Human Cloning Ban: Remarks by the President on Human Cloning Legislation,* Apr. 10, 2002. The president noted a difference between "reproductive cloning" and "research cloning": the former creates embryos for implantation and childbirth, whereas the latter creates embryos for research and stem cell derivation.

168 H.R. 534, 108th Cong. (2003) (passed in the House Feb. 27, 2003). The same bill passed in the House of Representatives during the 107th Congress as well, but it stalled in the Senate. Numerous bills aimed at prohibiting human cloning have been introduced since 2003, but none were passed. H.R. 1050, 111th Cong. (2009) was introduced in March 2009, but is still pending. *See* http://www.govtrack.us./congress/bill.xpd?bill=h111-1050.

169 This group was created after President Bush's statement on stem-cell research in August 2001. *See* Executive Order 13237, 66 Fed. Reg. 59,851 (Nov. 30, 2001).

170 *See* President's Council on Bioethics, Human Cloning & Human Dignity: An Ethical Inquiry (July 2002), www.bioethics.gov/reports/cloningreport/index.html.

Index

E

H

O

P

T

NOTES

NOTES

NOTES

NOTES

NOTES

NOTES

NOTES

NOTES

NOTES

NOTES